Web Survey Methodology

SAGE was founded in 1965 by Sara Miller McCune to support the dissemination of usable knowledge by publishing innovative and high-quality research and teaching content. Today, we publish more than 750 journals, including those of more than 300 learned societies, more than 800 new books per year, and a growing range of library products including archives, data, case studies, reports, conference highlights, and video. SAGE remains majority-owned by our founder, and after Sara's lifetime will become owned by a charitable trust that secures our continued independence.

Los Angeles | London | New Delhi | Singapore | Washington DC | Boston

Web Survey Methodology

MARIO CALLEGARO, KATJA LOZAR MANFREDA
& VASJA VEHOVAR

Los Angeles | London | New Delhi
Singapore | Washington DC | Boston

Los Angeles | London | New Delhi
Singapore | Washington DC | Boston

SAGE Publications Ltd
1 Oliver's Yard
55 City Road
London EC1Y 1SP

SAGE Publications Inc.
2455 Teller Road
Thousand Oaks, California 91320

SAGE Publications India Pvt Ltd
B 1/I 1 Mohan Cooperative Industrial Area
Mathura Road
New Delhi 110 044

SAGE Publications Asia-Pacific Pte Ltd
3 Church Street
#10-04 Samsung Hub
Singapore 049483

Editor: Katie Metzler
Assistant editor: Lily Mehrbod
Production editor: Ian Antcliff
Copyeditor: Neville Hankins
Proofreader: Sharon Cawood
Marketing manager: Sally Ransom
Cover design: Shaun Mercier
Typeset by: C&M Digitals (P) Ltd, Chennai, India
Printed and bound by CPI Group (UK) Ltd,
Croydon, CR0 4YY

Library of Congress Control Number: 2014951360

British Library Cataloguing in Publication data

A catalogue record for this book is available from
the British Library

MIX
Paper from
responsible sources
FSC® C013604
www.fsc.org

ISBN 978-0-85702-860-0
ISBN 978-0-85702-861-7 (pbk)

At SAGE we take sustainability seriously. Most of our products are printed in the UK using FSC papers and boards.
When we print overseas we ensure sustainable papers are used as measured by the Egmont grading system.
We undertake an annual audit to monitor our sustainability.

Contents

Preface

ABOUT THE *WEB SURVEY METHODOLOGY* BOOK

Web surveys appeared soon after the web was launched, at the beginning of the 1990s, and today they are the prevailing mode of survey data collection. With them, it has become very easy to create a survey, almost as simple as writing and sending an email. Correspondingly, sometimes it appears that basic computer literacy is not only the necessary, but also the sufficient, skill for conducting a web survey.

However, conducting web surveys raises numerous practical and conceptual questions: Is a web survey suitable for my research problem? How do I recruit respondents from the general population? Can I generalize the obtained results if survey participants come from online social media? How many people can I expect to answer my survey? Which strategy will assure enough cooperation? How much time can a web questionnaire take? Should respondents be forced to answer every question? How do I select the right web survey software? How do I adapt to respondents answering from a smartphone?

There are hundreds of questions like these and competent responses require the understanding of many issues, from changing technologies to various methodological specifics. Very often, there are no simple answers. Common sense alone is not enough for many of these situations. A recipe book would not suffice either, because there are too many issues and they are often too complex. Instead, knowledge and broader understanding of the subject matter are needed to provide the right orientation and the proper grounds for developing methodologically sound solutions, which then effectively respond to specific web survey circumstances with corresponding creativity. Providing such knowledge and understanding is the very aim of this book.

The book presents a dedicated treatment of web survey methodology, bringing evidence-based and comprehensive insight into all aspects of the web survey process. This is different from many other publications in this field, which often address only selected parts of web survey methodology, or discuss it only as a specific issue within a broader methodological treatment.

The book starts with introductory definitions and a conceptual outline of the web survey process (Sections 1.1 and 1.2). This is supplemented by further clarification of the context and evolution of computer-assisted survey information collection (CASIC), as well as by examples of the practical implementation of web surveys (Section 1.3). The three core chapters follow, which address the essential steps of the web survey process. Chapter 2 provides a systematic overview of web survey preparations, ranging from mode elaboration, sampling and questionnaire preparation to technical issues, nonresponse strategy and general management. Chapter 3 discusses actual data collection, which includes recruitment, measurement and corresponding support for fieldwork processing and monitoring. Chapter 4 reviews activities which follow after the data are collected: namely, data preparation, preliminary reporting and data exporting. These three chapters, together with the introductory one, provide an essential conceptualization of the subject, important structuring of the related processes and clarification of the terminology. We believe that these chapters are the main added value of the book and also that they will not immediately date due to rapid technological advances. This contrasts with Chapter 5, which addresses topics that depend to a much larger extent on continuous technological progress, thus making the related topics of web survey methodology very turbulent and fluid. New technological developments and related methodological research are appearing on a daily basis and continuously bring about substantial modifications of the landscape of contemporary web survey methodology. Within this context, Chapter 5 addresses three rapidly changing, but extremely important aspects of web survey implementation: namely, multiple devices, online panels and web survey software. Chapter 6 deals with broader methodological, management and professional frameworks, Chapter 7 concerns an outlook on future trends and Chapter 8 concludes the book.

The WebSM website (www.websm.org), which accompanies this book, contains various supplementary material, where concepts are further elaborated with examples (e.g. sample size calculations) and illustrations (e.g. interactive insight into question types), additional literature reviews, as well as some practical rules, recommendations and highlights in manual-like formats.

Throughout the text our overriding aim was to make sure that, for every issue discussed, we presented not only the key concepts and an up-to-date literature review, but also an articulated reflection on the related state of the art, as well as recommendations for practice. This was often very demanding, particularly where empirical evidence is weak, inconclusive or contradictory. As a result, the book provides overall an evaluation of and guidance on all important aspects of web survey methodology so it can therefore serve as a reference manual for methodological issues arising in web survey practice.

We have sought a delicate and sometimes impossible balance of combining an academic writing style with the applied practitioner style, taking advantage of the different backgrounds and positions of the three of us in both the business world and the academic sector. Besides conceptualizing the web survey process, we thus also address all key practical problems, from selection of the question format to technical settings for sending email invitations. We should add here that the applied style of a manual of guidelines was not the aim of this book; however, the corresponding guidance is being gradually developed on the WebSM.

Another difficult balance was sought by focusing on general web survey methodology principles, which are equally relevant for simple web surveys, as well as for complex settings in dedicated survey data collection organizations.

We should make it clear that web survey methodology is firmly rooted in general survey methodology, so its corresponding essential concepts are also introduced in the book, while for a broader insight we refer to relevant methodological textbooks. Our aim is to include general survey methodology issues to a sufficient extent so that the book can serve as a stand-alone textbook on web survey methodology.

While knowledge at the level of introductory courses in methodology or statistics is assumed as a general prerequisite, the concepts are introduced gradually and sections which assume more statistical and methodological knowledge – as well as sections which assume familiarity with web survey practice – are provided with supplementary material on WebSM. The book should therefore be suitable also for readers with little formal education in methodology or statistics but with rich experience of web surveys, and for readers who have a formal education but lack corresponding practice. Within this context, we will use the term *novices* to denote either of these two groups and direct them to the corresponding supplementary material.

The book can be used by students, as a textbook for their methodological education and research projects, but it also targets scholarly researchers in dealing with the state of the art on specific topics. In addition to academic usage, practitioners form the broadest audience, both professionals in marketing research and official statistics and users in numerous areas where web surveys are used, particularly human resource management, health studies, psychology, sociology and various other (social science) fields. The book is also suitable for do-it-yourself (DIY) users who have found themselves in the situation of conducting serious web surveys without much previous methodological education or experience.

A basic understanding of web survey methodology is increasingly essential for any research involving modern survey data. We expect further expansion of web surveys in the future, with extensions to new areas and usages. More innovations and turbulence related to the advance of technology are expected, particularly with respect to new devices and the integration of the entire survey research process. We believe that soon there will be almost no survey without at least some elements related to the web survey methodology framework. These factors place a high degree of importance on the subject we explore in this book.

ABOUT THE *WEB SURVEY METHODOLOGY* WEBSITE

To date (2015), approximately 20 years have passed since research started on how to conduct web surveys. Compared with other modes of survey data collection, such as telephone surveys, this research is scattered throughout a much wider array of resources, disciplines and publications. In order to pull together all these resources on web survey methodology, Vasja Vehovar and Katja Lozar Manfreda launched the WebSM in 1998 and have maintained it continuously since. In 2003–2005 their work was supported by the EU framework project WebSM (HPSE CT 2002 50031), and in 2009 they received the *AAPOR Warren J. Mitofsky Innovators Award* for WebSM. Since 2011, the work on this site has been partially supported by WebDataNet (Cost Action IS1004).

The aim of the WebSM has been to provide professional information on web survey methodology and the impact of new technologies on survey data collection. The website collects and publishes related news, information on scientific and professional events, web survey software and, most importantly, bibliographic details of web survey methodology and issues. At the beginning of 2014 the related WebSM database included 8,323 authors and 6,890 bibliographic entries.

This comprehensive website has been an important stimulus for writing this book. In addition, WebSM now serves as the companion website for the book. The bibliographic entries on the website are additionally structured according to the corresponding chapters. The website also contains various supplementary material for each of the chapters of the book. Readers are invited to follow the updates at http://www.websm.org.

Acknowledgements

While preparing the manuscript, we utilized research grants (J5-5538, J5-4159, J5-4177 and J5-6817) from the Slovenian Research Agency, awarded to the research team at the University of Ljubljana. Similarly, considerable funding was enabled through the support of four PhD students working on various aspects of web survey methodology. We also thank WebDataNet Cost Action IS1004 for the opportunities that allowed us to travel between London and Ljubljana to discuss and coordinate preparation of the book.

In addition to the above funding, we want to acknowledge those people who helped us to write this book. Katie Metzler at Sage helped us along the way, smoothed out difficulties and other writing issues, and encouraged us to complete this work. Patrick Brindle, our first editor at Sage, initiated the project and if it were not for his persistence, we would not be writing these words. We truly believe that Sage is a special publisher with specific added value.

Mario is grateful for the stimulating discussion on the Google internal 'survey mailing list', where challenging questions led to the refining of some sections of the book, and to digging deeper to find evidence for some hypotheses.

Katja and Vasja are grateful for the support of the Faculty of Social Sciences, University of Ljubljana, Chair of Social Informatics and Methodology, where they teach statistical and methodological courses. Current and past PhD students were very helpful, particularly Gregor Čehovin and Nejc Berzelak, whose contributions almost deserve a co-authorship, and also Andraž Petrovčič, Anže Sendelbah, Ana Slavec and Vesna Dolničar. Many other colleagues provided useful comments, particularly Valentina Hlebec on questionnaires, Jaroslav Berce on management and Irena Vipavc Brvar on archives.

Finally, Katja and Vasja also express their thanks to Professor Anuška Ferligoj, who encouraged them into this area of methodology, in which they started their professional careers. In addition to her dedication to scientific excellence, Professor Ferligoj had the vision and energy to establish a group of methodologists at the Faculty of Social Science, University of Ljubljana, which is now globally recognized.

Valuable feedback was obtained from Zenel Batagelj from Valicon and we also took advice from Tim Macer on mobile surveys.

We also need to acknowledge our families. Mario wants to thank his wife Ana Villar for the numerous discussions on web survey methods and issues and for sharing her experiences in conducting web survey experiments for the European Social Survey (ESS). Katja wants to thank her husband Marko and their parents, who helped and sometimes took over her role as a mother while she was working and travelling. Vasja is grateful for the warm support of his wife Darinka and for precious feedback from Aljoša, Miha and Natasha.

Of course, despite all this support, any remaining deficiencies of the book are attributable to the authors.

Mario Callegaro
Katja Lozar Manfreda
Vasja Vehovar
London & Ljubljana, January 2015

About the authors

Mario Callegaro is senior survey research scientist at Google, London, working on web surveys, on measuring customer satisfaction and on consulting survey design, questionnaire design, sampling and reporting. Before that he worked as a survey research scientist for Gfk-Knowledge Networks, which handles a US probability-based online panel. Mario holds a PhD in Survey Research and Methodology from the University of Nebraska, Lincoln. He is associate editor of *Survey Research Methods* and on the editorial board of the

International Journal of Market Research. He has published extensively in the areas of web surveys, online panels, telephone and cell phone surveys; question wording, polling and exit polls; the event history calendar; longitudinal surveys; and survey quality. He recently published (May 2014) an edited book entitled *Online Panel Research: A Data Quality Perspective.*

Vasja Vehovar and Katja Lozar Manfreda are professors of statistics and methodology at the Faculty of Social Science, University of Ljubljana, Slovenia, where they also earned their PhDs. They are pioneers in web survey research and began their web survey experiments in 1996. They have published more than 100 scientific papers, monograph chapters and other bibliography units on web surveys, some of high international importance. The most cited work (Lozar Manfreda et al., 2008), a meta-analysis on the field of web survey methodology, is already becoming a citation classic.

Since 1998 they have handled the most authoritative web survey methodology reference database WebSM, which also received the AAPOR Warren J. Mitofsky Innovators award in 2009. Their research and related publications focus on the methodological problems of web surveys: questionnaire design, nonresponse, mode effect, online measurement of ego-centric social networks, optimization of survey errors and survey costs, mixed-mode surveys, and data quality. They are also involved in the development of the web survey software tool 1KA.

Katja holds the first (2001) doctoral thesis in the field of web survey methodology (co-supervised by Mick Couper). She was the president of the Research Committee on Logic and Methodology RC33 at the International Sociological Association (2010–2014) and is a member of the core group and a working group leader of the Cost Actions WebDataNet (2011–2015). She is a member of the scientific committee of *BMS (Bulletin de Methodologie Sociologique)* and an associate editor of ESRA *Survey Research Methods*. She teaches the web survey methodology course at GESIS summer school.

Vasja has supervised four PhD students in the area of web survey methodology. In addition, his research focus spans a broad range of areas of Internet research (e.g. the Better Internet project, the Research on Internet in Slovenia project, digital divide studies), survey methodology (e.g. sampling, survey nonresponse, substitution in surveys, weighting for Europeans Social Survey) and specific statistical methods (e.g. time distance).

List of acronyms

AAPOR	American Association for Public Opinion Research
ABS	Address-Based Sample
ACASI	Audio Computer-Assisted Self-Interview/Interviewing
AoIR	Association of Internet Researchers
ARF	Advertising Research Foundation
BBS	Bulletin Board System
BCC	Blind Carbon Copy, Blind Copy Circulated
CAI	Computer-Assisted Interviewing
CAPI	Computer-Assisted Personal Interview/Interviewing
CASI	Computer-Assisted Self-Interview/Interviewing
CASIC	Computer-Assisted Survey Information Collection
CASM	Cognitive Aspects of Survey Methodology
CASRO	The Council of American Survey Research Organizations
CATI	Computer-Assisted Telephone Interview/Interviewing
CC	Carbon Copy, Copy Circulated
CESSDA	Consortium of European Social Science Data Archives
CRM	Customer Relationship Management
CSAQ	Computerized Self-Administered Questionnaire
CSS	Cascading Style Sheets
CSV	Comma Separated Values
CTR	Click-Through Rates
DBM	Disk-By-Mail
DDI	Data Documentation Initiative
DIY	Do-It-Yourself
DOI	Digital Object Identifier
EFM	Enterprise Feedback Management
ELIPSS	Étude Longitudinal par Internet Pour les Sciences Sociales
EMS	Electronic Mail Survey
ESOMAR	European Society for Opinion and Marketing Research
ESRA	European Survey Research Association
F2F	Face-to-Face (Interview)
FAQ	Frequently Asked Question
FFRISP	Face-to-Face Recruited Internet Survey Platform
FOQ	Foundation Of Quality Initiative
GOR	General Online Research
GPS	Global Positioning System
GRS	Graphic Rating Scale
GUI	Graphical User Interface
HCI	Human–Computer Interaction
HRM	Human Resource Management
HTML	Hyper-Text Markup Language
IBR	Introduction Breakoff Rate

ICT	Information and Communication Technology
ILB	Item Level Breakoff
INR	Item Nonresponse Rate
iOS (also iPhone OS)	a mobile operating system developed and distributed by Apple Inc.
IP	Internet Protocol
IRB	Institutional Review Board
ISO	International Organization for Standardization
ITV (also iTV)	Interactive TV
IVR	Interactive Voice Recognition
KPI	Key Performance Indicator
LISS	Longitudinal Internet Studies for the Social Sciences
MAR	Missing At Random
MCAR	Missing Completely At Random
MRIA	Marketing Research and Intelligence Association
MSE	Mean Squared Error
NMAR	Not Missing At Random
NOPVO	National Dutch Online Panel Comparison Study
OECD	Organization for Economic Cooperation and Development
P&P	Paper and Pencil questionnaire
PAPI	Paper and Pencil Interview/Interviewing
PSW	Propensity Score Weighting
QBR	Questionnaire Breakoff Rate
QR code	Quick Response Code
QUAID	Question Understanding Aid
RDD	Random Digit Dialing
RR	Response Rate
SaaS	Software as a Service
SAS	Statistical Analysis System
SD	Standard Deviation
SE	Standard Error
SMS	Short Message Service
SNS	Social Networking Site
SPSS	Software Package used for Statistical Analysis
SQP	Survey Quality Prediction
SRS	Simple Random Sample
SSL	Secure Sockets Layer
TBR	Total Breakoff Rate
TCP/IP	Transmission Control Protocol/Internet Protocol
TDE	Touchtone Data Entry
TQM	Total Quality Management
TSE	Total Survey Error
UBR	Unit-level Breakoff Rate
UCR	Unit-level Completeness Rate
UIN	Unit-level Item Nonresponse
UIT	Unproctored Internet Testing
UMR	Unit-level Missing-data Rate
URL	Uniform Resource Locator

UX	User Experience
VAS	Visual Analogue Scale
VCASI	Video Computer-Assisted Self-Interview/Interviewing
W3C	World Wide Web Consortium
WAP	Wireless Application
WCSC	Working Conditions in Slovenian Science
WWW	World Wide Web
WYSIWYG	What You See Is What You Get
XML	Extensible Markup Language Protocol

1

CONTENTS

Survey research and web surveys

In this chapter we first provide important initial definitions, conceptualizations and contexts of web surveys (Section 1.1), which will serve as a terminological and conceptual basis for further discussions. Next, we address the web survey process (Section 1.2) and its structure, which also outlines the core three chapters of this book (Chapters 2, 3 and 4). In Section 1.3 we provide further clarification of important technical aspects, additional insights into the evolution of web surveys and illustrations of web survey practice.

1.1 DEFINITION AND TYPOLOGY

Web surveys are basically surveys with certain specifics, so general survey methodology principles fully apply. Correspondingly, we often refer to the general survey methodology textbook of Groves, Fowler, Couper, Lepkowski, Singer & Tourangeau (2009), which we also recommend to readers for a broader overview. Still, the aim of this book is to provide a stand-alone treatment of web survey methodology, so besides web survey specifics we also include necessary discussions on essential general methodological aspects.

In this section, we introduce the general survey context and related notion of survey mode (Section 1.1.1). Next, we define the specifics of web surveys, structure their uses (the Section 1.1.2) and outline an important typology of web surveys based on related sampling characteristics (Section 1.1.3).

1.1.1 Surveys and Web Surveys

The notion of a *survey* relates to a method of systematic data collection, where we ask people questions by using standardized questionnaires for the purpose of quantitatively analysing some *target population* (Fowler, 2014; Groves et al., 2009), which is the population of interest. Typically, survey data are collected only from a sample of the target population, although we may collect data from the entire population, also called a *census* (e.g. all employees of a particular

organization). Surveys can be mandatory, which is extremely rare (e.g. some official surveys in certain countries), or voluntary. We focus here only on the latter.

Traditionally, surveys were administered by an interviewer, who recorded answers from respondents on paper, either in telephone or in face-to-face (F2F) interviews. Self-administered surveys, where respondents fill in the questionnaire by themselves, were traditionally also based on a paper and pencil questionnaire (P&P), usually delivered in the post and which we will denote hereafter simply as *mail surveys*. In the last few decades, the evolution of information and communication technology (ICT) has altered each of these *traditional survey modes*: answers are now recorded electronically and computers enable numerous other improvements. Furthermore, some entirely new methods have emerged.

With the rise of the Internet – particularly with the expansion of modern web browsers in the mid-1990s – web surveys have rapidly evolved to become the prevailing type of survey data collection with respect to the number of questionnaires that are filled in daily and also to the number of survey projects carried out (ESOMAR, 2013; Macer & Wilson, 2014).

We will use the term *survey mode* to describe specific characteristics of the survey measurement process. By measurement we denote here the essential stage of *data collection*, where respondents actually provide responses by filling in the questionnaire. We will use the term measurement to avoid – as much as possible – the notion of *data collection*, which is often related to a broader understanding of the survey data collection process.

We speak about the *web survey mode* as a self-administered mode, where the web is involved in the measurement process. Correspondingly, we talk about *web surveys* whenever the web survey mode is used. When the involvement of the web survey mode results in specific outcomes at the measurement stage, we talk about the *web survey mode effect*. For example, in the web survey mode respondents may admit more socially undesirable activities (e.g. gambling, smoking) compared with interviewer-administered surveys. The survey mode effect is a specific type of *measurement error*, which relates to the difference between a survey response and the true value. We discuss details of web survey mode effects further in Sections 6.1.1–6.1.3.

Of course, the measurement stage is part of the broader survey implementation process, which includes other components, such as sampling, recruitment and data preparation. Although all these components are closely related to the survey mode, and also highly relevant for the survey process, they can be regarded as separate and to a certain degree independent parts. For example, when we use the web survey mode at the measurement stage, various sampling or recruitment approaches can be used. Because these components of the survey process are often very specific in the web survey mode, we address them extensively. This is particularly true for the problems and related errors of *non-coverage* (where some segments of the target population were not included in the survey, e.g. non-users of the Internet), *nonresponse* (where responses were not obtained from segments included in the survey, e.g. refusals) and *self-selection* (where there was no control over the process of how respondents were recruited). Other *survey errors* can also appear and we will refer to their broadest context with the general notion of *survey data quality*, discussed in more detail in Section 6.1.2.

We restrict our focus in this book predominantly to a *basic web survey mode*. We define it as a survey mode using computerized self-administered questionnaires, stored on a specific computer connected to the Internet (i.e. *server*), which respondents access via a web browser. Respondents predominantly use desktop or notebook computers, but recent developments have led to the increased use of smartphones, tablets and Internet TVs. Respondents read questions visually displayed on the screen, and provide their answers using a keyboard, a mouse, a touch screen, or some other *manual electronic device* (e.g. pointer, stylus, etc.). No interviewer is present to guide the respondent, but the process can still be *interactive* in the

sense that questions can be displayed depending on previous answers. Similarly, respondents may get an immediate prompt if a question is left unanswered. Responses to questions are automatically transmitted, usually page by page, to a database on a researcher's server. As the server controls the entire process, we say that it is *server based*.

We should add here that we use the notion of *researcher* for the person, but also for the organization, that compiles the questionnaire and runs the entire web survey process. It is true, however, that in practice the role of researcher is often split into the sub-roles of (a) setting aims and conceptualizing the survey (usually done by a client, who orders the survey), (b) financing (also usually done by the client, but can be done by some other funding body which does not interfere with the conceptualization), (c) sponsoring (besides financing bodies, this can be any other entity formally supporting the survey), (d) elaboration of the methodology (the original researcher can further subcontract the survey to some research organization, which then handles the methodological aspect and runs the survey), (e) implementation (a specialized web survey provider can also be hired to conduct the web survey) and (f) supporting web survey software, because the majority of web surveys run on software which is supported by specialized suppliers offering this as a service together with web hosting (however, hosting itself can be separated as another sub-role). Due to our methodological focus, we do not elaborate any further on these institutional and organizational aspects, although they can be extremely important for the implementation of web surveys.

Further specifics and complexities may appear with various technological extensions, such as those arising from voice recognition and speech technologies, as well as from expanded use of video, multimedia, animations (e.g. virtual interviewer) and other applications. We exclude these aspects from our main focus on the basic web survey mode, which is currently by far the prevailing implementation for contemporary web surveys. Correspondingly, for practical purposes we will denote the basic web survey mode simply as web survey mode, unless explicitly labelled differently. We address some of these extensions in concluding Chapters 5, 6 and 7.

Another prevailing restriction of our elaboration concerns the type of survey design. When surveys are independent and the sample is drawn for the purposes of one survey only, we call this a *cross-sectional design*. If we want to observe changes in time, we may use a *repeated cross-sectional design*, where the same questionnaire is used on a new independent sample. Typical examples are traditional public opinion polls, which usually track the trends of political support with independent monthly surveys. Alternatively, we can observe changes with a *longitudinal design*, where the same sample of respondents is surveyed on the same topic sequentially, several times or even regularly (e.g. monthly). This enables a deeper insight and more precise observation of changes related to some important issues, such as unemployment, income dynamics or media consumption. The longitudinal design is also applied in so-called cohort studies, where we follow and repeatedly survey (e.g. annually, decennially) some specific population, such as the sample of an entire school generation.

Longitudinal design is closely related to the notion of panel design, which is sometimes even used as a synonym. However, we will use the term *panel* only in specific contexts, where a set of respondents serves as a frame for repeating selection in independent surveys, which can address related or entirely unrelated topics. The latter is also the main difference to longitudinal design, where we usually focus on only one specific issue. Here it is essential that panel members initially agree to participate and that they also provide socio-demographic information. Historically, this approach evolved from marketing research, where established household panels of thousands or even millions of households served for various independent surveys. Today, with so-called online panels, this approach is becoming essential for web surveys and is discussed in Section 5.2.

1.1.2 The Users of Web Surveys

The general development of ICT, the widespread adoption of the Internet, the continuous decline in ICT-related costs and the increasing speed of the Internet are some of the key factors driving the shift towards expanded usage of web surveys. However, this shift differs across segments of researchers.

We encounter the most intensive and advanced implementation of web surveys in marketing research, which is very indicative also for the entire commercial sector. The money spent on different survey modes in quantitative research for 77 countries (ESOMAR, 2013) has been increasing significantly over the past decade where web surveys are the dominant category. Figures also show a considerable drop for F2F surveys and a slight decline for telephone and mail surveys. Similar trends were described by GreenBook[1] and by Macer & Wilson (2013), confirming that in marketing research web surveys already account for the majority of all survey-related revenue. See detailed trends and figures in *Internet statistics*, Supplement to Chapter 2, at http://websm.org/ch2.

The usage of web surveys in official statistics – and in the government sector in general – is somehow lagging. This is mainly due to the need for high-quality samples of the general population, to privacy and confidentiality concerns, as well as to technical complexities. A certain obstacle also lies in the rigidity of large organizations and long-established processes. In addition, concerns exist about methodological issues and data quality. The problems may appear particularly in longitudinal surveys, where switching from traditional modes to web surveys can threaten the comparisons and related time-series data. Nevertheless, national statistical institutes in many countries are now faced with serious budget constraints, which can lead to the reduction of expensive F2F and telephone surveys (Bethlehem, 2009b; Cobben & Bethlehem, 2013). In enabling cheaper and faster access to large groups of potential respondents, web surveys therefore offer a promising alternative. This is especially true for *business surveys* (i.e. surveys of companies, organizations and institutions, also called *establishment surveys*), where almost complete Internet coverage is usually available, at least in developed countries.

For similar reasons web surveys are adopted relatively slowly in academic research and some key academic social surveys (e.g. the US General Social Survey, the European Social Survey) are still very cautious about the introduction of the web survey mode, although methodological investigations are currently on their way (Ainsaar, Lilleoja, Lumiste, & Roots, 2013; Villar, 2013).

In addition to their use in professional survey data collection organizations (in the commercial, government, and academic sectors), web surveys also make important contributions to the general democratization of survey research. Due to their lower costs and the availability of inexpensive and user-friendly web survey software, anyone with an Internet connection, a computer and basic ICT skills could create and implement a web survey. Sometimes no further education and skills in survey research are required and also no funds. This allows anyone to raise questions in the form of a web survey and then publish results. We call this *do-it-yourself* (DIY) research, with the common denominator that such researchers often have no or little methodological education/training in web surveys and surveys in general. However, DIY research is not without controversy. Very often, because these researchers do not have the necessary methodological knowledge, the quality of their surveys suffers. Low quality and the high volume of such surveys lead to 'over-surveying' the population, which can be very damaging to professional standards and to the web survey industry.

The share of DIY web surveys is not known exactly; however, it likely represents the largest portion of web survey questionnaires filled in daily by various respondents. This probably holds true even if we exclude numerous trivial polls, entertainment surveys, quizzes, etc. The DIY segment includes surveys conducted by students, pupils, bloggers, members of numerous Internet communities and many other curious citizens. Furthermore, there are countless small businesses, organizations, communities, associations and other groups that often run web surveys by themselves, outside the professional setting of dedicated survey organizations. While many of the web surveys in the DIY segment are relatively simple, a substantial part is complex and advanced, so their authors are among the key target audiences of this book.

The four segments above (commercial, official, academic and DIY) are often very specific, particularly with respect to the types of web surveys they use, the methodological problems they face and the web survey software features they require. Users of web surveys are thus not homogeneous. Still, we predominantly focus in our discussion on aspects which are common to all these segments.

1.1.3 Sampling Aspects of Web Surveys

Any discussion of web surveys, especially their advantages and limitations, should be made in the context of their type and function. A particular type of web survey may give high-quality results for a certain purpose, but have no scientific value for another. Within this context, besides the user segments discussed above, the typology based on sampling characteristics is another essential aspect for understanding the web survey context. Here, we detail two key sampling characteristics particularly important for our discussion.

Firstly, we need to define *probability* samples – which also determine the notion of probability surveys – where each *unit* (i.e. member of the target population) has a known and positive (non-zero) probability of selection into the sample. The units are then chosen for the sample according to these probabilities, using some *randomized procedures*, which basically resemble lottery drawing. On the other hand, *non-probability* sample surveys include all other surveys that do not follow the probability sample criterion. This distinction is of course not specific to web surveys, but relates to any survey mode.

Statistical inference, which refers to procedures that enable the generalization of results from the sample to the target population, is only possible with probability surveys, which for this reason are sometimes also called scientific sample surveys. Despite the advantage of statistical inference when using probability samples, for various practical reasons – particularly speed, price and convenience – we very often encounter web surveys with non-probability samples.

Secondly, we need to distinguish between list-based and non-list-based web surveys, as this dictates many other design characteristics. A survey is considered *list-based* when a list of units from the target population is available in advance, while all other surveys are *non-list based*. A list-based web survey can be a probability or non-probability one, as in Table 1.1, where we have provided some examples.

We therefore speak about probability list-based web surveys when the list adequately covers the target population and a probability method of sampling selection is used. One example is web surveys of specific populations that have high Internet penetration and an available list of members, suitable for use as a sampling frame (e.g. students, employees, subscribers/customers, registered members of an online group, etc.), which is then used for probability sample selection. Other examples are probability list-based web surveys of the general population, where units are recruited into the sample using traditional modes (mail, F2F, telephone). In addition, online panels can also rely on probability sample selection.

A list-based web survey is a non-probability one when the probabilities for inclusion of the units into the sample are not known or are known to be zero for some units, such as when important parts of the target population are missing. A typical example is the list of email addresses (hereafter *email*) obtained by using some non-probability recruitment methods, such as an open invitation on the web.

When the list of sample units is not available beforehand, we then have non-list-based web surveys, and usually these are also non-probability web surveys. Various examples exist in the popular segment of *unrestricted web surveys* (also referred to as *self-selected* or *open access* web surveys), where anyone who sees an invitation or a link (e.g. on some online forum) can participate without restriction. Here, of course, strong self-selection is in place, which means that the respondent decides – usually by some unknown mechanism – on inclusion in the sample, instead of the sample selection mechanism being controlled by a researcher. Often we encounter unrestricted online polls in the form of 'question-of-the-day' polls, which are used predominantly for entertainment and some simple insights.

Non-list-based, but still probability web surveys are rarer. One example is the probability *web intercept survey*, where randomly selected visitors to a certain website receive an invitation to a web survey, typically by some pop-up window. Of course, this procedure needs to comply with some additional restrictions to be truly treated as probability based.

In conclusion, it bears repeating that we have defined the web survey mode as having no genuine link to sampling. As shown in Table 1.1, web surveys can be combined with any type of sampling. A clear conceptual understanding of this independence is still not trivial and particularly in the early years of web surveys they

Table 1.1 Examples of web surveys according to key sampling characteristics

	Probability sampling	Non-probability sampling
List-based surveys	Probability surveys of specific Internet populations Probability-based web surveys of the general population Probability-based online panels	Web surveys with incomplete lists of the target population Web surveys based on lists collected by self-selection Non-probability online panels
Non-list-based surveys	Probability web intercept surveys	Unrestricted web surveys (self-selection)

8

were automatically associated not only with non-probability samples, but also with lower data quality. It is therefore advisable, particularly when presenting and disseminating results from web surveys, to attach explicitly the corresponding label denoting the type of sampling, such as probability web survey, non-probability online panel, probability web intercept survey, unrestricted web survey, etc. The mere notion of a web survey means only that the web survey mode was used for measurement but has no direct implication for the corresponding sampling approach, which is, however, one of the major determinants of data quality.

1.2 WEB SURVEY PROCESS

A web survey is implemented through the web survey process. We can structure the related activities into a few common steps, which usually appear in a sequential manner. The activities predominantly related to methodology and to the specifics of the web survey mode will be denoted as a *core web survey process*, which we separate from various other general research activities, such as preliminary conceptualization of the research problem or substantive analysis and publication of results, because they are typically independent from the survey mode. Consequently, a detailed discussion of these aspects is out of our scope, although we should never forget that they are still a very important part of the broader empirical research context. This is particularly true when a web survey is not a stand-alone project, but part of a larger research endeavour (e.g. customer satisfaction surveys can be just a small part of complex marketing research activities).

We outline the web survey process in Figure 1.1, where the focus is on the core web survey process. The corresponding structure is very important, because it determines the structure of Chapters 2, 3 and 4, where we elaborate on the activities of all *stages*, which are denoted in Figure 1.1 in boxes. Correspondingly, at this point, for a rough conceptual introduction we

provide only an initial brief description of these 12 stages. For novices this introduction might appear too abstract, so we recommend consulting the additional illustrations and practical examples in Section 1.3.

The web survey process starts with the step of *preliminary research activities*, which are undertaken before web survey specific methodological preparations start. This is a general research activity (see Section 6.1.5 for more details), independent from any survey mode, and thus formally outside of the core web survey process. It is typically related to the development of research objectives, outlining concepts and performing substantive tasks, such as preliminary desk research, qualitative investigation or expert consultations. We also conduct here various other preliminary activities of general project management and administration, including potential subcontracting, when we may hire an external agency to run the web survey.

Contrary to the substantive, managerial and administrative issues, which dominate the preliminary research activities, the main focus within the core web survey process is on methodological aspects related to web surveys.

We structure the core web survey process into three *steps*. The central and most essential step deals with collecting answers from respondents and relates to activities which are often labelled as *fieldwork*. This is a term originating from F2F surveys, where the collection of answers meant that interviewers had to go out into the field to obtain responses. Correspondingly, we call this step a *fielding*; it involves stages of *recruitment* (i.e. contacting and inviting potential respondents), measurement (i.e. data collection in a sense of questionnaire completion) and related *processing and monitoring*.

Of course, before fielding, thorough preparations are needed, so we actually start the core web survey process activities with the *pre-fielding* step, which includes the following stages: *mode elaboration*, dealing with decisions about the mode of measurement and mode of recruiting, *sampling*, encompassing work on defining the population, sampling frame, sample size and sample design, as well as selection of the sample; and *questionnaire preparation*, which includes questionnaire development, computerization and testing. In addition, pre-fielding also encompasses *technical preparations* related to database and case management, as well as to various privacy, security and email settings, and *nonresponse strategy*, which covers contacting and other means to achieve the desired cooperation, while *general management* includes overall management, administration, communication and some other activities.

After fielding, when data are collected, the *post-fielding* step begins with the stage of *data preparation*, which includes the specific activities of editing, coding, imputation and weighting. In addition, *preliminary results*, consisting of reporting and dissemination (e.g. summary statistics can be automatically generated and then disseminated online), are produced. Similarly, some preliminary *data exporting and documentation* can also be integrated into the web survey software and thus considerably support the archiving function.

We include the post-fielding stages in the core web survey process only to the extent to which integrated ICT support of the web survey software is provided. Of course, this border might be rather vague, because these activities are supported by web survey software to varying extents. Still, as we will further elaborate, advanced web survey software – which we have in mind when talking about the potential of ICT support – actually does support all three stages of the post-fielding to a considerable extent. At this point we can perhaps observe more clearly the essential role of ICT for the core web survey process. That is, not only is this process closely supported and integrated with ICT, but the corresponding ICT support also defines the borders of the process.

On the other hand, we exclude from the core web survey process all general research activities which follow the post-fielding, particularly the substantive analysis, activities independent of web survey specifics and activities fully conducted with some external web survey software. This step typically relates to (a) *advanced analysis*, run within specialized software, which is closely related to report writing and substantive interpretations, further (b) *processing* of the data, such as inclusion in some customer relationship management (CRM) database, or merging with and matching some external data, as well as (c) *valorization*, a term that covers *dissemination* (i.e. from traditional publishing to digital channel distribution) and *exploitation* (i.e. various uses and incorporation of the results).

The steps and stages of the core web survey process are clearly separated in Figure 1.1. Correspondingly, we address them separately and sequentially in the following key chapters of the book: pre-fielding (Chapter 2), fielding (Chapter 3) and post-fielding (Chapter 4). We may also add that the related arrows in Figure 1.1 illustrate only the essential flow of the processes. Of course, many other interactions across the various stages exist.

Note that the steps and corresponding stages cannot always be separated that sharply. The pre-fielding stages may overlap with the preliminary research activities, because some decisions specific to web surveys (e.g. selection of a specific mode, provision of an existing sample or draft questionnaire) may have already been made at the time of the initial request from a client or during the early conceptualization of the project. Similarly, some pre-fielding activities may overlap with the fielding; for example, when preparation of the questionnaire includes extensive field testing, or when part of the fielding is run earlier so that some corrections can still be made. Overlap between fielding and post-fielding may also occur, for example when preliminary reports are required urgently during the fielding. It is also sometimes difficult to separate some activities of data preparation or the documentation stages of post-fielding from activities that concern further analysis, processing and valorization, particularly because they are supported differently by various web survey software.

In the next three chapters, we discuss the simplified flow of the core web survey process, as outlined in Figure 1.1, but excluding the step of preliminary research activities and the step

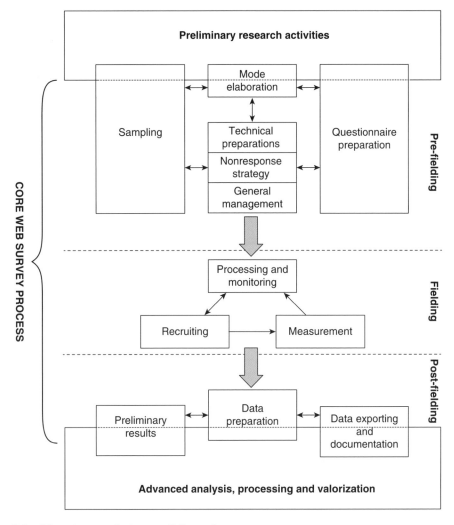

Figure 1.1   The steps and stages of the web survey process

of advanced analysis, processing and valorization. We further restrict our discussion to the context of independent, cross-sectional and stand-alone web survey projects. This means we assume only one questionnaire and a single measurement (i.e. questionnaire completion) session, without repetitions, recursions, iterations, loops or other complexities which often arise in the reality of the research environment. We address further extensions and complexities within broader methodological discussion in Chapter 6.

1.3 EVOLUTION OF WEB SURVEYS, APPLICATIONS AND RELATED PRACTICES

In this section we provide further elaboration of web surveys. We first separate web surveys from related notions which are often used in similar contexts, such as Internet surveys, email surveys, online surveys, digital surveys (Section 1.3.1). Next, we address the historical development of web surveys, from their precursors (Section 1.3.2) to the rise of modern web surveys (Section 1.3.3).

This is then followed with a discussion on survey modes and their taxonomy across type of administration (interviewer vs self-administered) and level of computerization (Section 1.3.4). We also overview the practical aspects of web surveys, which can be particularly useful for novices in web survey methodology. We look at the strengths and weaknesses which are usually related to web surveys (Section 1.3.5). We then present a series of examples and applications of web surveys in different research areas (Section 1.3.6). We end with a summary of practices which are related or similar to web surveys (Section 1.3.7), such as administrative forms, Internet testing and psychological experiments on the web. These three areas share much communality with web surveys but are generally not considered in the general literature of web surveys.

1.3.1 Web Surveys vs Internet and Online Surveys

The *web*, more precisely the World Wide Web (WWW), was launched in 1990 after a decade of development. This was almost three decades after the invention of the *Internet*, which is an electronic network of computers using standardized communication protocols (TCP/IP). The building block of the web is the hyper-text markup language (HTML), which is used to present and structure content for the web. It enables users to access remotely – via the Internet using special software (i.e. a *browser*) – the corresponding content in HTML-formatted web pages. Currently, the fifth revision, HTML5, is recommended by the World Wide Web Consortium (W3C), which brings further standardization across operating systems, as well as increased support for interactivity, graphics and video.

With a certain *web page* we understand the corresponding HTML content to have a unique web address (i.e. URL, Uniform Resource Locator) residing on a computer connected to the Internet (i.e. a server). The notion of a single web page is sometimes confused with a *website*, which typically has its own domain (e.g. websm. org) or sub-domain (e.g. book.websm.org) and contains numerous web pages.

A special subtype – today we prefer to talk about a component – of a web page is a *web form*, which enables the user – besides passive access – to also enter some data on the same web page and then transfer the content to the server. In the case of web surveys, the *web questionnaire* is actually a special type of web form, filled in by users (i.e. respondents), where the input (i.e. survey answers) is transferred to a researcher's server. The web form is thus the basis for the collection of web survey data. Within this context, standard HTML elements are defined as HTML controls in the technical specifications[2] of the W3C, the main international organization establishing web standards. The standard HTML elements, which appear extensively on the web (e.g. in bookings, administrative forms, shopping, registering, etc.) and also configure the basic building blocks of web survey questionnaires, are as follows: radio button, checkbox, drop-down menu and text input.

The notion of *Internet surveys* is broader than web surveys. This also holds for some other similar terms – typically not precisely defined – such as *surveys via the Internet* or *Internet-mediated surveys*. All these terms basically refer to surveys where the Internet is the medium for delivering (transmitting) responses from respondents to a researcher. Of course, delivery via the Internet can also be done without the web, as with email, which is another service that operates across the Internet.

The term *online survey* is usually also poorly defined, but in general has a broader scope than an Internet survey, although it is often used as a synonym. However, here we will be more precise and introduce a distinction between the two by exposing two essential determinants of online surveys. The first is related to computerized survey questionnaires where some electronic network supports the exchange of data between computers (i.e. between the respondent's device and a researcher's server). Besides the Internet, other telecommunication networks can be used in online surveys as well, such as a fixed telephone network (e.g. telepanel surveys), mobile telephone network (e.g. SMS surveys) and various other computer networks internal to some organizations. The second determinant is related to the automatic delivery of computerized questionnaires: respondents do not need to perform any additional activities (except pressing a button) to transmit their responses to a researcher. The questionnaire is received via email as a text file, and is thus not an online survey, because after completion the respondent needs to save it, attach it and return it to the researcher via email.

Note that the terms *digital surveys* and *electronic surveys* also sometimes appear in the context of web surveys, but we do not use them in the book due to their rather imprecise meaning. This can range from ordinary computerization of the questionnaire in some text processor, which can be isolated from any electronic network, to the synonym for online surveys.

Today, web surveys constitute the vast majority of Internet surveys (and also the majority of online surveys). The remaining 'non-web' segments of Internet surveys belong predominantly to email surveys. We discuss email surveys below, within the context of early precursors to web surveys, together with electronic mail surveys (EMSs) and computer-assisted panel research or telepanels.

The notions of web research, Internet research or online research – as well as digital or electronic research – are much broader than web, Internet or online surveys. They include, besides survey data collection, corresponding extensions to numerous other quantitative and qualitative research techniques.

1.3.2 Precursors and Alternatives to Web Surveys

In this section we review the historical formats of web surveys, paying special attention to two alternatives to web surveys, which are today undergoing a certain amount of revival: namely, email surveys and client-based questionnaires which run as applications on the respondent's computer.

The first online surveys via electronic networks began with the *electronic mail survey*

(EMS) in the mid-1980s. An electronic (computerized) questionnaire as a software file (application) was simply attached to an electronic mail communication (using TCP/IP or some other communication protocol). This was more likely to occur where respondents belonged to the same organization (Ramos, Sedivi, & Sweet, 1998) and all had the same electronic mail system. Alternatively, the questionnaires were sent via (telephone) modems – typically using the so-called bulletin board system (BBS) – directly to the respondent's computer. In any case, after running the application and filling in the questionnaire the respondents needed to send it back to a researcher as an attachment.

With the rise of the standardized email service over the Internet in the late 1980s and the 1990s, a unified form of email appeared and expanded rapidly, also stimulating the use of *email surveys*. Formally, email surveys are a subset of EMS; however, we often restrict the label EMS to early developments before standardized email surveys appeared.

With email surveys, in addition to a software file attached to an email message (the same as in early EMS), two more options appeared: a questionnaire embedded in the body of the email message and an electronic text document attached to an email (such as an MS Word, Excel or a PDF file; Porter, 2008). The first of these two new options now prevails in the understanding of an email survey. Initially, plain (ASCII) text was used and embedded into an email message. These text-based email surveys generally took the form of a paper questionnaire (Schonlau, Fricker, & Elliott, 2002, p. 20), where text was formatted in a simple way to retain consistency across email clients (systems). Generally, the respondent was asked to participate by replying to the email message. Answers were noted by typing an X next to the chosen response option(s), which were marked by square brackets [ ], or by typing a number or letter corresponding to the response option (for an example, see Sheehan & Hoy, 1999). This approach was so primitive that Grossnickle & Raskin (2001) wrote in one of the first online marketing research handbooks: 'The only reason we can think of to conduct a survey via email is if the population you're surveying has access to email but not to the Web' (p. 140).

The above approach can be considered an interim survey solution (e.g. Schaeffer & Dillman, 1998) to modern email clients that can handle HTML (Porter, 2008). This enabled a certain revival of email surveys. That is, with modern HTML-based email surveys the look and feel of the questionnaire is identical to one using a web browser, despite the fact that the email survey uses neither the web nor a browser. All types of data input available in HTML are available here, such as radio buttons and check-boxes, drop-down menus and text boxes. The embedded HTML forms also ensure the automatic recording of responses into a database. Although HTML-based email surveys formally do not belong to the web survey mode, most of the web survey methodology principles can be fully applied here.

In any case, these HTML-based email surveys are still similar to text-based email surveys due to the fact that they cannot handle branching or validations; they are not as interactive as web questionnaires. For this reason, they are suitable only for short and simple questionnaires. Another disadvantage is that the display of the questionnaire within an email message on smaller devices can be problematic if not handled properly. Similarly, harmonization across different email systems can be difficult, causing technical problems with the extraction of responses (Krasilovsky, 1996). Nevertheless, HTML-based email surveys have one important advantage over web surveys: the respondent does not need to open the questionnaire to see the questions, as required in the case of web surveys with an email invitation that includes the survey URL. Instead, the respondent is immediately presented with the first survey question. This may increase his or her cooperation, especially if the first question is simple, attractive and appealing. Despite serious disadvantages, we may to a certain extent expect increased use of HTML-based email surveys in future in specific situations concerning very simple and short questionnaires (e.g. on consumer satisfaction).

We direct the reader to Mesh (2012) or Porter (2008) for examples and for an advanced discussion of the advantages, limitations and recent research on the use of email surveys.

Attaching text-processing documents (e.g. MS Word), spreadsheets (e.g. Excel) or other document formats (e.g. PDF) to an email message is another way of delivering a questionnaire over the Internet. These documents can be specially adapted for data collection (e.g. locked instruction text and marked open input area). An important advantage is the potential for better formatting – in terms of graphics and standardization – compared with email (text- and HTML-based) surveys, but also compared with web surveys, where we do not fully control how various web browsers present the questionnaire to respondents. In addition, data extraction can be automated more smoothly and, in the case of PDF files, some consistency checks (e.g. range validations) can also be programmed (Donald, 2010). One disadvantage is the high burden on respondents where they have to save the file, fill in the questionnaire and send it back to the originator as an attachment to an email message. Nevertheless, attaching an editable form (i.e. text document) can be a good solution for business surveys, where the same questionnaire is filled in by multiple respondents, so it is easy to circulate it. Modern web survey software provides such an option in a much superior format, but for some researchers it might be easier and cheaper to prepare a corresponding form.

When the interactive questionnaire completion runs on the respondent's computer (i.e. client computer), we say it is *client based*. From the point of view of questionnaire design, the EMS and email surveys with an electronic questionnaire as a software file attachment (i.e. *application*) have some advantages over web surveys that are usually server based (i.e. the interactivity of the computerized questionnaire is run by a server). For example, client-based surveys traditionally have a much finer control of the questionnaire (Saris, 1991, pp. 40–49) in terms of the standardized appearance, branching, validation and randomization, as well as increased speed and flexible graphics/multimedia. However, unlike web surveys (running on a server via web browsers), they require an executable file to be run on the client (respondent's device). Respondents sometimes reject these types of surveys because they do not know how to run the file or they fear their computers will be infected with a virus (Porter, 2008). Sometimes this application, to be successfully run, requires additional software, which might not yet be present at the client, or a *platform*, which involves the operating system plus other related software and hardware features. The most frequent examples are *Flash* (multimedia software for displaying graphics and animations that is available for most web browsers as a plug-in) and *Java* (software that allows users to run programs written in the Java programming language). Another related issue concerns the size of the attachment, which – if too large – will be rejected by some email systems.

Today, however, most of these technological limitations of client-based application questionnaires have disappeared, and the entire questionnaire, including the automatic online transmission of responses (via the web or email) back to a researcher, should run smoothly. Compared with server-based web surveys, such modern client-run questionnaires therefore place no extra burden on the respondent, while providing increased speed (due to no interaction with the server when completing the questionnaire), larger multimedia flexibility (beyond the potential limitations of a browser) and independence from specific web browser characteristics (which are beyond a researcher's control in such surveys).

Nevertheless, the benefits of the standardized web browser interface, which is already supported by all devices, and the high costs of the corresponding tailor-made production of the applications, which often needs to be done outside the user-friendly and capable web survey software and programmed separately for different operating systems, seem to prevent client-based application questionnaires from becoming more than a negligible alternative compared with web surveys, at least for desktop or notebook computers. Another decisive factor in the decline of client-based approaches was the

development of powerful browser scripts that run on the client computer, which then extended the functionalities of browser-based web surveys and enabled more functionality of the client-side survey applications. We may add that, formally, client-based survey applications do not belong to web surveys, because the questionnaire can be filled in without using web browsers. They also run without interaction with the server, which is a defining feature of the (basic) web survey mode.

Nowadays, however, tablet and smartphone client-based survey applications are becoming more and more popular, so the client–server dilemma reappears and we discuss it further in Section 5.1.

Computer-assisted panel research, or the *telepanel*, is another precursor of web surveys, more specifically of what is now called an online panel. Traced back to its inception in the 1980s, where one of the first attempts was in the Netherlands (Saris, 1998), the idea was to recruit and survey a nationwide probability-based sample of households by providing them with a desktop computer and a telephone modem, so they could run a computerized self-administered questionnaire. Of course, at that time this was all run without the Internet, web and web browsers, so we cannot talk about web surveys. In 1999, more than 10 years after the first telepanel, Knowledge Networks started a similar national probability-based online panel in the United States. The firm recruited households via *random digit dialling* (RDD) and provided each one with a WebTV as the technology to deliver the questionnaire (Krotki & Dennis, 2001), enabling modern web surveys. Since their first appearance, we have seen important developments in the methodology of recruiting and maintaining online panels and in the selection of devices offered to panellists. See Section 5.2 for a detailed description.

1.3.3 Rise of Modern Web Surveys

The precursors of web surveys (EMS, email surveys and telepanels) in the 1980s could already run online computerized surveys without using the web (or even the Internet). The web as a survey medium was fully operational only when modern web browsers appeared, accompanied by advances in web browser graphical interfaces. These started when the Netscape browser was launched in 1994, which also boosted the general use of the Internet. Correspondingly, local web surveys were quick to expand, as well as global ones (e.g. GVU surveys)[3]. Email remained an important technology for contacting respondents. We may recall here that currently (2015) the browser market[4] is dominated by Chrome, Firefox, Internet Explorer, Safari and Opera.

The very first web surveys in the 1990s were rather static, using sequences of web forms (i.e. plain HTML forms) with questions arranged one after another on a single web page. They were, in essence, just computer (electronic) versions of P&P questionnaires, usually without any of the advanced features of computerized questionnaires – apart from Internet delivery (i.e. automatic transfer of answers to a researcher's database via the Web) – and as such should have been short, simple and without branching.

With further development of popular web browsers with flexible graphical features from 1994 onwards, web surveys, which started to involve interactivity, have relied prevailingly on server-based interactions. There, each web page (i.e. a separate HTML form) was sent to the server where it could be immediately validated and – depending on answers – the next page would appear. This interactivity is a very important feature and we have included it in the initial definition of the basic web survey mode. We might add that we usually assume – unless explicitly specified differently (e.g. in email surveys) – that computerized questionnaires in general are also interactive.

In recent years, particularly from the 2000s with the introduction of web 2.0, validations (e.g. range validations) and various interactive actions (e.g. feedback conditioned by responses on the same web page) have also been enabled at the client side (i.e. on the respondent's device) with the use of special browser scripts. Currently this is predominantly done with *JavaScript*, an object-oriented computer programming language commonly used to create interactive effects within web browsers. It can add functionalities to a client's device, which can – without interacting with the server – perform question validations, branching, prompts, etc., and thus enhance feedback and interactivity of the questionnaire screen. This greatly increases the speed because it eliminates many interactions with the server and provides much more flexibility in the design of the interface, particularly the interactive features. The increased client-based interactions of web surveys (i.e. JavaScript) have further reduced the advantages of the full client-based questionnaires, which run as an application (e.g. Java) and thus present an important reason for the decline of the client-based approach. Today almost all web surveys are server based and usually require JavaScript to be enabled on the respondent's side to function properly.

Initially, web surveys were accessed and answered by respondents using their desktop, laptop or notebook computers. In special cases, like the Knowledge Network panel mentioned previously, WebTV units were also used for this purpose. In the last decade, however, small portable devices such as smartphones and tablets have been increasingly used to access the Internet and also to participate in web surveys. This has generated new issues in the design of web questionnaires, such as how to deal with a much smaller screen for presenting survey questions as compared with that of the desktop or notebook. We discuss these issues further in Section 5.1.

Together with the expansion of web surveys, the corresponding software support has also developed rapidly and enabled the convenient implementation of web surveys. Initially, the web survey software supported only the basic and most browser-compatible elements available in HTML forms: namely, radio buttons, drop-down menus, check-boxes, tables, text boxes and graphical images. These elements are still the core components of web questionnaires today. Of course, modern web survey software has gradually expanded and Section 5.3 presents a full overview of web survey software.

1.3.4 The Context of Survey Modes

Survey modes differ across several dimensions (Biemer & Lyberg, 2003), the most essential ones being the absence or presence of an interviewer (interviewer-administered vs self-administered surveys) and computerization of the questionnaire (P&P vs electronic format), whenever we talk about computer-assisted survey information collection (CASIC) (Table 1.2).

Modern survey research – which is roughly about a hundred years old (J. M. Converse, 2009) – started with P&P surveys, first with interviewer-administered F2F and also with self-administered mail surveys, followed by interviewer-administered telephone surveys. Computerization of survey data collection only began in the 1970s with various computer-assisted interviewer-administered surveys (computer-assisted interviewing or CAI). Firstly, computer-assisted telephone interviewing (CATI) emerged due to the development of mainframe computers capable of handling the questionnaire and management of the sample (Couper & Nicholls II, 1998). In the mid-1980s, with the introduction of portable computers, it was also possible to conduct computer-assisted personal interviewing (CAPI) (Couper & Nicholls II, 1998; Saris, 1991, p. 5), sometimes in combination with computer-assisted self-interviewing (CASI) for part of the questionnaire (de Leeuw & Nicholls II, 1996). In the latter case – where an interviewer introduced the respondent to some form of computerized self-administered questionnaire – in addition to the standard visual (text) format, the questions could be delivered to the respondent in an audio (ACASI) or video format (VCASI).

Computerized self-administered questionnaires (CSAQs), where a respondent administers the entire process of answering the questionnaire without the involvement of an interviewer, also started to appear in the mid-1980s (Ramos et al., 1998). CSAQs may take different forms. An early form of CSAQ was disk-by-mail (DBM) where respondents received a diskette by mail to be run on their computer. The diskette contained an executable program (application) that handled the questionnaire and recorded the responses. Once the questionnaire was completed, the data were saved on the diskette, which was then sent back to the data collection agency, again by mail (de Leeuw & Nicholls II, 1996; McNaughton, 1999).

Two other forms of CSAQ data collection methods – namely, touchtone data entry (TDE) (Clayton & Werking, 1998) and, later, interactive voice recognition (IVR) (Miller Steiger & Conroy, 2008) – took advantage of telephones to conduct short self-administered surveys in which respondents listened to a recorded questionnaire and entered their responses using either the telephone keys (i.e. TDE) or an automatic voice recognition system (i.e. IVR). So-called *robo-surveys* are an extreme form of this approach where the telephone dialling is also automated (i.e. robo-dial), thus representing a specific example of interviewer-free (self-administered) and paper-free (computerized) data collection. With the advent of mobile phones, another form of CSAQ also appeared, namely SMS surveys.

The most important trend in CSAQs – and in survey data collection in general – is the use of the Internet to collect survey data, which started to expand in the 1990s. As mentioned, electronic mail surveys and email surveys first appeared, followed by web surveys which today dominate the survey industry in all developed countries with good Internet coverage and a certain level of computer literacy. With the convenience of self-administration, lower costs and high speed, these surveys have become promising alternatives to F2F and telephone surveys, both of which have had continuously declining response rates (Brick & Williams, 2013; de Leeuw & de Heer, 2002).

We should add that – after the initial enthusiasm, turbulence and excessive expectations about this new 'replacement technology' (e.g. Black, 1998) – web surveys are now becoming mature. Similarly, as the Internet did not eliminate other media (radio, TV, newspapers), but rather repositioned, transformed and integrated them, web surveys did not cancel out the other survey modes, but rather introduced a complex transformation in the entire data collection process.

Table 1.2 Administration and computerization aspects of survey modes

	Computerization	
Administration	**Paper and pencil (P&P) surveys**	**Computer-assisted survey information collection (CASIC)**
Interviewer-administered surveys	P&P interviewing (PAPI): • Face-to-face P&P surveys • Telephone P&P surveys	Computer-assisted interviewing (CAI): • Computer-assisted personal interviewing (CAPI) face to face • Computer-assisted telephone interviewing (CATI), via fixed or mobile telephone
Self-administered surveys	Self-administered P&P surveys: • Mail surveys • Self-administered P&P surveys, handed over by interviewers • Fax surveys	Computer-assisted self-interviewing, introduced by F2F interviewer (CASI, ACASI, VCASI) Computerized self-administered questionnaires (CSAQs): • Disk-by-mail (DBM) • Telephone self-interviewing: touchstone data entry (TDE), interactive voice recognition (IVR), robo-surveys, SMS surveys • Electronic mail surveys (EMSs) • Email surveys • Web surveys (on various devices) • Mobile survey apps

Table 1.2, inspired by Biemer & Lyberg (2003) and Groves et al. (2009), summarizes the basic classification of survey modes, where the evolution goes from the upper left to the bottom right corner, from P&P interviewer-administered surveys to CSAQs. The web surveys are at the bottom right and thus belong to the broader CSAQ family. At this point we should mention that we reject use of the term computer-assisted web interviewing (CAWI) because the notion of 'interviewing' implies some form of interviewer involvement/presence, which is not the case with web surveys. We provide further insight into survey modes in Section 6.1.1.

1.3.5 Overview of Advantages and Limitations

Web surveys are quite robust and particularly in the early years of their adoption some aspects were praised uncritically. On the other hand, there are also some weaknesses. Both aspects should be treated realistically, without exaggeration. We present an initial critical review of the main characteristics of web surveys. This will provide various holistic insights into the problems of web survey methodology and thus facilitate the discussion in subsequent chapters where we provide a systematic and detailed overview of the methodological issues.

1.3.5.1 Costs

One of the most appealing advantages of web surveys is the cost, when compared with mail, telephone and F2F surveys. For example, Greenlaw & Brown-Welty (2009) surveyed members of an association and showed that the cost per response was $0.6 for the web survey (with email invitations) vs $4.8 for the mail and $3.6 for the mixed-mode option. A similar study comparing web vs P&P for a sample of practising dentists demonstrated that the web option (with email invitations) was 2.7 times more cost-effective than the paper option (Hardigan,

Succar, & Fleisher, 2012). Strabac & Aalberg (2011) reported similar results when making a telephone–web comparison in the United States and Norway: the price per respondent for the web survey (with email invitations) was three to four times lower than for the corresponding telephone survey. We do not at this point detail the cost comparisons with F2F where costs per respondent may amount to hundreds and even reach thousands of euros/dollars.

Web surveys have a fundamentally different cost structure compared with other survey modes. Variable costs of data collection, which depend on sample size, are usually very small. For mail surveys, the variable costs per unit involve envelopes, questionnaire printouts, stamps, mail-back stamps and envelopes, as well as data entry. For telephone surveys the corresponding variable costs depend on the interview time (i.e. costs of interviewers and telephone charges), while with F2F costs additionally increase due to travel and in some cases also due to the initial process of locating households (e.g. area sample, random walk). For web surveys with email invitations all these variable costs practically disappear. Sending 10 or 10,000 email invitations costs the same, and obtaining 10 or 10,000 completed questionnaires costs almost the same. Costs for additional contacts (reminders) or for sending out related material (instructions, project background and results) in digital form do not increase with sample size either. What does increase are the costs of incentives and/or mail invitation letters and reminders, if used.

On the other hand, there are not many differences among the modes with respect to the fixed costs of questionnaire development and testing, while other fixed costs are often relatively small for web surveys. In a typical case of DIY web surveys we may have the costs of a server and some special web survey software, subscriptions to which can nowadays be inexpensive (see Section 5.3), while other survey modes typically have many more fixed costs, particularly for training and monitoring (interviewer-assisted modes) or for administration procedures (mail mode).

In a simplified example of a web survey with email invitations (assuming no nonresponse), the costs per unit are basically proportional to F/n, where F stands for fixed costs and n for sample size, while they equal $(F/n + c)$ for other modes, where c stands for variable cost per unit. The comparative advantage of web surveys is thus more than trivial and obviously increases with sample size. However, we can make four critical remarks on these observations:

- When fixed costs (F) include, for example, the maintenance of an online panel of the general population (especially a probability one), the costs per completed web questionnaire quickly increase and may become comparable with telephone or mail surveys. In small countries, where online panels are small and relatively expensive, the costs may also compare with F2F, particularly if labour costs are relatively low. This is in fact an excellent example against over-simplified discussions on the inherent cost advantages of web surveys.

- Comparably lower costs for web surveys should not necessarily result in just financial gains for researchers or clients, but should also be transformed into higher survey data quality. The comparable savings with web surveys can thus enable larger sample sizes, incentives, more promotion, etc., all of which could lead to higher data quality.

- Specific elements to consider when implementing web surveys are the costs for respondents. In some cases, respondents have to pay extra for Internet access specifically related to completion of the questionnaire (e.g. data transmission charges when responding via a mobile phone).

- In reality, as with any other service, we should never discuss costs separately from quality. When the quality of survey data – given certain fixed costs – is the same or better, web survey preference is trivial. When the web survey performs worse, we should first consider the difference in budget. It is an unfair comparison if we are evaluating lower data quality in web surveys, when the costs are radically lower than with other, more expensive alternatives. When data quality is involved – and in fact it should always be involved – the costs become a very complex issue (see Section 6.1.4).

1.3.5.2 Speed of Data Collection

The next appealing advantage of web surveys is the speed of the data collection process. This is especially important for time-sensitive studies where actionable decisions need to be made quickly, such as political studies during election campaigns. Similarly, in marketing research, a brief web survey can be up and running in a matter of days, even within hours with immediate access to results. If electronic media are used for survey invitations (email or banner ads), thousands of people can be reached in an instant, and responses start to arrive almost immediately. Of course, if a researcher (organization) is not yet experienced in web surveys or invitations via mail, telephone or F2F are used, these advantages may decrease.

The advantage of web surveys in terms of speed of returning responses is so obvious that recent published studies rarely report this topic. However, results from earlier studies can illustrate this not only for email (Shannon & Bradshaw, 2002; Truell, Bartlett, & Alexander, 2002) and fax invitations (Cobanoglu, Warde, & Moreo, 2001; Weible & Wallace, 1998), but also when mail invitations are used (Kwak & Radler, 2002a; Weible & Wallace, 1998). One extreme difference was reported by Aoki & Elsmar (2000): the average response time for a mail questionnaire in a survey of marketing managers was 50 days compared with 3 days for the identical web survey with email invitations. Similarly, Nadler & Henning (1998) reported that 4 days were needed in a web survey compared with 20 days in a telephone survey to obtain the same number of responses, while Heiervang & Goodman (2011) reported that the field period for the web survey was only a quarter of that needed for F2F surveys.

In any case, compared with other modes of data collection and invitations, responses in web surveys with email invitations begin to accumulate much more quickly. Figure 1.2 illustrates a typical response pattern from a 2011 survey on Working Conditions in Slovenian Science (WCSC). In this case, 4,551 email invitations were sent, followed by two reminders. The list

of email addresses was obtained from the official registry of Slovenian scientists. We can see that the majority of clicks occurred immediately on the invitation day and to a lesser extent on the days of the reminders. We may add that, at the end, altogether 1,104 usable responses were obtained. Detailed information can be found in *Case study on working conditions in Slovenian science*, Supplement to Chapter 1 (http://websm.org/ch1).

In addition, web surveys in general – but still not always – also save time for respondents. The gains occur in comparison with many F2F (e.g. Heerwegh & Loosveldt, 2008) and telephone interviews (e.g. Lindhjem & Navrud, 2011), and also with self-administered P&P questionnaires (e.g. Hertel, Naumann, Konradt, & Batinic, 2002). It appears that, for experienced users, taking surveys using a keyboard, mouse and computer screen makes answering a web questionnaire much easier and quicker than writing responses by hand or giving their answers to an interviewer who then records them. However, savings in time for questionnaire completion may also indicate that respondents pay less attention to the survey questions, which may result in a lower level of data quality.

To summarize, web surveys are typically faster than traditional survey modes, especially when email invitations are used, which is a salient (i.e. of high interest) point for time-sensitive studies, such as political polls of voting intentions. We nevertheless provide three critical comments:

- As with costs, we should not forget that speed is just one aspect of data quality. Sometimes it is essential, but it can also be entirely unimportant and even damaging, being outweighed by some other deficiencies.
- We should warn about the observational and quasi-experimental nature of the above-mentioned research evidence. Let us consider an experiment where, say, email and (mobile/fixed) telephone contact information is equally available for the entire sample of the general population, and where we compare web surveys with email invitations and telephone surveys with a correspondingly

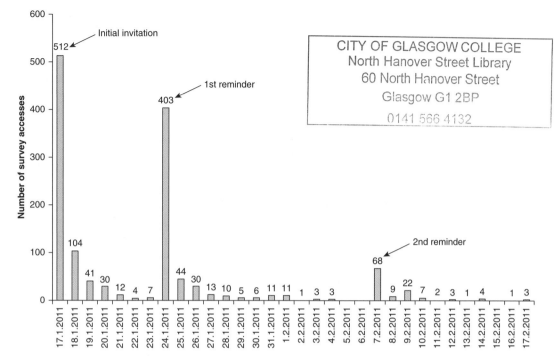

Figure 1.2 Access to the web questionnaire for the WCSC survey, 2011

tailored calling strategy. Will the responses in the web survey be collected faster? Perhaps they will be, but the response rates might be substantially lower (e.g. 10% vs 40%), which may be essential for the study.

• We have discussed above only the speed advantage of the questionnaire completion stage (fielding step), though many more important advantages of web surveys can appear in survey preparation (pre-fielding) and with instant access to the results (post-fielding).

1.3.5.3 Ease of Implementation

Today, web survey software increasingly enables convenient user-friendly data collection and in a similar way it also integrates various other stages of the web survey process. As a consequence, researchers with no programming skills and even with limited computer literacy are now able to implement a (web) survey. Together with simplified access to potential respondents on the Internet, this makes the ease of implementing web surveys superior to traditional survey modes and also to other CAI modes. This holds true not only for simple surveys and the DIY segment, but also for complex web surveys with advanced questionnaires, complex implementation and rigorous methodology. There, of course, the entire survey process remains very complex, requiring teams with various skills (programmers, sampling experts, etc.), but to a much lesser extent than traditional survey modes.

We should not underestimate the problems related to the initial adaptation and launch of a web survey system as an integrated data collection service in a dedicated survey organization. However, from all viewpoints this is still much easier than the introduction of complex systems for telephone, F2F or mail surveys.

Ease of implementation is perhaps one of the rarer characteristics of web surveys, which presents almost an absolute advantage, at least for computer-literate researchers. It cannot disappear in any circumstances nor can it be outweighed by other aspects.

1.3.5.4 Computerization of the Questionnaire

Web surveys belong to CASIC with its numerous features which stimulate higher data quality than P&P modes (de Leeuw, Hox, & Snijkers, 1995). To list some examples: branching errors (e.g. errors in question order, skips, loops) can be prevented; data can be validated immediately (range, consistency, nonresponse validations, etc.); questions and/or answers can be randomized to eliminate question order effects; adaptive questionnaires (assigning earlier answers of the participant) are enabled; randomization of questionnaires, questionnaire modules for participants is easily achievable; and there is no separate data entry phase and consequently there are no mistakes in data recording.

In addition, time stamps of every respondent's action (e.g. access to the questionnaire web page) and other data on the survey process (see Section 2.4) allow recovery from eventual system failures, and enable better management of the survey process.

Of course, computerized questionnaires need to be properly programmed. There are ample anecdotal reports of lost or mixed-up data due to errors in programming. However, besides these, proper (optimal) methodological tailoring of the questionnaire to the web survey mode (and CSAQ in general) is also required. For example, from the methodological point of view a researcher should be careful in programming hard prompts for validations (i.e. the respondent cannot continue until the question is answered), as this may damage the quality of data in various other ways. Another example of an inadequate methodological approach is the use of unequal spacing in each response option in tables (this may happen in some web survey software), which leads to measurement error. See Section 2.3.1 for more details on these issues.

The other precondition for a web survey (and any CSAQ) to achieve higher data quality is its acceptance by respondents. Generally, respondents like CSAQ (e.g. Beckenbach, 1995).

Computerization of the questionnaire typically also reduces the respondents' burden, especially because automated branching is involved. In addition, the questionnaire may allow respondents to leave it and resume at a later time precisely where they had left off. On the other hand, in the case of computer literacy problems (Olson, Smyth, Wang, & Pearson, 2011), unpredictable errors may occur.

To summarize, computerized questionnaires in principle increase data quality and the satisfaction of respondents. However, this holds only when the questionnaire is designed to be respondent-friendly, free from programming errors and based on sound methodological principles. We discuss the design of web questionnaires further in Section 2.3.

1.3.5.5 Multimedia

In addition to the above general benefits of computerized questionnaires, which typically relate to the questionnaire response process, multimedia capabilities deserve separate attention, since they enable extended and innovative interfaces for web survey questionnaires (and CASIC in general). Different visual and audio stimuli – background and font colours and types, innovative question displays and particularly various embedded programs (e.g. animations, soundtracks, video clips, virtual interviewers, etc.), a personalized approach, three-dimensional pictures of products and other advanced design features – can extend the scope and nature of survey questions. Various types of questions can now be asked remotely (e.g. evaluation of a video clip) and can replace 'real' physical stimuli (i.e. show card or actual product in F2F surveys) used in product and advertising testing (e.g. differentiation of brands, logos, company names). In addition, these can make surveys much more appealing for respondents and motivate them to participate. However, various warnings can be given here:

- One problem is the compatibility of respondents' equipment, its graphical resolutions and required download times. Respondents may become frustrated if they have to wait too long for extraneous features to load, or they may not even be able to access the questionnaire or see parts of it because their software does not support these features. For this reason, researchers should use only verified techniques in web surveys. A study by Dillman, Tortora, Conradt, & Bowker (1998) comparing a fancy and a plain web questionnaire design found that the plain one obtained a higher response rate, was more likely to be fully completed, and took respondents less time to complete. Fortunately, due to the development of ICT infrastructure and software, these technical issues are becoming less and less of a problem, particularly when a standard desktop or laptop and high-speed Internet connection (which is becoming a standard in developed countries) are used. However, this currently remains an important issue when small handheld devices, such as smartphones or tablets, are used for answering web questionnaires (Callegaro, 2010; see also Section 5.1 for more information).

- Another concern is how these features affect results, because graphical images may unpredictably affect respondents' answers (see Section 2.3.3). Therefore, caution should be used when choosing multimedia features to motivate respondents or to illustrate questions, since unpredictable effects may occur. A basic guideline is to use these features only when they are essential.
- In an extreme case, the survey instrument can become more like a game than a questionnaire. We discuss these issues further in Section 2.3.4.

1.3.5.6 Time and Geographic Flexibility

Time and geographic flexibility are very obvious advantages of web surveys. They are apparent when web surveys (or web survey software services) are praised with claims like 24/7 data collection, independence of time zone, no geographic limitations, instant access to the web questionnaire from any place in the world.

We can add here the benefits for international surveys and comparative research. The questionnaire can be programmed and tested in the reference language at a central location, taking care of all the branching, validations and other features of CSAQ, including visual design. The translated questions and text of error messages, navigation buttons and other system messages can be added separately. These all result in considerable time and cost savings and, very importantly, in fewer errors.

Web surveys also allow for easy access to special and low-incidence populations at lower costs. Other survey modes require expensive screening of large populations and of ones that are widely dispersed geographically, a factor that for F2F or mail surveys often prevents collection of any data.

On the other hand, the lack of geographic boundaries can be a drawback when a survey of a population within a specific region or country is of interest. In web surveys, it is harder (although not impossible)[5] to impose geographic restrictions. In addition, when we expect (and want) respondents from different regions, additional efforts for providing language options and proper translation of the questionnaire and system messages are needed.

1.3.5.7 Self-administration

As with all self-administered surveys, web surveys are convenient for respondents because they can answer the survey at their own pace, whenever and from wherever they choose. No scheduled telephone or F2F appointments are required. In some cases (depending on the questionnaire design) respondents even have the capability to navigate the questionnaire in its entirety, in a manner comparable with flipping through the pages of a P&P questionnaire. They may be able to scroll forwards and backwards to correct responses at any time. If sufficiently motivated, respondents can take the time to seek out records and documents for accurate completion of the questionnaire (Callegaro & Wells, 2008). This is especially important for business surveys where the respondent might need to look up answers in a file or consult someone who knows the answers, or where the respondent may experience workplace interruptions. If programmed, the questionnaire can allow respondents to answer it partially, stop and then return to it at a later time.

The lack of a human interviewer can be an advantage because interviewers may introduce specific bias and/or interviewer's variance. In an interviewer-administered survey, the interviewer's mood, prejudices and attitudes can be reflected in the data. Since web surveys have no interviewers, responses are free from potential errors of this nature. Correspondingly, better data quality regarding sensitive topics can be obtained. Web respondents may have a greater sense of privacy when answering the questionnaire, thus potentially giving answers that are less socially desirable. Several studies have shown that less socially desirable answers are obtained more often via web surveys compared with P&P questionnaires (e.g. Booth-Kewley, Larson, & Miyoshi, 2007; Joinson, 1999), telephone surveys (Chang & Krosnick, 2009; Kreuter, Presser, & Tourangeau, 2008; Lozar Manfreda, Couper, Vohar, Rivas, & Vehovar, 2002), IVRs (e.g. Kreuter et al., 2008) and F2F (e.g. Heerwegh, 2009). In addition, it is possible to explore delicate subjects online – which are considered difficult to measure offline – such as alcohol and drug use (e.g. McCabe, 2004; McCabe, Boyd, Couper, Crawford, & D'Arcy, 2002), health risk behaviour (e.g. Crutzen & Göritz, 2010) or sexual behaviour (e.g. Ross, Månsson, Daneback, Cooper, & Tikkanen, 2005). The range of social desirability bias in web surveys also depends on the level of perceived anonymity or the personalization of the correspondence with respondents. For example, Joinson (1999) found more socially desirable answers in a non-anonymous survey compared with an anonymous one, and Heerwegh & Loosveldt (2007) found more socially desirable answers in a web survey where personalized correspondence with respondents was used in comparison with one that was not personalized.

On the other hand, the lack of human contact in web surveys may also have some negative effects on data quality. Severe self-selection bias can occur, or respondents may need clarification or may not be motivated enough to participate or to complete an entire questionnaire without interaction with another person. A meta-analysis of response rates in web compared with other survey modes actually showed that response rates in web surveys are lower than in interviewer-administered surveys (Lozar Manfreda, Bosnjak, Berzelak, Haas, & Vehovar, 2008). Also, web respondents may be simultaneously involved in other activities (e.g. multitasking on the web or in offline activities) that disturb their concentration when answering the web questionnaire. Furthermore, probing is not possible as in a F2F or telephone context; this can be particularly problematic for questions with multiple responses (e.g. Smyth, Christian, & Dillman, 2008), for open-ended questions and for general omissions (e.g. Heerwegh, 2009; Roster, Rogers, Albaum, & Klein, 2004; Stephenson & Crête, 2011). Due to the unobserved process of data collection, it is also not known whether respondents understand and follow the given instructions. In addition, environmental factors such as heat, noise and the respondent's mood, fatigue level or substance consumption are also not under a researchers' control. Although this is true also for other survey modes, in some cases, such as in F2F interviews, the environmental factors can at least be measured. Also absent is contextual information, such as facial expressions, body language, tone of voice, clothing, etc., that might be of added value.

Lastly, many survey organizations are moving to mixed-mode data collection for very long questionnaires (one hour or more of an interview in CATI or CAPI), but there is insufficient literature at this stage to know the effects of mixed-mode data collection on drop-out rates and response rates. In other words, can web surveys replace an interviewer-administered hour-long survey and still collect data of the same quality? The typical recommended length for web surveys is sometimes reported as 20 minutes, similar to telephone interviews (Macer & Wilson, 2013), and which is also the length used in probability-based online panels (e.g. Gesis Internet panel, LISS panel). See also the discussion in Section 5.2.

Further, self-administration can be a drawback due to inexperienced Internet users and users with special needs, who may encounter problems when answering web questionnaires, for example deaf people with specific reading comprehension problems (Fontaine, Jacquemain, & Italiano, 2013), or people with Down's or Williams' syndrome (Marcell & Falls, 2001). Completing the questionnaire using a computer can thus be problematic for some people, such as the physically (e.g. blind) challenged, but also older or less experienced users, due to difficulties in hand–eye coordination in terms of using the keyboard and mouse along with viewing the monitor. Therefore, while computer questionnaires may appear to provide more objectivity than P&P questionnaires, for some people they can be frustrating and can negatively influence their decision to participate (Couper, Tourangeau & Smith, 1998, p. 435).

1.3.6 Applications of Web Surveys

We present the most typical examples of contemporary use of web surveys, together with an explicit description of the related type of sampling. This can help clarify the relationship between the survey mode and the characteristics of sampling. In addition, these examples contribute to a better understanding of the following chapters (2, 3 and 4), because we discuss practical illustrations of many essential methodological dilemmas.

We discuss applications of web surveys within eight typical segments, which we identified according to their general appeal and recognition. The 'classification' thus lacks clear underlying dimensions and formal criteria. Instead, it is a mixture of several overlapping characteristics of web surveys that appear in the implementation. Besides the type of sampling, these other criteria relate to the types of respondents, researchers and clients (sponsors), but also to the survey topic and methodological specifics.

1.3.6.1 Web Surveys of Highly Covered Specific Populations

Web surveys work very well when specific target populations are (almost) entirely connected to the Internet and there exists a sampling frame with contact information (preferably an email address) for the entire population. In such a case, it is easy to draw a sample or to send an email invitation to everyone (census). In either case we have potentially a high-quality probability list-based web survey.

There are several examples of such surveys. One such example is organizational surveys, which take advantage of the fact that employees/ members of many organizations and associations are reachable online. The best example of this is a web survey of company employees (e.g. a human resources survey) where each worker has a company-issued email. In this case, the company itself or an external provider can draw a sample of email addresses and invite the employees to participate in the survey. Often a census approach is used here. With this type of survey, it is considered best practice to promote the survey strongly and encourage a 100% response rate, so reporting can be done at a very fine level of detail, for example at lower managerial levels.

Another typical example is a web survey of university students (i.e. student survey). This seems like an ideal population for web surveys (due to complete Internet and email coverage), but problems are often encountered. One is the inaccuracy of student contact information in the registrar's office. This is often not up to date due to the nature of the student population, whose mail and (multiple) email addresses and telephone numbers frequently change. Although this problem has been dealt with in different ways, one solution has been to require that students use a university-issued email account that needs to be checked regularly. Another issue that arises in student web surveys relates to confidentiality.

Because the university collects students' contact information for its own purposes, it is not always permitted to use it (or pass it on) to individual (academic) researchers.

The third example relates to members of certain (e.g. professional) associations, which are generally reachable via email. However, in addition to the problem of recorded emails (which may be wrong or not updated), sometimes members join an association without providing any email address. In this case – if the whole population is targeted – some or all members should be surveyed in another mode, for example by mail.

1.3.6.2 Customer Satisfaction Surveys

We treat customer satisfaction web surveys independently, although they can also be considered as another type of web survey of highly covered (Internet) populations. Here, we deal with a special case of the target population (i.e. the customer list as the sampling frame) and with very specific content (i.e. customer satisfaction). Customer satisfaction surveys (collecting data on satisfaction, loyalty, engagement) – often as part of the voice of customer activities – are frequently used by companies to collect feedback, and web surveys provide an efficient (much faster) and low-cost alternative to telephone, mail and IVR customer satisfaction surveys. Typically, these surveys are highly standardized, often of huge volume, and are integrated into the broader information systems of companies (e.g. customer relationship management, sales support system, enterprise resource planning). Sometimes this is treated in the context of an *enterprise feedback management* (EFM) system. Customer satisfaction surveys are perhaps the most common survey experience to which any person is exposed. For an introduction to these types of surveys the reader can consult Hayes (2008) and Roman (2011), and, for a discussion on the timing of the measurement and measurement errors, Dillman, Smyth, & Christian (2009, p. 353).

There are two kinds of customer satisfaction surveys: transactional and tracking. For transactional surveys, an invitation (ideally, by email or SMS) is sent soon after a transaction (related to a purchase or a service) with the company has been performed. The main advantage of web surveys in this case is that the feedback used to improve the quality of the transaction is immediate. Tracking satisfaction surveys – usually longer than transactional ones – are used as a kind of 'pulse taking' of the population of customers. They are generally sent to a sample of the entire customer base and focus on overall satisfaction with the company, its products or its services. Recently, the concept of loyalty has been measured more often than satisfaction. To monitor the level of satisfaction/loyalty, companies can repeat the survey, using either a cross-sectional or a longitudinal design. In both cases, customers receive an email invitation with a link to a web survey. Lately, especially in the United States, we have seen more and more instances of the use of HTML-based email surveys for this purpose.

Among the key advantages of web surveys for customer satisfaction research is the speed, which offers the possibility of immediate customer feedback. Additionally, the cost savings in comparison with offline methods are substantial. However, the greatest advantage lies in the availability of the sampling frame. The list of customers (in an ideal case this would include emails) can be considered a panel, and regular email invitations to web surveys can be sent. Other existing customer data can be matched to individual responses for further analysis and segmentation (if legal and ethical issues are settled).

Careful monitoring of the share of customers who have not provided email addresses is very important when generalizing the results to the entire population of customers. If this share is large and some evidence exists that the customers covered may be different from non-covered ones, the company or service provider should consider moving to mixed-mode surveys or conduct additional non-coverage error studies to estimate the amount of bias.

We may add here that companies often build so-called proprietary panels where their own customers are regularly included in research, and also by participation in online community panels (see Section 5.2).

1.3.6.3 General Population Surveys

The increase in Internet penetration generates some optimism that web surveys can replace other data collection modes for probability surveys of the general population (Smyth & Pearson, 2011). This is, however, still not the case, even though the percentage of the population with Internet access has been increasing (in 2013, it had risen above 75% in both Europe and the United States, and has reached 90% in some countries).

Another related issue is that Internet users and non-users are not randomly distributed in terms of socio-demographic characteristics and lifestyle. The difference in speed of access and broadband vs dial-up is also a factor in many countries, which has led to discussions about a second form of digital divide, namely fast vs slow Internet connection or the 'adoption gap' (Economic and Statistics Administration & National Telecommunications and Information Administration, 2010).

In addition to the serious potential for non-coverage error, the absence of a readily available sampling frame of email addresses (which would be the most effective means of contacting the general population) is another major problem for these surveys. Email addresses are not as structured as telephone numbers, so it is not possible to generate randomly a meaningful list of email addresses for a specific country, as is the case with telephone numbers for RDD. Thus, standard and expensive recruitment is still needed here (e.g. mail, telephone or F2F invitation).

The third issue concerns ethics and country-specific regulations that prevent contact with a potential respondent using an email address unless a prior relationship exists (e.g. CASRO, 2011). Contacting someone via email without prior consent or some sort of relationship is otherwise akin to an unsolicited personal visit by the interviewer, sending a letter with the questionnaire in the mail, or a 'cold call' for RDD telephone samples, where an interviewer calls a household without any previous contact. Interestingly, these unsolicited non-Internet contact strategies are usually not restricted by any regulations, which is not the case for email invitations. The reason for this apparent inconsistency lies perhaps in the fact that email invitations cost nothing (much different to mail, telephone or F2F) and could potentially generate an extreme volume of invitations to web surveys, which is then closely related to spam problems.

The above problems do not totally preclude the general population from being surveyed via the web. Such surveys can be built in a mixed-mode fashion. Most often, a mail invitation to a sample from the general population is used, giving an initial option of answering the web questionnaire for any respondent willing and able to do so. A P&P questionnaire is then offered to nonrespondents in the reminder. This strategy is being used more and more frequently in the United States, for example as a way to avoid non-coverage error due to mobile-phone-only households in telephone surveys (e.g. Smyth, Dillman, Christian, & O'Neill, 2010), or in Scandinavian countries with high Internet penetration where this strategy works well for salient topics (e.g. Gelder, Bretveld, & Roeleveld, 2010).

Another strategy for surveying the general population is to use probability online panels. Here, participants are invited to join a panel via another survey mode (e.g. mail, telephone or F2F) based on a probability sample of households. The non-Internet households are given a device (e.g. desktop/laptop/notebook, smartphone or tablet) and an Internet connection in order to answer surveys by the panel organization on a regular basis. Examples are the Longitudinal Internet Studies for the Social sciences (LISS) panel in the Netherlands (Scherpenzeel, 2011), the Étude Longitudinal par Internet Pour les Sciences Sociales (ELIPSS) panel in France (Lesnard, 2011), the German Internet Panel in Germany (Blom, Gathmann, & Krieger, 2013) and the GfK (Knowledge Network) panel in the United States (Callegaro & DiSogra, 2008). Another option is the mixed-mode approach where non-Internet households are surveyed in another mode (e.g. mail or telephone). Examples of such panels are the Gesis panel in Germany (Bosnjak, Haas, Galesic, Kaczmirek, Bandilla & Couper, 2013) and the Gallup panel in the United States (Rao, Kaminska, & McCutcheon, 2010).

Note that, recently, several research-coordinated initiatives have been raised to emphasize the importance and study the feasibility of web surveys for surveying the general population (e.g. the GenPopWeb project[6] and WebDataNet Cost Action IS1004[7]).

1.3.6.4 Business Surveys

Business or establishment surveys (Snijkers, Araldsen, Jones, & Willimack, 2013) are usually very different in nature from surveys of individuals in households or in organizations. In business surveys, the information collected rarely concerns respondents themselves, but rather their employers or their company. In other words, the respondent acts as a *proxy*. In addition, business surveys rarely ask about attitudes but rather focus on factual questions with definite answers. The originator of the survey request is also different. It usually comes from a statistical agency, a federal agency or a financial institution, but also from marketing research agencies and other businesses.

For business web surveys we usually have good sampling frames, at least mail addresses, which in principle enable probability sample selection. Email invitations are of course beneficial, but they also involve many complexities (accuracy of address, within-company forwarding of the request, etc.), thus mail invitations are still often used.

Several peculiarities of web business surveys – one is the use of the term *form* among practitioners instead of questionnaire – should be kept in mind when designing the measurement instrument. The process of answering a business survey (regardless of whether it is online or offline) is different from that of a personal survey (Snijkers & Morren, 2010), resulting in different measurement errors

(Bavdaž, 2010). For example, there is generally a formal approval process from persons authorized to release the survey information to the data collection agency (S. W. Edwards & Cantor, 1991). Very often a paper copy of the questionnaire is used together with the web questionnaire as a rough draft before entering the data into the online questionnaire. Unique to web business surveys is the fact that more than one respondent is often required since it is very unlikely that one person knows all the answers or has access to all the sources necessary to formulate the answers. For this reason an easy login mechanism should be provided, enabling different respondents to access the survey. In addition, with business surveys there can be many sessions; therefore, having a function to save the entered data at any point in time will simplify the respondents' tasks. For the reasons mentioned earlier, sending the survey questionnaire as a PDF, MS Word or Excel file attached to an email invitation is one option to be considered. Since these questionnaires (forms) are generally not filled in sequentially, it is also important to design the web questionnaire to allow easy navigation among the different sections. Furthermore, the ability to print the questionnaire with the data already entered will simplify the task of retrieving information from multiple sources. Business surveys generally ask for a lot of quantitative data; thus, online data validations and prompts, such as constant sums or consistency checks against data entered in previous questions or even in previous surveys, should be provided to assist the respondents and, at the same time, collect data of better quality. Lastly, for many businesses security is of the utmost importance, so measures need to be taken when designing the survey that will ensure secure transmission of the data, which may contain confidential and/or proprietary information (Snijkers & Morren, 2010).

Snijkers & Morren (2010) provide an example of how a typical business survey was completed. Using data from the Annual Dutch Structural Business Survey, they were able to measure how businesses completed the survey. It took, on average, one hour and seven minutes to complete, but it was open for about eight days. In all, 43% of respondents printed the survey during the process, 29% saved information and 65% used the backward function of the instrument. On average, 270 actions were performed during the sessions. These data show that designing and answering a business survey is much more complex than other types of web surveys. In fact, the business survey is perhaps the most complex web survey to administer because it needs to follow all the rules for web surveys, plus the specifics that we delineated above, as well as internal organizational rules. To make matters even more complicated, all these features and specifications are generally not common to standard web survey software (see Section 5.3); thus, survey organizations often need to build in-house systems to deal with these specific demands. For example, the US Census Bureau has been using an in-house system called Census Taker, more recently called Centurion, to collect business survey data (Morrison, Dillman, & Christian, 2010).

1.3.6.5 Online Panels

Web surveys using individuals from online panels are the most frequently used types of web surveys in marketing research (Macer & Wilson, 2013). We provide only a short introduction to online panels here, which, however, deserve much more attention because of the high frequency and revenues, and the huge potential for future survey research. We thus present in a special section of this book (Section 5.2) a more detailed discussion on the types of online panels, building and maintaining them, implementing individual surveys from them, and data quality from such surveys.

There are basically two types of online panels, probability and non-probability ones. The probability panels are pre-recruited by mail, F2F or telephone from representative samples of households or individuals. To overcome the non-coverage problem of the general population, the non-Internet households are offered a device and Internet connection in exchange for participation in surveys on a regular basis, or they are surveyed in another mode (e.g. by telephone or mail). These panels are a tool to survey the general population via web surveys (see the above discussion on general population surveys). However, they are relatively rare due to the high costs involved in establishing and maintaining the panels.

The non-probability online panels (also called volunteer, opt-in or access panels) are much more common, much larger and of very different quality than probability online panels. Individuals join a panel on a voluntary basis and usually receive incentives for their participation. Although incentives are used by some probability online panels too, in non-probability ones they are almost a must. These panels represent large pools of participants to sample for marketing research and public opinion polls and allow access to very specific (rare) groups of individuals. Quota sampling and weighting techniques are used in these cases to mimic representativeness.

1.3.6.6 Online Community Surveys

Online communities have attracted much attention from social scientists over the last two decades. From the early beginning of the BBS in the late 1980s, through discussion boards and web forums in the 1990s and virtual environments (e.g. Second Life) in the 2000s, to the recent diffusion of social networks sites, researchers have explored the social, psychological and cultural aspects of these communities. Several research approaches have been used for this purpose, for example virtual ethnography, data mining with 'big data', and social network analysis (Preece & Maloney-Krichmar, 2005), but web surveys seem to be a frequently used approach as well. Using a web survey to study online communities is often very convenient since the target population – participants in online communities – can easily be contacted when they visit the website(s) of these communities or, when available, via lists of registered users. Different recruitment and sampling strategies for surveying online community participants have been developed. The most common ones use a pop-up window or a banner ad with an invitation to the survey on various targeted websites, but also posts (messages) with an invitation to the survey (e.g. in forums), or advertising with an invitation to the survey published on the wall of the social network site of interest. Usually, these are all examples of non-probability, non-list-based web surveys. In virtual worlds (e.g. Second Life) additional specifics may arise, where responding units (i.e. avatars) need first to be virtually approached and then 'attacked' with an invitation to the survey (Hill & Dean, 2009). On the other hand, owners of online communities may also use email invitations for registered website users, thus affording a probability list-based web survey. Similarly, certain types of pop-up invitations or banner ads may also provide probability sample selection (i.e. intercept surveys).

Drawing on the conceptual framework introduced by Preece (2001), two groups of studies of online communities can be distinguished. The first deals with the sociability dimension, which, according to Preece, refers to software, policies and practices to support social interaction online (p. 349). Consequently, these studies of online communities attempt to understand what people do in online spaces, how they express themselves and what motivates them, how they govern themselves, why some people prefer to observe rather than contribute, etc. (Preece & Maloney-Krichmar, 2005). The second group is concerned with the various facets of online community usability (user experience or UX). While sociability deals with how members of a community interact with each other via the supporting technology (in our case the Internet), the usability of communities is primarily concerned with how users interact with technology itself (Preece, 2001, p. 349). Usability of online communities is thus concerned with how intuitive and easy it is for individuals to learn to use and interact with the online technology supporting the community. Of course, in addition to these two specific topics, online community web surveys can also be used for any other general issues.

One of the most cited studies of online communities using a web survey is the Andrews, Nonnecke, & Preece (2003) study, which examined lurkers in asynchronous online communities. Among the increasing number of recent studies on social networking sites, we may mention Chou (2012) who studied the integration of Facebook as a class website using a web survey of students, and Woolley & Peterson (2012) who used a web survey to study the impact of a health-related Facebook fan page on health-seeking actions, thoughts and behaviours.

1.3.6.7 Website Evaluations

In website evaluations the aim is to measure visitors' or members' characteristics that are of interest to website owners or to advertisers, such as socio-demographic background, products/services usage and lifestyle choices. Such evaluations are sometimes integrated with website visitation measurement or web analytics, which provides industry standards for websites' reach. Visitation measurement is usually done with automatic technical approaches via code at the whole website involved in the measurement. The results can then be matched with a web survey, which provides insight into the profile of the visitors. Of course, serious legislation and confidentiality issues arise here: Would respondents allow matching web survey responses with data about the websites visited? Are they sufficiently informed about this? On the other hand, needless to say, such matched data are very valuable when advertisers make decisions about buying advertising space.

Recent examples of website evaluation surveys are those by Elling, Lentz, de Jong, & van den Bergh (2012) who used a standardized website evaluation questionnaire to evaluate governmental websites and, similarly, by Witt, Rowland, & Wilkinson (2012) who used a web survey to examine the views and needs of users of a charity website.

The focus here lies mostly on usability and diagnostic information on website usage (e.g. website-specific questions about how users use and rate particular pages or functions, and how they understand the main functional uses of the website). These websites sometimes use usability tests with split screens where the respondent answers a web questionnaire in one screen, while in the other screen the corresponding web pages of the evaluated website appear (navigated and synchronized with the web survey running on the other screen). Special survey instruments, such as Software Usability Measurement Inventory or SUMI (Kirakowski & Corbett, 1993), Web Analysis and MeasureMent Inventory or WAMMI (Kirakowski, Claridge, & Whitehand, 1998), System Usability Scale or SUS (Brooke, 1996), have been developed for this purpose.

1.3.6.8 Entertainment Polls, Questionnaires and Quizzes

There is little to be said about the methodological aspects of these surveys, except that they seek interaction and provide feedback and potentially interesting or entertaining results. Sometimes they may provide useful insight; however, very often they have no substantive or scientific value, nor can the results be generalized to the entire population. Commonly found on news websites, these types of surveys are used so frequently that they have sometimes become the lay population's notion (perception) of what web surveys are. Unfortunately, this mistaken belief sullies the reputation of legitimate web surveys, especially as the quality of the question wording and format in this case is low, as shown by an analysis of journalistic websites in Slovenia (Ličen, Lozar Manfreda, & Hlebec, 2006).

1.3.7 Related Practices of Web Surveys

Administrative forms, Internet testing and online psychological experiments share a lot of commonalities with web surveys. Web survey practitioners can learn a lot from these related practices and, the opposite, several principles of web surveys are useful for these related practices too. We are going to present some of them here.

1.3.7.1 Administrative Forms on the Web

An administrative form on the web is formally not a survey because it does not serve the purpose of describing the population observed. (Refer to our definition of a survey in Section 1.1.1.) Rather, it requests information to be used for some administrative processes. Examples of administrative forms are manifold: employment applications, event registrations, orders or purchase forms, loan applications, tax forms, reservation forms, etc. In some countries, web forms are also used for electronic voting (Herrnson, Niemi, Hanmer, Bederson, Conrad & Traugott, 2008). All these administrative web forms often pose issues similar to those of web surveys in terms of usability and various questionnaire layout aspects.

Sometimes the line between an administrative web form and a web survey is blurred, particularly because the terminology is often unclear. We initially used the notion of a form in the context of a web form being a special type of web page enabling some input from the respondent (Section 1.3.1). However, the notion of a web form often – especially in the usability profession (see Jarrett, Gaffney, & Krug, 2009) – includes short (typically one-page) web surveys. Similarly, in the context of web survey software a form typically denotes a short one-page survey (e.g. event evaluation). To increase confusion, we already mentioned that with business surveys the term form is routinely used instead of the term questionnaire.

1.3.7.2 Internet Testing

Educational and psychological instruments for testing and assessment use questionnaires mostly with closed-ended questions to be answered by individuals and have procedures very similar to those of surveys. Testing was traditionally administered using P&P questionnaires until about a decade ago when the Task Force on Psychological Testing over the Internet (Naglieri, Drasgow, Schmit, Handler, Prifitera, Margolis & Velasquez, 2004) realized the fundamental cost difference between P&P and Internet testing. The latter is scalable in the sense that 'adding volume results in very little additional cost' (p. 151). Another advantage of Internet testing is the decentralization of the test-taking experience enabled by the Internet.

Web testing serves specific administrative purposes (e.g. job hiring, student enrolment, carrier counselling, team building, etc.) instead of population inferences as in web surveys. Still, there is considerable methodological overlap, especially in the possible modes of administration, questionnaire design and confidentiality issues.

There are four possible modes of test administration over the Internet (Bartram, 2006), which also have parallels with the implementation specifics of web surveys:

Unproctored tests of two types:

- Open mode: tests can be accessed by anyone over the Internet, and there is no verification of the identity of the test taker, nor is there human supervision.
- Controlled mode: the test taker is provided with a login and a password, but there is no human supervision.

Proctored tests of two types:

- Supervised mode: a level of human supervision is assumed, although not necessarily in person (i.e. can be remote). A test administrator or proctor logs in the candidates and verifies that the test was completed, together with ensuring that test materials are kept secure.
- Managed mode: generally entails the use of physical test centres where there is control on the identity of the candidates and proctoring during the test to prevent cheating. The computers in these centres run special software that blocks any feature that could facilitate cheating, such as opening new browser windows to utilize a search engine, saving or printing the test contents, and/or communicating with persons outside the testing centre.

The most common testing on the web runs as unproctored controlled mode type, known also as Unproctored Internet Testing (UIT) (Tippins, Beaty, Drasgow, Gibson, Pearlman, Segall, & Shepherd, 2006), for example for hiring new personnel. According to recent overviews (Beaty, Dawson, Fallaw, & Kantrowitz, 2009), UIT is used for this purpose by two-thirds of employers. It has the advantage of being a cost-effective solution for testing a large number of widely dispersed candidates, providing more consistency in administration, scoring and recording compared with many employment offices. UIT also allows candidates who cannot get to an employment office during business hours to take the test in their own time. The entire hiring process can therefore go much faster. The main disadvantage of UIT is its susceptibility to specific cheating – in the form of assistance from others who previously took the test or from others during the test, substitution of test takers and alteration of test scores in the database (Tippins, 2009). We may add that cheating is possible and occurs during proctored testing as well (Drasgow, Nye, Guo, & Tay, 2009).

Various approaches to mitigate or prevent cheating in UIT have been developed: the use of remote cameras, the test taker's webcam, keystroke analysis, browser lockdown, statistical detection and a two-step process, by which a second battery of questions is administered in a proctored way for the candidates who passed the first test. These can all be used also for web surveys where there is evidence or fear that respondents might use fake identities.

The literature on online testing warns a researcher about another issue that might arise when taking an online test (and is relevant for web surveys too): distractions. Best practice in test taking suggests creating an environment that facilitates good performance on the test because distractions and interruptions can profoundly affect performance (Tippins, 2009). To draw parallels with web surveys, multitasking on the web can create distractions and interruptions that affect the performance of web survey respondents as well.

To conclude, the guidelines from The International Test Commission (2006) and the special issue of the *Journal of Industrial and Organizational Psychology* (Sackett, 2009) are good starting points to examine all the issues in computerized Internet testing which might be relevant to web survey practitioners too.

1.3.7.3 Psychological Web Experiments

Psychological web experiments are the natural extension of computer laboratory psychological experiments (Reips, 2002b). Participants access an online computer laboratory (practically a web server) via a web browser and interact with the experiment in the same way as they would in a laboratory, using a monitor, mouse and keyboard. Different from web surveys, where the aim is to infer characteristics of the target population, the purpose here is only a specific study of causality.

Web experiments have grown in popularity in the past few years (Reips, 2007). One reason for this newfound popularity is that they can be far more efficient than traditional laboratory experiments (Reips & Krantz, 2010). Web experiments can test a large number of subjects very quickly and it is possible to recruit a large sample with heterogeneous characteristics and, in many cases, rare populations. They are also cost-effective in terms of time, space and labour (Reips & Birnbaum, 2011).

There are literally hundreds of sites where a participant can enrol in an online psychological experiment, for example the website Psychological Research on the Net, which is maintained by Hanover College's Psychology Department[8] and the Web Experiment List[9] (Reips & Lengler, 2005), produced by the University of Deusto. Little software for web experiments exists (Reips & Birnbaum, 2011) and, among what there is, little of it is freely available (Reips, 2007). We can add that standard web survey software (see Section 5.3) increasingly supports features such as randomization or time stamps, thus enabling web experiments to be handled too.

Well-known authors on this topic suggest that – compared with laboratory experiments – the advantages of web experiments outweigh the disadvantages (Reips, 2002a; Reips & Krantz, 2010) and that the disadvantages have solutions (Reips, 2002a). Especially if cross-fertilization were to occur across the fields of web experiments, the previously mentioned Internet testing and web surveys, knowledge in all areas could be enhanced.

NOTES

1 http://www.greenbookblog.org/grit/
2 http://www.w3.org/
3 http://www.cc.gatech.edu/gvu/user_surveys/survey-04-1995/
4 http://www.w3schools.com/browsers/browsers_stats.asp
5 Some web survey software can restrict the geography by eliminating or flagging the IP address of devices connecting from a non-eligible region.
6 http://www.natcenweb.co.uk/genpopweb/
7 http://webdatanet.cbs.dk/
8 http://psych.hanover.edu/research/exponnet.html
9 http://www.wexlist.net/

CONTENTS

Pre-fielding

The core web survey process, as defined in Section 1.2 (Figure 1.1), starts with a pre-fielding step, which involves activities specific to the preparation of web surveys. We usually start pre-fielding with decisions related to survey mode (Section 2.1), sampling (Section 2.2) and questionnaire preparation (Section 2.3). We also look at technical issues (Section 2.4), nonresponse strategy (Section 2.5) and general management (Section 2.6).

2.1 MODE ELABORATION

We have already introduced the web survey mode as the mode where a web questionnaire is part of the measurement stage (Section 1.1.1). The web survey mode can be used as a stand-alone mode or in combination with other CASIC (see Section 1.3.4) or traditional survey modes. Considerations of the survey mode need to be among the very first ones and sometimes this decision is made already during the initial request for the survey project within preliminary research activities. The decision on the survey mode can be very complex, because it involves other stages of the pre-fielding, particularly sampling and questionnaire development. We thus advise the reader, particularly novices, to return to this section after reading the entire book, because discussing the survey mode inevitably includes many of the concepts discussed later (e.g. nonresponse, non-coverage, measurement, data quality, data preparation, etc.).

We first discuss issues related to the decision for web survey mode (2.1.1) and then address the corresponding mixed-mode context (2.1.2).

2.1.1 Selecting the Web Survey Mode

The decision for the web survey mode may be very trivial, for example when we have a simple questionnaire for a closed group (e.g. members of an association) and we also have email addresses at our disposal. On the other hand, sometimes a competent decision requires

considerable knowledge and experience, as well as a profound understanding of specific survey circumstances, including the nature of the research problem.

When considering the web survey mode, the following questions can be helpful, which we present as a simple, non-exhaustive and unstructured list:

- Is a web survey suitable for surveying our target population? Can we identify and contact the target units? Do we have an appropriate list of units? Is the target population able (i.e. skilful enough) to answer a web questionnaire? Is the target population motivated enough to fill in the web questionnaire properly?
- Is the web survey mode appropriate for the topic under investigation and the type of data to be collected? Can we measure the desired concepts with this self-administered mode? Are there some privacy and confidentiality issues? Is the questionnaire short and simple enough for self-administration? Does the questionnaire require interviewer assistance, in terms of motivation, clarification or physical intervention?
- What level of survey quality is required? Do we require probability sampling? What level of nonresponse and non-coverage is expected and tolerated? Do we expect problems with nonresponse or non-coverage?
- What are the requests and limitations with respect to resources and support (infrastructure, software, personnel, administration, finances and management)? Can we afford mail invitations or only email ones? Can we afford measures for nonresponse conversion (e.g. incentives, reminders, switching modes)?
- How much time flexibility do we have?
- What are the potential legal restrictions for web-based data collection?
- What are the technical options and limitations of the available web survey software?
- Are there other aspects that affect the decision on the survey mode?

Answers to the above questions concern the dilemma of selecting the right mode in a very complex way. In Section 1.3.6 we have reviewed the different types and applications of web surveys, together with corresponding examples.

They provide a basic insight into the dilemma regarding the selection of the appropriate mode. However, for a competent decision on the mode in our survey, it is essential to review similar research projects conducted in the past and also to observe the broader methodological context (see Section 6.1).

We should make it clear that with the above set of questions we predominantly address aspects that are linked directly to the survey mode as the mode of the measurement stage (i.e. questionnaire completion). However, this is closely interwoven with the mode of contact in the recruitment stage (i.e. invitation to survey). For contacting we can use various communication channels, from online posts, banners and pop-ups with links to the questionnaire URL, to email, mail or SMS invitations and leaflets. Contacts can even be done in person, by telephone or F2F, or via public media; (i.e. print, TV, radio). Most typically, however, we use email or mail invitations and reminders when we talk about personal contacting for web surveys (Dillman & Messer, 2010; Grady, 2010; Kaplowitz, Hadlock, & Levine, 2004; Porter & Whitcomb, 2007). In order to increase coverage and cooperation, it is a common strategy to use more modes in the recruiting stage, namely combinations of communication channels. Hereafter we denote such a situation as *multimode contacting*. The decision about selecting the right mode(s) of contact depends on various factors, such as the availability of contact information from the sampling frame, and then on time, budget and other specifics, including various quality requirements, where the nonresponse issues usually play an essential role. See Sections 2.5 and 3.1 for further discussion on the mode of contact, while below we restrict the discussion predominantly to the mode of measurement.

2.1.2 Mixed-Mode Setting

Web surveys are increasingly combined with other survey modes. We first clarify the terminology here, then warn about related problems and provide an overview of the most frequent mixed-mode settings for web surveys.

2.1.2.1 Mixed-Mode Surveys, Multimode Contacting and Mixed-Mode Systems

We initially (Section 1.2) restricted our discussion to the web survey mode as a single survey mode used in independent cross-sectional surveys. We will denote this context also as a *stand-alone* web survey. However, the web survey mode can also be combined with other survey modes. Despite our predominant focus on stand-alone web surveys, due to its importance we also address here the alternative option of involving more survey modes.

When more survey modes are combined in the measurement stage, we talk about a *mixed-mode* measurement, or alternatively about mixed-mode data collection. We will hereafter denote it simply as mixed-mode and the corresponding surveys and designs as mixed-mode surveys and mixed-mode designs respectively.

We repeat that we use the notion of mixing or combining survey modes only in relation to the measurement stage (i.e. questionnaire completion) and exclude other aspects of the survey process (e.g. recruiting). Accordingly, using multimode contacting – which is related to various sequences of email, mail, telephone and other channels of communication for recruiting potential respondents into a stand-alone web survey – does not mean a mixed-mode survey, but just a stand-alone web survey with multimode contacting.

For a more general term encompassing several activities, stages, decisions and consequences related to the combinations of different modes across the recruiting and measurement stages of the survey process we follow Biemer & Lyberg's (2003, p. 208) notion of *mixed-mode systems*. This general term covers not only mixed-mode situations where more modes are used in the measurement stage, but also multimode contacts for recruiting into a stand-alone (web) survey, as well as situations when the (single) mode of contact differs from the corresponding (single) mode of data collection, such as a mail invitation to a web survey.

We thus use the term mixed-mode systems as a general umbrella term for combining modes in measurement and in recruiting, and restrict the notion of mixed-modes only to combinations of modes within the measurement stage.

2.1.2.2 Problems with Mixed-Mode Surveys

When we decide to mix modes in the measurement stage, we have to carefully consider each mode involved, its fieldwork synchronization, administration and combination. Database management, archiving, documentation and nonresponse calculation also become much more complex when more modes are involved. This increases the required resources for administrative, methodological and management tasks. Serious methodological work is particularly needed for the adaptation of advanced and potentially problematic survey questions (see Section 2.3) to various survey modes. Different modes may also introduce specific mode effects. A typical example is the *primacy* effect in the web survey mode, where respondents are inclined to select the response options from the beginning of the list, as opposed to the so-called *recency* effect in the telephone survey mode, where they are prone to selecting options from the end of the list. We also need to consider carefully the proper and comparable handling of 'don't know' options, problem of nonresponse to certain questions and various strategies for respondents who may look for quick and easy ways of responding, which we discuss in detail in Section 2.3.4.

All of this requires additional resources for elaboration and testing, otherwise the survey questions may not be equivalent across the modes. Very often, some modifications to questions are needed when switching to another mode. For example, when adapting a questionnaire for the European Value Survey from F2F to the web, Bennink, Moors, & Gelissen (2013) report that certain wording modifications were needed for

156 out of 256 questions. Similarly, the transformation of the European Social Survey from CAPI to a web questionnaire required some changes in 85% of the questions (Ainsaar et al., 2013). Despite these efforts, certain mode-specific measurement effects may remain. For example, with sensitive topics (e.g. AIDS, drugs, health; see Tourangeau & Yan, 2007), respondents may report more risk-related behaviour in the web mode than in F2F, so a proper combination is then very problematic for estimation and analysis.

Mixing modes therefore raises serious issues of data integrity (de Leeuw & Hox, 2011). Luckily, there is considerable evidence that results are often robust and perform equally well – we talk here only about measurement differences (and not about nonresponse and sampling effects) – across the different survey modes. Many studies demonstrate that web surveys perform equivalently or better compared with traditional modes in terms of validity and reliability (e.g. Börkan, 2010; Chang & Krosnick, 2010; Mangunkusumo, Duisterhout, de Graaff, Maarsingh, de Koning & Raat, 2006; Miller, Neal, Roberts, Baer, Cressler, Metrik, & Alan, 2002). However, mode differences can appear with specific combinations of question topics, formats and characteristics (Bennink et al., 2013) and are especially common with questions related to socially undesirable issues (e.g. smoking, gambling, drinking). It is thus only when there is no evidence of specific measurement effects related to some mode (i.e. mode effects) that we can safely combine and analyse data from mixed-modes (de Leeuw & Hox, 2011). Efforts towards principles of so-called *unified* (or unimode) design (Dillman et al., 2009, p. 326) may be helpful for designing questionnaires, which would be robust across different modes. Nevertheless, to assure *mode equivalence*, that is comparable results across different modes, some mode-specific adaptation and tailoring are typically required (de Leeuw & Hox, 2011).

According to all of the above problems, very good reasons must exist to undertake the challenge of combining the web survey mode within mixed-mode designs. These reasons are usually related to lower costs and faster data collection, but also to specific aspects of data quality (e.g. reducing non-coverage and nonresponse) or to specific requests for delivering incentives.

2.1.2.3 Web Surveys in Mixed-Mode Setting

General mixed-mode combinations have been discussed by various authors (e.g. Berzelak, 2014; Bethlehem & Biffignandi, 2012; de Leeuw, 2005; de Leeuw & Hox, 2011; Dillman et al., 2009; Groves et al., 2009). Below we outline the most frequent mixed-mode survey situations where the web mode is involved in the measurement stage:

- Web assigned as a parallel mode of questionnaire completion: Different modes can be used for different sample segments within the same phase of data collection. This is mostly used to reduce the coverage problem of web surveys, but to a certain extent also nonresponse. For example, one part of the target population with Internet access is assigned to the web survey and the other part to a mail survey (e.g. Rookey, Hanway, & Dillman, 2008). We also encounter this option in international surveys, where the web mode is used in countries or regions with a high Internet penetration and other modes elsewhere (e.g. Blyth, 2008; De Beuckelaer & Lievens, 2009). In the above examples, the web segment is completely separated. However, these segments and corresponding sampling frames may also overlap, as is the case with *dual frames*. For example, Internet users are contacted based on a certain sampling frame containing email addresses, while at the same time the entire target population (including Internet users) is also included in a mail survey based on a general sampling frame of mail addresses.
- Web as a self-selected parallel mode of questionnaire completion: Different modes can be used for the same phase of data collection by allowing respondents to select the preferred option, instead of the above pre-assignment by the research design. For example, a mail invitation letter with a paper questionnaire sent to potential respondents may ask them to return the attached paper questionnaire, call a toll-free number to perform a telephone interview

or complete the survey via the web. See Medway & Fulton (2012) for a web and mail combination and ORC Macro (2003) for a web and telephone combination. However, there is considerable empirical evidence that offering more options and leaving selection of the mode to respondents reduces response rates (Medway & Fulton, 2012), because it complicates the decision process. Another reason for rather pre-assigning the mode by survey design is the fact that self-selection often interferes with the characteristics of specific respondents, as well as with measurement, nonresponse and non-coverage errors.

- Sequential mixed-modes for web nonrespondents: We may sequentially assign the nonrespondents from the web survey to another mode of questionnaire completion. We use this approach predominantly to increase response rates and reduce costs. Most typically, we start with the web as the cheapest mode and then proceed with more intrusive and expensive modes, such as telephone (Dillman et al., 2009; Greene, Speizer, & Wiitala, 2008), mail (P. D. Converse, Wolfe, Huang, & Oswald, 2008; Kroth, McPherson, Leverence, Pace, Daniels, Rhyne … Prime Net Consortium, 2009; Millar & Dillman, 2011; Vehovar, Berzelak, Lozar Manfreda, & Belak, 2009), or F2F (McMorris, Petrie, Catalano, Fleming, Haggerty & Abbott, 2009). However, the apparent expectations for cost savings might fail here due to increased implementation complexities and problems with data quality.
- Web mode for nonrespondents in traditional survey modes: Here the web is a follow-up mode for nonrespondents in initial phases. The approach is used only in specific circumstances when various traditional modes are initially used, for example telephone (Greene et al., 2008), F2F (McMorris et al., 2009) or mail (P. D. Converse et al., 2008), and the nonrespondents are then invited to a web survey.
- Web mode in specific waves of data collection: When we have two or more separate parts of data collection – e.g. the waves in longitudinal studies – respondents may be surveyed at different points in time using different modes. The reasons for this are usually the costs or specific convenience of a certain mode. For example, Nigg, Motl, Wong, Yoda, McCurdy, Paxton, … Dishman

(2009) described a study where a telephone survey was used initially, while follow-up participants were given the option of completing the questionnaire on the web.

- Recruitment to (probability) online panels: A very specific, but extensively used case is recruitment for online panels, particularly probability ones. This is often done via F2F interviews, as in the LISS panel in the Netherlands (Scherpenzeel, 2011). Alternatively, mail invitation packages can be sent to households, offering respondents the option of replying to the invitation by mail, web or by calling a toll-free number, as in the GfK Knowledge Networks panel in the United States (DiSogra, Callegaro, & Hendarwan, 2010). After successful recruitment, email is then used to invite respondents to a web survey for each subsequent wave of data collection. Non-Internet households may be given an Internet device, surveyed with alternative traditional modes, or simply excluded from the sample.

While all the above options relate to mixed-mode data collection for the entire session of questionnaire completion, the web can be used for only one part of such a session:

- Web assigned to part of a data collection session: For various reasons, such as privacy or cost savings, parts of a data collection session can be conducted via an alternative mode. For example, in F2F interviews the respondents may be given the option of answering sensitive questions on the web. Similarly, some consumer satisfaction surveys can be done in part by telephone (e.g. for essential or complicated issues), while the remaining part of the data collection session is done on the web.
- Web as an option in respondent mode switching: In principle, we may offer respondents within one session the opportunity to switch deliberately between certain modes of data collection (e.g. from the web to CATI and back), within the same questionnaire. This might be rare and technologically demanding, but can be a realistic option for some complex surveys.

At this point we can go no further in discussing the comparisons and specifics of various survey modes involved in a mixed-mode setting. For a general discussion the reader can consult Groves et al. (2009), who present key dimensions of survey modes (i.e. interviewer involvement, interaction with respondent, privacy issues, communication channel and technology used) and their consequences for measurement, sampling, coverage and costs. Biemer & Lyberg (2003) also provide a systematic overview of characteristics of various modes, while de Leeuw & Hox (2011) and Bethlehem & Biffignandi (2012) consider these issues within the context of web surveys. An excellent treatment of mixed-modes can also be found in Dillman, Smyth, & Christian (2014).

To conclude, we can say that mixed-modes introduce very radical changes into the survey process. As a consequence, many direct and indirect disadvantages may appear at various stages of the survey process. Particularly problematic is the increased complexity in management and administration, as well as measurement errors due to mode effects. We thus suggest a very conservative approach and careful consideration. The potential involvement of experts is also advised, because decisions related to the survey mode can be the most complex and difficult in the entire web survey process.

Unfortunately, these decisions are also among the very first to be made in the web survey process. Correspondingly, we address mode aspects at the very beginning of the pre-fielding step, although we discuss various mode-related aspects later, particularly in relation to nonresponse (Section 2.5) and fielding (Chapter 3). These other considerations are important and should also be taken into account when deciding on survey mode.

The broader context of mixed-modes is discussed further in Section 6.1.5, the definition of the web survey mode is revised in Section 6.1.1, and problems with the evaluation of mode effects are reviewed in Section 6.1.3.

2.2 SAMPLING

The notion of a *sample* relates to a subset of units from the target population, which is included in the survey with the aim of learning about the entire target population.

We also need to introduce here the term *variable* which is a statistical notion and refers to a quantity related to certain characteristics of our interest and to all units in the target population (e.g. gender, age, certain attitude). Variables are usually denoted by one-letter symbols. We use lower case letters when we discuss units in the sample (e.g. y, x, p) and capitals when we talk about units in the population (e.g. Y, X, P).

Variables take a certain *value* at each unit, which in the case of survey variables and for the responding units in the sample is simply the corresponding answer from the respondents. Also, units can be assigned other variables directly (e.g. external information about the region of the unit).

Variables can have certain statistical properties (e.g. minimum, maximum, mean, variance), which can be obtained by certain calculations. When performed on units in the sample, these calculations are called *sampling statistics* or *estimates*, because they serve as estimations for the characteristics of the population, which are called population *parameters*. For example, the percentage of women in the sample is $p = 50\%$, which can alternatively also be expressed as a share (proportion), 0.50. This is then used as an estimate for the corresponding parameter P, which denotes the share of women in the population. Ideally, the sample is a scaled-down version of the population, mirroring every characteristic of the population (Lohr, 2010, p. 3). Within this context, we often use the notion of a *representative sample*, which means that the characteristics of interest (e.g. socio-demographics) in the population can be estimated from the sample to some known accuracy.

In the sampling stage of pre-fielding we first consider the definition of the target population (Section 2.2.1). Next, we discuss the sampling design aspects: sampling frame, sampling methods, sample size and the selection of units into the sample. We build here on the initial classification of sampling approaches (Section 1.1.3, Table 1.1) and address sampling design separately for probability (Section 2.2.2) and non-probability web surveys (Section 2.2.3). In addition to designing the samples – which is only one part of the sampling – we also address (Section 2.2.4) the estimation part of the sampling (i.e. statistical inference), which we define as a set of procedures that enable results to be generalized from a sample to the target population. In this context we additionally elaborate on the dilemma of whether and when to use non-probability web surveys instead of probability ones. Within the sampling stage, we also discuss the eventual non-coverage problem (Section 2.2.5), where some segments of the target population are not included in the survey (e.g. Internet non-users).

Many of these issues depend strongly on the research objectives and may already be specified within preliminary research activities, particularly the definition of the target population and decision for probability sampling.

Similar to other pre-fielding stages, we limit the discussion to stand-alone web surveys, omitting the complexities of mixed-mode systems. We predominantly focus on aspects specific to web surveys. Nevertheless, we also cover the essential general sampling principles to a certain extent, in order to provide a stand-alone treatment of sampling issues.

2.2.1 Defining Populations

The units and target population, as well as target variables, are often outlined at the initial request for the survey, within preliminary research activities. In web surveys, as in any other surveys, the target population can span broadly from students to the general population and various specific segments, such as owners of exotic animals. Many examples have already been illustrated in Section 1.3.6.

For sampling purposes we need to elaborate the target population much more precisely, compared with the conceptual outline within the general setting of research objectives. For example, in a student evaluation survey, various student statuses exist, according to formal enrolment criteria or according to attendance, and we need to specify precisely which units are our targets. We call them *eligible units* and distinguish them from *ineligible units*, which do not belong to the target population, but may for various reasons still appear in the sample (e.g. a person died but was not removed from the list). In the case of student evaluations, if we focus on domestic students, then foreign students are ineligible. These redundant ineligible units – denoted sometimes as *overcoverage* – simply need to be ignored.

For practical purposes, instead of the target population we often focus on a narrower *survey population* which is more realistic for surveying than the theoretically defined target population. That is, the resources needed to include some narrow segment of negligible size might be disproportionate to the added value of their inclusion. For example, in student evaluation surveys we may survey only students present in the classroom and eliminate absentees. Similarly in general population surveys (e.g. election studies), we typically omit people in institutions (prisons, care homes, the military, etc.).

Of course, we need to be very careful with these simplifications. If for whatever reason some eligible units cannot be included – such as Internet non-users in the web survey of the general population – we need to openly address this problem (see Section 2.2.5 on non-coverage).

In web surveys the low costs of data collection may encourage us to survey the entire population (i.e. a census). Especially with small target populations, this may be a convenient solution, because it eliminates all procedures related to sample design and statistical inference. Nevertheless, the above discussion about defining the target and the survey population is equally relevant.

2.2.2 Sampling Design Principles in Probability Web Surveys

The preceding discussion on the target population relates to all web surveys, while we discuss sampling design issues separately for probability and non-probability approaches. We start with the probability setting, where we focus predominantly on list-based samples, because they are far more frequent than non-list ones. The latter are very rare and were introduced in our initial discussion (Section 1.1.3), together with the related example of probability web intercept surveys. Nevertheless, with respect to sampling design principles, the same concepts as those developed for list-based probability surveys apply, so we do not discuss them separately; the specifics of the practical implementation for intercept surveys can be found in Poynter (2010).

We review the key sampling design principles of list-based probability web surveys: namely sampling frame, sampling technique and sample size. To a considerable extent these issues hold true for any survey mode and are not specific to web surveys. Nevertheless, we discuss them in a somewhat more extensive manner, because their understanding is very important for web surveys.

We should add that the sampling design principles of probability samples discussed below are often also applied in non-probability settings, despite various risks and unknown effects which accompany such an implementation. In our discussion we will therefore occasionally make specific comments on this issue, while a dedicated discussion on the implementation of probability sampling principles in non-probability settings follows in Section 2.2.3.

2.2.2.1 Sampling Frames

Regardless of whether we survey the entire population or only a sample, with list-based probability web surveys we need a sampling frame, which is basically a list of elements that enables us to identify and contact the eligible units of the survey population. We discuss here the prevailing list-based situation, where the sampling frame is prepared in advance, either from some commercial (e.g. customer list) or administrative file (e.g. students on a university register), or with a preliminary procedure (e.g. web recruitment).

Ideally, sampling frames provide corresponding contact information (email or mail address, telephone number) and reflect the survey population with a one-to-one match between eligible units and elements of the sampling frame. We may come very close to this situation with population registers of voters for surveying populations of voters, or with the list of all enrolled students from the university registration office for surveying the students.

Once a list serving as a sampling frame is obtained or constructed, we should assess its quality. Some initial questions to ask are as follows:

- What is the share of eligible units that are missing (i.e. non-coverage)? The share and the characteristics of these units are perhaps the most essential and most critical questions related to the sampling frame, on which we elaborate further in Section 2.2.5 on non-coverage.
- How many duplicates are on the list? In the case of unique entries (e.g. email addresses), duplicates are easily identified and can be deleted. However, when the same units are listed under different entries in email lists, this is more difficult. Some external information, expert evaluation, small preliminary surveys or qualitative investigation may help here. Sometimes, we can estimate the share of duplicates only for units after they have been surveyed, and we compensate for this with weighting, which is a procedure in post-fielding (Section 4.1.4)where we assign the units different factors (i.e. weights) to compensate for inclusion probability or to improve representativeness of the sample. For example, a respondent with multiple entries (e.g. two email addresses) in our sampling frame should receive a weight inversely proportional to the number of entries (e.g. weight proportional to one-half).
- Do we have clusters of units behind a certain entry in the list? In such a case we should include the entire cluster. If we include only one unit, we need to compensate that with weighting – the responding unit receives a weight proportional to the size of the cluster.

In a survey of online purchase events, where we have a list of customers and not the list of purchases, a customer with multiple purchases forms a cluster. If we select customers with equal probabilities, we then typically subsample one purchase event and assign a corresponding weight to this unit (e.g. a customer with five purchases receives a weight proportional to five).

- How up to date is the list? Outdated entries in the sampling frame additionally increase non-coverage problems and introduce inefficiencies in data collection. It should thus be clearly documented when the list was last refreshed (with the so-called *reference date*) to estimate its quality properly.
- What proportion of units has missing or invalid contact information? Depending on the contact strategy, we may need various types of contact information, such as email address, telephone number, name, etc. We can roughly check and estimate the corresponding quality of these entries by inspecting a subsample of units.
- What is the percentage of ineligible units? If it is possible to identify them in advance, they should be eliminated from the sampling frames. Sometimes, however, they can be identified only when actually contacted. In any case it is important to obtain some estimates for their share, so that we can increase the initial sample. The units that turn out to be ineligible simply need to be ignored.
- What additional information is at our disposal? The quality of the sampling frame dramatically increases with other information. The name and title (Mr, Ms, Dr) can be used for personalization, while substantive variables (e.g. age, gender, education) can be used for controls and improved efficiency of the sample design (e.g. stratification) and adjustments (e.g. weighting).

In addition, we provide below three main approaches (email lists, traditional frames and online panels) for obtaining or building sampling frames for probability-based web surveys. In principle, these guidelines also hold true for non-probability samples, so we will not repeat them later in our discussion of those samples.

2.2.2.1.1 Email Lists as the Sampling Frame

A list of email addresses, potentially also with other information, is the expected and desired sampling frame in web surveys, particularly when surveying populations with high Internet coverage (e.g. students, employees, members, clients, businesses, etc.).

Email lists may already exist for some administrative, business or other reason, and if there are no legal, ethical or technical restrictions, we can happily use them. Increasingly often, however, explicit permission is required or the legal act related to the establishing of a certain list (or register) needs to formally allow the use of the list for a specific survey.

Sometimes only the list of names exists, without the corresponding email addresses, so we may have to use various search strategies on the web to obtain them. Of course, such a search may take a lot of time and sometimes the matching email might not be found with certainty, if at all.

The email list can also be compiled from scratch by using information available on the web. For example, if we want to survey scholars at a certain university, we may collect their publicly available addresses. However, having publicly available email addresses does not mean in some countries that we can use them for survey invitations. This is often very different to publicly available telephone numbers and mail addresses, which can be legally and legitimately used for traditional survey recruitment. In the early days of web surveys, these simple 'harvesting' approaches were also acceptable for publicly available email addresses to be extracted manually from the web or via an automated procedure, and used for web surveys (e.g. Swoboda, Mühlberger, Weitkunat, & Schneeweiß, 1997). However, this has now changed and in most developed countries various legal restrictions exist, as well as ethical codes applying to the survey profession, which prevent these practices. Such unsolicited contact might still sometimes be possible with some business email addresses – which are in principle open for any marketing, commercial and research purposes – but not for private ones. Similarly, for some very specific target populations, where the target population list is available online (e.g. various professionals, hobbyists, practitioners, owners of very specific items, plants or animals, etc.), publicly available private emails might still be conditionally used for invitations in non-commercial surveys, but this is usually not the case for the commercial context or in the case of the general population. Nevertheless, in many countries this is getting increasingly restricted.

Unless a certain survey is legally foreseen in regulation, a consent from potential respondents is thus in principle required to use email addresses for invitations into a survey. Such consent is now being increasingly required when we register to buy a product or a service (e.g. an explicit opt-in checkbox for receiving follow-up customer satisfaction surveys) or when applying for membership of some associations, clubs or communities.

Legislation can be particularly strict in some countries (e.g. Slovenia), where creating a database and storing personal data (e.g. email) on it requires a formal legal basis or explicit consent from the units on the list. If this is not the case, the corresponding information commissioner can charge substantial fines.

An exception where advanced consent is usually not needed are the lists of closely related social ties, which can be treated as a population of units that belong to the circle of a certain respondent; thus in DIY research we can typically invite our broader family, colleagues and friends, as well as social media 'friends', to join the survey.

In the case of email lists, additional contact information is very useful for combining the contact strategies (e.g. mail pre-notice, SMS reminder). Some other information can also be very precious (e.g. gender, age, region, education) for optimizing sample selection. Unfortunately, email lists often lack additional information because they were established for purposes other than surveying.

Given the increasing restrictions, it is becoming more and more difficult to obtain email addresses for web surveys, so it is not surprising that various specialized companies sell email addresses – of varying price and quality – which can then be legally used for surveys, since the owners of the addresses have given their consent. However, it is also true that in the majority of examples these email lists are not probability-based samples.

Sometimes, when we obtain, buy or build large datasets of email addresses, a separate sample is drawn from this dataset for each survey. In a probability sample setting, this approach is discussed within the context of so-called two-phase sampling (Lohr, 2010).

2.2.2.2.2 Traditional Sampling Frames

When a sampling frame of email addresses does not exist or cannot be effectively constructed, we need to rely on the sampling frames of traditional survey modes (F2F, telephone, mail). This can be the case for various specific populations (students, customers, employees, members) and also for the general population. A typical example is F2F recruitment into probability-based online panels (e.g. Scherpenzeel, 2011), where email addresses are obtained in the F2F interview. The high costs of F2F are then compensated for later with continuous (e.g. monthly) participation of the respondents in web surveys. More promising – in terms of costs – is a sampling frame of telephone numbers serving as a basis for short recruitment telephone interviews, during which email addresses are obtained, and which is then followed by a longer web questionnaire based on an email invitation (e.g. Bethlehem & Biffignandi, 2012, p. 241). Unfortunately, this may prove to be expensive, and suffers from low cumulative response rates across the web and the telephone phase.

The most frequent and convenient sampling frame option for recruitment into web surveys is the use of mail addresses. Thus the corresponding mail invitations contain the URL of the web questionnaire, which respondents need to type into their browser. With the right approach (e.g. incentives, multiple contacts, mixed-modes), acceptable costs and reasonable response rates can be obtained (Dillman et al., 2009, p. 235; Tijdens, 2014; Vehovar et al., 2009).

The above-mentioned traditional sampling frames can have – in addition to higher costs – their own problems, which we will not discuss here. We refer the reader to Lohr (2010) and Groves et al., (2009) for a general discussion of sampling frames in survey research.

2.2.2.2.3 Panels of Units

Another alternative sampling frame for web surveys is online panels. These are large and rich databases of units, where specific samples for different survey projects are selected each time. We typically have a considerable set of additional information from the recruitment phase at our disposal. We return to the same units repeatedly (e.g. monthly), so we call this a panel. The units within the panel can either be from a specific target population (students, consumers, employees) or from the general population of households or persons. We previously mentioned an example of recruitment into probability-based panels. However, most online panels today are of the non-probability kind, which we discuss further in Section 5.2.

2.2.2.2 Sampling Techniques

In survey research we usually study *samples*, which are a part of the population, because research goals can typically be achieved with a number of units that are much smaller than the population. However, it was only when the corresponding sampling theory was implemented in the 1930s that a major breakthrough in the development of modern surveys occurred. The cornerstone of this theory is *randomization*, which means that a researcher controls selection of the units into the sample with a randomized process, which conceptually resembles the drawing of a lottery. This usually also requires that the probabilities of selection are known in advance for all units (i.e. probability sampling), when selecting n units into the sample from the population of N units. As a consequence, huge cost savings are achieved, because with properly selected samples we can accurately measure the characteristics (e.g. specific attitudes) of a population of a hundred million with a sample size of just a few hundred. The price for these spectacular gains is a risk that by chance we did not select a good sample, because there are many potential samples and they oscillate randomly in quality.

We quantify this risk with *sampling errors* and express it with a confidence interval, which is related to the difference between the true population mean and the estimates we would obtain if we repeat our sampling procedures.

We assume here that the reader is familiar with the basics of inferential statistics (e.g. population variance, sample variance, confidence interval, standard error (SE), standard deviation (SD), significance level, etc.), so we will not elaborate on them further. However, as researchers without such knowledge also conduct web surveys, we outline on WebSM the essential principles in *Basic statistics* and *Sampling aspects in web survey practice*, Supplements to Chapter 2 (http://websm.org/ch2), together with examples and some practical rules of thumb.

The sample can be selected by using a rich array of sampling techniques. With web surveys and email recruitment, *simple random sample* (SRS) selection – which fully reflects a lottery draw, where all units in the population have the same probability of selection – typically prevails. We particularly recommend its approximation of *systematic sampling*, where we first select a random start and then select units using a fixed sampling interval. In addition to simplicity, the advantage here is the potential for implicit stratification. For this purpose, we first sort the units in the sampling frame across important control variables which might be at our disposal (e.g. region, age, gender), so when the sampling interval is implemented, the selected units are spread much better across all parts (strata) of the frame. Stratification according to regions is particularly frequent.

Sometimes SRS does not suffice and complex designs are needed, particularly when cost issues or mixed-modes are involved, which means that we consider using explicit stratification, stages, clusters, phases, etc. We do not discuss these designs further here, as they are not specific to probability web surveys (see Bethlehem & Biffignandi, 2012, Chapter 3), but instead point to the general survey (e.g. Groves et al., 2009) or sampling literature (Lohr, 2010).

We should also be aware that sampling is a highly specialized component of survey research, so considerable training and experience are needed for competent judgement in the case of complex sample designs, as well as in other complicated cases; expert advice is recommended in such circumstances.

2.2.2.3 Sample Size

The sample size is an essential element for achieving our research goals (e.g. substantive analysis of the target population), as well as for ensuring certain data quality standards (e.g. precision). The cost considerations have often limited the sample size in traditional survey modes, but this is not so much the case in web surveys. As a consequence, researchers sometimes implement large web samples simply because they are affordable or because they wrongly assume that increasing the sample size can compensate for the lack of quality of the sampling frame and other sampling deficiencies, as was often the case in the early years of web surveys (Lozar Manfreda, 2001). We strongly advise against unnecessarily large samples, since a high number of web questionnaires contributes to over-surveying, which in the long term might lower the general willingness of respondents to participate in web surveys. Unnecessarily large samples also violate professional ethics (Dillman et al., 2009, p. 358).

Determining the sample size is extremely important and sometimes also the only sampling dilemma we face in probability-based web surveys, as well as in non-probability ones. Unfortunately, various inadequate rules of thumb frequently appear, so samples are often too small or too large.

In the sampling literature, the basic approach for determining sample size builds on the required absolute *precision* reflected in corresponding *confidence intervals*. As an illustration, for variables on a scale of 1–5 with an SRS of, say, size $n = 100$, and with typical sample mean value $\bar{y} = 3.0$, corresponding standard deviation $SD(Y) = 1.0$ and standard error $SE(\bar{y}) = 0.1$, we obtain the usual 95% confidence interval

[3.0 ± 0.2]. This may already be enough for our needs, but sometimes we may need just a very rough orientation, and even $n = 30$ will do, giving a confidence interval of [3.0 ± 0.4]. At the other extreme, with $n = 1,000$, the corresponding interval [3.0 ± 0.06] might be unnecessarily narrow and beyond the precision we actually need. Careful evaluation of our needs is thus extremely important here.

Of course, there are some other variable types (e.g. shares) that might require much larger samples. Further refinement of this approach lies in the use of the relative precision and coefficient of variation, which we further elaborate on in *Sampling aspects in web survey practice*, Supplement to Chapter 2 (http://websm.org/ch2).

The above approaches tell us only the required sample size for estimates related to the entire sample. However, we usually also need estimates for domains (e.g. regions) and subgroups (e.g. age–gender classes), so it is very important that we clearly identify them in advance, because we then need to achieve a certain sample size in each subgroup. Often, the minimum is set to 20–30 units, but this depends strongly on the required level of precision and on the nature of the variables. For shares and important estimates, we may need $n' = 100$ units or more, while $n' = 10$ is often treated in practice as the absolute minimum. With requests for more detailed analysis (i.e. with increased precision and an expanded number of subgroups) the sample size increases rapidly. For example, if we set the subgroup minimum to $n' = 20$, with two gender categories, three for age and with 10 regions, we have 60 cells and $n = 2 \times 3 \times 10 \times 20 = 1,200$.

Different questions may require different sample sizes and in web surveys we can easily optimize for that. For example, out of 100 questions, we may ask all units only 10 essential questions and split the remaining 90 into two blocks of 45 questions, each randomly assigned to half of the sample (e.g. according to even and odd record numbers of the units). Of course, we assume here that for those 90 questions a sample of $n = 500$ units is sufficient. Instead of 1,000 units answering 100 questions and spending,

say, 20 minutes each, we thus have 1,000 units answering 55 questions and spending, say, 12 minutes. Alternatively, if we keep the same 20 minutes for all units, it enables us to include many more questions, for example 180 instead of 100, without changing the length of the response time. Of course, this split can be much more complex. In any case, this approach is often forgotten and considerably underused, although in our view it is one of the key recommendations for conducting effective web surveys; we discuss it further in the questionnaire preparation stage (Section 2.3.3).

Whichever sample size we determine, we should also inflate it for anticipated nonresponse and share of ineligible units. For example, if we estimate that 30% of units are ineligible (e.g. invalid email addresses) and that the response rate (e.g. due to refusals and non-contacts) is expected to be around 20%, we need to invite $300/(0.7 \times 0.2) = 2,143$ units if we wish to end up with 300 respondents.

We may also mention that some web survey software provides simple calculations of sample sizes, together with some stopping rules when the survey is closed after certain conditions are met. These rules are typically related to the precision of the estimates or to the structure of the sample expressed in quotas (e.g. we may require 50 females below the age of 30, etc.). With complex samples, mixed-mode systems and sequential sample selection, sample size optimization can require certain models that involve costs and errors (see Section 6.1.4).

The final sampling activities relate to the sample selection process, where the sampling design principles discussed above are applied to the corresponding sampling frame, so that the actual sample of units is selected, to be used in the fielding step. From a technical standpoint, the selection itself is usually done with some external statistical software, but web survey software also increasingly offers related database management features (e.g. sorting, merging, joining), as well as the corresponding sample selection procedures (e.g. SRS).

We may add that at this phase of sample preparation we could also prepare an additional sample – also called a *supplement sample* – in case low response rates in the fielding step require a larger sample. This sample should be independent and selected by the same principles as the main one. For such situations it is very important to have a sample ready instead of improvising during the fieldwork.

We do not elaborate any further on the issue of sample size, since web surveys have few specifics, so the standard textbooks (e.g. Lohr, 2010) should be consulted for in-depth study. However, as mentioned earlier, due to the practical importance of this issue we provide some additional guidelines and practical examples for novices in *Sampling aspects in web survey practice*, Supplement to Chapter 2 (http://websm.org/ch2).

2.2.3 Sampling Design Issues in Non-Probability Web Surveys

We now turn to the non-probability context, where the probabilities of the inclusion of the units into the sample are not known. This is of course very problematic, because all sampling principles discussed above (randomization, sampling frame, sample selection, sample size) have been developed for the probability context, where there is also a long tradition and accumulated knowledge in theory and applications, as outlined in the previous section and in any of the textbooks mentioned there.

We begin our discussion with a review of the recruitment procedures for non-list samples since these samples prevail in a non-probability setting. The corresponding recruitment replaces here the process of sample selection, which in list-based samples is done by a selection from the sampling frame. With respect to list-based non-probability samples, as already mentioned in our initial discussion on sampling frames (Section 2.2.2), the non-probability context adds nothing new here, so we do not discuss them separately.

Regarding sampling design principles in non-probability samples, the approaches from probability sampling discussed above are basically applied here, so we only deal with the corresponding implementation issues. Formally speaking, without knowing the probabilities of selection, such implementation involves many implicit assumptions, which are usually not checked, but often are also difficult or even impossible to check (e.g. verifying whether the unknown selection mechanism is random). Nevertheless, this may still preserve many of the benefits of probability samples and we systematically present the corresponding practice, approximations and recommendations, when probability sampling design principles are used in a non-probability setting; the statistical inference part of the problem is discussed in Section 2.2.4.

2.2.3.1 Recruitment for Non-List-Based Web Surveys

In non-list-based web surveys the sample selection does not really appear as a separate stage, but is merged with recruitment. The sample of respondents thus builds up together with the recruitment process. Below, we briefly examine the main approaches for recruiting into non-list-based, non-probability web surveys.

An invitation to such a survey can be posted on the web, as well as offline, either on some leaflets or via traditional media (TV, radio, print, billboards, etc.), where various invitations or advertisements appear. We labelled all these types of web surveys as unrestricted web surveys (Section 1.1.3), because anyone who notices such an invitation can participate. This approach is closely related to the notion of *convenience sampling*, where subjects are selected because of their accessibility and proximity, rather than through randomization applied to the target population. The corresponding sampling selection mechanism is thus outside a researcher's control and is usually unknown. We might hope that it still brings some randomization, but this is rarely the case. Instead, it typically reflects the salience of the topic and various other unknown drivers.

Recruitment into non-list-based, non-probability web surveys is predominantly conducted on the web, using various *online recruitment* methods. We list here the most common approaches:

- The simplest approach is the use of invitation texts, such as 'click me' or 'take a survey', which are embedded on a web page (e.g. online forum), together with the URL of the web questionnaire.
- Various types of banner advertising are particularly common and can be considered a form of display advertising, by which researchers buy space on particular websites where members of the target population are expected (e.g. a survey for cooking enthusiasts would be advertised on websites related to cooking and recipe sharing).
- Sometimes invitations are in a form of so-called 'pop-up' windows, where the survey invitation pops up on the respondent's screen. These may additionally include graphical animations and various multimedia files (e.g. sound, video). As this approach intercepts users invasively, it is often referred to as an intercept survey, and is parallel to offline mall intercepts, where we address consumers while shopping. The pop-ups typically cover only part of the screen, but can also be full-screen.
- A variation of the pop-up approach concerns floating banner ads, where such an ad appears more or less intrusively on the screen within the active browser tab and disappears or is repositioned in a corner of the website after a predefined time if no action is taken.
- Extreme cases of pop-ups may block the premium content of a web page that the user wants to access. Users are first asked or even forced to answer a web survey, and only then is access allowed to the desired content. This approach, also called interrupting traffic (Henning, 2013, p. 30), can be seen as a form of exchanging visitor's time (i.e. filling in a web survey) with the access to premium content. A similar philosophy is sometimes used in student evaluation web surveys, where students are not allowed to apply for an exam unless they first fill in the course evaluation web survey. Since respondents are forced to take a survey, they might see it as an unnecessary burden and not provide optimal answers.

- Search engine advertising is also a form of paid advertising, but has some specifics. The idea is to use information on what individuals are searching for to attract them into the survey, either by including the invitation at the top of the hits, or with a banner ad which typically appears to the right of the screen. For example, users who enter the search term 'dog' in a search engine may be exposed to paid advertisements inviting them to take a survey about issues related to dogs (food, protection, legislation, etc.). Search engine advertising is particularly useful for surveys that are specific to hard-to-reach populations. For example, Nunan & Knox (2011) bid on specific keywords to find respondents for a consumer engagement survey with private-sector health services in the UK.

The above approaches basically invite potential respondents to click on the invitation, which leads them to the first page of the web questionnaire. However, the number of clicks is typically very small compared with the number of visitors presented with such invitations. The corresponding ratio, also called the *click-through rate* (CTR), is often measured in decimals of percentages. Of course, more aggressive approaches (e.g. pop-ups) perform better. When payment is involved, it is usually charged for each click on the invitation (e.g. banner ad, link, pop-up window). We may add that the price per click typically starts around a few (tens of) cents. However, as users who click on the invitation and come to the first page of the questionnaire may not necessarily proceed with it, we may typically end up with prices up to a few (tens of) euros/dollars for a completed questionnaire, which may still be a reasonably cost-effective option.

Online recruitment methods can serve for one-time cross-sectional surveys, for online panel recruitment, but also as a supplement to online panels. In the latter case, we assume, and hope, that they will improve representativeness (R. P. Baker, Brick, Bates, Battaglia, Couper, Dever, … Tourangeau, 2013), increase diversity (Henning, 2013) and obtain respondents that are 'fresher', in the sense that they are less used to taking online surveys (Poynter, 2010, p. 9), in comparison with existing panel members.

These online recruitment methods can be combined among themselves, as well as with other approaches – particularly with email invitations, offline promotion and marketing strategies – so they can appear in various combinations and complex implementations. We present here a few of the most frequent examples, namely crowdsourcing, online social media recruitment, network sampling and guerrilla recruitment.

Crowdsourcing is a general way to solicit services from a large pool of people. The term is mostly used in reference to Internet communities, where users are willing to perform tasks for a fee (e.g. MTurk, Craigslist). Due to its cheap availability, it is becoming popular also as a method of recruiting paid participants for surveys or psychological experiments (Buhrmester, Kwang, & Gosling, 2011).

Online social media provide new and specific recruitment potentials, because of the increased engagement of units in online forums, communities, blogs, social network sites (SNSs), video/photo sharing services, multiple-person/group communication, virtual worlds and other collaboration platforms. An important advantage is the potential availability of auxiliary information from users' profiles, such as membership of interest groups, posts and links among them. Of course, we mean information that is part of so-called 'public social media' (ESOMAR, 2011b). By searching profiles, posts and network ties, it is possible to effectively find – with relatively few resources – very narrow target populations (Wejnert & Heckathorn, 2008), to which individual invitations can be sent. Of course, explicit and available sampling frames typically do not exist and often the email addresses we seek are not posted publicly. And even if they are, ethical and legal restrictions may limit their use for survey purposes. Thus, the main approach to sampling and recruitment in online social media is a direct invitation, which can be done by a researcher (e.g. posting a message), by the website administration (e.g. the administrator sends the invitation to all registered members) or by an advertisement, which often has a very strong advantage in narrow targeting done according to

the profiles of the users (e.g. age, gender, location). For example, Fenner, Garland, Moore, Jayasinghe, Fletcher, Tabrizi, … Wark (2012) successfully used such targeted advertising on Facebook to survey young females in a region of Australia for a health study. Another successful strategy is to form a special user group within certain social media sites, which invites and involves users in the study, and is also promoted within the realm of social media (i.e. stimulates users to invite their friends) and across websites (i.e. posting the invitation to join this group). Brickman Bhutta (2012) reported on the establishment of a Facebook group to study baptized Catholics. The participants differed from the general population in basic demographics, but the associations and in-depth analysis provided very similar results to a probability sample.

The **network sampling** approach uses social links between networked individuals to locate and add additional units to the sample. This approach is particularly convenient for sampling people with rare characteristics (e.g. rare diseases and behaviour). A variety of approaches have been developed, such as standard snowball sampling (e.g. Baltar & Brunet, 2012), where a researcher obtains a list of network contacts from the respondent and then proceeds with recruiting from this list. An important improvement comes with respondent-driven sampling (RDS; Heckathorn, 1997). This was further extended to the web environment by WebRDS (e.g. Schonlau & Liebau, 2012; Wejnert & Heckathorn, 2008), where the respondents – and not a researcher – recruit further respondents in waves, typically by passing coupons, all of which can considerably alleviate confidentiality concerns. If done carefully, that is with proper selection of seeds and controls in further steps, this approach can also be treated as probability sampling.

Guerrilla recruitment means we combine online recruitment methods in a very aggressive or very creative way. On the one hand, this includes extensive and systematic activities of posting invitations on various news websites, a range of online social media sites and other suitable virtual venues. Basically, we hire a person to work systematically on this aspect. This may be suitable for some research purposes, such as for the invitation in online forums to participate in a survey about online hate speech (Vehovar, Motl, Mihelič, Berčič, & Petrovčič, 2012), but might be problematic if, for example, a survey on wild animals is published on cooking forums. On the other hand, viral marketing approaches can also be used here. This is typically based on attractive and appealing multimedia content – which includes the invitation to the survey (plus some incentive) – being redistributed across the web by users themselves, typically via email or social media.

With respect to online recruitment, sometimes a notion of *real-time sampling* or *river sampling* also appears. The latter is defined as an opt-in web-based sampling approach which uses various attention-catching techniques, such as pop-up boxes, hyperlinks and banner ads (e.g. Baker et al., 2013, p. 18). This definition roughly overlaps with the notion of online recruitment, but it is sometimes unclear if it truly includes all the approaches mentioned above (e.g. all variants of interrupting traffic or all types of guerrilla recruitment).

Numerous case studies show that selection of the right recruitment approach depends strongly on specific circumstances (e.g. culture, context, research problem, target population). Nevertheless, the social media recruitment approach has often demonstrated comparable advantages in recent years (e.g. Antoun, Zhang, Conrad, & Schober, 2013; Wilkerson, Shenk, Grey, Rosser, & Noor, 2013). However, this advantage may change or even disappear over time, because future developments in web services may provide new opportunities for online recruitment.

With this we conclude our discussion of recruitment in non-list-based, non-probability samples and proceed with general issues related to implementation of probability sampling design principles in the non-probability context.

2.2.3.2 Sampling Design Approximations in Non-Probability Setting

Non-probability samples can be non-list based, when we use the recruitment approaches described above, but can be list based as well. The latter situation occurs when the list is built with procedures (e.g. self-selection) which do not control or provide inclusion probabilities (e.g. non-probability online panels). This can also occur when we have a very deficient sampling frame. The border where deficiencies (e.g. non-coverage, nonresponse) transform a certain sampling frame – from being suitable for probability sampling – into a list which can serve only for non-probability samples is extremely blurred and depends on various circumstances and perceptions.

In non-probability samples we basically try to follow, as much as possible, probability sampling design principles. We thus want to obtain the features which are inherent to probability samples, particularly the randomization, as well as the related representativeness. This can be achieved indirectly or directly, so we will systematically review both strategies.

2.2.3.2.1 Approximating Probability Sample Designs

In non-list-based, non-probability samples, the essential sampling design recommendation is to spread the sample recruitment as broadly as possible. In practice, this means that we do not stick to just one recruitment channel (e.g. to only one online community or only to advertising on a single website). Instead, we combine several recruitment channels (e.g. recruit youngsters on multiple online venues). A successful example is the Wage Indicator project, implemented in more than 30 countries, which uses an elaborate recruitment strategy and posts invitations to its unrestricted web survey across a wide range of websites (Tijdens, 2014). Similarly successful are broadly disseminated (i.e. banners on hundreds of websites) and unrestricted web surveys on Internet usage (e.g. project RIS 1996–2006[1]) and on online hate speech in Slovenia (Vehovar, Motl et al., 2012), where units were recruited from a large number of online forums.

Another indirect strategy for non-list-based, non-probability samples is to shape them so that their structure reflects the structure of the survey population as much as possible. This idea is often related to the notion of 'representative samples' and is traditionally based on various quota rules, where we typically control for socio-demographic features (e.g. gender, age, education, region) so that the sample obtains the characteristics of the population. The quotas are typically applied on recruitment or at the screening phase. For example, to achieve gender balance when we have already reached the quota for women, we might reject self-recruited women (or provide them with a brief entertaining survey) and proceed to the web questionnaire only with men. Alternatively, we might intensify the online recruitment channels that attract more men (e.g. advertising on sports websites).

Whenever we have a sampling frame with additional information on the units, as in some list-based non-probability samples (e.g. online panels), in principle we use similar strategies as described above for non-list-based samples. However, this time we have the benefit of disposing of all the units from a list, so this can be done much more effectively since we usually have more information on the units. We can therefore control the spread of the sample and define quotas in advance. This can be further facilitated, or even fully replaced with fine stratification, by preselecting units according to the target population's structure (i.e. age, gender, education, region, etc.). An extreme example, which is fully effective only when we have a very large database of units available, as in large online panels, is individual matching, where we first design a 'normal' sample from some ideal or high-quality control source and then search for units in our database (e.g. online panel) which most closely resemble the desired units (Rivers & Bailey, 2009). Concepts and solutions from so-called causal inference for observational data and propensity score modelling are also often applied here (Terhanian & Bremer, 2012).

2.2.3.2.2 Direct Incorporation of Probability Sampling Principles

Whenever possible, we should also directly introduce randomization and probability sampling principles into the related sample designs or recruitment processes. Sometimes the components of probability sampling selection can be directly introduced into the early steps of the sampling process. For example, in probability sampling with quotas, we might first select a probability sample of schools, we then recruit pupils with unrestricted banner ad invitations according to some quota (e.g. age, gender, year of schooling). Similarly, elements of non-probability samples (e.g. quotas) can be added as an additional restriction to probability model-based sampling (Berzofsky, Williams, & Biemer, 2009). Another example is randomization, which can be incorporated into online recruitment by pop-up invitations, so that the recruitment is spread across days or hours, so it can even approach probability web intercept surveys.

Of course, none of the above approaches can ensure that, after applying these sampling design approximations, the corresponding statistical inference will be equivalent to the situation with the formal probability sample. In the above example of the wage indicator, the final estimates of wages for the Netherlands (even after weighting), were improved but still with some biases in comparison to the official data from Statistics Netherlands (Steinmetz, Bianchi, Tijdens and Biffignandi, 2014). However, it is also true that these approaches usually bring certain improvements. Practitioners have developed many other approaches here, which work with various success rates across different circumstances, research problems and target variables. We discuss the potential of these procedures for statistical inference in the next section.

2.2.4 Statistical Inference in Probability and Non-Probability Surveys

We mentioned at the beginning of Section 2.2 that sampling has two closely related parts: sampling design, which is the main concern of the pre-fielding step; and estimation, which is related to statistical inference formally conducted in post-fielding and later, in data analysis. However, as both parts are closely linked, we discuss statistical inference here to provide a more complete picture. This also supports the related sampling decisions which need to be made in pre-fielding. We first summarize statistical inference in probability samples. Next, we address the problems when using this approach also in a non-probability setting. We then present recommendations on the probability–non-probability sampling dilemma.

2.2.4.1 Statistical Inference with Probability Samples

By the very definition of the sample survey (Section 1.1.1), its goal is to infer about the target population. We should therefore be aware that, whenever we use samples, we also need to present results – at least the key ones – within the inferential context. This means we need to quantify the fact that we studied only a sample instead of the entire population, which is usually done by measuring the risk of being wrong due to random oscillations in the quality of the selected sample. For example, rather than a point estimate of $p = 30$ for population percentage P, we report the corresponding 95% confidence interval, which among other factors strongly depends on sample size, so it can take values in the intervals [30.00 ± 0.05], [30.00 ± 0.50] or even [30.00 ± 5.00]. In each of these cases, the corresponding interval provides a good indication of precision, which is certainly something the user needs to know. For example, a confidence interval of [30.00 ± 5.00] means that on average in 19 of 20 samples of this type and size, such an interval will contain the population value P. Similarly, when we run statistical tests or statistical models, we report the significance levels, the power of the tests, the fits of the models and other inferential diagnostics.

Various approaches to statistical inference exist and almost all of them assume probability sampling. However, in this book we routinely refer to perhaps the most popular *frequentist approach*, which assumes that certain true (fixed) population values (parameters) exist and which builds on the sampling distribution of the estimate across all possible samples.

The estimation and entire statistical inference process can be very simple, as in the case of the sample mean in SRS settings, while complex samples (e.g. clusters, strata) and complex estimators (e.g. ratio, regression, calibration) require dedicated statistical work, particularly when weighting is involved. In any case, many elaborate inferential procedures have already been developed for probability sampling (J. F. Healey, 2011; Lohr, 2010), on which we do not elaborate further.

The calculation of the standard error (SE) is the basis for evaluation of the precision of the estimates. Less precise estimates can be put into brackets with corresponding methodological comments, while in the case of extremely low precision – e.g. statistical inference based on less than 10 units – we rather avoid publishing the estimates and use a dot '.' instead, meaning that the estimated value is *non-zero, but unreliable*. Many users are otherwise prone to using even the most unreliable estimates, regardless of methodological warnings.

Another issue that sometimes confuses statistical novices is when we have the census (e.g. all students, members, customers, employees, etc. of the target population). Nevertheless, once we have a census, all inferential statistical risks disappear and are redundant. There is no need for confidence intervals and hypothesis testing, because we already measured population values. Sometimes, particularly when we test certain models, we may still behave as if our population was only a sample implementation of some infinitely large artificial super-population. Such an approach can be acceptable, nevertheless this needs to be clarified and justified. Of course, other data quality issues, such as nonresponse, remain.

The Supplement to Chapter 2, *Sampling aspects in web survey practice*, at http://websm.org/ch2, provides further illustrations on these issues.

It is worth noting that the above holds true for an ideal implementation of a probability survey. We treat various deviations due to non-coverage (Section 2.2.5) and nonresponse (Section 2.5.3) separately, while other components of data quality are addressed in Section 6.1.2.

2.2.4.2 Statistical Inference with Non-Probability Samples

With non-probability samples the inclusion probabilities are unknown. As a consequence, without further assumptions – which are usually risky and impossible to verify – in principle this prevents any standard statistical inference calculations. In addition, non-probability samples often have a certain selection bias (Bethlehem & Biffignandi, 2012). For example, Internet-savvy respondents typically volunteer to participate in non-probability samples disproportionally more frequently, so the usage of various Internet services is typically overestimated.

In practice we often apply the same statistical inference procedures that were developed within the probability sampling setting in non-probability samples, although there is no guarantee whether and how this will work. For example, we can use standard procedures to calculate a 95% confidence interval from a non-probability sample and obtain, say, [30.0 ± 0.5]. However, the risk that this procedure will produce a confidence interval that will not contain a true population value (over repeating sampling) is no longer 5% – as it would be with probability sampling – but is unknown. Very likely, this risk is much higher than 5%, but we have no grounds to calculate it.

Nonetheless, researchers often and even routinely apply the standard statistical inference approaches with non-probability samples in exactly the same way as with probability samples, although in principle this could not and should not be done, because the basic assumption (i.e. known probabilities) is not fulfilled. When this is done without any consideration of the assumptions and with no warning, it might be denoted a problematic practice, so it seems reasonable to consider using a distinct terminology to separate it formally from the probability setting. Correspondingly, we might use the term *indications* instead of estimates (Baker et al., 2013).

In practice, three streams of factors may work in a researchers' favour when using standard probability-based statistical inferential procedures in a non-probability sample setting:

- In almost all non-probability samples, there exists a certain level of 'natural' randomization, which varies across circumstances and from sample to sample, and which can in extreme cases strongly resemble SRS selection.
- This can be further accelerated with measures that researchers undertake to improve non-probability sampling designs, which we discussed in Section 2.2.3 (spread, randomization, quotas, matching).
- In addition, powerful advanced techniques exist in post-survey adjustment (imputation, weighting) and estimation (complex estimators, statistical models). We discuss this in Section 4.1.

These three streams together can be very effective in practice. The study on online hate speech (Vehovar, Motl et al., 2012) is a typical example of a successful non-probability web survey. Comparisons with a parallel probability telephone sample confirmed the principles, which often hold for 'well-spread' non-probability samples:

- Estimated means on rating scales are usually very robust and in this study they completely matched for the two samples.
- The same is true for the correlations, ranks and subgroup analysis, which are also fully preserved.
- The estimates for shares (percentages) are usually more vulnerable and in this study they were higher in the non-probability web survey (e.g. respondents in the non-probability web survey showed more involvement). Nevertheless, the ranks and relations between categories were fully preserved.

This pattern is very typical. Correspondingly, some successful results from non-probability samples are reported for online panels (Rivers, 2007) and have already become the prevailing approach for web surveys in marketing research (Macer, 2014). In addition, we have increasingly observed that scholarly papers calculate confidence intervals for non-probability samples, as stated in Rivers (2010), who also lists three essential arguments in favour of non-probability samples:

- The first argument arises from the above-mentioned advances in sample selection and estimation procedures.
- The second argument relates to the weakness of many probability samples, arising from non-coverage and nonresponse, potentially resulting in de facto worse sampling quality compared with some high-quality non-probability sampling.
- The third argument builds on parallels with some neighbouring areas, where inference from non-probability sampling is already fully accepted, such as experimental and quasi-experimental studies, evaluation research, observational studies and medical research.

Another indirect argument concerns those clients who pay money for non-probability surveys. If the results from inexpensive non-probability samples justify their price in the long run and fit their purpose, this clearly points to the conclusion that the added value of expensive probability samples would simply be too low in these situations.

On the other hand, opponents insist that, without knowing the inclusion probabilities, there are no grounds to infer from non-probability samples (Langer, 2013; Lohr, 2010). Similarly, scholars often compare the two approaches (Yeager, Krosnick, Chang, Javitz, Levendusky, Simpser, & Wang, 2011), and the probability setting always proves to be superior. In Section 5.2 we provide more evidence that shows the considerable problems and variations in the quality of the estimates from non-probability online panels. Of course, such comparisons are limited only to statistical aspects and exclude comparisons of speed, costs and various other aspects.

In any case, whenever we use, run or discuss non-probability samples, we should clearly differentiate among them, as huge differences exist. Some samples carefully recruit and spread the units (e.g. strata, quotas, matching), while others simply self-select within one narrow sub-segment. The same is true for procedures applied in the post-fielding step (imputation, weighting, calibration,

estimation). The specifics of the target variables and the research problem are also very important here. We have already mentioned that shares are usually the most vulnerable, but problems with correlations exist as well (Pasek & Krosnick, 2010). On the other side, some topics are more robust, so they can be successfully dealt with even with low-quality non-probability samples – which is often the case with variables in marketing and opinion polling – while some topics require strict probability sampling, such as employment or health status.

All in all, we are inclined to recommend more open acceptance of the realities of using the standard statistical inference approach in non-probability settings. Nonetheless, we offer two warnings:

- Firstly, the sample selection procedure should be clearly described, presented and critically evaluated. We support the AAPOR recommendations (Baker et al., 2013) that sampling, collection and adjustment methods should be described in even greater detail as in the case of the probability sample. This also holds true for reporting on data quality indicators.
- Secondly, we should have elaborated on the assumptions and models used, as well as providing explanations about conceptual divergences, risks and limitations of the interpretations. When standard statistical inference is applied straightforwardly to whichever non-probability sample we have, the minimum requirement is clearly to acknowledge that estimates, confidence intervals, model fitting and hypothesis testing may work improperly or not at all. Of course, if some empirical evidence supports that inference from certain non-probability samples repeatedly worked, this should be used as an additional justification.

Strictly, and formally speaking, the probability sampling and related randomization are not necessary preconditions for valid statistical inference, because specific modelling approaches can also do the work. However, these modelling approaches have not been developed into general inferential procedures, which would then enable straightforward practical implementations, such as producing the estimates of descriptive statistics for all variables in the sample. (We use the notion of *standard statistical inference* for these approaches.) Instead, these specific modelling approaches predominantly focus only on certain target variables, involving specific auxiliary information, certain modelling assumptions and various external inputs, such as relations among variables from the past and the implementation of a tailored statistical model. A typical example is the elaboration of estimates for election outcomes, where data from a non-probability sample are only a small input component into some prediction models, which are increasingly successful (e.g. the 2013 US presidential elections)[2]. Another example is the focus on relations, as in the case of causal inferences, which can also be run in a non-randomized setting (Rosenbaum & Rubin, 1983). Nevertheless, due to their specific and narrow targeting, we exclude these approaches from the main thrust of our discussion, which is focused only on general inferential approaches. Of course, we do not underestimate by any means the corresponding achievements of these approaches.

2.2.4.3 Deciding on the Probability–Non-Probability Sampling Dilemma

As there is little theoretical basis for running statistical inference with non-probability samples, the corresponding justification relies predominantly on the accumulation of anecdotal practical evidence. If a certain approach repeatedly proved to be successful, this became the essential basis for the legitimacy of its support. Of course, in some circumstances a certain non-probability sampling approach repeatedly works sufficiently well, while in others it does not. Similarly, sometimes a very deficient (e.g. response rate of a few per cent) probability sampling outperforms the best non-probability samples, but it can also be the opposite. In any case, only repeated practical evidence within specific circumstances can justify non-probability sampling. Usually, after many successful repetitions, with the corresponding trials and errors, practitioners can also predict the differential effect of the variations in sampling designs and inferential procedures.

Thus, when deciding between probability and non-probability sampling, the first stream of consideration is to profoundly review all the past evidence. Whenever possible, we should inspect the distributions of the variables and also compare them with external controls when they are available. This will give us an impression of how the non-probability samples resemble probability ones in terms of randomization and population controls ('representativeness').

Another stream of consideration should systematically evaluate the broader setting. That is, instead of focusing only on the probability–non-probability issue, we should consider the accompanying features related to non-coverage, nonresponse, mode effect and other measurement errors, as well as the characteristics of costs, timing, comparability, etc. Extreme care is needed here to separate the genuine problem of non-probability sampling (i.e. selection bias) from other features. Rejecting a non-probability sample selection will be of little help if in fact it does not create a problem, when the issue is actually due to, for example, the mode effect.

We thus rarely decide on the probability–non-probability component in isolation, but simultaneously consider a broad spectrum of features. For instance, in a survey on youth tourism, we may choose between a probability-based telephone, mail or web survey and a non-probability online panel or a sample recruited through online social media. The decision involves the consideration of several criteria, where all of the components (nonresponse, non-coverage, selection bias, mode effect, costs, timing, comparability, accuracy, etc.) are often inseparably embedded (e.g. the social media option might come with not only high non-coverage and selection bias, but also with low costs and convenient timing etc.). In this context, the selection bias itself, arising from the use of a non-probability setting, is only one element in the broad spectrum of factors and cannot be isolated and treated separately.

Choosing a combination of approaches can sometimes be a good solution. Thus, we may obtain population estimates for key target variables with an expensive probability survey, while in-depth analysis is done via non-probability surveys. For example, in a study of online hate speech (Vehovar, Motl et al., 2012), key questions were put in a probability-based omnibus telephone survey, while extensive in-depth questioning was implemented within a broadly promoted self-selected web survey.

Situations also occur where probability sampling might not be an option, because we do not have the required time, budget or sampling list. However, we should still apply the above considerations in order to optimize the procedures, as well as to elaborate on whether the non-probability sample is worth conducting at all.

A nice example of how not to use non-probability web surveys was a survey on school uniforms, a hot public topic in Slovenia in 2014. The web survey was launched in cooperation with the corresponding ministry to indicate the attitudes among key segments. All schools were asked to post links on their websites with invitations to the web survey, and an impressive number of responses (20,731) was obtained for a country of 2 million. All three segments (teachers, parents, pupils) were against uniforms,[3] roughly with a ratio of 60:40. The extent to which these results were then used in a process of actual rejection of the school uniform project illustrates very well the danger of such samples. That is, it might be that the segments against school uniforms were simply 'louder' and more motivated to participate. A probability sample might show the opposite situation. The improved approach to non-probability sampling could also provide better results. That is, the sampling design could introduce more elements of randomization. For example, around 30 schools might have been randomly selected with some stratification, instead of self-selection offered to all schools. Next, in the selected schools a stronger campaign could have been prepared. Post-survey adjustments could also have been introduced, based on general (age, gender, social class, region) and specific (school type and year) controls, as well as with a question on attitudes towards clothing brands, for which a national survey might exist.

To conclude, we warn again that non-probability samples can easily be a waste of resources or can even cause damage by producing incorrect estimates. It therefore bears repeating that we need convincing evidence that the procedures we want to implement have repeatedly worked well in the past for similar contexts, making it highly likely that they will work also for our implementation. Luckily, this evidence is growing increasingly, so we need to make efforts towards finding it, using it and referring to it.

2.2.4.4 Concluding Remarks on Non-Probability Web Surveys

When introducing sampling techniques for probability samples (Section 2.2.2), we stated that almost a century ago they helped make spectacular gains in survey practice. We can now state the same for the advantages arising from non-probability web surveys. That is, thousands of web survey projects were enabled, which would not have been possible otherwise, and millions of web survey projects were facilitated to run dramatically faster, simpler and much less expensively. However, this change occurred more gradually and almost unnoticeably, but today we could still say that non-probability web surveys truly revolutionized the survey landscape.

We said (or hinted) on many occasions that formally, in a non-probability setting, probability sampling principles and standard statistical inference could not be applied. This is formally true, unless we treat these results as indications and approximations which are yet to be evaluated. It is also true that they cannot be evaluated in advance (ex ante), as in a probability setting, but only afterwards (ex post) and only to a certain extent. However, these evaluations are still very valuable, because we can then improve the corresponding sampling and estimation procedures, or at least recognize and consciously limit certain non-probability sampling and estimation procedures to just the types of problems for which this works.

By definition there is basically no standard statistical inference outside probability sampling, because standard statistical inference is inseparable from inclusion probabilities. When they are unknown, as in non-probability sampling, the corresponding inferential procedure implicitly assumes them. For example, applying the usual sample mean (i.e. simple average, arithmetic mean) calculation will implicitly assign to all units in the sample the probabilities for inclusion in the sample of n/N, where N is the population size and n the sample size. It then depends on corresponding evaluation procedures to judge the quality of such an 'estimate', which should perhaps be better called an 'indication' or 'approximation', as we have already mentioned.

With this we basically abandon the science of statistical inference and enter into the art and craft of obtaining optimal practical procedures. The experience based on trial and error is thus essential here, as well as the intuition of a researcher. Correspondingly, particularly with complex problems and large projects, expert advice or a panel of experts with relevant experience can be extremely valuable.

All of this may sound very unscientific, so some hardcore statisticians may experience doubts or even professional disgust towards procedures where inferential risks cannot be quantified in advance. However, is this not the very essential characteristic of applied statisticians – which separates them from 'out-of-reality' mathematicians – that is, to stop hesitating and accept the procedures which will bring them close enough for all practical purposes?

We should add that these issues are nothing new, in the sense that they are not issues which would appear only with web surveys, because from the very beginning of probability sampling (almost a hundred years) researchers have been trying various alternatives to simplify expensive probability sampling procedures. Wherever this worked sufficiently well, they abandoned strict probability sampling, as in the majority of marketing research, where large, self-selected, non-probability household panels were routinely used decades before web surveys appeared.

It also bears repeating that there is no inherent relation between non-probability sampling and the web survey mode. Just because the majority of web surveys are of a non-probability nature, this is not a characteristic of web surveys per se. By definition (see Section 1.1.1), the web survey mode is independent of the sampling, so non-probability sampling equally appears with traditional surveys (e.g. convenience surveys on a street corner, mall intercepts, call-in telephone surveys, magazine mail-in surveys), while many web surveys are probability based. Thus the problem of the inference from non-probability web surveys is only a manifestation of the old quest to replace expensive and complicated probability samples with less expensive non-probability ones. Web surveys expose this problem so intensively because they are so inexpensive, convenient and popular.

We may also add that this probability–non-probability dilemma is not that frequent in practice. Instead, it is rather embedded in the dilemma between non-probability samples with more or less elements of randomization, which usually also means more or less expensive non-probability samples. As usual in this context, the answer to this dilemma depends on practical aspects specific to certain settings (Galesic, 2009).

Further discussion of these problems can be found in the AAPOR report on non-probability samples (Baker et al., 2013), which cautiously and exhaustively addresses selection, weighting, estimation and quality measures, as well as notions of '*fit for purpose*' and '*fitness to use*'. We agree with this report that there is much more to investigate. However, our impression is that there is perhaps relatively little room for improvements in sampling design procedures or in post-survey adjustments. On the other side we expect improvements with respect to modelling and particularly to standards (e.g. reporting), classifications (e.g. types of non-probability samples) and diagnostics (e.g. quality indicators). These issues are also essential for the broader contemporary survey research agenda (e.g. Callegaro et al., 2014; Chang & Krosnick, 2009; Yeager et al., 2011).

We reiterate these issues in Section 4.2.1 (Preliminary reporting), when we discuss the implementation of inferential principles.

2.2.5 Non-Coverage Problem

Non-coverage refers to the situation where a considerable part of the eligible units is excluded from the sample. As a consequence, some units have zero probability of selection, which is against the principles of probability sampling, so the standard statistical inference cannot be done properly. This problem is usually dealt with at the start of the sampling stage discussions, but we treat it at the end of the sampling section because we want to introduce first all of the key sampling concepts (e.g. sampling frame, statistical inference).

In web surveys, non-coverage is often an important deficiency, due to Internet non-users, who are by definition excluded from any web survey. However, this type of non-coverage is slowly disappearing, at least in developed countries where younger generations are increasingly computer literate. Other non-coverage issues still remain whenever the sampling frame does not cover the entire target population.

In the remainder of this section we will focus on non-coverage in list-based probability samples, but the corresponding principles apply equally to non-list probability samples (e.g. probability web intercept surveys). With respect to the non-probability context, these principles hold as useful recommendations and function there as approximations, similar to other sampling principles.

Let us first discuss non-coverage due to Internet non-users, which was a particularly strong problem in the 1990s for developed countries, when Internet users were a very specific minority. At that time, the pressure and expectations of new methods which could solve the non-coverage issue and enable full exploitation of cheap and convenient web surveys were considerable. However, despite all efforts, no sampling and weighting methods were found to help generalize findings from such a small and specific segment to the entire population (Vehovar, Lozar Manfreda, & Batagelj, 1999).

Figures on Internet penetration change rapidly and we provide further evidence in *Internet statistics*, Supplement to Chapter 2, at http://websm.org/ch2. We can say that there is considerable variation even among developed countries; for example, according to Eurostat, in 2013 the average penetration for households in Europe was 79%, but ranged from 49% for Turkey to 96% for Iceland. Many other developed countries have a high percentage around 80%, such as the United States, Japan and Australia, but as of 2014 the majority of the world's countries are still around or below 30%.

Even when Internet penetration is close to or above 80%, the remaining Internet non-users are usually not a random subsample of the general population and the characteristics of Internet non-users, established in 1990s, still hold true today even in the most developed countries. According to US[4] and EU[5] official statistics, the elderly, non-caucasian, certain minorities, less educated and low-income segments are more likely to be non-users of the Internet. These differences are sometimes referred to as the basic digital divide (Vehovar, Sicherl, Hüsing, & Dolničar, 2006), but other divides are also emerging, such as those according to the type and structure of technology usage, which sometimes raises questions about the definition of Internet user (e.g. is the user of an interactive TV an Internet user?)

The other reason for non-coverage in web surveys relates to various deficiencies of the sampling frame – for example, we may not have email addresses for certain segments of students, members, customers, etc., so general issues about the effect of non-coverage exist. Decades ago, with telephone surveys, the general view was that if coverage was below 80% (Groves, Biemer, Lyberg, Massey, Nicholls & Waksberg, 2001), some measures needed to be undertaken, such as the dual frame approach involving the F2F mode for covering the missing units. Similarly, the national readership survey in the Netherlands (Petric & Appel, 2007) – despite Internet penetration above 80% – still required an F2F supplement to the web survey, because Internet non-users were very specific in their reading habits.

In general, however, the acceptable level of non-coverage depends on the characteristics of non-coverage bias, which is defined as the difference between the true population value and the expected estimate in the sample with non-coverage. For variable y we denote the expected bias of the corresponding mean $\bar{y}$ as Bias$(\bar{y})$. In certain circumstances some variables show no bias even with very high non-coverage, whenever the missing units have no specifics in relation to key variables. The situation is thus very similar to the above discussion on general robustness of the estimates in non-probability samples.

The bias of the estimate due to non-coverage is generally proportional to the non-coverage rate (W_n), which is defined as the ratio between the number of units in the population that cannot be included in the sample and the total number of units in the population. It also depends on the difference between the survey estimate in the covered $(\bar{Y}_c)$ and the non-covered population $(\bar{Y}_n)$. The non-coverage bias can be expressed as (Biemer & Lyberg, 2003, p. 69)

$$\text{Bias}(\bar{y}) = W_n \times (\bar{Y}_c - \bar{Y}_n)$$

If the difference between $\bar{Y}_c$ and $\bar{Y}_n$ is negligible, the level of non-coverage has no impact on the bias. Similarly, if non-coverage (W_n) is negligible, we will not be concerned with even high differences between the two segments.

The problem is that very often we do not know in advance any of these parameters (W_n, $\bar{Y}_c$, $\bar{Y}_n$). Nevertheless, it is still advisable to experiment with the above formula, and use it for guessing and simulating various options to see what can be done to be on the safe side. For example, with the expected $W_n = 40\%$ non-coverage and population shares $\bar{Y}_c = 0.20$ and $\bar{Y}_n = 0.30$, we will have Bias$(\bar{y}) = 0.4 \times (0.2 - 0.3) = -0.04$, because we use $\bar{Y}_c$ instead of the true value, which is $\bar{Y} = 0.24$.

Instead of the Bias $(\bar{y})$, it is more informative if we calculate the relative bias, Rbias$(\bar{y}) =$ Bias $(\bar{y})/\bar{Y}$, which is in this example Rbias $(\bar{y})$ = 0.17 (0.04/0.24 = 0.17), after disregarding the negative sign of the bias. This means that our estimate ($\bar{Y}_c = 0.20$) misses the true value ($\bar{Y} = 0.24$) by 17%. This is a very high discrepancy, because 5% and 10% are sometimes the benchmarks for relative bias. Consequently, for many purposes such bias would be unacceptably high; however, the tolerance level depends on the survey topic and other circumstances.

The bias needs to be compared also with sampling variability (see Section 2.2), expressed as the standard error, SE$(\bar{y})$. We then obtain standardized bias, Sbias$(\bar{y})$ = Bias$(\bar{y})$/SE$(\bar{y})$, which may very roughly, assuming an SRS, reflect the t-test value of the bias, where the value around or above $t = 1.96$ hints at the presence of statistically significant bias. If in our case we have SE$(\bar{y})$=0.03, this will result in Sbias$(\bar{y})$ = 0.04/0.03 = 1.3. As this value is very low we cannot talk about a statistically significant bias (despite high Rbias). More examples can be found in *Internet statistics*, Supplement to Chapter 2, at http://websm.org/ch2.

The above calculations, simulations and further investigations of the parameters are essential when deciding on non-coverage. In this respect we have the following options:

- We can conceptually restrict the target population to the narrower survey population which can be reached with our web survey. We may thus focus only on Internet users rather than on the entire population. Of course, the question reappears if such a restriction is in line with the initial aim of our research. For example, if we investigate public opinion, this approach may not work, because Internet non-users also vote and may vote differently from Internet users.
- The same 'do-nothing' approach in sample design can also be used by keeping the focus on the entire target population, but still omitting the units in the non-coverage segment. For example, in case of the general population, we include only Internet users in the web survey and then still generalize to the entire population using various post-survey adjustments (e.g. weighting, imputations), which may correct for non-coverage. The effects of this adjustment are usually

positive but otherwise relatively small (see Section 4.1.4). They are extensively used in non-probability samples in general, in order to compensate for non-coverage, nonresponse and self-selection (Callegaro et al., 2014c).

- An active approach for coping with non-coverage involves more expensive recruitment strategies to attract the missing segment. Typically this means involving a mixed-mode system, where we approach the missing units with some alternative mode, as discussed in Section 2.1.2. Most typically for web surveys, this means combining them with mail surveys, but can also involve dual frames, where independent and also overlapping samples are used (e.g. sample of mail addresses and sample of emails).

Non-coverage is also one of the important challenges in web survey methodology which is being increasingly explored in the scholarly literature (e.g. Bethlehem & Biffignandi, 2012; Smyth et al., 2010), in national and cross-national general population surveys such as the European Social Survey (e.g. Ainsaar et al., 2013), in various research networks such as the NCRM network[6] or Cost Action WebDataNet,[7] and in the various national probability online panels that are being increasingly established (see Section 5.2).

To summarize, we should keep in mind that we have discussed non-coverage only in a probability sampling context. With respect to non-probability samples, these principles can be applied only as an approximation. Of course, we should be aware of the fact that non-coverage already constitutes an important cause for the non-probability nature of a certain sample. Also, we need to emphasize that non-coverage issues in web surveys are especially critical when surveying the general population. Despite increasing Internet penetration, even in developed countries, in 2014 we still typically have 20–30% of Internet non-users and very few countries have surpassed the 90% benchmark. However, we believe that in a few years this specific problem of Internet non-coverage will disappear in developed countries (e.g. OECD countries). In the rest of the world, this process will be much slower.

2.3 QUESTIONNAIRE PREPARATION

Preparation of the questionnaire is usually the lengthiest stage of pre-fielding and typically also requires the largest amount of resources. As with other stages, we predominantly focus on aspects specific to web surveys; however, we cover related general issues to a larger extent in this section, because they are essential for the quality of web questionnaire preparation.

We first provide a general overview of questionnaire development issues (Section 2.3.1), then discuss question types (Section 2.3.2), questionnaire structure, computerization and layout (Section 2.3.3) and engagement aspects (Section 2.3.4). We conclude with questionnaire testing (Section 2.3.5) and integration of questionnaire preparation activities (Section 2.3.6).

2.3.1 General Issues

In this section we present a general introduction to survey questionnaire development by reviewing the main definitions, classifications and concepts.

2.3.1.1 Typologies of Survey Questions

The literature often structures survey questions according to their *content* (Bradburn, Sudman, & Wansink, 2004; Groves et al., 2009; Presser, Rothgeb, Couper, Lessler, Martin & Singer, 2004). When a respondent is asked about observable information, we talk about *factual questions*, ranging from simple demographics and other characteristics to complex issues related to behaviour. On the other hand, *non-factual questions* relate to attitudes, opinions, intentions, expectations, beliefs, perceptions, self-classifications, assessments, evaluations, etc. In addition, there are *psychographic* and *knowledge questions*, which are often treated outside the survey context, within psychology and educational testing. With respect to content we can also distinguish questions according to their *sensitivity* or *threatening nature*. That is, in some cases questions can make respondents uncomfortable, because they invade their privacy, confidentiality or intimacy (e.g. income, sexuality, health) or relate to *socially undesirable* behaviour (e.g. lying, stealing, cheating, etc.).

Another typology often met in the literature is based on the *response format* (Alwin, 2007; Krosnick & Presser, 2010; Saris & Gallhofer, 2014). With the *closed-ended* question format the respondent selects an answer from a list of predefined response categories (e.g. gender, region). In contrast, the *open-ended* question format requires the respondent to type a text (e.g. open comment on some service) or numeric response (e.g. entering a certain value for money).

An essential distinction relates also to *measurement level*, which is determined by the nature of response options offered to the respondent. Due to its importance, this is discussed in almost all methodological and statistical textbooks. For example, respondents can express their degree of happiness – which is a concept related to their inner state – with certain response values which may be expressed with different measurement levels. The corresponding options can range from offering respondents a very unstructured open-ended text format to highly structured measurement level, where respondents select some number, say, on a scale of 1–5. The corresponding measurement level of the question can be nominal, ordinal, interval or ratio:

- For questions with *nominal measurement*, responses can only be distinguished among themselves, but there is no intrinsic ordering in the measurement level itself, so they cannot be sorted. Examples are closed-ended question formats asking about gender, region, religion, as well as open-ended text formats asking for some descriptions.
- *Ordinal measurement* allows response categories to be sorted (e.g. we can say that daily usage is more frequent than weekly usage, or that the response category 'happy' means more happiness than 'unhappy'), but does not allow comparing the differences between categories.
- In *interval measurement*, distances between categories of responses can be compared (e.g. we can say that the difference between years 1994 and 2004 equals the difference between 2004 and 2014).
- *Ratio measurement* in addition includes a zero point, enabling the calculation of ratios (e.g. 40 years is twice as much as 20 years).

The measurement levels are extremely important for our discussion. Readers who are unfamiliar with these concepts can find further explanations and illustrations in *Measurement levels*, Supplement to Chapter 2 (http://websm. org/ch2). They can also consult books on basic survey methodology (e.g. Groves et al., 2009) or the statistical literature (e.g. Kirk, 2007).

We should add that the measurement level of the survey question, which is related to the process where respondents are providing answers, is usually reflected in the corresponding measurement level of the variables in the analysis stage, where it is often labelled as the *scale of the variable*. However, the measurement levels of the question and the scale of the variable are still two separate issues and they do not match automatically. For example, responses obtained with questions using the nominal measurement level can be coded and analysed as ordinal scale variables, or responses obtained with questions on the ordinal measurement level can be treated as interval scale variables in the analysis stage.

Understanding different types of questions according to content, response format and measurement level is essential for the survey questionnaire development process and also for the preparation and organization of the survey *datafile* (Section 4.1), which is a term we use for denoting the file with responses. Usually this is a rectangular matrix, where the respondents (units) are in rows and responses (variables) in columns.

2.3.1.2 Question Development Process

The question development process starts with the conceptualization and operationalization of the theoretical constructs that we wish to measure with the survey. While textbooks from different fields (social, marketing, health research, etc.) approach and structure this process in different ways (Bradburn et al., 2004; Iacobucci & Churchill, 2015; Neuman, 2009; Saris & Gallhofer, 2014), we refer to the very general and simplified description of this process provided by Hox (1997). The questionnaire development process starts with an elaboration of a certain *theoretical construct* or *concept* and the definition of its sub-domains, which we also call *dimensions*. We refer to this process as *conceptualization*. For example, in an employee survey the concept would be 'job satisfaction', while further dimensions (sub-domains) could be 'satisfaction with salary', 'satisfaction with managers', 'satisfaction with working conditions'. This is then followed by *operationalization*, where *empirical indicators* for each concept or dimension are searched for and then translated into the actual *survey questions*.

More complexity occurs when several empirical indicators for each dimension are defined. For example, the dimension 'satisfaction with the salary' can be further operationalized with different empirical indicators, such as 'satisfaction with the actual amount received', 'satisfaction in relation to average salary in organization', etc. In the language of survey questions, we typically name these indicators as *items*. Of course, in case we only have one indicator for a certain dimension, such a dimension matches with a corresponding item. In fact, for sake of simplicity in the discussion, we will assume hereafter that dimensions have only one indicator.

Another complication arises when each concept or its dimension is measured for different *subjects*; for example, respondents are answering questions on job satisfaction for themselves and for their partners. In such cases we have separate items for each dimension of each subject.

Questions can be visually presented to respondents as stand-alone questions, or as questions with several sub-questions, typically grouped into tables. The notion of item here covers both stand-alone question and sub-question, whenever it measures a single dimension of a certain concept for a single subject. In statistical terminology the item corresponds to the concept of the variable introduced in sampling (Section 2.2).

Several questions or tables of questions can be further structured into *blocks*, which usually denote a set of questions that form an entity of content-related questions (e.g. a block of socio-demographic questions, a block of job satisfaction questions, etc.). In self-administered survey modes, including web surveys, the questionnaire usually spans across several pages. Each *page* can contain one or more questions, which is a very important methodological decision.

2.3.1.3 Question and Questionnaire Design Principles

The basics of question wording and questionnaire design are covered extensively in the literature (e.g. Brace, 2008; Bradburn et al., 2004; Krosnick & Presser, 2010; Saris & Gallhofer, 2014). We summarize here some recommendations from Krosnick & Presser (2010), who provide general suggestions regarding question wording: use simple words (rather than technical terms, jargon or slang), simple syntax, specific and concrete wording, and comprehensive and mutually exclusive response options. Questions should measure one dimension at a time, rather than being double barrelled. Words with ambiguous meaning, leading questions, negations – single and particularly double negatives – should be avoided.

More specific suggestions are related to question types according to their content, which can be found in corresponding topic-specific literature. For example, with behavioural questions, attention to memory and recall problems is needed. Many specifics exist also for sensitive issues, proxy responses (where the respondent answers for another person), longitudinal research and specific groups (e.g. children).

Another set of principles deals with the design of the questionnaire as a whole, from the structure of the questions, issues of context and the order of the questions to formatting, writing instructions, visual layout, etc.

2.3.1.4 Measurement Process and Measurement Errors

When the questionnaire is implemented in the measurement stage (i.e. when responses are filled in) random or systematic *measurement errors* can appear (Biemer, Groves, Lyberg, Mathiowetz & Sudman, 2004; Lyberg, Biemer, Collins, de Leeuw, Dippo, Schwarz & Trewin, 1997). Measurement errors are defined as the differences between an observed value and a true value. The correlation between the two values is often expressed by the concept of *validity*, which relates to the problem of whether we truly measure what we aim to measure (Saris, 2012, p. 537). The concept of *response bias* is closely related to validity, which reflects the systematic difference between the responses and the true values (Groves et al., 2009, p. 279). On the other hand, the concept of *reliability* expresses random oscillations related to the stability of the responses across repeated measures (e.g. are the attitudes on general life satisfaction stable if asked again in 20 minutes or the next day?), which is also closely related to response variance (Groves et al., 2009, p. 282). Standardized information about validity and reliability scores often exists, for example for questions in the ESS (Survey Quality Predictor tool)[8] or for marketing research questions (Bearden, Netemeyer, & Haws, 2011).

2.3.1.5 Cognitive Aspect of the Response Process

When answering a survey question, respondents need to perform specific cognitive processes to provide an answer. Research on these processes started in the 1950s (Biemer & Lyberg, 2003, p. 123) and since then numerous models that structure the response process into several components have been proposed (for an overview see Tourangeau & Bradburn, 2010). The most widely recognized is the model by Tourangeau, Rips, & Rasinski (2000), which comprises four cognitive components:

comprehension of the question; *retrieval* of the relevant information from memory; *judgement* of the retrieved information; and finally *response,* with the selection and reporting of the answer. These components also form a basis for studying measurement errors due to respondents and for the development of questionnaire testing approaches, such as cognitive interviewing.

An important descendant of the cognitive approach models is the *satisficing* model (Krosnick, 1999), which deals with various deviations that may occur during the response process. According to this theory, respondents can *optimize* their response behaviour by carrying out all cognitive steps with the necessary effort to come up with an appropriate answer. On the other hand, s*atisficing* occurs when respondents perform one or more of the steps superficially. *Strong* satisficing implicates ignoring retrieval or judgement steps, so respondents interpret the question superficially and provide an answer that appears reasonable in the situation, selecting an easily defensible response, such as a status quo option, no opinion, random selection or responses without much differentiation. *Weak* satisficing implicates carrying out all of the four cognitive steps, but less carefully and thoroughly, such as selecting the first acceptable option or showing acquiescence (tendency to agree).

2.3.1.6 Specifics of Non-Substantive Responses

In addition to the open-ended response format or substantive response options in the closed-ended questions, we can also offer respondents the option of selecting a *non-substantive response* (e.g. 'don't know', 'no opinion'). However, this can fuel satisficing and other forms of low-quality responding (Krosnick, 1991; Krosnick, Holbrook, Berent, Carson, Michael Hanemann, Kopp, … Conaway, 2002; Thomas, Uldall, & Krosnick, 2002), with no evidence of an increase in reliability (e.g. Alwin, 2007, p. 199). We thus follow here the recommendation of Krosnick & Presser (2010) that non-substantive responses should in principle be avoided, particularly with non-factual questions. Exceptions can be made when such a response is considered an important and legitimate option in a specific setting (Manisera & Zuccolotto, 2014) or a question is related to the respondent's knowledge (Sturgis, Allum, & Smith, 2008). Similarly, non-substantive responses may be needed when questions are mandatory, so that respondents are required to select answers to closed-ended questions. When a non-substantive response option is used, it must be visually separated from the substantive response categories (Tourangeau, Couper, & Conrad, 2004), otherwise respondents can mistakenly perceive it as another substantive response category. In web surveys the decision about non-substantive responses closely interacts with the strategy related to reminding or even forcing respondents to reply to certain questions.

2.3.1.7 Question Banks

Before starting our question development, it is important that we thoroughly check the work done in the past in the related area. Data archives have thousands of questions from official and academic surveys that have already been used and tested. This is particularly handy for demographic questions, where there is not much new that we can invent that would prove more valid and reliable. In addition, various academic and government agencies have developed resources dedicated to this issue (e.g. Q-Bank[9] or the Survey Question Bank[10]). Similarly, numerous sources and handbooks with lists of questions exist in the field of marketing (Bearden et al., 2011) or psychometric measurement (Spies, Carlson, & Geisinger, 2010), where validity and reliability scores are reported in addition to the wording. We may add that web survey software suppliers are increasingly developing libraries with rich question banks, sometimes even in multiple languages.

2.3.1.8 Specifics of Web Questionnaires

Web surveys have few specifics in the early stages of questionnaire development, where we deal with conceptualization and operationalization. However, when it comes to question wording and the layout of the questionnaire, the specifics of the web survey context become increasingly important, especially the issues of self-administration and computerization.

Due to *self-administration*, the web questionnaire is the main communication tool in a researcher–respondent interaction. Its task is not only to measure, but also to convey the legitimacy and importance of the survey, to provide instructions and to ensure motivation. Self-administration also generally increases the sense of privacy, with potentially positive effects on disclosure of the required information. Web questionnaires require general and computer literacy, which may be a problem for certain population segments. The visual communication is very powerful, so careful elaboration of instructions, format and layout is needed (see Dillman et al., 2009).

Another specific of the web questionnaire arises from *computerization*, which brings numerous advantages, including interactivity and the option of integrating multimedia elements. Specific aspects are related to reading habits: on the web we tend to scan web pages, picking up individual words and sentences (Nielsen, 1997) and read in an F-shape pattern (Nielsen, 2006). This also applies to web questionnaires, as eye-tracking studies report that respondents spend more time at the top of the questionnaire page (Garland, Chen, Epstein, & Suh, 2013), at the beginning of the response options list (Galesic, Tourangeau, Couper, & Conrad, 2008), and answer in a more dispersed way compared with a P&P questionnaire (Fuchs, 2003).

The changing nature of the *technological environment* is indirectly related to computerization, where devices, interfaces and browsers are being continuously transformed, with important consequences for the user experience. Web survey software increasingly incorporates these advances, which makes web questionnaires even more specific. This software is thus particularly important for web questionnaire development, because it may or may not offer elaborate question types, advanced features, fine formatting options, question banks, guidance throughout the process, etc.

In summary to Section 2.3.1, we can say that the development of a survey questionnaire can be a very complex process, where simplifications, shortcuts, rushing and a lack of professional care can severely damage the entire project. We should thus carefully consider the above-mentioned general issues, as well as the particularities of web surveys, which we systematically review in the next sections.

2.3.2 Question Types

We first present key question types used in web questionnaires, together with recommendations on when to use them and in what layout format. We address the general methodological aspects and not the content of questions, which is otherwise an alternative approach for discussing question types, used in various content-specific literature (e.g. Bradburn et al., 2004).

Throughout our discussion we restrict ourselves to the basic web survey mode, as defined in Section 1.1.1, which means the visual display of the questions on the screen and the limited use of multimedia and animation. It also means that respondents provide answers using a keyboard, mouse, touch screen, or some other manual electronic device (e.g. pointer, stylus, etc.). We further limit the manual electronic output of respondents to words and numbers (i.e. to letters and digits). This excludes situations where the respondent is asked to draw something, as well as other alternative methods of survey measurement (see Groves et al., 2009, p. 150) where the respondent is asked to attach a file, take a photo, enclose scans, receipts, etc., This also excludes automatic measurement (e.g. GPS) and various recordings, such as the inclusion of data from external administrative (e.g. results of exams) or business records (e.g. financial data). We briefly reflect on these alternative survey measurements at the end of the section, not because they are unimportant, but because they are not subject to the classification discussed here.

Within this context we understand a survey question as a specific survey measurement method, based on set of words forming a sentence, which then serves as a stimulus for the respondent to address the corresponding concept.

As a result, the respondent then provides an answer through the related cognitive process.

Our approach is to classify questions according to methodological criteria. We thus initially (first level) separate questions with respect to their methodological complexity:

- *Single item questions* address one dimension of one concept for one subject at a time. In this case we have one survey item also matching one column in the datafile and one variable in the statistical analysis. An example would be a question on the age of the respondent in years.

- *Questions with multiple items* can be more or less complex. In the simplest case, we have a table with several sub-questions of the same format addressing more dimensions for a single subject. For example, we can measure the respondent's general satisfaction on three dimensions, such as 'satisfaction with job', 'satisfaction with family life', 'satisfaction with health'. In this case we have three survey items, which then match with three columns in the datafile and with three variables in the statistical analysis. A similar situation occurs when respondents evaluate one dimension of more subjects (e.g. 'satisfaction with health' for three family members). Again, this results in three survey items, three columns in the datafile and three variables in the statistical analysis. More complex combinations are also possible. For example, a table can consist of sub-questions addressing several dimensions of a certain concept for several subjects, such as three dimensions of job satisfaction for the respondents and for their partners. This results in 3×2 survey items matching six columns in the datafile and six variables in the statistical analysis. Of course, even more complex combinations are possible, with more dimensions and more subjects. However, we still assume here that the respondent deals with each item separately in a sequential manner.

- In addition, *other question types* also exist. Some of them require the respondent to process more items simultaneously. For example, a question may address a concept or several subjects (e.g. ranking more products across some quality dimension). Specific questions also appear in relation to various other combinations, as well as with the extensive use of graphics.

We will further classify single and multiple item questions (second level) according to the measurement level, where we separate the nominal, ordinal, interval and ratio measurement levels as discussed above.

In the next step (third level) we structure each measurement level with respect to key layout implementations of the questions (hereafter denoted simply as *layout*), which depend on the response format, interactive features and graphical appearance of the question. For example, the question about gender on the nominal measurement level can be asked by offering respondents: (a) open-ended text entry to describe their gender; (b) two radio buttons (male/female); (c) a dropdown menu with two options (male/female); (d) numeric entry (e.g. '1' for woman, '2' for man); as well as (e) a graphical layout (e.g. selection of the picture of a man or woman). It would be less appropriate for the situation of the nominal measurement level where we seek dichotomy (male/female), to use (f) scale. However, in some research we may ask respondents to express the perception of their own gender on some scale (e.g. 1–100, 1–10 or 1–5), between the extremes of male and female self-perception.

The literature on web surveys often begins the classification of question types according to the standard HTML elements (e.g. Bethlehem & Biffignandi, 2012; Couper, 2008; Tourangeau, Conrad, & Couper, 2013), which are involved as response options to certain question: radio button, checkbox, drop-down menu and text input. We acknowledge the importance of these HTML elements too, but we consider them only at the final (i.e. third) level of question type classification, when we discuss the layout. Here, due to the prevailing methodological approach of this book, we have rather decided to conceptualize single item questions primarily according to their measurement level. There are four main reasons for this:

- Firstly, it fully corresponds to the substantive activities of the question development process, where the measurement level is initially selected according to the research aims and according to the content of the question. Often, the research aims and the content already determine the measurement level. Only when the latter is selected can we start discussing the layout, which then includes a dilemma about the response format (open- or closed-ended questions), the selection of HTML elements and other graphical aspects.

- Secondly, the measurement level is important because it also reflects the essential specifics of cognitive processes on the respondent's side. The respondent needs first to understand what kind of measurement precision is required (nominal, ordinal, interval or ratio). Each of these levels then requires a specific cognitive process, while the layout has relatively little impact.

- Thirdly, the measurement level determines to a considerable extent the format and structure of the related variables in the datafile, and consequently also the nature of post-fielding processing. All this is extremely important for automatic analysis in preliminary reporting. For example, the means cannot be calculated for nominal measurement.

- Fourthly, the measurement level has permanent conceptual features, rooted in the nature of human cognitive processing, while the role of HTML elements changes with usability and technological developments. This is particularly true for devices that use smaller screens, where the role, importance and perception of HTML elements are modifying.

In the following discussion we identify key question types, classified as described above, address their essential methodological aspects and provide guidance for their use in web surveys.

We are fully aware how difficult it is to follow a discussion on question types without corresponding examples. We have provided an interactive overview of this in *Questions and layouts in web surveys*, Supplement to Chapter 2 (http://websm.org/ch2), which also includes a default statistical analysis related to certain question types.

2.3.2.1 Single Item Questions

The simplest type of survey question addresses a single dimension of a single concept for a single subject, which then results in one item. According to the response format, these questions can be open- or closed-ended. With open-ended questions, the respondent is in principle free to write any kind of response in *text* or *numeric* form, while with the closed-ended format, the respondent needs to select one answer from a list of categories which should be exhaustive and mutually exclusive. The selection can be done with a click (touch), but also by entering the corresponding number (or letter) that denotes the selected option.

Closed-ended questions, where the respondent selects one answer from a list, are also called *single answer questions.* They are different from *multiple answer questions*, where respondents can choose more than one answer from the list of categories, often in the format of checkbox. However, this is essentially a question with multiple items, because each of the response options counts as an item and needs to be treated by respondents separately. Each response option also gets a separate column (i.e. it is a variable) in the datafile (typically with values '1' when selected and '0' when not selected). As such it is thus addressed within the discussion of questions with multiple items.

2.3.2.1.1 Questions With Nominal Measurement

With nominal measurement, responses belonging to a question can be distinguished, but they cannot be sorted according to some substantive dimension, which would be intrinsic to the question. As a consequence, when transferred into the measurement level of the corresponding variable, very limited univariate statistical analysis can be done besides compiling a frequency distribution. The separation between open-ended text entries and the closed-ended format (with different layouts) is particularly critical here.

Open-ended text entries Open-ended text entry questions allow for the collection of responses in text format. We can ask for a *longer narrative answer* (e.g. comments, explanations), for a *shorter narrative answer* (e.g. name) or even for *non-narrative answers* (e.g. URL, email address, CAPTCHA codes, etc.).

Open-ended text entries are the least structured measurement level of survey responses.

We could even say that formally they hardly belong to the nominal measurement level.

As a consequence this type of question can also be exempted from the discussion on the nominal measurement level (Saris & Gallhofer, 2014). That is, it is difficult to talk about the nominal level of measurement because when the respondent is providing answers, there are no categories related to nominal measurement to assist the measurement process. Similarly, when we are dealing with data in a raw format (before cleaning and coding), the responses to the open-ended text entry questions can only be distinguished among themselves. Usually, every response is different, so the number of different responses simply equals the number of respondents (i.e. number of units). Thus, we do not obtain nominal values, which can be statistically analysed as a frequency distribution. This is only possible after a researcher has cleaned and coded the answers into a smaller number of categories in the post-fielding step. The measurement level usually remains nominal, but it can also change. For example, if we rate the open-ended responses according to certain criteria (e.g. less to more favourable) during coding, we may end up with ordinal measurement. However, this occurs only in post-fielding: at the measurement stage itself the question offers no measurement levels to the respondent.

The coding process for open-ended text entries means we assign the same number code to the same characteristics of responses. For example, in questions asking the respondent to comment on a new service, all responses which praise the speed of a new service receive the same code. We discuss coding in Section 4.1.5 of the post-fielding step. Below we only present a few approaches which can be undertaken when formulating and formatting the open-ended text entry questions and which can facilitate the coding:

- We should ask the open-ended questions in a structured way whenever possible. For example, we ask respondents to fill in their first name and their family name as separate entries. Similarly, it is advisable to ask about advantages and disadvantages separately.

Sometimes it is also useful to ask respondents to write down, say, three key advantages and three key disadvantages.

- Explicit requests for structuring can also be formalized with separate entry fields, in particular when we look for lists (e.g. for naming three top restaurants, we present the respondent with three separate entry subfields). However, this is then already a multiple item question.
- Open-ended text entries can suggest a certain structure with additional specifications. For example, the respondent can be asked to complete a sentence.
- For text entries related to specific non-narrative answers, we can impose further structuring and formatting with symbols and subfields (e.g. two fields with @ in between for the email address), various input character restrictions, labelling, instructions and validations, including external ones (e.g. checks with a database of ZIP codes or URL domains). As respondents are sensitive to the visual layout of questions, a careful design of visual layout encourages answers in the desired format. Couper, Kennedy, Conrad, & Tourangeau (2011) and Dillman et al. (2014) provide further practical guidelines for the presentation of open-ended text entry fields, such as labelling of input fields, structuring questions into components, providing templates, etc.
- Open-ended text entry can also be used as a supplement to closed-ended questions. Unless we have a list of all possible categories (e.g. administrative regions), it is useful to add the open-ended option 'Other, please specify'. For example, when asking about the respondent's favourite fruit, we identify 15 of the most popular fruits and capture others with the open-ended option.

The entry fields for open-ended text questions can be of different sizes. When only one or a few words are expected (e.g. name, favourite fruit), the entry field can be shorter and one full line is enough (e.g. 30 characters), which is called a *text box*. A text box is also used with the 'Other, please specify' option, offered as a final category in various closed-ended response formats. When we expect longer text (e.g. comments, explanations), more width (e.g. 60 characters) and more lines

(e.g. five) can be offered. The enlarged text box is commonly known as a *text area*. Web survey software usually allows for the specification of the number of rows of the text entry field, its width and a maximum number of characters allowed.

The size of the text entry field is important for the respondent. It has been determined (Dennis, de Rouvray, & Couper, 2000; Smyth, Dillman, Christian, & Mcbride, 2009) that larger entry fields in web questionnaires increase the length of the narrative response. However, when a respondent is faced with a larger text field, the perception of the burden and the related nonresponse may increase (Zuell, Menold, & Körber, 2015). Alternatives to this are the auto-adjustment of the text field size, also called scrollable boxes (where additional lines automatically appear when the respondent comes to the bottom), or the option for respondents to expand the size of the text field by dragging its lower right corner. The size of the box can be also customized according to previous answers (Emde & Fuchs, 2012b). Unfortunately, these options may not be supported by all software and have not been extensively tested.

Other strategies to obtain richer responses in web questionnaires are strong motivation statements (Smyth et al., 2009) or follow-up probes (Holland & Christian, 2009; Oudejans & Christian, 2010). For example, after providing an open-ended answer, the respondent receives a message acknowledging the response and at the same time is also asked a follow-up question about whether the respondent would like to add any other issues.

Studies have confirmed the advantage of text entries in web questionnaires, which produce longer, more detailed and more revealing responses compared with self-administered P&P questionnaires (Barrios, Villarroya, Borrego, & Ollé, 2011; Kiernan, Kiernan, Oyler, & Gilles, 2005).

We should be aware of the fact that open-ended text entries generally increase the respondent's cognitive burden and require a longer time to respond. This may then impact on the number of low-quality responses (e.g. invalid answers), breakoffs (preliminary terminations of surveying) or item nonresponse (omission of response to certain question), although evidence shows that this does not happen more often with web surveys than with P&P self-administration (Barrios et al., 2011; Kiernan et al., 2005; Kwak & Radler, 2002). Furthermore, text entries limit the quantitative analysis and involve coding, which is inconvenient, subjective, time consuming and expensive.

Whenever an exhaustive list of response options can be specified – and respondents know all of them – we recommend using a closed-ended format. Of course, there are cases when open-ended text entries are unavoidable. Typical situations include too many response options (e.g. names), a degree of complexity that is too high to be structured (e.g. complex sequence of certain actions), or when the options are impossible to foresee (e.g. preliminary enquiry about the most important problems in a certain context). Thus, the decision to use this question type requires a researcher to carefully consider substantive and methodological circumstances; a useful discussion can be found in Krosnick & Presser (2010) and in Saris & Gallhofer (2014). We also caution that this decision should be taken very responsibly, because it can affect different outcomes. For example, Reja, Lozar Manfreda, Hlebec, & Vehovar (2003) found considerable differences when the question of the most important Internet-related problems was asked with an open-ended text entry type compared with a closed-ended one.

Radio buttons Radio buttons are the default option with closed-ended questions requiring one answer from a list of answers for nominal measurement; this is also the default option to be considered with nominal measurement level in general. Radio buttons are the visual equivalent of the P&P questionnaire format and are thus preferred for the *unified design* used in several survey modes (Section 2.1). An additional advantage is that this is an HTML element which appears in many other web contexts (e.g. forms, bookings, payments, etc.) and respondents instantly recognize its function for the selection of only one option. The problem with the HTML radio button format is its

rather small size, which cannot be increased or changed. The selection can require a high degree of precision with the mouse, which can be problematic for certain purposes and populations (Lumsden, 2007). With respect to further layout possibilities, radio buttons can be presented horizontally below or alongside question text, with response option labels usually placed to the right (at least in Western cultures), but can also be placed below or above the radio buttons. The radio buttons can also be placed vertically, which is usually the only option for small screens. To maintain comparability across screens this is then the default recommendation whenever possible. Research has shown that these variations (i.e. horizontal–vertical) have few effects (Toepoel, Das, & van Soest, 2009) even with ordinal measurement, so with nominal ones we can expect them to be even fewer. The same research also showed that grouping response options in more columns of radio buttons is not beneficial; however, we may not be able to avoid it with a large number of categories. The alternative in such a case is an *answer tree*, which means structuring the responses in more steps (e.g. we first select a continent and then the corresponding country).

With radio buttons it is advisable to have a feature that allows unchecking (deselection) when needed. However, not all software supports this, so once the respondent selects a certain radio button, it may not be possible to unselect it and leave the question unanswered.

We may add that when we have items with only two response options, also called *dichotomy* (e.g. YES/NO), a specific alternative of a checkbox layout appears. Here, marking the checkbox means YES and leaving it unmarked implicitly means the answer is NO. While a stand-alone checkbox can be used in registrations and administrative forms, it is highly inappropriate as a layout for web survey questions, because of ambiguities when left unchecked. On the other hand, this can be a specific layout alternative for certain series of dichotomous questions. We therefore discuss this layout later, in the context of multiple item questions.

Drop-down menu   A drop-down menu, also known as a pull-down menu, drop-box, drop-down list or pull-down box, is another popular format for displaying a list of possible responses in closed-ended questions with nominal measurement. It appears in many CASIC modes, but has no comparable option in P&P modes. It is also a standard HTML element commonly used in everyday web browsing, so respondents are familiar with it. It is especially suitable for handling very long lists (e.g. hundreds of countries, year of birth) and should be considered when a radio button layout cannot fit on one typical screen.

Drop-down menus can be time consuming, especially when they include very long lists (B. Healey, 2007). The *autocomplete function* – also called *database lookup*, which is a feature predicting a word or phrase from the list in the drop-down menu after typing in the first few letters – can help here with rapid access to the desired response. For example, Couper, Zhang, Conrad, & Tourangeau (2012) successfully implemented this function in selecting medication from a list of thousands of entries.

When designing questions in the drop-down menu format, it is very important that the initial visible part of the responses is limited to the first line which is labelled 'click here' or 'select from the list', rather than being empty or filled with dashes '---', while offering the first response option should not be used at all.

In case of a very large number of response options the drop-down menu can use a series of related questions where each subsequent question is displayed conditionally on the answer of the previous one. For example, to select a model of car, the respondent first selects the brand, then the model within the selected brand. Here, the drop-down menu of the 'model' adapts interactively to the options selected in the 'brand' menu. This can be done in a single line, instead of tens of lines with an alternative 'answer tree' layout of radio button questions, which requires a sequence of conditional pages. This layout is sometimes referred to as a *drill-down* menu.

In comparison with the radio button layout, drop-down menus have several limitations. When used as a standard HTML element, we cannot add the open-ended option 'Other, please specify' nor the *content search*, which is very valuable if we have many options and the respondent knows the answer (e.g. country of residence). Additional scripts and browser functionalities (such as a combo-box for editable drop-down menus, where respondents can add an option that is not on the list; Couper, 2008, p. 120) can handle these deficiencies, but it is sometimes unclear if users always recognize these extra options.

A more serious problem with this layout format is related to the fact that the respondent does not see all the options in advance before the menu opens, which can be critical when the respondent is not very familiar with all the options.

Studies show a series of disadvantages with drop-down menus in terms of data quality: from stronger primacy effects, by which respondents more often click on response options at the top of the list (Couper, Tourangeau, Conrad, & Crawford, 2004), to increased response times due to the additional click needed to display the list (B. Healey, 2007). In common situations, when we have enough space and not too many response options, drop-down menus provide no advantages over radio buttons (Tourangeau, Conrad, & Couper, 2013, p. 93), so there is very little justification to use them.

Numeric entry   Sometimes we can use closed-ended questions with a numeric entry, where the respondent enters a number that corresponds to a certain response category at the nominal measurement level from a closed set of options. An example would be entering a certain well-known number that denotes a region, postal number or ZIP code. We may also ask respondents to put corresponding numbers (e.g. '1' for male and '2' for female), but very good reasons should exist for this, because it is much less convenient than the alternative with radio buttons. Nevertheless, specific benefits may also exist in situations when the mouse cannot be used effectively, or when the web questionnaire serves for the purpose of recording observations with an external code list. This is commonly used with data entry of P&P questionnaires, as well as in CAPI and CATI surveys.

Compared with the selection of categories with a click (or touch), entering a number is slower, prone to errors and less intuitive. In addition, entries outside the range of response options should be disabled, which we discuss in more detail with interval and ratio measurement, where an open-ended numeric entry is the default layout format. We may add here that instead of digits, we can also enter letters to denote a selected category (e.g. 'A', 'B' … for school grades, or 'M' for male and 'F' for female).

Advanced graphical presentation Closed-ended questions with nominal measurement can be implemented also by using various graphical presentations. For example, radio buttons can be replaced with special visually designed buttons (e.g. larger images of radio buttons) or other images (e.g. stars). Alternatively, verbal descriptions of the answers can be fully or partially replaced by certain graphical or multimedia elements (e.g. audio, video), for example when selecting the best video, the best logotype, etc.

In extreme examples, both the radio buttons and the verbal answers can be replaced with direct visualizations of response options (e.g. pictures of different types of fruits when selecting the best fruit), where the selection is done with a direct click on a specific picture (without the radio button). A specific case is a question with image area selection, *clickable image maps*, where the respondent selects a point on a prespecified area of the picture, for example a region from a map or a body part from a picture of a human. This format is particularly frequent in education (e.g. quizzes, e-learning) and marketing research, where it is sometimes called *hotspot question*.

An advanced graphical option is the use of *drag and drop* functionality, which is very specific and also popular in web surveys, particularly in marketing research. In the case of the nominal measurement level this would require the respondent to select a certain category (subject, usually presented with a picture) with the mouse, and drag and drop it into some preselected location. In this specific example there is an obvious increase in the mouse movements needed, compared with the simple

alternative of one-click selection of the corresponding category. The arguments for using it are usually related to increased involvement and engagement of the respondents.

While radio buttons are commonly presented across different technologies (devices, browsers and interfaces) in a standardized manner, the alternative graphical presentations may not be uniformly supported. Nevertheless, we have observed an emerging trend of new graphical question formats, especially with mobile devices.

We will present further examples later on when discussing the extensive use of graphics, where special care is needed with regard to the possible unintended effects of graphics on respondents' answers.

2.3.2.1.2 Questions with Ordinal Measurement

There are substantive and also methodological differences between a closed-ended category response at the nominal measurement (e.g. select a country of residence) or at the ordinal measurement, such as frequency (e.g. never, sometimes, often …) or agreement (strongly disagree … strongly agree). In contrast to the nominal measurement, the ordinal measurement enables the calculation of a median, a minimum, a maximum and Spearman's correlation coefficient. In practice, results from ordinal measurement are sometimes even treated as if they come from interval measurement, so that a mean and variance can also be calculated. If we further assume a normal distribution for the responses, a full array of multivariate statistical methods can be applied.

However, this important difference is not necessarily reflected in the visual layout of survey questions. For example, the same question layout with radio buttons is used in both cases. Below, we highlight the methodological specifics of the same layout implementations, but when used for the ordinal measurement.

With the ordinal measurement level, both factual and non-factual questions can be used. With non-factual questions (e.g. attitudes), we frequently encounter questions labelled as *rating scales*, where respondents rate (i.e. assign values from a closed list of ordered categories) an underlying concept. We distinguish between *unipolar* concepts (e.g. strength, from low to strong) and *bipolar* concepts (e.g. agreement, ranging from extreme agreement to extreme disagreement).

We may add that the rating scales are often labelled as Likert scales, particularly when denoting a 5-point rating scale. However, we avoid this labelling as it is too often used differently from what Likert originally intended (Neuman, 2009, p. 207).

In practice, rating scales with five response categories or more are often treated in the analysis as the interval measurement level. The prerequisite for this is that the visual distances between adjacent categories are equal, so as to resemble the interval measurement level. Within this context, efforts should be made also to obtain a normal distribution. For example, if all respondents tend to 'strongly agree' when asked about agreement with the statement 'The food was very good', we may consider rewording the question to a stronger assertion: 'The food was exceptionally good'.

Our discussion of question layout implementations within the ordinal measurement level will predominantly focus on rating scales; however, it will also cover other possibilities within the ordinal measurement related to factual questions (e.g. frequency, observed ranks, etc.).

Radio buttons   Radio buttons are the prevailing layout format for rating scales and for the ordinal measurement in general. Radio buttons share all the characteristics we discussed in the context of nominal measurement. In addition, rating scales also face many general methodological dilemmas that originate in traditional survey modes, but still have certain specifics in the case of web questionnaires. As they are very important for scale constructions, we briefly present their essential characteristics:

- Response categories can be numbered (e.g. 1, 2, 3, 4, 5) or can be verbal (e.g. agree, disagree …), or both labelling principles can be used. In specific situations, when numbers are used, they can also be negative (e.g. −2, −1, 0, +1, +2), although this is generally not recommended

because the respondent may tend to avoid negative values (Toepoel et al., 2009). Other combinations exist, for example only end points can be labelled (strongly agree and strongly disagree), while the remaining points are not labelled. The decision depends on the situation, but in general full verbal labelling takes precedence (Dillman et al., 2014; Krosnick & Presser, 2010, p. 275).

- There is an indication that the vertical layout of response categories is recommended over horizontal ones (Krosnick, 2013), but the question of whether this outweighs the required additional space remains.

- In the vertical format, a decreasing order of response categories (e.g. from good to bad) is recommended, because respondents expect positive things first, and because it is more conventional and thus imposes less cognitive burden on respondents (Holbrook, Krosnick, Carson, & Mitchell, 2000; Tourangeau, Couper, & Conrad, 2013). This would mean in principle that we should start with a positive category also in a horizontal format. However, this is contrary to the analogy of the coordinate system used in mathematics and also in the everyday practice of measuring length, time, weight, etc., where the scale goes from low to high (e.g. from 0 to 100). There is little evidence that the orientation of response categories is important for the horizontal layout. However, Toepoel et al. (2009), for example, found small, yet significant differences, with some evidence of primacy effects for the vertical format.

- An odd number of points is recommended (e.g. 5 or 7) so that a mid-point response option exists (Krosnick & Presser, 2010), except in specific circumstances.

- With respect to the number of categories, research has shown that more than seven categories result in smaller gains in data quality, or even in deteriorated quality: see Malhotra, Krosnick, & Thomas (2009) who recommend 5-point scales for unipolar concepts (e.g. from low to high strength) and 7-point scales for bipolar concepts (e.g. from extremely dissatisfied to extremely satisfied). However, in certain circumstances, other alternatives may be justified, particularly 2-, 3-, 4-, 6-, 10-, 11- and even 101-point scales. Some important surveys (e.g. the ESS)[11] use 11-point scales. The research is still inconclusive, since justification exists for a low number (e.g. Alwin, 2007) as well as for a high number of points (e.g. Saris & Gallhofer, 2014).

With respect to verbal labels, it often seems very practical to use wording with commonly used scales (e.g. agree–disagree), although research (Krosnick & Presser, 2010) sometimes shows certain advantages (less acquiescence, higher reliability and validity) of content and construct-specific scales. For example, instead of asking for agreement (disagree–agree) with the statement that the food was tasty, we ask the respondent to rate the tastiness from extremely un-tasty to extremely tasty. The same is also true for other question types, so natural metrics should be used instead of general ones. For example, we ask about the frequency of some events specifically (daily, weekly, monthly …) instead of using commonly used categories (very often, often, not so often …).

The above issues originate in the P&P self-administered questionnaire, but are equally relevant for web surveys. Special care is needed when it comes to the visual presentation of questions and response options, because respondents also consider spacing between categories (i.e. radio buttons) when interpreting distances between them. So, if we plan to use the responses from the ordinal measurement with radio buttons as interval ones in the analysis, equal spacing between categories should be ensured (Tourangeau, Conrad, & Couper, 2013, p. 79). This can be compromised if web survey software adapts the width of the columns to the width of the response labels and therefore introduces unequal widths across the scale.

There are additional specifics in web surveys as regards questions with non-substantive responses ('don't know', 'no opinion'), due to the potential interaction with real-time validations and prompts, which we discuss in Section 2.3.3.

Various rating scale subtypes exist, such as *compare one against another* (when two options are offered horizontally), *semantic differential* (where only end-point options on a horizontal bipolar scale are verbally labelled, such as ugly–beautiful) or *Stapel scale* (unipolar 10-point vertically oriented scale, numerically labelled from −5 to +5 without a middle point).

Drop-down menu   Drop-down menus share the same reasons against their use as outlined in the discussion on nominal measurement, but to an even greater extent. Since the number of categories is usually relatively small in rating scales and other questions with ordinal measurement, one of the key justifications for the use of drop-down menus – the convenience when having a large number of categories – disappears.

Numeric entry   As with nominal measurements, respondents can enter their answers in closed-ended numeric entries also for the ordinal measurement. The same limitations and specifics as with nominal measurement apply. However, in some situations, entering the numbers, such as school grades (e.g. 1, 2, 3, 4, 5), is very simple and intuitive. Of course, entries outside the range of response options should be disabled.

Advanced graphical presentation   The graphical presentation of questions with ordinal measurement is the same as in the nominal measurement when graphics and multimedia can replace radio buttons, response labels, or both. However, more specific alternatives appear here, such as smileys or thumb fingers. For example, faces with different expressions (from least happy to most happy) can be used to present satisfaction with a service. There are some positive reports on using images in rating scales, particularly in psychological research measuring pleasure, arousal and dominance (SAM scales), where images were found useful (Bradley & Lang, 1994). On the other hand, Emde & Fuchs (2012a) did not find any considerable advantages of using faces in web surveys, just delays and problems in response distributions. We raise further concerns against the use of various graphical presentations in the general discussion on graphics and multimedia later on.

Another graphical option used to present possible responses in ordinal measurement is graphical lines or ribbons, with a discrete number (e.g. five) of points in a graphical format on a line, where values can be selected. By this we do not mean a full continuous scale, because this is used for the interval and ratio measurement level, as discussed below.

2.3.2.1.3 Questions with Interval and Ratio Measurement

Here, we jointly discuss questions with the interval and ratio measurement level. In comparison with ordinal measurement, interval measurement enables us to compare differences among values. Ratio measurement relates to numeric quantities (e.g. age, income, weight, height, speed, time, etc.) where – in addition to the characteristics of the interval level – there is also a zero point, which enables the comparison of response values as ratios. In principle, the ratio is the most preferred measurement level, because it enables the broadest array of statistical methods and because, in addition to general univariate and multivariate statistics, relative measures can be used (e.g. coefficient of variation).

The reason why we jointly discuss the two measurement levels is that additional specifics of ratio measurement over interval one are very small, at least at the measurement stage. There are also almost no methodological specifics and differences between the two measurement levels in terms of question development and layout implementation.

We have already mentioned that interval measurement can sometimes be assumed in the analysis stage for rating scales and other questions on the ordinal measurement level.

Open-ended numeric entry Open-ended numeric entry, where responses are typed in as digits, is the most common layout option for questions at the interval and ratio measurement, because it provides high precision. In principle, we expect here numeric entries of infinite possibilities (e.g. salary). However, in reality the border between open-ended and closed-ended numeric questions – where we actually enter a number from a rather closed set of options (e.g. year of birth) – is sometimes blurred.

The size and format of entry fields are very important here, as in open-ended text entries. Tailored entry fields (e.g. a two-digit entry field instead of a ten-digit field, if we ask for the number of children) can result in more precise answers (Couper et al., 2011; Couper, Traugott, & Lamias, 2001). It is thus useful to structure and elaborate the entry fields by specifying the format (e.g. explicit currency signs $, €, £ ...), decimal points, length and subfields (e.g. year–month–day, hours–minutes–seconds). Real-time validations (see Section 2.3.3) are essential here to prevent numeric entries outside the range (e.g. an age of 572 years).

Radio buttons and drop-down menus Closed-ended response formats, such as radio buttons and drop-down menus, are in principle inferior to the open-ended numeric entry, which is usually more precise and neutral (Krosnick & Presser, 2010, p. 267) when it comes to interval and ratio measurement (e.g. salary). However, when we have a very limited number of response categories (e.g. number of children), the radio button layout can be faster. With a higher number of categories (e.g. age), a drop-down menu can be more error-free. In addition, sometimes we may consider categories with aggregated values across the expected range of the scale. For example, knowing that we will only use the age variable coded into three age groups (e.g. <30, 30–49, 50<) in the analysis (thus only at the ordinal measurement level, which means that we lose measurement level precision) it is better to offer immediately a closed-ended question with the three age groups instead of asking for the year of birth and recoding answers later. In general, closed-ended questions are also considered less burdensome for respondents. However, any grouping of values in advance needs to be done very carefully, since there is plenty of evidence on how improper categorization of numeric quantities in the closed-ended format can skew the results (Dillman et al., 2014, p. 161).

Continuous scale A continuous scale can be used in principle only when the response values formally take an infinite number of values on some continuum, instead of a finite number of closed-ended response categories. More specifically, the respondents need to be able to observe and express answers on very detailed interval and/or ratio measurement levels, which is however rarely the case. With attitudinal questions this can be a very controversial issue, so a researcher has to decide whether certain concepts belong to the ordinal or interval measurement. Of course, as soon as we implement a continuous scale, we assume that we have an item on interval or ratio measurement level.

Presentation of the continuous scale requires a simple graphical option where respondents denote their position on a line. The approach originated and raised controversies in traditional surveys in the form of the so-called *line production* (Saris & Gallhofer, 2014, p. 109), with the aim of providing better precision and particularly for avoiding the rounding of numbers (e.g. multiplies of 10 or 5), which often occurs when we ask for numbers in the open-ended numeric format. The advantage in web surveys is that the graphical response is automatically transformed into a numeric value (e.g. 1–100), which can be optionally displayed to respondents in real time.

In web questionnaires the continuous scale most frequently appears as the *visual analogue scale* (VAS) – predominantly in health or marketing research – with a horizontal line and two end-point verbal labels (e.g. agree–disagree). The respondent clicks with the mouse on the selected point (Reips & Funke, 2008). When we add labels (e.g. weak pain, medium pain, strong pain) to other parts of the line, or divide it into numbered segments, this is called a *graphic rating scale* (GRS). The selected position can be additionally marked with a handle so that the respondent drags it left or right. This is sometimes called a *slider bar*. Presentation of the slider bar can be problematic if the handle is positioned anywhere in the scale before the respondent selects an answer (e.g. in the middle of the scale). In such cases the intentional middle response cannot be distinguished from the situation where the respondent omits a response (Funke, Reips, & Thomas, 2011, p. 223).

Continuous scales are sometimes reported to be superior to radio buttons (Funke & Reips, 2012; Reips & Funke, 2008; Torrance, Feeny, & Furlong, 2001), because they are more precise and provide fewer extremes and mid-point answers. Continuous scales are also advocated by Saris & Gallhofer (2014), however, they also advise caution when it comes to implementation, where care should be taken whenever respondents differ strongly in their perception of the question. There is also research that shows the disadvantages of continuous scales. For example, Couper, Tourangeau, & Conrad (2006) showed that continuous scales took longer to complete than using a radio button layout, had higher breakoffs and a higher level of missing data, as well as a higher level of rounding when numeric feedback was provided. Similar problems were found in psychological research (Flynn, van Schaik, & van Wersch, 2004) and in Funke et al. (2011), especially with less educated respondents.

It thus seems that continuous scales may work well only with fully computer-literate respondents and for concepts where respondents can truly separate very fine nuances. Other than that, in general, continuous scales have few advantages and various disadvantages, so their usage requires very explicit justification.

Advanced graphical presentation The continuous scale itself already involves graphics; however, in addition to simple VAS, GRS and the slider bar, described above, many other graphical presentations can be included, from pictures replacing verbal descriptions and figures that appear on the scale to various animations and multimedia. In general, as with other question types we advise caution when implementing graphics.

With this we conclude our review of key layout formats for the corresponding measurement levels with single item questions. Table 2.1 summarizes the possible combinations. Filled circles mark the options which in our discussion are to be considered as default ones, while the open

Table 2.1 Key layouts for single item questions across levels of measurement

Level of measurement	Key response layouts					
	Open-ended text entry	Radio button	Drop-down menu	Numeric entry	Continuous scale	Advanced graphics
Nominal	○	●	○	○		○
Ordinal		●	○	○		○
Interval/ratio		○	○	●	○	○

circles mark the options that may be suitable in certain circumstances but their use requires some explicit justifications. Other options are not considered possible or reasonable (e.g. continuous scale for nominal level of measurement).

Some of the combinations related to open circles are very rare, such as numeric entry for the nominal level, while others are more frequent, such as open-ended text entry for the nominal level. With the latter we may repeat that, so far, we have discussed only single item questions, which excludes any series of open-ended text entries (e.g. for collecting the lists). Similarly, we referred here to the measurement level at the stage of obtaining answers from respondents and not to the measurement level at the stage of statistical analyses (i.e. scale of the variable) where, for example, responses in open-ended text entry questions can be further coded and treated as the ordinal scale. The same situation occurs when data are collected with ordinal measurement, but the corresponding variables are then treated in statistical analysis as being on an interval scale.

2.3.2.2 Questions with Multiple Items

In practice we often group questions with single items to save space or to speed up the respondent's task. The idea of saving space originates from the P&P mode, with the goal of reducing printing costs. In web surveys, space itself is no longer a direct limitation. The increased speed, together with the alleged decrease in the respondent's burden when similar questions are grouped together, remains the main argument for grouping questions. In addition, we may group

questions to add the same context to them. The potential advantages need to be weighed against the danger of lower data quality, which might result from increased complexity, compared with sequences of single item questions.

The grouping of single item questions results in questions which contain sub-questions; we thus talk about questions with multiple items. Such groups of questions are sometimes labelled as a *matrix* (Dillman et al., 2009, p. 179) or *grid*. However, this latter term often denotes a narrower combination of items with the same response options (Tourangeau, Conrad, & Couper, 2013, p. 72). A closer look at the discussions on grid questions reveals that they predominantly address the rating scales with the radio button layout. Another alternative labelling for a series of items with the same response option is a *battery* of questions (Alwin, 2007; Saris & Gallhofer, 2014, p. 86). We prefer to use here the most general notion of a *table* to denote any grouping or combination of questions.

Tables present many methodological challenges. We first discuss *simple tables* with a series of homogeneous questions for several dimensions or for several subjects, where individual questions measuring one item at a time, using the same implementation layout, are grouped together. The term roughly matches practical usage of the notions of battery and grid mentioned above. We thus discuss simple tables with homogeneous questions. For the sake of simplicity – unless explicitly denoted differently – we will talk simply about tables. Later we will reflect on more complex table types.

Again, examples and illustrations for the tables discussed below are presented in the Supplement to Chapter 2, *Questions and layouts in web surveys* (http://websm.org/ch2).

2.3.2.2.1 Tables with Questions at Nominal Measurement

We first observe the grouping of similar single item questions which use nominal measurement. The layout is very important here, as it determines the format of the tables.

Tables of open-ended text entries   When similar items with open-ended text entries are combined into a single row (or column), we get a one-dimensional table, so we prefer to talk about a *series* or an *array* of text entries. For example, we can put three text entries in one line for name, family name and address. In this way we measure three items, resulting in three columns in the datafile and three variables in the analysis. The advantage is that this saves space and eliminates the need to repeat the introductory question text. The labels (e.g. name …) can be added close to the corresponding entry field. When a series of text entries is repeated for five family members (subjects), each in a separate row, we have a two-dimensional table of text entries. In the case of five persons, we have $5 \times 3 = 15$ items measured (15 columns in the datafile and 15 variables in the analysis), packed into a neat interface, which saves a lot of space and is intuitive and user-friendly. Such layouts often appear in household rosters or in social network measurement as the *alter-wise* layout, because we take each alter (e.g. friend) and then assign corresponding answers (values) for all items (name, family name, address). An alternative is the *item-wise* layout, where we have rows for each item (e.g. name, family name, address) and we then assign values for all alters (e.g. friends). Unfortunately, it is not entirely clear whether – and for what complexity – the table layout with open-ended text entries provides an overall higher or lower data quality compared with the corresponding series of individual questions for each family member (Dillman et al., 2009, p. 180).

Tables of radio buttons   When respondents select their employment status from three available categories (e.g. employed, unemployed, retired) in a horizontal radio button layout, this is a single question measurement for one item. Reporting the same category for more subjects, for example five family members, can be conveniently done in a table, with family members listed in separate lines. We then need only one introduction and one set of response labels on top. Although this appears as a two-dimensional table with $5 \times 3 = 15$ radio buttons, only one dimension (employment status) is measured on five subjects (family members) and thus only five entries are required. Therefore, only five items are measured, resulting in five columns in the datafile and five variables in the analysis. Compared with five separate questions, this approach seems faster for the respondent and saves space in the questionnaire. Nevertheless, these advantages might be deceptive, because increased complexity can reduce the attentiveness of the respondents. We return to this issue when discussing tables with ordinal measurement. Of course, this danger also increases if we squeeze in more dimensions to obtain so-called *double tables* or *triple tables* of radio buttons, for example by adding radio button questions for gender for five family members to the same table. This is then a real two-dimensional table measuring $5 \times 2 = 10$ items (two socio-demographic characteristics for five family members).

Tables of drop-down menus   If we put employment status in the above example into a drop-down menu layout, this will rarely be advantageous, as already discussed with drop-down menus measuring only one item. However, if we need to save space, the drop-down menu layout enables clear presentation of additional dimensions in a row. For example, we can have a row with drop-down menus for employment and gender for each subject (e.g. family member). As above, this results in a two-dimensional table measuring $5 \times 2 = 10$ items. This is a very complex layout with a realistic fear of excessive burden and reduced attentiveness among respondents, so good justification is needed.

Tables of numeric entries Employment status in the above example can also be entered with the corresponding numeric entry (e.g. '1' for employment, '2' for unemployment, '3' for retirement) in a series of closed-ended numeric entries for each family member. However, this could be difficult to justify, due to the objections we have already raised in the discussion of questions with single items. To a lesser extent – due to effective space-saving – the same disadvantages hold true for 5×2 table of closed-ended numeric entries (two dimensions for five subjects), where the above discussion on drop-down menus also applies.

Series of dichotomous questions When we have a set of questions with a dichotomous status (YES/NO) – typically asking about evidence or possession of certain goods, characteristics, experience or agreement – it is particularly convenient to group them together. For example, we can ask whether a respondent visited each of the four countries listed by displaying the question text only once and listing the four countries as sub-questions. There are several possible layout options for doing this: a series of YES/NO radio buttons, a series of checkboxes, or a multiple selection box.

The first possibility is the *series of YES/NO radio buttons* in the form of a simple table of radio buttons discussed above. In this case, each country is put in a separate line, while two (YES and NO) radio buttons are positioned on the right. This seems much simpler than repeating the same question and response options separately for each country. However, with a question about last year's visit for 28 EU countries or for the 50 US states, this is not a good solution because a high number of redundant clicks on the option NO is usually needed.

The *checkbox* is another layout alternative for a series of radio buttons in the case of dichotomy. Similarly to radio buttons and drop-down menus, the checkbox is also a standard HTML element. As already mentioned, a stand-alone (single) checkbox is rarely used in web questionnaires, because the unchecked option with the implicit meaning NO is unclear compared with an explicit selection of NO in the corresponding radio button layout. That is, the unchecked option can be the result of an omission or refusal. Rather than for survey questions, checkboxes can be thus used in web surveys to get informed consent from respondents (e.g. 'Check if you agree to the conditions of the study and are willing to participate') or allow them to sign up for results (e.g. 'Check if you would like to receive the results of the study').

On the other hand, putting a *series of checkboxes* together is very common in web questionnaires. This layout is often labelled simply as a *checkbox question*, a *check-all-that-apply* or a *multiple answer question*. In the above example, a list of countries with a checkbox adjacent to each country would appear. The respondent selects (checks) only the countries visited, but is spared responding on the unvisited ones. Such questions do not belong to the group of single item questions, as might appear at first sight. Here, one concept (visit) across several subjects (countries) is measured, resulting in as many items as there are subjects, which also includes the corresponding number of columns in the datafile and variables in the analysis.

We may add that a situation with a checkbox question where the number of options is limited (e.g. only two selections are allowed) brings much more complexity (because, to select only two options, all options need to be considered simultaneously) and already belongs to ranking, which we discuss later.

Despite the checkbox being an HTML element – so respondents generally know that it gives the possibility of selecting more than one option – an explicit instruction that several answers may be selected is strongly recommended, as this may not be clear to some respondents.

A potential advantage of the checkbox is that it is quicker to complete in some situations (Callegaro, Murakami, Tepman, & Henderson, 2015) and also takes up less space than the alternative of YES/NO radio buttons. In the latter case, the respondent is explicitly faced with all options and needs to select an answer for each of them, so this is sometimes also called a *forced choice question*.

However, checkboxes also have serious disadvantages (Bradburn et al., 2004, p. 171). Firstly, problems can appear with mixed-mode surveys, since the standard way of asking multiple answer questions in auditory modes (like telephone surveys) is in the form of YES/NO items. Conversion to checkboxes for the web mode actually changes the context of the question and may introduce methodological differences among modes.

Secondly, an unchecked item in a series of checkboxes can have multiple interpretations. We usually assume that an unchecked item denotes the answer NO. However, the respondent might have missed that option or refused to answer, which in fact denotes item nonresponse. Likewise, respondents might not be sure, so the unchecked item actually means 'don't know'. This limitation can be avoided by adding the option 'none of the above' or 'other, please specify' to the end of the checkbox items, which may help in identifying some item nonresponse.

A meta-analysis of several randomized experiments that compared the layout of a series of checkboxes and YES/NO radio buttons (Callegaro et al., 2015) found that the YES/NO format uniformly provides higher endorsement rates. Nevertheless, the rank and the relative ordering of the items still remain the same in both formats.

To summarize, we prefer a series of YES/NO radio buttons, since it gives us a clearer interpretation of item omissions, respondents might consider each item more carefully, and it is more comparable across survey modes. Explicit reasons should thus exist for using the checkbox question. One such situation is when we have a few very clear and understandable categories (e.g. race origin question). Another is when our main focus is on ranks and relationships between items, and not so much on their precise absolute shares (i.e. exact endorsement rates or market shares). In such situations, the pressure to minimize the respondents' survey time can make the checkbox question more favourable. The same is true when we have a large number of categories and only a few of them relate to each respondent.

The *multiple selection box* is another alternative for a series of dichotomous YES/NO questions. Sometimes it is also called the multiple selection drop-down menu, multi-select or even combo-box question. Visually, it resembles an opened drop-down menu; however, the respondent can select several responses from the list, by holding down the CTRL key, which is not possible with the standard drop-down menu. Visually, a multiple selection box differs from the drop-down menu because more options are immediately visible without any action from the respondent. In the case of several options, a clearly visible scrollbar is available, and is used to see other options. In the above example of countries visited, instead of a series of YES/NO radio buttons or a series of checkboxes, one single multiple selection box could be used to select all countries visited. An explicit instruction for pressing the CTRL key is strongly recommended here, since this option might not be familiar to all respondents. Due to the complicated interface and reduced familiarity, explicit justification is needed to use this layout. Similar to drop-down menus, it might be practical for a large number of categories and extreme space limitations. A very important improvement here arises when all the potential categories appear in one box on the left, and are then moved into another box on the right with the drag and drop function.

Tables of checkboxes and multiple selection boxes In all the above examples of layout implementation of a series of dichotomous questions, we discussed the measurement of a single concept across several dimensions. In the case of country visits, we have four countries, resulting in four measured items (four columns in the datafile and four variables in the analysis). In a more complex situation, we may have the same question, but repeated for more subjects (e.g. five family members). Using a series of checkboxes (a *table of checkboxes*) we obtain a two-dimensional table with $5 \times 4 = 20$ items.

Using a multiple selection box for each of the subjects – which means a *table of multiple selection boxes* – further increases the main advantage of a multiple selection box: it takes up even less space, since a single column with five multiple selection boxes will do, one for each family member. We could even add another column of multiple selection boxes: for example, which of the listed languages (English, Italian, Slovenian) each family member speaks, producing a total of $5 \times 4 + 5 \times 3 = 35$ items. Needless to say, the disadvantage of multiple selection boxes in terms of unfamiliarity among the respondents becomes even more pronounced, particularly because a layout with drag and drop into another box is not possible in this case.

2.3.2.2.2 Tables with Questions at Ordinal Measurement

Similar to single item questions, our discussion of tables with questions at ordinal measurement predominantly focuses on rating scales. Here, this is even more justified, since a lot of research has been conducted with tables of rating scales, also labelled as matrices, batteries or grids.

Let us stress that many aspects (e.g. number of rows and columns) as discussed here in relation to tables with rating scales relate to the layout of tables in general.

Tables of rating scales with radio buttons The radio button layout prevails in tables with ordinal measurement, where each item – that is, each dimension (sub-question) of the measured concept(s) or each subject – is presented in a separate line. For example, we can ask the respondent to rate an overall travel experience for four countries on a 5-point rating scale. Typically, the question wording is placed on the left and the repeating response options (i.e. the radio buttons) on the right, while a reverse orientation – lines belonging to response categories and dimensions in columns – is generally inferior (Galesic, Tourangeau, Couper, & Conrad, 2007). Labels for response options are displayed only once, in the header at the top of the response columns. As already shown in the discussion on tables with nominal measurements, we have here only a series of single rating scales.

As with items on rating scales, we should be careful about column spacing among the response options in tables, because uneven spaces may affect response distributions (Tourangeau, Conrad, & Couper, 2013, p. 79).

Care is needed when the number of columns and rows is high, which is a general issue for all types of tables. We should avoid horizontal scrolling (left–right), even if this requires a reduction in the number of scale points (e.g. from 7 to 5). Vertical scrolling (up–down) is less critical, but is still best if it is avoided, due to disappearing top column labels when scrolling down a long table. To display the entire table on a typical computer screen, we can limit the number of dimensions in rows (items) per table to 8–10. Another solution is a programming feature where the header of the table is fixed and only items are scrolled, or the header labels are repeated after a certain number of items. However, as long tables also increase the respondent's fatigue, they are generally detrimental.

Marking the lines in the table with alternate shading is recommended for better separation among them. For example, Crawford, McCabe, & Pope (2005) suggested using light-grey background shades in alternating rows to improve readability. Dynamic shading – the font colour of the row changes or shading is provided after a response has been selected – was also successful in reducing item nonresponse (Galesic et al., 2007), though pre-selection shading and mouse-over highlighting can be detrimental (Kaczmirek, 2011). In general, however, when formatting the tables we should avoid any redundancy and visual clutter, so that the design of the table can fully serve its basic purpose: enabling respondents to provide quality answers in a user-friendly manner.

As summarized in Lozar Manfreda & Vehovar (2008), tables of rating scales with radio buttons save space, make the questionnaire look shorter, and are convenient to create. They often require less effort from the respondents, as there are fewer instructions and response labels. Mouse movement is also reduced, as well as the response time. On the other hand, such tables can have serious disadvantages, as shown by various studies:

- When the complexity of tables increases the respondents' cognitive burden, they can react with various satisficing strategies (e.g. smaller differentiation of answers), resulting in lower data quality (Fricker, Galesic, Tourangeau, & Yan, 2005; C. Zhang, 2013).
- There is evidence (e.g. Lozar Manfreda, Batagelj, & Vehovar, 2002; Toepoel et al., 2009) and concern (e.g. Couper, Tourangeau, Conrad, & Zhang, 2013, p. 113) that tables increase item nonresponse in comparison with a sequence of single item questions.
- Tables may change the nature of questions, because the items are placed in a comparative framework, which may result in context effects. These effects are weak but still present in web surveys (e.g. Tourangeau et al., 2004).
- Tables are often reported as being the most critical point at which respondents abandon the survey (e.g. Henning, 2011; McMahon & Stamp, 2009).

We lack systematic research where potentially negative effects (e.g. lower data quality) of tables of rating scales with radio buttons would be compared with actual disadvantages (e.g. increased time and length) of a series of single radio button questions as the alternative format. One reason for this deficit is the perplexing factors that can appear. For example, the effect of a table layout on breakoffs can differ at the beginning and the end of the questionnaire. Similarly, the effects of table layout on satisficing strategies can differ for 'professional' respondents in online panels and

for novices. We also advise caution regarding research on response times, which is often influenced by the effects of page design, where each item is placed on a separate web page as an individual question. Minor differences in response times were found when tables were compared with a sequence of single item questions on the same page (Bell, Mangione, & Khan, 2001), despite the fact that the latter option resulted in a questionnaire that was doubled in length. On the other hand, having each question on a separate page can cause an increase of over 50% in response time (Callegaro, Yang, Bhola, Dillman, & Chin, 2009), which is mostly due to the effect of page breaks and not directly related to the specifics of the table layout.

Unfolded tables – horizontal scrolling matrix The *horizontal scrolling matrix* (HSM) is an alternative layout for presenting sub-questions in tables with rating scales using radio buttons. The sub-questions (i.e. items) appear on the screen one by one, with responses (radio buttons) in either a vertical or a horizontal layout. The respondent sees only one sub-question at a time. The next question is automatically presented after the previous one is answered; there is no need to click on the 'Next' button. Navigation with an item counter and a visual bar provides control over the number of questions answered and progress. This format shows promising results with respect to context effects and reduced complexity (Klausch, de Leeuw, Hox, de Jongh, & Roberts, 2012). The approach is particularly suitable for devices with small screens (e.g. smartphones) and certain web survey software automatically transforms tables into such separate questions whenever a small device is detected (see Section 5.1).

Other tables with questions at ordinal measurement Drop-down menus, open-ended numeric entries and advanced graphical layout are alternative implementation layouts not only for simple tables with the rating scales, but also for other questions with ordinal measurement. The discussion of their limitations was covered in single item questions and with tables of rating scales, and they are also fully relevant here. Similarly, all the general problems with table layout apply too.

2.3.2.2.3 Tables with Questions at Interval and Ratio Measurement

The specific features of radio buttons, drop-down menus, numeric entries and continuous scales, serving as potential layouts for single item questions in the interval and ratio measurement levels, apply to corresponding tables as well. With respect to the layout itself, the general principles already discussed in relation to tables also hold true. We may only add that the cumbersome appearance of tables of continuous scales – compared with a more familiar radio button layout – can potentially reduce participation in general population surveys.

The *open-ended numeric entry format*, as the default table layout for the interval and ratio measurement levels, is closely related to those issues concerning open-ended text entries, as discussed with tables at the nominal measurement level. Namely, a series of open-ended numeric entries (e.g. height, width and length) strongly resembles a series of open-ended text entries (e.g. name, family name, address).

A date entry, which is basically a simple series of three numeric questions, often serves as a typical case for discussing how variations in the layout implementation of questions affect the responses. To summarize, a simple series of three numeric entries for the year, month and day with symbols 'DD', 'MM' and 'YYYY', added close to the entry field, can be a good solution (Christian, Dillman, & Smyth, 2007; Couper et al., 2011b), but drop-down menus can be used as an alternative too (Couper et al., 2011b).

2.3.2.2.4 Combined Tables

In all the above cases, questions of the same measurement level and of the same implementation layout are combined in the form of tables, resulting in what we call simple tables. However, the complexity of tables can increase with *combined tables* (sometimes also called 3D tables), which combine more measurement levels and layout formats. An example is household rosters, where

for each person we may have an open-ended text entry (name), an open-ended numeric entry (age) and a drop-down menu (gender) in one line. In addition, such lines are combined together in a table for members of the whole household. In general, we should be cautious about adding such complexity and should consider splitting such a table into sets of simpler tasks. However, situations exist where the savings in space and time may outweigh the potential disadvantages. This is particularly true for factual questions, which are extensively used in business surveys (e.g. financial sheets with entries for items by years). Another situation is where combined tables are required to reflect fully the parallel P&P forms, although this may not be the optimal solution for web questionnaires. Certain general usability principles were developed for this setting by Morrison et al. (2010), and should be carefully implemented in web questionnaires.

In conclusion, should tables in web questionnaires be used or not? As usual, there is no uniform solution, but we can still summarize certain conclusions. Although these are predominantly based on the most commonly used simple tables with rating scales, we believe they can be largely generalized to other table layouts as well. In the majority of situations, a well-designed table can save space. But an improper implementation can seriously affect data quality. Even when properly designed, there are indications that tables can cause problems (e.g. context effect, item nonresponse, satisficing). On the other hand, there are no clear indications about the advantages of using tables, with the exception of the unverified belief that – due to the obvious reduction in space – tables directly save response time and allegedly increase response rates and data quality. Consequently, a general recommendation would be to avoid – or at least minimize – the use of tables whenever possible. As tables importantly make the questionnaire more difficult, they may cause more damage to data quality than slightly lengthier alternatives with simpler questions (Burdein, 2014). In any case, despite considerable past research, we still lack a comprehensive study that compares tables with the alternatives (i.e. sequences of single questions) and simultaneously addresses all key aspects of data quality.

2.3.2.3 Other Question Types

In addition to the above question types, which relate to single item questions or their combinations in (simple) tables, various other question types exist. They are relevant when the respondent needs to consider more items (dimensions, subjects) simultaneously or when extensive graphics are involved, as well as when questions are combined and implemented in very specific contexts. Due to their complexity, we do not structure them systematically, but we illustrate below some common examples.

2.3.2.3.1 Ranking

Ranking mimics the card sorting technique used in F2F interviews, where respondents sort a set of cards (subjects) according to a single criterion (conceptual dimension), for example brands according to their preference. A similar approach is *grouping*, where respondents group certain subjects, for example grocery products, clothing products, etc. Respondents can be asked to select or rank only certain subjects, for example the top three subjects. The ranking task can also be split into several steps, as in *paired comparisons*, where not all, but pairs of subjects are compared/sorted at a time, or in *maximum difference scoring* (MaxDiff), where only the extreme subjects are identified, such as the most important and the least important.

Usually we have only one dimension; ranking according two dimensions is also possible, but very rare (Bradburn et al., 2004, p. 176).

Ranking questions can be implemented using the list of short numeric entries, into which a respondent enters a rank for each subject. Another possibility is to drag and drop subjects from one list to another in a preferred order, or to reorder the subjects within the same list. Blasius (2012) found the drag and drop layout superior to all alternatives (numeric entry, movement with arrows, most–least selection) in terms of the response time and item nonresponse. However, the drag and drop technique may be problematic for some users, due to technical limitations, particularly if mobile devices are used to access the web questionnaire.

The ranking task is cognitively very demanding, though it appears as a simple ordinal measurement question. However, an important specific of ranking is that two subjects cannot be assigned the same rank value from the available ordinal categories. As a consequence, the respondent needs to consider more subjects simultaneously, which is already demanding with five subjects, and becomes very difficult with more than ten.

Serious controversies about ranking vs rating already exist in traditional survey modes, but have been reinforced with the potentials of drag and drop in web questionnaires (Neubarth, 2010). However, the dilemma remains relatively under-researched. The rating ensures independent responses for each subject, higher validity, richer statistical analyses and lower cognitive burden compared with ranking. In addition, once we have the ratings, we can always sort the subjects to obtain the ranks. Nevertheless, ranking may be preferred when we have very small differences in ratings or when we cannot accept more subjects with the same rank. For example, a respondent may endorse four products with the highest rating (e.g. score 5 on a 1–5 rating scale), yet we would like to know the respondent's decision about purchasing only one or two. For this purpose, we need them to be sorted with the ranking approach.

2.3.2.3.2 Constant Sum

A *constant sum* question – sometimes also called a *running tally* – denotes a series of open-ended numeric entry questions (e.g. hours spent daily on certain activities), where responses are additionally restricted to a certain fixed sum (e.g. daily number of hours to 24). This is another example of a cognitively demanding question, where respondents need to consider and process more dimensions or subjects (items) at the same time. Implementing a real-time automatic sum, accompanied by certain prompts, in this case clearly increases the data quality (Callegaro,

DiSogra, & Wells, 2011; Conrad, Tourangeau, Couper, & Zhang, 2010).

2.3.2.3.3 Extensive Use of Graphics

Graphics are a very powerful feature of web surveys. Although we mostly focus on the basic web survey mode, where the use of multimedia (images, audio, video, animations) is limited, we nevertheless present below some of the possibilities of using extended graphics for survey questions, and discuss them briefly in relation to data quality. We return to this issue later when we address the entire visual layout of the web questionnaire and gamification (Section 2.3.4).

Graphics for illustrating survey questions. The use of graphics to illustrate survey questions in web surveys is attractive, easy and inexpensive, compared with other modes. However, a general concern exists in academic (e.g. Couper, 2008), as well as in marketing research (e.g. Poynter, 2010, p. 55) about the weak level of control researchers have on corresponding effects. Firstly, various technical difficulties may slow down download time, produce a different appearance of colours and fonts, and prevent appropriate functioning on certain devices and browsers. For example, Lozar Manfreda et al. (2002) report that when brand logos were added to questions in web questionnaires, the breakoff rate increased. Secondly, while technical problems are diminishing with increased Internet connection speeds and technical standardizations, this is not the case with unpredictable effects on responses.

When graphics are the essence of the question – as in a question on logotype preference – little can go wrong. However, when they are used merely as an additional questionnaire element (e.g. as an attempt to make the questionnaire more attractive), unpredictable side effects may occur. This is particularly problematic when graphics are inconsistent with the verbal context, which generally takes precedence over the visuals (Toepoel & Couper, 2011). A typical example is a picture of a healthy or a sick person next to a question on respondents' health, which then generates differences (3.4 vs 2.5 on a 7-point scale) in responses, with additional effects depending on the size and position of the picture (e.g. previous page, header, question side) (Tourangeau, Conrad, & Couper, 2013, p. 88). There is little evidence that adding non-essential pictures will improve data quality or increase satisfaction with the questionnaire (Toepoel & Couper, 2011), which is otherwise a frequent idea behind the use of graphics. No advantages of pictures were found also by Deutskens, de Ruyter, Wetzels, & Oosterveld (2004) and Ganassali (2008).

In general we should use additional graphics very carefully and thoroughly think about the possible side effects. In case of doubt, a conservative approach is recommended, particularly in prevailing situations when there is no research evidence to support the advantages of additional graphical elements. Such an attitude may seem unusual, conservative and even out of date, because graphics and multimedia are essential advantages of the web survey mode. Nevertheless, without evidence of advantages and corresponding guidelines, it is better to be on the safe side.

Graphics for simulating social presence. Pictures or video of interviewers may be used in web questionnaires to simulate social presence with the idea of increasing motivation and data quality, as successfully shown by Półtorak & Kowalski (2013). Experiments on this issue have replicated the effects from interviewer-administered surveys, particularly gender (Fuchs, 2009; Tourangeau, Couper, & Conrad, 2003) and the ethnicity of the interviewer (Krysan & Couper, 2006); thus, their use should be treated with caution.

Graphics forming new question types. Apart from the use of graphics as an additional element illustrating survey questions, graphics also provide opportunities for new question types and alternative layouts to existing ones. We have already presented some examples in our discussion (drag and drop, images replacing radio buttons, hotspots and continuous scales) and below we provide some more illustrations of questions in web questionnaires which take functional advantage of graphics:

- *Calendar layout* as a graphical interface for date format is an alternative layout asking for the date. Pop-up calendars are used in this case, and selecting a date from the calendar fully replaces the need for numeric entries or drop-down menus. Their use in various other contexts (e.g. online booking) makes this format increasingly advantageous for many situations in web surveys. More complex versions of online calendars are used in life history measurement, with graphical representations of dates, including certain landmarks, in order to simplify complex recall tasks (Glasner & van der Vaart, 2013).

- Selection of subjects in a *virtual reality environment* is an extension of ranking; for example, in a virtual supermarket products are picked up, inspected and placed in a certain order into a shopping basket using the drag and drop function (Brace, 2008, p. 169).
- *Heat-map* questions rely on a graphical interface, where respondents click on a point in the picture, according to a certain dimension (e.g. most important, attractive or unattractive part). There are no predefined areas here as with graphics discussed in the nominal measurement level (e.g. selecting regions). As each point matches the two-dimensional coordinates at the ratio measurement level, this enables very fine analyses. The results of corresponding heat-map analyses are density focuses presented by coloured graphs, similar to reporting on eye tracking or mouse movement. The majority of applications of this layout relate to usability and evaluation studies.

More examples of graphics forming new question types can be obtained on various marketing research websites (e.g. GMI).

2.3.2.3.4 Content-specific Implementations

We initially restrict our discussion on question types in relation to methodological aspects and exclude various content-specific questions (e.g. job satisfaction), which are sometimes also protected by copyright (e.g. Q12 questions for measuring employee engagement by Gallup Consulting; Harter, Schmidt, Killham, & Asplund, 2008). We also exclude specific combinations of questions closely related to certain research methods. These aspects essentially bring no new question types, but they do create very specific implementations. We thus highlight a few examples which typically illustrate their extensions in the web survey context:

- **Ego-centric social network questions** collect lists of people (alters) built with name generator(s). Respondents (egos) then answer the same questions (e.g. on age, gender, relation) for each alter from their network (e.g. friends). The *name generators* are formally a series of open-ended text boxes, where respondents identify the names of network members. The same layout can be used to generate lists of products, services, destinations and other subjects, especially in marketing research. Research on the most appropriate and standardized implementation layout of such questions in web questionnaires is still in progress (e.g. Lozar Manfreda, Vehovar, & Hlebec, 2004; Vehovar, Lozar Manfreda, Koren, & Hlebec, 2008). Major challenges are related to the graphical interface and format of the name-collecting text boxes, where the sequential appearance of text boxes, with the next box displayed only after the previous one is filled in, seems to be preferred (Hogan, Carrasco, & Wellman, 2007). For collecting data on alters, a series of questions for each alter can be used, either item-wise or alter-wise (Coromina & Coenders, 2006; Vehovar, Lozar Manfreda et al., 2008). The potential of the graphical interface to replace survey questions for social network measurement presents a further challenge (Hogan et al., 2007; Koren & Hlebec, 2006; Lackaff, 2012).
- **Conjoint analysis questions** integrate ranking questions into a series of questions with potential decisions (e.g. the purchase of a product). A carefully designed setting is used here, with different levels (ranks) of characteristics. This layout then enables us to apply a conjoint analysis approach. For example, respondents need to decide – among other variations – between a fast, cheap and small car vs a slow, expensive and large one. This approach can also use rating scales.
- **360°** or **multi-rater feedback** is a variation of the social network questionnaire used in human resource management (HRM), where each employee rates (evaluates) a list of persons from the higher (managers), lower

(subordinates) and peer (coworkers) levels. The web is particularly convenient for this task, but raises numerous methodological challenges (LeDuff Collins, 2009).

2.3.2.3.5 Questions Including Observations and External Data

Data from respondents in web surveys can also be collected by other methods (Groves et al., 2009, p-150), using recordings, plug-ins or file uploads. In this way audio recordings, drawings, signature scans (receipt payment), barcode or QR code, photographs (e.g. selfies), videos, biomarkers (e.g. measuring weight), media channel recognition (e.g. radio, TV) or GPS location can be collected. These possibilities represent an extremely important advantage of web surveys, particularly with the use of mobile devices. However, we will not go into more detail because we initially restricted the discussion to basic web survey mode.

With this we conclude our overview of question types in web questionnaires (Section 2.3.2). We followed the classification according to the methodological conceptualization, starting with complexity and then with measurement level and layout variations.

However, when we are creating web questions, we typically encounter the structure of question types provided by the web survey software used, which is determined to a large degree by the technical nature of selecting sub-settings and sub-options. At the very first level, web survey software usually separates single item questions and tables, open and closed-ended questions, questions with more answers, etc., which are closely related to HTML elements. This first level navigation for the question-selecting process in web survey software also depends on the frequency of use of various question types. Thus, the most frequent types (i.e. radio buttons, checkboxes, open-ended text and numeric entries, simple tables of rating scales with a radio button layout) are usually more easily available. See details in *Frequency of appearance of question*

types in web surveys, Supplement to Chapter 2 (http://websm.org/ch2).

In sum, selection of the most appropriate question type is often a very complex decision that needs to be guided by considerations of question content, clarity of presentation, technical requirements, and the task difficulty it imposes on the respondent. It is especially important that a specific type is not used simply because it is available or because it looks innovative and interesting – the primary criterion of use should be the data quality it provides for our research purpose.

2.3.3 Questionnaire Structure, Computerization and Layout

A survey questionnaire is much more than just a sequence of questions. Especially in the self-administered modes, such as web surveys, it can be regarded as a medium of conversation between respondents and researchers (Schwarz, 1996). The questionnaire's role is to ensure the flow of this conversation. This is achieved through the questionnaire's structure, interaction with the respondent and visual layout.

2.3.3.1 Structure of the Questionnaire

Decisions related to the structure of the questionnaire involve a broad spectrum of factors that we briefly address here: order of questions, distribution of questions across pages, inclusion of non-question pages, navigation, division of the questionnaire into sections and blocks of questions, and the use of special layouts for specific purposes.

2.3.3.1.1 Question Order and Context Effects

It is well known that the order of questions within the questionnaire is important and may guide their interpretation and the provision of answers. When one question affects the processing and answering of other questions, we talk about *context effects*. These effects have few specifics for web surveys and many studies report on their occurrence (Couper et al., 2004; Ester & Vinken, 2010; Malhotra, 2008; Nielsen & Kjær, 2011; Siminski, 2008), including questionnaires on mobile devices (Mavletova, 2013; Peytchev & Hill, 2010). The general principles of survey methodology can be thus directly applied to web questionnaires (Krosnick & Presser, 2010, p. 264): questions should be grouped by topic, starting with those mentioned in the invitation, and then proceed from the most to the least salient; within each topic there should be a flow from general to more specific questions; questions should also be grouped by format and logic (e.g. chronology of events); starting questions should be simple and attractive, while demographic and sensitive questions should be left to the end.

Context effects can be prevented by avoiding tables and by increasing the number of page breaks to separate the questions visually. Furthermore, question order effects can be handled with randomization, which we describe further in this section. More information on context effects can be found in general textbooks, such as Krosnick & Presser (2010, p. 291), Dillman et al. (2009, pp. 157–165) and Tourangeau et al. (2000, p. 197).

2.3.3.1.2 Page Breaks and Paging vs Scrolling

Questions can be distributed across questionnaire pages in different ways. Two extreme approaches regarding the number of questions per page are a *one-page design* (also named *scrolling*), where all questions are presented on a single page, and a *one-question-per-page design* (also named *paging*). The comparison of these two approaches was the focus of some of the first web survey experiments (Lozar Manfreda, Batagelj & Vehovar, 2002; Vehovar & Batagelj, 1996). These experiments found no differences in break-off rates for a 7-minute survey on general topics, but the scrolling design had more questions that were left unanswered. On the other hand, it was faster and showed lower response times. The latter difference was in large part due to the slowness of the Internet connections at the time. Nevertheless, even today it seems that these essential findings still hold true, although weakly.

The paging design has the advantage of resembling interviewer-administered questionnaires, where respondents are presented with only one question at a time. It also has an advantage of easier and more robust server-side implementation of interactive features, which are only executed after the respondent moves to the next page. However, the need to move to the next page after each question increases the burden for the respondent and typically expands response times slightly (Couper et al., 2001; Lozar Manfreda, Batagelj & Vehovar, 2002; Thorndike, Calbring, Smyth, Magee, Gonder-Frederick, Ost & Ritterbrand, 2009; Toepoel et al., 2009; Tourangeau et al., 2004).

Weak support for interactivity is one of the key deficiencies of scrolling. For example, branching, which means that the respondent skips over some questions (e.g. if gender is male, than the questions on childbirth are skipped), can be implemented by including hyperlinks, accompanied by written instructions (e.g. Peytchev, Couper, McCabe, & Crawford, 2006), which is rather awkward and burdensome for respondents; it also increases the response times. Alternatively, client-side scripts to perform *dynamic branching* – also called *hybrid* (Dillman et al., 2009, p. 202) – can be used, so that a click on a certain response option instantly (on the same page) invokes an additional set of questions. However, Peytchev et al. (2006) found that skips in scrolling design can cause avoidance of those response options that lead to a display of a large number of additional questions. Another disadvantage of scrolling is that the majority of web survey software saves answers only when proceeding to the next questionnaire page. Scrolling thus requires completion of the questionnaire in one session and does not save responses in case of break-offs. Furthermore, since all questions are visible to the respondent at once, the likelihood of context effects may increase.

On the other hand, the absence of page breaks in scrolling reduces the number of required clicks and also the response times. It also provides the respondent with insight into the entire questionnaire and thus more closely resembles a P&P self-administered format.

With respect to differences in substantive results, studies generally found no additional effects of paging vs scrolling design (Thorndike et al., 2009; Toepoel et al., 2009). It is true that in the case of simple web questionnaires, certain disadvantages of scrolling design disappear, but this still does not mean that scrolling has any advantages. According to Toepoel et al. (2009), differences in response times among four 10-item-per-screen pages and a scrolling design with all 40 questions per screen were negligible, while the increase in satisfaction with scrolling was very small, from 7.06 to 7.37 on a 10-point scale. The only real advantage of scrolling might appear when the context is required (e.g. all questions should be available on one screen for respondents to see all of them) or when it is essential that it resembles a P&P version.

In practice, we often use approaches somewhere in between these two extremes. We define a *modified scrolling* design as when page breaks appear only when this is necessary for the execution of server-side features such as branching, for reducing the context effect and for intermediate saving of responses. In an alternative approach, which we call a *modified paging*, each page contains a limited number of questions that fit on a typical screen without further scrolling. Given that studies found only small differences between the full paging and the full scrolling design, we can expect them to be even smaller for modified paging and modified scrolling.

We can conclude that we almost cannot go wrong with the modified paging strategy, while modified scrolling might still suffer from some of the scrolling problems mentioned above, especially from less frequent saving of responses into the database and problems with skipping. In addition to this general conclusion, we need to consider the advantages and disadvantages of each approach within the context of a specific survey.

Finally, we should point out the changing role of scrolling in the last decade, due to blogs, social networks and mouse devices. These all caused major changes in web usability principles (Nielsen, 2000a), which were very much against scrolling in the early years of Internet development. Scrolling has been additionally reinforced lately with mobile devices (smartphones, tablets) (Mavletova & Couper, 2014). All these might soften the disadvantage of scrolling designs.

2.3.3.1.3 Non-question Pages and Sections

In addition to questionnaire pages with survey questions, we sometimes include pages or questionnaire sections without questions. They contain introductions, additional instructions and other information relevant for respondents before they proceed with the questionnaire. Certain types of non-question pages listed below are commonly used, while the content of others is more usually presented next to other questions on the same page, especially if it is relevant only for specific questions and is relatively short:

- *An introduction page (splash page, welcome screen)* is a separate first page which introduces the survey to the respondent. It is omitted only in very short surveys (e.g. evaluation forms). The introduction page has the role of convincing the respondent to participate in the survey. Many respondents access the introduction page, but are not persuaded to continue with the survey, which makes this page a common place for major break-offs. Its content and design are therefore very important: it must be appealing and respectful, professional and polite. It should not jeopardize research ethics, so essential information therefore needs to be conveyed fairly to the participants: namely, the survey sponsor, purpose, content, privacy issues, contact information and expected time needed to complete the questionnaire. It is also important to stress additional encouragement for the respondents' participation, like the importance of the survey, the benefits for respondents, incentives, and so on. We further discuss these aspects of ensuring survey participation in Section 2.5 on nonresponse. At the end of the introduction page, it is also necessary to provide instructions for starting participation in the survey. This may include a simple instruction, 'To proceed click on the "Next" button', or additional guidance for entering a survey access code. In general, the page should be kept short and simple. Certain research has shown (e.g. Bauman, Jobity, Airey, & Hakan, 2000) that replacing a lengthy introduction page with dense text in 'cover letter' style with a shorter and more concise presentation increased cooperation. When mail or email invitations are used, the content of the introduction page needs to be in line with the invitation in order to avoid unnecessary repetition (Section 2.5.7).

• A *transition page* introduces respondents to a new topic. Some research shows the positive effects of transition pages without raising break-off rates (Callegaro et al., 2009). They can be used to slow down the pace of the questionnaire and ease the transition from one questionnaire topic to another.

• *Instruction pages* are used to provide respondents with the necessary information for completing the more complex survey tasks (e.g. how to perform a ranking task). When the required instructions are not long and complex, it is not necessary to present them on a separate page, and they may be included directly next to the question to which they apply.

• An *incentive* or *raffle page* can be used to give additional information about incentives for completing the questionnaire, for example by showing a picture of the incentive or stating the odds of winning the lottery incentive. Respondents may also collect incentives, such as online coupons and other electronic incentives.

• A *file upload page* or *section* is sometimes used to obtain pictures, text documents or other files from respondents. For example, a respondent can be asked to upload a photo of a defective product to which the questions refer. This can appear as a special page or, more often, as a specific request for an upload listed among other questions, although we can hardly talk about such a request being a survey question.

• A *thank you page* is the last page of the questionnaire and is used mainly to acknowledge the respondent's participation in the survey. It may also contain other elements, such as links to external websites (e.g. the website of the survey sponsor or the website with content related to the topic of the questionnaire) and information about the availability

of results. Sometimes respondents may be asked for contact information in order to receive the results by email, participate in further surveys or join an online panel. The completed questionnaire, as filled out by the respondent, may be enclosed (e.g. in PDF format) so that the respondent has an archive of the responses.

• In addition to non-question pages and sections, we can also have non-question sentences which are part of the questionnaire pages (e.g. introductions, explanations, encouragement, thank you notes).

2.3.3.1.4 Questionnaire Navigation

A respondent usually moves back and forth in the questionnaire using dedicated navigation buttons in the questionnaire. Here, the *'Next'* button is obligatory, while the *'Previous' button* is optional. The latter gives respondents some control over the questionnaire and allows them to correct answers (as in a P&P questionnaire). Sometimes this is regarded as undesirable behaviour and the option is removed, but this can then lead to an increase in breakoffs (R. P. Baker & Couper, 2007). We provide more details on the formatting of these buttons in the discussion on visual layouts further in this section.

Sometimes, *automatic forwarding* is used to avoid the need for the 'Next' button. Here, the selection of any responses automatically leads to the next page of the questionnaire. One problem with this approach is that it can create navigational confusion, since it can be implemented only with closed-ended single answer questions. Hammen (2010) also showed an increased tendency to satisfice in case of automatic forwarding, so very specific circumstances must exist to justify it, for example with the horizontal scrolling matrix presentation of tables of items (Section 2.3.2).

2.3.3.1.5 Blocks of Questions

The questionnaire is often structured into parts or sections, technically formatted as blocks. In longer questionnaires these can be visually separated by subtitles, running heads, introductions and encouragement, which provide respondents with some orientation and motivation. Top-level blocks can be presented even as navigation, visible throughout the entire questionnaire in the form of tabs, which then enable respondents to switch between different topics. This approach is more commonly used in business surveys, where different people may complete different parts of the questionnaire. However, navigation through the questionnaire should not be made too complex because it may confuse respondents (Blanke, 2011).

2.3.3.1.6 Special Layouts

Web questionnaires usually run in a separate browser window or tab, which can be maximized and resized by the respondent. However, for very specific purposes, alternative questionnaire layouts can be used. One such specific implementation is an *embedded questionnaire*, which is integrated into an existing website and appears as part of a certain web page, such as a consumer satisfaction survey on a certain page of an online store website. The main disadvantage of this approach is the limited space that can be allocated for the questionnaire. It is also less appropriate for more complex questionnaires, due to possible technical problems with some interactive and dynamic features that rely on client-side technologies (e.g. JavaScript).

Another example of a special questionnaire layout is a *split-screen* presentation, commonly used for website evaluations. In this case, a web questionnaire is usually presented in the lower browser window, while the evaluated website can be simultaneously used and inspected in the window above it.

2.3.3.2 Computerization, Interactivity and Dynamics

At a certain point in the questionnaire development process, we need to transform the fixed and static content of the draft questionnaire versions – which are often prepared on text processors (e.g. MS Word, Google Docs) or even on paper – into an online version of the questionnaire in the chosen web survey software. Alternatively, we can start developing the questionnaire directly in the

dynamic format of the web survey software, on the condition that the software supports the required features (Vehovar, Čehovin, & Močnik, 2014). In both cases, we then face the same essential challenges of dynamics and interactivity: skipping the questions (branching), randomizing questionnaire elements and providing various interactive feedback to respondents.

2.3.3.2.1 Branching

We talk about *branching* – also called *routing, filtering, skipping, conditions, IF sentences* – when a certain question is asked conditionally, based on previous responses (e.g. number of births is asked only if the reported gender is female). Compared with written instructions in P&P questionnaires, web surveys are superior and can automatically handle very complex conditions. A specific type is *loop branching*, where we repeat the same set of questions for each of the previously reported items. For example, for each country which was checked as being visited, a set of further questions appears. As in paging and scrolling discussed above, in server-based web surveys the branching process runs on a server and the conditional questions can only appear on separate pages. An alternative that can be implemented without interacting with the server is dynamic branching, allowing a dynamic appearance of questions within the same page. It relies on client-side technologies (JavaScript). As mentioned in the discussion on scrolling design, this enables the next question to appear on the same page (e.g. a question about the number of births appears on the same page as the gender question, immediately after clicking on the female gender option). This might work well for a few questions, but the danger for nonresponse and satisficing exists once the respondent realizes that some responses lead to larger sets of additional questions.

Support for branching is one of the important aspects where web survey software considerably differs in its capacities and even more in the usability of the user interface through which the branching logic is defined.

2.3.3.2.2 Randomization

Randomization enables manipulation of the presentation of questions, response options, layouts, blocks of questions, etc., between different respondents, according to some random mechanism. For example, we can use odd and even record numbers of the respondents accessing the web questionnaire to form two random groups.

The first type of randomization affects the order of questions, items or response options presented to the respondent. This can be done by random ordering of (a) response options in closed-ended questions with the nominal measurement, (b) sub-questions in a table, (c) questions on a page or within a block of questions, and (d) the blocks of questions themselves. Of these, the random order of response options is most commonly used, because it can handle response order effects. In web surveys this is especially important due to potential primacy effects, where respondents first consider the few options on the list more thoroughly (Galesic et al., 2008), and are also more likely to choose answers at the beginning of the list. There is also some evidence that respondents think more positively about the first options (Tourangeau, Couper, & Conrad, 2013). Such randomization does not change the problematic behaviour of respondents, but only spreads the effect randomly across all response options or sub-questions. In order to truly prevent primacy effects, other strategies need to be considered, such as increasing the respondent's motivation by appropriate instructions and tooltips (Kunz & Fuchs 2013).

Another type of randomization is an experiment where – different to the above randomization of the order where all respondents receive all options – each respondent is randomly assigned to one of the predefined questionnaire elements (response option, question or block of questions, implementation layout, etc.). A typical example is a so-called *split-sample* experiment with two random groups, which allows us to explore which question wording or implementation layout provides better data quality. We have already discussed experiments in Section 1.3.6, while further recommendations are offered by Reips (2007).

Similar principles of randomization can be used to reduce the respondent's burden. For example, certain questions can be randomly assigned to only half of the respondents and the remaining questions to the other half (see also discussion in Section 2.2.2). This approach, sometimes called *matrix sampling*, can increase the number of questions in the questionnaire without increasing the burden on the respondents. Of course, splitting can be used only for questions that will not be analysed together. Matrix sampling can be extended to *modular surveys* (Johnson, Siluk, & Tarraf, 2014) and *split-questionnaire designs* (Raghunathan & Grizzle, 1995), where additional imputations using data fusion (statistical matching) are then used in an attempt to complete the missing part of the responses.

Randomization can also be used in many other contexts which are otherwise beyond the questionnaire development context, for example the random selection of persons in a household.

2.3.3.2.3 Real-Time Validations and Prompt Messages

Web questionnaires can react to the respondent's answers and other actions by performing real-time validations and providing feedback in the form of prompt messages. This can be used for various purposes (Peytchev & Crawford 2005), including (a) prompts about items that are left unanswered and thus present item non-response, (b) controls to assure proper provision of answers according to question types, formats, length and range, and (c) consistency validations, where the consistency of responses is verified against some other data from the same survey (e.g. consistency of reported education and age), previous surveys of the same respondents, or external data from the sampling frame or other sources. Other types of validations and prompts also exist, including feedback based on paradata, such as notifications about responding too quickly. Certain system messages issued by the operating system or the web survey software may be relevant as well, for example notifications about lost Internet connection or notifications of an expired browser session in the case of long inactivity.

Interaction based on the validation is achieved by error messages and other forms of feedback to the respondent. Technically, the process can run on a server, so the feedback is provided when the respondent attempts to continue to the next page. Alternatively, client-side technologies can be used to enable real-time feedback on the same questionnaire page. Validations can generate three possible reactions: (a) *no prompt* for the respondent, who can normally proceed, but some indicator of a potential invalid answer may be recorded in the datafile; (b) a *soft prompt* where the respondent is notified about the error, but can still proceed without making the requested correction; and (c) a *hard prompt*, where the respondent cannot proceed without correction.

Since validation messages interfere with the respondent's completion of the surveying task, they may be considered intrusive and annoying. It is therefore important to implement them by relying on professional standards, as well as design and usability principles (Couper, 2008; Nielsen, 2000a). It is most important to keep the messages polite and respectful. Their content needs to state clearly what the problem is and how to fix it. They also need to be tested thoroughly.

Below, we take a closer look at the item nonresponse prompt as one of the most typical, important and frequent validation examples. The main principles remain the same for other types of validation messages.

2.3.3.2.4 Item Nonresponse Prompts

When a respondent decides not to answer a certain question (we call this an item nonresponse), a researcher can use a soft prompt, a hard prompt or do nothing. In practice, hard prompts are often used, especially if respondents obtain incentives for participation. However, academic researchers (Couper, 2008, p. 266; Dillman et al., 2009, p. 309) strongly advise against the use of hard prompts if they are not essential for further surveying, for example when a question is a key

question on which branching in the remainder of the questionnaire depends. The first reason for avoiding hard prompts is ethical, since survey participation is generally voluntary and respondents should not be forced to answer any question (AAPOR, 2010). The second reason against hard prompts is a methodological concern that they may lead to breakoffs or false responses. Unfortunately, we lack convincing empirical evidence to support this. Although both hard (Albaum, Roster, Wiley, Rossiter, & Smith, 2010) and soft prompts (e.g. DeRouvray & Couper, 2002) decrease item nonresponse, the effect of hard prompts on breakoffs was found to be insignificantly higher compared with soft prompts (Albaum et al., 2010; Couper, Baker, & Mechling, 2011; Heerwegh, 2005). Even more lacking is research on the effects of hard prompts on false responding and other aspects of response quality. Nonetheless, this does not mean that negative effects do not exist.

On the other hand, hard prompts apparently have great benefits: they eliminate item nonresponse, permit immediate analysis and save lots of resources, compared with situations where we need to deal with missing data in the post-fielding. Hard prompts may also discipline respondents at the outset, so they might take the survey task more seriously. It is thus not surprising that in online panels – and in marketing and commercial research in general – hard prompts are almost uniformly used, except perhaps for open-ended text entry questions. Special attention is needed with hard prompts to avoid generally inappropriate situations where respondents are forced to select only from response options that do not apply to them.

Item nonresponse prompts are closely related to approaches for dealing with non-substantive response options ('Don't know', 'No opinion', etc.) which we have partially discussed already in the introduction to questionnaire development (Section 2.3.1). There we followed Krosnick & Presser (2010) in not recommending the inclusion of such options unless explicitly needed. Another alternative is that non-substantive response options are displayed only after the respondent does not answer a question, so they are offered together with the prompt for an item nonresponse. If these three basic alternatives for handling non-substantive options (offered, not offered, offered after a prompt) are combined with the three approaches to item nonresponse prompts (none, soft, hard), a researcher would theoretically have nine alternative strategies. In addition, an important insight into the matter – which further increases the number of combinations – can be obtained with the *familiarity pre-question*, which then enables us to pose a question only for respondents familiar enough with the topic, or with the *certainty post-question*, which asks how sure respondents were about the provided responses.

We cannot discuss all of these combinations here, since the research evidence is very limited. In general, we can say that the prevailing practice in marketing research seems to use hard prompts for item nonresponse. On the other hand, academic and governmental research seem to prefer soft prompts or no prompts for item nonresponse, with or without non-substantive responses. When we want to mirror interviewer-administered surveys (F2F and telephone modes) – where non-substantive response is initially not offered, but interviewers record it if explicitly volunteered by the respondent – displaying non-substantive response only after the corresponding item nonresponse soft prompt might be the appropriate selection (Ainsaar et al., 2013).

Practical importance and inconclusive results place these issues among the top priorities for future investigation. Ideally, future research will consider all combinations of item nonresponse prompts and approaches to handling non-substantive options in various essential settings: that is, prompting for all questions or only for certain questions, comparing different types of respondents (general population, specific population, or trained online panellists), various levels of topic salience, different question types, as well as the importance and position of questions. It is also crucial to evaluate different aspects of data quality, namely reliability, validity, item nonresponse, breakoffs, satisficing, response times, as well as engagement and satisfaction levels. Furthermore, it is important to consider the comparability of these approaches with standard procedures in interviewer-administered surveys instead of solely optimizing the interactive advantages of the web mode. Conceptual perception towards non-substantive responses as a legitimate response category – instead of being treated as 'lazy responses' or 'masked nonresponses' – is also important. The familiarity pre-question and the certainty post-question should be included in such an investigation, because they address the essential substantive aspects of the problem.

Additionally, capable software support is also very important here. For example, adding the 'don't know' category option to the substantive responses on the same page only after an item nonresponse occurs can pose a problem for a lot of the software.

2.3.3.2.5 Data-Piping

Data-piping (or *fills*) enables the use of responses from previous questions, previous surveys or external databases (e.g. sampling frame). It is commonly used to establish clearer instructions about what the question demands from the respondent (e.g. 'What is your relationship with the person you named Mark?'). In addition, it can provide personalized introductions to increase the respondent's engagement. For example, if the name of the respondent is known, it can be included in motivating statements. Use of this feature can be advantageous, but certain care with its implementation is required, especially with personalized messages included directly in the questionnaire, which may undermine the respondent's sense of privacy.

2.3.3.2.6 Progress Indicator

A progress indicator offers respondents orientation about how much of the questionnaire they have already completed. It is often used with the aim of keeping them engaged in order to prevent breakoffs. Its position and format vary greatly:

it can be immediately visible or presented on demand/click; displayed on every page or only at certain key transition points; in graphical (e.g. typically a progress bar) or text format (e.g. 60% or 5 out of 10 questions/pages/sections). There is little research evidence on the performance of these variations.

The problems with progress indicators appear in complex questionnaires, with skips of a large number of questions, which cause the progress indicator to advance inconsistently. For example, if several pages are skipped due to branching, the progress indicator may 'jump' from 10% to 35%, but then move very slightly across subsequent pages without skips. These effects of branching are computationally very hard to calibrate (Kaczmirek, 2009, p. 146).

When a progress indicator is not used, respondents complain about its absence (Lozar Manfreda, Batagelj & Vehovar, 2002), but studies have shown that its use generally does not contribute to a reduction in the breakoff rate, and it can even slightly increase the breakoff problem. This was established in a meta-study of randomized experiments for medium to long web surveys with a median time of 18 minutes (Villar, Callegaro, & Yang, 2013).

We can conclude that the progress indicator, especially when a lot of branching is used, has no benefit for medium or long web questionnaires. However, it can be appropriate for shorter and simpler questionnaires, where it moves linearly at a consistent and detectable rate. The inclusion of the progress indicator also presents an interesting ethical dilemma: from the respondent's perspective, the basic orientation of progress is advantageous, but it brings no gains and may potentially introduce problems for a researcher.

2.3.3.2.7 Other Interactive Features

Some examples of other interactive and dynamic features have already been mentioned in the discussion of question types (e.g. dynamic shading in tables), and we present some more in the next section on visual layout. However, web questionnaires can offer a number of other possibilities (e.g. occasional encouragement) that can improve the flow of questionnaire completion and are not mentioned in this review. In general, it is important to consider whether and how the use of these features is beneficial for the respondent and data quality and to weigh this against their potential drawbacks. With a lack of relevant research, reliance on common sense and a somewhat conservative approach may be the best choice.

2.3.3.3 Visual Layout

In F2F surveys we expect interviewers to be decently dressed, behave pleasantly and professionally, and provide engagement, motivation and support whenever needed. Similarly, in telephone surveys, we train them to be polite and convey questions in a non leading way, with a neutral voice. In web questionnaires such good practices of interaction with respondents need to be achieved using the visual layout of the questionnaire.

This layout usually follows some basic design principles. For example, in Western culture, the top and left positions are often treated as 'more frequent' or 'more positive', and visual distances may reflect distances in perception (Tourangeau, Couper, & Conrad, 2013). There is also a hierarchy from verbal presentation, which dominates, to numeric and visual presentation. Verbal descriptions are thus preferred. When numbers and graphics are nevertheless added (as in rating scales), consistency is required. We should also comply with basic web design and usability principles, and refrain from writing text in capital letters (Nielsen, 2000a; Schriver, 1997). In addition, we should visually highlight what is important, keeping the rest hidden in the background or shown only upon request.

The majority of web survey software already offers certain predefined professional visual designs, called *themes*, *skins* or *survey templates*. When they are in line with basic web design principles, little or no additional intervention is usually required or recommended. If it is necessary to customize profoundly the overall questionnaire layout, it is advisable to involve someone with sufficient web design experience. The visual layout is technically defined by a special visual design language, called CSS (Cascading Style Sheets), which ensures a consistent look and format across web pages. Changing it usually requires design as well as some programming knowledge. However, researchers are not expected to be completely competent in the task of visual design, apart from minor adaptations, such as the inclusion of logotypes.

A researcher or programmer can make changes to the CSS file by direct modification of the code or by using a graphical user interface (GUI) if provided by the software. Depending on the software, some interfaces may allow modification of a variety of design elements (e.g. background colours, fonts, page structure) in a user-friendly way.

In addition to direct intervention in the basic visual layout, a researcher can also change structural elements, such as layout settings (e.g. logotype position, display of progress indicator, etc.), page structure (breaks, sections, blocks, etc.), formatting of instructions, definitions, help features, and other non-question sentences or pages. Specific editing of question text is also important, but should be done very carefully, particularly when the text editor allows changes to the font and size of the characters, numbers and symbols. Within this context, the size, structure and settings for pictures are also important.

Below we present some key elements, without going into further detail on the visual principles. More discussion on the subtle role of visuals can be found in Tourangeau, Conrad, & Couper, (2013, p. 88), Couper (2008, p. 84) and Dillman et al. (2009). We should keep in mind that checking and testing the look and feel of the web questionnaire in all key browsers, devices and operating systems is essential, particularly when making modifications to the standard visual layout.

2.3.3.3.1 Basic Layout

Elements of the basic visual layout of the questionnaire include font types and size, text width, spaces, colours, structure, and other common visual elements of web pages. They should not deviate much from the conventional styles used on other web pages. A general recommendation is to use a white or lightly shaded background, clearly visible standard fonts (e.g. Arial, Verdana, etc.), a professional look and feel, and keep the design consistent throughout the questionnaire. Couper (2008) provides more detail on all these issues. Despite their importance, there is little research on the basic layout specifics of web surveys, apart from some initial evidence that simple designs outperform 'fancy' ones (e.g. Dillman et al., 1998). Here, we should not forget that the quality of responses is the priority, and aesthetics should be used to foster this rather than increase the possibility of distraction. Within this context, Casey & Poropat (2014) explicitly demonstrated that classic aesthetic quality outperformed expressive aesthetic quality and had a positive correlation with the perceived ease of use of the web questionnaire, as well as with trust in the web survey researcher.

2.3.3.3.2 Logotypes

Logotypes increase legitimacy and remind the reader about the survey sponsor, survey organization, research project or online panel membership. They should be consistent with the whole visual layout, properly sized and positioned somewhere in the corner of the pages, in order to prevent a cluttered impression. They should not distract from the response process.

2.3.3.3.3 Position and Navigation of Other Action Buttons

The position and navigation of other action buttons that enable respondents to move from one screen to another are important. When Couper, Baker & Mechling (2011) manipulated the position of the 'Previous' button, they found no impact on breakoff rates, but increased use when positioned to the right of the 'Next' button. One explanation is that the increased use is due to mistakes, since such positioning opposes the general approach in surveys, other web pages and devices where 'Backward' is commonly to the left of 'Forward'. There are certain arguments that it may be beneficial to position the 'Previous' button below the 'Next' button or to the right of it in the form of a hyperlink. However, to be on the safe side, prevailing practice is to have (a) both buttons, (b) close to each other, (c) placed at the bottom of the questionnaire on the right or in the middle of the page, (d) with sufficient space between them, and (e) with 'Next' on the right.

Sometimes other action buttons are used for special purposes, such as the 'Save and continue later' button that allows respondents to answer the web questionnaire in multiple sessions, or the 'Print' and 'Save' buttons, used particularly in business surveys. The recommendation is that their visibility and position should be consistent with the navigation buttons, but also reflect their importance.

2.3.3.3.4 Position and Formatting of Additional Instructions

Additional instructions about how to answer a particular survey question are sometimes needed. They are usually presented in a format that distinguishes them from the main question text (e.g. by using smaller or differently coloured fonts). The number of additional instructions and the level of detail provided are important dilemmas here. For example, we need to decide if we can assume that respondents understand that checkboxes denote the selection of more answers, or whether this should be explained in further instructions. In this specific case, the latter option may be more appropriate (i.e. a brief note in every question), although we generally recommend reducing instructions to a minimum and to situations where they are really needed. The overuse of instructions can lead respondents to start ignoring them. Of course, this all depends on the context and the target respondents, but in any case we need to balance the importance with the visual exposure.

2.3.3.3.5 Position and Formatting of Definitions

Definitions of terms used in the survey questions share the same recommendations and dilemmas

as instructions. Peytchev, Conrad, Couper, & Tourangeau (2010) showed that increased visual exposure of definitions also increases their use. The study found the highest use of definitions when they were presented immediately after the question text, followed by a mouse-over appearance, and the lowest use when an additional click was required to display the definition.

2.3.3.3.6 Visual Layout of Help and Other Survey-Related Information

It is generally recommended to include a help email address, a toll-free number or a link to a help web page. Additional information, such as copyright, disclaimers, general information and FAQs, is also sometimes needed. In general, the visual layout of these elements should express their importance, for example by using smaller fonts, less prominent colours, and a non-central position at the top or bottom to avoid distractions. Details may be provided on hyperlinked pages.

2.3.3.3.7 Adaptability to Various Screen Resolutions

Because a web questionnaire is typically accessed on a variety of computers and other devices, it is important to ensure a robust visual appearance. The size and position of all questionnaire elements (including text, tables and pictures) should be defined using relative specifications and be flexible enough to adapt to the screen resolution. It is also important to ensure a proper appearance of navigation buttons, prevent horizontal scrolling, ensure proper positioning of pictures and prompts, etc. (Callegaro, 2010). A large part of the responsibility for this lies with the web survey software, but researchers should carefully verify its functioning.

To conclude the discussion of possibilities and issues regarding the visual layout of the questionnaire, it is important to remember that a careful and detailed evaluation of the visual elements is essential. This includes the verification of their perception by respondents, as well as a proper presentation across commonly used browsers, devices and operating systems. We address these issues further in Section 2.3.5 on testing.

2.3.4 Ensuring Survey Engagement

In order to obtain quality responses, we need to make sure that respondents not only start participating in the survey, but also maintain the necessary survey engagement. In this section we start with a general overview of survey engagement, then continue with a discussion of closely related issues relevant for questionnaire preparation (gamification, questionnaire length and satisficing), before presenting the related nonresponse aspects later in Section 2.5.

2.3.4.1 Engagement, Flow and User Experience

The notion of engagement is closely related to the concept of *flow* (Csikszentmihalyi, 2009), which is defined as a genuine mental state where a person is completely focused on and motivated by a certain activity. The concept of flow can appear in a broad range of human activities, and elaborated measures of flow already exist, for example a flow state scale (Jackson & Eklund, 2002). *Engagement* is sometimes considered a slightly more passive state, that is without the full 'absorption' or without losing awareness of the outside world (O'Brien & Toms, 2008).

Another approach to conceptualizing engagement comes from the field of *user experience* (UX), which is a term encompassing the behaviour and inner states of a person using a certain service or product. In the context of software applications, engagement relates to cognitive, affective and behavioural aspects, which 'make the user want to be there' (O'Brien & Toms, 2010, p. 3). The components of the corresponding concept of 'engaged use' are focused attention, perceived usability, aesthetics, endurability, novelty

and involvement. We may add that O'Brien & Toms (2008) successfully measured these components in the general context of computer applications.

Unfortunately, to our knowledge, none of the above conceptual approaches were applied to survey contexts. We only encounter a mention of the engagement as an implicit component of optimizing behaviour in satisficing theory (Krosnick, 1999). On the other hand, engagement frequently appears in practical investigations on how to increase survey cooperation, particularly in marketing research. Nonetheless, the concept of engagement is not fully elaborated in the survey context; at most, it is discussed as the intercept of usability and motivation (McMahon & Stamp, 2009).

In the absence of a theoretical elaboration of engagement within a specific survey context, consistency checks often serve as a measure of engagement, particularly with the use of various so-called *trap questions*, where the respondents are occasionally asked certain trivial questions (e.g. to select a certain response category in some artificially added question). It is recommended that these questions are not too demanding, boring, strange or insulting (Baker-Prewitt & Miller, 2009). According to some studies, usually much more than 10% of respondents fail to respond properly to such questions (Thomas & Barlas, 2014).

Another indirect insight into engagement can be obtained with evaluation questions at the end of the questionnaire, which enquire about satisfaction, perceived complexity and similar aspects. It is worth mentioning that Downes-Le Guin, Baker, Mechling, & Ruyle (2012) found that increased satisfaction with visually more attractive and interactive questionnaires had no effect on engagement, measured in the study with consistency checks.

Technical measurements may also serve as an indicator of engagement, especially paradata (such as response times, clicks or mouse movement), eye tracking, and brain wave recordings that detect emotional engagement when answering web questionnaires (e.g. Coombe, Jarrett, & Johnson, 2011). Various other studies occasionally note that certain aspects of the questionnaire have a negative impact on engagement, particularly the presence of cognitively demanding questions, such as tables, continuous scales and open-ended text questions (Peytchev, 2009).

Due to weak conceptual elaboration, we did not introduce the notion of engagement earlier in the discussion of questionnaire features. Nevertheless, engagement is the umbrella concept behind many aspects presented in the previous discussions related to question types, questionnaire layout, and interactivity. The notion of engagement is also important in the context of survey breakoffs, as part of the discussion on the nonresponse process (Section 2.5). We introduce this notion at this point because the remaining issues we discuss below (gamification, questionnaire length and satisficing) are closely related to the concept of survey engagement.

Survey engagement has an impact on measurement errors, which we typically observe from validity and reliability indicators, the number of non-substantive responses, invalid answers in open-ended questions, inconsistent responses, and various specific indications of satisficing (e.g. non-differentiation).

Survey engagement also has an impact on the potential occurrence of nonresponse errors, which is usually estimated by item nonresponse and breakoff rates. We will use the term *quality of responses* (Ganassali, 2008, p. 25) to denote the indicators of measurement and nonresponse problems, which can be caused – directly or indirectly (through suboptimal solutions in questionnaire development) – by low survey engagement. Of course, quality of responses is only one component of a broader methodological concept of data quality, which we introduced in Section 1.1.1 and upon which we reflect further in Section 6.1.2.

We have listed above a set of indicators related to the quality of responses. Unfortunately, the research on engagement – particularly in the context of questionnaire length, gamification and satisficing – is often focused on only one

isolated aspect of the quality of responses. This is not sufficient for a thorough evaluation and thus several issues below are discussed only partially and the formulation of more decisive judgements is therefore prevented.

2.3.4.2 Survey Gamification

The idea behind *gamification* is to bring features of games into various non-game contexts. This seems to be generally beneficial in many areas (Hamari, Koivisto, & Sarsa, 2014) and is being increasingly explored in the context of surveys (C. Roberts, 2013). Game thinking and game mechanics are expected to increase engagement and fun, which then hopefully also increase response quality (Puleston, 2011, 2012; Sleep & Puleston, 2011).

Web survey questionnaires and online games seem to be similar in many respects. The same visual and interactive elements often appear in both contexts, with the purpose of increasing engagement. The degree of inclusion of such elements can vary. The most basic elements are decorations and simple interactivity, such as slider bars and drop-down menus instead of radio buttons (Downes-Le Guin et al., 2012). More advanced approaches include various graphical and interactive elements related to invitations (e.g. reminders and incentives), question layouts that use pictures, and questionnaire layout elements such as encouragement and progress indicators. While all these elements are normally used in both contexts, the extreme end of game mechanics – such as animations, avatars, strong narrative context, point collection, badges, progress levels, time limits and excessive graphics – rarely appear in surveys. In addition, the gamification approaches use various qualitative techniques, including personalization, projection and role-playing to increase involvement, which can sometimes be used to create more attractive survey questions.

Despite this apparent similarity, a serious conceptual difference exists between games and surveys. We could say that surveys aim to measure reality, while games are designed for fun with the aim of escaping reality. It is therefore not surprising that academic researchers typically disregard survey gamification, while the gamification advocates treat web questionnaires as a subset of online games – 'just rather dull ones' (Puleston, 2013).

We can mention here the similar notion of *surveytainment*, which relates to layout and usability-driven enhancements. The aim is to increase the engagement of respondents by providing them with enjoyment and entertainment from visually attractive and appealing surveys, using graphics, visuals and interactivity (Półtorak & Kowalski, 2013). Obviously, this is a very similar notion to gamification; however, it is narrower because it relates specifically to web surveys. It is also somehow less aggressive in involving advanced game mechanics and focuses more on entertainment. Humans can be entertained for hours, while cognitively demanding activities, including answering surveys, may hold people's attention for only a short time.

Unfortunately, comprehensive empirical research on gamification in the survey context is rare and inconclusive. The use of various visual and interactivity elements – such as avatars, 3D environments, exposed feedback, narrative contexts, time pressure and awards – under the label of survey gamification is often reported to produce excellent results for certain aspects of quality of responses (Cechanowicz, Gutwin, Brownell, & Goodfellow, 2013). This is particularly demonstrated by richer open-ended responses, increased satisfaction, improvement in intercultural effects (Puleston & Rintoul, 2012) and sometimes much better response rates (Puleston, 2012). On the other hand, some studies (e.g. Chien & Chang, 2012; Ewing, 2012) found that animated questions generated unpredictable differences in responses, while others (e.g. Downes-Le Guin et al., 2012) found no effects from animations. In addition, the latter study also reported that animations increased breakoffs and programming costs, while no improvement was found regarding the engagement measured by trap questions.

The problem with studies that praise survey gamification is usually their narrow focus on a few isolated aspects of the quality of responses, while the overall consequences remain unexplored. Particularly critical are validity and reliability. Validity can be, for example, threatened if 'playing' unpredictably changes what we actually measure. Reliability is threatened because gamification effects tend to diminish, sometimes after just a few questions (Cechanowicz et al., 2013).

To summarize, we should acknowledge that graphics, interactions and contextualization are already standard elements of web questionnaires, so there is no need to treat them under the umbrella of gamification. The same is true for achieving respondents' engagement by promising them a certain level of 'fun', which is a long-standing and legitimated component in the *social exchange theory* of survey participation (Dillman et al., 2009). We thus recommend remaining within the survey context when talking about visuals and interactivity for increasing survey engagement and avoiding immediate reference to survey gamification. Gamification is a relatively unclear and ambiguous term; for example, a continuous scale can already be perceived as a gamification element for some researchers, but not for others. Nevertheless, we have to admit that we can learn from the creative use of visuals and interactivity from so-called survey gamification attempts, particularly because the role of visuals and interactivity within the survey context is largely unexplored.

Due to this inconclusive research, a conservative approach regarding gamification is recommended. We generally advise against unnecessary or excessive use of visuals, interactivity and contextualization, unless certain research explicitly demonstrates their benefits. The latter is perhaps already the case for some specific circumstances, such as avatars for surveying children, animations for scenario comparisons, question time limits (e.g. five seconds) for knowledge questions, or role-playing for surveys related to qualitative marketing research.

2.3.4.3 Questionnaire Length

In general, longer questionnaires have a negative impact on all components of survey engagement, causing fatigue (Krosnick & Presser, 2010, p. 292) and a lower quality of response. Of course, the perceived and actual length of the questionnaire may differ considerably (Galesic & Bosnjak, 2009). Respondents can react to a questionnaire that is perceived as too lengthy either by quitting (breakoff) or by bad performance (satisficing). Questionnaire complexity and the level of required cognitive effort are also crucial, because a simple and relatively long questionnaire may outperform a shorter, but cognitively demanding one in all aspects of the quality of responses (Burdein, 2014).

The factors that affect survey engagement also affect the perception of questionnaire length. It is therefore not surprising that recommended questionnaire lengths vary strongly. In marketing research, experience often suggests that short web questionnaires taking a few minutes should be used, particularly with mobile devices. On the other hand, a common denominator of many studies using web questionnaires (e.g. Cape, 2010; Couper, 2008, p. 298; Macer & Wilson, 2014; McMahon & Stamp, 2009) is that response quality starts to deteriorate after around 20 minutes, which is an attention span that is reported in many other human activities. However, there are reports of long questionnaires performing well online, for example the ESS web questionnaire, which is almost an hour long (Ainsaar et al., 2013; Villar, 2013).

If we observe only the relation to breakoffs as one specific indicator of the quality of responses, doubling the questionnaire length often increases breakoffs roughly by half, for example from 21% to 34% in Ganassali (2008), or from 17% to 24% in Deutskens et al. (2004). Similarly, Galesic (2006) compared 10-, 20- and 30-minute questionnaires and found breakoff rates of 32%, 43% and 53%, respectively. Similarly, Vehovar & Čehovin (2014) established that short questionnaires with up to 10 questions on average had questionnaire breakoff rates of

6%, while with a few hundreds of questions the breakoff rates increased to an average of 18%. According to this study, each newly added item increased the breakoff rate by 0.06%[12] on average, which is similar to findings by SurveyMonkey.[13] Both studies were observational and should be used with caution.

With respect to the impact of the announced length, Galesic & Bosnjak (2009) found that it has a certain effect on a proportion of respondents who started the survey: the announced length of 10, 20, 30 minutes resulted in response rates of 75%, 65%, 62%, respectively. Similar effects were also found in research by Crawford, Couper, & Lamias (2001), where the announcement of 10- vs 20-minute questionnaire durations created 63% vs 68% unit nonresponse, but was then countervailed with higher breakoffs in the shorter version. An even smaller effect was found in the study by Kaplowitz, Lupi, Couper, & Thorp (2012) for announced 10- vs 30-minute questionnaires and by Walston, Lisstiz, & Rudner (2006), who compared the announced length of 5 vs 15 minutes.

There is less evidence about when and how questionnaires that are shorter than 5 minutes outperform longer ones; however, if we offered incentives, we would perhaps not select such a short questionnaire anyway. In addition to the danger of breakoffs, lengthy questionnaires have other disadvantages which manifest with other indicators of the quality of responses. For example, there is evidence that some questions positioned later in the questionnaire additionally suffer from a lower quality of responses (Galesic & Bosnjak, 2009).

We may add that different languages and cultures require different questionnaire lengths. In international marketing research the length of the same questionnaire can vary by 50%, from the shortest in Japan to the lengthiest in Latin America.[14] Within this context the correct estimation of the length can also be important. Good web survey software can provide accurate estimates here, but various approximate rules of thumb also exist, from 2.5 seconds per word (24 words per minute).

To summarize, many factors and circumstances determine the acceptable or optimal length of a web questionnaire, particularly the sponsor, topic salience, incentives and overall quality of the questionnaire. A very general and rough benchmark for the maximum length is around 20 minutes, after which the quality of responses often deteriorates rapidly. Longer questionnaires thus require an advanced mix of the above-mentioned factors and, with that, they can then enable sessions up to around an hour; above this point, more sessions are perhaps needed. Additional questions diminishingly contribute to cumulative breakoffs and similarly the announced length has a relatively low and diminishing impact.

Further, we can add three specific recommendations regarding questionnaire length in web surveys. Firstly, randomization (i.e. split questionnaire or matrix sampling; see Section 2.3.2) should always be considered in order to shorten the questionnaire. Secondly, real-time online diagnostics should be used, particularly the monitoring of the performance of individual respondents, so that appropriate interventions can follow. For example, a sharp decline in the quality of responses can be detected before a breakoff occurs (Galesic, 2006), so prompts, help, encouragement, alternative branching or even modifications of the questionnaire might be arranged. This is particularly important if certain respondents are ready to complete a longer questionnaire, while others are willing to do only shorter ones (Garland et al., 2013). Thirdly, regardless of the length, researchers should always remain ethical by giving respondents – at least from time to time – some information about their progress through the questionnaire, as well as by announcing a (realistic) survey length.

2.3.4.4 Survey Satisficing

We have already defined survey satisficing in Section 2.3.4 as an alternative behaviour choice for respondents who lack survey engagement, but who for whatever reasons (such as a contract, incentives, embarrassment, habit or curiosity) still participate in a survey.

Similar to engagement, satisficing is closely linked to the quality of responses; however, it focuses on a narrower set of factors. For example, item nonresponse may be caused by 'suboptimal respondent behaviour' (Thomas, 2014), which is related to low engagement, but this is generally not considered a consequence of satisficing, because the respondent provides no answer at all. Indicators of survey satisficing usually relate to encountered response order (e.g. primacy) effects, non-substantive responses (e.g. 'don't know'), speeding, inconsistent responses and specific response patterns such as random selection, endorsing status quo, non-differentiation and straightlining at its extreme form, and acquiescence (tendency to agree). Studies on satisficing in web surveys typically focus on only a few of these indicators, create various satisficing indexes and may find certain evidence of satisficing (Barge & Gehlbach, 2012; Garland et al., 2013; C. Zhang, 2013). In addition to the engagement level (including motivation) and the properties of the survey questionnaire (difficulty of the task), the likelihood of satisficing also depends on the respondent's cognitive ability (Krosnick, 1991). Indirectly, the survey experience (Toepoel, Das, & van Soest, 2008), education (Malhotra, 2008) and cultural difference are also important. Fang, Wen, & Prybutok (2013) further found that in individualist cultures (as in the United States), satisficing happens more often than in collectivistic ones (like China).

We can expect more satisficing in web surveys, compared with interviewer-administered modes, due to the absence of an interviewer, increased privacy, anonymity, and multitasking opportunities (e.g. online chatting, checking emails, simultaneous browsing, etc.). The interviewer's role of providing motivation and clarifications is also difficult to replicate fully with the web questionnaire layout and interactive features. Web questionnaires are in principle also cognitively more demanding and assume a certain level of reading and computer literacy. Studies thus consistently report that satisficing behaviour appears more often in web surveys compared with F2F surveys

(Heerwegh & Loosveldt, 2008; Lindhjem & Navrud, 2011) and sometimes also in telephone surveys (Fricker et al., 2005; Klein, Havens, & Thomas, 2009). The situation is less clear with self-administered P&P questionnaires. While certain studies found more satisficing in the web mode (Fang et al., 2013), others report the opposite results (Linchiat Chang & Krosnick, 2009).

In general, we still lack more comprehensive research that would simultaneously address all aspects of the quality of responses, not merely a few isolated satisficing indicators. Furthermore, the potential for visual and interactive features of the web questionnaire to reduce satisficing has not yet been fully explored. Below we discuss some approaches to the reduction of satisficing in all three steps of the core web survey process:

- **Pre-fielding.** This is by far the most important step in reducing the occurrence of satisficing. General efforts need to be made to achieve overall quality of the pre-fielding activities in order to ensure respondents' proper engagement. A very abbreviated recommendation could be to keep questionnaires short and questions simple, and occasionally ask respondents to justify their answers (Krosnick & Presser, 2010, p. 281). A classic set of measures to maximize respondent motivation, minimize task difficulty and minimize response effects caused by satisficing is described in Krosnick (2000). The maximization of motivation can be achieved by ensuring the importance of the study, asking respondents for their commitment to careful deliberation, monitoring response quality using random probes, keeping the questionnaire simple, and placing the most salient questions early in the questionnaire. To simplify the task of survey participation, the following approaches can help: reduction of question wording complexity, avoidance of questions about events that may be difficult to remember, decomposition of complex questions into simple ones, labelling response alternatives, and other general approaches to question and questionnaire presentation that we have discussed in this chapter. Finally,

the minimization of response effects can be achieved with the randomization of response options or questions, avoidance of agreement questions that may lead to acquiescence, minimization of the use of tables, and not using non-substantive response options. Furthermore, the above discussions on engagement, gamification and questionnaire length are also highly relevant.

- **Fielding.** Satisficing can also be addressed in the measurement stage (the questionnaire completion phase). For example, whenever real-time speed or consistency measures indicate a low quality of responses, we can intervene by notifying the respondent. Human-like dialogues (e.g. through voice or video) can also prove beneficial, as found by Conrad, Schober, & Coiner (2007) and Tourangeau, Couper, & Steiger (2003). One should, however, not over-rely on the response time measurement to detect satisficing. While faster respondents can truly show more response order effects (Malhotra, 2008; Smyth, Dillman, Christian, & Stern, 2006), 'don't know' answers (Lindhjem & Navrud, 2011) and straightlining (C. Zhang, 2013), respondents can satisfice at very different speeds. The study by Garland et al. (2013) found no correlation between speed and satisficing measured by inconsistency of responses. Nevertheless, an extensive study of 18 online panels found that top speeders (around 5% of respondents) provide lower response quality, in part also due to higher satisficing (Thomas & Barlas, 2014).
- **Post-fielding.** Detection of satisficing is often postponed to the post-fielding step, where evidence of satisficing can be used to improve the data (Section 4.1). For example, some responses or entire units can be removed due to high satisficing, or imputations can be used to replace answers that were likely affected by satisficing.

Finally, we should point out the role of web survey software here. The software is essential for developing quality visual and interactivity features to increase engagement and prevent satisficing. It also has an important role in supporting the monitoring of the quality of responses and providing eventual interventions (further discussion on software appears in Section 5.3).

2.3.5 Web Questionnaire Testing

In the questionnaire preparation process, the activities of questionnaire development are iterated with testing. We regard *questionnaire testing* as a set of explicit and formal evaluation methods applied through pre-planned phases of the questionnaire preparation. In addition to formal testing, which we discuss here, *informal feedback* is also used and relates to the internal crafting, drafting and commenting of interim versions at various phases. This is usually done by a researchers themselves, who test and evaluate the draft questionnaire during its preparation. Other people can also be asked for informal and ad hoc help and advice (e.g. the research team, coworkers or people from the close social network). Nevertheless, this informal feedback is treated as an integral part of the questionnaire development process and is therefore not the focus of the testing approaches we discuss.

Formal questionnaire testing is an indispensable phase of questionnaire preparation. A classic work in this field by Bradburn et al. (2004, p. 314) determined that nobody can write a questionnaire in one go without the need for further testing and revision. Furthermore, these authors even claim – and we fully agree – that without resources for formal testing, a survey project should not be undertaken at all.

In the testing we mainly try to identify potential sources of measurement and nonresponse errors. Testing procedures have already been elaborated on for traditional survey modes. Comprehensive overviews can be found in Madans, Miller, Maitland, & Willis (2011) and in Presser et al. (2004). Campanelli (2008) also provides a brief practical insight with essential templates of rating forms, criteria for systematic reviews of questionnaires, coding schemes and other testing-related materials. Saris (2012) presents a very useful conceptual structuring of 13 approaches to questionnaire evaluation, according to the amount of additional data collected and according to subjective vs empirical evaluation criteria. Most of these approaches are included in our overview of traditional testing approaches below.

Web surveys share many aspects of testing with other survey modes. For example, each web survey needs to be tested for issues of question wording, question order and questionnaire length. However, the testing of a web questionnaire needs to include various other aspects that are more specific to the web mode, including visual layout (e.g. screen layout, navigation, question implementation layout), interactive and multimedia features, and technical issues (such as the proper functioning of branching and appearance under different devices). Overall testing of the web questionnaire should thus address:

- substantive issues related to content and validity;
- methodological and cognitive aspects of questions (understanding, wording, format, design, etc., including respondent's competence and social desirability) and of the questionnaire (layout, structure, interactivity, length, etc.);
- technical issues (appearance, as well as programming, branching, randomization and skips, etc. across devices, browsers, operating systems, Internet speed); and
- the overall usability of the questionnaire.

In practice, the amount of testing required depends on resources (budget, personnel and time), specifics of the web questionnaire (including the presence of complicated questions, measurement of some complex concepts), its length, the number of questions previously tested in other surveys, familiarity with the web survey software, the target population (e.g. elderly, children, businesses), importance of the survey, as well as other factors.

In this section we discuss systematically only the most important testing approaches, while in the next section (2.3.6) we address the relation to questionnaire development and the aspects of practical implementation.

2.3.5.1 Traditional Testing Approaches

A number of testing approaches relevant for web surveys have already been developed for traditional survey modes. They are typically used in the earlier phases of questionnaire development and can be directly implemented for web questionnaires. We therefore deal especially with those aspects that are highly relevant for web questionnaires.

Conventional pre-testing historically prevailed in the F2F context (Presser et al., 2004, p. 100), usually in the form of partial 'dress rehearsals'. Here, a few respondents were selected by convenience sampling and approached by experienced interviewers who conducted F2F interviews with formal debriefings at the end (see also Campanelli, 2008). Although little justification accompanied this common-sense practice, it was believed that at least 12–25 interviews sufficed to reveal major weaknesses in the questionnaire. Such an approach can still prove to be useful in the early phases of the web questionnaire development to identify various substantive and cognitive issues.

Expert evaluation involves *topic experts* evaluating substantive issues and *survey methodologists* focusing on cognitive and other methodological aspects of the questionnaire (DeMaio & Landreth, 2004). Various expert forms, appraisal systems and checklists were developed for this purpose (see Campanelli, 2008; Groves et al., 2009, p. 261), although entirely unstructured feedback can be provided as well. The recommended number of methodological experts (at least one) is usually smaller than the number of substantive topic experts (at least a few), because methodological issues are more standardized. In the case of web questionnaires, *technical* and *human–computer interaction (HCI) experts* can also be involved, as discussed later. Web questionnaires offer an important opportunity for the more integrated online provision of feedback in the form of online commenting (described below), which greatly contributes to the efficiency of the expert evaluation procedures.

Cognitive interviews address cognitive processes used by respondents to answer survey questions. Typical techniques include 'think-aloud' procedures, probing, retrospective thinking, paraphrasing, confidence judgements, vignettes and others (K. Miller, Chepp, Willson, & Padilla, 2014). The cognitive interviewing sessions typically take around an hour, require a trained interviewer (see Campanelli, 2008) and are typically run in laboratory settings. Interviewing techniques can be implemented in various different ways and sometimes even produce different results (DeMaio & Landreth, 2004). Sample sizes are often between 5 and 15 respondents, although some studies suggest that this number is too low and may fail to identify more than half of all problems (J. Blair & Conrad, 2011). Although cognitive interviewing is usually performed F2F, the interviewer can also be involved remotely, using chat, audio or video conferencing, or even virtual environments (Dean, Head, & Swicegood, 2013). With web surveys, cognitive interviews can also be performed online and be entirely self-administered in principle. For example, after answering a question, respondents are asked to describe how they came to the answer, and to provide their comments in writing or by audio recording. These qualitative data can be complemented with paradata, such as response times and screen capturing (Chaney, Barry, Chaney, Stellefson, & Webb, 2013). Nevertheless, while self-administered or web-mediated cognitive interviewing sessions can help save substantial amounts of resources, they are likely to be less informative than live F2F interaction, which can ensure higher motivation and depth. As for now, online approaches to cognitive interviewing remain largely under-researched and infrequently used (e.g. Behr, Bandilla, Kaczmirek, & Braun, 2013).

Respondents' debriefings relate to simple field test interviews, which are – in contrast to cognitive interviews – always conducted outside the laboratory. They are usually implemented in the later phases of questionnaire development to obtain additional insights about respondents' interpretation of questions. Open-ended or closed-ended follow-up evaluation questions are an essential tool for this approach. They are typically asked at the end of the questionnaire, but often also after certain individual questions. A specific approach concerns *vignette* questions, which we have already mentioned among cognitive interviewing methods, where a hypothetical situation is presented to the respondent (E. Martin, 2004, p. 154). For example, when clarifying the meaning of 'work', the respondent is asked to comment on whether the person conducting voluntary work in a hospital is treated as a working person. For web surveys, this technique can be transferred easily to the self-administered online environment (Aviram, 2012).

Focus groups typically involve 5–12 potential respondents who participate in a semi-structured discussion. Professional moderation is needed for these sessions, which typically last around an hour. They are particularly useful in the preliminary phases of questionnaire preparation for the clarification of essential concepts, but can also be used later on to evaluate draft versions of the questionnaire. In addition to respondents, focus groups can be attended by experts or interviewers. Typical sessions are conducted in a laboratory using standard focus group methodologies (Stewart & Shamdasani, 2014). However, online focus groups are becoming increasingly popular (Gaiser, 2008), particularly with the developments in video conferencing systems and modern software support.

Behaviour coding is a reliable and replicable technique where respondents (and interviewers) are observed – usually also video recorded – and their behaviour coded to learn about problems with question understanding and answering. This is based on an assumption that respondents' reactions and body language can express misunderstandings and problems (Ongena & Dijkstra, 2006). The sessions are typically done in a laboratory, but, with web surveys, a remote video conferencing system can also be used.

Experiments are used to split respondents randomly into several groups to observe the effects of different variations in questionnaire implementation on estimates, distributions, various indicators of the quality of responses, and usability evaluations. These are commonly used to test the appropriateness of question wording and visual layout, effectiveness of invitations and incentives, and many other factors. Conducting experiments introduces very specific methodological and statistical dilemmas about the number of experimental groups, considerations of the combined effects of different manipulations, and the establishment of valid causal relationships. Therefore, this approach requires a deliberate professional treatment (Tourangeau, 2004). With web questionnaires, the experiments are particularly convenient as their technical implementation is relatively simple and the required resources are relatively low (Reips & Krantz, 2010).

The approaches discussed above – from conventional pre-testing to experiments – are typically used in the earlier stages of questionnaire development and rely on a certain level of feedback from respondents or experts. As such, they are different from the remaining three approaches described below: in a pilot study we conduct testing using the very final draft version of the questionnaire, while with self-assessment and statistical modelling, no additional data are required from respondents or experts.

Pilot studies use a small sample of the target population to evaluate the final questionnaire in a real setting, which serves as a 'dress rehearsal'. Certain standard evaluation questions can be added at the end of the questionnaire (e.g. 'How easy was it to answer the questionnaire?') in order to obtain additional feedback from respondents. Analysis of the obtained data, particularly response distributions and paradata, is an essential component of pilot testing. Pilot studies are indispensable also because they can be used to test other aspects of fielding (e.g. sampling, recruitment, response rate, length) and post-fielding (e.g. datafile recordings, quality of responses). Pilot studies typically include up to a few per cent of the target sample. Various rules of thumb regarding the minimum sample size exist, usually around 15–30, which still enables a rough inspection of response distributions. On the other hand, hundreds of cases might be needed when the aim of the pilot is to test the measurement characteristics of questions across various subgroups. We may add that when research design features (like response rates or incentives) – and not the questionnaire itself – are the main focus of testing, some authors (Bradburn et al., 2004, p. 319) discuss this separately from the pilot studies and call it a *field trial*.

Statistical models are used on a complete set of survey data collected as part of a pilot study or previous studies. The aim is to provide insight into various types of errors, particularly reliability and validity, which is then used for the implementation of further improvements. Commonly applied approaches to statistical modelling include latent variable models (e.g. factor analysis, latent class analysis), scaling procedures (e.g. item response theory), quasi-simplex design and model, and multi-trait, multi-method designs (Saris, 2012).

Questionnaire assessment tools can help a researcher to evaluate the questionnaire according to certain rules or procedures. This can be done by reviewing the compliance of the questionnaire to simple checklists and expert schemes (Campanelli, 2008; Groves et al., 2009, p. 261), but can also involve evaluations on the basis of more complex conceptual approaches, such as the three-step question development procedure of Saris & Gallhofer (2014). Specialized software can be used for certain aspects of self-assessment and can provide features of automatic or semi-automatic diagnostics. Two examples include the Survey Quality Prediction (SQP) system, which estimates the validity and reliability of survey questions (Saris & Gallhofer, 2007), and QUAID (Graesser, Cai, Louwerse, & Daniel, 2006), which analyses the linguistic aspects of questions (such as the presence of infrequently used or technical words).

2.3.5.2 Specific Testing Approaches for Web Questionnaires

In addition to the traditional approaches described above, web surveys also use specific evaluation methods. Some were developed for other CASIC modes, while others are exclusive to the web mode.

Questionnaire technical testing is an integral part of questionnaire computerization. It is essential to ensure the correct functioning of the questionnaire and the avoidance of technical problems that can lead to serious nonresponse and measurement errors. The corresponding strategy, criteria, resources and planning need to be specified in advance, in order to enable a systematic evaluation process. Tasks related to the technical testing of the web questionnaire commonly include:

- *Checking for technical correctness and debugging.* Technical problems can originate from errors in the questionnaire specification or occur due to discrepancies between specification and actual programming. One of the critical components is the accurate implementation of branching, where minor errors in the definition of conditional statements can lead to serious problems with questionnaire branching. For simple questionnaires, a screen-by-screen inspection of the questionnaire may suffice to identify and resolve such issues. However, more complex questionnaires that use a lot of branching, randomizations, calculations, auxiliary data, combined tables and other advanced features require an elaborate formal strategy. To a large degree this overlaps with standard procedures for testing software applications, where simple observations of application functioning ('black-box testing') typically do not enable sufficient identification of programming bugs and need to be extended with further inspection of internal programming structures ('white-box testing', Baker, Crawford, & Swinehart, 2004a, p. 369). A systematic review of errors, methods and the corresponding management for computerized questionnaires is provided in Tarnai & Moore (2004). Additional benefits are offered by features of certain web survey software that enable the automatic generation of artificial datafiles and test entries.

- *Stability across browsers, operating systems, devices.* While commonly used web browsers offer a relatively standardized web browsing experience, variations in questionnaire display and interaction can occur due to various factors, especially different screen sizes, support for client-side scripts (particularly JavaScript) and input methods (mouse, touch pad or touch screen). To identify such problems, we should first identify the technology commonly used by respondents, for example by analysing device-type paradata (see Section 2.4.2) from similar or previous surveys and by checking the corresponding market shares of different devices, operating systems and browsers. The main focus should be on checking the visual display, functioning of interactive features and performance of advanced aspects of the web questionnaire (e.g. multimedia, advanced question types, external links, specially programmed features). To verify the specific performance of the software used for web surveying, we can also create a master test questionnaire with all question types, standard layouts and interactive features, and regularly test its performance on various platforms. web survey software of high quality makes an important difference and can eliminate a large part of these issues.

- *Compliance with standards.* When designing a web questionnaire, it is often beneficial to follow specific technical standards, which can also cover other aspects of survey preparation and implementation. We take the opportunity here to discuss all aspects related to standards. Standards can focus on narrow technical aspects (such as the W3C standard), but also on questionnaire layout and presentation (e.g. Dillman et al., 2009), usability (e.g. Nielsen, 2000a) and various other specific aspects, such as web accessibility, particularly for visually impaired respondents, where elaborate strategies exist (e.g. Kaczmirek & Wolff, 2007). In addition, a standard corporate visual identity can be established by integrating visual design solutions, such as font size, background colours and logotypes. Research organizations sometimes establish specific standards of questionnaire implementation, for example approaches to using hard and

soft item nonresponse prompts. The standard use of language (e.g. grammar, spelling, proofreading) and overall quality assurance policies are also extremely important. See Baker et al. (2004, p. 369) for examples of such standards in a marketing research organization. Once such standards are established, each web questionnaire is checked for compliance with them during the testing process.

- *Other technical aspects.* In addition to the technical aspects discussed above, we may also need to check for proper data recording, required Internet connection speed, various aspects of the technical infrastructure on which the survey is implemented (capacity of servers, backup and security policies, etc.) and other specific issues.

Electronic observations relate to technical recordings that are used to reveal respondents' behaviour, which points to certain problems. The recordings can be used as standalone data collection methods for the purpose of testing, but more often are implemented as support for the other testing approaches presented above. These methods include the following:

- *Analysis of automatically collected paradata* relies on computer traces that respondents leave while answering the questionnaire, such as time stamps, mouse movements and navigation paths through the questionnaire. Analysis of time stamps is frequently used in web questionnaire testing and is historically related to so-called *response latency studies*, which started in the 1990s when CASIC modes enabled automatic and detailed time recordings. The idea comes from cognitive psychology, where long delays between stimulus and response may signal a problem. Several studies on time analysis in web questionnaires have been published (e.g. Callegaro et al., 2009). We discuss paradata collection and use further in Section 2.4.2.

- *Screen recording* and *respondents' video sessions* are becoming increasingly available. Tracking of screen sequences and videotaping the respondent's behaviour can be studied alone or integrated into other testing approaches, particularly usability testing and various qualitative techniques. It can also be used as part of online cognitive interviewing, presented above.

- *Eye tracking* devices record points at which a respondent is looking at the screen (eye gaze on the parts of the questionnaire), corresponding fixations and the sequence of eye gazes (Galesic & Yan, 2011). Results are typically presented with heat maps and can be further analysed (Coombe et al., 2011) to enable improvements in the visual exposure of some elements (e.g. highlighting the instructions or response options). Eye tracking is typically considered a technique which is also used in the general context of web usability testing (Nielsen & Pernice, 2009).

- *Brain activity* measurements can be used to provide insight into various aspects of the respondent's engagement, flow, arousal and attention while answering the questionnaire. A variety of methods exist, including electroencephalography (EEG) and functional magnetic resonance imaging. Although rarely used, due to their very high costs and incomplete understanding of the relationship between brain processes and behaviour, some studies have already shown their potential for future survey testing applications (Coombe et al., 2011).

Online commenting can be used to collect feedback on questions, pages or the questionnaire as a whole, while answering or inspecting the web questionnaire online. Although the commenting itself is nothing new in survey testing and is routinely used as a part of traditional testing approaches, web surveys bring enormous convenience with their online implementation. This is done by adding simple commenting text fields to the testing version of the web questionnaire (positioned below or beside the questions) or a linked option to collect general comments. The commenting system needs to be incorporated in a user-friendly manner into the *testing mode* of the web survey software. The comments can be collected from the research team, experts or respondents. This can be implemented as part of informal feedback collection, stand-alone formal testing or as support for other online testing approaches (e.g. respondent debriefing, cognitive interviews, expert interviews, focus groups). The commenting and review process can be supported by a general management system to handle replies, follow-up discussions among researchers and to-do lists. Unfortunately, little web survey software provides this simple and powerful option and even less offers it in an advanced and user-friendly format (Vehovar, Slavec, & Berzelak, 2011). Due to its importance for testing and questionnaire development, this option is definitely one of the most essential features when selecting web survey software.

Usability evaluation refers to usability as the degree of simplicity and efficiency (a good fit) of use of software, hardware or anything else for the people who use it (Kaczmirek, 2006). Paraphrasing this definition, we can define the usability of a web questionnaire as the degree to which it is easy to answer and generally fits the respondent's tasks. In general, questionnaire usability can be achieved through the questionnaire design principles addressed in this section, including the proper selection of question types, questionnaire structure and layout, navigation and the provision of engagement. However, when it comes to the evaluation of usability, this overlaps to a certain extent with some of the testing approaches already discussed above. In a narrower sense, it is closely related to the principles of human–computer interaction (HCI), which can be applied to web questionnaires as a specific type of interactive system. The general principles of web usability (see Nielsen, 2012; Roe, 2008) can also be considered and applied to web questionnaires. Within this context, Kaczmirek (2006) provides an introduction and overview on how the usability of web questionnaires is linked to HCI and the usability principles of the ISO 9241-10 standard on ergonomic requirements for office work with visual display terminals.

Usability evaluations can use various techniques in an experimental or non-experimental setting, and can be done in the field (e.g. at the respondent's home) or in a laboratory. Some of the most commonly used approaches are think-aloud protocols and other observational and cognitive techniques.

Further, usability evaluation can be done simply by analysing paradata collected during the pilot or even the main study (i.e. observing response times, breakoffs, error counts, navigation behaviour), or by the evaluation carried out by HCI experts. The latter is an expert evaluation, also called *heuristic evaluation*, where experts typically follow certain structured heuristic criteria (such as simplicity of navigation, readability of fonts or overall clarity of visual presentation).

The most frequently applied usability evaluation approach is formal *usability testing*. By this we usually understand procedures of asking respondents to perform specific tasks according to predefined scenarios and then observing, recording and analysing their success. A major stream of usability testing of web questionnaires occurs in a laboratory setting, with respondents performing various *usability tests*. Overall, the methods of general usability testing largely apply (e.g. Nielsen, 2000a), including various rules of thumb. For example, a relatively small sample of five testers is often considered sufficient to find 80% of usability problems (Nielsen, 2000b). In very simplified circumstances, the think-aloud protocol with a few respondents who fill in the questionnaire and comment on the process can provide sufficient information to improve the questionnaire. In more advanced settings, around 10 respondents are typically used, sometimes separately at various phases of questionnaire development. Baker et al. (2004) practise three steps: the respondent is first observed while answering the entire questionnaire, then asked standard evaluation questions, and finally involved in a screen-by-screen discussion and specific tasks. Hansen & Couper (2004) provide further examples of advanced case studies.

Usability evaluation is often integrated with the methods of electronic observations discussed above. This is increasingly facilitated by inexpensive laptops with integrated video cameras and screen recording software. An attractive alternative is to perform testing in the respondents' natural setting (e.g. at home), using some video conferencing software with screen casting and communication between a respondent and a remote moderator (Stettler, 2013). Self-administered remote sessions can also be useful, using either online commenting systems or *remote unmoderated usability testing* software (Mccloskey, 2014), which enables the specification of tasks and video recording of the respondent's performance. A general insight into online usability testing is provided by Albert, Tedesco, & Tullis (2009).

Although usability evaluations are a well-researched field, the literature on specific implementation in web surveys is scarce and case oriented. In addition to the studies cited above, only a few more case studies exist (e.g. Da Costa, Schmoelz, Davies, di Pietro, Kupek & de Assis, 2013; Kaczmirek, 2011; Potaka, 2008). While it is true that the usability evaluation of web questionnaires brings relatively few specifics compared to general usability approaches, more guidance on practical implementation is needed. Some common dilemmas include whether to have only one usability testing session at the end of the questionnaire development or at several interim occasions; to use novices or experienced respondents; to have a laboratory or a remote setting; to use moderated or non-moderated sessions; and so on. Important dilemmas also relate to the optimal sample size, levels of structuring of the interaction (scenario vs natural flow), priority focuses (wording, visuals, interactive features, navigation, etc.) and the development of standardized performance indicators. Finally, a detailed study of approaches and added value of paradata and screen recordings for questionnaire usability testing is also needed.

Integrated automated diagnostics build on statistical modelling, but are – unlike the questionnaire assessment tools mentioned above (e.g. SQP or QUAID) – integrated into the web survey software and support the entire process of online questionnaire development. These diagnostics can help to detect various questionnaire-related issues. In their simplest form, they can provide notifications about potential problems that are rather straightforward to identify, for example an exceedingly large number of sub-questions in a table. To detect more complex issues, the automated diagnostics need to rely on advanced approaches, such as data mining for the automated estimation of question validity and reliability, language technologies for the identification of unclear words, and even artificial intelligence approaches based on semantics to provide suggestions for question wording. Some tools also produce summary scores of questionnaire quality (Nallan, 2012); however, the interpretation of these scores requires careful evaluation of the methodology used for their derivation in order to understand their limitations. In a very advanced form, automated systems could competently guide a researcher through the entire questionnaire development process.

All the testing approaches – traditional and web survey specific – discussed above should be regarded as complementary, although some of them are already very closely interrelated and can sometimes be merged. The selection of the right mix of testing approaches is a complex issue, which we address in the next section.

It is also important to note that web-specific testing approaches require specific *software support*. This may or may not be integrated into web survey software used for questionnaire development. We have already discussed some of these features in the different testing approaches above and we briefly summarize and extend them below:

- *The questionnaire preview* option exists in all web survey software and is used regularly during questionnaire development. Advanced preview settings are desirable, since they can improve testing performance by allowing us to ignore skips and conditions, jump between questions and pages, switch between paging and scrolling design, and so on. This option is very useful also for documenting the questionnaire at the stage of data publication and dissemination because a preview URL can be provided to users of the data even after the survey is deactivated.
- *The test questionnaire* differs from the questionnaire preview, since it additionally enables the test entry of answers. The test questionnaire is usually linked to the main questionnaire URL address and test responses are usually stored in the survey datafile. However, the answers provided are explicitly marked as test entries in order to enable simple removal from the datafile when they are no longer needed.

- *Real-time programming controls* can help to identify logical or technical errors in the specification of branching (conditions), question loops, randomization, and other dynamic questionnaire elements.
- *Response simulations* can perform artificial completion of the questionnaire (e.g. by generating a random answer to each question) and serve to evaluate the proper functioning of the questionnaire logic. For example, a conditional question that has no simulated response may signal that this question never appears due to an error in branching.
- *Paradata* can be used to collect a broad range of data about respondents' actions during completion of the pilot questionnaire and can be used for various diagnostics of questionnaire-related problems.
- *The online commenting system* enables respondents and experts to provide their feedback online, while researchers can effectively process and manage the comments.
- *Automated diagnostics* can be used to evaluate the appropriate implementation of a broad range of questionnaire characteristics, including the number of sub-questions in tables, estimation of length, and language problems with question wording.
- *Integration of the support for capturing and processing screenshots or videos*, as is the case with the standard usability procedures for web applications, can strongly facilitate formal testing. See, for example, Blaise Tools[15] for a discussion of these options.

While the main testing focus of the above approaches is on the survey questionnaire, we should not forget that other aspects of the survey process also require testing. We will discuss further the general technical pre-testing conducted within technical preparations (Section 2.4.4) and we have already elaborated on the role of pilot studies and field trials for the evaluation of fielding and post-fielding procedures, not just those related to the questionnaire. In Section 3.3 we also discuss the so-called *soft launch*, which can serve in some situations as a testing tool at the very start of fieldwork.

2.3.6 Integration of Questionnaire Development, Computerization and Testing

The process of web questionnaire preparation, covered in this section (2.3), consists of several phases and activities that need to be integrated. Question development is at the core of this process, ranging from initial conceptualization and operationalization to the final wording and layout presentation of questions. A set of questions is then integrated into the questionnaire through activities related to defining the questionnaire structure, layout and computerization. The quality of implementation of each phase is then ensured through testing, using various methods covered in the previous section (2.3.5). The implementation of all these phases is iterative by nature, with each iteration resulting in *draft versions* and/or some other outputs, which are then subject to further evaluations and necessary modifications.

Computerization of web questionnaires allows the important perspective of external software support to be included in the questionnaire preparation process. Early drafts of the questionnaire are usually prepared using standard *text processors* (e.g. MS Word, Google Docs) and are then exchanged among researchers and clients by email or some file sharing web services. Written instructions and specifications for questionnaire programmers, like branching, randomization and validation, are also part of these drafts. Sometimes, in large organizations, specialized external questionnaire documentation and development tools are used for this purpose (Lorenc, Biemer, Jansson, Eltinge, & Holmberg, 2013). We define all of these approaches to questionnaire preparation

as *external questionnaire development*, because it is done outside the web survey software.

However, at a certain point we need to shift to the web survey software in which we actually implement the web questionnaire. Correspondingly, all activities of questionnaire development and testing done with the support of the web survey software are denoted as *integrated questionnaire development*. With future developments of this software, we can expect an increase in integrated support for all phases of the questionnaire preparation process, from the initial specifications of concepts and outline to final testing. Vehovar, Petrovčič, & Slavec (2014) describe the steps in this direction. Nevertheless, it is likely that the external approach will remain in use to a certain extent, especially for more complex and large-scale survey projects.

The complexity of the questionnaire preparation process, as observed from the methodological perspective, is illustrated by Figure 2.1. The key activities of questionnaire development and testing are denoted by the bold boxes and capital letters in Figure 2.1. They are conceptually integrated into the iterating sequences, where each iteration usually develops a draft version of the questionnaire (boxes with cut corners in the figure), which is then subject to testing and subsequent further development.

The activities related to external questionnaire development appear in the shaded area at the top right of Figure 2.1. They are less structured in Figure 2.1 than the remaining activities of integrated questionnaire development because they are not within our main focus, but also because they may involve various other features related to the development and testing of the questionnaire in a specific external environment. In most situations, however, this external environment basically means some text processor.

As mentioned above, the questionnaire preparation process often results in draft versions. Note that, before a certain version is then tested, some additional questionnaire preparation activities are also needed, which are explicitly denoted in boxes in Figure 2.1. We may add that their importance is often overlooked and underestimated.

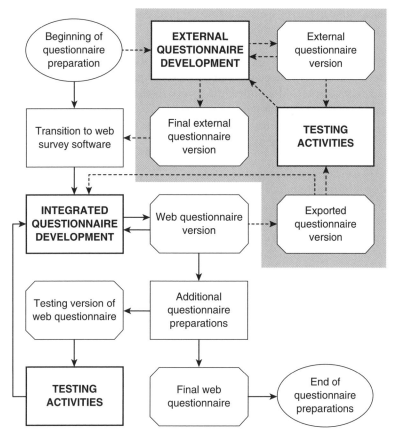

Figure 2.1   The flow and structure of the questionnaire preparation process

For the purpose of testing, for example, we need to include special introductory texts, instructions for testers and provision for question feedback. Sometimes, for specific tests, the questionnaires may need to be prepared also in printed format. In preparing the final version of the questionnaire, additional work may be required on final proofreading, final changes in visual layout, and other minor corrections that do not affect the methodological aspects.

The draft web questionnaire can sometimes also be exported to print, PDF or text processor format for further integrated development (e.g. the corresponding changes are then still made in the web survey software) or for external development (e.g. another cycle of questionnaire development with the external tools).

Formal testing – which can use various approaches discussed in the previous section (2.3.5) – is usually conducted sequentially. After one specific testing method is used, further questionnaire development to eliminate any identified issues is conducted before moving on to the next testing approach.

Alternatively, different testing approaches can be used in parallel within the same phase of questionnaire testing. However, available resources typically do not allow for this. Furthermore, there may be problems of redundancy due to various methods identifying the same issues, but potentially also conflicting results from different methods (e.g. Lenzner, 2012; Yan, Kreuter, & Tourangeau, 2012). Such discrepancies may simply reflect the complex and multidimensional nature of survey questionnaire development rather than serious problems and inconsistencies with different testing methods. However, decisions about how to include the contradictory results in the revision may become problematic and very complex. More often, different approaches complement each other (e.g. Hughes, 2004), suggesting that it may actually be beneficial to use several testing approaches simultaneously in certain phases.

The decision to end questionnaire testing after a certain iteration is often determined by external constraints, such as time and resources. Alternatively, it is useful to define beforehand certain decision rules for ending testing, since there is almost always some room for improvement. To stop an endless journey towards the perfect questionnaire, we may, for example, examine the number and severity of errors discovered during the last test. If there are a lot of problems or if problems are essential for the quality of the questionnaire, we may need another test run; otherwise, it is time to move on to the final version of the questionnaire.

The process in Figure 2.1 can be implemented in many combinations of different testing methods and their sequences; it therefore can become very complex. Nonetheless, such conceptualization can be useful to help identify and structure all the required questionnaire development phases and aspects, particularly the number of testing circles and evaluation methods that are to be used. Consequently, it can help to foresee the required effort and resources for these testing activities. We should stress that the resources needed for testing and additional questionnaire preparation are often substantial and should not be underestimated or even overlooked.

This conceptualization also presents the basis for the establishment of related timing and management plans. Of course, these all need to be elaborated very early in the pre-fielding step (Section 2.6). Further, within the broader project management context (Section 6.2), the key activities of questionnaire development and testing, as denoted in Figure 2.1, can be directly transformed into the corresponding work packages

or their components. For complicated situations and complex surveys, it is reasonable to consult experts regarding the optimal mix of sequences and procedures.

At this point we may repeat again that web surveys should not be undertaken without plans and resources allocated to formal testing. At the very minimum, testing should include the following:

- Initially it should involve two formal evaluation components: expert evaluation (by at least one survey methodologist or experienced practitioner) and some respondent debriefings or think-aloud cognitive interviews. For additional convenience, both components could be implemented remotely, using online commenting systems.
- Basic usability evaluation is also an indispensable testing activity, which can – in extremely simplified cases – be integrated within the formal evaluations mentioned above.
- Essential questionnaire technical testing is another compulsory part of questionnaire preparation.
- A pilot survey with some real respondents is also needed.
- If there is a sponsor or a client, their feedback will usually need to be obtained.

Even this minimum set of testing procedures may easily require five or more formal versions of the questionnaire, while, with complex surveys, particularly international ones, the number of versions may increase rapidly. Let us conclude with an example reported by Vehovar, Petrovčič, & Slavec (2014). They describe the preparation of a 30-minute master questionnaire in English – to be later translated and implemented in seven countries – that required six preliminary external versions in a text processor and a further 13 computerized online versions in web survey software with an integrated online commenting system. Four initial draft online versions were also exported back to the offline text processor to facilitate external commenting, while the last seven draft online versions were prepared after the pilot study. Additional versions of the questionnaire appeared after this point due to proofreading, translations, back-translations, design and formatting.

This example clearly shows the importance of and need for integrating questionnaire development, testing and computerization, for which sufficient additional resources should be allocated in each web survey project.

2.4 TECHNICAL PREPARATIONS

In addition to the essential methodological preparations related to mode, sampling and the questionnaire, the pre-fielding step also includes some other activities, which we structure in technical preparations, nonresponse strategy and general management.

We start with technical preparations, which are predominantly concerned with capturing and organizing data (Section 2.4.1), and proceed with handling paradata (Section 2.4.2), dealing with the technical aspects of security and privacy (Section 2.4.3) and technical pre-testing (Section 2.4.4).

2.4.1 Preparations for Capturing and Organizing Data

We need to clearly foresee which data to record, so that the corresponding technical support is organized with respect to preparing the database, tracing respondents, email settings and sample management. These activities are greatly determined by the chosen web survey software, but there are still many decisions to make and options from which to choose. In addition, understanding these issues can play an important role in selecting the right software.

2.4.1.1 Database Preparations

By *database* we mean a collection of structured files, which include all the data that were collected, obtained or produced in pre-fielding (e.g. contact information), fielding (e.g. survey responses, paradata) and post-fielding (e.g. weighting). Formally, the database can be organized into more components (sub-databases).

Understanding the components, format, structure, hierarchy and levels is essential for effective technical preparation. We need to distinguish between four types of primary data:

- *Questionnaire data* are collected in the measurement stage for each responding unit. They include *substantive responses, non-substantive responses* (e.g. 'don't know') and records of missing data (e.g. item nonresponse, break-off). Questionnaire data, which is the most essential database component, was already referred to as a datafile (Section 2.3.1), so as to separate it from the general notion of a database.
- *Paradata* are data about the process of answering the survey (Couper, 2000a), and are collected at the unit level. The main sources of paradata are *log files*, which include standardized traces (e.g. time stamps, type of action) after each action of the respondent. The *call record data*, which include all information about the contacting process, are also important here, as well as some other paradata types (e.g. screen recording).
- *Auxiliary data* are characteristics of units (e.g. gender, region, email address) obtained from a sampling frame or some other external source.
- *Metadata* are data obtained externally or assigned by a researcher. They can be at the level of the survey project (e.g. description of the project, fielding dates, etc.) or at question level (e.g. sensitivity, salience, measurement scale).

In addition to these four types of primary data, the database stores various types of *derived data*, such as weights or recoded or calculated values.

This is obviously a lot of data, with a complex structure across various levels: units, pages, questions and variables. Let us repeat that by variable we mean a statistical term which denotes a single column (sometimes also a line, depending on orientation) in a datafile, and which also corresponds to an item, while a question is a methodological term, denoting a building block of the questionnaire, which has its own characteristics (e.g. measurement level, content type, complexity, sensitive) and can include more items/variables (e.g. as in the case of tables).

Of course, except for survey data, it is not necessary to collect, store and analyse all the different types of data described above. This primarily depends on the goal and scope of the research. In general, we should not collect and store more data than needed, since this can lead to unnecessary complications and costs.

Moreover, we have relatively little impact on the database structure of specific web survey software and – once selected – no impact on the features offered. Web survey software varies considerably in its database performance according to:

- *capability* (e.g. What is the maximum number of questions or units? Which data are exported and in what format? Are paradata produced in a friendly manner? How do we change the questionnaire during fieldwork? How do we upload the auxiliary data? How do we input and export the metadata? What is the database structure?);
- *flexibility* (e.g. Can we change the settings for paradata collection? What are the options in data export and data import? Can we copy, merge and sort the datafile?); and
- *speed* (e.g. What is the technical speed when creating a questionnaire, when filling in responses and when generating reports? What happens to the speed in the case of numerous variables or units?).

While most of these are determined in the selection of the web survey software, a researcher is still responsible for certain questionnaire (e.g. defining the type of variables) or paradata settings (e.g. turning cookie collection on), as well as for foreseeing and preparing the procedures to organize the data needed for the analysis.

2.4.1.2 Respondent Tracing and Unique Identifiers

We address here the technical aspects of tracing units in list-based and in non-list-based surveys. Various reasons exist for tracing the units included in a sample. For example, if we want to send reminders only to nonrespondents, we first need to trace the response status of all units.

List-based web surveys invite individual units and then trace them by using a *unique identifier.* Email serves well for this purpose, but, due to privacy concerns, we prefer to generate a special and unique ID number or *ID code*, which allows a researcher to control the access (e.g. prevent unwanted access or disable multiple completions per unit). Support is also given for the 'pause and continue later' option for respondents who intentionally decide to postpone completion of the web questionnaire, so that, when they return, they can take up the survey from where they left off. Similarly, ID codes facilitate the process of reminding break-off units, since we may also ask them to proceed from their breakoff point.

ID codes can be used with automated or manual login. In the case of *automated login*, a unique URL is prepared for each respondent, to which an ID code is added as an extension to the basic URL of the web questionnaire. This individualized URL is then sent in the email invitation to the units from the list. When the recipients open the email invitation, they can access the web questionnaire simply by clicking on their individualized URL.

In the case of mail or other traditional invitations, *manual login* is needed, where sample members first use the initial URL address of the web questionnaire from the invitation. Next, they are asked to enter the ID code that they also received in the invitation. The process is split into two stages because the entire individualized URL address would be too long.

The initial URL should be simple and short, preferably with some content customization (e.g. www.researcher.com/projectname), instead of a default technical link generated with web survey software. In addition, with traditional invitations (e.g. mail), we should also make sure that this initial URL address appears at the top of the search engine hits, because many respondents – by mistake or intentionally – enter the URL address into a search engine and not into the web browser address bar.

With manual login there is the possibility that an incorrect URL or ID code is entered. To avoid this, the URL needs to be simple, while the password needs to be short, but still complex enough to make it difficult to guess. An increasing set of neighbouring numbers is therefore not suitable. Instead, a scattered random allocation is required, including letters and digits (e.g. 2X0A11). Pairs of ID codes should differ in at least two characters to avoid typing errors or random guessing. We can also have a combined *semi-automatic login* procedure, where an individualized URL is sent by email, but the respondent is still required to type in the ID code manually, either the one from the individualized URL or another one, in order to strengthen security.

Group passwords are sometimes used, often based on some easy-to-remember word (e.g. name of the organization), which is communicated offline (e.g. within an organization or in a classroom). However, this can serve only to separate respondents from different groups and not as an ID code. In addition, good software enables the separation of URLs for groups without using a group password.

An automated login, which can accompany email invitations, reduces respondent burden and helps avoid typing errors, while manual login increases the sense of personalization and decreases perceived anonymity. A higher quality of answers (fewer breakoffs, more answers to open-ended questions) due to increased personalization has sometimes been observed with manual login (Heerwegh & Loosveldt, 2002, 2003). However, these effects were weak and not confirmed in some other studies (e.g. Crawford et al., 2001). As expected, less disclosure to sensitive questions also occurs with manual login (Joinson, Woodley, & Reips, 2007), as well as lower response rates compared with automatic login (30% vs 35%). In general, we therefore recommend automatic login, but this further depends on other factors, particularly those showing clear evidence that manual login brings positive effects.

In any case, we should prepare carefully and also test the instructions for respondents to access the web questionnaire, which need to be much more detailed in case we use mail invitations. Additional elaboration is needed (e.g. attached screenshots) if respondents are less familiar with Internet usage (see Dillman et al., 2009, p. 287). Instructions should be brief and written in an accessible and non-demanding language. With email invitations, we may offer explicit alternative options for accessing the web questionnaire (e.g. 'type in the URL address', 'click on the link', 'copy and paste the address into your web browser').

Non-list-based web surveys do not enable unique identifiers. Consequently, the problems with controlling access to the questionnaire are more serious. One alternative to unique identifiers in this situation is the *IP address*, which is a number assigned to all devices logged on to the Internet, including the respondent's device. However, dynamic IP addresses also exist, by which a different IP can be assigned to the same device (e.g. computer) when it logs on to the Internet at different times. Similarly problematic are organizational IP addresses, where all devices in an organization appear with the same IP. If we were to allow only a single respondent per IP address, only one respondent from such an organization would be able to complete the survey. Still, blocking multiple responses from the same IP address – combined with time stamps (e.g. a large number of accesses from the same IP address in a short time interval) – can be helpful in preventing some simple frauds (e.g. fake responses) or server attacks coming from a single device.

Another alternative are *cookies*, which are small text files sent from the server hosting the web questionnaire, and then stored on respondents' devices. The server assigns its own unique code to the cookie, together with information on the time stamp, last question answered, etc. (ESOMAR, 2011a, p. 10). The next time the respondent visits this same web questionnaire, the web survey software recognizes this unit, which can be used to prevent repeated access or to enable proper continuation from the eventual pausing or breakoff. However, cookies are related to the browser used, so the respondent can still fill in the questionnaire several times by using another browser on the same device, by using another device or by deleting cookies. Cookies face serious problems due to increasing ethical and legal restrictions, as well as because some users decide to block them. For these reasons cookies serve poorly as a replacement for the ID code.

Cookies are usually temporary files and can be set to last as long as the browser session of the user, but can also last an hour, a day, a month or even permanently. With some software they may be needed as technical support for answering the questionnaire and expire when the session terminates (completion, breakoff, pause). Cookies that last longer than the questionnaire session can be subject to legal restrictions and may require explicit confirmation from the user, which additionally complicates the response process.

In general we do not recommend using IPs and cookies to restrict access to the survey, because they can cause various expected and unexpected problems. They are typically excluded from the default options of web survey software. Nevertheless, as described above, in some specific situations they can be useful, particularly if we know that none of the above problems emerge in our target population.

As a consequence of these limitations, cookie-free web surveys without individual IP number tracking are increasingly becoming the prevailing approach.

In non-list-based surveys, it is difficult to prevent multiple entries from the same person, but certain solutions can be applied in post-fielding (Section 4.1), where we can detect and remove them (e.g. if all responses are the same for two units). With respect to 'pause and continue later', the IP address or cookies can be more helpful, particularly if we assume the majority of respondents use them without any of the problems discussed above. If this is not the case, the option 'pause and continue later' requires the respondent to provide an email at the pausing point, so as to be reminded later about continuing the survey.

In non-list-based web surveys, we may also first recruit units to obtain their email addresses, which are then used for the invitations; in such cases, the features of list-based surveys fully apply.

2.4.1.3 Email Settings

List-based surveys with email invitations are the default object of our discussion and within this context the technical settings of email invitations are essential.

The simplest way for a researcher is to use a *default email system*. Addresses are entered into the BCC (Blind Carbon Copy) line of the email header and not in the CC (Carbon Copy) line, where all recipients then see the entire list, which is highly inappropriate for ethical and legal reasons.

Of course, this is a very limited approach and can only work with up to a few hundred addresses, while problems with the email system limiting the massive sending of emails can appear with larger numbers. With popular email services (e.g. Yahoo, Gmail, MS Outlook, etc.), the default limit is usually set to around a few hundred emails sent per day,[16] while with internal organizational email systems, the limits can be higher, up to a few thousand or even with no limitations.

More serious restrictions can occur on the recipient's side, where email systems use increasingly sophisticated spam-detecting filters, which may reject email messages with a large number of addresses in the CC or BCC lines. They are also sensitive to various technical settings of the outgoing email server, as well as to the subject line and content of the invitations (see Section 2.5.7 for the formatting of email invitations).

An important improvement in spam perception is the use of script[17] for sending each email separately, instead of CC or BCC packages. This also enables a researcher to use personalized invitations (e.g. including the name in the email) and can increase the number of emails sent above the limits related to CC and BCC.

Sending a few hundred emails from a researcher's default email can be a good practical solution when using one email invitation, plus another email with both the 'thank you' message for those who have already answered and a reminder for nonrespondents. We will often refer to this approach and hereafter call it the *two-email setting* to denote the specific situation where we do not track nonrespondents, but rather send both emails to the entire list.

However, for frequent usage and large lists, professional tools are usually required. These can be *dedicated external mass email services*, which have been developed predominantly for various alerts, newsletters and direct marketing. These tools are very effective in avoiding spam and have elaborate functionalities, such as personalization, detection of email status (e.g. email message sent, delivered, opened), management of email lists, graphic design of the invitation, unsubscribe (opt-out), etc. This represents a good alternative if our web survey software provides weak or no support for sending email invitations. However, with respect to detecting breakoffs, paused and partial respondents, this approach creates problems, because it is separated from the web survey software.

The prevailing and most elegant option is use of the *integrated email support of the web survey software*, which hopefully supports the same features as dedicated email applications and also integrates them with tracking based on unique ID. Within this option three alternatives exist:

- Where a web survey software supplier offers a hosting service (SaaS), a researcher typically uses the corresponding email address (e.g. survey@supplier.com) as the sender's email. Unfortunately, the most that the majority of suppliers allow is for a researcher to customize the 'name' in the prefix (e.g. name@supplier. com) or add a 'researcher' sub-domain (name@ researcher.supplier.com). However, also changing the domain (e.g. using '@researcher.com' instead of '@supplier.com') would require special procedures, which web survey software

rarely offer. Without them the fact that the domain name of the outgoing server (also called the domain key, which in this case is 'supplier. com') differs from the email domain (e.g. @ researcher.com) increases the probability that email invitations will be treated as spam. The usage of supplier domain (e.g. @supplier.com) is thus the prevailing approach.

- Where a researcher has the software installed to their own server, there is full flexibility to shape the sender's email address, because the two domains (email address domain and server domain key) do now automatically match (e.g. researcher.com).

- The process of sending email invitations through the web survey software email system, when installed on a dedicated server (e.g. SaaS), can be integrated into the email system of a researcher or research organization. This is a very useful option, and it enjoys the full benefits of the web survey software email system (e.g. tracking, separate email sending), while at the same time taking advantage of the benefits of sending emails from a researcher's own email account (e.g. personalization of the sender, increased legitimacy). Of course, this alternative suffers from the potential restrictions (e.g. number of emails sent, slow speed) of a researcher's server. However, commercial web survey software suppliers rarely offer this option.

The first option might have some technical advantages due to the continuous professional support from the supplier. However, this approach can be accompanied by methodological disadvantages related to the role of the sender's email in motivating the respondents. That is, the decision to participate is often made in seconds, and the email domain of the sender can play a very important role in this decision. This makes the third integrated option very advantageous, because a researcher controls the domain.

Often, we may have no alternative when it comes to the above options, but when we do have, we should carefully consider the potential effects of using the email domain or sub-domain names of the supplier, researcher (or research organization), subcontractor or sponsor. Of course, this decision fully depends on circumstances. Sometimes, an email invitation from a well-known web survey software supplier (e.g. info@supplier.com) or from a large marketing research provider has lower recognition and reputation in the eyes of recipients than an email invitation from a researcher or from a certain sponsor. However, it can be the opposite, too.

In addition, we should optimize the email prefix. Usually, when it pertains to a researcher, an individualized prefix (e.g. 'researchername@') or a specific project (e.g. 'projectname@') can be better than a general email prefix, such as 'info@'. The format of an email invitation is otherwise discussed in Section 2.5.7.

Care should be taken also to include the 'unsubscribe' option, also called 'opt-out' or 'remove from list', because this is often stipulated by legal and ethical restrictions. In addition, it can also channel the emotions of annoyed and reluctant respondents. For instance, they may alternatively label the email invitation as spam, which can then permanently and globally affect the quality of the sending email address.

We also need to ensure technical support, so that returned emails are redirected to a researcher and not to a general email account to which a researcher has no access. These returned emails should be assigned to the corresponding web project and linked to the corresponding units. With email invitations in list-based samples, we should be able technically to identify the following final email statuses: (a) error in sending email due to technical problems of outgoing email server; (b) email name or domain is unknown or non-existent; (c) mailbox full; (d) automatic reply (e.g. absence notice); (e) other messages that email was not delivered (e.g. various problems with the recipient's server or device), as well as tracking diagnostics that (f) email was successfully delivered or (g) email was opened. In addition, (h) the explicit unsubscribe option should also be recorded when selected. In the calculation of nonresponse indicators, we then assign to this technical situation corresponding nonresponse statuses (see Section 2.5).

To conclude, we can speculate that in the near future – due to growing technical complexities and anti-spam restrictions – the quality support of web survey software will become the most essential factor for processing effective email invitations.

2.4.1.4 Sample Management

Sample management integrates database preparation, tracking of the units and email settings for list-based web surveys. The default situation appears when web survey software is used for sending email invitations and for tracking ID codes. We then typically have the following steps:

1. Import a list of sample units with contact information (email address, name, title, etc.).
2. Mark the sample units to which an email invitation should be sent.
3. Send out email invitations with ID codes.
4. Track the response status of sample units through IDs.
5. Track bounced emails and classify them properly (incorrect address, certain out of office replies, etc.).
6. Mark nonrespondents or other units (e.g. auto-replies) for sending out reminders.
7. Send out reminders with ID codes.
8. Track the response status after reminders have been sent out using ID codes.
9. Treat bounced emails and classify them properly (incorrect address, out of office reply).
10. Repeat steps 6–9 for further reminders.

If we decide not to track response statuses and use only one invitation or a two-email setting, then we use only some of the above steps. Similarly, modifications are needed if we use an external email service, mail invitations or multimode recruiting (e.g. email, telephone).

Sample management in online panels requires additional tasks related to panel maintenance, assignment of individual survey projects to respondents, etc. Complications arise also with mixed-mode surveys, where the tracking of units across modes becomes increasingly complex, and which is sometimes treated within the context of *case management*.

Good web survey software is essential for effective case management; it keeps track of email invitations, reminders and contacts for each unit, including archives of each email invitation (e.g. who, when and what). The data produced by this administration are also special types of paradata, called call record data (see below). Support for database operations, such as merging, combining, creating and deleting various sample lists, is also extremely important, as is the feature of identification and elimination of duplicate units.

2.4.2 Paradata Collection[18]

Paradata usually refer to recordings about the fieldwork process (Couper, 1998). They are particularly important with web surveys, because they are very rich and easy to capture. They mostly relate to various digital recordings and traces left in the fielding step.

We talk about *direct paradata* when they are recorded automatically – with web survey software or with some integration of external script – as a by-product of the fielding processes. They can be structured into three broad classes: *contact info* paradata, *device-type* paradata and *questionnaire navigation* paradata.

On the other hand, we talk about *indirect paradata*, which require additional external equipment – such as a video recording system, a brain wave monitoring device, an eye tracking setup – or the involvement of some external human observations, as in behaviour coding. These indirect paradata are predominantly used in testing and were discussed in Section 2.3.4.

The notion of paradata predominantly relates to the actions of a respondent, but a researcher's actions from the fielding step usually belong to contact info paradata (e.g. sending of email invitations), which we have already denoted as call record data.

Within this context we may also point to further digital traces of a *researcher's actions* in the pre-fielding step (e.g. changes in the questionnaire:

who changed what and when) and in the post-fielding step (e.g. calculations of derived values or changes to responses: who changed what, when and how). All of these are very important for documentation, clarification and archiving purposes, as well as for the eventual optimization of these processes. The corresponding support for capturing these data is also one of the features of advanced web survey software. However, we usually treat these traces outside the notion of paradata.

In the case of mixed-mode systems, an additional array of paradata appears, from multimode contacting, interviewer characteristics and interviewer observations to additional audio or video recordings (Kreuter, 2013).

In the remainder of this section, we focus only on direct paradata. We first present typical examples and then address issues related to the software, analyses and ethics.

2.4.2.1 Contact-info Paradata

The contact-info paradata include information about contact attempts for respondents. They are very similar to traditional call record paradata in telephone or F2F surveys. Some examples follow.

Outcomes of an email invitation can be recorded and then structured in the manner described above (e.g. email delivered, email not delivered, error in sending email, etc.).

Access to the questionnaire introduction page is further essential paradata, which can serve to remind respondents who have not yet responded, as well as those who only entered the introduction page and left immediately after. These paradata are also essential for calculating response rates.

Last question answered before breakoff determines response completeness status, as well as the decision on whether the unit can be used in the final datafile (see details in Section 2.5). It can also be used for sending more sophisticated reminders, which direct the respondents to continue from the point where they left the survey.

2.4.2.2 Device-type Paradata

The device-type paradata consist of technical information about the device the respondent is using while answering the web questionnaire. Key ones are as follows.

User agent string is generated when a respondent accesses a web questionnaire and the respondent's browser sends a string of text to the server. The information contained in this string can be immediately used to provide tailored content and formatting (e.g. to adapt the questionnaire to a smartphone version). It can also later be used for methodological purposes (e.g. evaluation of data quality across browsers, device types, operating systems, screen sizes, etc.). For instance, Callegaro (2010) analysed a customer satisfaction survey in the United States, which was optimized for desktop/notebook computers, and showed that respondents on mobile devices were three times more likely to break off. Today, with the rise of smartphones, insight into the basic device-type statistics (desktop/notebook, tablet, smartphone) is becoming a routine diagnostics.

Detection of JavaScript and Flash signals to see whether the respondent's browser supports JavaScript and/or Flash, which we defined in Section 1.3.2 and Section 1.3.3. Advanced web questionnaires often rely on JavaScript, which is generally enabled by default in all browsers and is also required for many essential Internet services. Nonetheless, a few of the units may have it disabled. Their share should be monitored and a researcher can then either invite them to enable this option, or design a questionnaire without JavaScript for them. The Flash technology is more problematic, because it requires installation on the respondent's device and not just an option setting. As a consequence, the share of Internet users without this installation is usually in double digits.

Cookie and IP recordings can be beneficial in web surveys, although they can also be problematic. Nonetheless, when the IP address is recorded separately and not directly linked to the unit, this can provide useful insight into geographic information (e.g. country, region), albeit approximate.

2.4.2.3 Questionnaire Navigation Paradata

Questionnaire navigation paradata are much more complex and appear in much larger quantities than the previous two types. A few common examples are discussed below, but many others also exist: for example, detecting respondents who clicked outside the window of the web questionnaire, or video capturing of the screen with the response process.

We illustrate below the most typical examples of corresponding paradata usage.

Time spent per screen or response latency is perhaps the most common type of paradata here, which is also featured in several publications. Couper & Kreuter (2013) provide a good review on paradata for response latency, particularly its use in shedding light on the response process. In the context of web survey research, longer response latencies have been linked to deeper cognitive processing, due to increased motivation or engagement (Callegaro et al., 2009), interruptions or multitasking (Stieger & Reips, 2010), increased complexity of questions (Yan & Tourangeau, 2008), as well as ambivalent attitudes in the case of opinion questions and lack of knowledge in the case of knowledge questions (Heerwegh, 2003). The study by Yan & Tourangeau (2008) also stresses the influence of respondent characteristics – respondents who are younger, more highly educated or more experienced with surveys needed less time to complete the survey.

Research on response latencies is more commonly concerned with *speeding*, i.e. response latencies that are so short that legitimate doubts can be raised about whether a respondent carefully read the questions and performed optimally in all stages of the response process (e.g. Beckers, Siegers, & Kuntz, 2011; Kapelner & Chandler, 2010; Zhang, 2013). Thus, such analysis relates to the detection of extreme frauds, anomalies and fake responding, but can also serve as an indication of potential threats to data quality. However, a precise border or benchmark of where a certain unit can be declared as a *speeder* – respondents that progress through the questionnaire unacceptably fast – can be technically complicated, since we usually have time stamps for pages and not for questions. Problems can arise also from various statistical complications, which are related to unusual distributions of response latencies (asymmetry, non-normality).

Various metrics have been developed for this purpose, ranging from simple approaches, such as calculating 2–3 deviations from the median or the mean (West & Sinibaldi, 2013), to more complex solutions, such as the 'Speeder index' (Steinbrecher, Roßmann, & Bergmann, 2013) or the definition of cutoff points based on the average reading speed (C. Zhang, 2013). A cutoff value of 0.4 seconds per word can be used to identify speeders, while a high cutoff value of 2.5 seconds per word can denote units that are excessively slow.

Reported figures on the prevalence of speeders thus vary from less than 2% (West & Sinibaldi, 2013) to up to 16% (Beckers et al., 2011; Gutierrez, Wells, Rao, & Kurzynski, 2011).

Lastly, we should keep in mind that speeding does not always mean lower data quality, because respondents can satisfice with very different speeds (Garland et al. 2013). Nonetheless, extreme speeding is usually correlated with low data quality (Thomas & Barlas, 2014; C. Zhang & Conrad, 2013). Similarly, forcing respondents to read slowly by putting words on the screen sequentially (e.g. 250 per minute) actually did reduce satisficing behavior (Kapelner & Chandler, 2010).

Keystrokes and mouse-clicks are related to special scripts which then capture large quantities of data. For example, Stieger & Reips (2010) captured 336,262 single actions of 1,046 participants in a web survey with 23 questions. This served as a basis for measuring the overall length of the mouse track (i.e. mouse movements as the respondent answers the questions) for each page, where 11% of respondents showed excessive mouse movements. The analysis also showed that 6% of respondents practised excessive clicking, 4% were associated with longer inactivity, while the majority were clicking through at least once, having answered without sufficient time spent on reading the questions.

Change of answers means that respondents have modified their initial answers, which can indicate potential confusion with a question. Stieger & Reips (2010) showed, for example, that answer changes do occur and that they are more frequent (5.4%) for opinion questions than for factual questions (1.5%).

Real-time validation messages appear whenever a respondent is alerted and reminded with a prompt message, usually as a pop-up (e.g. for item nonresponse or for invalid entry). The corresponding analysis can provide additional insight into respondents' behaviour. We can also use a *quality index*, as proposed by Haraldsen (2005), for comparing all activated error prompts with all possible ones, which can help us improve questionnaire design and thus indirectly decrease the number of activated prompt messages. An example of a quality index calculation can be found in Callegaro (2014b).

2.4.2.4 Software for Collecting Paradata

To capture paradata, researchers can write their own script, use specialized paradata software or use the corresponding features of the web survey software, if they exist.

Specialized paradata software ranges from basic scripts such as Client Side Paradata (CSP)[19] and Universal Client Side Paradata (UCSP) (Kaczmirek, 2009)[20], to various advanced paradata external tools, as used in Stieger & Reips (2010), while support within the web survey software is relatively scarce. Vehovar, Čehovin, Kavčič, & Lenar (2012) reviewed a large number of web survey software suppliers and only a few of them provided easy collection and access to paradata. By default, 30% offered paradata for the total time of filling in the questionnaire, 4% had paradata for time spent per page of the questionnaire and 1% enabled tracking the respondent's movements back and forth across questionnaire pages.

From the viewpoint of paradata collection, we can distinguish *basic paradata*, which are routinely collected and reported. They either are automatically collected as part of the survey process (e.g. information that email invitations were sent) or require minimal additional effort (e.g. time stamp, user agent string, IP address), and are thus typically included in the default settings of the (advanced) web survey software. More *advanced types* of paradata – such as exact number of mouse-clicks, keyboard entries, prompt recordings, mouse scrolling, screen capturing, exits from the window tab of the questionnaire – require the activation of special options in web survey software or the involvement of external scripts. In both cases, this may slow down the measurement process and produce enormous amounts of data. We should therefore exclude the collection of advanced paradata when we have no intention of using them.

2.4.2.5 Analysis of Paradata

The analysis of paradata can be done at four levels of aggregation (Kaczmirek, 2009, p. 83):

- *The first level paradata* contain the individual actions of respondents, such as the time stamp or mouse-clicks. These data are usually recorded sequentially, because the number of individual actions on a certain screen cannot be predetermined. These first level data thus generate a complex (non-rectangular) dataset, which makes data analysis difficult from the outset. Eventual invitations (time stamp, content of invitation or reminder) and other call record paradata also belong to the first level.
- *The second level* paradata are the first level data aggregated across single actions within the same respondent, such as, for example, the total number of mouse-clicks on a page or the number of changes to answers per question. These data can be structured into a rectangular matrix and are easier to analyse.
- *The third level* paradata are the second level data aggregated across respondents or variables. At this level, we can compute the average number of answer changes per respondent (for all questions) or per question (for all respondents).
- *The fourth level* paradata are the highest level of aggregation, where aggregation occurs across respondents and variables. It provides

a single number per survey, such as the average survey length (in seconds) or item nonresponse rate.

The first-level paradata are the most essential and can be organized in various ways. When combined with metadata, auxiliary data and questionnaire data can be organized into a number of relational sub-datasets, where characteristics are assigned to the corresponding levels of the survey, unit, page, question, variable and individual response entry. For the latter we can also distinguish the status of sub-stantive response, non-substantive response or various missing values. These sub-datasets can be accompanied by response option labels, variable labels and question texts. How these disaggregated sub-datasets will be organized for the analysis depends on a researcher's aim. For many practical purposes, the data can be used as a matrix, where one line includes all data related to the actions of a certain respondent on a certain page. Of course, many other options also exist.

2.4.2.6 Paradata Privacy and Ethics

When paradata are treated as personal information (e.g. the IP number from the user agent string), they are protected by law and require special treatment. For example, the ESOMAR Guideline for Online Research requires compliance with the relevant local regulations, since it classifies, similarly to the EU legislation, IP addresses as personal data (ESOMAR, 2011a, p. 6). While this is not formally the situation in the United States, there too – at least in the psychology literature – often an agreement exists that if the IP address is recorded and integrated into the datafile, then a researcher should not claim that the study is completely anonymous (Barchard & Williams, 2008).

Paradata also raise ethical concerns and practical dilemmas about how to inform respondents about the collection of paradata. We may require explicit consent or provide only an acknowledgement in small print in the general conditions. We could simply not mention the issue at all; however, this can be considered unethical. In a series of experiments, Couper & Singer (2013) showed that any mention of paradata lowered respondents' willingness to participate in a survey (e.g. from 65% to 55%), although to a lower extent when consent was mentioned at the end of the survey.

We can conclude that paradata can give great insight into the response process, which is particularly valuable not only for testing, but also for understanding the nature and quality of responses. Although we initially stated that direct paradata are rich in information and easy to collect, we agree with Couper (2005, p. 494) and Nicolaas (2011) that analysing paradata is in fact extremely challenging. While basic paradata (call record, device string, time stamp) are captured by default and their analysis is already resolved into standardized diagnostics, the situation is very different with non-standardized analysis and with advanced paradata, particularly when they are not sufficiently structured, so additional resources might be required to prepare them for analysis. Careful consideration of the corresponding added value is thus needed, as well as realistic planning of resources.

2.4.3 Preparations to Support Security and Privacy

With web surveys, sensitive and confidential information is often collected and exchanged. A researcher is required to *secure* the data and the corresponding processes, which need to be reliable, safe from attack and protected from third-party access. Securing can be related to data *transmission* and means protecting the communication between a client (respondent's computer) and a server (hosting the survey questionnaire), as well as the handover of the datafile to clients or users. Securing the *storage* of data relates to securing access to the server, where web survey software runs, while securing the *archiving* of data refers to the protection of data when stored on other computers, servers and devices.

These concerns need to be specified in corresponding contracts that regulate the relations between all involved parties (client, researcher, subcontractors, web survey software supplier, etc.). This is particularly critical in marketing research, where the results of an expensive web survey can be confidential and should not end up in the hands of a competitor. Similarly, in official and academic surveys the questions on pre-release embargo and the primary right to exploit the data are closely related to securing the corresponding data and processes.

Security problems, which we discussed above, overlap considerably with concerns for the privacy of respondents. This is otherwise a very complex issue, stretching across various legal and technical aspects. Cho & Larose (1999) exposed the key dimensions of privacy that are relevant in the context of survey research. In addition to the above security issues being applied to individual responses, specific problems emerge with respect to *anonymity*. Anonymity refers to the linkage of personal data (*identifiers*) with survey responses and with controls over the conditions under which personal data are released. Another specific privacy aspect is the *confidentiality of individual responses*, which is concerned with secondary uses of personal information for purposes that were not originally foreseen. Other aspects of confidentiality also exist (e.g. strict business confidentiality), so the datafile can be confidential without any threats related to the confidentiality of respondents' answers.

Ensuring security and privacy is only partially in the hands of a researcher, because it depends strongly on the web survey software used, the technical specifications of the server, and the hosting environment. Still, considerable responsibility is left to a researcher and other entities working on surveys (e.g. institutional review boards), who are required to have certain technical knowledge. For this purpose, we briefly present the key issues related to privacy and security. We avoid discussing conceptual definitions and theoretical clarifications, as well as in-depth technical details. Instead, we focus on practical recommendations that are relevant for researchers. Additional treatment of this topic is available in Corti, van den Eyden, Bishop, & Woollard (2014) and in Section 6.3, where we offer a broader legal, professional and ethical treatment.

2.4.3.1 Securing the Server

Web surveys can be collected from servers hosted internally in a company or research institution, but also externally as SaaS solutions, a prevailing option among web survey software suppliers. External hosting also includes situations where a researcher installs, for example, open source software on an external server which is not primarily dedicated to survey data collection. Nevertheless, the same security guidelines apply for all cases. However, many researchers perceive that it is safer to host the data internally, based on the assumption that an organization knows and controls all persons with access to the server. Further, from the technical aspects, once the servers are connected to the Internet they are exposed to the same risks. The SaaS solutions might be even safer, because security is a part of their core business and they can dedicate more resources and knowledge to security issues than a small company or a university. This is in fact paradoxical, because many researchers (i.e. organizations) unconditionally reject – due to security concerns – any external hosting and thus also any web survey software that does not provide options for internal installation.

In addition to the dilemma of server location, there are some other critical aspects, which we briefly review in the form of questions adapted and further expanded from Buchanan & Hvizdak (2009):

- Does the hosting server provide third-party security certification? If so, how often is it updated?
- Can third parties access the data and what are the procedures? What are the screening, monitoring and controls for staff with access to the data?
- How often are penetration tests ('pentest') performed, which simulate attacks on a server to find security weaknesses?
- What measures are in place to safeguard data at the physical location of the server (e.g. electricity/power, fire, burglary)?

- For SaaS solutions, where (physical location, country) is the company storing the data and their backups? Are there any specifics in local regulations which might be relevant?
- What happens – and what are the procedures (including communication and timing) – when there is a fallback (when a server crashes and another server takes over)? Are the data transferred to the new server in an encrypted form?
- What happens to the data after a researcher completes the work? When and how are the data being removed? How long will the data be stored on the server and does this contradict the time frame indicated by a researcher or institutional policies?
- How is the data mirroring process provided during the fielding? How frequently are backups performed and archived?
- Who is responsible – and what is the nature of the responsibility – if data are lost or exposed due to a security breach? What mechanisms are in place to alert a researchers in the event of data loss or intrusion?
- How secure is the survey platform against attacks during data collection? More specifically, what are the prevention and recovery procedures for so-called DDOS (Distributed Denial of Service) attacks, where a large number of requests are sent to the server? For example, in 2014 these attacks disabled some of the largest SaaS web survey software suppliers for a number of days. What is the uptime, the percentage of time the server is working: 99%, 99.9% or 99.99% (which is becoming the industry standard)?

The above questions need to be evaluated with the assistance of ICT personnel, who should clarify the technical aspects and also make sure that the answers reflect current security standards. Of course, the depth of their elaboration depends on the importance of the survey. For simple DIY surveys, all this may be redundant and irrelevant, as general trust in a SaaS supplier is enough, while more security requires more resources. Having security certified by ISO standards, such as ISO 27001 (Information Security Management), ISO 27002 (Code of Practice for Information Security Management) and/or SAS 70 (Statement on Auditing Standards No. 70 Service Organization), is definitely a step towards having security processes and documentation in place.

2.4.3.2 Securing the Web Survey Response Process

The process of filling out a questionnaire (i.e. measurement session) raises various security concerns. One issue is ensuring secure communication between the respondent's device and the server. This should be encrypted (e.g. by the Secure Sockets Layer (SSL) Protocol), so that third parties cannot use it, even if they gain access to it.

Another aspect is vulnerability of the web survey software to attacks through the registration procedure, with direct access to subpages or files and measurement sessions, where damaging scripts can be entered as responses to open-ended questions.

Additionally, bugs in the programming of a certain survey are a potential problem, which is also true for potential bugs in web survey software. Sometimes an unexpectedly large number of responses (including scripts and robots) can cause problems. All this can result in the web survey response process slowing down or even being brought to a stop. These types of problems can appear only within our specific survey, while other surveys and the entire server will still be doing fine. Sometimes it is difficult to locate the exact source of the problem that caused the web survey to stop working.

In any case, we need to specify procedures for addressing these problems. In particular, we need to know in advance how fast and in which way technicians – and also a researcher – will learn that the web questionnaire is not working properly. Usually we expect the prespecified automated procedures to discover this and alert the technicians immediately (e.g. via SMS), which very often allows them to resolve the problem in a few minutes. A researcher is then alerted (e.g. by email) if the technician establishes that an immediate solution is not possible, so that crisis management dictates further action. In the case of new web survey software, or with server hosting solutions that are not fully specialized (e.g. the server is not dedicated exclusively to web surveys), it might be useful for a researcher to check access to the web survey from time to time.

2.4.3.3 Technical Aspects of Anonymity

When we dispose of or collect personal data, special care is required. This is particularly true when we explicitly guarantee confidentiality and anonymity to our respondents, which is almost always the case. This mainly refers to direct identifiers, which enable us to identify a person and form a link to survey responses and other personal data. Identifiers can be obtained not only from the sampling frame (e.g. username and password information, name, contact information, name, contact information), but also from administrative records, previous surveys and the survey itself (e.g. we ask for email addresses). As mentioned previously, in some countries (e.g. EU countries), certain paradata, such as IP addresses, are also treated as personal identifiers. Many of these identifiers are indispensable for fieldwork processes, such as sample management, incentives, access to the questionnaire, multiple completions and tracing of nonrespondents.

It is essential to store these identifiers separately, without a direct link to survey responses (see also Barchard & Williams, 2008; Thiele & Kaczmirek, 2010); they should therefore be excluded from the datafile which was exported for analysis. This is increasingly becoming a legal requirement and a recommendation in professional codes of conduct. Many web survey software packages automatically separate these two files.

Strategies that utilize time stamps or record numbers to identify the units need to be disabled as well. In online panels, personal identification is particularly powerful, because it links responses in all surveys, so it should not be used externally under any circumstances. Personal identifiers also need to be permanently deleted as soon as they are not needed for administrative purposes in the fielding and post-fielding steps.

We also need to pay attention to *statistical disclosure*, where respondents can be identified through combinations of variables (e.g. region, gender, occupation) in cross-tabulations or in publicly released datafiles; this is a concern we deal with in the post-fielding step (Section 4.3.2).

At certain points in fieldwork, anonymity cannot be assured, as is the case in all list-assisted surveys, where case management links ID codes, personal identifiers, invitations and responses. The respondents know that a researcher actually disposes of personal information and in principle there is no anonymity. In such cases, confidentiality plays a key role, and respondents need to be able to trust a researcher to undertake all steps to assure confidentiality – not just procedures to provide anonymity, but also a series of other security measures. This is particularly important with sensitive topics (e.g. health) and with social desirability topics (e.g. gambling), but also in human relation surveys (e.g. student evaluation surveys, employee satisfaction surveys) and in business surveys (e.g. financial data).

2.4.3.4 Securing Physical and Electronic Access to the Datafile

Sometimes the datafile may raise no privacy or confidentiality concerns and can be freely accessed and distributed. However, usually this is not the case, and in addition to access to the server, controls need to be established also for other types of digital storage. In many instances, corresponding procedures are already elaborated upon within the research organization's security rules. These typically include securing the computers (desktop/notebook) of researchers, the external communication (e.g. web browsing) and external storage (e.g. CD, USB key). We support Thiele & Kaczmirek (2010) in their recommendation to additionally encrypt the entire hard disks to secure the data and particularly to increase the protection of personal data. Another set of security measures is to make sure that the corresponding computers are up to date in terms of security patches for the operating system, the web browser, as well as with respect to the antivirus and antispyware software.

When data are exchanged, the files should be additionally encrypted (Barchard & Williams, 2008) and equipped with access codes. Similarly, when sending data via email, Thiele & Kaczmirek (2010) suggest encrypting the entire email communication. Another option is to use cloud-based secure storage services when sharing the files among colleagues, users or clients. When distribution over the Web is used, the SSL protocol and encryption for the transmission of files should also be included.

In addition to technical protection, a special security policy is needed to ensure responsible behaviour of the relevant personnel. This is usually resolved within organizational rules and protocols, while in non-institutional research (e.g. DIY), it is recommended that a *statement of confidentiality* is signed by all involved parties, where the purpose, protection, duration and legal responsibilities need to be specified. A similar practice is also recommended when confidential data from an organization are given to a researcher.

2.4.3.5 Access Auditing

One aspect which often gets overlooked is auditing individuals with access to a datafile and other confidential data (Corti et al., 2014, p. 88). This could be structured into the following questions for ICT personnel or the SaaS supplier:

- Who has direct access within the web survey software to a certain survey and what are the exact levels and authorities (e.g. viewing only or accessing full functionalities or limited access)?
- Who else has general access to the questionnaire and the datafile of a certain survey, as well as to the web survey software and the corresponding space on a server (e.g. system engineer, senior authoring personnel in an organization)?
- What is the time span for this access – temporary or permanent? How often are access control lists reviewed?
- How is access granted? Who manages it (e.g. adding another user, changing the password, deleting user accounts)?
- Who has access to log files on the server and who manages them?

- Are these accounts individual or group accounts? In the latter case, special procedures are needed.

These questions are particularly critical when there are more users with various levels of authority, as in enterprise feedback systems (see Section 1.3.6). However, a basic check is useful even for the simplest DIY web surveys.

2.4.3.6 Relation to Legislation and Professional Standards

An important aspect with respect to security and privacy entails staying up to date with the key relevant legislation and professional standards (see also Section 6.3). In international research, this is additionally demanding, because countries differ in terms of regulation on personal identifiers, storage, responsibility, paradata, rules for surveying minors, etc. The ESOMAR Guideline for Online Research (ESOMAR, 2011a, sec. 6) further defines key legislation issues regarding data privacy and security around the world, which is a great starting point. To get an impression of how sophisticated these issues have become, it is sufficient to check the security and privacy policy, as well as terms of usage for any SaaS web survey software supplier.

Learning and interpreting legislation can be a long and daunting process. A researcher should seek help by engaging the local statistical, survey and marketing research associations, which can provide basic assistance to their members on this matter. More complex cases may require specialized legal consultants.

Various initiatives can help keep us up to date; we present here a few that are relevant for researchers implementing web surveys. The Workshop on Ethics in Computer Security Research (WECSR) had its first conference in 2010, and brought together ethicists, members of institutional review boards, researchers, lawyers and the ICT community. Of particular interest is the Ethical Impact Assessment document (Kenneally, Bailey, & Maughan, 2010), which can serve as the initial discussion guide for ethics, data security and data

privacy for any data collected online. Although its scope is broader than web surveys, it tackles critical issues and is becoming widely adopted (Kenneally, Stavrou, McHugh, & Christin, 2011). Another good source to follow is the IEEE CS Security and Privacy (SP) workshops,[21] especially the Web 2.0 Security & Privacy (W2SP).

2.4.4 Technical Pre-testing of Web Survey Software

Technical preparations need to be made as early as possible, which means they run in parallel with the activities of sampling and questionnaire preparation. A researcher is faced with two streams of decisions.

The first decision needs to be made very early and relates to the decision or reconfirmation of whether to use certain web survey software. If serious technical deficiencies exist, it is better to learn about them early. The most critical issues are perhaps those related to security and to essential software features (capability, flexibility, speed). Once a researcher selects, accepts or reconfirms certain web survey software (more on the software selection process can be found in Section 5.3), another set of decisions emerges on the corresponding settings and preparations for capturing and organizing the data.

In any case, we need to plan and run some formal technical pre-testing of the software, where we check all of the above-mentioned technical issues, foresee potential problems and prepare solutions. The core activity here is creating an artificial questionnaire, which should cover the essential question types we use. This is then used to simulate all pre-fielding, fielding and post-fielding procedures which have some technical implications. An essential component of this process is also to produce responses, so as to test the processes and investigate the datafile. Some of these test entries (responses) may need to be done manually, while some aspects require a large number of responses, so automatic procedures are needed. Software often has the feature of automatic internal generation of artificial responses. In addition, it is also useful to launch an external script (i.e. robot) to fill in the prototype questionnaire, because this then fully simulates the real measurement session.

With simple surveys the main focus of such pre-testing are perhaps the speed, the inspection of how responses are recorded, as well as the standardized reports and exports. Key features needed in questionnaire development are also important in this pre-testing, particularly question layouts and interactivity.

Of course, if we already know and trust the technical features of the web survey software from past experience or from very reliable recommendations – and if our survey has no further specifics – this technical pre-testing may not be needed.

We should add that technical evaluations of the software cannot replace a technical testing of the questoinnare (Section 2.3.5), which in many aspects is a similar undertaking, but done much later in the web survey process; it is also conducted with a real questionnaire and with real data. Similarly, a pilot study cannot replace the technical evaluation and pre-testing of the web survey software, which should be done very early in the survey process.

2.5 NONRESPONSE STRATEGY

For various reasons, we may not obtain all the expected responses from units included in the survey in the fielding step. For example, some units may be absent or refuse cooperation. So we may miss important segments of the target population (e.g. people who are busier, older, richer, etc.). As a consequence, incorrect estimates can appear. We call this problem *nonresponse*, and the related notion of *nonresponse strategy* encompasses activities which we need to undertake to prevent the occurrence of nonresponse.

Certain nonresponse remedies can be applied also in the post-fielding step – which we discuss in Section 4.1 – but this can hardly replace real answers from real respondents during the fielding step. Prevention of nonresponse and

preparations required in the pre-fielding step are thus the focus of our discussion here.

Researchers have to be familiar with the general nonresponse principles in order to grasp competently the nonresponse aspects in the specific web survey and to prepare an appropriate nonresponse strategy. Correspondingly, we first provide a general introduction to nonresponse issues (Section 2.5.1), nonresponse indicators (Section 2.5.2) and nonresponse bias (Section 2.5.3). Next, we discuss approaches to prevent nonresponse: web survey design characteristics (Section 2.5.4), incentives (Section 2.5.5), contacting process (Section 2.5.6) and format of the invitations (Section 2.5.7). Finally, we summarize and outline the nonresponse strategy (Section 2.5.8).

2.5.1 General Issues in Web Survey Nonresponse

Nonresponse denotes a failure to obtain responses from eligible units included in a sample. Our initial focus here is on *unit nonresponse*, where we collected no responses (or at least no usable responses) from a certain unit.

The reasons behind nonresponse are typically structured into three streams (Groves et al., 2009): *non-contacts* (unable to contact a unit), *refusals* (unit was contacted but declined participation) and *other reasons*. The latter typically presents a small share that is very fragmented, from specific circumstances (e.g. a third-person intervention), to various health, language, administrative and technical problems. With web surveys we usually have very limited insight into these causes, as opposed to interviewer-administered surveys.

We also address *item nonresponse*, where we lack responses only for a specific *item* (question or sub-question) from an otherwise eligible and cooperating unit. The notion of *breakoffs* is related to the situation where an eligible unit starts answering the web questionnaire, but then leaves the survey prematurely, before concluding the questionnaire.

Completeness status, related to eligible units which have started to respond, is also very important. We can distinguish between units with *complete responses* or *completes*, when a unit meets some prespecified criteria for completeness (e.g. response to 80% of questions) and units with *partial responses* or *incomplete responses*, or simply *partials*, when a unit fails completeness, but still complies with criteria for a minimal set of responses (e.g. response to 50% of questions). We call the remaining units with insufficient responses, which fail to meet the minimal standards for inclusion in the analysis (e.g. responded to less than 50% of questions), *unusable responses* or *unusables*. The criteria differ among surveys, which can be a problem, since completeness status is closely related to nonresponse indicators which are compared across surveys.

We will further elaborate on these statuses later in our discussion. We have defined them here as an introduction to a general overview of nonresponse issues, specifics of the web survey nonresponse process and nonresponse factors.

2.5.1.1 Nonresponse Theories

The issue of survey nonresponse became prominent at the same time as modern survey sampling in the first half of the previous century (Singer, 2006) and has become increasingly important in the last few decades, due to declining *survey participation* (Groves et al., 2009, p. 186). Nonresponse affects all survey modes, but is particularly critical for self-administered surveys, where there is no external motivation or social pressure from an interviewer. It is much easier to decline cooperation when interacting with a machine (e.g. computer) than rejecting a human being standing on the doorstep asking – or even begging – for an interview. Web surveys usually exhibit lower levels of cooperation than other survey modes (Lozar Manfreda et al., 2008), although in some settings (e.g. organizational research), they outperform mail surveys (Baruch & Holtom, 2008). We should immediately add – and also remember whenever we encounter similar comparisons – that these studies usually disregard costs. Thus, they may lead

to unfair conclusions regarding the web survey mode, as they compare inexpensive web surveys with expensive alternatives, instead of allocating cost savings of web surveys into the development of a more elaborate nonresponse strategy (e.g. more incentives).

There is an extensive general nonresponse literature (e.g. Albaum & Smith, 2012), particularly for household interview surveys (Groves & Couper, 2008), mail surveys (Dillman, 1978; Goyder, 1988), telephone surveys (Dillman, 1978) and also for a variety of self-administered and mixed-mode surveys (Dillman et al., 2009).

Several general theories have been implemented in the survey context; see Fan & Yan (2010) for an overview. The most utilized in the case of web surveys is perhaps the *social exchange theory* (Ekeh, 1974), which is at the heart of the Tailored Design Method (Dillman et al., 2009), and the theory of *planned behaviour*, an extension of the *theory of reasoned action* (Ajzen, 1991), applied by Bosnjak, Tuten, & Wittmann (2005), Fang, Shao, & Lan (2009), Haunberger (2011a) and Heerwegh & Loosveldt (2009). Various other theories are sometimes used: namely, economic exchange theory (Biner & Kidd, 1994); the norm of reciprocity (Gouldner, 1960); the social psychology approaches (Groves, Cialdini, & Couper, 1992); transactional analysis (Comley, 2006); leverage–salience theory (Groves, Singer, & Corning, 2000); and specific theories such as cognitive dissonance, self-perception and commitment/involvement (Albaum & Smith, 2012; Heerwegh & Loosveldt, 2009).

Another very specific theoretical approach is related to *cognitive aspects of survey methodology* (CASM), which focuses on the psychological and communication processes underlining survey responding (Schwarz, 2007). This can be particularly useful in explaining the item nonresponse. The theory was conceived in the 1980s and has developed into an interdisciplinary field, sometimes dubbed the CASM movement.

Although there is a general consensus that theoretical understanding of the nonresponse process in web surveys is important, Fan & Yan (2010) state in their overview of 300 empirical nonresponse studies in web surveys that nonresponse studies were rarely guided by a set of theoretical principles, but rather focused on one or two nonresponse factors. Cook, Heath, & Thompson (2000) produced one of the rare studies providing an insight into a relationship among the factors. Further, conceptual discussions on nonresponse in web surveys are usually only indirect, hidden within general overviews of web surveys (e.g. Couper, 2000b), while empirical studies addressing specific nonresponse aspects strongly prevail. Among the few studies dedicated to conceptualization of the nonresponse process in web surveys are those by Vehovar, Batagelj, Lozar Manfreda & Zaletel (2002) and Fan & Yan (2010).

2.5.1.2 Nonresponse Process in Web Surveys

Following Vehovar et al. (2002), we will observe the nonresponse process in web surveys at the contacting phase and at the cooperation phase. We initially conceptualize here the process for list-based web surveys using email invitations, but this process can be adapted also to other types of web surveys.

The contacting phase starts with email invitations that are sent to all units. For reasons of simplicity, we initially assume that all emails relate to eligible units. The email messages are then expected to be absorbed by the network (i.e. the Internet). However, this may not occur due to (a) various technical problems, from typos and invalid email addresses to errors and technical problems with the outgoing sender's email server, infrastructure or email system. Usually, such emails are returned as undelivered, but this may occur also without notifications.

After it has been accepted by the network, the email invitation needs to be properly processed and delivered to the email inbox of the unit, where another set of (b) technical problems may prevent delivery of the email, related to issues with communication paths of the email or due to problems with the incoming recipient's email server. Even when the email successfully arrives to the recipient's email server, (c) organizational or personal email system settings may cause problems, from spam filtering and automatic forwarding to forgotten or incorrect subfolders or to other email accounts, down to various technical problems of the recipient's device (e.g. hardware issues, email software problems, mailbox full).

Only when the technical process of email delivery is successful can we start analysing the role and behaviour of the unit (potential respondent). The first problem is (d) the absence of the unit (e.g. illness, holidays, etc.) during the entire fieldwork period. Sometimes an automatic email alerts a researcher; however, more often than not a researcher does not receive any clarification. Further, the unit might be available, but (e) does not check his or her emails for other reasons (e.g. specific patterns of checking email, mismatch of multiple email accounts), or even checks the emails but for some reason never notices the invitation. Sometimes the unit is briefly aware of the email notification, but the email message is (f) then overlooked or omitted in a hurry.

Once the point of explicit awareness of the email invitation has been reached, the unit can start the cognitive process of dealing with the invitation. This is usually done in two steps. The unit first needs to decide on the corresponding abbreviated incoming information about the email in the message list. This is typically related to one or two lines in the email inbox message list and includes some relevant email information; exactly what information is included depends on the personal settings of the email system. Usually this line contains at least the information on the sender (name and/ or email), the delivery time and the subject. Sometimes the opening line of the email message is also shown, or even the entire message. Additionally, the email message may appear with a mouse-over movement. For simplicity's sake, we do not further elaborate on these specifics, but focus only on current mainstream email software, where the user is first exposed to a single line in the inbox message list. At this point in the process, the email invitation can easily be perceived as spam, a marketing teaser or deemed irrelevant for other reasons (e.g. unattractive subject). As a result, such an email invitation is never opened, but (g) omitted, deleted, abandoned or otherwise ignored based on this single line in the message list.

This line might also be deemed as potentially interesting and relevant by the unit, and can even be flagged and saved for later consideration, but this then never occurs, so that the email message (h) unintentionally sinks into extinction.

Only if the unit clicks on the line in the message list and opens the body of the email message (text) is there a possibility that the message is read. It can still be opened, but not truly read. Consequently, it is (i) abandoned without actually being properly considered. Finally, the invitation can be read and cognitively processed, but recognized as not relevant enough and (j) rejected, that is ignored, deleted or even explicitly refused (e.g. selecting the opt-out option or sending a reply with a refusal). In addition, the unit may read the email invitation and decide to participate, but postpones entry to the web questionnaire, which is then (k) forgotten.

The cooperation phase of the process begins with a click on the URL address of the web questionnaire. The web survey software records this information and at this point the unit starts the response process. Unless this click occurs, we usually know very little or nothing about the exact phase and status of the above contacting process. It is true that certain types of software provide an insight into the status of successful delivery of the email or the email being opened. However, this depends on the email system of the recipient, which can impose restrictions on such feedback, so this is of limited use.

After the unit has clicked on the web questionnaire, further nonresponse problems await in the form of breakoffs, which we have already defined. Here, we will further distinguish between introduction breakoffs and questionnaire breakoffs: (l) introduction breakoffs occur at the web questionnaire introduction page or on the first page of the questionnaire; these are then usually classified as unit nonresponse. When the breakoff occurs later within the web questionnaire, we talk about (m) *questionnaire breakoff*, which can also be classified as unit nonresponse, depending on the criteria used in a specific survey.

Above we have listed 13 points ((a)–(m)) at which unit nonresponse can occur, but we could also organize them further, according to technical subtypes ((a), (b), (c)), substructure of non-contacts ((d), (e)), further postponing subcycles ((h), (k)) and more precise questionnaire breakoff locations ((l), (m)). Given so many occasions for nonresponse, it is not surprising that response rates can be very low for web surveys. However, not all points are equally dangerous; we believe that with a legitimate survey with a salient topic, a target population that regularly checks its emails, a professionally designed email invitation, accurate email addresses and good technical infrastructure, the majority of unit nonresponse can be classified as implicit refusals when considering the email invitation ((g)–(j)) or as breakoffs ((l)–(m)).

Very similarly, but with less contacting phase structuring, the nonresponse process can be described also for list-based web surveys with mail, SMS or telephone invitations, as well as for non-list-based web surveys.

2.5.1.3 Factors Affecting Web Survey Nonresponse

As mentioned already at the beginning of this section, there have been only a few attempts to conceptualize factors influencing nonresponse in web surveys, and we follow and upgrade here the work done by Vehovar et al. (2002), who discussed topics related to the social environment, technology, respondents' characteristics and survey design. Nevertheless, our intention here is to provide only a brief overview.

The socio-technical context is a very important factor affecting participation in web surveys. On the one hand, this impact is indirect, through general culture, economic development, educational system, legitimacy of social institutions, degree of social cohesion, urbanism, infrastructure, etc. On the other hand, the general survey climate, public attitudes towards surveys, perception of direct marketing, legitimacy of web surveys and their sponsors, privacy legislation, data protection scandals, number of surveys conducted, etc., have a more direct influence on participation. Specifically for web surveys we can list the following:

- **Over-surveying**, that is the expansion of the web survey industry, particularly online panels and DIY research, may have caused a certain fatigue. While responses in online panels are in large part attributed to various types of 'professional respondents', who actually amount only to a small share of the total (Internet) population (Fulgoni, 2005), DIY research running on free or inexpensive SaaS platforms recruits citizens from all segments. The largest web survey software services deliver millions of web questionnaires daily. For example, in Slovenia, a country with 2 million inhabitants, the largest web survey software service[22] alone delivers more than a million survey questionnaires every year (as of 2014), mostly non-commercial and DIY, and outside of the professional survey industry. In addition to invitations to genuine web surveys – from the public, academic, private and DIY sectors – citizens are also bombarded with invitations to various entertainment polls, quizzes, short marketing surveys and brief individual enquiries, particularly on general, leisure and entertainment websites and social network sites. Further, surveys of all types compete for online attention with numerous other streams, from direct marketing to charity, gaming, gambling and various sophisticated forms of advertising. Unfortunately, Internet users have a hard time clearly separating requests for genuine research and various marketing noise. For further discussion and evidence of the problem of over-surveying, see Weiner & Dalessio (2006) for organizational research and Adams & Umbach (2012) for research in higher education. Where the respondents are especially exposed to over-surveying, we may thus expect increased difficulties with participation. Peytchev (2011), for example, showed

that students invited to multiple web surveys in a short period of time were more likely to be nonrespondents.

- **Spam and viruses** seem to be decreasing for end users, but studies still report that three out of four email messages were filtered as spam messages in MS Outlook email systems (Microsoft Corporation, 2013). This is particularly damaging for web surveys with email invitations, which may be automatically intercepted by spam-blocking tools, or subjectively considered by the respondent as spam. It is very difficult to estimate how many email invitations to web surveys are not delivered due to spam-blocking tools, which also results in problematic calculations of response rates (Dobrow, Orchard, Golden, Holowaty, Paszat, Brown, & Sullivan, 2008). Various measures to fight the problem of spam exist, from proper formatting of the message to the use of spam analyser tools (see Section 2.5.7). In addition, respondents may not want to click on the URL address sent by an unknown sender due to fear that this will send them to a 'phishing' website, that is a fake website resembling legitimate ones and designed to acquire usernames, passwords, credit card details, or sites that are hosting malware or viruses.

- **Internet privacy** is closely related to physical, informational, psychological, legal, economic and interactional aspects of privacy (Cho & Larose, 1999). It may cause Internet users to become reluctant to reveal personal information over the web. Hence, general attitudes towards privacy and subjective perceptions of risk, harm and benefits are becoming increasingly important when considering survey participation (Couper, Singer, Conrad, & Groves, 2008) and self-disclosure (Joinson, Paine, Buchanan, & Reips, 2008) in web surveys. Increasing evidence exists that privacy concerns have a negative effect on the level of disclosure of sensitive information in web surveys (Heerwegh, Vanhove, Matthijs, & Loosveldt, 2005; Joinson et al., 2007). In addition, such concerns may affect different segments of the target population differently. The more sensitive segments are usually more educated and older users (Sheehan, 2002), less experienced users and users from countries with stricter privacy regulation (Bellman, Johnson, Kobrin, & Lohse, 2004).

Information–communication infrastructure is critical for the successful implementation of web surveys. Considerable differences can be observed across different countries with respect to Internet penetration, as discussed within non-coverage section (Section 2.2.5). In addition, the quality of the Internet infrastructure (speed of Internet connections), Internet costs, and differences in systems used (email clients, browsers, devices) may additionally affect nonresponse, especially with complex questionnaires or technically advanced questions (e.g. mobile devices utilizing location data). Other ICT-related aspects are also important, from the nature and density of free Wi-Fi points to the prevalence of tablets and smartphones.

Respondents' characteristics have a strong impact on nonresponse. Common determinants are socio-demographic categories (age, gender, education, urbanity), but also survey experience, interest in survey topic, personality traits and other personal reasons. With web surveys, computer literacy, attitudes towards computer use and Internet usage patterns are also important. The intensity of computer and Internet use has been deemed the most important predictor of cooperation in a web survey, even when controlled for socio-demographic characteristics (e.g. Batagelj & Vehovar, 1998; Kwak & Radler, 2002; Payne & Barnfather, 2012). When computer use is not controlled for, it manifests via the usual characteristics of ICT users, which appear to be younger, educated, male, with higher social status (Batagelj & Vehovar, 1998; Diment & Garrett-Jones, 2007; Payne & Barnfather, 2012), but also more likely to be a student (Shih & Fan, 2008), and work in ICT or related sectors (Diment & Garrett-Jones, 2007). Sometimes ethnicity also plays a role (Couper, Kapteyn, Schonlau, & Winter, 2005). In general, technologically advanced users are more willing or able to participate. For example, fewer breakoffs were observed in a web survey using Java by those having the technological know-how (Stieger, Reips, & Voracek, 2007). Of course, characteristics of the target population as a whole have importance too; the general

public usually has high nonresponse, but the highest nonresponse rate may occur with various types of executives or celebrities. Regarding the factors defined by different theories, other specific predictors of web survey participation were found: time resources, fear of data misuse, salience of the topic, perception of burden (Haunberger, 2011b); moral obligation, frequency of past survey behaviour (Haunberger, 2011a); attitudes towards participating in web surveys, internalized social pressure, perceived behavioural control, extent of moral obligation towards participation (Bosnjak et al., 2005); personal web invitation and trust in sponsor (Fang et al., 2009). In addition, nonrespondents in one survey will likely be nonrespondents in another, unrelated, survey (Peytchev, 2011). We also believe that the general observation (e.g. Goyder, 1988) that overall higher social interactions and social involvements correlating with the survey participation holds true also for web surveys.

Web survey design is the only aspect affecting nonresponse that is within a researcher's control. It spans broadly across survey sponsor, topic salience, countless aspects of the questionnaire design to incentives, contacting and the format of invitations. We discuss all these aspects in Sections 2.5.4–2.5.8.

2.5.2 Defining Nonresponse, Breakoffs and Completeness

Unit nonresponse is closely related to breakoffs and also to the completeness status of the units. Corresponding indicators need to be defined clearly, because they are important for later phases of fielding and post-fielding, for providing comparisons across surveys, as well as for preventing potential manipulations in making response rates artificially higher.

Our discussion here conceptually follows the one on sampling (Section 2.2), where we first discussed probability list-based samples with email invitations and then approximated these principles for other types of samples.

2.5.2.1 Indicators of Unit Nonresponse

Following the above discussions on the nonresponse process, we use unit nonresponse indicators to reflect on nonresponse at the contact phase, while indicators related to breakoffs, item nonresponse and completeness reflect nonresponse at the cooperation phase. We start with a discussion on unit nonresponse and then proceed to other indicators, all of which are closely interrelated.

As a general reference for this discussion, we can point to Smith (2002) and particularly to the AAPOR (2011) Standard Definitions Report, from where we closely follow the final disposition codes in the section titled 'Internet surveys of specifically named persons' (p. 32). Some other sources are also useful, particularly with respect to online panels (e.g. Callegaro & DiSogra, 2008; ISO, 2009).

The literature generally agrees that the *response rate* (RR) is the key nonresponse indicator, defined as the ratio of responding units to all eligible units:

$$RR = \frac{\text{Responding units}}{\text{Eligible units}}$$

The implementation of this expression depends on how exactly the statuses are defined. For the purpose of our discussion, as well as for practical approximation, it is sufficient to separate effectively four key statuses: unit nonresponse from *ineligible units* and *responding units*, with the latter consisting of *completes* and *partials*.

We can also add that the RR lies in the interval (0–1); however, we will often express it in the alternative form of a percentage, which is of course in the interval (0–100%). The same is true for some other rates that we discuss in this section.

Web surveys have many specifics when it comes to the statuses listed above. The first set of specifics is related to the establishment of eligibility for those units that have not started the questionnaire (have been invited but never clicked on the URL of the questionnaire). This is relatively easy for units that provide an explicit reply (e.g. the respondent explains the reasons for refusal by email by which eligibility can be determined). The same is sometimes true for automatic email replies (see the discussion on possible outcomes in Section 2.4.1). Based on this feedback we then determine eligible (e.g. auto-reply denoting temporary absence) or ineligible status (e.g. auto-reply denoting death, move or permanent absence). Sometimes, even after the email reply message, eligibility is still unknown (e.g. auto-reply denoting an incorrect email address). In such a case we face a similar situation as with other units where nothing is returned, which is in fact usually by far the most frequent response status in web surveys with email invitations. In practice we often treat all units with unknown eligibility simply as eligible. Only when we have strong evidence to the contrary do we use an estimate to split them between eligible and ineligible statues. We should remember that, by definition, when an eligible unit provides no response, we have a unit nonresponse.

Another set of clarifications relates to eligible units that at the very least clicked on the URL of the web questionnaire. The introduction breakoffs also belong to unit nonresponse by way of definition. More complicated it is to separate unit nonresponse from questionnaire breakoffs and other partials, because this involves specific criteria for defining completeness statuses, which vary across surveys. We discuss this problem later on, after elaborating further on breakoffs, item nonresponse and completeness status.

Nevertheless, at this point we can already mention a simple *technical status* alternative, by which we treat all questionnaire breakoffs as partials. We can therefore use two approximations: 'nothing returned' units are treated – together with introduction breakoffs – as unit nonresponse, while questionnaire breakoffs are treated as partials. With this simple approximation, which is – as we will see – very realistic for most practical situations, we can obtain a simple estimation of the above RR. That is, we need to identify only the four statuses mentioned above in order to roughly estimate the corresponding AAPOR standard RR2 (Response Rate 2). Nevertheless, as the formal AAPOR standard for probability list-based web surveys (AAPOR, 2011) has 22 final statuses, instead of just four, we denote our approximation as RR2'. The AAPOR RR2 should of course be used for official documentation and reporting, however, the approximation of RR2' works well for the vast majority of situations and is suitable also for conceptual discussion, as can be seen from the two examples below.

First, in a survey of Slovenian scientists (WCSC from Section 1.3.5), 4,551 emails were sent out and nothing was returned from 3,185 of them. There were also 149 introduction break-offs and 113 units with no answered questions, which gives an estimate of 3,447 unit nonrespondents. On the other hand, there were 103 partials – the default technical approach was used here to identify partials – and 1,001 completes, thus 1,104 responding units. This gives RR2' = 24.3% (1,104/4,551). When all disposition codes were treated in full and in accordance with AAPOR guidelines, the comparable result was only negligibly different.

Likewise, Petrovčič, Lozar Manfreda, & Petrič (2013) elaborated on the AAPOR disposition codes – using survey-specific criteria (at least 50% of items answered) to define a partial – in a survey of the registered members of an online health forum. They obtained RR2 = 9.7%, which only slightly differed from the approximation RR2' = 9.9%.

Further elaboration of these two examples appears in *Examples of response rate calculations*, Supplement to Chapter 2 (http://websm.org/ch2).

To obtain more general insights into the level of nonresponse in list-based web surveys, we additionally present results from a study of 37 list-based web surveys with email invitations from 2011 to 2012 (Lozar Manfreda, Berzelak, & Vehovar, 2012), which reports that the share of complete respondents (defined as answering more than 90% of items presented to respondents) among all invited participants was 27%. There were on average also 18% partials, 41%

'nothing returned' units and 14% introduction breakoffs – so unit nonresponse presents 55% of eligible units – which gives the average of RR2' = 45%. This is relatively high, and can be attributed to the specifics of these surveys (i.e. short and with high salience).

Other meta-content studies confirm a similar range of response rates in web surveys (Anseel, Lievens, Schollaert, & Choragwicka, 2010; Baruch & Holtom, 2008; Mitra, Jain-Shukla, Robbins, Champion, & Durant, 2008; van Horn, Green, & Martinussen, 2009). We can typically expect a response rate (RR2) roughly within the range of 30% to 40% for list-based web surveys with email invitations, but only with surveys that have a sound methodology, a good sponsor and a salient topic. When one or more of these features are missing, we easily end up with a one-digit response rate. Only in some special circumstances (e.g. extremely high salience, rich incentives and/or aggressive reminders) do we approach or surpass 60% (Murphy, Hamel, Harrison, & Hammer, 2011).

We previously assumed that all units with an unknown status (e.g. 'nothing returned') are eligible, which means they are unit nonresponses. This is also the AAPOR assumption for the calculation of RR2. If they are all classified as ineligible and thus excluded from the denominator of RR, AAPOR denotes the corresponding calculation as RR6. But when they are split (based on some specific estimation) between nonresponses and ineligible, this is classified as RR4. Further variants (RR1, RR5 and RR3) are respectively obtained if we exclude partials from the numerator and keep only completes.

The response rate is a very important indicator of data quality – as well as its complement (1 − RR), called the *nonresponse rate* – and it is comparable across surveys. In addition, many other comparable, but more specific, nonresponse indicators exist. With traditional surveys, *cooperation rates* and *refusal rates* are very important, because they communicate the reasons for nonresponse (non-contact, refusals), but they seem less suitable for web surveys. For instance, for 'nothing returned', we cannot distinguish between non-contacts and refusals.

The *contact rate* compares units that show at least some reaction to an email invitation (e.g. click on questionnaire, explicit refusal) to all eligible units. In this case, the complete or partial respondents, the breakoffs and some other minor categories, such as explicit refusals, are added to the numerator. Similar is the *click-through rate* (CTR), which expresses the share of units that performed the desired action (i.e. accessed the web questionnaire) among successfully delivered email invitations.

Instead of limiting the units in the denominator to eligible ones, we can also include all units to which an invitation was sent, resulting in so called the *participation rate* (AAPOR, 2011). When all units are eligible, this of course equals RR.

To evaluate the quality of the email list, Vehovar et al. (2002) introduced the *absorption rate*, which is the share of units with no signs of an undelivered status among all emails sent. The complementary measure is the *failure rate*, that is the share of unsuccessfully delivered invitations.

What we have described until now applies to cross-sectional probability list-based web surveys with email invitations. Let us briefly comment on possible adaptations to other types of web surveys:

- **Probability list-based samples with mail invitations** use similar principles, but the contacting statuses can be taken from AAPOR rules for mail surveys. The same holds true for telephone recruitment.
- **Repeated probability surveys**, that is specific longitudinal surveys or probability online panels, use the same principles, but also require the calculation of the overall response rates. With probability-based online panels, we multiply the *recruitment rate* (referring to initial respondents among eligible invitations) by the *profile rate* (respondents who completed the introduction profile survey among initial respondents) and the response rate of the specific survey (AAPOR, 2011, p. 12). Here we also need to consider the *attrition* (i.e. panel members who sign off from the panel or simply no longer cooperate). Consequently, the *cumulative response rates* in online panels rarely exceed 20% and can often be below 10% (DiSogra & Callegaro, forthcoming). Only

the most advanced non-commercial probability-based panels come close to 40%, such as FFRISP (Krosnick, Ackermann, Malka, Sakshaug, Tourangeau, de Bell & Turakhia, 2009) or LISS (Scherpenzeel, 2011).

- **Non-probability list-based web surveys** are not based on the probability sample of the target population, so the denominator referring to eligible units in the response rate calculation has no meaning. Consequently, the participation rate is recommended instead. This is particularly relevant for non-probability online panels, where the participation rates are often only a few per cent (Tourangeau, Conrad, & Couper, 2013, p. 41).
- **Non-probability non-list web surveys**, such as unrestricted samples, have no proper denominator, so we can hardly calculate anything. For banners or with hyperlinks to web surveys, we may talk about CTRs, which is an online advertising concept comparing clicks on the banner/hyperlink to all page views. In practice, these rates are usually in decimals of a percentage point (e.g. 0.03%).
- **Probability non-list-based samples**, such as intercept web surveys, can use the number of website visitors exposed to the pop-up window with the invitation as the denominator in the response rate calculations.

2.5.2.2 Breakoffs

We have also defined breakoffs as eligible units that started the web questionnaire, but then left prematurely, that is before answering the last question in the questionnaire. We avoid using alternative notions of *dropout*, *abandonments* or attrition, as they may also have other meanings. We also warn that breakoffs are sometimes used in traditional survey modes to denote residual eligible units, after eliminating partials and completes (AAPOR, 2011), which is not our understanding here.

We have also defined *introduction breakoffs*, which occur due to initial reluctance, rooted in a broad range of reasons from survey characteristics (e.g. sponsor, salience) to situational circumstances (e.g. time pressure) and specifics of the invitation (e.g. frequency, timing, content of the introduction and other formats). Very different reasons are responsible for *questionnaire breakoffs* later in the questionnaire. These might range from the respondent's situation (e.g. fatigue, distractions, etc.) to questionnaire characteristics (e.g. design, length, content, question types, etc.). Correspondingly, three rates can be computed (IBR, QBR, TBR).

It is also interesting to observe questionnaire breakoffs among all responding units (units starting the questionnaire), which can be labelled as *gross questionnaire breakoffs*, where the corresponding rate, denoted as QBR′, is also the product QBR′ = QBR × (1 − IBR).

$$\text{IBR(Introduction Breakoff Rate)} = \frac{\text{Introduction breakoffs}}{\text{Units starting the questionnaire}}$$

$$\text{QBR (Questionnaire Breakoff Rate)} = \frac{\text{Questionnaire breakoffs}}{\text{Units starting the questionnaire} - \text{Introduction breakoffs}}$$

$$\text{TBR (Total Breakoff Rate)} = \frac{\text{Introduction breakoffs} + \text{Questionnaire breakoffs}}{\text{Units starting the questionnaire}}$$

Complementary to breakoff rates are *retention rates* (Göritz & Crutzen, 2012). For example, the *total retention rate* equals (1 − TBR), with a nice characteristic: (1 − TBR) = (1 − IBR) × (1 − QBR).

Let us give some examples on breakoff rates from several meta-content studies. In a meta-study of 5,752 web surveys (mostly done by students and DIY), Vehovar & Čehovin (2014) obtained the following averages: IBR = 33%, QBR = 11% and TBR = 40%; the corresponding retention rates were 67% (units that made it past the introduction), 89% (units that made it to the end among those who made it past the introduction) and 60% (units that made it to the end among all that started). Of course, in some surveys we may also have TBRs of a few per cent and in others retention rates of a few per cent. We may add that in the Vehovar & Čehovin (2014) study the obtained TBR is somewhat higher than those reported in meta-studies a decade ago, namely from 16% to 34% (Lozar Manfreda & Vehovar, 2002; Musch & Reips, 2000).

Overall, the above figures illustrate well the reality of web surveys, particularly in the DIY segment. Academic and government surveys have lower breakoffs, very often in the one-digit range. For example, Ainsaar et al. (2013) reported a TBR of 7% in an ESS web experiment in Estonia. Probability-based online panel LISS reports TBR rates of 10% to 15% (Scherpenzeel, 2011). Marketing research surveys have a broad spectrum, but are typically comparable with or even worse than DIY surveys. This is true also for many non-probability online panels, where the range is very broad. The meta-study by Vehovar & Čehovin (2014) also indicated that the majority (83%) of breakoffs occur as introduction breakoffs (IBR > QBR′). The opposite situation (QBR′ > IBR) may appear in surveys with high legitimacy and with a good invitation, but a problematic, non-salient, difficult and/or long questionnaire, as in Petrovčič et al. (2013), where the introduction breakoffs amounted to only 24% of all breakoffs. The length of the questionnaire is particularly important determinant of breakoffs, as discussed in Section 2.3.4, as well as other questionnaire characteristics, such as design, complexity and topic (Peytchev, 2009).

We may add that breakoffs can be − besides above indicators at survey level − calculated also at the item (variable) level, as *item level breakoff* (ILB), which then expresses the share of values (units) per item (variable) that are missing due to breakoffs. For example, if half of respondents quitted the questionnaire before arriving at certain items, we have ILB = 0.5. Similarly, the *unit-level breakoff rate* (UBR) expresses the share of items per respondent that are missing due to breakoffs. For example, if the respondent left after only 10% of the questionnaire, we have UBR = 0.9. Both indicators have various variants and refinements, but we do not elaborate this further. Additional insight can be found in *Examples of response rate calculations*, Supplement to Chapter 2 (http://websm.org/ch2).

2.5.2.3 Item Nonresponse at the Question Level

Item nonresponse occurs when a respondent is exposed to an item (question or sub-question) for which we expect an answer, but do not get one. We measure it by the *item nonresponse rate* (INR) at the level of a specific item (survey question or sub-question):

$$INR = \frac{\text{Number of units with item nonresponse}}{\text{All eligible units exposed to the item}}$$

Here, the denominator contains only eligible units exposed to the item, thus completes and partials (but only those who were still completing the questionnaire at the particular item). The units not exposed to a certain item due to branching, randomization, preliminary breakoffs and other possible reasons are excluded here. In the numerator we need to exclude non-substantial answers ('don't know', 'other', etc.), which are legitimate responses, while explicit nonresponse options (e.g. 'refuse' or 'prefer not to answer') need to be added to the numerator.

In online panels, as well as in marketing research surveys, very often there is no item nonresponse, because hard prompts are applied rigorously to all questions, except perhaps for open-ended text entries. Social scientists in academia, on the other hand, do not endorse this strategy, as elaborated on in Section 2.3.3.

One important reason for item nonresponse is the sensitive nature of questions, for example on income, sexuality, social stigma behaviour, health, etc. Alternatively, this problem can also manifest as excessive responses such as 'don't know', middle point, more socially desirable answers, etc. The techniques available for handling sensitive questions, from item count, randomized responses and question wording techniques to other tactics (Tourangeau & Yan, 2007), can be used to prevent item nonresponse here. However, studies show that the web – and computerization and self-administration in general – reduce this problem (see illustrations in Section 1.3.5).

Item nonresponse can also be an indirect aspect of the general indication of a lack of engagement (see Section 2.3.4), which can in particular appear in complicated (e.g. tables), long, boring, frustrating and/or poorly designed questionnaires, so strategies to increase engagement can be helpful.

Question types also affect the level of item nonresponse. Open-ended text questions are especially problematic: the study by Vehovar & Čehovin (2014) showed that INRs are often above 90%, particularly when questions are optional (e.g. 'Do you have any other comments?'), but can be much lower, even below 10%, when they are essential (e.g. 'Describe your job position.'). Supplementary open-ended text options to questions with a closed list of responses (e.g. 'Other, please specify:') can have an even higher INR, typically above 95%. On the other hand, questions with numeric entries and closed-ended questions with a predefined set of response categories usually have an INR of up to a few per cent.

INR indicators which are primarily calculated for individual items, can be observed also for groups of questions or for all questions in the questionnaire, where range, mean and median can be calculated and compared across surveys (e.g. mean item INR across all items in the questionnaire).

2.5.2.4 Item Nonresponse at Unit Level

Above, we observed the nonresponse in relation to a certain item across all units. In addition, item nonresponse can be observed also at the unit (respondent) level, as the share of items answered among all items to which a certain unit was exposed. We call this the *unit-level item nonresponse* (UIN):

$$UIN = \frac{\text{Number of all item nonresponse for a certain unit}}{\text{Number of all items to which a certain unit was exposed}}$$

According to this expression, for example, an empty unit, where all question were 'answered' as item nonresponse, has a UIN = 1, while a unit with responses to all items has UIN = 0.

However, the above expression makes full sense only for respondents who conclude the questionnaire, as those who breakoff have further missing data to items to which they were not exposed. Thus, in case of breakoffs, the unit-level breakoff rate (UBR) should be combined. The total share of missing items per respondents can then be expressed as the *unit-level missing-data rate* (UMR):

$$UMR = UBR + (1 - UBR) \times UIN$$

with the *unit-level completeness rate* (UCR) as the corresponding complement:

$$UCR = (1 - UMR)$$

In the case of UBR = 0.9 with, say, half of the responses on the remaining 10% of items which were exposed to the respondent (i.e. UIN = 0.5), we have UCR = 0.05. UCR is an extremely important indicator of the data quality, because it can be decisive for the definition of complete, partial and unusable units.

2.5.2.5 Completes, Partials and Unusable Units

When we introduced completeness status (complete, partial, unusable), we specified that they are defined by some arbitrary and survey-specific rules. As these rules interfere with important unit nonresponse indicators, we devote extra attention to the matter.

With traditional survey modes, sometimes a completeness benchmark of 50% of all items answered per respondent is mentioned (e.g. AAPOR, 2011) to distinguish partials from unusable units. Various measures of completeness of the units can be used to estimate this share; the UCR above is one possibility, which we will also use further in this context. Nevertheless, we are in general inclined towards less formal and rather more substantive criteria for defining partials. For example, we suggest defining a set of key survey-specific items and only when this minimal set is not complete are the units classified as unusable; otherwise they are partials.

Let us repeat the essential characteristics of unusable units: they are excluded from the statistical analysis, archives and from all further usage, where only the complementary set of *usable units* is processed. We took the notion of usable and unusable units from the elaboration in the corresponding ISO standards (ISO, 2009, 2012). We may add that usable units basically match, what we called responding units or units with responses, and thus usually include all partials and all completes.

The unusable units can be defined as units that are below the minimal completeness benchmark (e.g. UCR < 0.50). In addition, they may include responses of insufficient quality (e.g. fake responses, fraud, excessive satisficing, etc.). We must keep in mind that we can calculate the completeness status only for eligible units that started to respond, so by definition the unusable units belong to unit nonresponse, mostly to the category denoted in AAPOR (2011) as 'Partial or breakoff with insufficient information'. This is conceptually clear enough and should suffice for all practical purposes. However, we may notice that unusable units are a very complex category, because nonresponse issues interact there with sampling (e.g. eligibility) and measurement (e.g. response quality) problems. Within this context we cannot elaborate on this problem any further.

Also arbitrary is the separation between partials and completes. We may again use the criterion of completeness level (e.g. UCR), for example a certain percentage of items with quality (i.e. usable) responses to define completes, such as 80% (AAPOR, 2011). However, we may again use a substantive approach, which we already recommended, and treat completes as units that provided quality responses to a pre-specified set of key questions.

All of the above completeness criteria thus rely on certain arbitrary rules, which vary from survey to survey and, in addition, are hard to implement in structured questionnaires, where units are exposed to a different number of items due to branching. We have already mentioned a very simple alternative for avoiding these problems, which is to define the completeness using *default technical statuses*:

a respondent accesses only the introduction page and then leaves;
b respondent proceeds to the initial page with questions and then leaves;
c respondent proceeds beyond the initial page with questions, but never responds and then leaves before the end (i.e. empty unit);
d respondent comes to the end of the questionnaire (i.e. concludes it), but provides no responses (i.e. empty unit);
e respondent provides some or all responses to questions to which he or she is exposed, but leaves before the end of the questionnaire;
f respondent provides some or all responses and concludes the questionnaire.

These statuses are very easy to establish with any given survey software. They were also the basis for an important classification of (non) response patterns in web surveys by Bosnjak & Tuten (2001), who identified various levels of lurkers and item nonresponses.

Building on the above statuses, we can easily form the categories (e) partials and (f) completes, while the remaining categories ((a)–(d)) can be declared as unusable. Of course, partials and completes may in this case also include units that responded to only one item, which is a serious disadvantage of this approach. On the other hand, its advantages are the ease of calculation and comparability across surveys. Using this technical approach, Vehovar & Čehovin (2014) observed the following structure in their meta-study:

- Partials (e): questionnaire breakoffs with at least some responses (7%).
- Completes (f): units that provided some responses and made it to the last page (57%).
- Unusable units ((a) + (b) + (c) + (d)): units that cannot enter into the analysis (36%), composed mostly of introduction breakoffs ((a) + (b) – 33%), with empty units presenting a minority ((c) + (d) = 3%).

Introduction breakoffs and empty units are unusable not only in this technical approach, but also in general, while the status of questionnaire breakoffs can be complete, partial or unusable (Table 2.2). The above technical approach, labelled in Table 2.2 by an asterisk (*), may thus differ considerably from other strategies, which use a certain value of the UCR as the criterion. Petrovčič et al. (2013) initially used the criterion of UCR = 0.5 for defining partials and UCR = 0.9 for completes. However, if the above technical approach had been used there, the number of partials would have increased by six times and the number of unusable units by one-tenth. Accordingly, in their case the estimate for RR2 would have increased from 9.7% to 11.0%.

Table 2.2 and the above examples illustrate well the complex and highly sensitive nature of establishing the completeness statuses in web

Table 2.2 Potential completeness status according to the number of items to which the unit has responded and the level of questionnaire completion (default technical statuses are denoted with an asterisk*)

Number of items responded to	Level of questionnaire completion		
	Introduction breakoff	Questionnaire breakoff	Concluded questionnaire
No item (UCR = 0)	Unusable	Unusable	Unusable
Some items (0 < UCR < 1)	–	Unusable Partial* Complete	Unusable Partial Complete*
All items (UCR = 1)	–	–	Complete

surveys, which is, however, extremely important, since it closely determines the nonresponse indicators. Further calculations and illustrations can be found in *Examples of response rate calculations*, Supplement to Chapter 2 (http://websm.org/ch2).

2.5.3 Relation Between Nonresponse Rates and Nonresponse Biases

When chasing high response rates, we may easily forget to consider the relation between response rate and nonresponse bias, which is in fact an essential aspect when preparing the nonresponse strategy. Due to its great importance, which is often neglected in the literature, we provide a more extensive insight into this critical matter. This is especially important for web surveys, because they usually suffer from considerable nonresponse.

We need to keep in mind that we discuss here only the probability sample setting and the discussion below is related to this assumption. With respect to the non-probability context, a similar approximate approach can be applied, as discussed in sampling (Section 2.2).

The difference between the expected estimate based on respondents and the true value is called the *nonresponse bias*, $\text{Bias}(\bar{y}) = (\bar{Y}_r - \bar{Y})$, where $\bar{Y}_r$ is the expected value of the estimate based only on respondents in the survey and $\bar{Y}$ is the 'true' (benchmark) value in the population

(Groves et al., 2009, p. 189). Of course, the nonresponse bias we discuss here is different from the non-coverage bias (Section 2.2.5). However, due to our separate treatment, we do not introduce a separate notation, such as $\text{Bias}_{NR}(\bar{y})$ and $\text{Bias}_{NC}(\bar{y})$, although we do bear this distinction in mind.

Certain nonresponse bias may be irrelevant for some research projects; however, when we make important population estimates (e.g. market share, unemployment rate, disease prevalence, etc.), or in the case of mixed-modes, it can become essential.

We need to be aware that any level of nonresponse raises suspicion about the nonresponse bias, because nonresponding units may differ from responding ones. For example, let us say that $\bar{Y}$ = 54% of all units in our population possess a smartphone (benchmark) and that smartphone users are also more likely to participate in a web survey on ICT usage. Due to the higher participation of smartphone users, their share in the survey is overestimated, say $\bar{Y}_r$ = 90%, which is painfully incorrect, with $\text{Bias}(\bar{y})$ = (90% − 54%) = 36 percentage points.

With some simplification we can say that we differentiate between respondents who always respond and nonrespondents who never respond. It can then be easily shown that the bias is proportional to the share of the nonrespondents (W_{nr}) and to the difference between the respondents ($\bar{Y}_r$) and the nonrespondents

$(\bar{Y}_{nr})$. When we rely only on respondents $(\bar{Y}_r)$, the bias can be expressed as

$$\text{Bias}(\bar{y}) = (\bar{Y}_r - \bar{Y}) = W_{nr} \times (\bar{Y}_r - \bar{Y}_{nr})$$

With a very small share of nonrespondents, W_{nr}, or a small difference $(\bar{Y}_r - \bar{Y}_{nr})$ between respondents and nonrespondents, the bias is not an issue. For the above case with $W_{nr} = 0.60$ and $\bar{Y}_r = 0.90$ and, say, $\bar{Y}_{nr} = 0.30$, we again obtain $\text{Bias}(\bar{y}) = 0.6 \times (0.9 - 0.3) = 0.36$.

It is more realistic, however, to assume that units become nonrespondents with certain propensities. This reveals that nonresponse bias essentially depends on the correlation between nonresponse propensity and the value of the target variable. In addition, the variances of both terms also increase the bias, as well as the inverse of the response rate. We do not elaborate further on this issue; an excellent treatment can be found in Bethlehem (2009a).

An improved insight into the nonresponse bias is obtained by calculating the relative bias, $\text{Rbias}(\bar{y}) = \text{Bias}(\bar{y}) / \bar{Y}$. In our case the corresponding $\text{Rbias}(\bar{y}) = 0.36/0.54 = 0.66$ is very high, as the bias represents 66% of the population value. We already mentioned in Section 2.2.5 that 5% and 10% are sometimes the benchmarks for relative bias that is still acceptable.

Further insight can be provided with standardized bias, $\text{Sbias}(\bar{y}) = \text{Bias}(\bar{y})/\text{SE}(\bar{y})$, which we conceptually introduced in discussion on non-coverage bias (see Section 2.2.5). In the above case, if we have $n = 400$ and a standard error of $\text{SE}(\bar{y}) = 2\%$, we obtain $\text{Sbias}(\bar{y}) = 0.36/0.02 = 18$, which is dramatically higher than $t = 1.96$, so we have statistically highly significant nonresponse bias.

In reality, nonresponse bias is usually unknown, because we do not know the true value $\bar{Y}$. That is, not knowing $\bar{Y}$ is exactly why we conduct a survey. Still, we may learn something about certain $\bar{Y}$ from a sampling frame (e.g. gender), some auxiliary sources (e.g. election outcome), or from other waves of the survey, such as a preliminary screening, a post-survey follow-up, a previous wave in a longitudinal study, or from comparisons of sequential efforts

(e.g. refusal conversion, increased contact). All of these can provide precious evidence about the pattern of nonresponse bias (Groves & Peytcheva, 2008).

If we ignore nonresponse, we implicitly assume there is no bias, which usually means that efforts to increase response rates would be a waste of resources, unless we need a high response rate only to increase the sample size. At the other extreme, we may, with or without much evidence, believe that every increase in the response rate will reduce nonresponse bias. When this turns out not to be the case in practice, we might again have spent resources unnecessarily.

Given its importance, studies dealing with the relationship between the response rate and nonresponse bias are surprisingly rare; at most they observe that the bias depends on a number of contacts (Vehovar, 1999). An excellent review of these studies can be found in Fuchs, Bossert, & Stukowski (2013). Sometimes these studies even compare different surveys, where the results are then mixed with countless other factors we cannot control for. As a consequence, little or even no correlation can be found between nonresponse bias and nonresponse rates (e.g. Groves & Peytcheva, 2008). This surprising finding can be explained by the fact that high response rates are usually pursued when dangerously high nonresponse biases are expected, which then creates a false (positive) correlation between response rates and nonresponse biases. At the level of a specific survey, where the nonresponse efforts are increased (e.g. adding more contacts), there is of course the opposite correlation, because a high response rate by definition gradually reduces the nonresponse bias to zero.

In Figure 2.2, the potential relationships between the nonresponse bias and response rate are illustrated for a certain item in a specific survey setting:

- Line A represents a strong relationship between nonresponse rate and nonresponse bias with the latter decreasing with increasing response rate.
- Lines B and C represent a weak relationship (nonresponse bias does not change significantly

with increasing response rate) and/or only moderate bias.

- Line D represents a situation where increasing response rates could even lead to higher nonresponse bias.

All lines finish at 0% nonresponse bias and 100% response rate which is a theoretical situation that in reality may never be reached.

Fuchs et al. (2013) elaborated on this relation in a very similar way to Figure 2.2, but for socio-demographic variables in selected ESSs. The contact paradata were used there to simulate nonresponse rates and nonresponse bias conditional on the number of contacts. Lines B and C were most observed in their study. We can also speculate further that in the case of substantive target variables (e.g. attitude towards government) – in this high-quality ESS with response rates close to or above 60% – the impact of response rate on nonresponse bias would be even much smaller, particularly if the weighting corrections were implemented (which might further reduce the bias).

Of course, each survey item may behave differently, requiring a separate line in Figure 2.2. Each line also relates to an item within a fixed and specific survey setting, within which we

hypothetically manipulate only with increased nonresponse efforts, such as sequential adding of waves of contacts, increased incentives, additional refusal conversion, etc. If we change some other survey setting factors (e.g. initial incentives or initial mode of data collection), we get a different survey setting with different lines. In principle, these lines can also be obtained in a corresponding experimental setting, as in Vehovar, Berzelak, & Lozar Manfreda (2010).

Figure 2.2 illustrates well the dilemma of whether to invest resources to obtain high response rates:

- In the case of a strong relationship between nonresponse rate and nonresponse bias (line A), we cannot afford low response rates. An example is the above case with an estimated share of smartphone users, where the 40% response rate produces $\text{Rbias}(\bar{y}) = 0.66$. More contacts, incentives, refusal conversion or additional mixed-mode options – serving as follow-up variation of a certain survey setting – may push the response rate towards 80% and move bias towards $\text{Rbias}(\bar{y}) = 0.10$.
- In the case of a weak relationship and/or only moderate bias, efforts to increase the response

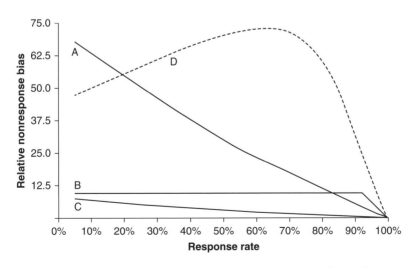

Figure 2.2 **Possible relationships between relative nonresponse bias and response rate**

rate may have little effect on the bias (lines B and C). Luckily, this model seems to prevail in reality. For example, in the Slovenian survey of scientists (WCSC), we may include only respondents after the initial invitation and before the reminder, to end with $n = 580$ respondents and RR = 13% instead of a final RR = 24%. However, none of the survey estimates would change significantly. When the RR was moved from 13% to 24%, the relative changes in estimates were all below 5% for all variables. Of course, we should not forget that with RR = 24% in this study, three-quarters of eligible units are still nonrespondents. However, studies in social and marketing research, which intensified the hunt for the last nonrespondents (e.g. Stoop, 2005), often concluded that expensive efforts to reach the 100% response rate would not change the estimates. Similarly, in the AAPOR membership survey, small differences in estimates were found when respondents from later waves had been included, although RR almost doubled (Murphy et al., 2011). It is also worth noting that in this membership survey, the first reminder pushed the cumulative response rate percentage for members from 20% to 30%, which is the usual effect, while two additional email reminders, accompanied by a mail and telephone follow-up, increased the response rate to 61%. The key question here is whether these extra efforts really paid off in terms of reducing nonresponse bias.

- Line D is a deliberate illustration showing that this relationship can assume almost any format, but it also reflects an authentic, although rare, situation described in Vehovar et al. (2010), where experiments with additional sequential nonresponse efforts in a mixed-mode survey (i.e. a €5 prepaid cash incentive in a mail invitation to a web survey) moved the response rate percentages from 33% to 74%. However, this attracted even more Internet users and thus increased the nonresponse bias for target variables related to Internet use. For example, the proportion of daily users for the experimental group without incentives was 62%, with incentives 76%, while official data report 56% of the general population.

It is also worth mentioning that even with the slightest indication of nonresponse bias, there is usually some contextual explanation behind it.

In the WCSC example above, the more successful scientists responded earlier and the responses from this first wave reflected the tendency in the estimates of scientific performance being slightly and consistently higher – although statistically not significant – than for respondents from later waves. For example, the scientific achievement level on a 1–7 scale for units responding after initial invitation was 5.0 vs 4.8 for units responding only after reminders. If we stopped after the initial email, this would create a very small nonresponse bias. Nevertheless, it is important to check whether the directions in the change of the estimate are contextually consistent, logical and reasonable.

Here we recall observations and references from Section 2.2.3, where we discussed the robustness of variables for deviations from probability sampling. Similarly, some variables are simply more robust (i.e. less vulnerable) when it comes to nonresponse. Here too, the percentages (shares) are in general more vulnerable than variables on scales, correlations and comparisons across subgroups. Similarly, with trends, the biased estimates are sometimes less important, as far as the trend change is properly reflected (e.g. declining satisfaction or declining market share).

2.5.4 General Web Survey Design Characteristics and Nonresponse

In the above sections, we introduced the key nonresponse issues and concepts, and will now focus on approaches to prevent nonresponse problems.

We start with the general characteristics of web surveys, where a researcher has relatively weak (sponsor, salience) or indirect (questionnaire design) control. We then continue with direct nonresponse interventions related to incentives (Section 2.5.5), the contacting process (Section 2.5.6) and the format of invitations (Section 2.5.7).

2.5.4.1 Survey Sponsor

We use the term *survey sponsor* for any entity that can be presented as an authority in the invitation or in the introduction page of the survey. This can be a researcher, a subcontractor, a partner, a client, some other organization, or individuals who can recommend the survey. The literature consistently states that legitimate authority increases trust and the odds that the survey will be perceived as benevolent, honest, and competent enough to protect privacy in traditional (Groves et al., 2009; Groves & Peytcheva, 2008) and web surveys (Dillman et al., 2009; Fang et al., 2009).

Empirical evidence on *willingness to participate* in web surveys shows that the reputation of and trust in the web survey sponsor affect the intention to participate (Bosnjak & Batinic, 2002; Fang et al., 2009; Fang & Wen, 2012). The same is true also for *actual participation*. This was confirmed in an example of a scientist and a student sending out survey invitations, where the difference in the response rate was extremely high: 55% vs 7% (Guéguen & Jacob, 2002). The effect of involving the university vice-president in a survey among faculty staff was also substantial, pushing the response rate from 33% to 43% (Kaplowitz et al., 2012). Similarly, in an unrestricted website evaluation survey, government sponsorship in a banner invitation increased the response rate from 11% to 15% for the banners in which the sponsorship was displayed (Walston et al., 2006). When differences in the sponsorship level were small or unclear, the effects disappeared, as in the director vs administrative assistant survey invitation (Porter & Whitcomb, 2003a), or with sponsors with high (sponsor – government department) vs low (research – university research centre) prominence (Boulianne, Klofstad, & Basson, 2011).

It is therefore very important that the sponsor is clearly represented, for example by a logo or a signature of the authority figures. On the other hand, placing a sponsor's logo on every questionnaire screen brings no added value, at least in preventing breakoffs (Heerwegh & Loosveldt, 2006). In addition to the response rate, sponsorship also has an impact on other aspects of data quality, as shown in a sexual harassment study, when the alternative sponsor was a feminist organization (Galesic & Tourangeau, 2007; Tourangeau, Groves, Kennedy, & Yan, 2009).

The effects of sponsorship vary strongly according to circumstances, particularly those related to cultural and organizational aspects, as well as survey design (e.g. email invitation or mail invitation, list-based or non-list-based web survey). Small differences in the perception of sponsors and the specific role of the sponsor are also important. In fact, Fang & Wen (2012) showed that the reputation of the survey sponsor or a client usually has a greater effect than the reputation of the research organization conducting the survey. On the other hand, a client with a weaker reputation may benefit from the higher reputation of a researcher.

In this context, we should also mention that, regardless of the type of web survey, publicity can also help to increase the general awareness of the survey among the target segment. For example, the presence of a researcher in traditional or online media, as well as any other mentions of the survey's importance in the media, can contribute to successful recruitment and cooperation. Similarly, a general plea outside the recruitment process from management, the hierarchy or other authority figures can stimulate participation, particularly in membership, student or employee surveys (Borg & Mastrangelo, 2008, p. 192). A formal awareness campaign can also be organized for large surveys, when the sample is a non-negligible part of the target population, such as for example in a census (Datta, Yan, Evans, Pedlow, Spencer & Bautista, 2012). Unfortunately, when it comes to paid promotion (e.g. advertising, public relations), the effects are poorly researched, since it is very difficult to conduct experiments in this area. Correspondingly, the potential effects, which are difficult to measure in any case, can be easily overestimated and resources wasted.

To conclude, very often we may have very limited options for involving a sponsor with a high reputation for our target population. Commercial or DIY web surveys can hardly involve government sponsorship. However, whenever this option exists, we should consider it. The opposite is also true: we should not use sponsors whose involvement may damage the reputation of our survey.

2.5.4.2 Topic Salience

Topic salience is defined as the association of importance and/or timeliness of a specific topic for respondents (C. Martin, 2004) and is considered as one of the key factors in survey participation, not only for the response rate, but also for survey engagement (see Section 2.3.4).

Empirical research confirms that salience is a positive predictor of participation, particularly in student surveys (Adams & Umbach, 2012; Porter & Whitcomb, 2005), while in online panels the effects are often small or non-existent (Tourangeau et al., 2009), although Keusch (2012b, p. 68) found that respondents interested in certain topics participated more often: in the high-interest group (79%), the participation rate was almost 7% higher than in the low-interest group (72%). In addition, the former provided a higher quality of responses. However, more exposed salience of the topic in the email invitation had no effect in this study.

In addition to the effect on unit nonresponse rates, breakoffs occur less frequently when respondents exhibit a high level of interest in the survey topic, as was established by Galesic (2006) in a banner advertisement web survey. Those more interested in the survey topic also give answers of higher quality (e.g. open-ended questions), as shown by Holland & Christian (2009). Emphasizing the salience of the topic in the communication with potential respondents can potentially be an effective strategy for increasing the response rate and the quality of answers in web surveys.

We may add that, in unrestricted surveys, such as customer intercept surveys (Comley, 2000), salience is even more important, as it is easier to advertise it on the web.

Salience has an even greater importance in specific populations. For example, even the most busy top executives may participate because of the high salience, as is the case in the monthly-based 'Business tendency surveys', which often achieve high response rates.[23] Implemented by the Statistical Office in Slovenia, they had an average 85% cumulative response rate in mixed-mode surveys since 2014; where more than half of respondents completed the web survey.[24]

However, stressing salience may also have negative effects on respondents with low topic interest (Keusch, 2012b), because salience reinforces self-selection, leading to potential nonresponse bias. Thus, we may end up with disproportionally more respondents greatly interested in the topic and with results biased towards this group, as in Hansen & Smith (2012), Chang & Krosnick (2009) and Faas & Schoen (2006) indicated that this is especially problematic for non-probability web surveys with self-selection of volunteer respondents, where salience primarily attracts respondents with extensive knowledge of the subject, causing so-called 'expert bias'. For this reason, sometimes we may intentionally avoid stressing the salience and prefer to hide it behind general labelling of the survey topic.

Similar to sponsorships, researchers cannot often exert too much influence when it comes to this since the survey has a fixed required topic. Little can be done to increase the perceived salience of a topic that has generated very little general interest. Nevertheless, we can – to a certain extent – use some direct marketing approaches and stress the most salient aspects of our survey in the title, invitation, introduction page and the questionnaire itself. We then need to strike a balance to avoid the negative effects of the disproportionate attraction of more involved respondents, which is a potential by-product of this technique.

2.5.4.3 Questionnaire Design

Questionnaire design does not have an overly strong effect on the initial decision to access the web questionnaire page (unit nonresponse), except when the first page with questions is visible at the very start, as with some unrestricted web surveys. Walston et al. (2006), for example, showed that the cumbersome appearance of sliders reduced response rates from 13% to 8%, compared with tables of rating questions with radio buttons. The impact of the questionnaire design – particularly the structure, layout, graphics, interactivity, question formats and length – is much stronger on questionnaire breakoffs, item nonresponse and other aspects of the quality of responses. We have discussed all these issues extensively within the context of survey engagement (Section 2.3.4). An additional review of general web questionnaire design aspects affecting nonresponse has been provided by Vicente & Reis (2010).

With this we conclude our overview of the role of general survey design characteristics in terms of nonresponse. In the next three sections (2.5.5 – 2.5.7) we discuss more specific nonresponse approaches, namely: incentives, contacting and invitation format.

2.5.5 Incentives in Web Surveys

Incentives have been shown to be effective in increasing the response rate in traditional survey modes (Singer, van Hoewyk, Gebler, Raghunathan, & McGonagle, 1999). The meta-analysis of Göritz (2006a) and other studies (e.g. Gajic, Cameron, & Hurley, 2012; Parsons & Manierre, 2013) confirm this also for web surveys. We first address general issues related to incentives in web surveys and then present a specific case of lotteries.

Incentives in web surveys can take various forms with different effects on unit nonresponse, breakoffs and the general quality of responses. Some general incentive principles also apply here:

- Unconditional incentives are more effective than contingent ones (Göritz, 2005).
- Prepaid incentives generally work better than promised ones, although in web surveys this effect seems to be weaker; studies often show no advantage (Bosnjak & Tuten, 2003) or a very modest effect (Downes-Le Guin, Janowitz, Stone, & Khorram, 2002).
- Monetary incentives typically outperform non-monetary ones, as in Vehovar et al. (2009), where the prepaid cash incentive of €5 pushed the response rate up from 33% to 74%, while a gift (the gift was a wallet for coins) – sent with the invitation letter – of similar value had almost no effect.
- Offering various services or transfers as incentives, such as access to special information,

memberships, charity donations, etc., rarely works and generally cannot be compared with cash. For example, a meta-analysis of 11 randomized experiments in mail and electronic questionnaires showed no increase in the response rate for the group offered study results vs not offering anything (Edwards, Roberts, Clarke, DiGuiseppi, Wentz, Kwan, … Pratap, 2009). Similar conclusions were drawn when participants in the probability-based online LISS panel were provided with elaborate multimedia results (Scherpenzeel & Toepoel, 2014). This seems to work only with extremely salient topics, such as providing tailored feedback on responses in health surveys (Balter, Fondell, & Balter, 2012).

- According to social exchange theory, the rule of thumb for symbolic appreciation is sometimes to offer the lowest monetary note (where coins end), e.g. €5 or $1. On the other hand, when we want to show appreciation for the respondent's time, the amount roughly reflects wages in a certain environment; in developed countries this is usually between €5 and €40 per hour.
- Very often the increased value of the monetary incentives has a very small effect, as shown in comparisons of €15 vs €25 (Downes-Le Guin, Janowitz et. al., 2002), $5 vs $10 (Boulianne, 2013) or ₤15 vs ₤35 (Villar, 2013). The two amounts in this latter study – an experiment with a web version of the ESS in the UK – were conditional on completion, but a ₤5 unconditional prepayment was used with the mail invitation. This two-step approach can be a good model for long and demanding surveys, but again this depends on the context; the above experiment produced a 20% response rate, while a similar study in Estonia (Ainsaar et al., 2013) reached a 40% response rate using only a symbolic non-monetary prepaid incentive. Also, Alexander, Divine, Couper, McClure, Stopponi, Fortman & Johnson (2008) found that a $2 unconditional prepayment and a $20 payment conditional on completion were optimal among the 24 incentive strategies studied.
- For web-specific incentive formats for the online environment (e.g. various forms of online payments, transfer to mobile accounts, online bookshop coupons) there is little published evidence, so it seems these potentials have not yet been fully exploited.

For online panels, monetary incentives, which are conducted indirectly by collection of points, have already become a standard way of showing appreciation. Their role in panel recruitment (Scherpenzeel & Toepoel, 2012) and in participation in individual panel surveys (Göritz & Luthe, 2013) has been studied extensively.

The effect of incentives also depends on the context of the web survey. A meta-content analysis of web surveys (Lozar Manfreda & Vehovar, 2002), which took into account several factors that influence response rates, showed that incentives, together with other measures, predominantly influenced the decrease of break-offs, but not the unit nonresponse. We caution against false association, which may appear in meta-studies, because incentives are more frequently used for long or tedious surveys, where response rates are expected to be lower anyway (Cook et al., 2000).

Similar to stressing the salience of a study, incentives may also disproportionally attract specific units – for example, those with lower incomes (Göritz, 2008) – which can then increase nonresponse bias (Parsons & Manierre, 2013). In addition, incentives may also make respondents more eager to please (e.g. provide favourable responses), but also to satisfy, or – when allowed – even to fill out the questionnaire more than once (Comley, 2000).

In general, incentives improve data quality, particularly the response rate, item nonresponse, rich responses to open-ended text questions, consistency of responses and decrease satisficing; at the same time, they usually show few problems in completion time or response styles (Göritz, Wolff, & Goldstein, 2008).

We should also check the legal and tax environments when it comes to incentives. For example, in some countries (e.g. Slovenia), the income tax for incentives over a certain amount needs to be paid immediately, which is extremely inconvenient for web surveys.

In web surveys, a special role is also given to lotteries or sweepstakes, where respondents are attracted by the promise of a random draw for a certain prize, which will be awarded to cooperative respondents. Given there is generally one or more prizes per survey, lotteries are much cheaper compared with prepaid or postpaid individual incentives, making them particularly attractive to researchers. Some studies also show that a large number of smaller prizes works better than a few large ones (Deutskens et al., 2004).

Again, we should be aware that lotteries are highly regulated by law. A researcher needs to follow national legislation and pay particular attention to the amount of paperwork in the international context. In the United States, for example, the Council of American Survey Research Organizations (2012) provides certain guidelines on this, and a more detailed explanation can be found in Lord & Miller (2009). A good starting point is to contact a local survey or marketing research association.

In a meta-analysis of experimental comparisons of incentives in web surveys, Göritz (2006b) shows that the effect of offering a lottery vs no incentive is small, with an average increase of 19% in the respondents' odds of responding to the survey. Studies of online panels show a similar effect (e.g. Göritz & Luthe, 2013; Tuten, Galesic, & Bosnjak, 2008). For single web surveys, the results follow a similar pattern, but with more variability: from no effect (e.g. Cobanoglu & Cobanoglu, 2003) to a medium effect (Heerwegh, 2006; Porter & Whitcomb, 2003b), up to 30% higher odds of responding (Sauermann & Roach, 2013).

We conclude the discussion on incentives with reflections on costs. Firstly, when considering alternatives (e.g. incentives vs no incentives, different types and values of incentives), it is essential to compare the total costs per respondent. That is, a 5% response rate with no incentives may cost more per respondent than using incentives which provide a 30% response rate (see Downes-Le Guin et al., 2002). Of course, price per respondent needs to be put into the context of the corresponding data quality. Secondly, when we use incentives, we should seek past evidence that they have already worked for our context. This can be done with a small experimental study, which may then show that they actually have no effect (as for example in Žagar & Lozar Manfreda, 2012).

2.5.6 The Role of the Contacting Process: Mode, Timing and Frequency

When discussing the contacting of potential respondents, we predominantly address – as when discussing sampling (Section 2.2) – the situation of list-based web surveys; we then adapt the principles to other contexts.

There are basically three types of invitation messages: the pre-notification, the main survey invitation and reminders. The *pre-notification* is sent a few days prior to the main invitation and may use a different communication channel than the main invitation (e.g. a mail or SMS pre-notification and email main invitation). The aim is to notify participants about the incoming invitation, to gain their interest and to increase the legitimacy and perception of importance of the survey. While the pre-notification is optional, the *main invitation* – typically in email or mail format – communicates the URL of the web questionnaire, as well as other content. The aim of the *reminders* is to increase response rates through the perceived importance of the study and repeated exposure to the stimulus (i.e. the survey invitation).

2.5.6.1 Mode of Contact

The potential mode of contact with respondents depends on circumstances. Very often we have no choice, as for example with the general population, where only a sampling frame of postal addresses exists (Smyth et al., 2010; Vehovar et al., 2009). Typically, only email is available, while we may also deal with both, and sometimes with telephone numbers. In the latter cases we face the complex dilemma of optimizing a multimode contacting approach.

Emails have an advantage over mail letters in the sense that they are fast, inexpensive and pose a low respondent burden, because a simple click is all that is needed to access the web questionnaire. In addition, they also enable convenient delivery of additional materials (e.g. leaflets, brochures) and communicate directly with the potential respondent, while mail addresses may interfere with other household members.

However, email has certain disadvantages, due to more frequent changes, typos, virus threats (e.g. users dare not click on a URL from an unknown sender), or spam perception. With mail invitations only a few of these problems exist (e.g. incorrect address, unsolicited mail), and to a lesser extent. In addition, mail is more effective in communicating the legitimacy of the survey request, in order to establish trust and to deliver potential prepaid incentives.

Empirical evidence shows that whenever a relationship between potential respondents and a researcher already exists, the email invitation may be equal to or more effective than the mail or postcard approach (e.g. Kaplowitz et al., 2012). On the other hand, when no prior relationship exists, a mail letter may look more legitimate and thus be more effective, as shown by Vehovar, Lozar Manfreda, & Batagelj (2001) for a business survey and Bandilla, Couper, & Kaczmirek (2012) for a survey of the general population.

When both email and mail addresses are available, their combination can be useful. Typically, we use a mail pre-notification in order to increase legitimacy of the survey and prevent perceptions of an unsolicited invitation, an email main invitation to simplify access to the questionnaire, and email reminders, since they are simple and inexpensive (i.e. Millar & Dillman, 2011). We may also do the opposite: that is, use email for the first few contacts and a follow-up mail or telephone contact for increasing the conversion of nonresponses (e.g. Murphy et al., 2011).

The use of SMS on mobile phones (also called text messaging) for contacting respondents can replace email and help to avoid spam perception and attract more immediate attention (an arriving message is usually indicated by the mobile device in an auditory and a visual manner).

With the increased use of smartphones, which also support email communication, the latter advantage may gain less importance. Still, SMS invitations are cheaper than mail and telephone contacts. Bosnjak, Neubarth, Couper, Bandilla, & Kaczmirek (2008) showed that a combination of SMS pre-notification and email invitation works well. Hansen & Pedersen (2012) showed that SMS recruitment for an online panel performed worse than telephone recruitment, but was comparable with mail recruitment.

2.5.6.2 Day and Time of Sending Invitations

In interviewer-administered surveys, the best time to contact respondents is typically during weekday afternoons (F2F) or evenings (telephone), and particularly at weekends. With invitations to web surveys, the situation is much more complex and varies greatly with circumstances (e.g. employees, students). Different studies report on very different best days of the week and best times of the day (e.g. Basso & Rathod, 2004; Faught, Whitten, & Green, 2004; Granello & Weathon, 2003; Sauermann & Roach, 2013; Shinn, Baker, & Briers, 2007; Survey Monkey, 2011; Trouteaud, 2004). The best general advice would be to time survey contacts in such a way that participants are not too busy when they receive the invitation. Observing respondents' habits when it comes to email use, but also the timing of responses during the current survey project, are of crucial importance for deciding on when to send the invitations.

Faught et al. (2004) found that Wednesday was the best day to send email invitations to US manufacturing firms, while some studies found that the day has no effect (e.g. Shinn et al., 2007). This was also the case for students in the Sauermann & Roach (2013) study; however, they were less likely to respond on the same day if an invitation arrived at the weekend. Trouteaud (2004) obtained a higher response rate for emails sent early in the morning than at lunchtime in a survey of large US companies. In research by Granello & Weathon (2003) on

employees of a large state agency, the most effective reminder was sent at 6.00 p.m., yielding the highest completion rate the next day, compared with a reminder sent at 3.30 p.m. For a Dutch online panel of 18–40 year olds, the process should preferably start on a Monday, or at least include a Monday, as Friday invitations are most likely to produce responses on Monday. The midday hours should always be included in the field period (Basso & Rathod, 2004). In an observational study conducted by Survey Monkey (2011) for over 100,000 customer satisfaction surveys and employee organization surveys, Monday was also the day with the highest response rate. Finally, in unpublished observational research conducted on 561,000 cases of the online panel Knowledge Networks (M. Callegaro & C. DiSogra, personal communication) in 2007, email invitations sent on a Sunday and Monday obtained the highest number of completes by the next day, while overall response rates converged to very similar rates when taking into account one email reminder sent three days after the initial invitations.

We can conclude that when we use reminders, the effects of different initial response rates by day or hour line up, so unless we need to conclude a survey very quickly or with a single email invitation, we should not expect too much from a specific timing.

2.5.6.3 Number of Contacts and their Scheduling

In traditional survey modes, a larger number of contacts means a higher probability of participation (P. J. Edwards et al., 2009). Similarly, in web surveys, the number of contacts is one of the most important factors in predicting response rates (Cook et al., 2000), which is also advocated by the tailored design method for self-administered surveys (Dillman et al., 2009).

Pre-notifications increase response rates in telephone and mail surveys. For example, de Leeuw, Callegaro, Hox, Korendijk, & Lensvelt-Mulders (2007) assessed that pre-notification letters in telephone surveys increase the response rate (RR1) from 58% to 66% on average, whereas the results published by Edwards et al. (2009) suggest an even larger effect for mailed surveys, where the odds of response in the case of pre-notification increase by almost 50%. This is in general confirmed also in web surveys (Dykema, Stevenson, Day, Sellers, & Bonham, 2011; Keusch, 2012a; Porter & Whitcomb, 2007; Wiley, Han, Albaum, & Thirkell, 2009), although some studies also show no effect (Felix, Burchett, & Edwards, 2011; Hart, Brennan, Sym, & Larson, 2009).

Similarly, experimental studies (e.g. Kaplowitz et al., 2004) confirm that reminders are effective in web surveys, which was also confirmed with meta-studies (Batanic & Moser, 2005; Göritz & Crutzen, 2012). The latter study warned that reminders may disproportionally attract respondents who then frequently break off.

Regarding the *number of contacts*, repeated follow-ups may have diminishing returns, especially email reminders. In addition, they may be considered as spam, irritating and annoying potential respondents, and making them resistant to future survey involvement. Very often the two-email setting (i.e. an invitation plus thank you note/reminder to all respondents) is enough, because it typically enables us to capture almost all respondents who could potentially be attracted. In such cases, additional reminders would not bring real added value. Of course, exceptions exist and Kaplowitz et al. (2012) reported that a second reminder (third email) increased the response rate from 32% to 40% for faculty and 15% to 19% for students. Similarly, the second reminder added around one-tenth of respondents in the study by Rao & Pennington (2013); however, these respondents had two very common characteristics: they changed the final estimates very little and they also provided a much lower quality of responses.

In addition to the number of contacts, the scheduling and time interval are important. When mail invitations to a web survey are sent, the timing may be similar to mail surveys, where reminders are sent a week after the initial mailing, assuming that this is right after the majority have responded to the initial invitation. With emails, it makes sense to compress this time interval, since responses to email invitations occur much faster, but also rapidly decline. Very often, the bulk of responses is obtained on the first day. After three days less than 10% (or even less than 5%) of responses related to a certain contact are obtained, which was also the case for the WCSC survey in Figure 1.2. On the basis of these data, sending reminders after three or four days is recommended. Crawford et al. (2001) found that more frequent reminders – one group received the first reminder after two days and the second reminder after another two days – yielded a higher and faster response rate (36% vs 33%) than the group with a single reminder after five days. On the other hand, Deutskens et al. (2004), Muñoz-Leiva, Sánchez-Fernández, Montoro-Ríos, & Ibáñez-Zapata (2010) and Sánchez-Fernández, Muñoz-Leiva, & Montoro-Ríos (2012) found no significant difference in the response rate when reminders were sent more or less frequently. However, in these studies, the time interval between the contacts was much longer (one week or more), indicating that a shorter time period between the contacts makes more sense.

2.5.6.4 Length of the Fieldwork Period

Longer fieldwork seems preferable, because we may get additional responses. However, beyond a certain point, this can only negligibly increase the number of responses, with no impact on estimates. Again, the case of the WCSC survey (Figure 1.2) is an excellent illustration of the prevailing situation in web surveys with an email invitation:

- most responses were obtained immediately after the invitation/reminder (after a week they practically disappeared);
- the first reminder added a very substantial increase in the response rate (from 13% to 23%), while the second reminder increased the response rate only from 23% to 24%;
- the observation of patterns gives the impression that another reminder would bring about less than 1% of additional units;

- the changes in the estimates were negligible compared with the data obtained before the first reminder, so from this aspect we could stop there (but a larger sample also has other benefits).

In online panels we may expect an even faster turnover. For example, in an online panel in the Netherlands (Basso & Rathod, 2004), respondents on average replied 1.75 days after the invitation, with approximately 60% of all respondents replying within the first 24 hours of receiving the invitation, and 80% after 2.5 days, while around 5% needed more than a week.

It is true that if we have enough time, we do not lose anything if we wait a bit longer. But when time is an issue, one week after the last reminder seems reasonable enough for the majority of web surveys with email invitations to close the fielding, while in the case of extreme time pressure, this may be reduced to three or even two days.

The question arises of whether it is worth waiting for the last respondents. Often, as we showed for the WCSC survey, we safely assume these respondents will bring no changes to estimates, which is particularly the case when measuring attitudes, and where their potential contribution is below 10% or even 5% of all units. When we observe shares related to factual characteristics or behaviour with potentially larger contributions, things may be different. For example, Kypri, Samaranayaka, Connor, Langley, & Maclennan (2011) and Kypri, Stephenson, & Langley (2004) found a higher prevalence of health risk behaviour and different alcohol drinking characteristics among the last fifth of responding students. Similarly, differences in ICT skills were observed by Irani, Gregg, & Telg (2004) in the last half of the respondents. In any case, daily monitoring of the number of responses gives us enough information to estimate the cutoff point and also about the potential of additional reminders. We must warn that there is no general rule about when to stop, since this depends on the relationship between response rate and nonresponse bias. We may add that telling respondents about the deadline can also help in some surveys (e.g. business ones).

2.5.7 Specifics of the Invitation Format

An invitation to a web survey must persuade respondents to start with the web questionnaire and also ensure the required motivation to complete the entire questionnaire. The classic survey literature states that the invitation to the web survey should provide basic information, legitimacy, instructions and motivation. It should clearly (Dillman et al., 2009, p. 149):

- state what is being asked of respondents;
- describe what the survey is about;
- provide information on how and why respondents were selected;
- state that data will be kept confidential;
- provide additional contact information (e.g. reply email) for any potential questions;
- give instructions on how to access the web questionnaire;
- in the case of email invitation also give alternative contact information – a telephone number and/or a mail address – to ensure legitimacy; and
- state the possibility to opt out of the list, as suggested by professional codes (see also Section 6.3.3 on ethical issues).

These key principles have general consensus and very specific circumstances may allow some of them to be omitted. We may still add some aspects from the *email marketing* literature, because the invitation to a survey resembles the situation where the potential customer needs to be 'moved' to perform the desired action. The corresponding marketing research literature exposes a number of factors which considerably overlap with actions a researcher needs to undertake to make the recipient open the email (subject line and sender of the email), pay attention to it (characteristics and attractiveness of the email) and click on the URL link (characteristics and attractiveness of the offer). The most frequent additional points in the marketing literature are that the invitation should convey a certain urgency and importance to make readers feel special, repeat the same call to action in multiple places in the email, use effective design, and offer an appealing and carefully designed subject line. More aspects and examples from this literature can be found in the Supplement to Chapter 2, *Overview of email marketing approaches* (http://websm.org/ch2).

The problem for a researcher is to shape all this into the right implementation. For this purpose we review below the essential aspects related to personalization, tone and design of the invitation to web surveys. We focus predominantly, but not exclusively, on email invitations.

2.5.7.1 Personalization of the Invitations

According to Dillman et al. (2009, p. 272), personalization of the contacts in web surveys establishes a connection between a researcher and the respondent, necessary to invoke social exchange, and increases the perceived importance of the respondent. The level of personalization depends on the contact information from the sampling frame. For example, if names are known, a personal name can be used in the salutation ('Dear [personal name]'), otherwise perhaps only 'Dear Madam' or 'Dear Sir' should be used, which is also the case when only email addresses are known. As discussed in the section on email setting (Section 2.4.1), emails should be sent separately and individually, which means that only the recipient's email address appears in the addressee line ('To:'), while the sender ('From:') needs to be carefully selected.

Meta-analysis by Cook et al. (2000) and Edwards et al. (2009) found personalization to have a positive impact on response rate in web surveys. A similar positive effect was found also in experimental studies on the use of 'Dear [Name]' vs a non-personalized salutation using email (Heerwegh et al., 2005; Joinson et al., 2007; Muñoz-Leiva et al., 2010; Sánchez-Fernández et al., 2012; Sauermann & Roach, 2013) and mail invitations (Sinclair, O'Toole, Malawaraarachchi, & Leder, 2012), and a study experimenting on sending invitations individually in comparison with sending them to a group (Barron & Yechiam, 2002). Exceptions are the studies by Porter &

Whitcomb (2003) and Mueller, Straatmann, Hattrup, & Jochum (2014) where personalization had no effect on response rates.

Personalization may also have a negative impact, because it further escalates the general situation in list-based samples, where respondents know that a researcher disposes of identification (unique ID code), so technically there is no anonymity. The quality of answers, such as more socially desirable answers, more item nonresponse and less disclosure to sensitive questions, may be affected in consequence. The empirical evidence of this relationship in the case of web surveys is still limited. Heerwegh et al. (2005) found that respondents receiving a personalized email invitation tended to respond with more socially desirable answers to sensitive questions, and Joinson et al. (2007) found that personalized salutations tended to increase the selection of 'I prefer not to answer' option.

Personalization thus has positive effects on response rate, but we should also consider its potentially negative impact on collecting sensitive topics. In such situations we may decide not to personalize, even when we can. Further steps would also be to use the same URL for all units, because respondents know that an email invitation with unique URLs for the web questionnaire identifies them, as does their name. Of course, the non-individualized URL approach enables only one or two email settings, because we cannot track nonrespondents. In addition, trust must be established that the respondent will not fill in the questionnaire more than once. We have some anecdotal evidence of how important anonymity is from unofficial student course evaluations, as well as from employee satisfaction surveys conducted at the University of Ljubljana, when we used the same URL for all units. We also stated in the email invitation that identification was not possible, as the URL link was obviously not individualized, which strongly increased response rates and provided more answers to open-ended questions. The higher trust was also confirmed with corresponding control questions in the survey, when this approach was used only as a second reminder, after initial emails with individualized URLs.

In addition, qualitative testimonials from respondents also confirmed very positive effects of this strategy. On the other hand, there were no signs of fake or multiple responses.

The problem of simultaneously keeping both unique IDs and full anonymity is otherwise hardly solvable. One possible solution is that respondents physically conduct a lottery drawing of the letters containing a random unique ID. However, this may be feasible only in schools or organizations.

2.5.7.2 Providing Motivation and Tone of Request

One of the major roles of the invitation message is to provide the motivation to respond. As already mentioned, several theories regarding motivation to respond can be found in the literature (see Section 2.5.1). According to social exchange theory (Dillman et al., 2009) we can motivate cooperation in (web) surveys by increasing the perceived rewards, reducing the perceived costs and establishing trust that the rewards will outweigh the costs of responding. We summarize those that refer to invitation letters in list-based web surveys:

- The *benefits* can be listed as follows: (a) results will be used to benefit the respondent and (b) society, (c) repeating a plea for help from a researcher can also increase a sense of reward, (d) expressing positive regards by saying 'thank you', (e) stressing group values, (f) letting the respondent know that others have responded and (g) telling respondents that opportunities to respond are limited.
- The *perceived costs* can be decreased by providing information and ways to make it (h) convenient to respond (e.g. providing a link to a web survey in an email invitation), by (i) avoiding subordination language and by (j) emphasizing similarity to other requests/tasks to which a person has already responded (so they are consistent in their attitudes, beliefs and actions).
- The ways of *establishing trust* through the invitation letter include (k) obtaining sponsorship from a legitimate authority, (l) including a token of appreciation in advance with the letter, (m) making the task appear important, and (n) ensuring confidentiality and security of information.

The above list of 14 potential elements in an invitation to a web survey is not exhaustive, but provides a good impression of the possibilities that we may select in our approach.

In the context of web surveys we illustrate some studies that elaborate on the effectiveness of these suggestions:

- *Pleading tone of the invitation*: Two studies (Felix et al., 2011; Trouteaud, 2004) report an increase in response rate when an email invitation with some 'pleading' sentences was used in comparison with no pleading condition.
- *Scarcity* (e.g. telling respondents that they are chosen from a small select group, or stating the deadline of the survey) was shown to increase responses in a web survey by Porter & Whitcomb (2003) and Henderson & Callegaro (2011) (but in the latter case only when revealing the deadline in a survey with an incentive, but not in a survey without an incentive).
- *Similarity to others*: a systematic review of experimental studies on response rates in electronic questionnaires showed that the odds of response were increased when including a statement that others had responded (P. J. Edwards et al., 2009).

2.5.7.3 Format and Visual Design of Email Invitations

With the absence of an interviewer, the format and visual design of the invitation are crucial factors that foster interest in the invitation before it is actually read. Regarding mail invitations, we may learn from the discussion on mail surveys (e.g. Dillman et al., 2009).

Regarding email invitations, some additional specifics are as follows:

- *Visual appearance* should be functional. Fancy email messages with different coloured backgrounds, different font types and sizes, and embedded graphics, usually do not work. Whitcomb & Porter (2004) showed increasing survey response in an experiment on a student sample, when moving from plain text email contacts without a header to text emails with a header and then to an HTML email with a white background and simple header. As far as images are concerned, Chittenden & Rettie (2003) confirmed the hypothesis that higher response rates in email campaigns correlate with more images, although it is not advisable for an email to include many images (average number of images in email was 1.7), since they can be problematic when viewed on handheld devices. In addition, a negative trend appears with fancier HTML email backgrounds and more complex headers (Whitcomb & Porter, 2004).

- *Length* of the invitations is usually recommended to be short and concise (Dillman et al., 2009), with one page for a mail letter and even less for an email (e.g. one screen). All additional information can be published on the questionnaire introduction page or the research project's website. However, in practice, Klofstad, Boulianne, & Basson (2008) did not find significant differences in web survey response rates when long or short email invitations were used, while Kaplowitz et al. (2012) even found longer text to have a positive effect in a web survey for faculty and staff, but not for students. This is contrary to the expectation that shorter invitations work best, given the arguments (e.g. Nielsen, 2000a) that Internet users do not read but just scan the text on the screen, as well as to general experience in email marketing. As Kaplowitz et al. (2012) have argued, longer text may convey 'seriousness' or 'importance' that accounts for the increased response.

- *Spam* is a challenge with email invitations. Standard approaches for avoiding spam are to check if the IP address of the sender has no spam attributers; use text rather HTML message format; send individual emails rather than group emails; avoid marketing words (free, cash, win, promo, prize); use spam analyser tools to examine the message for common content that is known to trigger spam filters; and so on. Such tools provide a spam score and allow changes to keywords and other aspects of the email message to lower the score. Even the use of the word 'survey' in the subject heading may be problematic and susceptible to spam filters. When members of the target population have email addresses from the same institution, it also makes sense to obtain the cooperation of the institutional gatekeepers in order to avoid mass rejection of the email invitations. Special attention should be paid to the email address from which the invitation and reminder emails are sent; it makes sense to use a domain that is recognizable by the email systems of respondents. Some evidence that changing the email address of the sender (a university instead of a research institute) can be successful in overcoming the spam filters has been given by Hartford, Carey, & Mendonca (2007). However, as mentioned in technical preparations (Section 4.1.1), the bulk of anti-spam responsibility is now increasingly moving to email software (or integrated web survey software) which can take professional care of this increasingly complex matter instead of a researcher.

- *Header of the email invitation – 'From' line* needs to convince the participant not to delete an unread email message, but rather that this is an important message from a reputable sender. This line should convey the legitimacy of the survey, so it should be selected carefully. A full formal name may work better than a nickname and an organizational email (e.g. organization.com or university.org) may outperform generic ones (e.g. Yahoo, Gmail, Outlook). However, this all depends on circumstances, particularly the reputation, recognition and relationships among the involved parties (sponsor, client, researcher, software supplier).

- *Header of the email invitation – 'Subject' line* should be informative and professional to distinguish the email survey invitation from spam and marketing messages, so as to gain interest. There is mixed empirical evidence regarding the type of appeal stressed in the subject line. Porter & Whitcomb (2005) showed that the effect of different text in the subject line is modest when sample members are hardly involved with the survey sponsor. Results on mentioning an incentive in the subject line are also not conclusive: while Henderson & Callegaro (2011), Smith & Kiniorski (2003) and Zhang (2011) found emphasizing the prize as positive, Kent & Brandal (2003) found the opposite – mentioning the prize decreases response rates. Kaplowitz et al. (2012) also found that a subject line with a request from an authority figure was more successful in obtaining responses than a subject line with the salient subject request. Henderson & Callegaro (2011) found a polite request in the subject line ('Please provide your feedback') to be more effective than a question ('Would you like to provide your feedback?').

To summarize, these elements need to be tailored to the circumstances (target population, topic and its salience, relationship with the sender, survey aims, etc.). A pioneering study of email survey invitations (Tuten, 1997) showed that the email message is deleted when the subject line does not interest respondents or when they do not recognize the name of the sender. Further elaboration can be found in Dillman et al. (2014, Chapter 9), as well as in the review of the email marketing literature in the Supplement to Chapter 2, *Overview of email marketing approaches* (http://websm.org/ch2).

2.5.8 Towards a Nonresponse Strategy

Fighting nonresponse in web surveys can be relatively simple, as is sometimes the case for list-based web surveys with email addresses readily available (e.g. students, employees, members, customers, etc.). There, often very few alternatives exist besides sending an email invitation plus a couple of reminders. The same is true when we have clear indications that potential nonresponse bias is negligible, so an expensive nonresponse strategy would be a waste of resources. On the other hand, when high response rates are essential, we may need to combine all of the approaches discussed above into an elaborate nonresponse strategy, which can be complicated, expensive and time consuming. This is often the case with online panels. With respect to non-list-based web surveys, similar to the discussion on sampling (Section 2.2), we approximate the principles we have discussed for list-based web surveys.

We need to be realistic in our expectations about the response rate in web surveys, which we mentioned to be around 30%–40% only in the case of a salient topic, good sponsor and with professional survey procedures. A higher response rate (above 60% or 80%) can be expected only in very special circumstances, such as an extremely salient topic (e.g. a post-event or a post-purchase evaluation), a very specific target population (e.g. an association with very dedicated members) or with very elaborate efforts (Murphy et al., 2011). We may also recall that we have many marketing and DIY web surveys where response rates are not only very low, but also irrelevant, as far as certain quotas are met or some key segments sufficiently targeted. Of course, we should also recall that in non-list-based, non-probability web surveys, the nonresponse rate cannot be formally calculated at all. Nevertheless, this does not mean that nonresponse and survey participation are not an issue there.

A researcher needs to deal with nonresponse issues across all three steps of the core web survey process. The pre-fielding step is the most essential, because at that point we define the nonresponse strategy. The activities can be structured into the following sequence:

- Collect empirical and expert evidence on the response rate and nonresponse bias in comparable surveys. Here, specifics across various settings are considerable; for example, surveying medical practitioners requires a very unique investigation (e.g. Pit, Vo, & Pyakurel, 2014) and corresponding experience from other medical surveys is of crucial importance.
- Evaluate potential differences between respondents and nonrespondents. Knowing nothing about this relationship is very risky for defining any nonresponse strategy (see Section 2.5.3 on nonresponse bias).
- Contemplate and simulate potential nonresponse bias, using the approximation Bias $(\bar{Y})$ = $W_n(\bar{Y}_r - \bar{Y}_n)$, under different survey designs, nonresponse strategies and response rate assumptions.
- Establish how important it is to achieve a high response rate and what response rate is required, but consider also that other criteria

may be equally or even more important, such as timing, data quality and costs, as well as the goal and mission of the web survey project.

- Calculate cost per respondent for alternative nonresponse strategies, considering also the data quality perspective. Know that a small sample of respondents can be more expensive per respondent than a large one, but can also provide higher data quality, better meeting the aims of the survey.
- When web survey measures for fighting nonresponse treat the nonresponse problem insufficiently, consider also larger changes in the survey design (Groves et al., 2009), such as isolating and treating problematic segments of the target population with different research designs and nonresponse strategies (e.g. in separate strata), using two-phase sampling, where we subsample nonrespondents and approach them with a more intensive (and usually more expensive and time-consuming) strategy, and implementing a mixed-mode design, or even reconsidering the use of the web survey mode.
- Allocate time and resources for the proper calculation of nonresponse indicators, their monitoring and also to foresee corresponding interventions (e.g. additional reminders in the case of low response).
- Outline the procedures, timing and resources for testing various aspects of the nonresponse strategy. For example, it is very important to specify in advance who will test the email invitation, when and how.
- Foresee the nonresponse related activities in the fielding and post-fielding steps.

We usually start with *simple nonresponse strategies*, which require no or few resources, but have been proven to have positive effects, such as pre-notification, elaboration of the invitation format, improved questionnaire design or reminders.

When this is not enough, we consider *advanced nonresponse strategies*, involving incentives, multimode contacting, mixed-modes or modifications of survey design (e.g. two-phase sampling). Of course, since such actions require another level of sophistication and resources, consulting experts or an experienced researcher is strongly advised.

The essential components of a nonresponse strategy can be formalized into a *recruitment implementation plan*. For list-based web surveys, this means specifying and elaborating the invitation instrument formats (mail, email, SMS) and specifying the contacting process (sequence, frequency, mode, timing). For non-list-based web surveys, the above approaches can be adapted; this also includes the elaboration of eventual recruitment procedures (e.g. banner advertising). There are also measures relevant to both types of web surveys, such as incentives, general promotion, elaboration of introduction page and corresponding technical, managerial, administrative and other types of support. Lastly, the expected benchmarks and actions need to be specified, including monitoring and the corresponding scenarios and interventions for the fielding step. It might seem that preparing all this will generate unnecessary formalization and paperwork, but in the post-fielding step, when we prepare documentation and report on methodology, we need to prepare this documentation anyway. Hence, outlining this in advance can save time and has the additional benefit of providing better preparations (see also Section 2.6 on management).

In the *fielding step*, these plans are implemented and the entire process is monitored. When serious deviations from expected benchmarks are detected, we run the prespecified actions and interventions. For example, we may change the timing, increase the initial sample size, modify our incentive strategy, contacting and invitation formats, etc. We detail these aspects further in Chapter 3.

Certain remedies of nonresponse can be done in the *post-fielding step*, predominantly with nonresponse adjustments. Another important activity is the preparation of the documentation and evaluation of nonresponse rates and biases (see Chapter 4).

In addition, certain nonresponse activities can range beyond the core web survey process. We may perform advanced statistical adjustments, or we may conduct a follow-up survey via mail, telephone or F2F, if our web survey ends up with serious indications of nonresponse bias.

In summary to Section 2.5, when dealing with nonresponse issues, we should be aware that, as in traditional surveys (Albaum & Smith, 2012; Lozar Manfreda & Vehovar, 2002), there is no particular nonresponse strategy that would work as a panacea for all web survey contexts. We should also recall that our discussion on nonresponse strategy stems from the practical purpose, sometimes at the cost of over-simplification of some issues. For example, different variables may require different nonresponse strategies. Similarly, additional complications can arise from the potential interaction of the nonresponse bias with other aspects of data quality, as well as with timing and resources.

2.6 GENERAL MANAGEMENT

Management is an organizational function which guides, organizes, coordinates, optimizes, controls and prepares the web survey activities across all stages. It runs continuously for the entire web survey, typically starting within the preliminary research activities, since a kind of project management plan is often drafted before the core web survey process starts.

Management aspects, particularly the organizational structure and control, are very important, because they form a central point that links all processes and all decisions. In a way we can say that management is often the key component of a successful web survey process. We have already mentioned in the final discussion on questionnaire preparations (Section 2.3.6) that good management is essential to steer the web survey process towards the predefined goal. Particularly with large or complex surveys, standard management approaches and optimization of business processes are extremely important. However, as our focus here is on methodology, we do not elaborate any further on these aspects at this point. We provide additional insight into specific project management issues within the broader context of web surveys in Section 6.2.

A very important managerial task is to prepare – or detail and revise if already prepared in the proposal – the general management plan. For simple web surveys, a detailed formalization might not be needed. Nonetheless, a basic *flowchart* with timing, key *milestones*, which denote the key events of the process, and a list of essential outcomes is very useful when formally prepared in advance, as well as a rough estimate of the required hours of work for the personnel involved and costs of other resources.

Within the specific context of the web survey process we can list the following essential managerial activities, which we need to take into account in our project:

- Management support for pre-fielding (Chapter 2) relates to all the pre-fielding steps, with special attention being paid to situations that interact, overlap or contradict.
- Management support for fielding (Chapter 3) relates to the tasks of recruiting, measurement, processing and monitoring, including any specific interventions a researcher may need to undertake (e.g. the decision to send another email reminder or to prolong the fieldwork period).
- Management support for post-fielding (Chapter 4) covers the activities of corresponding stages, particularly the specifications for data preparation (advanced editing and validation procedures, imputation, weighting), for derived data procedures (coding, recoding) and for the level of integrated reporting, dissemination of results, archiving and exporting.
- The overall management also supports coordination across stages and steps, general monitoring and corresponding interventions, internal and external communication (strategy, plans, rules and activities), administrative support, quality assurance, fulfilling internal and external standards, documentation and archiving, as well as compliance of activities with the general goals of the project.

Special care is needed to coordinate and optimize activities, which stretch across more stages. For example, testing appears as technical pre-testing in technical preparations (Section 2.4), but also as questionnaire testing and field trials within questionnaire preparation (Section 2.3) and as soft launch in fielding (Chapter 3).

Of course, management activities span across the entire web survey process and continuously interact with all the other stages. Correspondingly – and different from other stages – their position in Figure 1.1 (Section 1.2) of the core web survey process does not properly reflect their conceptual role. Nonetheless, the best point at which to discuss these issues is here, following an overview of all the pre-fielding steps.

It is also here, in the management stage, where all pre-fielding preparations are formally elaborated and coordinated, which means that plans and documentation for pre-fielding, fielding and post-fielding procedures are described in writing. Within this context, we should be aware that in almost every survey certain documentation needs to be prepared. A considerable amount of this further depends on circumstances such as external requests from a sponsor or a client. This material then usually appears in the methodology section and/or in the appendices of the corresponding report. It is therefore strongly recommended that we prepare this documentation about processes, methodology and management – at least at the level at which it will appear in the final report – as a by-product of the corresponding preparations within certain stages of pre-fielding. In addition to plans and documentation related to the preparation – which are predominantly located in the stages of pre-fielding – we should not forget about reporting on the implementation of these activities in fielding and post-fielding, such as reports on fieldwork timing, nonresponse indicators, weight computation procedures, fieldwork interventions, eventual changes of plans, etc. We should add that the systematic and centralized production, formatting and archiving of this documentation are coordinated within the management stage, especially in the case of complex web surveys.

Having this documentation in writing as soon as possible is also useful because it clarifies procedures (e.g. sample selection), reinforces the quality of preparation plans (e.g. coding or weighting approaches), helps solve implementation ambiguities (e.g. fieldwork interventions), clarifies responsibilities (e.g. in the case of delays or security problems), strengthens researcher promises in relation to the client or sponsor, as well as saves time when writing the documentation in post-fielding, when we might be busier.

For the effective preparation of this documentation, it is advisable to make a corresponding plan early in the core web survey process, preferably as part of a general management plan. The minimum extent of this preparation is to structure in advance the index and the content of the corresponding methodological chapter and related appendices in the final report. This allows us to manage the preparation of documentation better, but also to specify in advance which of the procedures will be elaborated on more explicitly and formally as stand-alone documents, which is particularly true for the recruitment plan, weighting approach and security policy. Further management formalization in specifying results, deadlines and responsible individuals for certain activities can be very helpful as well.

It is also extremely useful to establish a system, preferably online, where a researcher or the research team (as well as the potential client or sponsor) can continuously record information about mistakes, lessons learned and proposals for changes and innovations in the entire process, in order to improve procedures for future web survey projects.

In addition to the standard managerial issues discussed above, as well as sampling, mode, questionnaire and technical preparations, some other preparatory activities may exist in the pre-fielding step. The spectrum is very broad: namely, special public relations campaigning, unique technical requirements (e.g. special archiving procedures), additional security monitoring, continuous attention to legal considerations (e.g. dealing with legal complaints), external requests related to administration (e.g. recording of specific time sheets, frequent and detailed managerial or statistical reporting), various integration with external processes (e.g. a customer satisfaction survey may interact with sales and direct marketing activities), etc. Formally, it is at this stage where we pay attention (plan, prepare, document, run, coordinate, report) to these activities.

The structure and format of management and other preparation activities vary enormously across web survey projects, but nevertheless we can extract some of the most critical aspects in the form of a checklist to be applied before the fielding:

- Has the web questionnaire been tested and does it run properly on all the main browsers, devices and servers, as well as across key types of respondents?
- Have we assigned the resources and responsibilities to monitor the fielding regularly? Have we clearly specified the corresponding monitoring frequency (daily, weekly, monthly)?
- If we run a preliminary analysis and automatic reporting during the fielding, do we have in place the corresponding resources, planning and regular monitoring?
- Do we have control of all essential managerial activities? For example, do we have pre-specified procedures and rules for all important managerial (e.g. a quality control system for approving outputs), communication (e.g. who responds to certain external enquiries about the survey), methodological (e.g. testing and evaluation of all of the important methodological solutions) and technical activities (e.g. security procedures)?
- Do we have the recruitment and the nonresponse strategy in writing?
- Do we have specifications for the methodology, procedures and timing of all the activities in the post-fielding step (editing, imputation, weighting, coding, reporting, dissemination, exporting, archiving)?
- Do we have a plan (who, what, how, when) for the collection of methodological documentation, preparation and reporting, as well as writing, formatting and archiving?
- Can the web survey software support the output in the format we need (e.g. for paradata)?
- Do we have archiving and tracing for every second of data collection (so we can reproduce

answer proofs for every questionnaire), as well as regular daily backups?
- Do we fully control the activation and deactivation of the web questionnaire, particularly in unrestricted web surveys?
- In the case of a web survey software hosting service (SaaS), do we have the contact information and support in case of emergencies?
- Do we have contingency plans (risk management) for potential technical problems (e.g. with a server) or for methodological mistakes discovered during fielding (e.g. some inadequate wording), as well as for some other problems that may appear, such as legal issues or public scandals brought about by a certain respondent (e.g. some privacy issues)?
- Do we have a crisis management plan in case of unexpected changes in our team or organization?
- If we appoint a subcontractor to run the web survey, or if we are the ones who run the survey for some client or sponsor, are the responsibilities clear, elaborated and documented?
- Do we have scenarios for situations where we obtain dramatically lower data quality (e.g. the response rate) than our expectations?
- If the monitoring of timing and resources shows serious problems, do we have the possibility to change the fielding or post-fielding plans? Do we have procedures to check whether we can still achieve targets with the available resources, or do we need to increase resources or change targets?
- In the case of serious delays in the fielding step, do we have an option for starting a substantive analysis before the end of the fielding?
- Can we ensure that the core web survey process interacts well with the overall management of the project, particularly with the activities which follow the post-fielding, namely advanced statistical analysis, processing, dissemination and report writing?

As mentioned earlier, in addition to the above discussion, which is related specifically to web surveys, we provide a brief reflection on project management issues in Section 6.2.

NOTES

1 http://www.ris.org

2 http://fivethirtyeight.blogs.nytimes.com/2012/11/10/

3 School uniform survey in Slovenia 2014, presentation of results: http://www.websm.org/db/12/17584/

4 Current Population Survey (http://www.census.gov/hhes/computer/).

5 Eurostat (http://epp.eurostat.ec.europa.eu/portal/page/portal/information_society/data/database).

6 http://www.natcen.ac.uk/genpopweb/

7 http://webdatanet.cbs.dk/

8 http://sqp.upf.edu/

9 http://wwwn.cdc.gov/qbank

10 http://surveynet.ac.uk/sqb

11 http://www.europeansocialsurvey.org/

12 http://www.websm.org/db/12/17443/

13 https://www.surveymonkey.com/blog/en/blog/2010/12/08/survey_questions_and_completion_rates/

14 http://question-science.blogspot.com/2012/07/how-to-calculate-length-of-survey.html

15 http://www.blaise.com/Tools

16 For example, the limitations for Gmail at https://support.google.com/a/answer/166852?hl=en

17 For example, mailmerge script for Gmail: http://www.labnol.org/software/mail-merge-with-gmail/13289/

18 This section on paradata draws partially from Callegaro (2013b).

19 Written by Dirk Heerwegh, https://perswww.kuleuven.be/~u0034437/public/csp.htm

20 Available on Lars Kaczmirek's homepage at http://www.kaczmirek.de/ucsp/ucsp.html

21 http://www.ieee-security.org/TC/SPW2014/

22 1KA at the University of Ljubljana, http://1ka.si

23 http://www.oecd.org/std/leading-indicators/31837055.pdf.

24 Kozina, Lea, and, Čertanec, Barbara. 2014. Presentation of the Business Trends Survey. Ljubljana: Statistical Office of the Republic of Slovenia.

3

CONTENTS

Fielding

When preparations in the pre-fielding step are done properly, there is relatively little work left for a researcher in the fielding step. This is particularly true for the measurement stage (Section 3.2), where – due to the self-administered nature of the web survey mode – a researcher/interviewer is completely absent and the respondent fills in the web questionnaire by him/herself. Measurement is closely linked to the corresponding recruitment (Section 3.1), as well as to fieldwork processing and monitoring (Section 3.3), where a researcher is fully involved.

As initially outlined in Section 1.2, the approach used in this book is to discuss issues within the stages in which a researcher is involved. In this chapter we therefore address only the implementation activities that a researcher undertakes in the fielding, while the corresponding preparations were extensively discussed in various pre-fielding steps, where a researcher actually needed to work on them. Consequently, this chapter is relatively short, because it links the results of various pre-fielding preparations, and highlights the most essential activities, together with their implementation specifics.

3.1 RECRUITING

Recruiting is a stage in the web survey process where units are contacted and invited to participate in the survey. It is a direct result of mode elaboration (Section 2.1), sample selection (Section 2.2), technical preparations (Section 2.4) and nonresponse strategy (Section 2.5). More indirectly, recruiting also depends on questionnaire preparation (Section 2.3) and general management (Section 2.6). Recruiting thus strongly relies on the issues we have already discussed in great detail across the stages of pre-fielding, so we will not repeat them here, and assume the reader is familiar with them.

Recruitment activities should follow the nonresponse strategy and corresponding recruitment implementation plan (Sections 2.5.8 and 2.6), where all the related elements (invitations, incentives, contacts, promotion, etc.)

have already been specified. Within fielding, a researcher runs these pre-assigned procedures and selects some variations and adaptations in the implementation, such as (a) enlarging the sample by launching additional pre-prepared supplement samples, (b) intensifying and modifying some aspects of online recruiting and promotion, (c) fine-tuning of the timing (e.g. when exactly to send the next reminder), (d) modifying the number of reminders (e.g. whether to send another reminder or not) and (e) refining the invitation formats (e.g. text in email or in banner ad). Other than these, there is not much else to add – unless we consider the advanced interactive fieldwork designs context (Section 6.1.6) – so below we provide just a few practical comments on implementation.

Let us recall that typical recruiting in list-based web surveys relies on email invitations, discussed previously within technical considerations (Section 2.4.1) and nonresponse strategy (Section 2.5.8). Due to practical importance, we reiterate the dilemma about using a researcher's own email (organizational one or of some popular email service, e.g. Yahoo, Gmail, MS Outlook) or an email from a dedicated web survey software system. We have somehow allowed for the former in some specific circumstances, but in general the professional email system integrated into the web survey software is preferred, because it can handle spam better and can also facilitate recruitment activities. For example, the advanced features of automated scheduling can enable control of the time for sending email messages (e.g. according to time zones).

In any case, before we send email invitations, one final check is recommended, which should focus on who we are sending the invitations to and how they appear to recipients in key email systems and devices. Similarly, it is recommended that we recheck the content of the email for typos or an incorrect URL link, which may be very damaging.

With respect to non-list-based web surveys, recruitment is actually done within the sampling stage, because sample self-selection is in fact also the recruitment. Here, we should stress the importance of the introduction page in the web survey questionnaire, which is treated as a kind of non-question screen when it comes to list-based web surveys (Section 2.3.3). In non-list-based web surveys (e.g. in the case of banner recruitment), the introduction page is much more important (see also sampling, Section 2.2.3), because it is the main place where essential information is communicated to potential respondents, so the discussion related to the format of the invitation letter (Section 2.5.7) should be taken into account. Here, too, a researcher needs to recheck – even when technical and field testing was properly conducted – how the invitation, URL link and questionnaire actually appear in all key browsers (e.g. Internet Explorer, Chrome, Firefox).

We may also recall the discussion on general publicity and promotion of the survey (Section 2.5.4), which can be done during the field-work, so whenever possible and reasonable, this type of promotion should be planned and then implemented. Of course, any ad hoc (positive) appearance in relevant media is also welcome.

3.2 MEASUREMENT

The measurement stage relates to the process of actually filling in the web questionnaire, once the respondent has decided to cooperate. Compared with other stages, the burden in this self-administered measurement session is fully on the respondent. A researcher interacts with respondents only indirectly via the design of the web questionnaire, which is now fixed in content and format. Correspondingly, we focus in this section exclusively on aspects that are directly related to the respondent, while potential interventions by a researcher in the measurement process are discussed in the next section on processing and monitoring.

Successful measurement depends on the quality of the previous stages, particularly questionnaire preparation (Section 2.3) and recruiting (Section 3.1). With proper preparations, the respondent should proceed smoothly, equipped with the needed engagement, providing quality responses with no pauses related to excessive thinking, wondering, confusion, rereading and uncertainty about what to answer, or looking around for explanations.

Nonresponse, motivation and engagement problems can manifest in the measurement stage as breakoffs, satisficing and other data quality issues, which were all extensively examined in discussions on the questionnaire (Section 2.3) and nonresponse (Section 2.5). In addition, specific concerns in the measurement stage can arise from various interruptions on the respondent's side. When these interruptions are linked to the simultaneous or sequential conducting of some other activities, we can talk about multitasking. This can be related to media activities, either on the screen of the same device (e.g. email, web surfing, etc.) or on another device – also called a second screen (e.g. TV) – as well as to various non-media activities (e.g. live socializing, food, various personal disturbances, etc.).

Interruptions and multitasking in web surveys are difficult to measure directly, as this would require a video camera to record the respondent. In reality, we may ask respondents at the end of the questionnaire whether they paused or were involved in other activities. Alternatively, we can use paradata to check whether the survey window was left (e.g. user switched to another window or program) or remained inactive for extended periods of time. Of course, we are not talking here about longer intentional interruptions of the questionnaire answering process – for which the respondent should be offered the option to 'pause and continue later' (Section 2.4.1) – but about various smaller delays and interruptions which still belong to a single web questionnaire session.

To a certain extent, the detection of these interruptions and multitasking can be related to response times and response latencies (discussed in Section 2.4.2). However, direct empirical evidence on the relationship between respondent multitasking and longer response latencies is limited, because, in response latency studies, the research focus is usually on detecting speeding and delays due to ambivalent attitudes, longer cognitive processing, usability problems, lack of knowledge or engagement (Olson & Parkhurst, 2013) and not on interruptions and multitasking. Nonetheless, substantially longer response times might indicate certain interruptions or engagement in multitasking, but can also indicate outliers or some specific patterns of behaviour of certain respondents. Various criteria have been used as benchmarks (Beckers et al., 2011; Callegaro et al., 2009a; Heerwegh, 2005; Stieger & Reips, 2010), which are, however, very often rather arbitrary, but also very specific and related to a particular survey. Nevertheless, certain types of multitasking can be conducted during questionnaire completion with little or even no reflection in response latencies (e.g. some young respondents may successfully fill in the questionnaire and chat simultaneously). In part, as mentioned, an alternative approach for detecting same-screen media multitasking is to observe the switching from the survey window to another window or browser tab (Callegaro, 2013b).

Estimates of the share of respondents in web surveys who interrupted the measurement session at least once depend on the specific survey and approach to measuring multitasking. It can range from a few per cent (Ainsaar et al., 2013; Stieger & Reips, 2010), to around 10% (Beckers et al., 2011; Stieger & Reips, 2010) and up to 50% (Heerwegh, 2005, p. 142; Vehovar, Slavec, & Sendelbah, 2014), as observed in surveys of students. The latter figure seems high, but we should mention that this is not far from the rate of multitasking in telephone interview surveys (C. Kennedy, 2010; Lavrakas, Tompson, & Benford, 2010), where multitasking was also found to be related to satisficing behaviour. It is, in fact, reasonable to expect more multitasking in web surveys, because various options (e.g. email, chat, social networks, TV, games and the entire web) are much more at hand on the same screen.

The approaches used to detect interruptions and multitasking in web surveys are obviously under-researched, as well as the reasons for and potential effects of such behaviour. The same is also true for measures to prevent, intervene or correct for these behaviours. This is another area where further research is needed, particularly with the emergence of portable survey devices.

3.3 PROCESSING AND MONITORING

We saw above that recruitment and measurement stages basically implemented the recruitment plan and the questionnaire, which was created in the pre-fielding step. The remaining actions required from a researcher in the fielding step are minimal, but still very important. On the one hand, they are related to some pre-approved strategies, plans and schedules, such as activating/deactivating the questionnaire (Section 3.3.1). On the other hand, they can be triggered by specific requests for help (Section 3.3.2) and interventions (Section 3.3.3) due to unforeseen problems. All require careful monitoring of the fieldwork processes (Section 3.3.4).

3.3.1 Activation, Soft Launch, Full Launch and Deactivation

The fieldwork is run to some pre-assigned plan, elaborated and integrated within the general management stage in pre-fielding (Section 2.6). Usually, this starts by activating the questionnaire, which enables respondents to access the web questionnaire and also to store the answers in the real datafile. Immediately after activation, recruitment can start (e.g. invitations are sent, URL is promoted), usually with some manual action commands from a researcher. It is very important to eliminate or denote clearly beforehand any test entries from the datafile, because later we may not be able to separate them from the real ones. This can be particularly damaging for paradata analysis, because the test entries may not use branching and can be done much faster without any substantive consistency. An alternative approach is to create a new copy of the questionnaire and start with an empty survey.

Before the full activation and launch of the survey, it is advisable also to have a soft launch, which involves a small subset of respondents. In list-based samples this usually means sending the invitation only to a part of the sample, while in non-list samples it means activating only limited promotion (e.g. banners only on a few websites).

A soft launch allows quality checking by collecting some responses and analysing them, and helps to ensure that there are no errors in the questionnaire programming, recruitment or any of the other fielding activity. It also allows us to obtain an estimate of actual questionnaire length, which can then be used in the communication for the full launch. Obviously, all these features resemble the pilot study in questionnaire field testing (Section 2.3.5); however, the key difference is that responses from the pilot study are not entered into the real datafile and analysis. On the other hand, the very essence of the soft launch is to replace or supplement a pilot study whenever there is not enough time to run it, which is in fact often the case, particularly in marketing research. Even when a pilot study is run properly, we still suggest starting with a soft launch before the full launch, and rechecking the procedures and preliminary results.

After the end of the measurement stage, the questionnaire needs to be deactivated, either at some pre-assigned date or according to certain *stopping rules*. The latter resembles the concept of sequential sampling, where we add the units to the sample until some statistical criteria are met (e.g. minimal number of units in a certain segment). In web surveys this is typically implemented by limiting the number of respondents, either overall or across certain parts, using various types of quota settings. A survey may be automatically deactivated after the stopping rule is met, but it is better if a researcher is first alerted that a stopping rule has been met, because closing the survey typically involves some other recruitment aspects (e.g. removing questionnaire URLs from the web, stopping promotional activities, etc.), in addition to the deactivation itself.

We need to avoid situations where a recruited unit that is willing or even eager to participate is faced with a notice that the survey has already been closed. Particularly in DIY research, we often encounter invitations to participate in web surveys that have already been deactivated, which can be very frustrating for respondents, and is also considered unethical. If links to the questionnaire cannot be removed (e.g. we post the URL in some forum), we may – if the web survey software allows for this – change the content at this link (i.e. replace the questionnaire with some other web content) or set up automatic redirection, so that the URL points to some web page with an explanation, information on results, follow-ups of the study, etc. Even worse is the situation – which happens because a researcher forgot to deactivate the survey or did not care about it – where a survey is actually closed, but the web invitations and links to the questionnaire are still active and responses are still stored. This is unethical because these responses are in vain – nobody will use them. For this reason most web survey software has a default activity duration setting (e.g. one or three months), which then needs an intentional action from a researcher to change it.

3.3.2 Providing Help

We have already discussed the instructions, definition and help in Section 2.3.3 on questionnaire layout. In addition, within the fielding step, we should also make sure we provide live help, so as to give feedback to questions from respondents. Respondents may encounter various technical issues, from slow Internet connection to forbidden access or problems with the questionnaire. In most cases a researcher is responsible not only for insufficiently pre-tested email invitations and questionnaires, but also for incorrect cookie or IP settings. However, sometimes respondents truly have some technical problems of their own. In any case, the above issues may raise questions from respondents which require some guidance and explanation. We need to prevent such questions from respondents as much as possible. For example, in the case of certain minimal technical requirements (e.g. JavaScript, Flash, etc.), respondents should automatically receive clarifications and instructions, which then eliminates the need to ask questions.

Clear contact information, containing an email address or a feedback form, should be provided for respondents, at least in the invitation, but also on the introduction page or in the footer of the questionnaire web page(s). It is also helpful sometimes to have some kind of help button with FAQs and contact information on every web page of the questionnaire. Adding telephone contact information in particular increases the legitimacy and credibility of the survey, but then also requires some resources for the corresponding support. Balance is needed to prevent too many enquiries, which can cause redundant communication.

Respondents may also have various other concerns and complaints, such as a wish to obtain their completed questionnaires for archiving, a demand for research results, a request to sign off from the invitation list (opt-out) or a desire to explain their reasons for explicit refusal. They may also wish to complain about and criticize the survey, both technically (e.g. font size) and methodologically (e.g. no progress indicator, no back button, unclear instructions, questions of low quality, etc.), as well as substantively (e.g. 'inadequate' questions, lack of open-ended questions to elaborate their thoughts, etc.). For salient topics in web surveys outside online panels we may expect that up to around 1% of respondents will provide some email reply (e.g. ask for results, comment on subject). This depends strongly on circumstances (e.g. extremely salient and controversial issues raise more feedback) and particularly on how explicitly the feedback option was offered and visually exposed. When telephone feedback is involved, we can typically expect much less reaction; nonetheless, roughly up to 0.1% may call. To prevent excessive feedback, we should provide sufficient online help, relevant FAQs, an exhaustive 'thank you' page and, in particular, an open comment question at the end of the survey for whatever comments respondents may have. Nevertheless, in the case of large samples or with problematic topics, a researcher should be ready to process more feedback.

When an external web survey software service or subcontracting research agency is involved, it may be useful to separate technical and substantive questions, which then requires a coordinated help and feedback strategy.

In any case, once a researcher promises help and interaction in the invitation, this should then also be organized, so that professional and rapid answering is provided. This is particularly true when telephone feedback is foreseen.

Although the provision of some interactive help to respondents is essential, the focus of a researcher should be on creating a good questionnaire and sufficient communication in the invitation and introduction page, instead of explaining, repairing, clarifying and apologizing for badly designed features.

3.3.3 Fieldwork Interventions

By fieldwork interventions we mean actions undertaken by a researcher because unexpected events occur in the fielding step. We thus do not talk about *implementation variations* and other modifications foreseen in advance by the scenarios of the recruitment plan, but about additional activities which a researcher performs to improve data quality (e.g. increase the response rate), and sometimes also to save the web survey project from serious problems (e.g. attacks on the server).

Most frequent interventions relate to additional recruitment efforts (e.g. prolongation of the fieldwork, additional invitations, extra promotion, etc.) which were not foreseen in the initial recruitment plan. In more serious situations, we may even change the entire research design (e.g. switch to mixed-modes).

Various requests for closing the survey or removing some of its parts can also appear due to allegations of legal violations (e.g. use of email without consent, privacy violations, spam evidence, illegal content). Similar requests can also be based on substantive, methodological or ethical concerns and can come from respondents, target population, general public, methodology experts, subject professionals or involved stakeholders.

An even more frequent issue is certain methodical problems. For example, serious errors in branching can be discovered in the middle of the fieldwork or essential errors can be discovered in the wording of the questions. Here, we then need to be very clear about the protocol and technical procedures required to modify the questionnaire during fielding.

Very serious reasons for intervention can arise from technical problems with the web survey software or the server, which can make a web questionnaire unavailable. A researcher can also intervene and additionally adjust the questionnaire for technical problems at the respondent's side, such as inadequate browser type (by providing support for that browser) or blocking due to an organization's security policy (by negotiating with the organization).

Needless to say, the majority of problems requiring intervention can be prevented by quality activities in pre-fielding, so they are very rare in professionally prepared web surveys. Nevertheless, we still need to be aware of these possibilities and ready to face them.

Again, we discussed above only interventions due to unexpected events, which then require some additional action from a researcher, while various other fieldwork interventions can be foreseen and automated in advance.

Thus, our discussion here exceeds changes in the questionnaire answering process, which are outside of its default flow. This potentially means specific intervention with respondents who progress too quickly (e.g. speeding), too slowly (e.g. cognitive problems), or when they provide otherwise problematic data quality (e.g. satisficing). In principle, many aspects of the quality of responses (e.g. item nonresponse, inconsistencies, validity, reliability, indication of satisficing) can be checked online during the measurement stage. Respondents could then be helped, stimulated, directed to a simpler version of the questionnaire, or their sessions postponed and rescheduled for a more suitable time. Of course, such online interventions can also be counter-productive, due to their intrusiveness and the 'big brother' effect.

Similarly, we exclude from our discussion here the specific fieldwork interventions related to interactive fieldwork design (see also discussion on engagement in Section 2.3.4), which we discuss within the broader methodological context (Section 6.1.5).

3.3.4 Monitoring of the Fieldwork Process

Product quality cannot be achieved without underlying process quality (Lyberg, 2012). Correspondingly, to achieve the goals of a web survey project and provide quality survey results, we need to ensure the quality of the web survey process, where monitoring is an essential component. Formally, monitoring the survey process is strongly related to response statuses (Section 2.5.2) and nested within general management (see Section 2.6).

It is very convenient if the most essential insights of the fieldwork process are offered to a researcher by the web survey software as a summary presentation of key indicators. When they are related to process performance, they are also called *key performance indicators* (KPIs), which need to be defined early in pre-fielding. When we observe them during fieldwork, they are usually summarized and presented on a single page provided by the web survey software, also called a *dashboard* page. The corresponding analytics and graphics in principle resemble the analytical tools for website visitor traffic, but they also have various specific features. The indicators automatically shown by the web survey software vary and a researcher is not limited only to them, but can also run additional calculations. Practical illustrations of typical dashboards are available in the Supplement to Chapter 3, *Examples of fieldwork monitoring and diagnostics* (http://websm.org/ch3).

The essential KPIs are related to real-time insights into the response process, which includes insights into the structure of the basic technical response statuses of the units and into nonresponse indicators, such as unit response rates, item nonresponse rates, respondent completeness rates and breakoff rates (see Section 2.5.2). Particularly important here is the corresponding graphical presentation of the response process in time (as in Figure 1.2 in Section 1.3.4).

In addition, many other KPIs can be useful. Firstly, the above response indicators can be filtered according to response status, time interval (months, weeks, days, hours) and separately for eventual versions of the questionnaire, based on language, target group or internal branching (e.g. random groups). Breakdown across key control variables (e.g. gender, age, region) or across variables from paradata (e.g. device type, monitor size, computer operating system, browser type) is also useful. Next, it is helpful to obtain formal calculations of AAPOR response rates (e.g. AAPOR, 2011; see also Section 2.5.2) or at least their approximations.

Various additional insights can be useful:

- The structure of referrals – that is, URL addresses of where the respondent came to the survey – and the geographical location of respondents (using IP numbers) are particularly valuable for non-list-based web surveys.
- In list-based web surveys with email invitations integrated into the web survey software system, we expect detailed statistics of sending email messages: what was sent, when and to whom. In addition to an insight into the overall structure of response statuses, inspection of each unit needs to be enabled (e.g. call record data).
- Monitoring the length of the survey and time spent per each page, where certain trimming needs to be applied to remove the extremes (e.g. 5% of extreme cases) when calculating averages. Comparisons with expected time can be useful for observing deviations and potential problems.
- The monitoring of appearance for various prompt messages (Section 2.3.3).

Ideally, the real-time insight should include details about the response quality of the units, such as unusable responses, fraud, extreme speeding, extreme satisficing and other problematic data quality aspects. Unfortunately, generating such information requires complex statistical procedures, which are usually run only at the data preparation stage (see Section 4.1). Nonetheless, any quality diagnostics are more than welcome here, such as the distribution of units (e.g. share of units that were straightlining). We believe that, in the future, web survey software will provide increasing sets of these diagnostics and their availability will become an important criterion for selecting software.

In addition to the above activities, an essential part of monitoring is to run basic summaries (i.e. frequency distributions, descriptive statistics) of all the variables in the questionnaire during the data collection process to check the distribution and deviations.

The above insights and indicators should be observed in certain contexts. Ideally, we first select the activities to monitor (e.g. participation of the units), then we select the corresponding indicators (e.g. response rate), evaluation criteria (e.g. benchmark of 40%) and also any corrective actions (e.g. sending another reminder). Let us illustrate a few examples of KPI usage in web surveys and the corresponding fieldwork interventions:

- When the response rate after two reminders is below the expected benchmark (e.g. 20% instead of 40%), we may consider another contact (reminder).
- When the questionnaire breakoff rate is above the expected benchmark (e.g. 40% instead of 20%), we may recheck the questionnaire, particularly the pages where breakoffs are occurring.
- When the number of certain prompts is excessively high (e.g. 40% of units entered the incorrect number), we may consider improving the question instructions.
- When there are no responses for a certain period (e.g. day, hours), we may check server performance and technical errors.
- When the socio-demographic structure of the respondents deviates from the expected one (e.g. too many women, 80% instead of 50%), we may change the recruitment strategy (e.g. promotion, additional contact, differential incentives). This is also true when the structure of referrals (e.g. we expected 50% of units

to come from Facebook, but we only have 20%) or IPs (we expected 30% from certain counters, but only have 3%) deviates from expectations.

We should separate fieldwork monitoring from the remaining diagnostics conducted in the post-fielding processes (Section 4.1), where we inspect each unit separately and then decide on its status (complete, partial, unusable) and potential remedies (e.g. imputations). Further illustrations are provided in the Supplement to Chapter 3, *Examples of fieldwork monitoring and diagnostics* (http://websm.org/ch3).

In conclusion, we should add that things get more complicated in the case of mixed-mode systems, online panels, longitudinal surveys and very complex surveys, as well as when an interactive fieldwork strategy replaces the implementation of more or less fixed recruitment plans with limited variations. However, as this extends beyond the basic survey mode, we briefly reflect on it only in Section 6.1.

CONTENTS

Post-fielding

Once we finish with fielding, the post-fielding step begins. Unless in some special situations, we do not collect any additional responses in post-fielding.

According to the structure of the core web survey process (Figure 1.1, Section 1.2), in the post-fielding chapter we discuss the activities of the following stages: data preparation (Section 4.1), preliminary results (Section 4.2) and data exporting and documentation (Section 4.3).

The criteria for separating the post-fielding step from advanced analyses, processing and valorization – which are outside of the core web survey process – are the focus on methodological issues instead of substantive ones and the integration of ICT support in the web survey software. Accordingly, certain activities related to post-fielding stretch beyond the core web survey process, either because they are related to substantive content aspects (e.g. report writing) or because external software support is involved (e.g. statistical analysis).

Despite the focus on web survey related aspects – for ensuring completeness of the treatment – in this chapter we also address certain essential post-fielding activities which are general and independent of the survey mode. As a consequence, we often refer to the standard survey methodology textbooks, such as Groves et al. (2009), Biemer & Lyberg (2003) and Iarossi (2006).

Similar to fielding, post-fielding activities need to be planned and prepared within the pre-fielding step (Section 2.6). However, with the activities of fielding, considerable resources are needed in the pre-fielding step for the preparation of related tasks, which are then simply implemented in the fielding (e.g. nonresponse strategy). The opposite is true of post-fielding, since the tasks related to post-fielding are predominantly conducted there. Preparations for post-fielding require relatively few resources, compared with their implementation.

We may add that in general the notion of post-fielding roughly overlaps with the concepts of post-survey adjustments, post-collection processing (Groves et al., 2009) and the data processing stage (Biemer & Lyberg, 2003).

4.1 DATA PREPARATION

Data preparation relates to the clarification of response statuses (Section 4.1.1), editing and validations (Section 4.1.2), imputation (Section 4.1.3), weighting (Section 4.1.4), and coding and recoding (Section 4.1.5). The raw input here is a datafile with web survey responses, as well as with other primary data (paradata, meta-data, auxiliary data), while the output is the *final database*, ready for statistical analysis, preliminary results, data export, archiving and further utilization.

Data preparation depends on the activities in the pre-fielding and fielding steps. Bad planning, overlooked aspects, questionnaire design errors, rushing, lack of resources, problems with management, weak fieldwork monitoring, etc., can all have painful consequences. They manifest in various aspects of lower data quality. At the data preparation stage we can fix some of these problems, but only to a certain extent.

Particularly critical are technical database preparation (Section 2.4.1) and questionnaire preparation (Section 2.3), especially the wording, selection of response categories, adequate layouts for various types of questions (e.g. allowing enough space for open-ended questions), error-free implementation of branching, proper handling of missing values and non-substantive responses, reasonable real-time validations, as well as properly elaborated definitions, explanations, help and instructions.

As in the entire post-fielding step, the data preparation activities need to be considered in overall management (Section 2.6). Planning and scheduling are particularly essential here, because data preparation – in addition to questionnaire preparation – is often the lengthiest stage of the core web surveys process.

4.1.1 Establishing Response Statuses

The very first activity is to establish and check the statuses of the units and individual entries (i.e. the respondent's answers to a certain item). This is the basis of all further data preparations, including response rate calculations and data quality diagnostics. In a broader sense, these clarifications belong to data editing; however, as the main focus here is only to ensure the exact status of the data and not to check, evaluate or edit them, we treat these aspects separately.

4.1.1.1 Eligibility, Completeness and Quality Status of the Units

The following issues are of key concern here: ineligible units, multiple submissions, unit non-response, completeness statuses and data quality diagnostics.

Ineligible units were defined within the discussion on sampling (Section 2.2) and we expect that they would have already been excluded in the sampling. However, in some cases eligibility can only be verified during fielding by asking appropriate questions (e.g. foreign citizens in a voting study) or acknowledging that a certain unit moved or died. Eligibility should therefore be rechecked, and if some units do not belong to the target population, we should exclude them from the final database or denote them correspondingly.

Multiple submissions bring more challenges. They occur when a unit responds or starts responding more than once. We discussed this issue in database preparation (Section 2.4.1). The situation is simpler if we have unique identification (ID code) of the respondent at our disposal. When this control is not used to prevent duplications, although we dispose of ID codes, we may end up with more records of the same respondent with the same ID code. The solution is simply to identify the multiple entries which belong to the same ID code, inspect them and keep only the highest quality entry. The problem is more severe when we do not have ID codes, as in non-list-based web surveys. There, at most we may use cookies and IP numbers, but both approaches have problems, as discussed in Section 2.4.1. Alternatively, we can discover duplicate units with statistical matching algorithms, which identify duplicates with some probability. Typically we match by socio-demographics (e.g. same

age, gender, etc.), key substantive responses and paradata (e.g. device, browser, etc.). We assume here that respondents attempted multiple entries because the initial entry was not completed or the respondent was not sure if the responses were saved, or due to some other misunderstanding. In the case of intentional falsification we face a very different problem, which we discuss later in this section.

Unit nonresponse identification was outlined in Section 2.5.2, where we elaborated on the nonresponse process for list-based samples with email invitations, and we discussed adequate technical preparations related to email settings in Section 2.4.1. Certain rules are needed to transform the emails in which the respondent did not click on the URL of the questionnaire (e.g. nothing returned, error in sending email, automatic reply, etc.) into ineligible, unit non-response and unknown statuses. Preferably, we can be even more precise and convert them into the AAPOR final disposition codes (AAPOR, 2011).

Completeness statuses can be problematic to establish. We focused on this in Section 2.5.2, where we discussed approaches to identifying complete, partial and unusable units. We can add here that paradata – for example, timing for each page, level of mouse movement, longer inactivity, changes of responses, excessive clicking, missing items (Stieger & Reips, 2010) – can help us to assess these statuses. For example, if a respondent finishes the questionnaire extremely quickly in comparison with the median time, we can assign the status of an unusable unit.

Quality response diagnostics rely on respondent data and paradata, which enable the calculation of various quality indicators of the units, such as the percentage of item nonresponse, satisficing indicators (e.g. straightlining), consistency levels, evidence of multitasking, etc. This diagnostics can be an integral part of web survey software, but dedicated external services also exist, especially for online panels.

Ideally, we develop a precisely defined and consistent approach to assign the exact statuses – or best possible approximations – to each unit in the datafile, using all the available data for the aspects of eligibility, completeness and data quality. Some of these statuses can be assigned automatically within the fielding step, while others need to be run with special procedures in post-fielding. In any case, each unit needs to have at least one general status assigned, which can have further subcomponents for eligibility, response status, breakoffs and completeness. In advanced web surveys, each unit should also have at least one quality status, which can have subcomponents related to the various data quality aspects discussed above.

4.1.1.2 Missing Values and Non-Substantive Responses

In addition to clarifying the status of the units, we also need to identify the status of each individual response. As well as the expected substantive responses, various types of missing and non-substantive responses also exist, sometimes called invalid or non-valid responses. Part of the coding of these responses is done automatically during fielding by the web survey software, while the rest needs to be done in post-fielding. In any case, we have to inspect and check the assignment of these statuses carefully.

The status of (a) item nonresponse needs to be coded differently from legitimate non-substantive responses, explicitly offered to respondents, such as (b) 'don't know', (c) 'prefer not to answer', (d) 'not relevant' (or any other non-substantive response). When the respondent is not presented with a certain question, this needs to be coded differently, according to the specific reason: (e) the 'not applicable' status appears due to questionnaire design (i.e. branching) and is very different from item nonresponse, (f) preliminary breakoff performed in the preceding questions, (g) questions that were added to the questionnaire after a certain unit began answering the questionnaire; or due to (h) an entirely empty questionnaire.

For example, if we first screen for smoking and then ask only smokers about the number of cigarettes smoked yesterday, the answer to this question can be any number of cigarettes (1, 2, 3, 4 …), including zero '0', which should be clearly separated from 'no answer', which means item nonresponse (a). We may also offer explicit refusal (c) or explicit 'don't know' (b). The 'not applicable' status (e) should be automatically assigned for non-smokers screened out in the first question.

In addition, we may reserve another set of statuses to label values removed due to low quality (e.g. inconsistency, fraud, satisficing). Ideally, each unit as well as each item and each individual entry in the datafile should have a related meta-variable labelling the descriptive and processing characteristics, such as the type and source of the variable and statuses of the units, together with the eventual edits, changes or imputations for units, and particularly for individual entries. This fits also into requests for the creation of a special data imputation flag (Heeringa, West, & Berglund, 2010), so the user can distinguish between the original value and the imputed one. In practice, however, the final database typically has only a one-dimensional variable for each item. In addition to substantive values, negative values are often used for missing values (e.g. -1, -2, …) and for non-substantive responses (e.g. -99, -98, …). This requires special treatment for rare situations, where substantive responses are also negative (e.g. temperature).

4.1.1.3 Reporting on Response Statuses

Only when all response statuses – at the unit level, as well as at the level of the individual entry – are properly set, can we determine various response indicators. This should include: (a) standard response rates (AAPOR, 2011), at least RR2 or RR1, but preferably also all final disposition codes; (b) a report on breakoffs, preferably separated into introduction breakoffs, questionnaire breakoffs and total breakoffs, as well as insight across questions where breakoffs appear; (c) completeness statuses of the questionnaires (complete, partial and unusable statuses, preferably according to technical and substantive classification); (d) distributions of item nonresponse (across variables and across units); and in advanced situations also (e) various other data quality diagnostics (e.g. speeding, satisficing, multitasking).

While in certain situations some of the above diagnostics may need to be calculated manually, the majority are often routinely reported in the survey dashboards of web survey software. There, we can also expect more detailed analytics of the key response statuses across fieldwork time, regions/countries (geographic locations of IP numbers), referrals and device types.

More can be found within the corresponding Supplements, *Examples of fieldwork monitoring and diagnostics* (http://websm.org/ch3) and *Examples of response rate calculations* (http://websm.org/ch2).

4.1.2 Validation and Editing

Validation and editing mean we inspect and sometimes also change the collected data to retain as much as possible the properties intended in the original measurement design (Groves et al., 2009, p. 345). In other words, we check (validate) and also correct (edit) for erroneous and inconsistent entries (Waal, Pannekoek, & Scholtus, 2011).

In web surveys, it is possible to perform all validations in real time, during questionnaire completion. Real-time validation produces prompt messages that invite or even force respondents to check their answers and correct them. However, it is often difficult to predict all possible validation rules in advance. Another reason for not performing all validations in real time is because this may result in many prompt messages that can annoy the respondent and potentially increase breakoffs. Below we discuss validation and editing issues from various aspects and levels.

Basic validations are the most essential data validations and are usually performed during fieldwork measurement. They predominantly relate to open-ended entries (text and numbers), such as preventing wrong types and formats (e.g. entering text in a number box) or range checks (e.g. age of 200 years). They also address key elementary consistency (e.g. a respondent of 12 years of age could not report voting) and simple calculations related to a single variable (e.g. constant sum question). These validations are essential and when they are not corrected in real time by respondents, they need to be performed at the data preparation stage.

Item nonresponse validation is usually the most frequent validation implemented during fieldwork measurement. It essentially relates to a prompt message that appears when the respondent proceeds without providing an answer; we have already discussed it in Section 2.3.3. However, this is in fact optional, because item nonresponse may not be an error, omission or inconsistency, but legitimate behaviour in a voluntary survey, so forcing a respondent to answer may be controversial. Nevertheless, researchers very often prefer to prevent or minimize item nonresponse by using various prompts. If item nonresponse nevertheless occurs in the datafile, this is dealt with by imputations, which we discuss in the next section.

Advanced validations are the core of the validation and editing activities, which are conducted at the data preparation stage. They usually involve more variables that are interrelated. These validations need to be systematic, and profound checks have to be made for all aspects that are deemed important by a researcher. The criteria depend on circumstances. For example, in business surveys, responses to different items need to be consistent (e.g. number of employees or turnover, when summed across organizational units, should not exceed the total institutional level). This may be checked with web survey software, with general statistical software (e.g. SAS, Stata, IBM-SPSS, R), by manually running various conditions, or with specialized software for data editing (Groves et al., 2009, p. 346).

When validations find a serious error or inconsistency, this is replaced (edited) either with a specific type of missing value (e.g. if respondents answered a question which was not applicable to them), or with some plausible alternative values (e.g. if reported expenditures exceed the reported income, then the income is replaced with the sum of expenditures).

The key is not to invest too much time in these validations and editing, but to accept that respondents can be slightly incoherent. The number of validations in simple attitude surveys is usually small, but can grow rapidly in the case of behaviour and factual questions (e.g. events, expenditures, income, travel, etc.). In this case many validations can turn into inefficient use of resources. In some business surveys, editing activities may even take up the largest part of the entire survey budget. In addition, excessive validations, also called over-editing, may not achieve noticeable quality improvements (Grandquist & Kovar, 1997).

Substantive validations include careful and systematic observation of univariate statistics for all variables: frequencies for questions with nominal and ordinal measurement and descriptive statistics (mean, median, variance, minimum, maximum) for variables with interval and ratio measurement, usually in combination with graphical distributions (e.g. histograms). Some key breakdowns may also be inspected (e.g. means across gender or age). These inspections require the methodological and substantive knowledge of an experienced researcher, in contrast to previous validations, which can be done purely technically. Substantive validations are very important, because they provide essential legitimacy to the survey data for further processing and use. A similar inspection is useful also in testing, as well as during fieldwork, in order to detect problems on time and provide appropriate interventions.

Further data inspection can be conducted and tailored to the needs of the users. Examples are advanced screening procedures for data quality assurance and fraud detection (Blasius & Thiessen, 2012) or various data cleaning procedures (Osborne, 2012), such as checking for normality or outliers. However, these typically fall beyond the post-fielding step of the core web survey process, because the results are usually not part of the final database, where we do our best to keep as much of the originally reported data as possible and make changes only for very convincing reasons.

We have seen that the validation details and overall editing strategy are very structured issues and as such need to be carefully organized, specified and planned at the data management stage of pre-fielding (Section 2.6).

4.1.3 Imputations

We have already presented a specific type of imputation related to editing, which arises from validations. However, the notion of imputations is typically defined as a general practice of inserting artificial values for missing data, predominantly for item nonresponse. The corresponding occurrences, causes, consequences, bias and prevention were dealt with extensively in Section 2.5.2, while here we focus only on compensations using imputations. In addition to item nonresponse, imputations can also be used for other types of missing values or even for non-substantive responses (e.g. 'don't know'), but additional assumptions and justifications are needed. For example, we need to demonstrate that 'don't know' answers were in fact surrogates for item nonresponse, as in the case of the Slovenian plebiscite survey (Rubin, Stern, & Vehovar, 1995).

When considering imputations for item nonresponse, we first need to assume that status assignments (see Section 4.1.1) have been conducted successfully. Thus, item nonresponse should be clearly identified and separated from other missing values, non-substantive responses, as well as from substantive responses (e.g. a value of zero). Similarly, we need to distinguish between respondent-level item nonresponse and item-level item nonresponse (Section 2.5.2).

Unlike validations, imputations have fewer specifics in web surveys. There are case studies addressing imputations on web survey data (e.g. Chang, Frost, Chao, & Ree, 2010), but almost no studies focusing on potential methodological specifics, to our knowledge. We provide a general overview here and talk about imputations for missing values, where we would otherwise have expected a response from an eligible unit.

Once the missing data and the corresponding indicators are identified, we first observe the patterns of missing data. These can be explored with standard statistical packages, which increasingly include such procedures (e.g. the command 'mvpatterns', which displays rates and patterns in Stata); this is true also for some advanced web survey software, or with specialized software for dealing with missing data.

There is no general agreement on how much data can be missing to avoid imputations. Some authors even propose 1% to 2% (Heeringa et al., 2010, p. 108), but this depends on why and how the data are missing, particularly on issues related to bias (see Section 2.5.3).

A default approach might be to ignore the missing data by using various 'listwise' procedures meaning that only complete cases are included in the analysis. However, this may result in a serious loss of data. For example, if we have 10 variables, with 10% of missing values appearing randomly for each, we end up with only 35% of complete units. Especially if we need to run some multivariate analysis (e.g. regression), this is perhaps an unacceptably high loss. Thus, we strongly advise against this simplified practice, particularly for key variables.

An appropriate imputation strategy depends on the type of missing data (see Little & Rubin, 2002), which can be *missing completely at random* (MCAR), where the probability of a missing value is unrelated to any other variable, *missing at random* (MAR), where the probability of a missing value can be explained with other variables which we dispose, or *not missing at random* (NMAR), where the probability of a missing value is related to the value of an unobserved variable(s) or to an unknown missing-data mechanism. It is therefore very important that we include rich and relevant variables in the survey, which can potentially explain the missing-data patterns (see Peytchev, 2012) and create the MAR condition.

The 'listwise' procedure mentioned above works only under the assumption of MCAR. However, in reality, MCAR is rarely the case, so it makes sense to also perform basic checks for MAR, simply by observing the variability of missing values in the target variable across other variables (e.g. age, gender, etc.). If we discover variations, this indicates that we may have an MAR situation, which can then be dealt with by standard imputation methods.

These methods vary from the least appropriate (e.g. when we simply impute the mean calculated from responding units) to more standard approaches (cold deck, hot deck, nearest neighbour, predicted value from some model, expectation–maximization (EM) algorithm) for MAR situations.

The most complete approach, which is also the most demanding, is based on multiple imputations (Little & Rubin, 2002), where we create more imputation values and thus also obtain more datasets. This approach has the advantage of providing proper calculations of the sampling variances for any variable. The underestimation of the variability is often a basic deficiency of single imputation strategies. Users are easily lulled into the belief that imputed values are real, while the effective sample size is actually much smaller than the artificial one that is built up with imputations. As a consequence, the confidence intervals are too narrow.

It is beyond the scope of this chapter to provide further description of imputation methods, so we refer the reader to the appropriate textbooks (e.g. Enders, 2010; Little & Rubin, 2002; Särndal & Lundström, 2005; Waal et al., 2011). We may also add that some simple imputation procedures are implemented in some web survey software, while fully elaborated procedures exist in all the main statistical packages, as well as in specialized software.

Unfortunately, applied statistics has not yet developed procedures by which a researcher can press a button and all the missing values will be properly imputed. Nonetheless, we are slowly approaching this situation. For now, the main problem with imputations is that they require time, resources and competences. Therefore very often it is the imputation strategy which most clearly separates advanced web surveys from simple ones. DIY approaches often provide no imputations. However, the reality is that imputations need to be performed and professional statistical advice is typically required for related actions, except for trivial surveys, surveys with negligible item nonresponse or surveys with clear MCAR patterns. When imputations are performed incorrectly, this can be very damaging for data quality. This is perhaps the most critical aspect of web surveys and refutes the impression that web surveys can be implemented 'easily'.

The best approach to avoiding resources for imputation is by preventing item nonresponse (de Leeuw & Hox, 2008), which we discussed in Section 2.5.2. Given the problems and complexities of imputation exercises, we might have a better understanding of why this prevention takes the extreme form of placing hard prompts on all questions in so many web surveys, despite the dangers of annoyance, breakoffs, satisficing and ethical concerns.

We may add that imputations can also be used for unit nonresponse, where they parallel weighting procedures (discussed below). A very interesting approach is the split questionnaire – already mentioned in the sampling (Section 2.2.2) and questionnaire stage (Section 2.3.3) – where questionnaire modules are randomly assigned to subsamples and then statistical matching (i.e. data fusion) algorithms are used to impute large portions of survey data for the units that were not presented with certain modules in the survey (Johnson et al., 2014).

4.1.4 Weighting

As with imputations, weighting has relatively few specifics in web surveys; however, a considerable literature dealing with this topic exists, not only on implementation, but also on methodological specifics in web surveys. The impetus came perhaps from the early years of web surveys, when large samples were collected inexpensively, but were skewed and non-representative. This created pressure to investigate weighting procedures

for solving this problem (Vehovar et al., 1999). Otherwise, the problem of fixing skewed samples with weights is not new, nor is it restricted to web surveys. We thus limit the discussion to a general overview and stress a few practical aspects related to web surveys.

Generally, we can identify three broad phases in weighting. Firstly, we establish base weights, which originate from the sampling selection design and are proportional to the inverse of selection probabilities. For example, in obtaining overall EU estimates from Eurobarometer surveys – which have around $n = 1,000$ units in each country – weights need to be used to incorporate large differences in the population size of the countries. With certain simplifications, we could say that each unit in $n = 1,000$ represents 2,000 citizens in a country of 2 million, and 20,000 citizens in a country of 20 million.

Next, we calculate nonresponse weights to compensate for unit nonresponse. For example, we can apply a weighting class adjustment when we obtain a 40% response rate in a certain age–gender class (e.g. women above the age of 50). We then use weights that are proportional to $1/0.4 = 2.5$ for all responding units in this class. With this, each respondent from that class represents 2.5 eligible units originally included in the sample.

Finally, using the product of weights from the previous steps, we further adjust the data to known population values with *population weighting*. With this our sample perfectly matches the controls (e.g. region etc.). This is very convenient for substantive users of the data, although typically it has relatively little effect on estimates, so it is sometimes also called *cosmetic weighting*. Various standard approaches (post-stratification, raking) are used here, as well as more complex ones, such as advanced calibration.

Weighting formally assumes ideal probability sampling, where the effects of the weighting are then usually small. With increased discrepancies from the ideal probability sample – due to nonresponse, non-coverage and selection bias – weighting can have a greater effect on the estimates. This is particularly true in the case of non-probability samples, where we can apply the philosophy from sampling

(Section 2.2) about implementing probability sampling principles in a non-probability setting.

The result in the majority of weighting practices is that the weighting has relatively little effect on estimates; however, this is typically still perceptible and worth doing. We should carefully observe the direction of the changes in the estimates after weighting, because the true value is often moving further in the same direction. At most, weighting removes up to half the bias, which has been confirmed in numerous studies, from Vehovar et al. (1999) to the recent meta-analysis on weighting in web surveys by (Tourangeau, Conrad, & Couper, 2013, p. 33).

A specific approach, often mentioned in the web survey context, is so-called *propensity score weighting* (Steinmetz et al., 2014). The idea originates from observational research by Rosenbaum & Rubin (1983) and was popularized extensively for non-probability web surveys. In the early years of web surveys, this approach sometimes appeared in marketing research as a magic wand that fixed problems arising from non-probability sampling, non-coverage and nonresponse (e.g. Taylor, Bremer, Overmeyer, Siegel, & Terhanian, 2001). Later, the method was studied extensively and sometimes in specific circumstances it truly showed certain advantages compared with selected alternatives (R. P. Baker et al., 2013). However, the differences were still very moderate and can by no means solve the issue of inference from non-probability samples.

We further comment below on a few practical aspects, which appear frequently with weighting in web surveys:

- With web surveys we often have samples, where specific base weights are not needed. This is particularly true in the case of a census and a SRS.
- In non-probability samples we have no base weights and also no nonresponse weights, but use population weighting to compensate for the selection, nonresponse and non-coverage at once.
- The weights result in an increase in sampling variance, which can be easily estimated with the variance (i.e. the square of the standard

deviation) of normalized weights, where the average weight equals 1.0. The increase is usually below 40%, which would otherwise mean that the confidence intervals are almost 20% broader. To limit this increase, we often cut the weights – after normalization – when they exceed a value of four or even two.

- Differences among various weighting approaches are usually very small, as long as they use the same amount and detail of auxiliary information.
- It is very important to include the right control variables in the weighting (and also into the survey), so we may consider obtaining control variables from other reliable surveys on the same topic.
- For this purpose we should use standardized socio-demographic questions and not invent new questions (e.g. for education).

A general introduction to weighting is the one by Groves et al. (2009) and specialized treatment is provided by Valliant, Daver, & Kreuter (2013), while a specific overview for web surveys is outlined in Bethlehem & Biffignandi (2012). As with imputations, some advanced web survey software already provides integrated support for certain approaches, while elaborate procedures exist in standard statistical packages and in specialized statistical software. The simplest practical approach is perhaps raking (Battaglia, Hoaglin, & Frankel, 2009), where we specify population margins and make our sample fit them.

As with imputations, weighting also requires time, resources and competence. When faced with complexity and complications, expert guidance is needed.

4.1.5 Coding and Recoding

In the data preparation stage, a researcher can produce various derived data (Section 2.4.1), which are then entered into the final database, and are thus available to all users.

Coding is the process of producing derived data by assigning numbers to open-ended text entries (e.g. words, phrases, comments), but also to multimedia entries (e.g. sounds, pictures, videos). The purpose of assigning numeric codes is to include them in the quantitative analysis, which can provide rich insight by calculating frequencies, correlations, bivariate analysis, segmentation, etc. We will focus predominantly on the coding of open-ended text entries (i.e. words, phrases, ideas), but the principles apply also for other types.

For coding we need a coding list of target values (categories), also called a coding scheme or a code structure. This sometimes exists in advance (e.g. official occupational codes), or we need to develop it specifically for our variable (e.g. open comments about a new service). A coding list should have categories with the following characteristics (Groves et al., 2009, p. 332): (a) a unique number for each category; (b) labels to describe all answers assigned to the category; (c) exhaustive categories, so that all answers can be assigned to a category; (d) mutual exclusion of categories; and (e) categories must fit the purpose of the research.

In the case of a large sample, we start with a small random subsample or stratified subsamples of answers (e.g. 100–300), writing down recurrent themes (categories, codes). If a considerable number of answers cannot be coded, a new category needs to be added. We might also introduce another level of coding for some of the most frequent categories. Sometimes each entry has more dimensions. For example, in the case of open comments on a new service, in addition to the topic (category), the intensity (scale) dimension could be added.

Once a preliminary coding scheme has been developed, it can be further applied and tested for its efficacy in coding the answers. When coding is done manually, it is considered best to have another coder check it over a small subset. Measures of intercoder reliability are then applied to assess the quality of the coders and the coding scheme (for details see Biemer & Lyberg, 2003).

The coding approach depends strongly on the nature of the problem. Hundreds of comments require a different approach than millions of ones (e.g. customer feedback for a global corporation service). In official statistics, staff are typically specifically trained for large coding exercises, while in the commercial sector, outsourcing is frequent and the label of *verbatim coding* often appears for these services.

A user-friendly interface is extremely important for the support of manual coding. This is also true for semi-manual coding, where the roots of words are automatically recognized as an identical code (e.g. apples and apple), but some manual control is still needed. In this regard, there are considerable differences between the coding of words (e.g. brands, names, fruits) from contextual coding, where concepts, themes and dimensions are extracted from a paragraph or long text. Fully automated coding – with or without pre-existing coding schemes – is also on the rise, due to natural language processing technologies, which build on developments in artificial intelligence, data/text mining and machine learning (e.g. Esuli & Sebastiani, 2010). Various specific approaches were developed for certain types of problems, such as sentiment analysis, and strong links were established to visualization and various types of big-data analysis.

Many specialized software packages for coding exist. In addition, coding is offered within the standard statistical packages (e.g. IBM-SPSS, SAS, Stata, R), as well as with some web survey software. The latter is extremely practical and time saving, to the extent that the integrated functionalities do not seriously lag behind the ones in specialized software.

There are several alternatives to coding in the post-fielding step. As discussed in Section 2.3.2, a frequent mistake with open-ended text questions is to use them where a closed-ended question would do. This is for example the situation when we have up to 20 options and all respondents know them well. Using closed-ended questions in these situations instead of open-ended ones can save a lot of coding resources.

In situations where the coding scheme is known in advance, another alternative is the interactive potential of the client scripts that can be used to stimulate real-time coding at the respondent's side. We have already elaborated on these approaches in Section 2.3.2, where we discussed answer trees, drill-down menus and autocomplete functions of drop-down menus. Another alternative is *text string matching*, used in occupational coding (Tijdens, 2011), where respondents type the word or first few letters of the word that is related to their occupation, and then they obtain a set of best matches from a pre-assigned database, so a final selection can be made from them.

In addition to coding open-ended text entries, we can produce derived data also by assigning additional values to other question types. This is usually called *recoding*, since categories (i.e. raw code options) already exist, but for whatever reason we want to change them. Here, however, only the most essential recoding fits into the data preparation stage. For example, 10-year age groups are often calculated by recoding the answers, where respondents report their year of birth.

Sometimes, more complex derived data can also be produced and assigned in the data preparation stage, for instance some scores, calculated from more variables (e.g. in knowledge or reading performance surveys).

Of course, each data analyst may then produce more derived data of his/her own for the purposes of specific analyses.

4.2 PRELIMINARY RESULTS

With respect to preliminary results, we talk here about corresponding reporting (Section 4.2.1) and dissemination (Section 4.2.2) to the extent that they are integrated into web survey software. Software features vary greatly, as well as the needs of users. Sometimes these preliminary results can already fulfil the needs of a researchers, clients or users, while very often additional in-depth analysis is required. Thus, we limit the discussion here to reporting and dissemination, based on intelligent automated statistical data analysis, supported

by integrated web survey software. Advanced analyses, which run on specialized statistical software, as well as various types of manual dissemination, are thus outside of the core web survey process.

4.2.1 Reporting

After the data preparation stage is concluded, preliminary reporting can provide an insight into substantive results. In addition, this can also support data validations and editing inspections (Section 4.1.2), serve as monitoring in the fielding step (Section 3.3.4), or can be an input for further use. Sometimes this preliminary reporting may already suffice for all purposes, especially with simple web surveys.

Preliminary reporting is increasingly becoming an integral part of the core web survey process, and 93% of web survey software already supports the automatic generation of univariate summary statistics (frequencies, descriptive statistics) and default graphs (92%), and half of them also offer cross-tabulations (Vehovar, Čehovin et al., 2012; see also Supplement to Chapter 5, *Web survey software analysis*, http://websm.org/ch5).

Here, measurement levels and question types are essential for selecting the default statistical analysis (J. F. Healey, 2011). Different analyses are suitable for nominal, ordinal or interval/ratio measurement of a single variable, as well as for tables and advanced question types. For examples of default reports for various question types, readers can consult the Supplements *Questions and layouts in web surveys* and *Measurement levels* (http://websm.org/ch2).

Some advanced web survey software already integrates powerful statistical features which resemble standard statistical packages. Nevertheless, advanced statistical work – done internally within the web survey software or externally with standard or specialized statistical packages – is no longer considered to be part of post-fielding, because it is predominantly a substantive exercise.

In our discussion on statistical inference (Section 2.2.4) we stated that probability samples can ensure appropriate estimates and that the results from any sample need to be reported in an inferential context, with standard errors, confidence intervals, etc. We may add here that typically we assume an SRS, which is also the default approach in all standard statistical packages. The same is true for simple sampling variance estimation formulae, which are used to calculate variances, standard deviations, standard errors and confidence intervals. This is often considered unacceptable simplification, particularly with complex samples (stages, strata, phases, replications, panels, weights, imputations) or complex estimators (e.g. ratio or regression estimator), which require special estimation procedures (Heeringa et al., 2010). Thus, whenever an SRS sample is assumed, but we have complex samples, weights, complex estimators, or even non-probability samples, we should be aware that we are entering the art of approximations. In such situations, firstly, a clear warning is needed and, secondly, the discussion from Section 2.2.4 fully applies here. This also includes the warning related to reporting unreliable estimates and to situations where we analyse all units (census) instead of a sample.

In addition, we need to be aware of the limitations brought about by the fact that data preparations (e.g. editing, imputations) may not be completed, or are not done at all, when preliminary reports are produced.

4.2.2 Dissemination

Dissemination of the survey results can be a complex and lengthy activity which needs to be carefully planned within the preliminary research activities (Section 2.6).

Web survey software provides some powerful features that enable a researcher, client and other users to obtain effective access to a rich array of preliminary reports. Not only can a specific preliminary report be disseminated automatically, but a real-time report can be generated online at the very time of the enquiry. The latter is particularly valuable for surveys where continuous real-time insight is required in the fielding step. In addition, target users can be automatically alerted according to certain criteria, such as regularity (e.g. weekly reports) or conditions (e.g. critical sample size achieved). Real-time insight into raw data can also be disseminated, which may be useful for reviewing open-ended text questions or when units with very specific characteristics appear.

Web survey software increasingly offers integrated tabulation features, where a rich supply of specialized tools already exists. Here we mean online access to a user-friendly interface that enables users to run interactive statistical analyses (cross-tabulations, segmentations, filters, graphs or even multivariate statistics). Compared with alternative offline analyses using standard statistical packages, integration into the web survey software has many advantages: access from any device, real-time data, no data preparation or transformation, no stage of transmitting the datafile to the user and no software installation. There also exists a rich control of differential levels of access to the system and increased data security. All these may also eliminate printed summaries, which are often the essential format of results.

Different levels of access are a very important feature enabled by advanced web survey software, where we can specify the functionalities (analysis, data, exports, editing, etc.) provided to various levels of users. The tools which support feedback from various stakeholders (customers, employees) in large organizations have especially elaborated functionalities. Namely, in such large, structured and hierarchical organizations access to information needs to be set and controlled very precisely. We have already illustrated this by the example of enterprise feedback management (EFM) in Section 1.3.6.

4.3 DATA EXPORTING AND DOCUMENTATION

In addition to preliminary reporting and dissemination, which essentially relate to the statistical results produced within web survey software, the other stream of outputs from the web survey relates to exporting the final database (Section 4.3.1) and taking care about statistical disclosure (Section 4.3.2), documentation (Section 4.3.3) and archiving (Section 4.3.4). This enables effective direct usage with external software (e.g. for statistical analysis) and general accessibility of data archives.

4.3.1 Data Exporting

With web surveys the data may not be exported at all, because the summary statistics, tabulations, graphs and all the other analyses can be sufficiently run within the integrated features of the web survey software. Nevertheless, exporting is usually still needed, either for in-depth statistical analyses or for external processing and archiving.

In any case, it is very important that the final database, as the ultimate output of the data preparation stage, possesses certain basic features, such as the initial description, versioning, authoring, time stamp and tracking of changes.

Preparations for data exporting start in the pre-fielding step when the technical aspects are dealt with, particularly when the database is defined (Section 2.4.1) and with technical testing (Section 2.4.4), as well as with pilot tests and field trials (Section 2.3.5). Through these activities we check how the actual data exporting is run, how standard export formats work (e.g. Excel) and how the complex data structure is exported (e.g. branching, modules, nested data). Special care is required when it comes to exporting variable names and labels, as well as measurement level and type properties of the variables, as these might not be preserved correctly after exporting. Limitations also exist sometimes with respect to the number of variables, number of cases, variable names (length, characters allowed) and the treatment of complex data structures. Special attention is also needed for identifier variables, which must be strictly separated from survey data. Depending on the project, specific paradata and metadata exports should also be checked: which paradata are included in exports (i.e. only basic and default paradata, such as time stamps and user device strings, or more advanced ones) and in what format (organized and ready for analysis or still in the form of strings).

Web survey software typically offers some standard exports, at least to Excel and CSV (character-separated values) format, meaning that tabular data (number and text) are stored in plaintext. Unfortunately, with the latter, some data might be lost in the process (e.g. labels). Nevertheless, this format is very common and should be offered as an intermediate option in case of problems with other more specific exports. That is, some variable types (e.g. combined tables, social network data) might not be recognized when exported directly to standard statistical packages (such as IBM-SPSS, SAS, Stata, R), because labels and data structures cannot always be fully preserved.

4.3.2 Statistical Disclosure

Respondents are generally provided with the assurance of privacy, which also includes the statement that their responses will be kept confidential and reported in an aggregated fashion only, not allowing identification. As already mentioned in technical preparations (Section 2.4.3), survey responses first need to be separated from personal identifiers, such as email addresses, names, physical addresses, respondent or customer identification numbers and detailed geographic information. Some device-type paradata, such as IP addresses, are also increasingly treated as personal information.

Another threat appears when summary statistics, cross-tabulations or survey datasets (microdata) are made public. The chances of indirectly identifying a respondent can become considerable, particularly in business and official statistics surveys. According to professional codes and ethical standards, a researcher is responsible for preventing statistical disclosure, which can also be a legal issue. Thus, we need to restrict the levels of control variables, such as age, gender, education, geographic information, etc., because when included in cross-tabulations or into the final database, this may allow disclosure of the respondents if the cells are too small. For example, we may eliminate ZIP codes and city names when it comes to geographic information, and keep only region, country or state, so that crossing with age and gender controls ensures enough units (e.g. 10) to prevent identification. Various approaches have been developed to prevent disclosure in cross-tabulation and in microdata. The reader can refer to Hundepool, Domingo-Ferrer, Franconi, Giessing, Nordholt, Spicer & de Wolf (2012) for an advance treatment of this subject. A good start is also the overview by Groves et al. (2009, p. 308) and Vehovar, Zaletel, & Seljak (2008).

4.3.3 Documentation

Data documentation is an extremely important and often overlooked stage of the core web survey process. Poor documentation leads to potential mistakes and misinterpretations. It may also unnecessarily waste the time of other users and analysts who will use and interpret the datafile. In addition, a researcher who authored the survey may forget many issues in a one-year time span.

To minimize this problem, special metadata describe the survey in a standard format. We expand below the key methodological information that needs to be documented (ICPSR, 2012): (a) sampling design and data collection method; (b) use of incentives; (c) information about the fielding of the survey, timing and data collection organization; (d) details on eligibility, eventual screening procedures, indicators of the response processes and other data quality indicators; (e) questionnaire preferably exported into a stable standardized format (e.g. XML) and, if applicable, the respective translations;

(f) codebook together with coding schemes, recoding procedures and eventual derived variables; (g) description of data imputation procedures and weighting procedures; (h) content summary and other reports produced with the dataset; and (i) URL of preview of the questionnaire to obtain insight into interactive features. In addition, for formal archiving, (j) other administrative data are needed, such as authors' contact information, targets, organization, principal investigator, conditions of use and also various archiving specific data. More formally, this description should reflect internationally accepted structure and standards, such as Data Documentation Initiative (DDI)[1].

Ideally, by reading the survey documentation, the user should be able to reproduce the results and findings without putting further questions to the team which collected the data.

The *codebook* (f) is particularly essential here and should contain standard information on survey questions, from the wording to response categories and related codes (Mohler & Uher, 2003). In web surveys, codes associated with response statuses, discussed in Section 4.1.1, are particularly important. Codebooks are often automatically produced by statistical packages and also by many web survey packages, which have recently started to produce advanced, interactive, user-friendly and hyperlink-type codebooks.

With respect to the questionnaire (e), in addition to textual files (e.g. PDF, RTF) and spreadsheet formats (e.g. one question per row), web survey software can often export it together with structures (e.g. branching). The eventual programming code should be exported separately. In addition, the URL of the questionnaire preview is also important, in order to see how the questions and the flow actually look and interact. Some web survey software can also produce a series of screenshots of the entire survey in PDF format.

As discussed in the section on management (Section 2.6), it is strongly recommended that documentation is collected during the prefielding and fielding steps, in order to save time, and used for clarification and management, as well as being a reminder of details.

4.3.4 Data Archiving

Data exporting and documentation are not enough to enable long-term survey usage. For this we need a stable archiving format and location.

However, first we need to distinguish internal archiving for a researcher or research organization from standardized external archiving run by a professional data archiving organization (e.g. listed within the global CESSDA archiving network). The latter is based on elaborate procedures and complex archiving standards, which may also require considerable resources. Typically these data archives predominantly contain surveys conducted with public resources, such as official and academic surveys. Certain differences exist across countries, so national data archives need to be consulted for further insight.

Commercial organizations typically have no intention of archiving surveys publicly, although some exceptions exist. Nevertheless, for quality archiving, they must also comply with the principles of the archiving profession. Various standards and certificates exist to support professional approaches (e.g. ISO, DSA[2]).

With many web surveys, special archiving procedures might not be needed at all, because web survey software services already keep the essential archives of the datafile, questionnaire versions, exports, outputs, dashboard with essential fieldwork activities and diagnostics, link to questionnaire preview, etc. This already fulfils almost all of the above documentation requirements ((a)–(j)), except for a few general descriptions, which cannot be produced automatically, but should be added manually. Of course, all this relates only to a corresponding specific web survey software format, which may not be available in the long run.

In addition to this, modern web survey software usually provides support for further copying and reuse of the questionnaires and questions. Thus, each user can build their own archive library of questionnaires and questions, while public libraries are also available by the web survey software.

It seems that web survey software already takes good care of archiving. However, if we think 5 or 10 years ahead, we do not know whether web survey software, used for specific web surveys, will still exist and support surveys in old versions. This is a very relevant issue for single DIY web surveys, and even more so for organizations. There is no doubt that it is valuable to keep data from past surveys, where so much effort has already been spent; however, the question of how much resources we are ready to spend for archiving procedures arises.

The data archiving profession already provides methodology, standards, formats and procedures which ensure long-term archiving (ICPSR, 2012). Some web survey software (e.g. Blaise) already implements some archive standards and uses them with exports. We should also acknowledge that the unique DOI (Digital Object Identifier) can be assigned to certain survey data. This ensures permanent identification for further referencing and enables the data citation index, which parallels the science citation index.

For further reading, as mentioned, data archiving organizations provide lots of information about their activities (ICPSR, 2012). Specialized books also exist (e.g. Corti et al., 2014) as well as simple online manuals (see for example a manual by UK Data Service[3]) where important basic guidelines are summarized, while in the case of external formal archiving activities, consultation with experts is strongly advised in the pre-fielding step. As with other post-fielding activities, archiving needs to be considered in pre-fielding (Section 2.6), particularly because archiving spans the entire web project (e.g. affects the selection of the variable names).

NOTES

1 http://www.ddialliance.org
2 http://www.datasealofapproval.org/
3 http://ukdataservice.ac.uk/media/440320/depositsurvey.pdf

5

CONTENTS

Selected topics in web survey implementation

In this chapter we tackle three special topics regarding the implementation of web surveys in practice: new devices that can be used to answer a web questionnaire, online panels and web survey software. Although these issues have already been mentioned in the core chapters of this book (Chapters 2, 3 and 4), they bring so many specifics and are of so much interest to survey practitioners that they deserve additional attention. We have decided to discuss them separately in a special chapter so as not to interfere with the core web survey process, where we presented a general discussion of the possible implementation procedures, which do not change as quickly as the variability of the devices used by respondents, the possibilities offered by online panels, and the web survey software available on the market.

In Section 5.1 we take into account the existence of a fast-emerging group of respondents who use their smartphones and tablets to answer surveys, either because they choose to do so or because the survey organization asks them to. We discuss current knowledge of the topic because nowadays we cannot design a web survey and expect all respondents to use a desktop/notebook to access and respond to it.

Online panels use web surveys to obtain information from their panel members. These panels account for a large portion of web surveys. They bring many benefits to researchers in terms of ease of data collection, speed and cost, but at the same time pose many challenges in terms of data quality and sample representativeness, as we discuss in Section 5.2.

Finally, a web survey cannot take place without web survey software, to which Section 5.3 is dedicated. We provide a taxonomy of this software and review some of the key features a researcher should be aware of when choosing and using it.

5.1 SMARTPHONES, TABLETS AND OTHER DEVICES

The shift towards answering web surveys on multiple devices, particularly smartphones, is perhaps the most obvious and also the most turbulent trend related to web surveys in recent years. We discuss this issue by first introducing general terminology, typology and trends in adopting new devices (Section 5.1.1). Next we address the strategies a researcher can undertake (Section 5.1.2) and the related specifics of these devices (Section 5.1.3). We also overview the basic recommendations for designing web surveys on mobile devices (Section 5.1.4) and discuss the issues brought by mobile survey applications (Section 5.1.5). We conclude with an overview of software specifics (Section 5.1.6) and future challenges (Section 5.1.7).

5.1.1 Introduction to Multiple Devices

At the beginning of web survey research, a major technical focus was to make sure that the web questionnaire – recall that we are talking about the basic web survey – was displayed correctly in different browsers and on different operating systems. The main assumption was that the respondent would be answering the survey using a desktop/notebook. In this chapter, we discuss a recent and fast-growing phenomenon, namely *web surveys for multiple devices*. With this notion we refer to web surveys that are answered on different devices that have access to the Internet but cannot be categorized as traditional desktop and notebook computers. In the first place these include *mobile devices* – small, handheld (portable) computing devices, typically having a display screen with touch input or a small keyboard. In this context we predominantly talk about *smartphones*, which are mobile phones with advanced computing capability and Internet connectivity, and *tablets*, which are small mobile computers that are primarily operated by touching the screen.

As of January 2014, 58% of US adults owned a smartphone, and 42% owned a tablet[1]. In the EU, during the same time period, 52% of people with a mobile phone also had a mobile Internet subscription (European Commission, 2014). More recent figures can be found in *Internet statistics*, Supplement to Chapter 2 at http://websm.org/ch2.

We may add that with respect to socio-demographic characteristic, the mobile devices repeat the pattern of Internet penetration. Users of smartphones, particularly early adopters, are younger, more educated, etc. (Peterson, 2012; Stapleton, 2011), in comparison with desktop/notebook survey respondents.

However, we should be aware that other mobile devices are also capable of accessing the Internet and enable web surveying. Within this context we should mention *feature phones* and *phablets*. Feature phones are mobile phones with more limited functions compared with smartphones, but they usually still allow web browsing. The restriction of features often relates to limitations in Wi-Fi Internet access, touch-screen capabilities and the potential to download applications. However, there is no clear and standardized way of distinguishing feature phones from smartphones, so we do not elaborate on this issue. Phablets are mobile devices designed to combine the functions of smartphones and tablets, with size somewhere in between the two. Examples of other mobile devices are *e-readers* (or e-book readers, which are mobile electronic devices designed primarily for the purpose of reading e-books and periodicals), *MP3 players* (portable digital consumer electronics devices capable of storing and playing digital media). In addition to mobile devices, Internet access is available also on *video game consoles* and *interactive TV (ITV)*, where various data services, such as on-demand delivery of content, online shopping and banking, are added to traditional television technology.

We may illustrate the proliferation of these other devices with 8% of all Internet users (age 16–74) in a Eurostat 2013 survey for Slovenia (which is around the EU average with respect to various ICT penetration rates),[2] who also use these other devices – besides desktop/notebook computers, tablets and mobile phones – to access the Internet. This is a considerable share, since all these other devices are designed for a single and very specific purpose (e.g. gaming or listening, reading, watching), being less likely to be used for general activities related to web surveys. At present, there is little empirical evidence that they are used for accessing web surveys beyond a negligible proportion. However, this may change in the future, particularly with increased use of ITV; despite being on the market for more than a decade. ITV is still in the early adoption stage due to various technical and commercial reasons. Different competing and overlapping concepts, solutions and products appear here, namely IPTV, Internet TV, web TV, smart TV, Apple TV, Chromecast, which are all related to the integration and convergence of TV with the Internet.

As the range of devices with access to the Internet is mushrooming, the possibilities of designing and answering surveys from different devices multiply. Expanding on Peterson's (2012) definition of intentional and unintentional usage of a certain device, *intentional and unintentional device-specific web surveys* could be defined, where the *intent* refers to that of a researcher (i.e. survey designer), not the respondent. In an intentional device-specific web survey, there is a one-to-one match between the device the questionnaire was designed for and the respondent's device. A web questionnaire designed to be taken on a desktop/notebook and actually completed on a desktop/notebook fits this definition. With unintentional device-specific web surveys, there is a mismatch between the device design and the respondent's device.

The most problematic combination is when a questionnaire designed to be completed on a desktop/notebook is completed on a smartphone. This is also the most common scenario with unintentional device-specific web surveys since an increasing number of respondents use smartphones to read and answer emails. For example, figures for the end of 2013 show that mobile devices have a share of email read of almost 50%.[3] Because an email invitation is the primary invitation method for web surveys, it is not surprising that many respondents also decide to complete a web survey just by clicking on the link on the screen of their smartphone.

By looking at the device used by respondents to access web surveys, the company Kinesis (2013b) reported that in the United States in the third quarter of 2013, 51% of web surveys served by its platform were initiated from either a smartphone or a tablet. For Europe, Kinesis reports a much lower proportion of 10%. Peterson (2012) found that the percentage of surveys initiated from a mobile device in the United States varies by target population and by topic, from a maximum of 30% to a minimum of 1%. Finally, in non-probability online panels, up to 20% of members use mobile devices (Fisher & Bernet, 2014), while in probability online panels this share is around 10% (Toepoel & Lugtig, 2014).

These figures illustrate the trends well, so we can expect that in developed countries, within a few years, when smartphones further improve and expand, they will be increasingly used for accessing web questionnaires. Therefore, they need to be considered as a serious option in almost every web survey.

The unintentional device-specific case is problematic because respondents have moved ahead of the survey industry in terms of adapting to the new technology. According to the 2011 technology survey of 230 marketing research companies in 36 countries, carried out by Meaning Ltd, only 15% of companies modified their questionnaires for smartphones, while many could not even provide a percentage of respondents using smartphones (Macer, 2012), suggesting that they did not modify their questionnaires. Similarly, at least 30% of companies did not know (or could not provide an estimate) if their respondents were accessing their web surveys via a desktop/notebook or smartphone or tablet in 2012 and 2013 (Macer & Wilson, 2014). Even the latest WebSM overview of web survey software (WebSM, 2014) shows that support for displaying simple web questionnaires is limited and very often the necessary adaptations are not done even for the most essential aspects.

Before entering into a more detailed discussion we clarify the basic terminology. Firstly, we will use the term *mobile surveys* to denote any survey, where a mobile device (most often a mobile phone) is involved in the survey measurement stage. These can be either interviewer-administered such as mobile CATI (also mCATI, a computer-assisted

telephone interview where respondents answer using a mobile phone) or mobile CAPI (also mCAPI, a computer-assisted personal interview where interviewers use a mobile device to administer the questionnaire), or self-administered. In the latter case we predominantly talk about web-related surveys. It is true that mobile devices can be used also for SMS surveys, which do not need the Internet to work, and that historically a specific Wireless Application Protocol (WAP) approach was used for surveys. However, since these two protocols are becoming outdated in web survey practice they will not be featured in our discussion.

We will use the term *mobile web surveys* to denote self-administered surveys answered on smartphones or any other mobile device with access to the Internet, where the web is involved in fieldwork data collection.

Within mobile web surveys we will further distinguish between *browser-based mobile web surveys*, which relate to the usual web surveys, where respondents use a mobile device to browse the questionnaire, and *mobile survey applications*, which actually stretch beyond the basic web survey mode, restricted to browser-based and server-based interactions. That is, mobile survey applications can run a questionnaire without a browser and can provide interactivity without interacting with the server. In the use of such applications, the web can be involved only to receive the questionnaire and, when completed, to send it to the server of a researcher.

The notion of *multiple device survey* will be used to emphasize that the survey questionnaire is potentially being answered using different devices and that a researcher has also intentionally modified the questionnaire to support this. On the other hand, we could say that, today, almost all web surveys are unintentionally multiple device.

We should also note that mobile surveys are part of a broader concept of *mobile research* which – in its broadest meaning – encompasses any research methods where a mobile device is involved: from mobile web surveys (including diaries), through mobile CATI and mobile

CAPI, to mobile qualitative methods (e.g. mobile ethnography), and especially a variety of approaches in marketing research (e.g. mobile shopper research, mobile advertising testing, etc.) and/or other non-survey approaches (e.g. location-based research, quick response (QR) code data collection).

5.1.2 Survey Strategies for Handling Mobile Devices

Callegaro (2010) suggested some possible actions to deal with respondents taking web surveys from a mobile device such as a smartphone or tablet. Couper (2013) provided a similar and complementary discussion with a comprehensive overview of corresponding studies conducted so far. In what follows, we further expand on and advance their initial elaborations on mobile web surveys into the following strategies.

1 *Doing nothing* means that we do not modify the web questionnaire according to the device used to access it, but at most identify and categorize these devices. This approach is the 'easiest' to implement but may incur problems in terms of data quality for smartphone respondents. Depending on the number of these respondents or other criteria, a researcher might decide to exclude such respondents from the analysis or to handle them carefully according to a set of clearly defined rules. When doing question-wording experiments, for example, it is very important to use information about device type in the data analysis to control different effects properly.

2 *Explicitly discouraging the use of a mobile device for surveying* can be introduced at various points:

2(a) *In the survey invitation:* Discourage respondents from using mobile devices in the survey invitation. This is another approach that requires little or no effort from a researcher. Unfortunately, it does not seem to work, as explained below.

2(b) *On the introduction page:* Discourage respondents at the very beginning of the web questionnaire. This strategy could

also be ineffective. For instance, in a short web customer satisfaction survey (6–7 minutes) Market Strategies randomized about 71,000 US customers into three conditions: (i) taking the survey from a smartphone was discouraged in the email invitation; (ii) taking the survey from a smartphone was discouraged on the introduction screen; (iii) a control group to whom the standard email invitation was sent (Peterson, 2012). The experimental conditions had no substantial impact on the percentage of respondents taking the web survey from smartphones, suggesting that, regardless of the message, the share of respondents who will switch to another device is unchanged. Slightly better results were obtained with a college student population, where half of the smartphone respondents were asked to switch to a desktop/notebook, while the other half were not. Of the prompted respondents, 14% switched devices in comparison with 7% of the control group, who did it spontaneously (Guidry, 2012).

2(c) *Blocking mobile device access:* This can be done by recognizing the user agent string of the browser used by respondents. Blocked respondents may be flagged and a tailored email reminder can be sent inviting them to complete the survey from an alternative device. Since this solution might lead to a high nonresponse rate, extreme caution and careful monitoring is needed. That is, this strategy may work where the share of these users is very small and adapting for them would allow only negligible improvements.

3 *Optimizing web questionnaire for mobile browsers:*

3(a) *Optimize the web questionnaire for the most common devices and corresponding operating systems:* We talk here about modification of the appearance of the questionnaire in mobile browsers, which is usually done automatically as soon as the mobile device is recognized by the server on which the web survey is run, although respondents are also often allowed to switch from this adapted mobile layout to the general web browser layout. Such optimization involves many methodological (e.g. turning horizontal scales to vertical ones) or technical changes (e.g. increasing the size of radio buttons). Firstly, however, we need to decide for what devices (i.e. which lines of smartphones or tablets) the questionnaire will be optimized. Such a decision often depends on the market penetration of a specific device in the survey target population (or the country they live in), but also on the available resources. If a researcher is developing and programming a stand-alone web survey from scratch – an unlikely, but nevertheless possible, situation – then there is a lot to optimize. More often this depends on survey software, which may or may not be optimized to handle mobile web surveys.

3(b) *Optimize the web questionnaire for all devices:* This solution is very demanding and almost impossible, since it requires web survey software that can handle all types of mobile devices and all types of related platforms (operating systems), together with all versions of the supported browsers. Mobile browsers are much less standardized than the standard browsers for desktop/notebook computers. Nevertheless, handling two of the most common platforms – Android and iOS (Apple) – for common screen sizes and key browser versions seem to currently (2013) cover more than 95% of the market.[4]

4 *Providing a questionnaire as a mobile application, developed for a particular survey (custom mobile survey application)* means that a questionnaire runs partially or entirely on mobile devices (i.e. client based). This can utilize many specific features of mobile devices (GPS location, alarms, photos and videos). However, this approach requires considerable resources, particularly because it has to be developed separately for different smartphone platforms. In addition, the application may need to undergo time-consuming procedures before it appears

in online stores (Google Play, Apple iTunes, Microsoft Windows Phone store). Finally, extra effort is required from respondents who need to download and install the specific application (Fernee & Scherpenzeel, 2013).

5 *Providing a questionnaire through a general application for surveying on mobile devices (general mobile survey application)* means that respondents download the corresponding general application for surveying only once and then automatically receive further questionnaires in an optimized way. Such a general application specialized for mobile surveys can be a stand-alone or supplementary application to existing web survey software, which already supports the basic web survey mode on desktops/notebooks. The use of a general application could be particularly suitable for web surveys with a long-term relationship between the surveyor and respondents, for instance in the case of an online panel.

5.1.3 Device Effects

In the remainder of this section we predominantly focus on mobile web surveys where a web questionnaire is answered using a smartphone, but provide a short comment on tablets and ITV at the end of the section. Many of the issues discussed below apply to almost all mobile devices.

The smartphone is emphasized because it is the most frequent mobile device used for web surveys. We should be aware, however, that it was only in 2013 that smartphones for the first time reached half of all mobile phone shipments[5], so feature phones still prevail.

It seems obvious that with a growing proportion of respondents taking surveys from mobile devices, every web questionnaire should be optimized for smartphones (strategies 3, 4 and 5 above). Yet, at the same time, if the same web questionnaire is answered on a desktop/notebook or on a smartphone – being optimized for the device or not – the answers may differ, so we can talk about specific *device effects*. It should be pointed out that with this notion we mean only the effects of a specific device used for surveying (e.g. a desktop/notebook or a smartphone) on the respondent's answers during the measurement stage of the survey process. Consequently, a device effect has to be distinguished from the mode effect that occurs due to the use of a certain survey mode (e.g. a basic web survey mode) for questionnaire completion. Studies looking at potential device effects by comparing smartphone and desktop/notebook web surveys found the following issues.

Faster reaction, but longer questionnaire completion times on smartphones: Peterson (2012) noted that, on average, smartphone respondents started completing a web questionnaire earlier than desktop/notebook respondents from the moment the email invitation was sent. At the same time, in spite of their optimization, surveys undertaken on smartphones may take 25% to 50% longer to complete compared with the same survey on a desktop/notebook. Similar results were also reported by Bruijne & Wijnant (2013), Grenville (2012), Schmidt & Wenzel (2013) and Wells, Bailey, & Link (2014). Longer completion time for smartphone respondents is likely to be associated with the speed of mobile Internet networks (generally lower than broadband connections) and usability issues. For these reasons some studies show that the scrolling design has certain advantages over paging with a smartphone (e.g. Mavletova, 2013).

Lower participation rates on smartphones: In studies where respondents were randomly allocated to different devices, a lower participation rate has sometimes been observed for smartphone survey takers. For example, in two studies conducted at the end of 2011 participation rates for smartphone web surveys were around half that for desktop/notebook web surveys (Mavletova, 2013; Mavletova & Couper, 2013). Likewise, in an experiment in the Netherlands, the completion rate for the smartphone respondents was 47%, and for desktop/notebook respondents it was above 60% (Bruijne & Wijnant, 2013). Such findings could be at least partially explained by the increased burden on respondents due to the longer time required to

complete a questionnaire on a smartphone and the small size of the device complicating the task. In addition, we need to be aware that web surveys for smartphones are still at the initial stages, so not all possible aspects of optimization have been explored and integrated.

Higher breakoff rates on smartphones: In three studies of professionals (i.e. online advertisers in Asia, Europe and North America) where the web questionnaire was not optimized for smartphones, Callegaro (2010) noted that breakoff rates for surveys taken on smartphones were 2–3 times higher than for those taken on desktop/notebook computers. In a customer satisfaction study, Stapleton (2011) found a breakoff rate of 3.3% for web respondents using a desktop/notebook in comparison with 16.9% for those with smartphone access. Similar results were found for a college student population (McClain, Crawford, & Dugan, 2012) and for two German online panels (Bosnjak, Poggio, Becker, Funke, Wachenfeld & Fisher, 2012; Schmidt & Wenzel, 2013). In particular, higher breakoff occurs when encountering tables, open-ended questions and Flash technology. For example, Jue & Luck (2014) noted many breakoffs when respondents encountered a 12-column by 10-row table in a 10-question web survey. For smartphone users, the breakoff rate on that page was double that of desktop/notebook users. However, this is an inordinate example which might be related to the absence of question optimization for smartphones. As Callegaro (2010) noted, tables are particularly problematic because the response options are laid out horizontally and thus difficult to complete on a smartphone given its small screen size. That is, the horizontal response options in many cases were not fully visible without horizontal scrolling. In a randomized experiment, Stapleton (2011) was able to decrease the smartphone breakoff rate by 30% when switching the table from a horizontal to a sequential vertical format. A web questionnaire with open-ended questions is another format that is more difficult to deal with on smartphones. Jue & Luck (2014) measured a 50% higher breakoff rate for smartphone users compared with desktop/notebook users in a web questionnaire with open-ended questions. Further, Flash technology does not work on certain smartphones (iPhones). Bosnjak et al. (2012) also noted a doubling of breakoff rates for respondents using a smartphone when Flash technology was used.

Shorter length of answers to open-ended text questions on smartphones: Most studies (experimental or observational) have shown shorter answers to open-ended questions for smartphone survey takers (Mavletova, 2013; Peterson, 2012; Wells et al., 2014). Peterson (2012) also observed that, after coding for open-ended text questions, the results were very similar despite the smaller number of characters among smartphone survey takers.

Mixed findings on social desirability: In an experiment where members of a non-probability online panel in Russia were randomized to either a desktop/notebook web survey (email invitation) or a smartphone web survey (SMS invitation), Mavletova & Couper (2013) found some social desirability bias for the smartphone group. The smartphone respondents reported less alcohol consumption than desktop/notebook respondents, even though there was no social desirability effect with other sensitive questions. In another experiment with a very similar design (e.g. random allocation of online panel members) no social desirability effect was found (Mavletova, 2013). One reason for the potentially higher social desirability bias in smartphone web surveys may be the actual reduction of sense of privacy when using smartphones – for example, if respondents are answering the questionnaire in a public place. Further, there may be a larger concern among the mobile phone users about privacy due to the (perceived) possibility of identification because the mobile phone is a personal device.

Unclear evidence on differential satisficing behaviour on smartphones: It is not yet clear whether satisficing occurs at a higher rate for smartphones than for desktop/notebook respondents. A number of studies, measuring different aspects of satisficing, did not find differences between the devices. Notably, Buskirk & Andrus (2013), Mavletova & Couper (2013) and Wells et al. (2014) did not find any difference as regards primacy

effects, Mavletova (2013) found no difference in the level of non-substantive responses, Wells et al. (2014) found no difference in relation to the use of the 'other' category, and Buskirk & Andrus (2013) found no difference in the item nonresponse rate. Conversely, item differentiation seems to be affected by the device used for questionnaire completion. In a web survey of college undergraduates, Guidry (2012) noted a doubled amount of item non-differentiation for smartphone takers (18%) compared with desktop/notebook respondents (9%) and tablet (i.e. iPad) respondents (8%).

However, all of the above results need to be considered with caution. We need to be aware that web surveys for smartphones are still at the initial stage, so not all possible aspects of optimization have been explored and integrated. Thus, the identified effects can be expected to decrease with technical and methodological advances. Smartphones are continuously improving and providing a better user experience with web browsing. These technological improvements also increase the speed of Internet access for smartphones based on an extended coverage of Wi-Fi access points and increasing support for new generations of mobile broadband networks. Likewise, the methodological and design optimization of browser-based surveys for smartphones is rapidly improving.

At the same time, the amount and range of tasks that users conduct daily on smartphones are also expanding, so answering a survey over the mobile device is likely to become an everyday practice.

In fact, the results of the study by Toepoel & Lugtig (2014) could provide strong support for such a suggestion. Using a 10-minute browser-based questionnaire, fully optimized for smartphones, they actually found no difference between smartphone and desktop/notebook versions with respect to response rates, breakoffs, item nonresponse, time to complete the survey, answers to open-ended questions, and the number of responses in a check-all-that-apply question.

For large tablets (e.g. iPads) with a screen size of about 10 inches (25 cm), studies show a very similar breakoff rate as for desktop/notebook users (Callegaro, 2010). Other research shows that the behaviour of tablet respondents in terms of item nonresponse may actually be more similar to desktop/notebook respondents than to smartphone respondents (Guidry, 2012). Taking these aspects into account, tablets appear to be a promising technology. In fact, some online panels have already considered offering tablets to panel members with no Internet access to participate in their surveys (e.g. the ELIPSS panel[6] in France). However, with the proliferation of smaller tablets (e.g. iPad mini, Nexus 7 and the like) more research is needed in order to measure potential device effects.

Another device with considerable potential for answering web surveys is ITV, where consumers – besides watching a TV programme – can also use it to vote, comment, purchase, play games or bid (e.g. auction, horse race, gambling), as well as for general browsing of the web. It is therefore reasonable to think that they could also fill in a web questionnaire. After all, this is what Knowledge Networks panel members did in the early days of online panels in the beginning of the 2000s. Panel members, using WebTVs obtained from the company, completed the surveys via a special remote control and a wireless keyboard (Huggins & Eyerman, 2001). Although ITV might in future – after essential commercial, technological and usability issues settle down – gain a considerable share among survey devices, this is not yet the case. The corresponding methodological challenges are unclear, but we can expect that they will relate to the privacy and to the specifics of the extended remote controller (e.g. pointer, mouse) which will be used to select survey responses.

To sum up, existing evidence (in 2014) seems to be far too limited to give any conclusive statements on exactly what kind of device will prevail with surveys, as well as what kind of effects we may expect from unintentional device-specific web surveys run on multiple devices. Discouraging respondents from using mobile devices to complete the questionnaire (strategy 2) would solve this problem but at the potential cost of losing many respondents.

Further, not considering and not adapting to new devices would in a way restrict the natural habitat of respondents in web surveys. Thus, we rather recommend adaptations to the changing survey environment described here. In the next section, we provide some design tips regarding adaptations of web questionnaire design for smartphones.

5.1.4 Designing Web Questionnaires for Smartphones

As Macer (2011) made clear, today we can still argue that for mobile web surveys there is relatively little consensus, little research and limited evidence of best practices. Nevertheless, we provide a couple of design considerations drawn from our experience and by summarizing the findings of Callegaro (2013a). These considerations are related to both survey design and survey software. On the one hand, survey design decisions relate to question wording, selection of question types, wording of email invitations, etc., which a researcher needs to make within a certain web survey software. On the other hand, considerations driven by survey software are also very important, especially those related to specific features of the software that affect the appearance of the questionnaire on mobile devices (see e.g. Mavletova, 2013).

We suggest the following *survey design considerations*, which should, however, remain within the principles of general questionnaire preparation (Section 2.3) and which are related to *intentional* and *unintentional* usage:

- Keep the subject, content and survey link short in the email invitation – which in unintentional design also affects non-smartphone users. Long subject lines and content will create multiple lines of text, requiring the respondent to scroll. It is also important to make the survey URL link visible as soon as possible. The URL should be short and, if possible, not stretch into multiple lines; URL shortening can also be used, although this hides the legitimacy of the domain.
- Remove or reduce all non-essential, non-question content in the question pages. Logos,

disclaimers and help links may be limited to the introduction page in order to have more available space for questions. Likewise, since the progress bar requires a lot of space and does not really help to reduce breakoffs for medium to long surveys, it can be avoided (Villar et al., 2013).

- Avoid questions in tables (e.g. table of radio buttons). Tables do not fit on smaller screens and require respondents to zoom and scroll horizontally just to read the text. Consider having a single question for each item. Most survey software nowadays already automatically *unfold tables* to a series of single questions when displaying them on a smartphone (e.g. Pferdekaemper & Batanic, 2009). An alternative solution is to transform the tables automatically into a series of drop-down menu questions, each placed on one line.
- *Decompose* questions and use single item question types with standard response formats and layouts (e.g. radio buttons); many advanced question types (e.g. ranking) may not work well on a small screen.
- Be very careful with drag and drop questions (e.g. ranking) and test them fully because they are extremely difficult to work seamlessly on touch screens and other small screens.
- Consider *splitting* long bipolar scales into two questions, first the main two options (e.g. satisfied or dissatisfied) and then the level within each option (e.g. extremely, very and somewhat). An example of this for questions with seven or more response options is given by Malhotra et al. (2009). On a smartphone, it is not always possible (depending on the length of the question text) to show a scale of more than five points.
- Avoid making the respondents scroll horizontally. In addition to the above modifications (e.g. decomposing, splitting, unfolding) this involves the transformation of horizontal scales into vertical ones, limiting the size of the text area and some other approaches.
- Arrange vertical scales so that response options at the top have a positive connotation while options at the bottom have a negative connotation, following the 'up means good' logic (Tourangeau, Couper, & Conrad, 2013) for Western language cultures.

- Consider not mentioning the response options in the question text (but only in response text) in order to save precious space.
- Avoid videos when possible, because they can be problematic and take a long time to load. Care is needed also with (large) pictures.

While these modifications are mostly based on a deliberate decision by a researcher and are not conditioned by the web survey software, the following *survey software considerations* usually cannot be done by a researcher and require modification of the web survey software:

- Optimize the font size and navigation buttons for usability with smartphones; this also includes potentially abandoning standard HTML elements and using graphics, where images replace the radio button or pictures replace the verbal description of the response options.
- Make sure Flash technology is not used because smartphones and tablets with the iOS operating system (e.g. iPhone, iPad) will not be able to support it.
- Customize prompts and error messages to be shown with the right font size and length for smartphones.
- Optimize the size of pictures for small screens and also the size of the text areas. Provide automatic unfolding of the grids into a horizontal scrolling matrix.
- Consider offering smartphone users the option to voice-record their answers when asking open-ended questions; some encouraging implementations already exist in marketing research practice.

These are only some general considerations and recommendations. It is important to thoroughly test the questionnaire on multiple devices and related operating systems to explore fully what might go wrong. We also suggest asking the developers of the web survey software about how they handle smartphones and tablets, and obtaining a list of automatic adjustments they provide for such devices.

Many of the above considerations coincide with usability guidelines for mobile websites developed by Nielsen & Budiu (2013). For instance, the distinction between mouse and fingers as input devices is important when thinking about designing a web questionnaire for multiple devices. The main difference is the precision of the mouse, which is much higher than touching with fingers. The mouse also does not obscure the view of the screen, while fingers do. Finally, a mouse has generally at least two buttons and a scroll wheel, while the control that a finger or even two fingers can have on a web page is much more limited. As a consequence, the size and the placement of questionnaire objects (e.g. radio buttons or checkboxes) should be different in the case of mobile web surveys. Moreover, with respect to the size of the screen, Nielsen & Budiu (2013) recommend designing websites where respondents do not have to scroll horizontally, keeping drop-down menus short, making sure the text is not truncated, handling error messages and prompts correctly, and properly formatting a mobile website. As described above, each of these recommendations could be successfully applied to web surveys on smartphones. We may even think in terms of the so-called 'mobile first' approach. Unfortunately, so far, we have not seen much cross-fertilization between usability designers and mobile web survey designers.

5.1.5 Browser-based Mobile Surveys vs Mobile Survey Apps

So far, we have predominantly discussed the case of having a basic web survey questionnaire that can be completed from some multiple devices using a web browser. We called this approach browser-based mobile surveys (strategies 3a and 3b). However, as mentioned above, surveys can be answered from mobile devices (e.g. smartphones, tablets) also by using special mobile survey applications (strategies 4 and 5). Software applications on mobile devices are usually abbreviated as *apps*, therefore we refer to them hereafter as *mobile survey apps*.

With technological progress browser-based mobile surveys are becoming more and more capable; this can be observed in the context of the general advancement of so-called *responsive design* and *responsive websites*, which

automatically adapt the interface to the specific device of the user. This strongly reinforces the standard advantages of browser-based mobile web surveys:

- Respondents can start answering the questionnaire from the email invitation without downloading anything. Of course, this advantage is somehow less prominent with online panels, where invitations delivered through a dedicated app convenient.
- Questionnaires using standard HTML elements can achieve higher coverage, since they are not dependent on the operating systems of different devices, platforms and browsers.
- It is much easier to administer certain questionnaires only to desktops/notebooks or only for smartphones/tablets than to develop and coordinate parallel questionnaires for different devices, platforms and browsers.

However, at present, browser-based mobile surveys still face certain limitations that often make the use of mobile survey applications more suitable:

- The Internet connection is necessary all the time to answer the questionnaire.
- Some technologies, which are needed to support advanced features (e.g. JavaScript and HTML5, not to mention Java and Flash), may not work properly – or do not work at all – on mobile devices.
- In order to leverage all the hardware capabilities of the device, such as capturing a location or taking a picture, the respondent is required to accept a prompt from the smartphone browser asking permission to do so, while with apps this might be required only once during the app installation.
- Integration of the mobile functionality, such as the detection of device movements, capturing the QR code, GPS location, or camera use, may not be fully supported.
- There may not be sufficient flexibility that may be required for some surveys (e.g. regular ringing/prompts in time use diaries).
- Support is required for surveys related to location-based services, where presentation of the questionnaire is triggered by the location of the respondent (e.g. after exiting a shop or when approaching a certain location), which is sometimes also discussed within the context of

so-called *geofencing* (based on GPS or mobile operator location identification techniques) or *beaconing* (based on Bluetooth technology).

- Support is required for surveys where continuous reporting and photos are collected at various locations, as in ethnographic studies.

On the other hand, mobile survey apps need to be downloaded to a mobile device by respondents from the web (e.g. Apple Store, Google Play). This can be done separately for a specific survey questionnaire (strategy 4) or there may be a general software application where the installation needs to be done only once. This then enables further questionnaires to be received and completed from a mobile device (strategy 5).

A very important distinction with mobile survey apps relates to two essential functionalities: displaying the questionnaire and data management. In a browser-based mobile survey both functionalities are run by the server and web browser. Of course, this is also the case for the basic web survey mode, used for desktops or notebooks. However, with mobile survey apps this is different, since the app can take control of both functionalities:

- *Displaying the questionnaire*: When the mobile survey app controls the appearance of the questionnaire, this can rely on the web browser installed locally on the device, or on the app that simulates the browser. This can be a very simple function, called *HTML container*, which reshapes the appearance of the HTML elements for a mobile device screen. For example, it can switch – as a functional device and not as a browser extension – the horizontal scale to a vertical one or resize the radio button. At the other extreme, this function can be expanded to be entirely independent of browser limitations and HTML elements. It takes full control of the presentation of the questionnaire to the respondent, as in advanced mobile applications. Examples are those of Facebook, Gmail or YouTube, which greatly improve the mobile GUI (though data exchange still relies on the server). The guidelines for mobile app developers produced by the mobile operating systems can be used for such purposes (Owen, 2013).

- *Data management*: However, even in cases of advanced mobile survey apps, we still need a server-based web survey with a permanent Internet connection when no support for data management is provided by the app. Only when data management is an integrated functionality does a mobile survey app become more or less independent of the continuous interaction with the web server. In extreme cases, such an app can unfold the CSAQ as a client application independently of the server, submitting responses to a researcher's server only at the end of the questionnaire or when the corresponding procedure is triggered by a researcher.

The support for displaying the questionnaire on a mobile device is a defining characteristic of mobile survey apps, which we call the *passive mobile survey app*, while for the case when the support is provided also for data management we can talk about the *active mobile survey app*. The main difference between the two types is that in the former the data connection is synchronous (always online), but asynchronous (online/ offline) in the latter. With active mobile survey apps, strictly speaking, we can no longer talk about the basic web survey mode because questionnaire completion can be done without a web browser and also without interaction with a server (see the definition of the basic web survey mode in Section 1.1). In this case, the web is used only to exchange empty and completed questionnaires, so active mobile survey apps belong to *web-related survey modes* (Section 6.1.1).

Drawing on Macer (2011, pp. 9–10), the following advantages of mobile survey apps – predominantly the active ones, though passive ones are increasingly expanding their capabilities due to the advances in browser-based mobile surveys – can be put forward:

- The questionnaire can work without an Internet connection. It is only necessary to download the questionnaire and to submit it, which may be done immediately after the response session or later.
- The app can integrate its own interactive functionalities, like prompts, sending messages, triggering alarms (e.g. vibrate or beep), and

can be 'active' at all times even without the Internet connection.

- The app can fully use the capabilities of a device, such as recording of GPS data, pictures (e.g. a survey question requires the respondent to take a picture), videos, voice recordings and barcode or QR code scanning.

In any case, both kinds of mobile survey apps are in general very suitable for various types of online panels, especially for travel studies, location services studies, multimedia data collection (voice, pictures, video) and continuous reporting as in diaries, biomarker collections and ecological momentary assessments (EMA). With respect to active mobile survey apps, we may add that they are also very convenient for CAPI interviews and for capturing data in various business processes.

On the other hand, mobile survey apps also have disadvantages:

- The app must be downloaded and installed on the device prior to answering the survey(s).
- It also needs to be reinstalled whenever the respondent replaces the device, which, unfortunately, can happen quite often. This increases the respondent's burden and reintroduces concerns about the safety of required downloads.
- The app needs to be programmed and designed for each specific operating system (at least for: iOS and Android, but potentially also for Windows phone), which substantially increases the cost and development time, at least for custom mobile survey apps (strategy 4). For general apps (strategy 5) this may represent a somewhat lesser issue, but still imposes a considerable additional burden, because the browser-based web survey usually needs to be developed in parallel.
- It might be more difficult and demanding to administer the same questionnaire via both an app and a web browser.

Considering the current state of the technology we may conclude that mobile survey apps are suitable when we are seriously faced with the above limitations of browser-based mobile surveys. However, we believe that in the future, when support for advanced scripts and HTML5 will be more widely available, browser-based mobile surveys will be able to handle much more advanced features than today. In fact, the difference between mobile survey apps and browser-based mobile web surveys will become more and more blurred, because the latter will increasingly simulate richer functionalities of the former. Buskirk and Andrus (2012) call one of the approaches in this direction *app-like* browser-based mobile surveys, which rely on JavaScript and HTML5.

5.1.6 Software for Multi-device Web Surveys and Mobile Survey Apps

As discussed previously, at the time of this writing, standard web survey software does not fully support multi-device surveys. The WebSM survey software study (WebSM, 2014) showed that many of the major web survey software suppliers still have surprisingly limited support for browser-based mobile surveys at the beginning of 2014. For instance, many have problems even with simple functionalities, such as automatic unfolding of the tables or automatic transformation of a horizontal scale into a vertical one. Nevertheless, as elaborated above, these problems will disappear in a few years. In the near future, the related client-side scripts, which are activated with browsers, may upgrade browser-based mobile surveys to the level where mobile survey apps will be needed very rarely.

With respect to the support for developing flexible questionnaires within the context of general mobile survey apps (i.e. a general authoring tool for creating these apps), we can say that this also has been improving rapidly, although it is still relatively weak in features compared with the rich array of functionalities in standard web survey software for creating browser-based web questionnaires for desktops/notebooks. As a consequence, complex questionnaires may still need to be programmed separately as custom mobile apps for every mobile platform.

Nevertheless, the number of mobile survey apps is increasing rapidly. In July 2012, the research magazine *Quirk's* listed 32 suppliers specializing in mobile web surveys (Townsend, 2012). Recent overviews of mobile apps available from iOS and Android app stores showed that there were more than 1,000 applications related to the notion of web surveys (WebSM, 2014). While a majority of them refer to respondents in an online panel, there are also many active and passive mobile survey apps that accompany some established web survey software, as well as apps for creating simple web surveys on mobile devices (e.g. for voting), as discussed below.

In addition to various types of mobile survey apps used by respondents, on which we have predominantly focused here, we have to distinguish sharply those apps providing support for a researcher. That is, many web survey software suppliers have developed special *mobile survey authoring apps* that support the creation of the browser-based web questionnaire on a mobile device. Usually, but not always, respondents can still access the questionnaire using a web browser. The main reason for providing dedicated mobile apps for survey creators lies in the complexity of the user interfaces of web survey software that makes their use on mobile devices practically impossible. Therefore, if a researcher wants to quickly create a simple survey (e.g. feedback form) on a mobile device, such an app can be very helpful by providing a special interface, where navigation and options are adapted correspondingly. Of course, this works as a completely independent application with no direct relation to the mobile survey app for respondents.

In any case, given this variety of survey-related mobile apps, we need to be very careful when talking about different types of such apps. We therefore recommend using explicit and additional labelling to denote whether we are talking about active or passive mobile survey apps, custom or general mobile survey apps, as well as whether the app is meant for the respondent or for a researcher.

5.1.7 Challenges and Conclusions

Even though surveys on smartphones and other devices have come a long way since the first experiments with SMS (Cooke, Nielsen, & Strong, 2003) and WAP surveys (Fuchs, 2008), many challenges still lie ahead. In developed countries we can expect that smartphones will achieve almost full coverage (90% or more) within a few years. Furthermore, in a considerable number of countries Internet penetration is growing primarily via smartphone adoption. This is the case for many countries in Africa and South America, where users are skipping the desktop/notebook Internet experience and embracing it directly via their smartphones.[7]

With this steadily increasing adoption of smartphones and tablets, the trend is for respondents to answer a questionnaire from whatever device they have at hand, 'without asking for our permission' (Peterson, 2012). Today it seems clear that the attempts to stop or redirect respondents to a different device do not work. The only viable solution for the future seems to be careful planning for multi-device web surveys. This paradigm shift is a combination of survey platform-driven design decisions and, very importantly, survey design decisions in terms of questionnaire design, content and email invitations.

However, some obstacles to the more widespread utilization of mobile web surveys still persist. Sometimes, users are charged for data transmission, so a researcher should always check if the target population can truly run cost-free web surveys on mobile devices. Furthermore, the capabilities of mobile browsers still lag behind their desktop counterparts, while the implementation of dedicated mobile survey apps is less convenient for both respondents and researchers. However, we can expect that improved availability and lower costs of Internet connection will provide stable and virtually always available connections to the web, and technical issues will be largely solved by app-like mobile browser approaches.

Experiences from the development of the basic web survey mode (Section 1.3.3) for desktops/notebooks show that methodological aspects will likely become essential only after key technical issues have been resolved. Drawing a parallel with the development of web surveys for desktops/notebooks, we can say that the turbulence of the first decade of web survey developments (1994–2004) was often related to the improvements in Internet speed – which was for a long time very limited by dial-up access – and client-side scripts (e.g. JavaScript). In the subsequent decade (2005–2014), technology became more stable with fewer technical changes, so the methodological effects were no longer linked substantially to technological specifics. While a similar pathway can be expected with mobile web surveys, the importance of related methodological issues has already been recognized and investigated. This also relates to the dilemma of whether to use browser-based surveys or mobile survey apps. This dilemma will very likely diminish due to technical progress, because there will be less and less difference for respondents between these two alternatives. (We further discuss possible future trends related to the corresponding software support for mobile surveys in the conclusion to Section 5.3 on software.)

In our review of various studies (Section 5.1.3) it seemed that surveys using mobile devices faced certain methodological difficulties, particularly with respect to nonresponse rates, breakoffs, question types, length of questionnaire and time required. However, it is important to note that many technical limitations, which have already been overcome today, may actually have interfered with these methodological deficiencies in those studies, conducted a few years ago with old-fashioned devices. In addition, the results from research with surveys using different devices need to be interpreted very carefully, because even in experiments it is difficult to randomize subjects across the devices used. Smartphone coverage can be much lower than desktop/notebook coverage, and if device selection is left to the respondent (which cannot be reliably prevented), a strong self-selection bias may occur. In such a case, device specifics interfere with those of the users, causing confusion about

where the effects are coming from. In addition, device effects may also be mixed up with other aspects, such as nonresponse. Isolation of mobile device effects is therefore very difficult to achieve and explore.

Another specific issue that requires careful treatment is related to the diversity of environments in which surveying can take place when a mobile device is used. The presence of other persons, inconvenient locations and multitasking may have an impact on the quality of responses. In addition, mobile web surveys, especially when implemented using survey apps, have powerful options of collecting other kinds of data from the respondents' devices (e.g. location or Internet traffic behaviour). Therefore, a clear and open communication with the respondent is crucial for addressing privacy and security (see Section 6.3).

In summary, there is an inevitable trend that more and more respondents will access survey questionnaires via mobile devices. This will require a substantial amount of new methodological work and resources to conduct high-quality web surveys. In this section we have laid down some key principles and presented findings from prior studies that provide some initial insights, despite the infancy of the research in this field.

Finally, we should stress that mobile surveys can be just one component of mobile research, (Poynter, Williams, & York, 2014). It is in marketing research (and related web survey software) that new mobile survey solutions are devised, such as in innovative formats for SMS or email surveys.

5.2 ONLINE PANELS

Online panels[8] are built primarily with the goal of having a set of pre-recruited respondents who are ready to be contacted to answer web surveys in a timely fashion. They consist of a group of registered respondents who, at the time of registration, agree to participate in web surveys on a regular basis. The panel providers invest a lot of resources to recruit and maintain their panels so that the entire data collection process is streamlined, and data for a particular survey are available in a matter of weeks if not days or even hours. Online panels are, in a way, the natural evolution of consumer (or household) panels, where surveys used to be administered via mail, telephone and F2F (Wansink & Sudman, 2002).

We use the term *online* here in the broadest sense (similar to the way we defined the difference between online surveys, Internet surveys and web surveys in Section 1.3.1). In addition, the term *panel* is used very specifically here, in the sense previously outlined in Section 1.1.1, and is related to the sampling frame of potential respondents who can repeatedly be included in various surveys. On the other hand, the more usual understanding of the term panel relates to longitudinal surveys where the same sample of actual respondents is repeatedly surveyed about the same topic (e.g. Labour Force Surveys), which is usually not the case here.

We first overview general issues related to terminology (Section 5.2.1), recruitment (Section 5.2.2) and maintenance (Section 5.2.3) of online panels. Next, we address specific aspects of online panel designs (Section 5.2.4) and data quality (Section 5.2.5). We conclude with discussion about buying online panel research (Section 5.2.6) and the future of online panels (Section 5.2.7).

5.2.1 Terminology and Typology

'Online panel' is a broad term for several different types in use. Panels can differ in their membership composition, in the kind of data they collect and how they collect them. The three most common types of online panels regarding membership composition are general population panels, specialty panels and proprietary panels (Baker, Blumberg, Brick, Couper, Courtright, Dennis, ... Zahs, 2010, p. 8). *General population panels* are the most common type of panels. In this case an attempt is made to include every possible type of respondent, including hard-to-reach populations. The panel is used as a frame from which a researcher draws a specific sample for the study requested by the client. *Specialty*

panels are built by recruiting specific types of people because of their age or other demographics (e.g. a panel of Latinos) or their profession (e.g. a panel of medical professionals), or by recruiting particular population groups (e.g. election panels where eligible voters are recruited and surveyed for months before and after an election to study their attitude formation). *Proprietary panels* are a subclass of specialty panels where members participate in research for a particular company. For example, researchers can use the email addresses of owners of a particular type of product to build a proprietary panel. Recently, these panels have also established a considerable overlap with *online community panels*, where panellists share some common virtual space.

Online panels can collect data in two ways: by web survey questionnaires (i.e. online survey panels) and by collecting online behaviours passively from the respondents. The latter are called *Internet ratings panels* (Napoli, Lavrakas, & Callegaro, 2014). They are set up to measure the Internet audience mostly in terms of market share, visitors' demographics and online advertisement. They differ from online survey panels in that they also measure another dimension: namely, the passive measurement of online behaviour. To measure this behaviour, the company conducting Internet ratings asks the panel members to install an online software meter on their devices. The software then tracks all Internet activity from the respondents' computers in a passive way.

In the rest of this section we focus only on online survey panels (called online panels for short) as those using web survey questionnaires to collect data.

5.2.2 Recruitment, Sampling and Selection

The main distinction among panel providers lies in their panel recruitment methodology. Applying our initial taxonomy of types of web surveys (see Section 1.1.3), online panels can be classified into two types: non-probability online panels and probability online panels.

Non-probability online panels, also called access, opt-in, volunteer panels, involve a self-selection process by the people who want to join the panel. Generally, almost anyone can opt to be a part of this type of panel. Panel members can also sign up friends and family or refer someone else. From a sampling point of view, a panel member has an unknown probability of selection because of the voluntary nature of the recruitment. As we will explain in detail later, these panels do not include the non-Internet population.

Probability online panels recruit panel members using a probability sampling mechanism, providing each member of the target population with known and non-zero probability of selection for the panel. Offline modes (telephone RDD, mail, and F2F recruiting) are typically used here for the initial recruitment. No respondent is allowed to join the panel voluntarily if he or she is not selected and recruited first by of the above methods. Panel members cannot refer friends, family or colleagues as members. To be representative of the entire population, probability online panels offer a device and/or Internet access to those recruited members who do not have an Internet connection (DiSogra & Callegaro, 2015).

5.2.2.1 Recruitment Methods for Non-Probability Online Panels

Researchers and companies who build non-probability online panels often do not disclose their recruiting methods because they believe this gives them a competitive advantage (Baker et al., 2010). For this reason, there is little published information on recruitment methods. The following inventory is based on a few sources (e.g. Baker et al., 2010; Comley, 2007; Postoaca, 2006) plus our personal experience in dealing with providers and by reading online panel websites.

Offline recruitment methods include recruitment from offline panels, recruitment at the end of an offline survey, recruitment from existing marketing databases of mail or email addresses, direct recruitment via telephone, mail or F2F, and offline media exposure, leaflets, etc.

Online recruitment methods are cheaper (see Section 2.2.3) than offline ones and have more variability. The easiest recruitment method is for the online panel to have volunteers sign up directly at their website or the panel portal. Banner ads are also used to recruit potential volunteers. They redirect potential respondents to a website where they can enrol. The banner ads can be targeted at specific websites, thereby recruiting specific groups of users based on their interests. Invitations to join a panel in newsgroups or mailing lists are also common and quite inexpensive. Search engine advertising (Nunan & Knox, 2011) seems to be used more and more by online panels to recruit potential members. Online social networks (such as Facebook, Twitter, etc.) are another way to recruit potential panel members. A co-registration agreement is one way to propose online panel enrolment when a user signs up for an online service at the same time. Portals as well as e-commerce, news and special interest websites are all examples of websites where co-registration agreements typically occur. Affiliate hubs, also called online panel consolidators, are websites that sign up individuals to one or more online panels at the same time, generally by promising money as an incentive. A member-get-a-member campaign uses current panel members to recruit their friends and family, generally by offering an incentive. Recruiting at the end of a web survey is another way to build a panel. Lastly, sending unsolicited emails to purchased mailing lists is another method, although it is not a likely recruitment method used by any reputable firm, at least those in the United States and Europe (Baker et al., 2010, p. 721).

5.2.2.2 Recruitment Methods for Probability Online Panels

Probability online panels use traditional offline methods to recruit potential members (Callegaro & DiSogra, 2008; DiSogra & Callegaro, 2015). A probability sample for the panel can be drawn as an address-based sample (ABS), a sample from a population register, an area probability sample, or an RDD sample. Potential panel members can be initially contacted via advance mail or directly by an interviewer. For example, the LISS panel in the Netherlands sent advance mail plus a panel brochure to potential households. For cases where an address could be matched to a telephone number, the interviewers contacted the household via the telephone. For any address that could not be matched to a telephone number, interviewers contacted potential panel members in person (Scherpenzeel & Das, 2010). In the United States, GfK (formally Knowledge Networks) uses an ABS frame (DiSogra et al., 2010) and sends a mail recruitment package to the sampled households. In the recruitment package, there are instructions on how to join the panel by mail, telephone or web (Knowledge Networks, 2011). RDD is used to recruit panel members in Canada by EKOS[1] and in the United States by the Gallup panel (Tortora, 2009). Finally, F2F recruitment using ABS was employed by the FFRISP in the United States (Krosnick et al., 2009).

For the panel to be representative of the whole population, a different method is needed to contact or survey households without Internet access. GfK (Knowledge Networks) and the LISS panel offer these non-Internet households a free computer and pay for their Internet connection, while other companies, such as EKOS and the Gallup panel (DiSogra & Callegaro, 2015) or the Gesis panel in Germany (Bosnjak et al., 2013), survey the offline population via telephone and/or mail.

A third way is to provide all panel members (and not just those without Internet access) with the same device and Internet connection. This is the case for the FFRISP which gave a notebook and broadband connection to all panel members (Krosnick et al., 2009) and the French ELIPSS which gave a tablet with data connection to all of its panel members (Legleye & Lesnard, 2013).

Finally, the panel company might decide not to recruit non-Internet households because, for example, the Internet penetration of that particular country is very high and the coverage error can be compensated for by adequate weighting (as in the online panel of the Social Science Research Institute in Iceland).

---

[1]http://www.probit.ca/

5.2.2.3 Sampling and Selecting Online Panel Members for Individual Surveys

Given that an online panel offers a frame of pre-recruited respondents, how does a company actually select respondents in order to be part of a particular study? Probability panels generally use traditional probability sampling methods, such as simple random sampling or stratified sampling.

Non-probability online panels generally use quota sampling methodologies (Rivers, 2007). This entails setting up quotas or maximum numbers of respondents in key subgroups, usually demographically defined, but sometimes behaviourally as well. Quotas are enforced during completion of a particular questionnaire. Once a quota is filled, new respondents who might qualify for that cell are screened out. Of course, large panels are in a much better position here, particularly panels with millions of members.

A number of panel companies also use more complex sampling methods designed to maximize sample representativeness. All these new methods tend to be proprietary. Among the best known, YouGov developed a *sample matching* method (Rivers, 2007) that starts with an enumeration of the target population using frames from commercially available databases (in the United States, Acxiom, Experian and InfoUSA, or lists of registered voters when the topic is election polling). A random sample is drawn from the frame and matched to panel members who share the same selected characteristics. Multiple panel members are then selected for each line in the pseudo-frame to increase the likelihood of getting a response. This method is used simultaneously for all open studies of the panel provider sharing the same sample specifications. If a panel member reaches a study and another closest match has already completed it, he or she is rerouted in real time to the second-best match study, and so not turned away.

Other methods used are Propensity Score Select or SmartSelect by Toluna (Terhanian & Bremer, 2012) and Global Market Insight's

Pinnacle methodology (GMI, 2012), explained in more detail by Callegaro et al. (2014). These alternative sampling and selection methods have not been extensively tested, and very few investigations of them are available in the literature.

5.2.3 Maintaining an Online Panel

Once a panel is built, sample maintenance methods are similar across probability and non-probability online panels (Callegaro & DiSogra, 2008). Maintaining the sample for online panels requires a lot of work because of the panel dynamics. As Callegaro and DiSogra (2008) explain, a panel changes constantly. Most of the panels continuously recruit new members. This is because all panels suffer from voluntary attrition, passive attrition, retirement, and attrition by mortality.

We define *voluntary attrition* as a proactive action by panel members to contact the company and asking to be removed from the panel. This is not as common as the other reasons for attrition. More frequently, panel members just stop answering surveys or change email addresses without notifying the company. In these cases we talk about *passive attrition*. Some panel companies also have a rule of maximum panel tenure (e.g. two years) and '*retire*' panel members when they reach that tenure. Lastly, *attrition by mortality* occurs when a panel member dies or is no longer physically or mentally capable of answering survey questions.

Knowing how many active panel members are available at a given time is a key statistic for each online panel. Unfortunately, the meaning of an active panel member varies considerably by providers in terms of definition and reference period. The ISO 26362 standard (ISO, 2009) defines an active panel member as a 'panel member who has participated in at least one survey if requested, has updated his/her profile data or has registered to join the access[9] panel, within the last 12 months' (p. 2).

There is much variability in the way companies manage passive attrition in their online panels. More aggressive panel management, for example

by purging less active members from the database, thereby increasing the participation rate of each survey (Callegaro & DiSogra, 2008), does come at a price. Such action reduces the active panel size, and there is a risk that more active panel members will have different response behaviours from average panel members. The attrition is particularly problematic in longitudinal study designs where the same panel members are surveyed over time. In this case, the reduction in available sample size can prevent specific analysis, and potential attrition bias can have an impact on data quality. The panel provider can tackle the problem of attrition with specific initiatives to try to reduce it (Kruse, Callegaro, Dennis, DiSogra, Subias, Lawrence, & Tompson, 2010), such as re-recruitment of members who have left the online panel and creating an incentive programme to keep members in the online panel for longer.

The incentive strategy is particularly important for potential attrition. Usually, an incentive per completed questionnaire is provided via some consumer point-collection plans. Typically, this amounts to a few cents or few tens of cents per minute of responding time. While monetary incentives seem to work best, other means are also used, such as lottery tickets, random prize draw and charity donations or symbolic presents (Göritz, 2010). In the case of online communities various activities can be used as incentives, including online or offline events.

We may add that the respondent's burden can also have an impact on attrition. It is difficult to know exactly how many survey invitations panel companies send on average. One way to obtain some information is to sign up to online panel portals that allow you to do so, and monitor the activity as a panel member. The company Grey Matter Research has used this approach. Staff and other volunteers signed up to 11 different US online panels and monitored the traffic for three months (Grey Matter Research, 2012). Surveys varied in length, but were on average 17.3 minutes long, and the average number of invitations was 20.4 per month with a range from 6.5 to a maximum of 51 invitations.

5.2.4 Online Panel Study Designs

Online panels allow for cross-sectional and longitudinal research (see definition in Section 1.1). In cross-sectional research, panel members participate in a variety of surveys on different topics. They can be done once (cross-sectional) or in repeated cross-sectional designs, where the same survey can be run multiple times, which is also called *tracking studies*. These studies are conducted on the same topic but with a different sample of respondents every time. A classic example of this is a brand awareness study, where a company monitors its brand awareness over time. Online panels can also be utilized for *longitudinal* purposes, where the same study subjects are interviewed at different points in time on the same topic to study change over time (Göritz, 2007). This type of design is the closest to the traditional concept of a household panel. In this design, each new survey is called a *wave*. In addition to tracking changes over time, asking the same question again at different points in time can be used also to study the validity and reliability of items (*test–retest*) and increase the overall data quality (Sikkel & Hoogendoorn, 2008). At the same time, it is possible to use a longitudinal design with a cross-sectional component where specific or thematic questions are asked only once, while other questions are repeated over time.

It is common for online panels to run thematic surveys on selected topics on the whole panel in a census fashion. This strategy is called *panel profiling* (Callegaro & DiSogra, 2008). These surveys are generally on characteristics, attitudes and behaviours that are considered stable and do not change too often, such as demographic information (which is collected at the beginning or at panel enrolment), health status, general political orientation and primary shopper status. There are several advantages of such profile surveys: (a) there is no need to ask these questions repeatedly in each client study, thus making the questionnaire shorter; (b) previously collected data can help in questionnaire branching for particular studies, making it more efficient; (c) profile survey data can be purchased by clients directly without even doing a survey; (e) when a client wants to conduct a study on a specific target population (e.g. respondents with a medical condition), the provider can take a sample of respondents based on profile survey data, called *targeted sampling* (Sikkel & Hoogendoorn, 2008) or *pre-screening* (Callegaro & DiSogra, 2008). Good panel management thus means collecting and maintaining multiple datasets per respondent and thus increasing efficiency by lowering the survey burden.

Another advantage of online panels (closely related to the concept of profiling) is the ability to reach niche and rare populations, in a way that would be cost-prohibitive in other modes of data collections (Boyle, Ball, Ding, Euler, Starcie & Lewis, 2013; G. Wright & Peugh, 2012).

5.2.5 Online Panel Data Quality

Among the different metrics of probability and non-probability online panel data quality, two are of key interest in this section: point estimates compared with the gold standard and relationships among variables[10]. When comparing point estimates it is particularly interesting to discuss the special case of election poll estimates. Other issues of quality are briefly discussed later on. Finally, we devote some space to the issue of weighting in online panels, which is a very controversial and highly debated topic.

5.2.5.1 Comparison of Online Panel Data Quality and Results

Since the beginning of online panel research, a typical data quality study has been to compare the results of online panels with known benchmarks, either population census data from official statistics or some other high-quality official statistical survey benchmarks. Given the number of studies produced in this respect, we focus on the largest comparisons and refer the reader to the book chapter by Callegaro et al. (2014c) for more details.

The most typical study is to run the same questionnaire at the same time across a large number of online panels and compare their results to known benchmarks. The first commercial large-scale study comparing different non-probability panels was the National Dutch Online Panel Comparison Study (NOPVO) (Vonk, van Ossenbruggen, & Willems, 2006). This study compared the results of the same survey on a sample of 1,000 respondents from 19 different online panels in the Netherlands. As a milestone in terms of study design, the NOPVO design was later repeated in other countries, from both commercial and academic organizations. For example, the Advertising Research Foundation (ARF) started the Foundation Of Quality 1 (FOQ1) initiative (Walker, Pettit, & Rubinson, 2009) which compared 17 US non-probability panel providers and an RDD telephone and one mail sample panel. A similar study was repeated in 2012 by ARF FOQ2 (Advertising Research Foundation, 2014) and by the Marketing Research and Intelligence Association (MRIA) (Chan & Ambrose, 2011) among 14 Canadian panels. The results of the above studies (NOPVO, ARF and MRIA) converge on the main findings that online panels are not interchangeable and that the same study conducted on different online panels will produce different results. When compared with known benchmarks, variations across panels are very high, as well as when focusing on a single panel survey. In other words, within the same survey for a given panel, the range of variations to known benchmarks is high.

On the academic side, Yeager et al. (2011) compared the results of an identical questionnaire administered via RDD with the results of six non-probability panels, one probability online panel, and one sample with data collected via river sampling (see Section 2.2.3) for a total of eight datasets. Results indicated that the RDD and online probability panel data were closer to the benchmarks than any other non-probability panel. In a new study with a similar methodology the results were very close to the previous findings in terms of higher data quality for the probability samples (Krosnick, MacInnis, Suh, & Yeager, 2013).

When looking at the relationship among variables the picture is not as clear as in the above

studies, which focused mostly on point estimates. In this case the number of studies is low. The research question would be whether we (clients, researchers) make different decisions or draw different conclusions when looking at the relationship among variables in different panels. Callegaro et al. (2014c) reviewed such studies, noting that most of them were in the area of political science. They found that – although it is generally believed that relationships and correlations among variables do not suffer much (i.e. they are *robust*) from non-probability sample selection – when looking at the signs of the coefficients, they are not always in the same direction and the strength of the relationships varies across samples. In other words, it is possible to make different decisions depending on the type of panel used, as Pasek & Krosnick (2010) highlight. We hope more studies will follow on this topic.

The special case of election polls. The advantage of election polls is that the main statistic of interest (i.e. the final election outcome) can be evaluated for all panels. In general, studies show that non-probability online panels can provide as good and sometimes even better accuracy than probability online panels. In the United States, for example, this goes back to the 2000 election (Taylor et al., 2001) and in the UK to 2001 (YouGov, 2011). Recently, in the 2012 US Presidential Election, non-probability online panels performed as well as and sometimes better than traditional probability polling (Silver, 2012). The conclusions on the performance of election polls are thus very different from the above studies which showed higher data quality in probability than non-probability online panels. There are several possible explanations for this discrepancy. For election polls we need to remember that they estimate mainly one variable (the election outcome), which is most of the time (depending on the country) a binary variable. Secondly, election studies are very often conducted in an environment where, weeks before the election, many other studies, generally telephone polls, are available publicly. In fact, unlike the majority of surveys, in election polls websites that poll the results in real time provide continuous guidance until the very end. This guidance allows for the constant refining of sampling, identification of likely voters, question wording, handling of undecided and nonrespondents, and weighting mechanisms. Thus differences in accuracy reflect more the differences in the mix of these survey aspects than differences in accuracy of non-probability panels overall. The data are also highly modelled, including lots of knowledge from previous elections and general knowledge on how to model election poll data. As the recent AAPOR report on non-probability samples states: 'Although non-probability samples often have performed well in electoral polling, the evidence of their accuracy is less clear in other domains and in more complex surveys that measure many different phenomena' (Baker et al., 2013a, p. 108). The case of election polls is nevertheless very interesting and the lessons learned from them have the potential of being applied to other domains.

5.2.5.2 Effect of Weighting on Online Panel Data Quality

The weighting used in the NOPVO, ARF FOQ1 and ARF FOQ2 and MRIA studies was mostly done on demographics variables, with small variations. This weighting technique (post-stratification on demographics), however, had little effect on bringing the estimates on the non-probability panels close to each other, thus signalling that other self-selection mechanisms are in place in non-probability online panels affecting data quality. In the FOQ2 study, adding behavioural variables such as frequency of internet usage, together with demographic variables, was proven to help in bringing estimates close to benchmarks. Yeager et al. (2011) used post-stratification weighting in their comparisons and noted that it increased the accuracy of the estimates from two probability samples, but sometimes increased and sometimes decreased the accuracy of the non-probability panels in a non-systematic way. Lastly, Tourangeau, Conrad, & Couper (2013) presented a meta-analysis of the effect of weighting on non-probability samples from online panels in order to reduce bias from coverage and selection effects. Among different findings, they concluded that the

adjustment removed at most up to three-fifths of the bias, that large differences across variables still existed and that the differences among weighting approaches were not substantial.

Another method that is gaining popularity in weighting online panels is *propensity score weighting* (PSW), also called *using a reference survey* weighting method. PSW is based on the assumption that the differences between the non-probability online panel and the 'true' target population cannot be compensated for by weighting on demographics only. As we discussed earlier, weighting by demographics does not solve the issue of panel members being different from the target population. In order to correct for these biases, extra covariates need to be added to the model, called *webographics* (Schonlau, Zapert, Payne Simon, Hayness Sanstand, Marcus, Adams, … Berry, 2004). To apply PSW, a reference survey is needed, generally coming from a high-quality probability survey, which is often a survey collected via telephone (RDD sampling) or F2F. The reference survey is used to calibrate or balance the online panel. The propensity score is the conditional probability that a respondent is an online panel respondent rather than a respondent from the reference survey (Schonlau et al., 2004). PSW has been applied in different areas with promising results, although the choice of which webographic variables to include in the model is still not clear (Steinmetz et al., 2014). See also discussion in Section 4.1.4.

5.2.5.3 Other Data Quality Issues in Online Panel Research

In the past 15 years of online panel research other data quality issues have been studied, a number of them completely new, while some were known from other data collection methods and are now discussed in the online panel literature. Due to space limitations, we provide the reader only with a discussion of the key concepts. One set of issues has to do with the fact that online panel members fill in a large number of surveys and spur the discussion about data quality, professional respondents, speeders and panel conditioning effects.

Given that panel members take many surveys over the course of their membership, does repeatedly filling out surveys increase or decrease questionnaire measurement error? From one point of view the act of answering questions can become better with practice. In other words, as Chang & Krosnick (2009) show, online panel members have higher reporting accuracy than comparable telephone interview respondents. From another point of view, and in the case of non-probability online panels where anybody can sign up, the issue of *professional respondents* and their threat to data quality arises. They are defined as experienced survey takers that seek to fill in a large number of questionnaires probably for the rewards associated with them, for example cash or points (Baker et al., 2010, p. 756). The evidence on the relationship of professional respondents to data quality is mixed. As Hillygus, Jackson, & Young (2014) discuss in their critical review of professional respondents, sometimes professional respondents provide data of high quality and sometimes not.

Related to professional respondents, *speeders* are respondents who complete a questionnaire well below the median completion time and for this reason probably provide answers of lower quality. Greski, Meyer, & Schoen (2014) show how the percentage of speeders is higher in non-probability-than probability-based panels. Their effect on data quality is, however, not of high magnitude.

Finally, and related to multiple survey taking, the old issue of *panel conditioning* re-emerges in the literature of online panels. Panel conditioning (Warren & Halpern-Manners, 2012) is related to longitudinal surveys where the same or similar questions are put to the same respondents multiple times, which then makes respondents adjust so that the quality of responses declines. There is some indication that panel conditioning effects are stronger for knowledge questions (Kruse et al., 2010) than other types of questions, but as Warren & Halpern-Manners (2012) remind us, studying panel conditioning is really complex and often interacts with the effects of attrition.

Other sets of data quality issues are studied in the areas of coverage, nonresponse errors and attrition. If the goal of a panel is to produce results representative of the entire population, coverage error is strongly related to country Internet penetration rates (Callegaro & Krosnick, 2014). As discussed in Section 5.2.5, probability-based online panels have different ways of dealing with coverage error (e.g. by giving respondents a device to complete surveys). For non-probability online panels, the only option to produce results with the goal of being representative of the entire population is by weighting, given that, by definition, non-Internet households or respondents do not take part in non-probability online panels.

Nonresponse has a completely different meaning depending on what panel type we are talking about. In the case of probability panels, nonresponse affects each stage of the panel, from recruitment to single survey completion (Lee, 2006). For non-probability online panels, it makes less sense to talk about nonresponse because of the lack of a sampling frame (Section 2.5.2). It also makes less sense to talk about nonresponse for a single survey, given that its completion rate depends more on the way the panel company manages and invites its panel members than anything else (Callegaro & DiSogra, 2008). Attrition is a problem from different points of view. In terms of costs, attrition reduces the size of the panel and forces the panel companies to keep recruiting members in order to keep the panel size stable. From a nonresponse point of view, attrition is an issue because it is almost never at random (i.e. different sets of respondents attrite at different rates) (Lugtig, Das, & Scherpenzeel, 2014). Lastly, attrition is particularly an issue for longitudinal study designs because it reduces the effective sample size and introduces nonresponse measurement errors.

5.2.5.4 Conclusions on Online Panel Data Quality

The evidence provided thus far raises questions about the online panel data quality and non-probability sampling. From the largest comparison studies we can learn how different decisions would be made using different online panels. At the same time it does not look like the situation is better now than it was years ago when Internet penetration was lower. We still have similar data quality issues in online panels.

We agree with Baker et al. (2013) that the available evidence points to the fact that 'the most promising non-probability methods for surveys are those that are based on models that attempt to deal with challenges to inference *in both the sampling and estimation stages*' (p. 101; italics added). For this reason, we believe that the research agenda of comparing across sample sources and to keep studying sampling and weighting strategies should not stop. An indication of research in this direction is given by two AAPOR task force reports (online panels and non-probability samples) (Baker et al., 2010, 2013), by the forthcoming study results of ARF FOQ2, and of a WebDataNet initiative comparing European probability online panels (WebDataNet Task Force 04)[11].

Other data quality issues such as professional respondents, speeders, panel conditioning and the effect on coverage, nonresponse and attrition in online panels have received particular attention in the survey literature but more work is definitely needed to move from measuring such effects to doing something about them.

5.2.6 Buying Online Panel Research

The studies reviewed so far have sparked a debate about online panel data quality. It is sometimes unclear what advice a professional association should give to its members when purchasing online panel research. Nevertheless, professional associations are doing something in this direction. ESOMAR is, for example, providing a set of 28 questions (to pose to the providers) that are aimed at helping a researcher during this process (ESOMAR, 2012). The Council of American Survey Research Organizations (CASRO) requires its members to adhere to the

Code of Standards of Ethics for Survey Research (CASRO, 2011), which contains eight rules of disclosure for various aspects of online panel research, such as panel recruitment practices, panel member activity and panel quality practices. Other local associations (e.g. Arbeitskreis Deutscher Markt, 2007) provide guidelines to their members when dealing with online panel providers. Although these guidelines are definitely useful in providing clients with a better understanding of what kind of sample they are buying, most online panel providers protect and do not reveal their recruitment and panel management practices. In practice the providers usually take into account the essentials of the above recommendations in the form of so-called *panel books*, which describe, document and promote their offers.

The concept of fit for purpose applies best in this context (Baker et al., 2013). In this respect, as buyers of online panels, we should ask ourselves the following questions: What other data collection methods could be afforded for the same price as the online panel? Is the goal to estimate a national or a regional statistic? Is representativeness really necessary? Are experiments within the online panel the main goal of the study? Are the results generalizable only to the Internet population or to the general population? Is the focus on correlations, which perhaps are more robust than point estimates?

If representativeness and generalizability are necessary, one strategy could be to add a few questions to the study where known benchmarks associated with the main research topic are available. In this way, it is possible to have a sense of how far the results obtained are from the benchmarks. With more and more public datasets readily available, this strategy seems possible for most studies.

5.2.7 The Future of Online Panels

As we stated in Chapter 1, more than half of marketing research survey-related revenues already come from web surveys, while third-party (non-probability) online panels already represent almost 35% of all samples (ESOMAR, 2013). Online panels are here to stay, and the decline of F2F and telephone surveys favours the shift. At the same time, online survey data quality is becoming a real issue. While non-probability online panels are becoming a commodity, this is not the case with probability ones. So often we must step back and consider which type of online panel we need, or whether methodologies other than web surveys are more appropriate, or whether primary data collection should be done at all.

We may also highlight a recent trend of mobile online panels, which is rapidly expanding with mobile apps. There, users become members by downloading the corresponding application for a smartphone or tablet which then delivers the questionnaires (see Section 5.1).

We have already mentioned various industry standards and codes for online non-probability panels (Arbeitskreis Deutscher Markt, 2007; CASRO, 2011; ESOMAR, 2012). For probability online panels, evidence based practices have also been published and are readily available (e.g. Scherpenzeel & Das, 2010). However, following these practices makes the online panel expensive to build (upfront initial cost) and maintain. Probably because of this reason, probability online panels are a minority in the overall online panel business. On the other hand, as Internet penetration increases and devices to browse the web become less expensive, the overall cost to build and maintain a probability online panel should decrease. In Europe, for example, more and more probability panels are being built (Das, 2012), promoted[12] or planned (Nicolaas, 2013). National statistics offices are also looking into building probability online panels (Amarov & Rendtel, 2013; Cobben & Bethlehem, 2013), although quality and representativeness are key issues here, raising much debate (Svensoon, 2013).

As already mentioned, we still have a lot to learn about sampling and weighting for non-probability panels, and we challenge our readers to design and conduct more research on online panel data quality. Unfortunately, the evidence so far shows that the advantages of online panel data collection in terms of cost, speed and reach of niche populations do not always correlate with data quality.

Finally, it is very important to remember that quality is related to cost. As the cost of a 'survey complete' for a non-probability online panel can be as low as $2 (Terhanian & Bremer, 2012), how can this be compared with the costs from a probability panel or a telephone interview, which can be 10 times higher, while an F2F interview may be even 100 times more expensive? Does such a price range truly reflect the differences in data quality? We briefly reflect on these issues in Section 6.1.4. We look forward to more research being conducted on online panel data quality and hope this section contributes to this discussion.

5.3 WEB SURVEY SOFTWARE

Some form of software is needed to run a web survey. In the early 1990s this was a custom-made computer program, created from scratch for the needs of a specific questionnaire, an approach we can still find today in some circumstances. Further, numerous web survey modules and plug-ins, usually with limited functionalities, exist within content management systems, e-learning platforms, social network sites and other web services. Finally, there is dedicated web survey software, our key focus here.

The scholarly literature rarely addresses web survey software; exceptions are Baker (2013), Crawford (2002), Kaczmirek (2008), Wright (2005) and Macer (2014). Some conference presentations, online evaluations, magazine reviews, blogs and forums also exist, which address these issues (see the WebSM overview of blogs)[13]. Publications and posts of authors from the survey software industry can also be helpful, but tend to be promotional (Bhaskaran & LeClaire, 2010), while independent experts are very rare.[14]

Despite the importance, it seems that complexity and changing dynamics prevent more thorough scholarly elaboration of this matter. Namely, there are hundreds of web survey software packages, with thousands of features and with a long array of evaluation criteria, from usability, communication, statistics and methodology to technical, legal, managerial and cost aspects. In addition, web survey software changes very quickly; many suppliers publish weekly improvements and newcomers appear continuously. Changes in the broader environment create additional turbulence, from developments of technology (e.g. SaaS, HTML5), survey design principles (e.g. adaptive design) and changes in usability principles (e.g. with web 2.0) to new services (e.g. social network sites), new devices (e.g. smartphones and tablets) and professional standards related to methodology (e.g. nonresponse coding), legislation (e.g. cookie/spam regulation) or security (e.g. ISO standards).

Correspondingly, the perception of 'must have', 'should have' and 'nice to have' features of web survey software (Kaczmirek, 2008, p. 238) is changing rapidly and today's best choice may become obsolete tomorrow, while 'tomorrow' can be as short as a year because about half of the marketing research companies have plans to change their platform for the collection and analysis of data in the next two years (Macer & Wilson, 2014).

In general, the ideal software saves resources, increases data quality and ensures satisfaction of the respondent, researcher and client/sponsor. The importance and value of selecting the right software often exceeds the decisions related to countless methodological issues which are extensively elaborated on in the literature and also in the previous chapters of this book.

Of course, different types of users make different demands on web survey software. Good software is particularly important for *professional* users, such as dedicated data collection organizations (statistics offices, marketing research agencies) and other survey-intensive institutions (research/academic/non-profit), as well as for advanced and complex types of web survey projects, such as online panels, very complex questionnaires (e.g. research experiments) and large (e.g. population census) or repeating (e.g. customer satisfaction) surveys. These professional users appreciate the nuances of advanced features and often highly value long-term liaisons. For them, a change in web survey software also brings serious technical, methodological and organizational complications and inefficiencies.

Needs may be somewhat smaller for *ordinary users*, who often implement simple or moderately advanced web surveys as part of their specific projects. This is usually only an accompanying or supporting activity, which may also be to a certain extent regular; however, it is still not an essential part of their business or professional activity, nor is it methodologically very advanced. At the lower end of this segment, there are many DIY users, who actually create the majority of today's web surveys and typically require only a limited set of functionalities. The ordinary user can also usually switch the software relatively easily.

We first look at the broader conceptual framework of web survey software (Section 5.3.1), then we review the web survey software market (Section 5.3.2), web survey software characteristics (Sections 5.3.3) and discuss two selected usability aspects (5.3.4). Finally, we address the software selection process (5.3.5) and future trends (5.3.6).

We predominantly focus on support for the core web survey process (Figure 1.1, Section 1.2) despite the reality which increasingly treats web surveys only as integrated into the broader social science research environment. This is sometimes covered under the umbrella of e-social science (Vehovar, Petrovčič, & Slavec, 2014) where ideally the entire research process is supported by one integral ICT solution, similar to e-learning platforms. On the other hand, the web survey process is also becoming an element within various application areas, such as marketing research, HRM, customer satisfaction, customer relationship marketing (CRM), business intelligence, direct marketing, sales, etc. The notion of enterprise feedback management (EFM) often emerges here in relation to customer (and other stakeholder) surveys in complex organizations, where multiple levels of users exist (e.g. questionnaire authors, data managers, reporters, translators, dashboard executives).

5.3.1 Integrated ICT Support for the Web Survey Process

Considering the core web survey process – pre-fielding, fielding and post-fielding – we would normally expect ICT to integrate the entire process. This is, however, not the case (yet) as seen from the overview summarized in Table 5.1, where levels of the integration of ICT support in today's web survey software were assigned to the stages of the web survey process. This assignment of levels was done based on our experience and according to exhaustive analyses of the web survey software market (Vehovar, Čehovin et al., 2012).

Strong support means that all web survey software supports and integrates a certain stage or sub-stage of the web survey process. One such aspect is the computerization of the questionnaire (2.3b), which is supported by all tools. Advanced software may offer some additional user-friendliness, guidance and diagnostics to this process, such as online help. Another stage in the full integration of ICT support is the measurement (3.2), where ICT fully supports filling in the questionnaire and saving data. This is also the most essential feature of web survey software and is thus fully supported by all software. Here, too, some advanced tools may provide additional features, such as real-time quality controls (Peytchev & Crawford, 2005), break & continue options, etc.

Moderate support means that the majority of tools already integrate these functionalities. Here we talk about recruitment (3.1), elaborated

Table 5.1   Stages of web survey process and levels of integrated ICT support*

Step in survey research process	Integrated ICT support
1 Preliminary research activities	None
2 PRE-FIELDING	
2.1 Mode elaboration	Weak
2.2 Sampling	Weak
2.3 Questionnaire preparation	
(a) Questionnaire development	Almost none
(b) Computerization of the questionnaire	**Strong**
(c) Testing	Weak
2.4 Nonresponse strategy	Weak
2.5 Technical preparations	Moderate
2.6 Management	Almost none
3 FIELDING	
3.1 Recruitment	Moderate
3.2 Measurement	**Strong**
3.3 Processing and monitoring	Weak
4 POST-FIELDING	
4.1 Data preparation	Weak
4.2 Preliminary results	Moderate
4.3 Data exporting and archiving	Weak
5 Advanced analysis, processing, valorization	None

* The first two levels in the table follow the section structure of the core Chapters 2, 3 and 4.

technical support (2.4) and preliminary reporting (4.2). The corresponding sections of our book discuss in detail various features that require the related ICT support. Recruitment and preliminary reporting are particularly important and they typically appear, together with both strongly supported stages (2.3b and 3.2), already in web survey software navigation menus, suggesting the basic stream of the process:

Create → Recruit → Measure → Analyse

We may add that in some web survey software the 'Recruit' and 'Measure' stages are merged into 'Collect'. In addition, of course, various different labels may be used instead of 'Recruit', such as 'Distribute', 'Publish' or 'Invite'.

Weak support means that some external ICT solutions are typically used and only rare, advanced web survey software may partially support the particular stage. This holds for support for mixed-mode surveys (2.1), which are rarely integrated with the web survey software (e.g. software that would support web and telephone surveys). In addition, this holds for sample selection (2.2), which is typically done with external data management tools, and testing (2.3c), where various external tools are usually needed for advanced questionnaire diagnostics (e.g. Survey Quality Predictor)[15], for capturing and analysing usability documentation (screenshots, paradata), for various questionnaire evaluation methods (Madans et al., 2011), etc. Only the most advanced tools (Stark & Gatward, 2010) partially integrate some of these aspects. Support for the nonresponse strategy (2.5) is also typically very limited and even response rates often need to be calculated manually, because unit response statuses are difficult to establish 'on the fly'.

Weak support also relates to fieldwork processing and monitoring (3.3). Web survey software usually provides limited insight into the web survey process and external calculations are required to support some decisions. Similarly, a detailed insight into the data quality (e.g. satisficing, unusable units, etc.) is not provided during the fielding step.

The same is true for data preparation (4.1), where only limited integration of ICT support exists. Instead, various external tools are usually involved for editing, coding, recoding, weighting, imputations, and also for data management (e.g. file sort, merge, update). These are all complex activities, especially if detailed documentation is required, such as audit trails (paradata) about changes (who, when, what) or checks for consistency of changes in the datafile. The same holds for data export and archiving (4.3), where elaborate paradata exports, archive production and export to standard library formats – except for some rare tools (e.g. Blaise)[16] – are typically produced externally or additionally on special request.

Almost no support means that external ICT services are typically needed to support some features at the particular stage and even the most advanced tools provide very little ICT integration. Here questionnaire development (2.3a) can be exposed as most typical, because, as discussed in the corresponding Section 2.3.6, it usually involves a combination of text processors (e.g. MS Word, Google Docs) or some specialized questionnaire specification tools and some asynchronous communication tool (e.g. email, web exchange) of the draft questionnaires. Vehovar, Čehovin et al. (2014), however, demonstrated that ICT integration of this stage together with computerization (2.3b) would require relatively few extensions (e.g. online editing, integrated questionnaire feedback via a commenting system, etc.). This approach then potentially also enables the full documentation of the questionnaire development process (i.e. tracking the changes) and enhances the involvement of interactive diagnostics in the process using language technologies (language quality of the question wording), data mining (looking for potential questions from a library) and artificial intelligence (formalizing and implementing the questionnaire development rules from the theoretical literature). This is without a doubt one of the key challenges for the future development of web survey software.

Having almost no integrated ICT support is also characteristic of general management (2.6), which usually requires external software support (e.g. BaseCamp, MS Project). The same is true also for internal (i.e. team) and external (i.e. sponsor/client) communication, which would ideally be integrated with management, as well as with web survey software. Today, however, the communication typically runs externally via email, forums, chat, or by some dedicated online collaboration tools (e.g. wiki). Here, too, some rare advanced tools now increasingly integrate communication and management functionalities, especially when they are structured across levels of users, multiple surveys, complex surveys or online panels.

No support means that none of the web survey software integrates the corresponding ICT support, either because the corresponding ICT services are external to the web survey software or because there is no such support at all. This is related (in Table 5.1) to preliminary research activities (1), where a set of separate ICT services is used, from email and video conferencing to special software for brainstorming, mind mapping, structuring ideas, computerized qualitative research and question bank systems (e.g. Survey Question Bank)[17]. The same is true for advanced analysis (5), where for example the statistical analysis is performed externally via spreadsheets or professional statistical tools (e.g. IBM-SPSS, R, Stata, SAS), as well as for advanced processing (e.g. integration into some CRM) and valorization (e.g. preparation for print).

All in all, we can observe a considerable fragmentation of the corresponding ICT support. In part this can be attributed to the lack of an integrated conceptual approach, which then causes the survey process to be perceived as being split into isolated components, each supported with separate ICT solutions. Such separation was historically established due to various technical limitations (e.g. web 2.0 appeared only a decade ago) which are now being increasingly removed, but also due to the historically prevailing engineering perspective of the software developers (Vehovar, Čehovin et al., 2014), where methodologists were not the key architects.

The ideal software would integrate ICT support for all steps of the core web survey process and we actually do observe a general trend in this direction. Of course, pre-fielding and post-fielding activities are very demanding to formalize and integrate, which is perhaps best illustrated in the various research papers presented at the Blaise user conferences.[18] We should also add that the integration we talk about is in fact strongly appreciated from the perspective of users who wish to design, collect, analyse and present survey data with just one tool (Macer & Wilson, 2014).

There are of course limits on how far dedicated web survey software can and should go with the integration of ICT support, instead of relying on the specialized external ICT solutions. The integration should take into account the huge differences among the stages, each having specific limitations, dynamics and challenges. For example, a highly specialized and powerful imputation feature might simply be too complex and expensive to be developed just as an integrated component of web survey software.

5.3.2 The Web Survey Software Market

From the very beginning, in the 1970s, the CASIC market has been very dynamic due to the shifts from mainframes to desktops, from MS DOS to MS Windows, and then also to the Internet. Nevertheless, the web survey software industry was already well-established by the late 1990s, and included some of today's leading suppliers, from complex commercial (e.g. Blaise, GlobalPark/Questback, Confirmit) or open source tools (e.g. PhPSurveyor/LimeSurvey) to inexpensive hosted platforms with a web GUI, all of which enabled the user-friendly creation of web surveys without any programming script (e.g. SurveyMonkey).

Nowadays, the dynamics of the market are strongly characterized by startups, venture capital, mergers and acquisitions.[19] The pressure for profit is further pushing the suppliers of web survey software to establish their own online panels and thus – in addition to software – also provide researchers with samples of respondents.

Consumers benefit from this competition as more and more software features become an inexpensive commodity. At the same time – as in other global ICT industries – market concentration is a trend. The big players are slowly suppressing the low-price end of the industry, where many players support only ordinary users. The market concentration also manifests at the high-price end of advanced tools for professional users, because high development and marketing costs require increasingly large numbers of customers.

We observe that suppliers who have been on the market for a decade or more are increasingly facing limitations in flexibility, arising from restrictions related to their initial software architecture. The move to SaaS, implementation of web 2.0 (e.g. drag and drop functions) and support for mobile devices are the most typical examples of where many suppliers have lost their competitiveness. At the same time, entry barriers to the web survey software market are increasing. Only a few new software packages were detected on the global market in 2013 and 2014 (WebSM, 2014). The same holds for in-house tools, created exclusively for certain organizations, which are increasingly being abandoned due to the inability to cope with continuous requests for modification and integration. Their share among marketing research companies is falling towards and below 10% (Macer & Wilson, 2014).

There are currently hundreds of specialized web survey software tools on the market. Due to their dynamics a comprehensive overview is increasingly difficult to maintain. We rely hereafter on the WebSM list of web survey software (WebSM, 2014), which is predominantly limited to English-language-based tools, but also includes key tools in Spanish, German and Russian. We do not believe there are many global tools outside this list, except perhaps in Asia. In 2013 the WebSM list included 350 active tools, with the majority of the suppliers located in the United States (42%) and Europe (35%). This structure applies to 2014 as well, because the number of active tools has remained almost unchanged (352 tools).

According to the 2012 WebSM study (Vehovar, Čehovin et al., 2012), the majority of web survey software (51%) are commercial tools intended for ordinary users, usually offering them fixed price packages. In addition, ordinary users are offered various free (3%) or open source tools (7%). A quarter (25%) of tools target professional users, while the remaining segment (15%) consists of tools which support web surveys only partially (e.g. event support, quizzes, forms, voting, HRM), as a by-product, and often have rather limited functionalities.

The weak presence of open source tools – as well as their prevailing limitation in capabilities – can in part be explained by the related request for their own server installation, which is often an insurmountable obstacle for ordinary users, but also for professionals who may lack the technical staff that can handle open source solutions. In addition, prompt and professional user support is extremely important for this specific web service, which is another advantage of commercial solutions over the open source ones. A recent study of open source web survey software confirms this, and there is a trend that these tools are now increasingly starting to charge for some of their services (e.g. installation, hosting) (see the open-source study in WebSM, 2014).

5.3.3 Characteristics of Web Survey Software

The most apparent distinction among web survey software is the *price*. Low-priced software typically targets ordinary users and includes the following packages (Vehovar, Čehovin et al. 2012):

- A free version (with various limitations, typically with up to around 100 responses or 10 questions per questionnaire and with limited features).
- A basic version in the range of a few tens of euros/dollars per month (but also as low as €3 per month), with limited features (typically, no support for conditions and advanced question types).

- One, two or even three versions (e.g. advanced, professional and corporate), where prices and features gradually increase, but usually stay within up to a few hundreds of euros/dollars per month.

The trend is towards a reduction in the number of packages per supplier. Sometimes only one flat rate (per month or year) is offered. Similarly, the price-per-respondent model is disappearing and only 12% of tools offered such a model in 2012. The corresponding price depends on the total number of respondents per month and ranges from €0.002 to €0.938 per respondent (average €0.194, median €0.145). An update in 2014 shows a very similar situation (see pricing study in WebSM, 2014).

The low-priced tools are extensively elaborated in Vehovar, Čehovin et al. (2012), while the corresponding overview of features with separate package levels can be found in Čehovin & Vehovar (2012a). A comparison with past studies (Vehovar, Koren, Lozar Manfreda, & Berzelak, 2005) illustrates how distinguishing features, such as advanced types of questions, support for conditions, real-time validations, randomization, data piping, etc., are increasingly becoming industry standards.

On the other hand, the high-priced web survey software targets professional users and it is not structured into packages. Instead, a quote is typically required; tailored specification is then provided, followed by negotiations. There are huge differences in the advanced *methodological features* (Vehovar, Čehovin et al., 2012) of high-end tools, which are typically not supported by the low-end tools for ordinary users. In general these features relate to all advanced aspects of the features discussed above in relation to Table 2.1. We provide below a more specific overview of the features and first expose six essential methodological characteristics that most clearly define the advanced web survey software:

1 Integrated *email system* with advanced features in database management (e.g merging email lists), design (e.g. elaborated formatting of email invitations), email diagnostics (e.g.

insight whether email was delivered/open), monitoring (e.g. powerful dashboard for detailed, tracking detailed response history of each unit), setting for sender's email (e.g. anyname@anyorganisation.com) and very strong spam prevention (see Section 2.4.1).

2 Integration of *mixed-mode surveys* (e.g. web, telephone, F2F, mail), including recruiting, case management and database synchronization.

3 Integrated support for *multiple devices* (desktop/notebook, smartphone, tablet, ITV), including full optimization for browser-based mobile surveys and integrated support for creating mobile survey apps, as well as for authoring apps for creating browser based web surveys (Section 5.1.6).

4 *Language and translations*: multilingual support for respondents, storage of multilingual responses in a single datafile, option for respondents to select the language, option to have different URLs for different languages, a capable translation interface with strict separation from changes of the questionnaire, flexibility for changing the default text of validation type messages and navigation buttons, multilingual question libraries, multilingual administrative user interface.

5 *Advanced questionnaire features* as outlined in Section 2.3.2 with strong question modification flexibility, advanced question types (e.g. 360°, social networks, conjoint analyses, biomarkers, multimedia, etc.), powerful support for graphics and multimedia, integration with location based services (maps, geographic information systems, GPS) and support for integrated questionnaire development and testing (e.g. elaborated commenting system).

6 *Support for longitudinal surveys*, including general features supporting sample and case management for longitudinal surveys, where units are surveyed more times (from sample selection to tracking of the units) and also specific support for online panels: from recruitment to panellist profiling, various process optimizations, management of incentives, fraud detection, post-survey adjustments, etc. See Macer (2014) for a detailed treatment.

Besides the above methodological issues, important distinctions between high-end and low-end web survey software also exist with respect to features related to *technical, managerial* and *administrative* aspects, which were discussed from a substantive point of view in various other sections of this book:

7   Data collection can be done at the *client* and also at a *supplier server* (SaaS), where each option has advantages and disadvantages related to security requirements (see Section 2.4.3).

8   In a desktop/notebook *installation* there can be an option for enabling offline questionnaire creation. Similarly, there can be an option for user-friendly creation of web surveys from mobile devices (see Section 5.1.5).

9   An important option is to add custom parts of programming scripts to existing code and the option of developing web questionnaires based on the stand-alone *programming language*, which can enhance speed and flexibility of programming for long/complex questionnaires (e.g. thousands of questions with complicated real-time validations).

10 Advanced technical features are related to *capacity* (e.g. no limitations for number of users, survey projects, responses), *privacy* (e.g. advanced IP and cookie settings), *security* (e.g. mirroring, replications, backups, tracking, cloud), *technical standards* (e.g. W3C) and web accessibility standards for people with disabilities (e.g. Section 508[20]).

11 Support for *multiuser hierarchy* assigning elaborated selective features and authority relates to various levels of users (e.g. EFM).

12 Advanced support for *administration, management, monitoring and reporting* can be offered, from automatic response rate calculations (e.g. AAPOR rates) and elaborated missing data documentation to various processing and project management reports, insights and intervention.

13 *Integration with business processes* is extremely important, from direct plug-ins (e.g. for selling) to general flexibility of linking with other software (e.g. for marketing, analytics, business intelligence, etc.) and particularly the ease and capability for integration and communication with internal data in the organization.

14 Support for *changing/switching of the tool* – particularly importing and exporting features – is extremely important to avoid being an unnecessary 'prisoner' of a certain tool (Kinesis, 2013a).

15 Quality of the *user support*, from manuals, documentation, tutorials to interaction (e.g. chat, phone, operating times, response time), is strongly related to the *level of localization*: (a) quality user interface in the language of a researcher (not only English interface), (b) question and questionnaire libraries in local language and (c) effective local support (telephone and live help, training, interventions and additional software development).

16 Transparent and elaborated *legal issues* and *financial terms* are very important and can strongly vary.

High-end solutions typically start with annual fees of thousands of euros/dollars and may easily reach six-figure numbers for professional users in dedicated data collection organizations. The high-end tools are thus already very clearly separated by price level and also with the absence of option of packages.

An easy but important and very specific delimitation feature between high-end and low-end tools – but also for structuring within the high-end tools themselves – is the presence/absence of one's own programming language (point 9 in the above list). Similarly distinctive is the compliance with formal accessibility standards (mentioned in point 10 in the above list).

Despite these differences the line between low- and high-end tools is becoming increasingly blurred: the former support more and more features needed by professional users, while some of the latter extend their supply and prices to approach ordinary users. In part, this is considerably due to the characteristics of web survey software, which address the issues of all tools and are related to user-friendliness, adaptation to new trends and usability:

17 *General usability* has many components (Nielsen, 2012), from design, general user-friendliness, number of clicks needed to perform operations, speed and overall sophistication (e.g. the tool might be unnecessarily technical) to architecture and navigation.

18 Capable *GUI*, which provides friendly support to handle complex operations

(e.g. conditions) and can thus to a considerable extent replace the need for scripts (i.e. written program code, see point (9)).

19   *Design flexibility* is related to the quality of default survey templates, friendly design builder interface (e.g. to change a logotype, a header/footer, fonts, colours), integrated CSS editor, capable external imports and also a powerful responsive web design feature to automatically adapt the layout to various devices.

An interesting trend in the level of *involvement of computer programmers* in the web survey process can be observed here. That is, computer programmers were historically included in the survey process as an inevitable collateral component of the CASIC revolution. Specifically, in order to create a computerized questionnaire, professional programming skills were needed to write the programming scripts which described and ran the questionnaire. This of course complicated the process substantially, because the programmers required elaborated specifications, feedback, communication and various levels of control. All of this introduced an additional stage into the process and also generated costs, complications, conflicts and prolongations. Only in the late 1990s did the web GUI enable non-programmers to create (simple) web surveys. After the web 2.0 revolution and other technological advances in the 2000s, GUI developments further enhanced this process. On the other hand, for very complex questionnaires the offline programming script – which of course requires certain computer programming skills – sometimes still seems to be more efficient. However, new tools are increasingly shifting these borders and thus re-establishing the pre-CASIC era, where survey researchers alone could create, finalize and control the questionnaires without any computer programmers.

5.3.4 Discussion of Two Selected Features

We elaborate further on the interface speed and critical features of the GUI – already included among the 19 aspects above (points 17 and 18) – both as an illustration of the complexity of these aspects and because they are often forgotten.

5.3.4.1 Interface speed

Within the general usability aspects of the web survey software the *speed*, in terms of page loading time when creating and editing a web questionnaire, may be a serious problem for a researcher during the process of creating the questionnaire. If the questionnaire runs offline on a desktop/notebook with a script, the corresponding response times are (almost) zero, which is an important advantage of such an approach. This speed advantage of offline editing – particularly when editing questionnaires with hundreds or thousands of questions – is one of the key reasons why some advanced web survey software may even rely exclusively on programming scripts instead of a web GUI. On the other hand, when the questionnaire is on the web, using the GUI, which is today's prevailing solution, speed may become an issue. The bulk of the delay is not created by the Internet connection – even overseas distances (e.g. Europe–United States) typically contribute a delay of up to 0.5 seconds for a simple task (e.g. adding a question) – but arises from the specifics of the web survey software running on a server.

Differences in speed are considerable, as observed in a study where 16 SaaS tools were compared (Čehovin & Vehovar, 2012b) for key questionnaire development commands: add, edit and delete a question; create, preview, save and delete the questionnaire; click on internal and external navigation buttons. The highest average delays were found for the questionnaire saving command (2.8 seconds), with a maximum of up to 8.7 seconds.

Another command with a large average delay concerned clicking on the outside features of the application (e.g. help, about, etc.) with an average of 3.0 seconds, though the slowest tool required 8.1 seconds. Other commands had averages mostly in the interval of 1–2 seconds, but with considerable variations.

In addition, the average Google PageSpeed Insights score (higher values are better and 100 is the maximum) for the 16 SaaS websites hosting the observed survey software included in the study was 77 out of 100 (minimum 57, maximum 99), while the measured average response time for the 'homepage' or 'first page' on those websites was 2.3 seconds (minimum 0.6, maximum 6.6).

Comparing these figures with standard benchmarks gives the impression that web survey software is in fact a relatively slow web service. As a general rule, we should acknowledge that humans typically do not notice delays below 0.1 seconds. After that the effect increases and becomes clearly noticeable – although non-problematic and usually still tolerable – until around 1.0 second (Nielsen, 1993). After this point annoyance slowly increases and can reach a critical level after 10 seconds, where users become increasingly impatient, nervous or think about abandoning the exercise. In web questionnaire development using a GUI we can easily approach these delays with large questionnaires (e.g. hundreds or thousands of questions). However, we should add that increasing technological developments are continuously improving the performances of GUIs.

All these benchmarks are based on pre-Internet times, established by research 30–40 years ago on human–computer interaction; however, they still hold, and this is true also for the elaboration of factors causing differential tolerance for various tasks and software types, as well as for the impact of these delays on productivity, which in our case is related to developing a questionnaire (see Shneiderman, 1984).

In any case, speed is easy to measure and also easy to compare with different tolerance levels, so when selecting web survey software a researcher may check for this feature, because considerable differences exist within SaaS solutions using a GUI for creating a questionnaire. We should again recall that when programming

scripts are used to describe the questionnaires, this problem disappears (delays are zero).

5.3.4.2 Critical Features of the GUI

Despite the above problems of speed, GUIs are becoming increasingly popular, particularly in the WYSIWYG (What You See Is What You Get) context. Decades of developments of text processors (e.g. MS Word, Google Docs, Open/Libre Office) may serve as a good parallel here, where considerable convergence and standardization have already occurred with respect to the corresponding GUI solutions (e.g. buttons with standardized position and functionality are used in all tools). Certain standardization was also achieved in the case of web survey software, so the structure of landing pages and that of the inner interface of competing tools is often very similar. However, several issues are still open, awaiting a final solution.

Currently it seems that researchers often select from options according to subjective personal preference. However, we believe that some alternatives are basically outdated and inefficient. Most of these relate to (a) the layout of the questionnaire, (b) basic procedures and steps for editing a question, (c) the interface for creating conditions (i.e. branching) and (d) information architecture and navigation. More insight into some of these dilemmas can be found in the corresponding Supplement to Chapter 5, *Characteristics of web survey software* (http://websm.org/ch5).

One simple check for the efficiency of the corresponding GUI is the *number of clicks needed to accomplish a certain task*. In principle, advanced and high-end tools with more features need more complex navigation and consequently more clicks. Nevertheless, important differences still exist within similar tools. A study of a homogeneous group of 27 tools, where a standardized questionnaire was programmed (Berzelak & Lozar Manfreda, 2009), showed that a wide range of clicks was needed to create a standardized questionnaire (from 149 to 524 clicks). A recent evaluation of some of the most popular web survey software showed that the range of average number of clicks for performing individual tasks when creating a standardized questionnaire goes from 3.1 to 6.3 (Čehovin & Vehovar, 2012b). Any user can repeat this task and check this number for corresponding software.

To summarize, these two aspects (speed and the number of clicks) can easily be measured in a standardized way and then compared with benchmarks in the above report. In addition, it is also advisable to perform a qualitative evaluation in a real setting with experienced users or usability experts, because these issues are often difficult to evaluate before the actual usage experience occurs.

5.3.5 Finding the Right Tool

Customers of any service or product face the problem of separating marketing noise from reality, while, on the other hand, it is sometimes difficult to find potentially good products, which are not excessively promoted. We face the same problem with web survey software. It is thus helpful to structure the process of finding web survey software into four phases, all of which are conceptually similar for professional and ordinary users.

Preliminary list of specifications. Firstly, the real and also realistic needs of a researcher have to be clarified. A preliminary step in this direction for ordinary users may be to check the preliminary list of standard package features (Čehovin & Vehovar, 2012a), while professional users should further elaborate on the 19 features of high-end tools mentioned above to articulate their needs and positions. A researchers performing the experiments are perhaps the most unique and non-standardized segment, with very specific requirements (e.g. they may require a particular paradata export, such as mouse movement tracking).

We should recall that, throughout this book, we have systematically elaborated all stages of the web survey process and discussed many methodological features, all of which require corresponding

ICT support. Very often we have also made explicit comments about the required features of web survey software. The best preliminary specification of required features can therefore be obtained by careful consideration of our discussion at various stages of the web survey process.

Here, we also need to caution that web survey software does not always use the same standard language to describe certain survey features, so sometimes it is difficult to understand if a particular function is supported, so additional efforts may be required.

Shortlisting the specifications and criteria. Among the features on the preliminary list we then need to identify the essential ones. We have the same situation here as when buying any other product or service. For example, if we were buying a car, we would first use a few simple and easy to identify essential criteria, possibly related to the budget and some other key characteristics (size, kilometres per year, maintenance costs, environmental concerns). This then determines our core level (e.g. a family saloon car), while from a substantive view of functionalities other details would be less important (e.g. colour, brand, additional features). With web survey software, the essential criteria are also linked to budget range and then to the scale, which relates here to the number of surveys, number of questions per survey, number of respondents, number of web survey software users and the number of hierarchical levels. Other criteria are more specific to our needs, and should be carefully identified from standard characteristics (Čehovin & Vehovar, 2012a) or from the above 19 advanced features. For ordinary users the usability aspects discussed above may have some importance, while professional users may focus more on SaaS specifics and the programming scripts.

Users may also have various additional preferences. For example, they may need easy and user-friendly interventions in the questionnaire during fielding (i.e. on the fly), or detailed online insight into the results/statistics, so the tool needs to support this. Similarly, if we require some advanced question types, such as very specific combined tables (Section 2.3.2), we need to check explicitly for this feature.

Shortlisting of the tools. Knowing what we need enables us to check the corresponding supply. This should start with an extensive – and preferably systematic and formally structured – consultation with peers, colleagues, partners, etc. This is the most powerful source of information, but only if done properly and extensively, otherwise we may end up with deceptive results (e.g. information from different, non-comparable or problematic users). We may also systematically perform our own investigation on the web. Unfortunately, no list (including the WebSM and Quirk's lists)[21] is fully exhaustive, structured friendly, and maintained frequently enough. For the SaaS solutions, the ranking of the tools according to approximate page visits (Vehovar, Čehovin et al., 2014) may provide some insight into established players; however, many deficiencies are associated with such a ranking.

Selection process. The final phase is a multi-criteria exercise, where a set of essential criteria established in previous phases is evaluated by key users (or evaluators or experts), who score each dimension (typically on a scale of 1–5), while the sum of the averages gives the 'winner'. For more elaborate cases some professional strategies from the area of group decision making related to the software selection process may be used (Lai, Wong, & Cheung, 2002). There, the importance of certain criteria and the evaluation according to these criteria are first measured and then combined.

When decisions relate to tens or hundreds of thousands of euros/dollars annually – and also have an essential impact on organization flows and satisfaction of the employees involved – the selection processes should be more elaborate. Investing in experts or an expert panel might be a very wise decision. Changing some complex software is a potential nightmare for any organization, given that there is no easy way to transform and integrate surveys from one software package to another.

5.3.6 Trends in Web Survey Software

We expect that increased ICT integration across pre-fielding, fielding and post-fielding will likely continue and also intensify, so support for more and more stages in the web survey process (Table 5.1) will move to a higher level. Users will get much better services for lower costs. In particular, the involvement of data mining, language technologies and artificial intelligence in all stages of the process is expected to increase (Vehovar, Petrovčič & Slavec, 2014).

We may also expect a general shift towards hosted solutions (SaaS), already preferred by the majority of ordinary users today. However, it is questionable whether large clients will – due to security and privacy reasons – fully accept this approach and give up their own installations.

We can also expect the web GUI to continue replacing programming scripts. However, just as GUIs for text processors did not prevent technical professionals and publishers – and also some researchers publishing in the technical disciplines – from preferring LaTeX programming tools for describing text, the niche of professional users will perhaps continue to use programming scripts for complex questionnaires.

With respect to web GUIs for questionnaire creation, a convergence – similar to text processors – may occur towards a standardized interface solution, which may follow online text processor interfaces with the additional integration of commenting tools and also with the provision of various view/mode options. We should stress, however, that online text processors currently still have certain drawbacks in speed and functionalities compared with the corresponding offline alternatives, so this process might be slow.

We can also expect further concentration and globalization of the market. In many aspects, only large suppliers will be able to provide effective support across the entire spectrum of devices and operating systems, as well as with respect to ICT integration across the stages of the web survey process. Equally demanding is the possible continuous integration of advanced algorithms into the questionnaire development process (data mining, language resources and technologies, artificial intelligence). On the other hand, it is also true that technological progress facilitates and simplifies the implementation of new solutions across platforms and devices (e.g. HTML5). However, many features, such as comprehensive multilingual support involving various aspects of localization, do require substantial resources, which only the large players can afford. Nevertheless, new technologies may still offer some opportunities to newcomers and for niche players, as was the situation in recent years when a number of new tools appeared and predominantly focused on mobile web surveys (Vehovar, Čehovin & Močnik, 2014)

Let us also briefly reiterate the issue of devices, because we are increasingly interacting with the web not only through desktop and notebook computers, but also through a series of other devices with very specific interfaces and screen sizes, and which are now being used to answer web surveys. As discussed in Section 5.1.2, this creates many complications, because these devices are in many respects much less standardized than desktop and notebook computers. Obviously, the web survey software should recognize the device and modify the questionnaire accordingly (e.g. omit drag and drop questions and mouse-over texts). This means, for example, automatic modification for small screens (e.g. splitting tables into separate items, arranging long horizontal options vertically, etc.). However, adapting for these specifics seems to be a relatively slow process, as discussed

in Section 5.1.6, where we showed that the majority of web survey software in 2014 still does not provide automatic smartphone adaptations for browser-based mobile surveys, even for the basic aspects, such as eliminating the need for zooming or horizontal scrolling (see mobile feature study in WebSM, 2014).

With respect to the mobile survey apps discussed in Section 5.1.5, we can expect a few more years of further turbulence before things settle down and stabilize, particularly with the expanded implementations of HTML5 standard and advanced browser-based scripts. We can recall here the late 1990s when client-based questionnaire applications started to appear for desktop computers (see Section 1.3.2) and gained momentum due to their superior design flexibility and speed over browser-based web surveys. However, Internet speed subsequently increased, browsers improved and client scripts were developed, so the client-based applications for desktops/laptops lost their advantages and almost disappeared. We believe that contemporary mobile survey apps, which are basically a type of client-based application, will also follow a similar trend. However, at this time somehow more exceptions might exist, related to situations that require location-based services.

NOTES

1 http://www.pewinternet.org/fact-sheets/mobile-technology-fact-sheet/

2 Uporaba informacijsko-komunikacijske tehnologije. Statistični urad Republike Slovenije. Retrieved September 1, 2014, from http://www.stat.si/tema_ekonomsko_infdruzba_informacijsko.asp

3 The ultimate mobile email statistics overview. Emailmonday. Retrieved September 1, 2014, from http://www.emailmonday.com/mobile-email-usage-statistics

4 Apple cedes market share in smartphone operating system market as Android surges and Windows phone gains, according to IDC. IDC Analyze the Future. Retrieved September 1, 2014, from http://www.idc.com

5 IDC Analyze the Future. Retrieved September 1, 2014, from http://www.idc.com

6 *ELIPSS*. Retrieved September 1, 2014, from http://www.elipss.fr

7 Seven ways mobile phones have changed lives in Africa. Retrieved September 1, 2014, from http://www.cnn.com

8 This section draws on some material from Callegaro et al. (2014a).

9 Note that for the ISO, access panels are 'a sample database of potential respondents who declare that they will cooperate for future data collection if selected' (p. 1).

10 For space reasons we omit here a third quality metric: test–retest reliability (running the same study at two close points in time on the same panel but with a different set of respondents)

11 http://webdatanet.cbs.dk/

12 GESIS Panel Roadshow 2013/2014. Retrieved September 1, 2014, from http://www.gesis.org

13 http://www.websm.org/blogs/

14 For example, http://www.meaning.uk.com/blogs/tim-macer/

15 http://sqp.upf.edu/

16 http://www.blaise.com/

17 http://surveynet.ac.uk/sqb/

18 http://www.websm.org/blaise

19 Mergers in web survey software & service industry. Retrieved September 1, 2014, from http://www.websm.org/merges

20 http://www.websm.org/508

21 http://websm.org/sw and http://www.quirks.com/directory/software/

CONTENTS

Broader context of web surveys

In previous chapters we focused on the essential methodological aspects of the core web survey process (Chapters 2, 3, 4) and on related implementations (Chapter 5), while in this chapter we will discuss the broader methodological (Section 6.1), managerial (Section 6.2) and professional (Section 6.3) contexts, which are all very important for understanding and managing the process of web surveys. We also overview the web survey bibliography (Section 6.4).

6.1 BROADER METHODOLOGICAL CONTEXT

We first address aspects that have considerable indirect methodological relevance for web surveys and provide a closer look at the definition of the web survey mode (Section 6.1.1), data quality (Section 6.1.2), web survey mode effect (Section 6.1.3) and costs (Section 6.1.4). In addition, we review the related activities that extend beyond the core web survey process (Section 6.1.5): the steps of preliminary research activities and advanced analysis, processing and valorization, as well as mixed-modes and mixed methods. We conclude with a discussion on adaptive, responsive and interactive designs (Section 6.1.6).

6.1.1 Web Survey Mode Revised

Our initial definition (Section 1.1.1) of the basic web survey mode served as an introduction to this mode, but now we can outline it more precisely. Firstly, let us say again that we conceptualized the survey mode as being entirely separate from the sampling and also from the recruitment process. When we defined it, we thus considered only factors with a direct impact on the measurement stage, where respondents fill in the questionnaire.

The literature typically defines the survey mode with certain attributes (dimensions, factors, characteristics) that are related to the

features and procedures of the measurement stage. These attributes define the basic mechanisms of communication, including information transfer between the respondent and questionnaire. While different authors (Biemer & Lyberg, 2003; Couper, 2011; Groves et al., 2009; Tourangeau & Bradburn, 2010) identified different dimensions of the survey mode, recently Berzelak (2014) defined the survey mode by six *inherent mode characteristics*. These are the characteristics that are all under a researcher's control, are stable across actual survey implementation and have an impact on the response process. We briefly outline them below, building on our discussions in Chapter 1, together with their options, where we <u>underline</u> those that relate to the basic web survey mode:

a *Interviewer involvement*: interviewer administered, <u>self-administered without the presence of an interviewer,</u> self-administered with the passive presence of an interviewer (e.g. CASI, see Section 1.3.4).

b *Usage of computer technology*: <u>interactive computerized questionnaire,</u> non-interactive computerized questionnaire, P&P recording (see Section 1.1 and Section 1.3.2).

c *Information transmission medium* (i.e. delivery of the completed questionnaire from the respondent to a researcher): F2F, telephone, mail, email attachment, email embed, <u>automatic online delivery</u> (e.g. via the Internet or some other electronic network, see Section 1.3.1).

d *Question presentation input channel*: auditory, <u>visual,</u> both (see Section 1.3.4 and Section 1.1).

e *Response output channel*: oral, manual handwriting, <u>manual electronic</u> (mouse, keyboard, pointer, stylus, touch screen) (see Section 1.3.4 and Section 1.1).

f *Closeness of the interviewer interaction*: physical, remote audio or video, pre-recorded audio or video, virtual audio or video (e.g. virtual interviewer), <u>no interaction.</u>

Moreover, there are also other survey mode characteristics, related to various *implementation and contextual specifics*, which are mostly out of a researcher's control and vary across implementations, interviewers and respondents. As such they do not define the survey mode, but rather the specific implementations in a particular survey. Examples include the pace of the interview, cognitive requirements, technology (e.g. device type, screen resolution, sound quality, etc.), environmental distractions, multitasking of respondents, sense of impersonality, and characteristics of the interviewer and the respondent. Implementations may also differ across various other technical aspects, which often have no or negligible impact on the survey process, such as the location of the server (e.g. SaaS), web survey software, as well as client-side (e.g. surveys run as mobile applications) vs server-based surveys. Correspondingly, the use of smartphones and tablets for answering web questionnaires does not introduce a new survey mode, and when a respondent is using a desktop/notebook, tablet or smartphone to answer the web questionnaire, we still speak about the web survey mode. This does not mean that the mobile device does not cause any specific device effects (see Section 5.1.3), or that we do not need to consider also the case of intentional device-specific web survey implementations (e.g. online panels using mobile survey applications). The six dimensions define hundreds of different survey modes. The underlined options in (a)–(f) above specify a survey mode, which has the characteristics of the basic web survey mode, but in fact relates to a broader family of *basic* online CSAQ (which we introduced in Section 1.3.2) survey modes, where the input (d) is restricted to the visual option and the output (e) to a manual electronic output. Within this context, the basic web survey mode is only a specific subtype of basic online CSAQ, with the following three sub-characteristics: the online transmission medium (c) is the Internet; server-based communication is used for interaction; and the interface is based on web browsers. Thus, the basic web survey mode excludes surveys which run within mobile applications, independent of browsers and the interaction with the server (see Section 5.1.5).

When we remove the restrictions for input (d) and output (e) channels, the remaining four

inherent mode characteristics – self-administration (a), interactive computerization (b), online delivery of responses (c) and absence of interviewer interaction (f) – define an even broader family of *online CSAQ* survey modes, where voice technologies are also involved. When the web is used specifically as the transmission medium for the automatic online delivery of responses, then we speak about the *web-related survey modes*. This is the case with some mobile survey applications, where the web serves only for receiving the questionnaire and sending it back to the server.

The above clarifications demonstrate the large variety of possible modes and show that the case of the basic web survey mode is in fact only a very specific example. Nonetheless, it bears repeating that the vast majority of contemporary web-related surveys are conducted with this mode. More detailed elaboration, examples and graphical presentations of survey modes can be found in the Supplement to Chapter 6, *Survey modes* (http://websm.org/ch6).

6.1.2 Total Survey Error and Survey Data Quality

The notion of *total survey error* (TSE) is an umbrella term covering all types of survey errors. Certain classification and terminological differences exist with respect to the treatment of TSE by various authors, as discussed in Groves & Lyberg (2010), and continuous revisions also appear, for example Smith (2011) provided a much elaborated typology of TSE components. Nevertheless, the following components of survey errors are most often exposed: sampling, coverage (frame), nonresponse, specification, measurement and processing (Biemer & Lyberg, 2003). Each type of error can have systematic and random components, expressed as bias and variance respectively. The TSE is defined and conceptually elaborated on only within a probability sampling context; however, in practice the approximations are also used, as outlined in Section 2.2 on sampling.

The *mode effect* is a specific subtype of measurement error and also a subcomponent of the TSE. It appears as a result of the influence of survey mode on estimates. The corresponding differences in response distributions are caused by inherent characteristics of the specific mode. They are obtained when administering the same question in different survey modes (e.g. F2F vs the web). Biemer & Lyberg (2003) used the more precise term *pure mode effect* to contrast a broader notion of the *mode system effect*, which also includes other related error sources potentially accompanying certain survey modes (e.g. sampling, nonresponse, recruitment, incentives, research design context). For example, these mode system effects refer to situations when a specific survey mode is not assigned to the units randomly, but is chosen by respondents through an unknown selection mechanism, which is then difficult to separate from the pure mode effect.

Each component of the TSE can damage the statistical quality of the estimates used to infer the population parameter. Most frequent indicators of these deviations are related to sampling precision (random oscillations, expressed with sampling variance), bias (difference between the true population value and the expected value of the estimate), reliability (consistency of responses in repeated measures) and validity (degree to which we actually measure the concept we truly wanted to measure).

Very often we also use the notion of *accuracy*, expressed by the *mean squared error* (MSE), which estimates various components of the TSE (Dietrich, 2008). The MSE is the sum of random variances and squared biases of the related components included in the TSE. However, it is difficult to deal with the random and systematic errors of all TSE components. In practice the discussion is most often reduced to the sampling variance and the biases arising from nonresponse or non-coverage. Minimizing the MSE can justify the use of web surveys which can afford inexpensive larger samples, and where smaller sampling variance then outbalances the potential bias, which often appears in web surveys due to higher nonresponse and/or non-coverage.

While survey errors integrated into the TSE relate to the statistical characteristics of the estimates (e.g. accuracy), the notion of *survey quality* is much broader (Lyberg, 2012). It includes additional aspects of survey outcomes (statistical results), such as *relevance, comparability, coherence, timeliness, accessibility* and *clarity*. An even broader framework of data quality involves trust and the *perception of the users*, as well as the characteristics of the related *production process* (Ehling & Körner, 2007). Similar processing components are included in the ISO (2012) standard on the survey process. Various general quality management approaches can also be applied here, such as Six Sigma statistical process control and total quality management (TQM). Dedicated survey data organizations (e.g. statistics offices) typically develop their own – often very elaborate – systems to monitor the data quality via standardized quality reports (e.g. Eurostat, 2009). Nevertheless, the specific mode effects are a component of these general systems on which rather little and weak elaboration is available in the literature, though we believe this will change with the increased usage of mixed-mode surveys.

Particularly for large and complex surveys as well as for decision support surveys, these broader survey quality aspects are very important. For example, a failure to deliver the results at a certain time (e.g. at a decision point) means the entire survey was useless, regardless of its accuracy and otherwise high quality. Researchers with a very narrow focus on the methodological details of the web data collection process may sometimes overlook these additional and very important components of data quality, and consequently forget to look at the big picture. Thus, it is advisable to include aspects of data quality explicitly in the conceptualization, operationalization and planning of web surveys, as well as in the regular managerial monitoring of the process.

6.1.3 Evaluation of the Web Survey Mode Effect

The complexities of the survey mode and its interaction with other types of survey errors make the empirical evaluation of mode effects very demanding. As a consequence, there are numerous studies in which we cannot truly isolate the pure mode effect. The mode effect can also be contaminated with a poorly designed questionnaire (e.g. incorrect scale format, excessive colours or pictures, etc.), respondent failures (e.g. low computer literacy), technical problems (e.g. device failure) and other mistakes in the web survey implementation. Most importantly, pure mode effects often interact with nonresponse, non-coverage and sample selection mechanisms, which are then very difficult to separate.

When comparing survey modes, one mode is usually declared (or implicitly assumed) to be the accurate one (i.e. the gold standard). Very often this is F2F. We need to be very careful about such situations and rather speak about the *between-mode effect* or, better, *between-mode difference*, unless we know the true value of the responses (e.g. via auxiliary data). The between-mode differences are usually observed as simple differences of estimates of means among alternative implementations, such as experimental groups. Further, mode effect studies can also focus on correlations or measurement equivalence (Revilla, 2013), reliability (Buchanan & Smith, 1999; Chang & Krosnick, 2009; Hertel et al., 2002; Mangunkusumo et al., 2006; Miller et al., 2002), latent structures (Buchanan & Smith, 1999; Deutskens et al., 2004; Roster et al., 2004) and so-called concurrent validities (Linchiat Chang & Krosnick, 2009; Hertel et al., 2002).

A typical example of a study comparing survey modes, but not isolating the pure mode effect, is the Spijkerman, Knibbe, Knoops, Mheen, & Eijnden (2009) study comparing results from a non-probability online panel ($n = 57{,}125$) with a probability F2F survey

(CAPI, $n = 7{,}204$) of the Dutch general population. They found considerably higher drug usage in the online panel (e.g. 39% vs 28% for ever using cannabis in the age group 15–24). However, it is unclear whether these differences come from the mode (respondents admit more drug use in the web vs F2F survey mode) or from differences with respect to nonresponse, self-selection, sampling, non-coverage or different populations involved. The mode effect in many studies is often confounded by frame problems (Burr, Levin, & Becher, 2001; Tomsic, Hendel, & Matross, 2000), different samples (e.g. Braunsberger, Wybenga, & Gates, 2007; Chang & Krosnick, 2009; Roster et al., 2004), the availability of email addresses (Deutskens, de Ruyter, & Wetzels, 2006; Griffis, Goldsby, & Cooper, 2003), and sequential mixed-mode designs for nonresponse reduction (Carini, Hayek, Kuh, Kennedy, & Ouimet, 2003). These uncontrolled differences can be wrongly attributed to pure mode effects.

A standard approach towards isolating the pure mode effect is to use experiments and randomly assign units to subsamples with different implemented modes. Nevertheless, nonresponse and considerable random errors still cannot be separated from the mode effect (Vannieuwenhuyze & Loosveldt, 2013). Population weighting might help, but only to a limited extent which is usually unknown (see Section 4.1.4). Some specific approaches (Vannieuwenhuyze, Loosveldt, & Molenberghs, 2010, 2012) which use single mode groups within the mixed-mode context may partially reduce this problem.

An even better research design is randomization in a laboratory, where the participants are randomly assigned to experimental groups only after arrival at the laboratory, as in Chang & Krosnick (2010). Similarly, Jäckle, Roberts, & Lynn (2006) reported an experiment where participants were recruited on the street and, after they agreed to cooperate, they were randomly assigned to one of four modes. With this approach we can additionally eliminate the potential differences in nonresponse.

However, external validity issues arise; that is, whether the findings in artificial (laboratory) experimental conditions also hold in real-life conditions.

An alternative approach to measuring the pure survey mode effect is *re-surveying* (test–retest or repeated measurement), which can effectively control for sample, coverage and nonresponse differences between groups. In addition, this sharply reduces the sampling variance, because we measure the same units in both waves, and dramatically increases the power of discovering potential differences (e.g. Alwin, 2007). However, practical implementation is complicated and expensive, as we can infer from the limited number of studies with this implementation (Mangunkusumo et al., 2006; E. T. Miller et al., 2002; Rivara, Koepsell, Wang, Durbin, Jaffe, Vavilala, ... Temkin, 2011). In addition, respondents may remember the same question from the first wave and some external effects/events between the two measurements may change the value of the target variable. To control for these, another experimental group would be needed (i.e. an 'after' control group without treatment of the first wave). An additional problem may arise due to the effect of the order in which survey modes are applied; to control properly for it, yet another experimental group would be needed with the opposite order of treatments.

Many studies demonstrate that the web survey mode is usually superior, or at least equivalent to conventional interviewer-administered (F2F, telephone) and also to P&P self-administered modes (e.g. Börkan, 2010; Braunsberger et al., 2007; Buchanan & Smith, 1999; Chang & Krosnick, 2009; Hertel et al., 2002; Mangunkusumo et al., 2006; Roster et al., 2004). More specifically, a meta-study by Tourangeau, Conrad & Couper (2013) showed that with respect to sensitive behaviour, which is usually under-reported in traditional survey modes, respondents tend to answer more realistically in web surveys, where no interviewer is present. We have already asserted (Section 1.3.5) that self-administration is advantageous for other reasons (e.g. respondents select their own time and pace when filling in the questionnaire).

On the other hand, specific web survey mode effects may sometimes appear in the negative direction, predominantly due to various forms of shortcutting: satisficing, excessive item non-response (or don't know) selection, speeding, inconsistent responses, etc. Most often this is a consequence of the absence of the interviewer, whose presence is sometimes indispensable for motivation (e.g. long surveys) and clarification (e.g. complicated questions). Nevertheless, a careful combination of incentives and interactive questionnaire design may compensate for the absence of the interviewer to a considerable extent.

6.1.4 Cost-Error Optimization

When discussing differences in survey modes and survey data quality in general, cost aspects are very often omitted. The question of whether it is accurate and fair to compare the web survey mode to the alternatives without controlling for costs then arises. That is, only comparisons under a fixed budget – and not under the usual practice of fixed sample sizes (e.g. $n = 1,000$ for each mode) – would possibly show that web surveys allow us to afford much larger sample sizes. Alternatively, the comparative savings from web surveys may be invested in incentives, mixed-modes and other improvements, which can substantially increase data quality and change the results of comparisons. The absence of cost considerations in the literature is even more surprising, because the cost is very often the most essential factor when we decide on which survey mode to use.

We have already mentioned certain specifics (Section 1.3.5) of fixed costs in web surveys, which are often relatively independent of sample size, while variable costs per unit are comparatively low and depend on sample size. The computation of *total costs per minute* of respondent time is a great tool to compare web surveys with traditional alternatives. For example, general population probability-based F2F surveys, such as general social surveys, have typical per minute costs of a few euros/dollars in developed countries, sometimes even above 5 or 10, while probability online panels often have total per minute costs roughly in the interval of 1–2 euros/dollars. Web survey responses from non-probability samples can have much lower costs per minute, which strongly varies, depending on the quality. The costs need to be balanced with data quality, which is a very complex problem, and can be additionally complicated when modes are mixed. Conceptually, these issues were addressed relatively early (e.g. Groves, 1989), but in practice we still lack effective operational criteria and procedures. An approach to optimizing cost and accuracy simultaneously – which means minimizing the product of costs and MSE – has been discussed by Vehovar et al. (2010). A specific approach was presented by Roberts, Vandenplas, & Stähli (2014) and Vannieuwenhuyze (2014), while Schouten, Calinescu, & Luiten (2013) discussed cost optimization within the context of responsive design, where cost-error optimization directly affects sequential fieldwork procedures.

6.1.5 Beyond the Core Web Survey Process

So far we have observed the core web survey process as being entirely isolated and within a simplified flow of pre-fielding, fielding and post-fielding. In reality this is rarely the case – web surveys are usually more complicated and nested in the larger research context, so we review a few of the most essential aspects below.

6.1.5.1 The Step of Preliminary Research Activities

We defined preliminary research activities in Section 1.2 (Figure 1.1) as preceding the core web survey process. What separates them from pre-fielding is that they are not directly related or involved in the specifics of web surveys. Instead, they are concerned with general preparations, which are independent of any survey mode. Nevertheless, they can be very important for the entire context of web surveys. These preliminary research activities typically – but now always – include the

following components, which we present in a simple, unstructured and non-exhaustive list:

- clarifications of general issues, such as initial research ideas, the broader (research, business, administrative) framework, basic paradigmatic and conceptual settings, problem formulation, goal identification and research problem definition, together with elaboration of the relation between the research problem (e.g. how to measure customer satisfaction) and the eventual decision problem (e.g. how to increase customer satisfaction);
- further elaboration of research design aspects, such as a more specific outline of the key concepts, operationalization of the constructs, development of research hypotheses, specification of research methods used, definition of the target population and sometimes the selection or elaboration of key questions;
- ethical considerations, which can also involve the potential formal approval process;
- key administrative, management and process quality issues, including essential aspects of timing, costs and other resources;
- in the case of complex research designs, certain forms of preliminary research activities are conducted here, particularly desk (secondary) research, qualitative studies and expert consultations;
- additional activities appear whenever the role of a researcher – whom we have treated so far as one entity – is split across the sponsor, the client, research provider, the software supplier, etc. (see Section 1.2), which then greatly complicates the preliminary research activities and requires additional actions, interactions and processes.

Although not all of the above activities appear in every survey, the majority of them do, at least in some unstructured and informal way. Even in simple DIY research, certain decisions and activities are needed for the majority of these issues to find corresponding solutions. In more complex research projects, the methodological aspects are usually elaborated in a formal *research design*, which specifies the research methods used, together with the stages, sequence and other specifics of the related research activities. In general, various qualitative and quantitative research methods can be involved, according to the exploratory, descriptive or causal nature of research. The role of the web survey needs to be determined within the general research design. Of course, some of the above preliminary research activities can overlap with pre-fielding to a certain extent, particularly the early elaboration of methodology (e.g. the questionnaire is already predetermined by the client).

Another type of formalization relates to a *research proposal*, which outlines all essential aspects of the proposed research, not just the methodological aspects. Examples of good practical elaborations can be found in the book by Iacobucci & Churchill (2015). Very often this proposal then undergoes a certain approval process from management, client, sponsor or other funding body.

A research proposal is particularly relevant in situations where the role of the research is split among various entities and their relationships need to be specified. In this context, various forms of tenders or research grant calls are very frequently involved, requiring additional and careful administrative elaboration (application forms, specification of processes, legal aspects, selection process and criteria). In addition to the price, quality indicators of the web survey process (e.g. response rate) should play a decisive role whenever a web survey is involved.

Since preliminary research activities are typically very complex, structured and survey specific, the literature rarely discusses them as one entity. Instead, various components or aspects are discussed separately (e.g. research paradigms, research methods, procurement procedures, legal aspects). For a more informed view of the methodological aspects of preliminary research activities, the reader can consult the general literature on survey methodology (e.g. Blair, Czaja & Blair 2014; Groves et al., 2009), social science methodology (e.g. Babbie, 2013) or discipline-specific literature (e.g. for marketing research; Iacobucci & Churchill, 2015). Other aspects are rarely elaborated specifically for survey contexts. Exceptions are the publications by Iacobucci & Churchill (2015), Iarossi (2006),

and Sue & Ritter (2012), which do provide some insight into the specifics of the tendering process.

6.1.5.2 The Step of Advanced Analysis, Processing and Valorization

We have already defined this step in Section 1.2 (Figure 1.1) as the one belonging to broad research activities, not directly related to the specifics of web surveys. Its activities thus follow the core web survey process and we also specified the corresponding separation from the post-fielding step in Chapter 4.

The corresponding activities predominantly relate to advanced *analyses*, which include reporting, statistical procedures, variance estimation, substantive interpretations and the preparation of reports and presentations.

This step also includes various advanced forms of post-survey *data processing*, such as integration into certain management and decision-making procedures within broader administrative or business processes. Survey data can be subject to further manipulations, from data merging, record linking, statistical matching (i.e. data fusion) and several other uses. These manipulations are increasingly becoming an important element in advanced research and administrative or business processes.

The valorization component includes further exploitation of results (usage and reusage in other research or decision processes) and dissemination of results by public archiving of the datafile and by distribution, promotion and publication of the findings (in newsletters, briefs, documentation, full reports, as well as in papers and books).

6.1.5.3 Mixed-modes

We introduced the notion of mixed-modes in Section 2.1 as a combination of survey modes in the measurement stage, and we used the term mixed-mode system to also encompass multi-mode contacts in the recruiting stage, as well as other aspects and consequences of using more communication channels in the fielding step.

In addition to this, we address certain broader implementation aspects.

Firstly, note that, with business surveys, the web survey mode and the P&P (or telephone) survey mode are often routinely combined, typically in a standard sequential manner, proceeding from the inexpensive (web) mode to the more expensive (mail, telephone) one.

Secondly, we should point out that, despite various claims and indices of the growing use of mixed-modes – understood as a combination of survey modes in the measurement stage – this in general is not the case, at least for marketing research and for the DIY segment. In marketing research (Macer & Wilson, 2013, p. 40), mixed-mode surveys have a relatively low share of revenue (6% for mixed-mode compared with 52% for web surveys). In addition, the share has already been very stable for the last seven years and no future increase is foreseen. This is not surprising, since high-quality mixed-modes are complicated and typically very expensive, compared with the stand-alone alternatives of web, mail or telephone surveys, which currently dominate in the field of marketing research.

The situation is different with expensive probability-based F2F household surveys. Here, due to problems related to sampling, recruiting, non-coverage and nonresponse, web surveys cannot simply replace traditional surveys modes, but can enter into the survey process through mixed-modes. However, as discussed in Section 2.1, this is methodologically complicated. Nevertheless, it seems that – after initial implementations (e.g. Beukenhorst & Wetzels, 2009) – mixed-modes involving a web survey mode are slowly becoming mainstream in these types of surveys (Buelens & van den Brakel, 2014).

An important mixed-mode challenge in official statistics relates to the Labour Force Survey, where continuous progress can be observed in terms of introducing web surveys as a mode of data collection, as in Körner & van der Valk (2011) or the DCSS project (Blanke & Luiten, 2014).

In academic surveys we can also observe progress in considering mixed-mode data collection, but with a high degree of caution, as shown in the ESS mixed-mode experiment in Estonia (Ainsaar et al., 2013) and the UK (Villar, 2013).

Let us present a typical example which illustrates well the problems with mixed-modes. A recent tobacco, alcohol and drug survey (average length 40 minutes) from the Slovenian Institute of Health[1] used a standard sequential mixed-mode survey approach (web → telephone → F2F) and obtained a cumulative response rate of 20% after the web, 45% after the telephone and 60% after the F2F wave. Response rates and cost savings were a big success compared with the standard alternative of F2F as well as the inclusion of segments which would not cooperate in traditional survey modes. However, mode effects remained unclear. For example, cannabis consumption (ever using cannabis) – after weighting for socio-demographic population for each mode segment – was 25%, 10% and 9% for the web, telephone and F2F mode segments respectively. The problem is that it is now impossible to isolate mode effects from selection (wave) of the mode, differential nonresponse bias, stage of survey process and differences in survey population. The future impact of the increasing percentage of responses collected via web surveys on trends is thus unclear. If the estimates of cannabis consumption increase, we might not know whether this is because people truly consume more, or only because more and more people respond on the web, where they may admit more consumption.

A possible solution to this problem would require parallel experiments where units would be surveyed only F2F, so that pure mode and between-mode effects could be estimated. Alternatively, re-interviewing the units with a different survey mode can be used. These approaches were studied in experiments run by Klausch, Hox, & Schouten (2014), where various mode effects were then isolated. A possible solution is also the involvement of advanced weighting approaches (Buelens & van den Brakel, 2014). It seems that we need to use both approaches, the involvement of some modelling assumptions based on external estimates (e.g. obtained by reinterviewing) of mode effects and also advanced weighting.

6.1.5.4 Mixed Methods

Mixed methods refer to the research design where we combine quantitative methods of primary data collection (e.g. surveys) with certain qualitative methods of primary data collection (e.g. in-depth interviews, focus groups, expert interpretations, story-telling, action research, ethnography and brainstorming). As with surveys, qualitative research techniques are increasingly moving to the web (e.g. online in-depth interviews (via chat) or online focus groups).

There exist extensive paradigmatic, conceptual and operational discussions about these issues, and sometimes mixed methods even stand as the third research paradigm, in addition to qualitative and quantitative research (Johnston, 2007). In recent years we can also observe an expansion of mixed methods in the literature and in practice (Morgan, 2013).

We should add that within the web survey process researchers already rely on qualitative insights for various methodological reasons when formulating a problem, developing a questionnaire or evaluating survey questions. For the substantive aspects researchers typically involve qualitative research in the interpretations, using expert evaluation or qualitative feedback from the target population.

The web is extremely suitable for the combination of approaches. With traditional survey modes, the combination of methods beyond two steps (e.g. focus group → survey) very often requires a lot of time and resources. In contrast, the web enables easy, inexpensive and rapid mixing of qualitative and quantitative methods. Lobe & Vehovar (2009) showed that sequences of qualitative (online chat) and quantitative (web survey) methods can iteratively sharpen the depth and quality of the research and can provide a comparable advantage: four steps (qualitative → quantitative → qualitative → quantitative) may thus outperform one step (either qualitative or quantitative) and also more standard two- (qualitative → quantitative) or three-step (qualitative → quantitative → qualitative) research designs within the resources provided.

Mixed methods are particularly convenient within the context of so-called crowdsourcing and various other approaches in online community studies, where corporations and marketing research companies establish and maintain an online community of the target population for their qualitative and quantitative data collection.

6.1.6 Towards Interactive Fieldwork Design

According to the initial scope of discussions (Section 1.2), we predominantly discussed cross-sectional web surveys in previous chapters, relying on a single measurement session. The fieldwork process is relatively simple in such situations, particularly when we have list-based web surveys, using an email invitation and a reminder that is sent to all units.

On the other hand, complexities can arise from more sophisticated designs. Survey data can be collected in a series of replications of an identical survey on independent samples, but also with sequences of complementary surveys on independent samples, and of course in various types of longitudinal designs. In addition, different external data can be iteratively incorporated into the web survey process, namely administrative (e.g. using a certain form or enquiry of a citizen), business (e.g. commercial transactions of consumers) or technical (e.g. log file information of certain actions performed by the user on the web).

Another level of complexity appears when a mixed-mode system is involved and particularly when various interactive fieldwork strategies replace more or less fixed recruitment plans with limited implementation variations, as discussed in the recruitment stage (Section 3.1).

Adaptive design (Schouten et al., 2013) builds on the fact that survey fieldwork in general faces many uncertainties, which could be reduced by using the data from the fieldwork itself. That is, very often all units in the sample receive the same *treatment*, which means the same number of reminders, the same modes of invitation and the same survey measurement mode. Certain auxiliary data (such as age, region, cost structure, estimates of response rates) are used to structure and optimize the sampling or the research design (e.g. stratification, multi-stage sampling, double sampling, repeated survey, mixed-modes). However, this is done in advance and does not incorporate feedback from the fieldwork.

Adaptive design is often discussed within the narrower context of *responsive design* (Groves & Heeringa, 2006), which additionally requires that the survey is structured in phases, where data from the previous phase are then used to improve the next phase (e.g. Wagner, West, Kirgis, Lepkowski, Axinn & Kruger-Ndiaye, 2012). Typically, certain subgroups may report low response rates, so with responsive design additional resources (e.g. more contact) are allocated in the next phase.

It is surprising that adaptive and responsive designs are mostly discussed with F2F or telephone surveys (Schouten et al., 2013), while implementations with web surveys are rather rare, despite the fact that rich paradata, flexibility, ICT support and elaborate monitoring actually provide a much more convenient setting (Bianchi & Biffignandi, 2014).

We extend here the notion of adaptive design to even more general *interactive fieldwork design*, which means any usage of data generated during (a) fieldwork at the (b) unit level – namely, survey data, paradata and external data (technical, administrative, business) – to improve the (c) real-time optimization of the fieldwork procedures related to the recruitment and measurement stages.

The line between implementation variability adaptations discussed in Section 3.1 and interactive fieldwork design can sometimes be very thin, as, for example, in the case where we pre-specified the exact criteria in the recruitment plan, when low response rates would require activation of a supplementary sample, sending additional reminders or launching an additional promotion. The main distinction is that interactive design also includes interventions at the unit level, not just at the level of segments. For example, it is not that a mail reminder is simply sent to all nonrespondents who have already received three email invitations, but that additional information at unit level is used to treat each unit separately and decide specific actions at that level.

Figure 6.1, updated from Vehovar & Batagelj (1996), conceptualizes the potential processes in interactive fieldwork design within the mixed-mode setting. The flow refers to information and data communication processes at the unit level, which is different from the conceptualization of the general web survey process in Figure 1.1 (Section 1.2). The centralized processing and monitoring interactively links the two essential fieldwork activities: recruitment and measurement (i.e. questionnaire completion). Different survey modes can be used to recruit respondents (i.e. multimode contacting) and contact attempts can be repeated until it is decided that a response is not possible (e.g. we learn that the unit is ineligible), the fieldwork time has finished, or it is not reasonable to try any further to contact a certain unit. The decision on the latter can depend on simple rules (e.g. a maximum of five contact attempts), on the nonresponse context (e.g. minimal response rate or minimal number of responses in a certain segment), on statistical parameters (e.g. required precision of certain estimates) or on certain complex cost-error criteria, which optimize the data quality by cost (e.g. product of costs and MSE).

Different decisions can be applied to different units in order to optimize timing, costs and data quality. For example, if there were units with no response after two email invitations, intelligent centralized processing – which disposes with all auxiliary information about the unit (e.g. age, gender) and also all fieldwork data, paradata and external data – might automatically decide, based on some optimizing algorithm, on the optimal timing, mode and format for the next contact attempt. It might be optimal to send the next email reminder in a week or two, or rather to send a mail reminder. Similarly, the most appropriate survey mode can be a P&P questionnaire instead of a web questionnaire.

The centralized ICT-supported processing can strongly improve integration, interactivity and optimization, particularly because it can incorporate experiences from past surveys and involve statistical and decision models. We may further optimize the structure of the measurement session at the unit level, which can be split into more sessions.

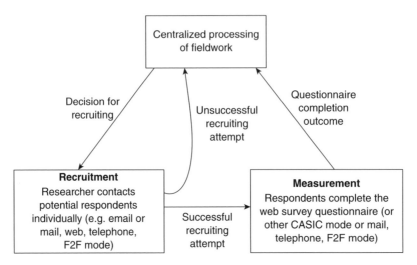

Figure 6.1 **Unit-level processes within an interactive mixed-mode fieldwork design for list-based samples**

In the above discussion and in Figure 6.1, we have talked about list-based web surveys, but in the case of non-list-based web surveys, this would change slightly: instead of direct individual invitations, a researcher interacts with the units using variations in the promotion strategy (e.g. banner ads), so the focus of interaction would be on modifying the online recruitment efforts (Section 2.2.3). For example, a researcher can decide to decrease direct banner advertising and increase promotion in online social media.

Interactive framework designs need to be considered in pre-fielding and can complement or replace the recruitment plan, where we additionally extend the set of design features related to timing, costs and data quality, as well as the set of monitoring indicators, which then point to situations requiring action or modification. As mentioned previously, real-time calculations can be integrated and expanded with intelligent ICT support.

Some aspects of the general optimization in a mixed-mode setting can be found in the literature (e.g. Schouten et al., 2013; Vannieuwenhuyze, 2014; Vehovar et al., 2010). Of course, the iterative fieldwork design can be further expanded beyond the involvement of mixed-modes by the incorporation of mixed methods and with the interaction of external administrative, business and/or technical processes.

6.2 WEB SURVEYS WITHIN THE PROJECT MANAGEMENT FRAMEWORK

In Section 2.6 we addressed management aspects that were specific to the core web survey process, while in this section we discuss the broader context of project management.

Web surveys can be treated as any other project, where general project management principles apply: a researcher needs to organize, plan and coordinate various activities to reach the goals within certain time and resource constraints. Professional project management standards were developed for these types of tasks and work, particularly when it is done once, for the first time, or repeated with different content.

Project management helps formalize the elaboration of *description of work* (DoW), structuring of the tasks and activities into *work packages* (WP) and the optimal allocation of resources. It also deals with planning and timing, including the specification of milestones (i.e. key dates) and *deliverables*, which is the term that denotes reports, results and other measurable outputs of the project in the project management context. The provision of control is also very important here, as well as supervision, coordination and interventions.

A researcher needs to coordinate many activities during the web survey project. We can deduce from the structure of the web survey process, illustrated in Figure 1.1 (Section 1.2), that the activities of all 12 stages interact among themselves. These stages can also be directly transformed into the structure of work packages within the project management plan. Considerable complexity arises already within the questionnaire preparation process (Figure 2.1 in Section 2.3.6), where testing and questionnaire development are linked to a complex management process. Additional complications come from preliminary research activities and other interactions with the environment that is external to the core web survey process.

Thus, there is a lot to plan, a lot to coordinate and also a lot that could go wrong. The managerial skills required can easily become equally important – or even more important – than the methodological skills for the successful running of web surveys. We can illustrate the project management tasks with a few examples related to levels of complexity:

- In a post-event evaluation survey – where we seek feedback from participants whose emails we are also disposing of – project management can be a straightforward sequence of preparing the questionnaire, arranging emails, sending invitations plus a reminder and then generating a preliminary report, which is disseminated online. All this may take only a few minutes for an experienced researcher with suitable software and with a standardized questionnaire at hand.
- In the above case, if we add new questions, which need to be developed and pre-tested, this involves more activities, so the entire project may require a few hours of a researcher's time. In any case, this example fully demonstrates the power of web surveys: namely, the extreme speed and convenience, especially if respondents reply immediately via a mobile device. The time and cost efficiency cannot be compared with any traditional survey mode alternative.
- Things get more complicated when we conduct a survey for a client or when the complexity of the web survey requires a project team, where additional interactions, communications and complications arise. A typical web survey project, which includes certain substantive preliminary investigations, implementation of the web survey and a final report, may already require a small team and a few hundred hours spanning a few weeks or months. All of this perhaps also requires formalized project management tasks, at least at a minimal level.
- With growing complexity the resources required for project management typically expand rapidly, while at the same time the core web survey process itself often takes up an increasingly smaller part. Running web surveys with budgets approaching or exceeding six digits (e.g. $100,000) is already a serious enterprise which requires formalized project management.
- With online panels, longitudinal studies, research conducted across many countries and research where partners from different organizations and sectors are involved, the importance of project management increases additionally. Within international research, the translation and back-translation alone is already a serious project management challenge.

Professional data collection organizations, regardless of the sector (commercial or public), typically have their own elaboration of project management rules. On the other hand, organizations not dedicated to survey data collection, particularly in the academic and non-profit sector, are also involved in conducting web surveys, and sometimes their researchers are not prepared for the management of complex web survey projects because management issues cannot be dealt with using only general knowledge and common sense. Below we outline typical project management issues that can cause problems when they are treated with insufficient resources and attention:

- Adequate format of project team meetings (i.e. structure, length, frequency), together with strict recording of minutes, their monitoring and reporting.

- Clear (i.e. written) separation of responsibilities among team members and the client, including the communication strategy (e.g. can the client talk directly to the web programmer?).
- Quality assurance criteria and corresponding evaluation procedures, which need to be formalized in advance in a stand-alone document, and where it is also useful to involve external expert monitoring or a steering committee, which regularly oversees the project (this is particularly relevant for new, lengthy or complex projects).
- Elaboration in advance of the essential management procedures, together with initial planning, contingency plans, risk management, crisis management and conflict resolution schemes.
- Formalized monitoring of the core web survey process, especially fielding (e.g. response rates, data quality).
- Regular control of resources, including hours spent, and monitoring of the timing via milestones, deadlines, critical paths and Gantt charts, which is a standard monitoring approach in project management.
- Platform for documenting, backing up, archiving and communication, which preferably goes beyond email attachments and enables online access to the most recent material (e.g. draft questionnaire).
- Clear regulation (e.g. contracts) regarding ownership of the data, intellectual property rights, and penalty clauses in the case of delays or mistakes in data collection.

All of the above hold true for any survey research project, while with web surveys there are many additional opportunities to shorten, simplify and optimize management tasks by using integrated web survey software and other online services.

The essential professional resources are related to specific management approaches where standards and certificates are also elaborated, for instance PMIbook,[2] IPMA[3] and PRINCE2[4]. There also exist many project management textbooks and guides, but there are surprisingly few dedicated treatments dealing directly with surveys (Stouthamer-Loeber & van Kammen, 1995) or indirectly (Lyberg et al., 1997). Likewise, survey methodology textbooks rarely have explicit chapters covering project management, although they may partially cover these issues in sections on survey administration. A more structured discussion of project management issues in surveys – not specifically geared to web surveys, but to surveys in general – can be found in Iarossi (2006) and Kennedy, Tarnai, & Wolf (2010).

6.3 THE WEB SURVEY PROFESSION

Conducting web surveys requires familiarity not only with survey methodology, but also with ICT, statistics, management, legislation and with the broader social context, including ethics. Related competences are found at the intersection of various professions. In addition, a question of whether we can talk about a separate web survey methodology profession arises.

Generally, we talk about a profession when the following elements exist: formal education programmes, explicit occupation profiles, professional journals, dedicated international associations and events, as well as certain general codes and standards. The majority of these attributes are missing for web survey methodology. However, they do exist for survey methodology in general, which is the field to which web survey methodology predominantly belongs.

On the other hand, various professional activities specific to web survey methodology do exist, from regular events, dedicated courses (particularly in various summer schools), numerous research projects, professional networks, specialized standards and textbooks. We may also mention dedicated conference tracks, thousands of scholarly papers, presentations and other materials, including numerous online resources, as well as hundreds of web survey software packages, which often include related methodological guidelines. WebSM (http://www.websm.org) provides an exhaustive overview of these aspects.

From this point of view, we can talk about a certain professional knowledge and the corresponding elements of the profession, of which this book is a testimony. In the remainder of this section, we first review the scientific disciplines where web surveys are applied and methodological research is conducted (Section 6.3.1). We also address the related legal (Section 6.3.2) and ethical issues (Section 6.3.3), formal codes and standards (Section 6.3.4), as well as informal guides and other materials (Section 6.3.5).

6.3.1 Related Disciplines

Web surveys are formally nested within the framework of survey research and within the broader context of social science methodology. In the narrowest sense, social science methodology often relates predominantly to sociology and to a somewhat lesser extent also to political science and communication studies. In any case, implementations of web surveys in these areas are highly relevant for web survey methodology.

In an even broader sense (e.g. OECD, 2002), the social sciences – and the implementation of web surveys – also include three other large streams: psychology, economics and educational science, as well as geography, urban planning, demography, management, public administration, law, management, organization science, and various specific areas such as evaluation research, social anthropology and linguistics. Marketing research, in particular, nested within the broader field of economics and business, is especially important for web surveys, because it is there that the majority of professional web surveys are conducted. A very important area of web survey implementation is also the specific cross-disciplinary context of so-called online research and Internet studies.

Besides the social sciences, web surveys appear in other sciences, especially in the humanities and medicine (health research), but also in various natural and technical sciences. The areas of statistics, computer science and informatics (e.g. HCI) are particularly relevant for web survey methodology.

To understand the role of web surveys in the various contexts, we should be aware that many disciplines have developed their own methodological approaches. Accordingly, the corresponding professions should be taken into account when implementing web surveys; see the relevant textbooks: Iacobucci & Churchill (2015) for marketing research; Eysenbach & Wyatt (2002) for health studies; Bocarnea, Reynolds, & Baker (2012) for organizational research.

A very natural methodological environment of web surveys is the social science methodology, which provides the broader methodological framework for web surveys (e.g. Babbie, 2013). In particular, this holds true for the issues related to problem formulation, research steps, relationship of decision vs research problem, the conceptualization and operationalization process, as well as for general familiarity with the implementation of qualitative and quantitative research methods. More specifically, the survey research context is particularly important here. Throughout this book we have referred to the standard textbooks in this field, of Groves et al. (2009) and Biemer & Lyberg (2003).

On the other hand, for various specific aspects, other disciplines need to be consulted. For example, survey data analysis requires statistical knowledge (e.g. Heeringa et al., 2010), while web usability involves expertise from HCI (e.g. Roe, 2008).

According to the above overview of the related disciplines, the aspects of web survey methodology are very scattered, which is also a characteristic of survey methodology in general. Therefore, we can find these aspects within various professional associations, mostly related to survey research (AAPOR, CASRO, ESRA, ESOMAR), but also to Internet research (AoIR, AAAS, APA), social science methodology (ISA RC33), statistics (ISI, IASS, AMSTAT, RSS) and marketing research (ESOMAR, AMA, MRS), as well as areas related to computer science and informatics (ASC, ACM, IFIP-HCC). Large organizations (e.g. Eurostat) may also run specific activities related to new technologies in data collection (e.g. the New Techniques and Technologies for Statistics (NTTS) conference). None of the above professional organizations is dedicated exclusively to web surveys, and the same is also true for the corresponding activities and events. Nevertheless, dedicated and continuous events related to web survey methodology exist: namely, the biannual Internet Survey Methodology Workshop[5] and the annual International Workshop on Internet Survey and Survey Methodology[6].

6.3.2 Legal Issues

Web surveys are closely interwoven with legislation, which can become very complicated particularly when we conduct international research. This is in general a very complex issue, and in our brief overview we will pinpoint and illustrate only the most essential aspects. More specific information and guidance can be obtained from local marketing, statistical or survey research associations.

Despite the trends towards global harmonization, legal settings vary considerably across countries, particularly with respect to criminal issues, privacy, intellectual property, telecommunication rules and consumer protection. Let us present a few of the crucial legal issues:

- Unsolicited email invitations: Can they be sent to private or business email addresses, which are public on the web?
- Cookies: How does legislation regulate them?
- Spam: What are the specific spam regulations?
- Incentive: What type and level of incentives are allowed and what administrative procedures accompany them?
- Lotteries or sweepstakes: How are lotteries or sweepstakes arranged from a legislation point of view?
- Privacy, confidentiality, anonymity: How are these issues legally regulated (for technical discussions, see Section 2.4.3)? How does one deal with situations where researchers take advantage of collected responses (e.g. for marketing purposes)?
- Paradata: Who has the right to capture, process, analyse, publish and archive them?
- Minors: How can children be involved in a web survey and what is the lowest age for their participation?
- Intellectual property rights: Is permission required to use a certain question? How is the copyright for certain questions established and protected?
- Archiving: Whose responsibility is it if data disappear? What are the data archiving procedures?
- Software: Whose responsibility is it if a software bug causes damage?
- Illegal content: Whose responsibility is it when illegal content is uploaded by a researcher or respondents to the web questionnaire?
- Disclosure: Who is responsible if tables or data that enable identification of personal information are released?
- Security: Whose responsibility is it if an unauthorized person accesses the data during the (non-)encrypted answering process, via a stolen account, or directly by breaking into the server?

When web surveys run as a hosted service (SaaS), the *cancellation policy* and *taxes* can also become an issue, as well as the relationship between the respondent, a researcher and the supplier of the web survey service. Additional complications arise when the hosting service is separated from the software supplier, not to mention situations when all these subjects and services are in different countries with different legislation.

It is not surprising that the terms of use and the related legal clarifications of web survey software are becoming increasingly lengthy, often with separate sections on privacy, spam, cookies, security, incentives, cancellation policy, etc. A good illustration of this complexity are the popular web survey software services, where we can find up-to-date examples of elaborations on legal issues (e.g. terms of use, privacy issues). However, such detailed treatments are still not standard. A WebSM study (Vehovar, Čehovin et al., 2012) found that only 60% of suppliers include a privacy statement on their main website, while only 44% list conditions of use.

6.3.3 General Ethical Concerns

Ethical dilemmas are present in all steps and stages of the web survey process. Generally speaking they address the question of whether data, procedures, actions and non-actions related to the web survey process may potentially harm other persons or groups. By harm we mean certain negative physical, psychological or societal experience and related negative feelings.

A typical problem, yet still a relatively light one, is whether to disclose the expected length of the web questionnaire in advance – when we know that it is above 30 minutes – and then run the risk of a decline in cooperation rates (Crawford et al., 2001; Galesic, 2006). Likewise, we have mentioned that seeking explicit consent that paradata can be captured substantially decreased cooperation (Couper & Singer, 2013), which is problematic for the entire *informed consent* approach (Losch, 2008) that requires respondents explicitly to agree – before undertaking the survey – that they are aware of the purpose, rights and potential harm of the research.

A more extreme example would be a web respondent reporting various problematic issues in a web survey, from illegal activities (e.g. stealing, drug trafficking, illegal gun ownership) and eventual critical inner states (e.g. depression, suicide attempts) to serious crime issues (e.g. attempted murder, paedophilia practices). In such cases, keeping the promise of anonymity and non-disclosure can become a very serious ethical dilemma for a researcher. We provide some illustration of typical ethical dilemmas in web surveys in the Supplement to Chapter 6, *Examples of ethical dilemmas in web surveys* (http://websm.org/ch6).

The treatment of ethical aspects varies across countries to a lesser extent compared with the variation of legal issues. However, a larger variation in ethical aspects is seen across different institutions and associations. Instead of inspections and juridical systems, various ethical committees and boards monitor the rules and may impose profession-specific sanctions (e.g. formal warning or even expulsion from a professional association). Sometimes (e.g. in health research) explicit pre-approval is required from an ethical body before the start of the survey. In the United States, for example, research in most institutions (academic, public and sometimes private) is subject to Institutional Review Boards (IRBs), and surveys are examined in order to ensure the protection of safety, rights and welfare of the respondents. The American Association for Public Opinion Research (AAPOR) maintains a special section on its website dedicated to IRBs and survey research practices.

We recommend familiarity with ethical codes before the start of a web survey project, in order to identify and address potential problems. The recommendation of which ethical code to read is less straightforward. Groves et al. (2009) provide a good starting point for the general survey research context.

6.3.4 Formalized Certificates, Codes and Standards

In previous sections we mentioned the general legal and ethical issues that need to be taken into consideration when conducting web surveys. More specific elaboration is usually found in various codes and standards for conducting research, which have been established by professional research associations within the context of formal certificates and standards. Since the methodological, legal, ethical and professional aspects are usually interwoven in such codification, we treat them all together in this section.

With respect to project management, we have already mentioned specific standards (e.g. PMI-book, IPMA and PRINCE2), and other quality management approaches and certificates (e.g. Six Sigma TQM). General management, administration and processing standards (e.g. ISO 9001) can be obtained from professional certification organizations (e.g. ISO[7] or BSI[8]). Some more specific standards may appear relevant for web surveys, as we mentioned in the related discussions on usability, security or archiving. Similarly, we referred to two survey-specific ISO standards:

- ISO 20252 Market, opinion and social research. Vocabulary and service requirements (ISO, 2012).
- ISO 26362 Access panels in market, opinion and social research. Vocabulary and service requirements (ISO, 2009).

Obtaining and maintaining these certificates confirms that an organization complies with certain standards and may also help to qualify a research organization for big clients. However, this is expensive (e.g. ISO or BSI).

In addition to these certificates, which are commercialized to a considerable degree, various other codes, standards and guides – directly or indirectly related to web surveys – exist and are typically freely available in the context of professional associations and organizations. These may be stand-alone documents dealing exclusively with web surveys or just explicit sections in some broader documents. The corresponding focus is typically coloured with the mission and specifics of the organization/association (e.g. survey methodology, marketing or statistics). A monitoring and/or appeal body may also exist to overview and clarify issues.

In terms of specific international treatment related to web surveys, ESOMAR is particularly a very rich source that provides several guidelines, including 'Guideline for online research', 'Guideline for social media research', 'Guideline for conducting mobile marketing research', as well as 'Questions to help buyers of online samples'. Similar guidelines are also provided by the Marketing Research and Intelligence Association in 'Ten questions to ask your online survey suppliers' (MRIA, 2013).

Ethical decision making and Internet research are also fully elaborated within the context of Internet research surveys (AoIR, 2012). International aspects of professional ethics are also provided by the Global Research Business Network (GRBN), which published a study comparing codes of professional conduct in Australia, Canada, Germany, the UK and the United States, with a specific section dedicated to Internet research.[9]

Specific web survey aspects are discussed in the CASRO 'Code of standards and ethics for survey research' (CASRO, 2011) and in the Council of German Market and Social Association's 'Directive for online surveys' (Rat der Deutschen Markt- und Sozialforschung eV, 2007).

We should also mention the resources provided by AAPOR with respect to standards and ethics, including the elaboration of disposition codes (AAPOR, 2011), as well as the annual review of new books (English language only) in public opinion, survey methods and survey statistics (Callegaro, 2014a).

With respect to general statistical aspects, Eurostat's professional code is very informative (Eurostat, 2011). Various other professional codes and standards exist, particularly within national associations and large organizations; an overview can be found at WebSM.

We may also recall here the importance of general W3C technical standards on the web (e.g. HTML or CSS code) and particularly the compliance with web accesibilty standards (e.g. the US Rehabilitation Act, Section 508[10]).

6.3.5 Informal Guides, Recommendations and Other Material

Despite the certificates, codes and standards discussed above, in practice there is still a considerable dearth of practical guidelines about how to run web surveys. This gap is filled in part by various informal guides, which predominantly appear on the web.

The main stream of these materials originates from web survey software suppliers. They understand that selling the software and related services represents only one part of their business and that providing methodological guides, hints, training and best practice material from the broader methodological field – and not merely support for specific software features – is an important part of their mission. These materials range from simple how-to-do checklists and systematic tutorials to special user conference events and profound methodological materials, including white papers and even books (e.g. Bhaskaran & LeClaire, 2010).

According to a WebSM study (Vehovar, Čehovin et al., 2012), out of 377 software suppliers, 67% offer basic methodological documentation on how to conduct surveys. 30% offer specific white papers, while 17% include extensive documentation and 9% have methodological documentation in a formalized PDF file. An overview of their recommendations is summarized in the Supplement to Chapter 6, *List of web survey software methodological recommendations* (http://websm.org/ch6).

Another stream, which fills the gap in popularizing the best practices in web survey methodology, is represented by the blogs and other regular postings on the web. There might be some promotional noise in these postings, but much valuable insight can be obtained on the current state of affairs in web survey methodology. The WebSM organizes blogs into four main categories:

- Expert blogs, which are maintained by survey methodology professionals and marketing professionals.
- Association and media blogs, which strive to discuss contemporary survey methodology objectively and are not directly involved in selling survey software or providing methodological advice.
- Web survey software supplier blogs, which are a part of the supplier's marketing and sales strategy, but also offer relevant information because they must be interesting to a broader audience to be successful.
- Research organization blogs from the private, public and non-profit sectors which deal extensively with web survey methodology.

In 2014, the WebSM database[11] contained around a hundred blogs and other online sources, which more or less regularly address issues related to web survey methodology.

6.4 WEB SURVEY BIBLIOGRAPHY

We introduced the WebSM website http://www.websm.org in the Preface and referred to it in all the chapters, particularly with respect to supplementary materials, the web survey software list, blogs and other information. However, the core mission of WebSM is its bibliographic database, established in 1998. The selection and inclusion

process is routinized and relies on a regular overview of around a hundred sources and also on an elaborated strategy to deal with new entries detected by search engines.

In WebSM the bibliographic entries are included according to three criteria: (a) the source is publicly available; (b) at least the abstract exists; and (c) the entry is based on research with relevance to web survey methodology. Since a methodological research focus is essential for establishing this relevance, various descriptive research project reports or marketing research conference papers are beyond the scope of the database. On the other side, some more general bibliographic entries are also included, because of their high indirect relevance for web survey methodology. They span from general social science methodology, general survey methodology, and CASIC, through usability research, HCI, online qualitative methods, Internet studies, research on online communities, e-learning to important case studies from different substantive fields where web surveys are used to collect data. This indirect criterion is more arbitrary, but we believe the approach has been consistent through the years.

The bibliography is structured according to scholarly entries (journal papers, books, edited books, book chapters) and other types (magazine papers, newsletters, conference proceedings, conference material, theses and diplomas, reports, business material, etc.). Each bibliographic entry is described with standard codes for publication type, title, author(s), source, year, abstract and source database for full text, and also with specific codes for scientific field, topic, country, target population and related topics.

We provide here some insights into the WebSM bibliographic database structure for publications dating up to 2013. The scholarly ones amount to 2,888 out of 6,890 entries, the remaining ones belonging predominantly to various conference materials, proceedings and other documents.

The 10 journals with the largest number of entries (journal papers) in the WebSM database – each journal having more than 10 entries – can be sorted in descending order as follows: *Quirk's Marketing Research Review, Public Opinion Quarterly, Social Science Computer Review, Journal of Official Statistics, International Journal of Market Research, Survey Practice, Behavior Research Methods, Computers in Human Behavior, Journal of Medical Internet Research* and *Marketing News*. These journals essentially reflect the structure of the related scientific fields and disciplines discussed in Section 6.3.1. The majority of the entries are from the social sciences, followed by marketing, health, Internet research, psychology and education, with a strong overlap with general social science methodology, computer science and statistics. Of course, this structure differs greatly from the structure of actual web survey projects, as well as from the structure of daily completed web questionnaires.

With respect to region, US-related research contributes the majority of entries (53%), while, for conferences, AAPOR has by far the most entries, followed by ESRA (European Survey Research Association) and GOR (General Online Research).

Regarding the trends shown in Figure 6.2, there seems to be a steady increase of new entries over two decades, following the initial publication year of 1994, when the very first scholarly publication directly related to web survey methodology appeared (i.e. Pitkow & Recker, 1994). After 2004, the increase in annual input has slowed down to around 500 entries per year, of which 150–200 are scholarly entries. An unexplained decline occurred in 2006. It is interesting to note that similar observations on trends were found by a meta-study of related publications on web survey research in China (Zhang, Shao, & Fang, 2008).

As for authors, there were 8,323 in the database by the end of 2013, of whom 4,741 contributed some scholarly input. In both cases the largest part (76% and 84% respectively) contributed only one entry. We might say that the entry level for publishing in this area is relatively low, but this is more likely due to the fact that the main research focus of the authors is outside web survey methodology.

In Figure 6.3, we illustrate a co-authorship network of authors in the field of web survey methodology using the Pajek tool for network

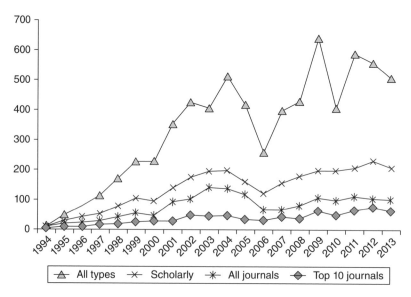

Figure 6.2 Bibliographic entries in the WebSM database according to publication year (1994–2013) and publication types

analysis (de Nooy, Mrvar & Batagelj, 2011). For this purpose we run additional analysis on November 2014 WebSM bibliographic database, including only scholarly publications with direct relevance to web survey methodology. In Figure 6.3 only 72 authors with five or more scholarly bibliographic entries appear and all together they produced 528 entries included in this analysis. Each author is presented with a circle and its size reflects the number of their entries in the WebSM database, for example Couper with 53, Reips with 42, and Dillman with 31 entries. Altogether, there are 25 authors with more than 10 entries. The weight of the lines linking the authors reflects the number of scholarly entries written in co-authorships, for example Couper-Tourangeau with 14 entries written in co-authorship.

We should not forget that this illustrates only bibliographic entries that are directly relevant for web survey methodology and that it excludes eventual other scientific bibliography of the authors.

It is interesting to note that 52 of the 72 authors in the figure present the largest component in the network (the largest sub-network of connected authors). Thus, this is a relatively small network and as we (the authors of this book) personally know almost all of these researchers, we observe that web survey methodology is a dominant research focus only for a few of them. The great majority are involved in general social science methodology, general survey methodology and various substantive fields (e.g. sociology, psychology).

The list of all bibliographic entries included in the above figure, together with some further statistics on the bibliographic entries (research topic, language, sources, etc.), can be found on WebSM as the Supplement *Statistics of WebSM bibliography database* (http://websm.org/ch6).

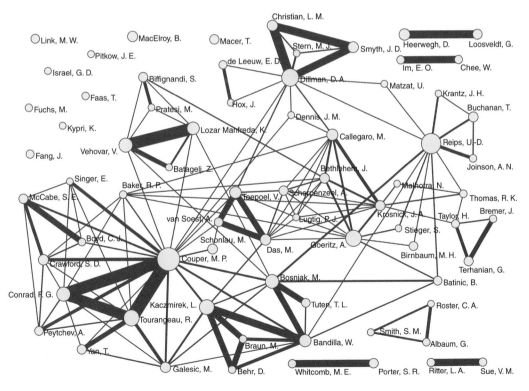

Figure 6.3 WebSM co-authorships for authors with five or more scholarly entries with direct relevance to web survey methodology, November 2014

We can conclude that professional activities related to web survey methodology have stabilized at a certain level. In future we expect that web surveys will become even more integrated into the general social science methodology context, as well as into the general management framework. The borders with survey methodology will become increasingly blurred, which we further discuss in Chapter 7 on future trends.

NOTES

1 See pages 20–21 in Institute of Public Health presentation on data aspects, available at http://www.websm.org/nijz13

2 http://www.pmi.org/PMBOK-Guide-and-Standards.aspx

3 http://ipma.ch/resources/ipma-publications/ipma-competence-baseline/

4 http://www.prince2.com/prince2-methodology

5 http://workshop.websm.org

6 http://kostat.go.kr/iwis/index.html

7 ISO standards: http://www.iso.org/iso/home/standards.htm

8 BSI certification: http://www.bsigroup.com/

9 http://www.websm.org/grbn12

10 http://www.websm.org/508

11 http://www.websm.org/blogs

CONTENTS

Future of web surveys

There can be little doubt that web surveys will continuously expand and at least certain aspects of web survey methodology will become increasingly relevant for almost every survey. In addition to this general observation, we discuss below a few more specific assertions. Some of them were scattered across previous chapters and so we only summarize them. Additionally, we incorporate certain observations and speculations about the industry, profession and science, as well as reflections based on our experience with web surveys, related events and professional networks.

Future trends can be structured roughly into four streams, which might also partially overlap: technological developments (Section 7.1), web survey software (Section 7.2), methodology (Section 7.3), and broader issues related to the profession, science, business and society (Section 7.4).

7.1 GENERAL TECHNOLOGICAL DEVELOPMENTS

General ICT trends will continue to provide cheaper, faster and better devices and services, e.g. from cloud computing to three-dimensional images (holograms). In addition, we expect that web surveys in the future will benefit especially from the following technological breakthroughs.

Voice input. Despite rapid developments in past decades, we are still waiting for a major breakthrough in voice recognition technologies to lead to an inexpensive standard commodity, at least for the major official languages. Among numerous other implementations, further developments can also enable respondents to answer web surveys in a specific user-friendly manner, simply by speaking to a device. Once this becomes fully operational, a certain share of web surveys may shift to this alternative way of answering surveys. We see this trend as especially useful for smartphone and tablet surveys.

Intelligent data analysis. This is another breakthrough for which we have been waiting for decades, but is continually postponed. Artificial intelligence implemented into statistical analysis – covering the entire spectrum from handling outliers to creating appropriate graphs – is particularly intriguing for web surveys, since it can be smoothly integrated into the web survey process to support real-time data quality diagnostics, data editing and imputations, fieldwork interventions, preliminary reporting, etc. This will hopefully help the integration of ICT support and also fulfil some of current needs for separate software for data quality diagnostics, iterative fieldwork designs, data cleaning, preliminary data analysis and automatic preparation of advanced dissemination materials. Elaborated dashboards can also take advantage of these developments and allow users to run real-time in-depth analyses of the collected data and share the results with other team members.

Online collaboration tools. We expect progress in the development of capable and user-friendly platforms – integrated into web survey software – in supporting all the collaboration and communication aspects of the corresponding research process. This will present more efficient alternatives to current reliance on email and text processors, especially for more complex survey projects, where coordination of numerous tasks and the people involved is needed.

Multiple devices. It is not difficult to predict that devices that have already become alternatives to desktop/notebook computers (e.g. smartphones, tablets, Internet TV) will further expand, become more diverse and integrate new features. Standard computers (desktop and notebook) may soon have only a minor share among devices used to complete questionnaires. Hardware developments and software standardization (e.g. platforms, browsers, HTML5) will thus have important consequences for web surveys and will dictate numerous changes and adaptations in web survey software and methodology.

Body as a language. Respondents have traditionally provided answers only orally or manually. This can be expanded in the directions already traced by gaming consoles (e.g. Xbox Kinect, PlayStation Move or Wii MotionPlus), where feedback can be delivered also as a specific body movement. This relates not only to moving the hand (e.g. signs for YES/NO), but also to any movement of any part of the body, including various eye contacts.

Development of electronic micropayments. Establishing a general standard for the easy and simple payment of small amounts – and particularly its increase in popular use in other contexts – may additionally foster the development of more effective incentive strategies for web surveys. This may then enable a respondent to receive an incentive with just one click.

Direct shift to smartphone web surveys in developing countries. Many developing countries skipped the landline telephone technology and went directly to mobile phones. We can expect a similar trend for the Internet: the desktop/notebook based on household Internet connection will be skipped in favour of mobile devices. This move depends on the available technology. In a majority of countries, where the market share is high for smartphones, they may prevail as a survey device.

7.2 WEB SURVEY SOFTWARE

Survey software is so essential for web surveys that we even used it to define the borders of the core web survey process (Figure 1.1, Section 1.2). While many ICT services (e.g. email, fixed telephone services, etc.) have already exhausted the majority of their essential developments, web survey software has a long way to go to reach its full potential. Language technologies, text/data mining, artificial intelligence and other advances will enable us to gain the maximum from existing knowledge and databanks, as well as from survey data, paradata and metadata, which will jointly support the integration and optimization of each step in the web survey process. More specifically, the following advances in web survey software are expected in the three steps of the core web survey process:

1 **Pre-fielding:** Technology will integrate, automate and facilitate the entire questionnaire development process. Intelligent interactive help will provide suggestions and will lead users through the process, from conceptualization and operationalization to question wording (with support from rich banks of questions), computerization and testing. Testing results will be processed and extracted automatically using various evaluation methods (e.g. mouse movement of testing users). Further, text processors will be integrated into the web survey software and include advanced support for the management of comments. With this feature, web questionnaire development will finally find its full support in its natural environment, which is online on the web. Questionnaire development will no longer reside in ordinary text processors, where feedback can be managed only by tracking changes, editing words in different colours and adding comments to the text, all of which are then exchanged by email or other Internet services.

2 **Fielding:** Benefits will arise from the automatic and real-time detection of low-quality responses and other potential problems, as well as from tailored interactive assistance to respondents, which will in considerable part replace the clarification and motivation role of the interviewer.

3 **Post-fielding:** Data preparation (editing, coding, imputation and weighting), which is currently often done externally, will be increasingly automated and integrated; the same holds true for the reporting and data export stage. This integration will then extend the borders of the core web survey process further into advanced analysis and exploitation.

In addition to advances in web survey software technology, we expect increasing horizontal integration among suppliers by mergers and acquisitions. Advances in web survey software and its integration require a critical mass of developers and users, where the minimal and optimal size of the required resources will further increase. It is unclear how long various local, national and small-scale survey software will exist to support certain user segments, but concentration is definitely a trend. This is reinforced with competitive prices, which require an increasingly large number of customers to ensure resources for marketing, support and development.

Vertical concentration is even more important with the integration of online panels and various business processes (e.g. measuring the voice of the customers), with web survey plug-ins integrated into popular content management systems (e.g. WordPress) and social network websites (e.g. Facebook), as well as with expanded support of office services provided by large ICT players (Microsoft, Google, Apple).

7.3 METHODOLOGY

In addition to the general and specific technological trends, we also expect important improvements in methodological developments. We include here also technical progress with direct methodological consequences.

Rise and decline of mixed-mode data collection. We do not expect that the mixing of survey modes will increase in the marketing and business sectors, since it is too expensive and too complicated for their specific needs. However, we do expect a temporary increase within the transition process when web surveys are introduced into official statistics and academic probability surveys. Ultimately, almost all telephone and F2F surveys will at least in part migrate to the web. In the first step, this will typically mean a shift into mixed-mode surveys. Due to the complexity of this transition, this will be one of the most interesting and challenging methodological exercises in the history of web surveys.

After this initial shift, perhaps in a decade or two, we expect an overall decline in mixed-mode surveys. This will be fostered by technological and methodological advances, software integration and further societal changes, when 'digital natives' will grow (i.e. people born into an environment where digital technologies are commonly used), Internet penetration will reach over 95% in most countries and the computer literacy level will increase. Very likely, the elaborated and tailored web surveys will eliminate the need for an interviewer and only for very few and rare surveys will the interviewer be indispensable.

Increased use of paradata. Given the fact that no interviewer is present in web surveys, paradata will also increasingly be used as a tool to better understand the question answering process and to shed light on web survey data quality issues.

Increased integration with qualitative research. Contrary to mixed-modes, the integration of web surveys with various qualitative approaches is expected to grow steadily. The so-called mixed methods approaches, where survey data collection is combined with qualitative data collection, are currently still relatively weakly explored, both from conceptual and methodological aspects, as well as from technical aspects (i.e. integrated software support). Once both approaches are fully integrated and supported on the web, new possibilities for their complementation and synergies will arise.

Technology-enhanced complementary data collection. We have already provided some illustrations related to smartphones, which can semi-automatically (e.g. bar-code) or automatically collect specific data (e.g. location, movement, distance, etc.). Similarly, data on exposure to radio and TV signals and to billboard advertising can be automatically recorded (of course, the respondents need to accept some wearable technology to detect the signals), so there will be less need to ask respondents about advertising in surveys. Considerable progress can be expected also with respect to biomarker data collection and other data collected through wearable technologies.

Technology-enhanced survey questionnaires. We can expect increased richness in the survey questionnaire's look and feel, from the multimedia expansion of questions and the questionnaire's visual layout (interface) to the introduction of gamification and advanced animation (e.g. intelligent virtual interviewer). In addition, the rise of 'the Internet of things', where objects (devices, appliances, consumer goods) will receive IP numbers and thus become integrated into the Internet, will also bring substantial changes. For example, with some regularity (e.g. once a year), a fridge may invite customers to a survey using its own voice or touch-screen features. Alternatively, the invitation to a survey can be shifted to other more convenient survey devices belonging to the same consumer (e.g. TV, smartphone, etc.).

Augmentation and integration of the survey data with big data. Survey data are increasingly being merged among themselves (e.g. statistical matching) and linked with administrative and business data, as well as with numerous electronic traces related to transactions and online behaviour. Modern technology further enables the capture, processing and analysis of enormous volumes of data (i.e. big data), which may potentially replace certain types of surveys (e.g. surveys on media consumption, retail purchases, movement and travel of the respondent). However, with some exceptions, all of this will not weaken the general requests for surveys, especially because asking people questions may still be simpler, faster and more valid in many cases than extracting that information from enormous amounts of non-structured data that were not collected for that specific purpose. On the other hand, this will definitely improve synergy in the integrated exploitation of various data sources.

The rise of customer panels and online communities. In addition to the expansion of general population online panels, more and more organizations are building their own online panels based on their target groups (customers, voters, members, clients, etc.). They are also increasingly establishing various types of online communities (e.g. via social media followers), where they conduct qualitative research, crowdsourcing and data mining, in addition to web surveys.

Social media recruitment, real-time recruitment and river samples. Some companies are already treating all Internet users as a pool of potential survey respondents and use a combination of different recruitment techniques in order to create an online sample in real time and administer a survey. Due to problems with response rates in traditional surveys, as well as in online panels, we can expect increased pressure to recruit respondents on the fly, using innovative approaches and incentive strategies.

Inference from non-probability samples. Non-probability samples already prevail in web surveys, so we expect important developments here. More elaborate rules and standards for non-probability surveys will be established, as well as a common understanding about their potential and limitations, particularly the development of conditions when this approach works. The corresponding skills,

which today replace scientific statistical inference, are also expected to be formalized and to generate scientific attention. As a consequence, we can also expect textbooks to appear on this matter, covering both conceptual and practical aspects.

7.4 BROADER BUSINESS AND SOCIETAL ISSUES

To a considerable extent the broader business and societal contexts also determine the role and usage of web surveys.

Further integration with administrative and business processes. Various administrative and business processes will increasingly integrate the collection of web survey data. This includes a variety of processes, from intelligence reporting via mobile apps (e.g. from bar-code scanning to photos and videos), customer relationship marketing (CRM) databases, support for the sales department, to human resource management (HRM) systems and various other evaluations and managerial applications.

Expansion of Do-It-Yourself (DIY) research. With web survey software providing increasingly intelligent support for all steps of the web survey process, basic computer literacy and common sense will be additionally empowered, not only to run simple surveys, but also to deal with many of the more advanced methodological issues. With this, the line between professional and DIY web surveys will become additionally blurred. Further expansion of DIY research will also be the main factor in the growth of web surveys, because new users will be increasingly enabled to run more sophisticated surveys.

Democratization of research. The expansion of DIY has already led to the democratization of research. Survey data collection used to require considerable resources (in terms of time, personnel and funds) that only professional survey organizations were able to afford. Today, anyone – even without respondents, funds or knowledge – can conduct web surveys, which increasingly opens up the research field to small players, to non-professional and to civil society in general, who may propose research topics that official, academic or marketing research players would never put on the agenda. We see no end to this trend: more and more subjects (persons, organizations) will be able to run more and more complex web surveys.

Decreasing participation in surveys. We mentioned in Section 2.5 the various reasons leading to a continuous decline in cooperation in surveys. We expect these trends to be reinforced in the future to some point where over-surveying will lead to critical saturation with web surveys. Within this context, we may in particular mention the role of increased social restrictions on web surveys, mostly due to privacy and confidentiality concerns, but also due to a rising general concern about unsolicited communication. As a consequence, the role of explicit informed consent for respondents will increase. Methodologists will need to respond to these problems predominantly with elaborated incentives, optimized iterative fieldwork designs and even friendlier web questionnaires, often involving elements of surveytainment and gamification.

Rise and decline of the web survey profession. Currently, it seems there are many unresolved issues related to web survey methodology. For example, we do not have the final verdict on very basic issues, such as a one-page or multiple page design, hard vs soft prompts, ways of handling 'don't know' answers, or even the optimal format for calendar date entry questions. In the future, various technological turbulences related to new devices and to the process of moving traditional surveys to the web will produce additional methodological challenges. Consequently, we can expect that the requests for professional support will increase, as well as the corresponding methodology research.

However, once almost all surveys are fully integrated into the family of web-related surveys, web survey methodology will increasingly become an integral part of survey methodology. Similarly we no longer discuss separately and at length the notion of information society, since ICT has already infiltrated every corner of modern society, therefore there is no modern society outside the information society.

In addition to the formal and rather terminological decline of web survey methodology, in the long run (e.g. more than a few decades), we may also expect its substantive decline. One reason is that much of the methodological turbulence that appeared in the last two decades was often only temporary, as web survey technologies (e.g. devices, web survey software, Internet speed) had not yet become stable and mature, but were subject to permanent technological improvements. This will all slowly disappear, once technological platforms and the related methodology become largely stabilized, as was the case with fixed telephone interview surveys. Consequently, we may also expect a certain decline in the survey methodology profession, because the majority of survey processes will be standardized and intelligently automated by machines. Of course, this is the very opposite of past trends, where the needs for methodologists to handle questionnaire development, nonresponse, non-probability sample selection and post-survey adjustment increased continuously.

Decline of the survey industry? We do not think that the sheer volume of surveys will be reduced in the future. Within this context, it is useful to recall speculations from the mid-1990s, following the initial increase of CASIC, that the survey industry will decline after 2020 due to the development of alternatives (e.g. automated data, models). While automated data collection and modelling are actually expanding very rapidly, we see today that this is not accompanied by a decline in surveys. On the contrary, we are seeing a rapid increase in the number of surveys, which is a trend that can be confirmed by suppliers, researchers and also by respondents. We can definitely expect that certain automatic data collection and processing will replace the need for surveys, so that the related services (e.g. business intelligence) will actually increasingly compete with services provided by the survey industry, particularly by its marketing research segment. Nevertheless, this shift will still not compensate for the expansion of web surveys due to other reasons, such as DIY expansion and increased requests for information. Particularly in business the concept of being more data-driven in order to make decisions is rapidly gaining ground. For this reason, we are witnessing more and more decision makers commissioning a survey as another data source to support business decisions.

The volume of web survey questionnaires completed daily will likely increase steadily. As mentioned above, at a certain point the expansion of the web survey profession may not follow these trends. It will undergo numerous changes, predominantly in the direction of increased integration with management, statistics, informatics and field-specific intelligence, which may further reduce the need for a specialized (web) survey methodologist.

Let us conclude with the extreme futuristic speculation that a true decline of the survey industry as we know it today may occur with some radical breakthrough in neuroscience, which would enable the direct detection of answers to survey questions. This could effectively lead to the automatic completion of survey questionnaires and a completely new way of data collection (e.g. scanning responses directly from brain waves, without requiring any active cooperation from the respondent). However, again this may not only reduce the extent of the conventional survey industry, but also further increase the volume of completed questionnaires.

8

Conclusions

Web surveys are a relatively new method for collecting survey data. Previously, research on web survey methodology has seen many developments that we have attempted critically to discuss, organize and present in this book.

Let us briefly summarize what web surveys have brought to the survey methodology field. Firstly, they have raised some of the issues previously debated in the literature on mail surveys. That is, we deal here with a self-administered mode with all of its advantages and disadvantages. This additional, essential and specific aspect of web surveys is that respondents need to interact with a device and also with the Internet in order to answer a questionnaire.

Web surveys have also reinforced the importance of visuals, where it has become clear that even a small modification to the layout of survey questions can seriously change the distribution of responses. A related specific of web surveys is that they share many characteristics of the common web experience, which respondents are used to from their browsing of the web for other purposes. Namely, elements such as radio buttons, checkboxes, input fields, etc., also appear in many other contexts besides web surveys.

Web surveys have additionally exposed the problem of sampling and recruiting respondents. The Internet has opened up the possibility to recruit an inexpensive pool of respondents quickly, but at the price of moving to non-probability samples. Although non-probability samples have already been used with other methods of data collection, online recruitment has opened up many new possibilities and also challenges.

Self-administration, the visual design and sampling are all essential aspects of web survey methodology and are interwoven throughout the chapters of this book, which is otherwise organized according to the flow of the web survey process (pre-fielding, fielding, post-fielding). Within our deliberations we have provided over 700 key references and hand-picked the best ones from the related WebSM bibliographic database, which at the beginning of 2014 contained 6,890 entries.

After years of research related to web surveys we know a lot about different sampling and online recruitment mechanisms, the effects of visual design, interactivity and the use of images in web questionnaires, incentives, multiple contacts and other ways to increase response rates, and now we also know a lot more about paradata. At various points of our discussion in this book we have needed to repeat the general phrase that 'more research is needed'. In this propulsive area, where technological and methodological changes unfold almost on a daily basis, ideas for potential research appear particularly frequently; however, let us emphasize again the key specific topics that especially need further research:

- elaboration of hard prompts for invalid or missing responses, as well as their interaction with the usage of non-substantive response options (e.g. 'don't know') and data quality in general;
- circumstances and criteria for using tables instead of series of individual questions;
- potential role of interactive and visual elements;
- web survey implementations using multiple devices;
- establishment of standards (indicators, reporting, documentation) for non-probability web surveys; and
- mixed mode systems.

While the research on web surveys started to build on the general knowledge originating from survey methodology, it turned out to be much more interdisciplinary than research related to traditional survey modes. One can get a good sense of this variety simply by browsing the WebSM, where implementations of web surveys span social science and marketing, health, education and Internet studies, and where contributions stretch from social science methodology to statistics, computer science, usability research and web design.

So where are web surveys headed? Following the discussion of potential trends in Chapter 7, we can be reassured that the use of web surveys will steadily continue to increase. As Internet penetration in many countries increases, more surveys will be done on the web, particularly with the recent global shift to mobile devices. On the other hand, there are also alternatives to the increased use of web surveys. Namely, automatic data collection, statistical modelling and big data, particularly in marketing research, create grounds for competitors from the business intelligence industry. Within this context, web survey methodology has a particularly important role in helping to provide a competitive product: that is, the inexpensive collection of quality survey data information.

Regarding the general research areas where we expect the most promising future developments, we can emphasize the further conceptual, methodological and technical integration of ICT support for the entire web survey process.

Similarly, we expect knowledge technologies to be increasingly included more in the process of questionnaire development, as well as in the diagnostics of the quality of responses. All this will enable important improvements in the quality of the web survey process.

Finally, we may add that the book does not end here. Updates and new material will be constantly added to the WebSM website (http://www.websm.org). Readers can already access various supplementary materials and other information there. Feedback can be sent to book@websm.org, so we can improve the supplementary materials and provide better future editions of the book.

Bibliography

AAPOR. (2010). *AAPOR code for professional ethics and practices*. Retrieved from http://www.aapor.org/.

AAPOR. (2011). *Standard definitions: Final dispositions of case codes and outcome rates for surveys*. Retrieved from http://www.aapor.org/.

Adams, M. J. D., & Umbach, P. D. (2012). Nonresponse and online student evaluations of teaching: Understanding the influence of salience, fatigue, and academic environments. *Research in Higher Education*, *53*(5), 576–591.

Advertising Research Foundation. (2014). *Foundations of quality 2.0: Launching what we've learned*. Retrieved from Presented at ARF's Symposium on FOQ2 Initiative. Retrieved from http://www.thearf.org/.

Ainsaar, M., Lilleoja, L., Lumiste, K., & Roots, A. (2013). *ESS mixed mode experiment results in Estonia (CAWI and CAPI mode sequential design)*. Report. Retrieved from http://www.yti.ut.ee/sites/default/files/ssi/ess_dace_mixed_mode_ee_report.pdf

Ajzen, I. (1991). A theory of planned behavior. *Organizational Behavior and Human Decision Processes*, *50*(2), 179–211.

Albaum, G., Roster, C. A., Wiley, J. B. Rossiter, J., & Smith, S. M. (2010). Designing web surveys in marketing research: Does use of forced answering affect completion rates? *Journal of Marketing Theory & Practice*, *18*(3), 285–294.

Albaum, G., & Smith, S. M. (2012). Why people agree to participate in surveys. In L. Gideon (Ed.), *Handbook of Survey Methodology for the Social Sciences* (pp. 179–193). New York: Springer.

Albert, W., Tedesco, D., & Tullis, T. (2009). *Beyond the usability lab: Conducting large-scale online user experience studies*. Amsterdam: Morgan Kaufmann.

Alexander, G. L., Divine, G. W., Couper, M. P., McClure, J. B., Stopponi, M. A., Fortman, K. K., … Johnson, C. C. (2008). Effect of incentives and mailing features on online health program enrollment. *American Journal of Preventive Medicine*, *34*(5), 382–388.

Alwin, D. F. (2007). *Margins of error: a study of reliability in survey measurement*. Hoboken, New Jersey: Wiley.

Amarov, B., & Rendtel, U. (2013). The recruitment of the access panel of German Official Statistics from a large survey in 2006: Empirical results and methodological aspects. *Survey Research Methods*, *7*(2), 103–114.

Andrews, D., Nonnecke, B., & Preece, J. (2003). Conducting research on the Internet: Online survey design, development and implementation guidelines. *International Journal of Human-Computer Interaction*, *16*(2), 185–210.

Anseel, F., Lievens, F., Schollaert, E., & Choragwicka, B. (2010). Response rates in organizational science, 1995–2008: A meta-analytic review and guidelines for survey researchers. *Journal of Business and Psychology*, *25*(3), 335–349.

Antoun, C., Zhang, C., Conrad, F. G., & Schober, M. F. (2013). *Comparisons of online recruitment strategies: Craigslist, Facebook, Google Ads and Amazon's Mechanical Turk*. Presented at the The American Association for Public Opinion Research (AAPOR) 68th Annual Conference, Boston, Massachusetts.

AoIR. (2012). *Ethical decision-making and Internet research*. Retrieved from http://aoir.org/.

Aoki, K., & Elsmar, M. (2000). Opportunities and challenges of conducting web surveys. Results from a filed experiment. *Proceedings of the Survey Research Methods Section, American Statistical Association, pp. 930-935*. (pp. 930–935). Alexandria, Virginia: AMSTAT.

Arbeitskreis Deutscher Markt. (2007). *Guideline for online surveys*. Retrieved from http://www.adm-ev.de/fileadmin/user_upload/PDFS/R08_E_07_08.pdf

Aviram, H. (2012). What would you do? Conducting web-based factorial vignette surveys. In L. Gideon (Ed.), *Handbook of Survey Methodology for the Social Sciences*. pp. 463–473. Berlin: Springer.

Babbie, E. R. (2013). *The practice of social research* (13th ed.). Bedford, CA: Wadsworth.

Baker, J. D. (2013). Online survey software. In *Online instruments, data collection, and electronic measurements: organizational advancements*. (pp. 328–334). Hershey, PA: IGI Global.

Baker, R. P., Blumberg, S. J., Brick, J. M., Couper, M. P., Courtright, M., Dennis, J. M., … Zahs, D. (2010). Research synthesis. AAPOR report on online panels. *Public Opinion Quarterly*, *74*(4), 711–781.

Baker, R. P., Brick, M. J., Bates, N., Battaglia, M. P., Couper, M. P., Dever, J. A., … Tourangeau, R. (2013). Report of the AAPOR task-force on non-probability sampling. Retrieved from http://www.aapor.org/.

Baker, R. P., & Couper, M. P. (2007). The impact of screen size, background color, and navigation button placement on response in web surveys. Presented at the General Online Research Conference (GOR), March, University of Leipzig, Germany.

Baker, R. P., Crawford, S. D., & Swinehart, J. (2004). Development and testing of web questionnaires. In S. Presser, J. M. Rothgeb, M. P. Couper, J. T. Lessler, J. Martin, & E. Singer (Eds), *Methods for Testing and Evaluating Survey Questionnaires* (pp. 361–384). Hoboken, New Jersey: Wiley.

Baker-Prewitt, J., & Miller, J. (2009). *Beyond 'trapping' the undesirable panelist: The use of red herrings to reduce satisficing*. Presented at 2009 CASRO Panel Quality Conference, New Orleans, Louisiana. Retrieved from http://www.casro.org/. http://www.burke.com/Library/Conference/Beyond%20Trapping%20the%20 Undesirable%20Panelist_FINAL.pdf

Baltar, F., & Brunet, I. (2012). Social research 2.0: Virtual snowball sampling method using Facebook. *Internet Research, 22*(1), 57–74.

Balter, O., Fondell, E., & Balter, K. (2012). Feedback in web-based questionnaires as incentive to increase compliance in studies on lifestyle factors. *Public Health Nutrition, 15*(6), 982–988.

Bandilla, W., Couper, M. P., & Kaczmirek, L. (2012). The mode of invitation for web surveys. *Survey Practice, 5*(3).

Barchard, K. A., & Williams, J. (2008). Practical advice for conducting ethical online experiments and questionnaires for United States psychologists. *Behavior Research Methods, 40*(4), 1111–1128.

Barge, S., & Gehlbach, H. (2012). Using the theory of satisficing to evaluate the quality of survey data. *Research in Higher Education, 53*(2), 182–200.

Barrios, M., Villarroya, A., Borrego, Á., & Ollé, C. (2011). Response rates and data quality in web and mail surveys administered to PhD holders. *Social Science Computer Review, 29*(2), 208–220.

Barron, G., & Yechiam, E. (2002). Private e-mail requests and the diffusion of responsibility. *Computers in Human Behavior, 18*(5), 507–520.

Bartram, D. (2006). Testing on the Internet: Issues, challenges and opportunities in the field of occupational assessment. In D. Bartram & R. K. Hambleton (Eds), *Computer-Based Testing and the Internet: Issues and Advances* (pp. 13–38). Chichester: Wiley.

Baruch, Y., & Holtom, B. C. (2008). Survey response rate levels and trends in organizational research. *Human Relations, 61*(8), 1139–1160.

Basso, L., & Rathod, S. (2004). Response and field period effects: *The effect of time in online market research and consequences for future online survey strategies*. Survey Sampling International White Paper. Retrieved from https://www.surveysampling.com/.

Batagelj, Z., & Vehovar, V. (1998). WWW surveys. *Advances in Methodology and Statistics (Metodološki Zvezki), 14*, 209–224.

Batanic, B., & Moser, K. (2005). Determinanten der rücklaufquote in online panels. *Zeitschrift Für Medienpsychologie, 17*(2), 64–74.

Battaglia, M. P., Hoaglin, D. C., & Frankel, M. R. (2009). Practical considerations in raking survey data. *Survey Practice, 5*(2).

Bauman, S., Jobity, N., Airey, J., & Hakan, A. (2000). *Invites, intros and incentives: Lessons from a web survey*. Presented at the The American Association for Public Opinion Research (AAPOR) 55th Annual Conference, Portland, Oregon.

Bavdaž, M. (2010). Sources of measurement errors in business surveys. *Journal of Official Statistics, 26*(1), 25–42.

Bearden, W. O., Netemeyer, R. G., & Haws, K. L. (2011). *Handbook of marketing scales: Multi-item measures for marketing and consumer behavior research* (3rd ed.). Los Angeles, CA: Sage.

Beaty, J. C., Dawson, C. R., Fallaw, S. S., & Kantrowitz, T. M. (2009). Recovering the scientist-practitioner model: How IOs should respond to unproctored internet testing. *Industrial and Organizational Psychology, 2*(1), 58–63.

Beckenbach, A. (1995). Computer-assisted questioning: The new survey methods in the perception of the respondents. *Bulletin of Sociological Methodology/Bulletin de Méthodologie Sociologique, 48*(1), 82–100.

Beckers, T., Siegers, P., & Kuntz, A. (2011). *Speeders in online value research. Presented at the General Online Research Conference (GOR)*, Düsseldorf, Germany.

Behr, D., Bandilla, W., Kaczmirek, L., & Braun, M. (2013). Cognitive probes in web surveys: On the effect of different text box size and probing exposure on response quality. *Social Science Computer Review*.

Bell, D. S., Mangione, C. M., & Khan, C. E. (2001). Randomized testing of alternative survey formats using anonymous volunteers on the world wide web. *Journal of the American Medical Informatics Association*, *8*(6), 616–20.

Bellman, S., Johnson, E. J., Kobrin, S. J., & Lohse, G. L. (2004). International differences in information privacy concerns: A global survey of consumers. *The Information Society*, *20*(5), 313–324.

Bennink, M., Moors, G., & Gelissen, J. (2013). Exploring response differences between face-to-face and web surveys: A qualitative comparative analysis of the Dutch European Values Survey 2008. *Field Methods*, *25*(4), 319–338.

Berzelak, N. (2014). *Mode effects in web surveys*. Ljubljana: PhD thesis. Retrieved from http://www.fdv.uni-lj.si/.

Berzelak, N., & Lozar Manfreda, K. (2009). *Relations between usability and functionality of web survey software tool: An empirical evaluation*. Presented at the 7th Internet Survey Methodology Workshop, Bergamo, Italy.

Berzofsky, M., Williams, R., & Biemer, P. (2009). Combining probability and non-probability sampling methods: Model-aided sampling and the O*NET Data Collection Program. *Survey Practice*, *2*(6).

Bethlehem, J. (2009a). *Applied survey methods: A statistical perspective*. Hoboken, New Jersey: Wiley.

Bethlehem, J. (2009b). Can we make official statistics with self-selection web surveys? *Proceedings of Statistics Canada Symposium 2008*. Canada: Statistics Canada.

Bethlehem, J., & Biffignandi, S. (2012). *Handbook of web surveys*. Hoboken, New Jersey: Wiley.

Beukenhorst, D., & Wetzels, W. (2009). *A comparison of two mixed mode designs: cati-capi and web-cati-capi. Presented at the European Survey Research Association Conference*. Presented at the European Survey Research Association (ESRA), Warsaw, Poland.

Bhaskaran, V., & LeClaire, J. (2010). *Online surveys for dummies*. Indianapolis, IN: Wiley.

Bianchi, A., & Biffignandi, S. (2014). Responsive design for economic data in mixed mode panels. In F. Mecatti, P. L. Conti, & M. G. Ranalli (Eds), *Contribution to sampling statistics*. (pp. 85–101) Berlin: Springer.

Biemer, P. P., Groves, R. M., Lyberg, L. E., Mathiowetz, N. A., & Sudman, S. (Eds). (2004). *Measurement Errors in Surveys*. New York: Wiley.

Biemer, P. P., & Lyberg, L. E. (2003). *Introduction to survey quality*. Hoboken, New Jersey: Wiley.

Biner, P. M., & Kidd, H. J. (1994). The interactive effects of monetary incentive justification and questionnaire length on mail survey response rates. *Psychology and Marketing*, *11*(5), 483–492.

Black, G. S. (1998). *Internet surveys: A replacement technology*. Presented at The American Association for Public Opinion Research (AAPOR) 53rd Annual Conference, St. Louis, Missouri.

Blair, J., & Conrad, F. G. (2011). Sample size for cognitive interview pretesting. *Public Opinion Quarterly*, *75*(4), 636–658.

Blair, J., Czaja, R. F., & Blair, E. A. (2014). *Designing surveys: A guide to decisions and procedures* (3rd ed.). Thousand Oaks, CA: SAGE.

Blanke, K. (2011). *Scrolling or paging – it depends*. Presented at the 5th Internet Survey Methodology Workshop, Hague, Netherlands.

Blanke, K. & Luiten, A. (2014). *Query on Data Collection for Social Surveys*. Deliverable for ESSnet Data Collection for Social Surveys using Multiple Modes. Luxemburg: Eurostat. Retrieved from http://www.cros-portal.eu/sites/default/files//Query_report_DCSS.pdf.

Blasius, J. (2012). Comparing ranking techniques in web surveys. *Field Methods*, *24*(4), 382–398.

Blasius, J., & Thiessen, V. (2012). *Assessing the quality of survey data*. London: SAGE.

Blom, A. G., Gathmann, C., & Krieger, U. (2013, July). The German Internet Panel: Method and results. Mannheim: Universität Mannheim. Retrieved from http://reforms.uni-mannheim.de/internet_panel/home/gip_concept/gip_overview_for_sfb_website.pdf.

Blyth, B. (2008). Mixed-mode: The only 'fitness' regime? *International Journal of Market Research*, *50*(2), 241–266.

Bocarnea, M. C., Reynolds, R. A., & Baker, J. D. (Eds). (2012). *Online instruments, data collection, and electronic measurements: Organizational advancements*. Hershey, PA: IGI Global.

Booth-Kewley, S., Larson, G. E., & Miyoshi, D. K. (2007). Social desirability effects on computerized and paper-and-pencil questionnaires. *Computers in Human Behavior*, *23*(4), 463–77.

Borg, I., & Mastrangelo, P. M. (2008). *Employee surveys in management: Theories, tools, and practical applications*. Cambridge, MA: Hogrefe.

Börkan, B. (2010). The mode effect in mixed-mode surveys: Mail and web surveys. *Social Science Computer Review*, *28*(3), 371–380.

Bosnjak, M., & Batinic, B. (2002). Understanding the willingness to participate in online surveys: the case of e-mail questionnaires. In B. Batanic, U.-D. Reips, & M. Bosnjak (Eds), *Online social sciences* (pp. 115–116). Seattle: Hogrefe.

Bosnjak, M., Haas, I., Galesic, M., Kaczmirek, L., Bandilla, W., & Couper, M. P. (2013). Sample composition discrepancies in different stages of a probability-based online panel. *Field Methods*, 25(4), 339–360.

Bosnjak, M., Neubarth, W., Couper, M. P., Bandilla, W., & Kaczmirek, L. (2008). Prenotification in Web based access panel surveys: The influence of mobile text messaging versus e-mail on response rates and sample composition. *Social Science Computer Review*, *26*(2), 213–223.

Bosnjak, M., Poggio, T., Becker, K. R., Funke, F., Wachenfeld, A., & Fisher, B. (2012). *Mobile survey participation rates in commercial market research: A meta-analysis*. Presented at the 6th Internet Survey Methodology Workshop, Ljubljana, Slovenia.

Bosnjak, M., & Tuten, T. L. (2001). Classifying response behaviors in Web-based surveys. *Journal of Computer-Mediated Communication*, *6*(3).

Bosnjak, M., & Tuten, T. L. (2003). Prepaid and promised incentives in web surveys: An experiment. *Social Science Computer Review*, *21*(2), 208–217.

Bosnjak, M., Tuten, T. L., & Wittmann, W. W. (2005). Unit (non)response in Web-based access panel surveys: An extended planned-behavior approach. *Psychology and Marketing*, *22*(6), 489–505.

Boulianne, S. (2013). Examining the gender effects of different incentive amounts in a web survey. *Field Methods*, *25*(1), 91–104.

Boulianne, S., Klofstad, C. A., & Basson, D. (2011). Sponsor prominence and responses patterns to an online survey. *International Journal of Public Opinion Research*, *23*(1), 79–87.

Boyle, J. M., Ball, S., Ding, H., Euler, G., Starcie, G., & Lewis, F. (2013). Understanding bias in probability and non-probability samples of a rare population. Presented at the The American Association for Public Opinion Research (AAPOR) 68th Annual Conference, Boston, Massachusetts.

Brace, I. (2008). *Questionnaire design: How to plan, structure and write survey material for effective market research* (2nd ed.). London: Kogan Page.

Bradburn, N. M., Sudman, S., & Wansink, B. (2004). *Asking questions: The definitive guide to questionnaire design for market research, political polls, and social and health questionnaires* (Revised.). San Francisco: Jossey-Bass.

Bradley, M., & Lang, P. (1994). Measuring emotion: The self-assessment manikin and the semantic differential. *Journal of Behavior Therapy and Experimental Psychiatry*, *25*(1), 49—59.

Braunsberger, K., Wybenga, H., & Gates, R. (2007). A comparison of reliability between telephone and web-based surveys. *Journal of Business Research*, *60*(7), 758–64.

Brick, J. M., & Williams, D. (2013). Explaining rising nonresponse rates in cross-sectional surveys. *The ANNALS of the American Academy of Political and Social Science*, *645*(1), 36–59.

Brickman Bhutta, C. B. (2012). Not by the book: Facebook as a sampling frame. *Sociological Methods & Research*, *41*(1), 57–88.

Brooke, J. (1996). SUS: A quick and dirty usability scale. In P. W. Jordan, B. Thomas, B. A. Weerdmeester, & I. L. McClelland (Eds), *Usability evaluation in industry* (pp. 189–194). London: Taylor and Francis.

Bruijne, M. de, & Wijnant, A. (2013). Comparing survey results obtained via mobile devices and computers: An experiment with a mobile web survey on a heterogeneous group of mobile devices versus a computer-assisted web survey. *Social Science Computer Review*, *31*(4), 482–504.

Buchanan, E. A., & Hvizdak, E. E. (2009). Online survey tools: Ethical and methodological concerns of human research ethics committees. *Journal of Empirical Research on Human Research Ethics: An International Journal*, *4*(2), 37–48.

Buchanan, T., & Smith, J. L. (1999). Using the Internet for psychological research: Personality testing on the World Wide Web. *British Journal of Psychology*, 90(1), 125–144.

Buelens, B., & van den Brakel, J. A. (2014). Measurement error calibration in mixed-mode sample surveys. *Sociological Methods & Research*. Published online before print.

Buhrmester, M., Kwang, T., & Gosling, S. D. (2011). Amazon's Mechanical Turk: A new source of inexpensive, yet high quality, data? *Perspectives on Psychological Science*, 6(1), 3–5.

Burdein, I. (2014). Shorter isn't always better. *CASRO Journal, 2014*, 5–42.

Burr, M. A., Levin, K., & Becher, A. (2001). Examining Web vs paper mode effects in a federal government customer satisfaction study. Presented at The American Association for Public Opinion Research (AAPOR) 56th Annual Conference, Montreal, Quebec, Canada.

Buskirk, T. D., & Andrus, C. (2012). Smart surveys for smart phones: exploring various approaches for conducting online mobile surveys via smartphones. *Survey Practice* 5(1).

Buskirk, T. D., & Andrus, C. (2013). Online surveys aren't just for computers anymore! Exploring potential mode effects between smartphone and computer-based online surveys. *Proceedings of the Joint Statistical Meeting, American Association for Public Opinion Research Conference* (pp. 5678–5691). Washington, DC: AMSTAT.

Callegaro, M. (2010). Do you know which device your respondent has used to take your online survey? *Survey Practice* 3(6).

Callegaro, M. (2013a). From mixed-mode to multiple devices. Web surveys, smartphone surveys and apps: Has the respondent gone ahead of us in answering surveys? *International Journal of Market Research*, 55(2), 317–320.

Callegaro, M. (2013b). Paradata in web surveys. In F. Kreuter (Ed.), *Improving surveys with paradata: Analytic use of process information* (pp. 261–279). Hoboken, New Jersey: Wiley.

Callegaro, M. (2014a). Recent books and journals in public opinion, survey methods, and survey statistics. *Survey Practice*, 7(2).

Callegaro, M. (2014b). Using Paradata to Improve the Quality of Web Surveys: Some Examples and Applications. Presented at the Conference on Paradata – From survey research to practice, Royal Statistical Society, London. Retrieved from http://www.southampton.ac.uk/s3ri/news/events/2014/06/26_paradata_from_survey_research_to_practice.page.

Callegaro, M., Baker, R. P., Bethlehem, J., Göritz, A. S., Krosnick, J. A., & Lavrakas, P. J. (Eds). (2014a). *Online Panel Research: A Data Quality Perspective*. Chichester, United Kingdom: Wiley

Callegaro, M., Baker, R. P., Bethlehem, J., Göritz, A. S., Krosnick, J. A., & Lavrakas, P. J. (2014b). Online panel research: History, concepts, applications and a look at the future. In M. Callegaro, R. P. Baker, J. Bethlehem, A. S. Göritz, J. A. Krosnick, & P. J. Lavrakas (Eds), *Online panel research: A data quality perspective* (pp. 1–22). Chichester: Wiley.

Callegaro, M., & DiSogra, C. (2008). Computing response metrics for online panels. *Public Opinion Quarterly*, 72(5), 1008–1032.

Callegaro, M., DiSogra, C., & Wells, T. (2011). How the order of response options in a running tally can affect online survey estimates. Presented at The American Association for Public Opinion Research (AAPOR) 66th Annual Conference, Phoenix, Arizona.

Callegaro, M., & Krosnick, J. A. (2014). Introduction to part I. In M. Callegaro, R. P. Baker, J. Bethlehem, A. S. Göritz, J. A. Krosnick, & P. J. Lavrakas (Eds), *Online panel research: A data quality perspective* (pp. 56–60). Chichester: Wiley.

Callegaro, M., Murakami, M., Tepman, Z., & Henderson, V. (2015). Yes-No answers versus check-all in self-administered modes. A systematic review and analyses. International Journal of Market Research. 57(2).

Callegaro, M., Villar, A., Yeager, D. S., & Krosnick, J. A. (2014). A critical review of studies investigating the quality of data obtained with online panels. In M. Callegaro, R. P. Baker, J. Bethlehem, A. S. Göritz, J. A. Krosnick, & P. J. Lavrakas (Eds), *Online panel research: A data quality perspective* (pp. 23–53). Chichester: Wiley.

Callegaro, M., & Wells, T. (2008). Do online respondents go the extra mile and take on inconvenient tasks? Retrieved from http://www.knowledgenetworks.com/ganp/docs/Do-Online-Respondents-Go-the-Extra-Mile-and-Take-on-Inconvenient-Tasks_6-25-08.pdf.

Callegaro, M., Yang, Y., Bhola, D. S., Dillman, D. A., & Chin, T.-Y. (2009). Response latency as an indicator of optimizing in online questionnaires. *Bulletin of Sociological Methodology/Bulletin de Méthodologie Sociologique*, *103*(1), 5–25.

Campanelli, P. (2008). Testing survey questions. In E. de Leeuw, J. J. Hox, & D. A. Dillman (Eds), *International handbook of survey methodology* (pp. 176–200). New York: Lawrence Erlbaum.

Cape, P. (2010). Questionnaire length, fatigue effects and response quality revisited. Retrieved from http://www.surveysampling.com/ssi-media/Corporate/white_papers/SSI_QuestionLength_WP.image.

Carini, R., Hayek, J., Kuh, G., Kennedy, J. M. & Ouimet, J. (2003). College student responses to web and paper surveys: Does mode matter? *Research in Higher Education*, *44*(1), 11–19.

Casey, T. W., & Poropat, A. (2014). Beauty is more than screen deep: Improving the web survey respondent experience through socially-present and aesthetically-pleasing user interfaces. *Computers in Human Behavior*, *30*(2014), 153–163.

CASRO. (2011). Code of standards and ethics for survey research. Council of American Survey Research Organizations. Port Jefferson, NY: Council of American Survey Research Organizations.

Cechanowicz, J., Gutwin, C., Brownell, B., & Goodfellow, L. (2013). Effects of gamification on participation and data quality in a real-world market research domain. In *Gamification 2013* (pp. 58–65). Stratford, Ontario.

Chan, P., & Ambrose, D. (2011). Canadian online panels: Similar or different? *Vue* (January/February), 16–20.

Chaney, B. H., Barry, A. E., Chaney, J. D., Stellefson, M. L., & Webb, M. C. (2013). Using screen video capture software to aide and inform cognitive interviewing. *Quality & Quantity*, *47*(5), 2529–2537.

Chang, L., Frost, L. Z., Chao, S., & Ree, M. J. (2010). Instrument development with Web surveys and multiple imputations. *Military Psychology*, *22*(1), 7–23.

Chang, L., & Krosnick, J. A. (2009). National surveys via Rdd telephone interviewing versus the Internet: Comparing sample representativeness and response quality. *Public Opinion Quarterly*, *73*(4), 641–678.

Chang, L., & Krosnick, J. A. (2010). Comparing oral interviewing with self-administered computerized questionnaires: An experiment. *Public Opinion Quarterly*, *74*(1), 154–167.

Chien, Y.-T., & Chang, C.-Y. (2012). Exploring the impact of animation-based questionnaire on conducting a web-based educational survey and its association with vividness of respondents' visual images. *British Journal of Educational Technology*, *43*(3), E81–E85.

Chittenden, L., & Rettie, R. (2003). An evaluation of e-mail marketing and factors affecting response. *Journal of Targeting, Measurement and Analysis for Marketing, 11*(3), 203–217.

Cho, H., & Larose, R. (1999). Privacy issues in Internet surveys. *Social Science Computer Review*, *17*(4), 421–434.

Chou, P.-N. (2012). The integration of Facebook into class management: An exploratory study. *Educational Research*, *3*(7), 572–575.

Christian, L. M., Dillman, D. A., & Smyth, J. D. (2007). Helping respondents get it right the first time: The influence of words, symbols, and graphics in Web surveys. *Public Opinion Quarterly*, *71*(1), 113–25.

Clayton, R. L., & Werking, G. S. (1998). Business surveys of the future: The world wide web as a data collection methodology. In M. P. Couper, R. P. Baker, J. Bethlehem, C. Z. F. Clark, J. Martin, W. L. Nicholls II, & J. M. O'Reilly (Eds), *Computer-assisted survey information collection* (pp. 543–562). New York: Wiley.

Cobanoglu, C., & Cobanoglu, N. (2003). The effect of incentives in web surveys: Application and ethical considerations. *International Journal of Market Research*, *45*(4), 475–488.

Cobanoglu, C., Warde, B., & Moreo, P. J. (2001). A comparison of mail, fax, and web-based survey methods. *International Journal of Market Research*, *43*(4), 441–452.

Cobben, F., & Bethlehem, J. (2013). *Web panels for official statistics*. Discussion Paper 201307. The Hague, The Netherlands: Statistics Netherlands.

Comley, P. (2000). Pop-up surveys: What works, what doesn't work and what will work in the future. In ESOMAR (Ed.), *Proceedings of the ESOMAR Worldwide Internet Conference: Net Effects 3*. Amsterdam: ESOMAR.

Comley, P. (2006). The games we play: A psychoanalysis of the relationship between panel owners and panel participants. Presented at the *Panel Research Conference*. Amsterdam: ESOMAR.

Comley, P. (2007). Online market research. In M. van Hamersveld & C. de Bont (Eds), *Market research handbook* (5th ed., pp. 401–419). Chichester: Wiley.

Conrad, F. G., Schober, M. F., & Coiner, T. (2007). Bringing features of human dialogue to Web surveys. *Applied Cognitive Psychology*, *21*(2), 165–87.

Conrad, F. G., Tourangeau, R., Couper, M. P., & Zhang, C. (2010). *Professional web respondents and data quality*. Presented at The American Association for Public Opinion Research (AAPOR) 65th Annual Conference, Chicago, Illinois.

Converse, J. M. (2009). *Survey research in the United States: Roots and emergence 1890–1960*. Piscataway, NJ: Transaction Publishers.

Converse, P. D., Wolfe, E. W., Huang, X., & Oswald, F. L. (2008). Response rates for mixed-mode surveys using mail and e-mail/web. *American Journal of Evaluation*, *29*(1), 99–107.

Cook, C., Heath, F., & Thompson, R. L. (2000). A meta-analysis of response rates in Web or internet-based surveys. *Educational and Psychological Measurement*, *60*(6), 821–836.

Cooke, M., Nielsen, A., & Strong, C. (2003). The use of SMS as a research tool. In R. Banks, J. Currall, J. Francis, L. Gerrard, R. Khan, T. Macer, … A. Westlake (Eds), *The impact of technology on the survey process. Proceedings of the Fourth International Conference on Survey and Statistical Computing* (pp. 267–276). Chesham, Bucks, UK: Association for Survey Computing. Retrieved from http://www.asc.org.uk/.

Coombe, R., Jarrett, C., & Johnson, A. (2011). Usability testing of market research questionnaires. Presented at the European Survey Research Association Conference. Presented at the European Survey Research Association (ESRA), Lausanne, Switzerland.

Coromina, L., & Coenders, G. (2006). Reliability and validity of egocentered network data collected via web: A meta-analysis of multilevel multitrait multimethod studies. *Social Networks*, *28*(3), 209–231.

Corti, L., van den Eyden, V., Bishop, L., & Woollard, M. (2014). *Managing and sharing research data: A guide to good practice*. London: SAGE.

Council of American Survey Research Organizations. (2012). *Rules for governing sweepstakes*. Port Jefferson, NY: Council of American Survey Research Organizations. Retrieved from http://c.ymcdn.com/sites/www.casro.org/resource/resmgr/docs/rules_for_governing_sweepsta.pdf.

Couper, M. P. (1998). Measuring survey quality in a CASIC environment. In American Statistical Association (Ed.), *Proceedings of the Joint Statistical Meeting, Survey Research Methods Section* (pp. 41–49). Washington, DC: AMSTAT.

Couper, M. P. (2000a). Usability evaluation of computer-assisted survey instruments. *Social Science Computer Review*, *18*(4), 384–396.

Couper, M. P. (2000b). Web surveys: A review of issues and approaches. *Public Opinion Quarterly*, *64*(4), 464–494.

Couper, M. P. (2005). Technology trends in survey data collection. *Social Science Computer Review*, *23*(4), 486–501.

Couper, M. P. (2008). *Designing effective web surveys*. New York: Cambridge University Press.

Couper, M. P. (2011). The future of modes of data collection. *Public Opinion Quarterly*, *75*(5), 889–908.

Couper, M. P. (2013). *Surveys on mobile devices: Opportunities and challenges*. Presented at the NCRM Conference: Web surveys for the general population: How, why and when?, London, United Kingdom. Retrieved from http://www.natcenweb.co.uk/genpopweb/documents/Mick-Couper.pdf.

Couper, M. P., Baker, R. P., & Mechling, J. (2011). Placement and design of navigation buttons in web surveys. *Survey Practice*, *4*(1).

Couper, M. P., Kapteyn, A., Schonlau, M., & Winter, J. (2005). Noncoverage and nonresponse in an Internet survey. *Social Science Research*, *36*(1), 131–148.

Couper, M. P., Kennedy, C., Conrad, F. G., & Tourangeau, R. (2011). Designing input fields for non-narrative open-ended responses in web surveys. *Journal of Official Statistics*, *27*(1), 65–85.

Couper, M. P., & Kreuter, F. (2013). Using paradata to explore item level response times in surveys. *Journal of the Royal Statistical Society, Journal of the Royal Statistical Society, Series A*, *176*(1), 271–286.

Couper, M. P., & Nicholls II, W. L. (1998). The history and development of computer assisted survey information collection. In M. P. Couper, R. P. Baker, J. Bethlehem, C. Z. F. Clark, J. Martin, W. L. Nicholls II, & J. M. O'Reilly (Eds), *Computer assisted survey information collection* (pp. 1–21). New York: Wiley.

Couper, M. P., & Singer, E. (2013). Informed consent for web paradata use. *Survey Research Methods*, *7*(1), 57–67.

Couper, M. P., Singer, E., Conrad, F. G., & Groves, R. M. (2008). Risk of disclosure, perceptions of risk, and concerns about privacy and confidentiality as factors in survey participation. *Journal of Official Statistics*, *24*(2), 255–275.

Couper, M. P., Tourangeau, R., & Conrad, F. G. (2006). Evaluating the effectiveness of visual analog scales: A Web experiment. *Social Science Computer Review*, *24*(2), 227–245.

Couper, M. P., Tourangeau, R., Conrad, F. G., & Crawford, S. D. (2004). What they see is what we get: Response options for web surveys. *Social Science Computer Review*, *22*(1), 111–127.

Couper, M. P., Tourangeau, R., Conrad, F. G., & Zhang, C. (2013). The design of grids in web surveys. *Social Science Computer Review*, *31*(3), 322–345.

Couper, M. P., Tourangeau, R., & Smith, T. W. (1998). Collecting sensitive information with different modes of data collection. In M. P. Couper, R. P. Baker, J. Bethlehem, C. Z. F. Clark, J. Martin, W. L. Nicholls II, & J. M. O'Reilly (Eds), *Computer assisted survey information collection* (pp. 431–454). New York: Wiley.

Couper, M. P., Traugott, M. W., & Lamias, M. J. (2001). Web survey design and administration. *Public Opinion Quarterly*, *65*(2), 230–253.

Couper, M. P., Zhang, C., Conrad, F. G., & Tourangeau, R. (2012). *Database lookup in web surveys*. Presented at the 6th Internet survey methodology workshop, Ljubljana, Slovenia.

Crawford, S. (2002). Evaluation of web survey data collection systems. *Field Methods*, *14*(3), 307–321.

Crawford, S. D., Couper, M. P., & Lamias, M. J. (2001). Web surveys: Perception of burden. *Social Science Computer Review*, *19*(2), 146–162.

Crawford, S. D., McCabe, S. E., & Pope, D. (2005). Applying Web-based survey design standards. *Journal of Prevention and Intervention in the Community*, *29*(1–2), 43–66.

Crutzen, R., & Göritz, A. S. (2010). Social desirability and self-reported health risk behaviors in web-based research: Three longitudinal studies. *BMC Public Health*, *10*(1), 720.

Csikszentmihalyi, M. (2009). *Flow: The psychology of optimal experience*. New York: HarperCollins.

Čehovin, G., & Vehovar, V. (2012a). *WebSM study: Overview of features of software packages*. Retrieved from http://www.websm.org/db/12/16586/.

Čehovin, G., & Vehovar, V. (2012b). *WebSM Study: Speed and efficiency of online survey tools*. Retrieved from http://www.websm.org/db/12/16583/.

da Costa, F. F., Schmoelz, C. P., Davies, V. F., di Pietro, P. F., Kupek, E., & de Assis, M. A. A. (2013). Assessment of diet and physical activity of Brazilian schoolchildren: Usability testing of a web-based questionnaire. *JMIR Research Protocols*, *2*(2), 1–15.

Das, M. (2012). Innovation in online data collection for scientific research: The Dutch MESS project. *Methodological Innovations Online*, *7*(1), 7–24.

Datta, R. A., Yan, T., Evans, D., Pedlow, S., Spencer, B., & Bautista, R. (2012, March 13). 2010 Census Integrated Communications Program Evaluation (CICPE). Retrieved from https://www.census.gov /2010census/pdf/2010_Census_ICP_Evaluation.pdf.

De Beuckelaer, A., & Lievens, F. (2009). Measurement equivalence of paper-and-pencil and internet organisational surveys: A large scale examination in 16 Countries. *Applied Psychology*, *58*(2), 336–361.

de Leeuw, E. (2005). To mix or not to mix? Data collection modes in surveys. *Journal of Official Statistics*, *21*(2), 1–23.

de Leeuw, E., Callegaro, M., Hox, J., Korendijk, E., & Lensvelt-Mulders, G. (2007). The influence of advance letters on response in telephone surveys. *Public Opinion Quarterly*, *71*(3), 413–443.

de Leeuw, E., & de Heer, W. (2002). Trends in household survey nonresponse: A longitudinal and international comparison. In R. M. Groves, D. A. Dillman, J. L. Eltinge, & R. J. A. Little (Eds), *Survey Nonresponse* (pp. 41–54). Hoboken, New Jersey: Wiley.

de Leeuw, E., & Hox, J. (2011). Internet surveys as a part of a mixed-mode design. In M. Das, P. Ester, & L. Kaczmirek (Eds), *Social and Behavioral Research and the Internet: Advances in Applied Methods and Research Strategies* (pp. 45–76). New York: Routledge.

de Leeuw, E., & Hox, J. J. (2008). Missing data. In P. J. Lavrakas (Ed.), *Encyclopedia of survey research methods*, pp. 468–472. Thousand Oaks, CA: SAGE.

de Leeuw, E., Hox, J. J., & Snijkers, G. (1995). The effect of computer-assisted interviewing on data quality: A review. *Journal of the Market Research Society*, *37*(4), 325–344.

de Leeuw, E., & Nicholls II, W. L. (1996). Technological innovations in data collection: Acceptance, data quality and costs. *Sociological Research Online*, *1*(4).

Dean, E., Head, B., & Swicegood, J. (2013). Virtual cognitive interviewing using Skype and Second Life. In C. A. Hill, E. Dean, & J. Murphy (Eds), *Social Media, Sociality, and Survey Research* (pp. 107–132). Hoboken, Ney Jersey: Wiley.

DeMaio, T., & Landreth, A. (2004). Examining expert reviews as a pretest method. In P. Prüfer, M. Rexroth, & F. J. Fowler (Eds), *ZUMA-Nachrichten Spezial Band 9, QUEST 2003. Proceedings of the 4th Conference on Questionnaire Evaluation Standards* (pp. 60–72). Mannheim, Germany: Gesis.

Dennis, J. M., de Rouvray, C., & Couper, M. P. (2000). Questionnaire design for probability-based Web surveys. Presented at The American Association for Public Opinion Research (AAPOR) 55th Annual Conference, Portland, Oregon.

de Nooy, W., Mrvar, A., and Batagelj, V. (2011). *Exploratory social network analysis with Pajek* (2nd Edition). New York: Cambridge University Press.

DeRouvray, C., & Couper, M. P. (2002). Designing a strategy for reducing 'No opinion' responses in Web-based surveys. *Social Science Computer Review*, *20*(1), 3–9.

Deutskens, E., de Ruyter, K., Wetzels, M., & Oosterveld, P. (2004). Response rate and response quality of Internet-based surveys: An experimental study. *Marketing Letters*, *15*(1), 21–36.

Deutskens, E., Ruyter, K. de, & Wetzels, M. (2006). An assessment of equivalence between online and mail surveys in service research. *Journal of Service Research*, *8*(4), 346–355.

Dietrich, B. J. (2008). Mean square error (MSE). In P. J. Lavrakas (Ed.), *Encyclopedia of survey research methods*, (pp. 456–458). Thousand Oaks, California: SAGE.

Dillman, D. A. (1978). *Mail and telephone surveys: The total design method*. New York: Wiley.

Dillman, D. A., & Messer, B. L. (2010). Mixed-mode surveys. In P. V. Marsden & J. D. Wright (Eds), *Handbook of survey research* (2nd ed., pp. 551–574). Howard House, United Kingdom: Emerald Group Publishing.

Dillman, D. A., Smyth, J. D., & Christian, L. M. (2009). *Internet, mail and mixed-mode surveys: The tailored design method* (3rd ed.). Hoboken, New Jersey: Wiley.

Dillman, D. A., Smyth, J. D., & Christian, L. M. (2014). *Internet, phone, mail, and mixed-mode surveys: The tailored design method* (4th ed.). Hoboken, New Jersey: Wiley.

Dillman, D. A., Tortora, R., Conradt, J., & Bowker, D. K. (1998). Influence of plain vs fancy design on response rates for web surveys. *Proceedings of the Joint Statistical Meeting, Survey Research Methods Section*. Dallas, Texas: AMSTAT.

Diment, K., & Garrett-Jones, S. (2007). How demographic characteristics affect mode preference in a postal/web mixed-mode survey of Australian researchers. *Social Science Computer Review*, *25*(3), 410–417.

DiSogra, C., & Callegaro, M. (2015). Metrics and design tool for building and evaluating probability-based online panels. *Social Science Computer Review*.

DiSogra, C., Callegaro, M., & Hendarwan, E. (2010). Recruiting probability-based web panel members using an address-based sample frame: Results from a pilot study conducted by Knowledge Networks. In *Proceedings of the Annual Meeting of the American Statistical Association* (pp. 5270–5283). Hollywood, FL: AMSTAT.

Dobrow, M. J., Orchard, M. C., Golden, B., Holowaty, E., Paszat, L., Brown, A. D., & Sullivan, T. (2008). Response audit of an Internet survey of health care providers and administrators: implications for determination of response rates. *Journal of Medical Internet Research*, *10*(4), e30.

Donald, E. (2010). Using a fillable PDF together with SAS ® for questionnaire data. Presented at the 23rd NorthEast SAS Users Group, Baltimore, MD. Retrieved from http://www.nesug.org/Proceedings/nesug10/cc/cc10.pdf.

Downes-Le Guin, T., Baker, R. P., Mechling, J., & Ruyle, E. (2012). Myths and realities of respondent engagement in online surveys. *International Journal of Market Research*, *54*(5), 613–633.

Downes-Le Guin, T., Janowitz, P., Stone, R., & Khorram, S. (2002). Use of pre-incentives in an internet survey. *Journal of Online Research*.

Drasgow, F., Nye, C. D., Guo, J., & Tay, L. (2009). Cheating on proctored tests: The other side of the unproctored debate. *Industrial and Organizational Psychology*, *2*(1), 46–48.

Dykema, J., Stevenson, J., Day, B., Sellers, S. L., & Bonham, V. L. (2011). Effects of incentives and pre-notification on response rates and costs in a national web survey of physicians. *Evaluation & the Health Professions, 34*(4), 434–447.

Economic and Statistics Administration, & National Telecommunications and Information Administration. (2010). *Exploring the digital nation: Home broadband internet adoption in the United States.* Washington, DC: US Department of Commerce.

Edwards, P. J., Roberts, I., Clarke, M. J., DiGuiseppi, C., Wentz, R., Kwan, I., … Pratap, S. (2009). Methods to increase response to postal and electronic questionnaires. *Cochrane Database of Systematic Reviews* 8(3). Chichester: Wiley.

Edwards, S. W., & Cantor, D. (1991). Towards a response model in establishment surveys. In P. P. Biemer, R. M. Groves, L. E. Lyberg, N. A. Mathiowetz, & S. Sudman (Eds), *Measurement errors in surveys* (pp. 211–236). New York: Wiley.

Ehling, M., & Körner, T. (Eds). (2007). *Handbook on data quality assessment methods and tools.* Wiesbaden: Eurostat.

Ekeh, P. P. (1974). *Social exchange theory: The two traditions.* Cambridge, MA: Harvard University Press.

Elling, S., Lentz, L., de Jong, M., & van den Bergh, H. (2012). Measuring the quality of governmental web-sites in a controlled versus an online setting with the 'Website Evaluation Questionnaire'. *Government Information Quarterly, 29*(3), 383–393.

Emde, M., & Fuchs, M. (2012a). Exploring animated faces scales in web surveys: Drawbacks and prospects. *Survey Practice, 5*(1).

Emde, M., & Fuchs, M. (2012b). Using adaptive questionnaire design in open-ended questions: A field experiment. *Proceedings of the Survey Research Methods Section, American Statistical Association.* San Diego, California.

Enders, C. K. (2010). *Applied missing data analysis.* New York: Guilford.

ESOMAR. (2011a). *ESOMAR guideline for online research.* Amsterdam: ESOMAR.

ESOMAR. (2011b). *Esomar guideline on social media research.* Amsterdam: ESOMAR. Retrieved from http://www.websm.org/db/35/17108/

ESOMAR. (2012). *28 Questions to help research buyers of online samples.* Amsterdam: ESOMAR. Retrieved from http://www.websm.org/db/35/17126/

ESOMAR. (2013). *Global market research 2013.* Amsterdam: ESOMAR.

Ester, P., & Vinken, H. (2010). Measuring attitudes toward controversial issues in internet surveys: Order effects of open and closed questioning. In M. Das, P. Ester, & L. Kaczmirek (Eds), *Social and behavioral research and the internet. Advances in applied methods and research strategies* (pp. 245–268). New York: Routledge.

Esuli, A., & Sebastiani, F. (2010). Machines that learn how to code open ended survey data. *International Journal of Market Research, 52*(6), 775–800.

European Commission. (2014). *Eurobarometer special surveys: Special Eurobarometer 414.* Brussels, European Commission. Retrieved from http://ec.europa.eu/public_opinion/archives/ebs/ebs_414_en.pdf.

Eurostat. (2009). *ESS standard for quality reports.* Luxemburg: Eurostat.

Eurostat. (2011). European Statistics Code of Practice. Luxemburg: Eurostat.

Ewing, T. (2012). Not just playing around. *Quirk's Marketing Research Review, 26*(3), 30–34.

Eysenbach, G., & Wyatt, J. (2002). Facilitating research. In B. C. McKenzie (Ed.), *Medicine and the internet* (3rd ed., pp. 211–226). Oxford: Oxford University Press.

Faas, T., & Schoen, H. (2006). Putting a questionnaire on the Web is not enough: A comparison of online and offline surveys conducted in the context of the German Federal Election 2002. *Journal of Official Statistics, 22*(2), 177–190.

Fan, W., & Yan, Z. (2010). Factors affecting response rates of the web survey: A systematic review. *Computers in Human Behavior, 26*(2), 132–139.

Fang, J., Shao, P., & Lan, G. (2009). Effects of innovativeness and trust on web survey participation. *Computers in Human Behavior, 25*(1), 144–152.

Fang, J., & Wen, C. (2012). Predicting potential respondents' decision to participate in web surveys. *International Journal of Services Technology and Management, 18*(1/2), 16.

Fang, J., Wen, C., & Prybutok, V. (2013). The equivalence of Internet versus paper-based surveys in IT/IS adoption research in collectivistic cultures: The impact of satisficing. *Behaviour & Information Technology*, *32*(5), 480–490.

Faught, K. S., Whitten, D., & Green Jr, K. W. (2004). Doing survey research on the internet: Yes, timing does matter. *Journal of Computer Information Systems*, *44*(3), 26–34.

Felix, L. M., Burchett, H. E., & Edwards, P. J. (2011). Factorial trial found mixed evidence of effects of pre-notification and pleading on response to web-based survey. *Journal of Clinical Epidemiology*, *64*(5), 531–536.

Fenner, Y., Garland, S. M., Moore, E. E., Jayasinghe, Y., Fletcher, A., Tabrizi, S. N., … Wark, J. D. (2012). Web-based recruiting for health research using a social networking site: An exploratory study. *Journal of Medical Internet Research*, *14*(1), e20.

Fernee, H., & Scherpenzeel, A. (2013). The smartphone in survey research: Experiments for time use data. *Survey Statistician*, *67*(January), 19–25.

Fisher, B., & Bernet, F. (2014). Device effects: How different screen sizes affect answer quality in online questionnaires. Presented at the General Online Research Conference (GOR), Cologne, Germany.

Flynn, D., van Schaik, P., & van Wersch, A. (2004). A comparison of multi-item Likert and Visual Analogue Scales for the assessment of transactionally defined coping function. *European Journal of Psychological Assessment*, *20*(1), 49–58.

Fontaine, S., Jacquemain, M., & Italiano, P. (2013). Specific mixed-mode methodologies to include sensory disabled people in quantitative surveys.Presented at the European Survey Research Association (ESRA), Ljubljana, Slovenia.

Fowler, F. J. (2014). *Survey research methods* (5th ed.). Thousand Oaks, CA: SAGE.

Fricker, S. S., Galesic, M., Tourangeau, R., & Yan, T. (2005). An experimental comparison of Web and telephone surveys. *Public Opinion Quarterly*, *69*(3), 370–392.

Fuchs, M. (2003). Kognitive prozesse und antwortverhalten in einer Internet-befragung (Cognitive processes and behavioral response in an Internet survey). *Österreichische Zeitschrift für Soziologie*, *28*(4), 19–45.

Fuchs, M. (2008). Mobile web surveys: A preliminary discussion of methodological implications. In F. G. Conrad & M. F. Schober (Eds), *Envisioning the survey interview of the future* (pp. 77–94). Hoboken, NJ: Wiley.

Fuchs, M. (2009). Gender-of-interviewer effects in a video-enhanced web survey: Results from a randomized field experiment. *Social Psychology*, *40*(1), 37–42.

Fuchs, M., Bossert, D., & Stukowski, S. (2013). Response rate and nonresponse bias: Impact of the number of contact attempts on data quality in the European Social Survey. *Bulletin of Sociological Methodology/ Bulletin de Méthodologie Sociologique*, *117*(1), 26–45.

Fulgoni, G. (2005). *The professional respondent problem in online panel surveys today*. Presented at the Market Research Association annual conference, Chicago, Illinois.

Funke, F., & Reips, U.-D. (2012). Why semantic differentials in web-based research should be made from visual analogue scales and not from 5-point scales. *Field Methods*, *24*(3), 310–327.

Funke, F., Reips, U.-D., & Thomas, R. K. (2011). Sliders for the smart: Type of rating scale on the web interacts with educational level. *Social Science Computer Review*, *29*(2), 221–231.

Gaiser, T. J. (2008). Online focus groups. In N. G. Fielding, R. M. Lee & G. Blank (Eds), *The SAGE handbook of online research methods* (1st ed., pp. 290–306). London: SAGE.

Gajic, A., Cameron, D., & Hurley, J. (2012). The cost-effectiveness of cash versus lottery incentives for a web-based, stated-preference community survey. *The European Journal of Health Economics*, *13*(6), 789–799.

Galesic, M. (2006). Dropouts on the web: Effects of interest and burden experienced during an online survey. *Journal of Official Statistics*, *22*(2), 313–328.

Galesic, M. (2009). *Comparing the results of web surveys on volunteer versus probabilistically selected panels of participants in Germany and the US*. Presented at the 4th Internet Survey Methodology Workshop, Bergamo, Italy.

Galesic, M., & Bosnjak, M. (2009). Effects of questionnaire length on participation and indicators of response quality in a web survey. *Public Opinion Quarterly*, *73*(2), 349–360.

Galesic, M., & Tourangeau, R. (2007). What is sexual harassment? It depends on who asks! Framing effects on survey responses. *Applied Cognitive Psychology*, *21*(2), 189–202.

Galesic, M., Tourangeau, R., Couper, M. P., & Conrad, F. G. (2007). Using change to improve navigation in grid questions. Presented at the General Online Research Conference (GOR), Leipzig, Germany.

Galesic, M., Tourangeau, R., Couper, M. P., & Conrad, F. G. (2008). Eye-tracking data: New insights on response order effects and other cognitive shortcuts in survey responding. *Public Opinion Quarterly*, *72*(5), 892–913.

Galesic, M., & Yan, T. (2011). Using eye-tracking for studying survey response process. In M. Das, P. Ester, & L. Kaczmirek (Eds), *Social and behavioral research and the Internet: Advances in applied methods and research strategies* (pp. 349–370). New York: Routledge.

Ganassali, S. (2008). The influence of the design of web survey questionnaires on the quality of responses. *Survey Research Methods*, *2*(1), 21–32.

Garland, P., Chen, K., Epstein, L., & Suh, A. (2013). Speed (necessarily) doesn't kill: A new way to detect survey satisficing. *CASRO Journal, 2012–2013*, 21–23.

Gelder, M. M. H. J. van, Bretveld, R. W., & Roeleveld, N. (2010). Web-based questionnaires: The future in epidemiology? *American Journal of Epidemiology*, *172*(11), 1292–1298.

Glasner, T., & van der Vaart, W. (2013). Life history calendars: A viable method for web-based data collection? Presented at the NCRM Conference: Web surveys for the general population – How, why and when?, London, United Kingdom.

GMI. (2012). GMI Pinnacle.

Göritz, A. S. (2005). Contingent versus unconditional incentives in WWW studies. *Advances in Methodology and Statistics (Metodološki Zvezki)*, *2*(1), 1–14.

Göritz, A. S. (2006a). Cash lotteries as incentives in online panels. *Social Science Computer Review*, *24*(4), 445–459.

Göritz, A. S. (2006b). Incentives in web studies: Methodological issues and a review. *International Journal of Internet Science*, *1*(1), 58–70.

Göritz, A. S. (2007). Using online panels in psychological research. In A. N. Joinson, K. Y. A. McKenna, T. Postmes, & U.-D. Reips (Eds), *The Oxford handbook of Internet psychology* (pp. 473–485). Oxford: Oxford University Press.

Göritz, A. S. (2008). The long-term effect of material incentives on participation in online panels. *Field Methods*, *20*(3), 211–225.

Göritz, A. S. (2010). Using lotteries, loyalty points, and other incentives to increase participant response and completion. In S. D. Gosling & J. A. Johnson (Eds), *Advanced methods for conducting online behavioural research* (pp. 219–233). Washington, DC: American Psychological Association.

Göritz, A. S., & Crutzen, R. (2012). Reminders in web-based data collection: Increasing response at the price of retention? *American Journal of Evaluation*, *33*(2), 240–250.

Göritz, A. S., & Luthe, S. C. (2013). Effects of lotteries on response behavior in online panels. *Field Methods*, *25*(3), 219–237.

Göritz, A. S., Wolff, H.-G., & Goldstein, D. G. (2008). Individual payments as a longer-term incentive in online panels. *Behavior Research Methods*, *40*(4), 1144–1149.

Gouldner, A. W. (1960). The norm of reciprocity: A preliminary statement. *American Sociological Review*, *25*(2), 161.

Goyder, J. (1988). *The silent minority: Nonrespondents on sample surveys*. Boulder, Colorado: Westview Press.

Grady, J. (2010, February 23). *Libraries nationwide receiving ALA-APA Library Salary Survey invitation*. Retrieved from http://www.ala.org.

Graesser, A. C., Cai, Z., Louwerse, M. M., & Daniel, F. (2006). Question understanding aid (QUAID): A web facility that tests question comprehensibility. *Public Opinion Quarterly*, *70*(1), 3–22.

Grandquist, L., & Kovar, J. G. (1997). Editing of survey data: How much is enough? In L. E. Lyberg, P. Biemer, M. Collins, E. de Leeuw, C. Dippo, N. Schwarz, & D. Trewin (Eds), *Survey measurement and process quality* (pp. 415–436). New York: Wiley.

Granello, D. H., & Weathon, J. E. (2003). Using web-based surveys to conduct counseling research. In J. W. Bloom & G. R. Walz (Eds), *Cybercounseling and cyberleaning: An encore* (pp. 287–305). Alexandria, Virginia: American Counseling Association.

Greene, J., Speizer, H., & Wiitala, W. (2008). Telephone and web: Mixed-mode challenge. *Health Services Research*, *43*(1 Pt 1), 230–248.

Greenlaw, C., & Brown-Welty, S. (2009). A comparison of web-based and paper-based survey methods: Testing assumptions of survey mode and response cost. *Evaluation Review*, *33*(5), 464–480.

Grenville, A. (2012). *Debunking mobile research*. Retrieved from http://www.visioncritical.com/system/files/ WHITE_PAPER_Debunking_Mobile_Research-Its_just_the_same_or_is_it.pdf.

Greski, R., Meyer, M., & Schoen, H. (2014). The impact of speeding on data quality in nonprobability and freshly recruited probability-based online panels. In M. Callegaro, R. P. Baker, J. Bethlehem, A. S. Göritz, J. A. Krosnick, & P. J. Lavrakas (Eds), *Online panel research: A data quality perspective* (pp. 238–262). Chichester: Wiley.

Grey Matter Research. (2012). *More dirty little secrets of online panel research*. Retrieved from http://www. greymatterresearch.com/index_files/Online_Panels_2012.htm.

Griffis, S. E., Goldsby, T. J., & Cooper, M. (2003). Web-based and mail surveys: A comparison of response, data and cost. *Journal of Business Logistics*, *24*(2), 237–258.

Grossnickle, J., & Raskin, O. (2001). *The handbook of online marketing research*. New York: McGraw-Hill.

Groves, R. M. (1989). *Survey errors and survey costs*. New York: Wiley.

Groves, R. M., Biemer, P. P., Lyberg, L. E., Massey, J. T., Nicholls, W. L., & Waksberg, J. (2001). *Telephone survey methodology*. New York: Wiley.

Groves, R. M., Cialdini, R. B., & Couper, M. P. (1992). Understanding the decision to participate in a survey. *Public Opinion Quarterly*, *56*(4), 475–495.

Groves, R. M., & Couper, M. P. (2008). *Nonresponse in household interview surveys*. Hoboken, New Jersey: Wiley.

Groves, R. M., Fowler, F. J., Couper, M. P., Lepkowski, J. M., Singer, E., & Tourangeau, R. (2009). *Survey methodology* (2nd ed.). Hoboken, NJ: Wiley.

Groves, R. M., & Heeringa, S. G. (2006). Responsive design for household surveys. *Journal of the Royal Statistical Society. Series A*, *169*(3), 439–457.

Groves, R. M., & Lyberg, L. E. (2010). Total survey error: Past, present, and future. *Public Opinion Quarterly*, *74*(5), 849–879.

Groves, R. M., & Peytcheva, E. (2008). The impact of nonresponse rates on nonresponse bias: A meta-analysis. *Public Opinion Quarterly*, *72*(2), 167–189.

Groves, R. M., Singer, E., & Corning, A. (2000). Leverage-saliency theory of survey participation: Description and an illustration. *Public Opinion Quarterly*, *64*(3), 299–308.

Guéguen, N., & Jacob, C. (2002). Solicitation by e-mail and solicitor's status: A field study of social influence on the web. *CyberPsychology & Behavior*, *5*(4), 377–383.

Guidry, K. R. (2012). *Response quality and demographic characteristics of respondents using a mobile device on a web based survey*. Presented at the The American Association for Public Opinion Research (AAPOR) 68th Annual Conference, Orlando, Florida.

Gutierrez, C., Wells, T., Rao, K., & Kurzynski, D. (2011). *Catch them when you can: Speeders and their role in data quality*. Presented at the 36th Midwest Association for Public Opinion Research (MAPOR) Annual Conference, Chicago, Illinois.

Hamari, J., Koivisto, J., & Sarsa, H. (2014). Does gamification work? A literature review of empirical studies on gamification. In *Proceedings of the 47th Hawaii International Conference on System Sciences* (pp. 3025–3034), Hawaii, USA.

Hammen, K. (2010). The impact of visual and functional design elements in online survey research. Presented at the General Online Research Conference (GOR), Pforzheim, Germany.

Hansen, J. M., & Smith, S. M. (2012). The impact of two-stage highly interesting questions on completion rates and data quality in online marketing research. *International Journal of Market Research*, *54*(2), 241–260.

Hansen, K. M., & Pedersen, R. T. (2012). Efficiency of different recruitment strategies for web panels. *International Journal of Public Opinion Research*, *24*(2), 238–249.

Hansen, S. E., & Couper, M. P. (2004). Usability testing to evaluate computer-assisted instruments. In *Methods for testing and evaluating survey questionnaires* (pp. 337–360). Hoboken, NJ: Wiley.

Haraldsen, G. (2005). *Using client side paradata as process quality indicators in web surveys*. Presented at the Exploratory workshop on Internet survey methodology: Towards concerted European research efforts, Dubrovnik, Croatia.

Hardigan, P. C., Succar, C. T., & Fleisher, J. M. (2012). An analysis of response rate and economic costs between mail and web-based surveys among practicing dentists: A randomized trial. *Journal of Community Health*, *37*(2), 383–394.

Hart, A. M., Brennan, C. W., Sym, D., & Larson, E. (2009). The impact of personalized prenotification on response rates to an electronic survey. *Western Journal of Nursing Research*, *31*(1), 17–23.

Harter, J. K., Schmidt, F. L., Killham, E. A., & Asplund, J. W. (2008). *Q12 meta-analysis*. Retrieved from http://strengths.gallup.com/private/resources/q12meta-analysis_flyer_gen_08%2008_bp.pdf.

Hartford, K., Carey, R., & Mendonca, J. (2007). Sampling bias in an international internet survey of diversion programs in the criminal justice system. *Evaluation & the Health Professions*, *30*(1), 35–46.

Haunberger, S. (2011a). Explaining unit nonresponse in online panel surveys: An application of the extended theory of planned behavior. *Journal of Applied Social Psychology*, *41*(12), 2999–3025.

Haunberger, S. (2011b). To participate or not to participate: Decision processes related to survey non response. *Bulletin of Sociological Methodology/Bulletin de Méthodologie Sociologique*, *109*(1), 39–55.

Hayes, B. E. (2008). *Measuring customer satisfaction and loyalty: Survey design, use, and statistical analysis methods* (3rd ed.). Milwaukee, WI: ASQ Quality Press.

Healey, B. (2007). Drop downs and scroll mice: The effect of response option format and input mechanism employed on data quality in web surveys. *Social Science Computer Review*, *25*(1), 111–128.

Healey, J. F. (2011). *Statistics: A tool for social research* (9th ed.). Belmont, California: Cengage Learning.

Heckathorn, D. (1997). Respondent-driven sampling: A new approach to the study of hidden populations. *Social Problems*, *4*(2), 174–199.

Heeringa, S. G., West, B. T., & Berglund, P. A. (2010). *Applied survey data analysis*. Boca Raton, Florida: Chapman and Hall/CRC.

Heerwegh, D. (2003). Explaining response latencies and changing answers using client-side paradata from a Web survey. *Social Science Computer Review*, *21*(3), 360–73.

Heerwegh, D. (2005). *Web surveys: Explaining and reducing unit nonresponse, item nonresponse, and partial nonresponse* (Unpublished doctoral dissertation). Katholieke Universiteit Leuven, Leuven, Belgium.

Heerwegh, D. (2006). An investigation of the effect of lotteries on web survey response rates. *Field Methods*, *18*(2), 205–220.

Heerwegh, D. (2009). Mode differences between face-to-face and web surveys: An experimental investigation of data quality and social desirability effects. *International Journal of Public Opinion Research*, *21*(1), 111–121.

Heerwegh, D., & Loosveldt, G. (2002). Web surveys: The effect of controlling survey access using PIN numbers. *Social Science Computer Review*, *20*(1), 10–21.

Heerwegh, D., & Loosveldt, G. (2006). An experimental study on the effects of personalization, survey length statements, progress indicators, and survey sponsor logos in web surveys. *Journal of Official Statistics*, *22*(2), 191–210.

Heerwegh, D., & Loosveldt, G. (2007). Personalizing e-mail contacts: Its influence on web survey response rate and social desirability response bias. *International Journal of Public Opinion Research*, *19*(2), 258–268.

Heerwegh, D., & Loosveldt, G. (2008). Face-to-face versus web surveying in a high-Internet-coverage population differences in response quality. *Public Opinion Quarterly*, *72*(5), 836–846.

Heerwegh, D., & Loosveldt, G. (2009). Explaining the intention to participate in a web survey: A test of the theory of planned behaviour. *International Journal of Social Research Methodology*, *12*(3), 181–195.

Heerwegh, D., Vanhove, T., Matthijs, K., & Loosveldt, G. (2005). The effect of personalization on response rates and data quality in web surveys. *International Journal of Social Research Methodology*, *8*(2), 85–99.

Heiervang, E., & Goodman, R. (2011). Advantages and limitations of web-based surveys: Evidence from a child mental health survey. *Social Psychiatry and Psychiatric Epidemiology*, *46*(1), 69–76.

Henderson, V., & Callegaro, M. (2011). *Increasing (or decreasing) response rate by changing the subject of email invitations*. Presented at the The American Association for Public Opinion Research (AAPOR) 6th Annual Conference, Phoenix, Arizona.

Henning, J. (2011). *Causes of survey incompletes: Why panelists say they abandon surveys*. Retrieved from http://blog.verint.com/.

Henning, J. (2013). Improving the representativeness of online surveys. *Alert!*, *4*, September.

Herrnson, P. S., Niemi, R. G., Hanmer, M. J., Bederson, B. B., Conrad, F. C., & Traugott, M. W. (2008). *Voting technology: The not-so-simple act of casting a ballot*. Washington, DC: Brookings Institution Press.

Hertel, G., Naumann, S., Konradt, U., & Batinic, B. (2002). Personality assessment via Internet: Comparing online and paper-and-pencil questionnaires. In B. Batanic, U.-D. Reips, & M. Bosnjak (Eds), *Online Social Sciences* (pp. 115–133). Seattle: Hogrefe.

Hill, C. A., & Dean, E. (2009). *Survey research in virtual worlds: Second life R as a research platform*. Presented at the European Survey Research Association (ESRA), Warsaw, Poland.

Hillygus, S. D., Jackson, N., & Young, M. (2014). Professional respondents in nonprobability online panels. In M. Callegaro, R. P. Baker, J. Bethlehem, A. S. Göritz, J. A. Krosnick, & P. J. Lavrakas (Eds), *Online panel research: A data quality perspective* (pp. 219–237). Chichester: Wiley.

Hogan, B., Carrasco, J. A., & Wellman, B. (2007). Visualizing personal networks: Working with participant-aided sociograms. *Field Methods*, *19*(2), 116–144.

Holbrook, A. L., Krosnick, J. A., Carson, R. T., & Mitchell, R. C. (2000). Violating conversational conventions disrupts cognitive processing of attitude questions. *Journal of Experimental Social Psychology*, *36*(5), 465–494.

Holland, J. L., & Christian, L. M. (2009). The influence of topic interest and interactive probing on responses to open-ended questions in web surveys. *Social Science Computer Review*, *27*(2), 196–212.

Hox, J. J. (1997). From theoretical concepts to survey question. In L. E. Lyberg, P. P. Biemer, M. Collins, E. de Leeuw, C. Dippo, & D. Trewin (Eds), *Survey measurement and process quality* (pp. 47–69). New York: Wiley.

Huggins, V., & Eyerman, J. (2001). Probability based internet surveys: A synopsis of early methods and survey research results. Paper presented at Research Conference of the Federal Committee on Statistical Methodology, Arlington, Virginia.

Hughes, K. A. (2004). Comparing pretesting methods: Cognitive interviews, respondent debriefing, and behavior coding. Statistical Research Division Study Series, Survey Methodology 2004(02). U.S. Census Bureau. Retrieved from http://www.census.gov/srd/papers/pdf/rsm2004-02.pdf.

Hundepool, A., Domingo-Ferrer, J., Franconi, L., Giessing, S., Nordholt, E. S., Spicer, K., & de Wolf, P.-P. (2012). *Statistical disclosure control*. Hoboken, New Jersey: Wiley.

Iacobucci, D., & Churchill, G. A., Jr. (2015). Marketing research: Methodological foundations (11th ed.). Nashville, TN: Earlie Lite Books.

Iarossi, G. (2006). *The power of survey design: A user's guide for managing surveys, interpreting results, and influencing respondents*. Washington, DC: World Bank Publications.

ICPSR. (2012). *Guide to social science data preparation: Best practice throughout the data life cycle* (5th ed.). Ann Arbor, Michigan: ICPSR Institute for Social Research University of Michigan.

Irani, T. A., Gregg, J. A., & Telg, R. (2004). Choosing to use the web: Comparing early and late respondents to an online web-based survey designed to assess IT computer skills perceptions of county extension agents. *Journal of Southern Agricultural Education Research*, *54*(1), 168–179.

ISO. (2009). *ISO 26362: Access panels in market, opinion, and social research – Vocabulary and service requirements*. Geneva: International Organization for Standardization.

ISO. (2012). *ISO 20252: Market, opinion and social research – Vocabulary and service requirements* (2nd ed.). Geneva: International Organization for Standardization.

Jäckle, A., Roberts, C., & Lynn, P. (2006). Telephone versus face-to-face interviewing: Mode effects on data quality and likely causes. Report on phase II of the ESS-Gallup mixed mode methodology project. *ISER Working Paper* 2006-41. Colchester: University of Essex.

Jackson, S. A., & Eklund, R. C. (2002). Assessing flow in physical activity: The flow state scale-2 and dispositional flow scale-2. *Journal of Sport & Exercise Psychology*, *24*(2), 133–150.

Jarrett, C., Gaffney, G., & Krug, S. (2009). *Forms that work: Designing web forms for usability*. Amsterdam: Morgan Kaufmann.

Johnson, E. P., Siluk, L., & Tarraf, S. (2014). Cyborgs vs monsters: Assembling modular surveys to create complete datasets. *CASRO Journal, 2014*, 49–54.

Johnston, M. (2007). Spoken and multimodal dialog systems for survey research. In *The Challenges of a Changing World*. Southampton, United Kingdom: Association for Survey Computing.

Joinson, A. N. (1999). Social desirability, anonymity, and Internet-based questionnaires. *Behavior Research Methods, Instruments, & Computers: A Journal of the Psychonomic Society, 31*(3), 433–438.

Joinson, A. N., Paine, C., Buchanan, T., & Reips, U.-D. (2008). Measuring self-disclosure online: Blurring and nonresponse to sensitive items in web-based surveys. *Computers in Human Behavior, 24*(5), 2158–2171.

Joinson, A. N., Woodley, A., & Reips, U.-D. (2007). Personalization, authentication and self-disclosure in self-administered Internet surveys. *Computers in Human Behavior, 21*(1), 275–285.

Jue, A., & Luck, K. (2014). Update: Participation of mobile users in online surveys. Retrieved from http://ww2.focusvision.com.

Kaczmirek, L. (2006). A short introduction to usability in online surveys. Presented at the IFD&TC, Montreal, Canada.

Kaczmirek, L. (2008). Internet survey software tools. In N. G. Fielding, R. M. Lee, & G. Blank. (Eds), *The SAGE handbook of online research methods* (1st ed., pp. 236–54). London: SAGE.

Kaczmirek, L. (2009). *Human survey-interaction: Usability and nonresponse in online surveys*. Cologne: Herbert Von Halem Verlag.

Kaczmirek, L. (2011). Attention and usability in internet surveys: Effects of visual feedback in grid questions. In M. Das, P. Ester, & L. Kaczmirek (Eds), *Social and behavioral research and the Internet. Advances in applied methods and research strategies* (pp. 191–214). New York: Routledge.

Kaczmirek, L., & Wolff, K. G. (2007). Survey design for visually impaired and blind people. In *Proceedings of the 4th International Conference on Universal Access in Human Computer Interaction: Coping with Diversity* (pp. 374–381). Berlin, Heidelberg: Springer-Verlag.

Kapelner, A., & Chanlder, D. (2010). Preventing satisficing in online surveys: A 'kapcha' to ensure higher quality data. Presented at the CrowdConf 2010, San Francisco, California.

Kaplowitz, M. D., Hadlock, T. D., & Levine, R. (2004). A comparison of web and mail survey response rates. *Public Opinion Quarterly, 68*(1), 94–101.

Kaplowitz, M. D., Lupi, F., Couper, M. P., & Thorp, L. (2012). The effect of invitation design on web survey response rates. *Social Science Computer Review, 30*(3), 339–349.

Kenneally, E., Bailey, M., & Maughan, D. (2010). A framework for understanding and applying ethical principles in network and security research. In *Proceedings of the 14th International Conference on Financial Cryptography and Data Security: Workshop on ethics in computer security research (WECSR)* (pp. 240–246). Tenerife, Canary Islands, Spain: Springer-Verlag.

Kenneally, E., Stavrou, A., McHugh, J., & Christin, N. (2011). *Moving forward, building an ethics community (Panel statement)*. Presented at the Workshop on ethics in computer security research (WECSR), Saint Lucia.

Kennedy, C. (2010). Nonresponse and measurement error in mobile phone surveys. University of Michigan.

Kennedy, J. M., Tarnai, J., & Wolf, J. G. (2010). Managing survey research projects. In P. Marsden & J. D. Wright (Eds), *Handbook of survey research* (2nd ed., pp. 575–592). Howard House, UK: Emerald Group Publishing.

Kent, R., & Brandal, H. (2003). Improving email response in a permission marketing context. *International Journal of Market Research, 45*(4), 489–503.

Keusch, F. (2012a). How to increase response rates in list-based web survey samples. *Social Science Computer Review, 30*(3), 380–388.

Keusch, F. (2012b). The role of topic interest and topic salience in online panel web surveys. *International Journal of Market Research, 55*(1), 59–80.

Kiernan, N. E., Kiernan, M., Oyler, M. A., & Gilles, C. (2005). Is a web survey as effective as a mail survey? A field experiment among computer users. *American Journal of Evaluation, 26*(2), 245–252.

Kinesis. (2013a). Online survey platform conversion: Processes, issues and projected costs. Austin, Texas: Kinesis Survey Technologies. Retrieved from http://www.kinesissurvey.com/wp-content/uploads/2013/09/OnlineSurveyPlatformConversion_KinesisWhitepaper.pdf.

Kinesis. (2013b). Online survey statistics for the mobile future. Austin, Texas: Kinesis Survey Technologies. Retrieved from http://www.kinesissurvey.com/2013/10/09/latest-mobile-survey-traffic-stats-q3-2013/.

Kirakowski, J., Claridge, N., & Whitehand, R. (1998). Human centered measures of success in web site design. In *Proceedings of the 4th Conference on Human Factors & the Web*. Basking Ridge, NJ.

Kirakowski, J., & Corbett, M. (1993). SUMI: The Software Usability Measurement Inventory. *British Journal of Educational Technology, 24*(3), 210–212.

Kirk, R. E. (2007). *Statistics: An introduction* (5th ed.). Belmont, California: Cengage Learning.

Klausch, L. T., de Leeuw, E. D., Hox, J. J., de Jongh, A., & Roberts, A. (2012). *Matrix vs single question formats in web surveys: Results from a large scale experiment*. Presented at the General Online Research Conference (GOR), Mannheim, Germany.

Klausch, L. T., Hox, J., & Schouten, B. (2014). Evaluating mixed-mode redesign strategies against benchmark surveys: The case of the Crime Victimization Survey. Presented at the General Online Research Conference (GOR), Cologne, Germany.

Klein, J. D., Havens, C. G., & Thomas, R. K. (2009). Comparing adolescent response bias between internet and telephone surveys. *Journal of Adolescent Health, 44*(2), S36–S36.

Klofstad, C. A., Boulianne, S., & Basson, D. (2008). Matching the message to the medium: Results from an experiment on internet survey email contacts. *Social Science Computer Review, 26*(4), 498–509.

Knowledge Networks. (2011). Knowledgepanel design summary. Retrieved from http://www.knowledge networks.com/knpanel/KNPanel-Design-Summary.html.

Koren, G., & Hlebec, V. (2006). Web application of Antonucci's hierarchical approach for measuring social networks. Presented at the SMABS-EAM conference, Budapest, Hungary.

Körner, T., & van der Valk, J. (2011). Mixing modes in the LFS: Computer-assisted, cost effective and respondent friendly. Presented at the 97th DGINS conference, Wiesbaden, Germany.

Krasilovsky, P. (1996). Surveys in cyberspace. *American Demographics: Tools Supplement, 11*(Nov–Dec), 18–22.

Kreuter, F. (2013). Improving surveys with paradata: Introduction. In F. Kreuter (Ed.), *Improving surveys with paradata: Analytic use of process information* (pp. 1–11). Hoboken, New Jersey: Wiley.

Kreuter, F., Presser, S., & Tourangeau, R. (2008). Social desirability bias in CATI, IVR, and web surveys: The effects of mode and question sensitivity. *Public Opinion Quarterly, 72*(5), 847–865.

Krosnick, J. A. (1991). Response strategies for coping with the cognitive demands of attitude measures in surveys. *Applied Cognitive Psychology, 5*(3), 213–236.

Krosnick, J. A. (1999). Survey research. *Annual Review of Psychology, 50*(1), 537–567.

Krosnick, J. A. (2000). The threat of satisficing in surveys: The shortcuts respondents take in answering questions. *Survey Methods Newsletter, 20*(1).

Krosnick, J. A. (2013). *Lecture at Web Surveys Day 2013, Faculty of Social Sciences*. Ljubljana, Slovenia.

Krosnick, J. A., Ackermann, A., Malka, A., Sakshaug, J., Tourangeau, R., de Bell, M., & Turakhia, C. (2009). *Creating the face-to-face recruited internet survey platform (FFRISP)*. Presented at the Third Annual Workshop on Measurement and Experimentation with Internet Panels, Santpoort, The Netherlands.

Krosnick, J. A., Holbrook, A. L., Berent, M. K., Carson, R. T., Michael Hanemann, W., Kopp, R. J., ... Conaway, M. (2002). The impact of 'no opinion' response options on data quality: Non-attitude reduction or an invitation to satisfice? *Public Opinion Quarterly, 66*(3), 371–403.

Krosnick, J. A., MacInnis, B., Suh, A., & Yeager, D. S. (2013). The accuracy of survey data collected by various American on-line survey firms: A 2012 comparison. Presented at the MESS Workshop 2013, Scheveningen. The Netherlands, Amsterdam: CenterData.

Krosnick, J. A., & Presser, S. (2010). Question and questionnaire design. In P. Marsden & J. D. Wright (Eds), *Handbook of survey research* (2nd ed., pp. 263–313). Howard House, UK: Emerald Group Publishing.

Kroth, P. J., McPherson, L., Leverence, R., Pace, W., Daniels, E., Rhyne, R. L., ... Prime Net Consortium. (2009). Combining web-based and mail surveys improves response rates: A PBRN study from PRIME Net. *Annals of Family Medicine, 7*(3), 245–248.

Krotki, K., & Dennis, J. M. (2001). *Probability-based survey research on the Internet.* Presented at the 53rd Conference of the International Statistical Institute, Seoul, Korea.

Kruse, Y., Callegaro, M., Dennis, J. M., DiSogra, C., Subias, T., Lawrence, M., & Tompson, T. (2010). Panel conditioning and attrition in the AP-Yahoo news election panel study. *Proceedings of the Joint Statistical Meeting, American Association for Public Opinion Research Conference* (pp. 5742–5756). Washington, DC: AMSTAT.

Krysan, M., & Couper, M. P. (2006). Race of interviewer effects: What happens on the Web? *International Journal of Internet Science, 1*(1), 17–28.

Kunz, T., & Fuchs, M. (2013). Reducing response order effects in check-all-that-apply questions by use of dynamic tooltip instructions. Presented at the General Online Research Conference (GOR), Mannheim, Germany.

Kwak, N., & Radler, B. (2002). A comparison between mail and web surveys: Response pattern, respondent profile, and data quality. *Journal of Official Statistics, 18*(2), 257–273.

Kypri, K., Samaranayaka, A., Connor, J., Langley, J. D., & Maclennan, B. (2011). Nonresponse bias in a web-based health behaviour survey of New Zealand tertiary students. *Preventive Medicine, 53*(4–5), 274–277.

Kypri, K., Stephenson, S., & Langley, J. (2004). Assessment of nonresponse bias in an internet survey of alcohol use. *Alcoholism, Clinical and Experimental Research, 28*(4), 630–634.

Lackaff, D. (2012). New opportunities in personal network data collection. In M. Zacarias & J. V. de Oliveira (Eds), *Human-computer interaction: The agency perspective* (pp. 389–407). Berlin: Springer.

Lai, V. S., Wong, B. K., & Cheung, W. (2002). Group decision making in a multiple criteria environment: A case using the AHP in software selection. *European Journal of Operational Research, 137*(1), 134–144.

Langer, G. (2013). Comment on summary report of the AAPOR task force on non-probability sampling. *Journal of Survey Statistics and Methodology, 1*(2), 130–136.

Lavrakas, P. J., Tompson, T. N., & Benford, R. (2010). Investigating data quality in cell phone surveying. Presented at The American Association for Public Opinion Research (AAPOR) 65th Annual Conference, Chicago, Illinois.

LeDuff Collins, M. (2009). *The thin book of 360 feedback: A manager's guide.* Plano, Texas: Thin Book Publishing.

Lee, S. (2006). An evaluation of nonresponse and coverage errors in a prerecruited probability web panel survey. *Social Science Computer Review, 24*(4), 460–475.

Legleye, S., & Lesnard, L. (2013, May 19). ELIPSS: Étude Longitudinale par Internet Pour les Sciences Sociales. Retrieved from http://www.cinis.fr.

Lenzner, T. (2012). An evaluation of two non-reactive web questionnaire pretesting methods. Presented at the General Online Research Conference (GOR), Mannheim, Germany.

Lesnard, L. (2011). ELIPSS: A new mobile web panel for social scientists. Presented at the MESS Workshop, Amsterdam, Netherlands.

Ličen, S., Lozar Manfreda, K., & Hlebec, V. (2006). The quality of survey questions published on Slovenian journalistic web sites. *Advances in methodology and statistics (Metodološki Zvezki) 3*(2), 355–368.

Lindhjem, H., & Navrud, S. (2011). Are Internet surveys an alternative to face-to-face interviews in contingent valuation? *Ecological Economics, 70*(9), 1628–1637.

Little, R. J. A., & Rubin, D. B. (2002). *Statistical analysis with missing data* (2nd ed.). Hoboken, NJ: Wiley.

Lobe, B., & Vehovar, V. (2009). Towards a flexible online mixed method design with a feedback loop. *Quality & Quantity, 43*(4), 585–597.

Lohr, S. L. (2010). *Sampling: Design and analysis* (2nd ed.). Boston, Massachusetts: Brooks/Cole.

Lord, T. H., & Miller, L. C. (2009). Playing the game by the rules: A practical guide to sweepstakes and contest promotions. *Francise Law Journal, 29*(1).

Lorenc, B., Biemer, P. P., Jansson, I., Eltinge, J. L., & Holmberg, A. (2013). Prelude to the special issue on systems and architectures for high-quality statistics production. *Journal of Official Statistics, 29*(1), 1–4.

Losch, M. E. (2008). Informed consent. In P. J. Lavrakas (Ed.), Encyclopedia of Survey Research Methods, pp. 335–337. Thousand Oaks, California: SAGE.

Lozar Manfreda, K. (2001). *Web survey errors.* PhD thesis. Ljubljana: University of Ljubljana, Faculty of Social Sciences.

Lozar Manfreda, K., Batagelj, Z., & Vehovar, V. (2002). Design of web survey questionnaires: Three basic experiments. *Journal of Computer Mediated Communication, 7*(3).

Lozar Manfreda, K., Berzelak, N., & Vehovar, V. (2012). *Paradata insight into survey response behaviour: An analysis of a set of hosted web surveys.* Presented at the General Online Research Conference (GOR), Mannheim, Germany.

Lozar Manfreda, K., Bosnjak, M., Berzelak, J., Haas, I., & Vehovar, V. (2008). Web surveys versus other survey modes: A meta-analysis comparing response rates. *International Journal of Market Research, 50*(1), 79–104.

Lozar Manfreda, K., Couper, M. P., Vohar, M., Rivas, S., & Vehovar, V. (2002). Virtual selves and web surveys. *Advances in Methodology and Statistics, 18*, 187–213.

Lozar Manfreda, K., & Vehovar, V. (2002). *Survey design features influencing response rates in web surveys.* Presented at the International Conference on Improving Surveys, Copenhagen, Denmark.

Lozar Manfreda, K., & Vehovar, V. (2008). Internet surveys. In E. De Leeuw, J. J. Hox, & D. A. Dillman (Eds), *International handbook of survey methodology* (pp. 264–284). New York: Lawrence Erlbaum.

Lozar Manfreda, K., Vehovar, V., & Hlebec, V. (2004). Collecting ego-centred network data via the web. *Advances in Methodology and Statistics (Metodološki Zvezki) 1*(2), 295–321.

Lugtig, P. J., Das, M., & Scherpenzeel, A. (2014). Nonresponse and attrition in a probability-based online panel of the general population. In M. Callegaro, R. P. Baker, J. Bethlehem, A. S. Göritz, J. A. Krosnick, & P. J. Lavrakas (Eds), *Online panel research: A data quality perspective* (pp. 135–153). Chichester: Wiley.

Lumsden, J. (2007). Online-questionnaire design guidelines. In R. A. Reynolds, R. Woods, & J. D. Baker (Eds), Handbook of Research on Electronic Surveys and Measurements, (pp. 44–64). Hershey: Idea Group Reference.

Lyberg, L. E. (2012). Survey quality. *Survey Methodology, 38*(2), 107–130.

Lyberg, L. E., Biemer, P. P., Collins, M., Leeuw, E. de, Dippo, C., Schwarz, N., & Trewin, D. (Eds). (1997). *Survey measurement and process quality.* New York: Wiley.

Macer, T. (2011). Making it fit: How survey technology providers are responding to the challenges of handling web surveys on mobile devices. In D. F. Birks, R. Banks, L. Gerrad, A. Johnson, R. Khan, T. Macer, … P. Willis (Eds), *Shifting the boundaries of research* (pp. 1–23). London: Association for Survey Computing.

Macer, T. (2012). Developments and the impact of smart technology. *International Journal of Market Research, 54*(4), 567–570.

Macer, T. (2014). Online panel software. In M. Callegaro, R. P. Baker, J. Bethleem, A. S. Göritz, P. J. Lavrakas, & J. A. Krosnick (Eds), *Online panel research: A data quality perspective* (pp. 413–440). Chichester, United Kingdom: Wiley.

Macer, T., & Wilson, S. (2013). *The Confirmit annual market research software survey, 2012.* United Kingdom: Meaning ltd.

Macer, T., & Wilson, S. (2014). *The Confirmit annual market research software survey, 2013.* United Kingdom: Meaning ltd.

Madans, J., Miller, K., Maitland, A., & Willis, G. B. (2011). *Question evaluation methods: Contributing to the science of data quality.* Hoboken, New Jersey: Wiley.

Malhotra, N. (2008). Completion time and response order effects in web surveys. *Public Opinion Quarterly, 72*(5), 914–934.

Malhotra, N., Krosnick, J. A., & Thomas, R. K. (2009). Optimal design of branching questions to measure bipolar constructs. *Public Opinion Quarterly, 73*(2), 304–324.

Mangunkusumo, R. T., Duisterhout, J. S., de Graaff, N., Maarsingh, E. J., de Koning, H. J., & Raat, H. (2006). Internet versus paper mode of health and health behavior questionnaires in elementary schools: Asthma and fruit as examples. *Journal of School Health, 76*(2), 80–86.

Manisera, M., & Zuccolotto, P. (2014). Modelling 'don't know' responses in rating scales. *Pattern Recognition Letters, 45*(August), 226–234.

Marcell, M., & Falls, A. (2001). Online data collection with special populations over the World Wide Web. *Down Syndrome Research and Practice*, *7*(3), 106–123.

Martin, C. (2004). The impact of topic interest on mail survey response behaviour. *International Journal of Market Research*, *36*(4), 327–338.

Martin, E. (2004). Vignettes and respondent debriefing for questionnaire design and evaluation. In S. Presser, J. M. Rothgeb, M. P. Couper, J. T. Lessler, E. Martin, J. Martin, & E. Singer (Eds), *Methods for testing and evaluating survey questionnaires* (pp. 149–172). Hoboken, New Jersey: Wiley.

Mavletova, A. (2013). Data quality in PC and mobile web surveys. *Social Science Computer Review*, *31*(6), 725–743.

Mavletova, A., & Couper, M. P. (2013). Sensitive topics in PC web and mobile web surveys: Is there a difference? *Survey Research Methods*, *7*(3), 191–205.

Mavletova, A., & Couper, M. P. (2014). *Mobile web survey design: Scrolling versus paging, SMS versus e-mail*. Presented at the General Online Research Conference (GOR), Cologne, Germany.

McCabe, S. E. (2004). Comparison of web and mail surveys in collecting illicit drug use data: A randomized experiment. *Journal of Drug Education*, *34*(1), 61–72.

McCabe, S. E., Boyd, C. J., Couper, M. P., Crawford, S., & D'Arcy, H. (2002). Mode effects for collecting alcohol and other drug use data: Web and US mail. *Journal of Studies on Alcohol*, *63*(6), 755–761.

McClain, C. M., Crawford, S. D., & Dugan, J. P. (2012). *Use of mobile devices to access computer-optimized web surveys: Implications for respondent behavior and data quality*. Presented at the The American Association for Public Opinion Research (AAPOR) 67th Annual Conference, Orlando, Florida.

McCloskey, M. (2014). Selecting an online tool for unmoderated remote user testing. Retrieved from http://www.nngroup.com/articles/unmoderated-user-testing-tools/?utm_source=Alertbox&utm_campaign=cd82fc86c0-Alertbox_email_06_02_2014&utm_medium=email&utm_term=0_7f29a2b335-cd-82fc86c0-24345537.

McMahon, L., & Stamp, R. (2009). *Questionnaire intelligence: New rules of engagement for online survey design*. Presented at the Worldwide Readership Research Symposia, Valencia, Spain.

McMorris, B. J., Petrie, R. S., Catalano, R. F., Fleming, C. B., Haggerty, K. P., & Abbott, R. D. (2009). Use of web and in-person survey modes to gather data from young adults on sex and drug use: An evaluation of cost, time, and survey error based on a randomized mixed-mode design. *Evaluation Review*, *33*(2), 138–158.

McNaughton, R. B. (1999). Disk by mail for industrial survey research: A review and example. *Industrial Marketing Management*, *28*(3), 293–304.

Medway, R. L., & Fulton, J. (2012). When more gets you less: A meta-analysis of the effect of concurrent web options on mail survey response rates. *Public Opinion Quarterly*, *76*(4), 733–746.

Mesh, G. (2012). Email surveys. In L. Gideon (Ed.), *Handbook of survey methodology for the social sciences* (pp. 313–325). New York: Springer.

Microsoft Corporation. (2013). Microsoft security intelligence report, Volume 15. Key findings and summary. Redmond, Washington.

Millar, M. M., & Dillman, D. A. (2011). Improving response to web and mixed-mode surveys. *Public Opinion Quarterly*, *75*(2), 249–269.

Miller, E. T., Neal, D. J., Roberts, L. J., Baer, J. S., Cressler, S. O., Metrik, J., & Alan, G. (2002). Test-retest reliability of alcohol measures: Is there a difference between Internet-based assessment and traditional methods? *Psychology of Addictive Behaviors*, *16*(1), 56–63.

Miller, K., Chepp, V., Willson, S., & Padilla, J. L. (2014). *Cognitive interviewing methodology*. New York: Wiley.

Miller Steiger, D., & Conroy, B. (2008). IVR: Interactive voice technology. In E. de Leeuw, J. Hox, & D. A. Dillman (Eds), *International handbook of survey methodology* (pp. 285–298). New York: Lawrence Erlbaum.

Mitra, A., Jain-Shukla, P., Robbins, A., Champion, H., & Durant, R. (2008). Differences in rate of response to web-based surveys among college students. *International Journal on E-Learning*, *7*(2), 265–281.

Mohler, P. P., & Uher, R. (2003). Documenting comparative surveys for secondary analysis. In J. A. Harkness, F. J. R. Van de Vijver, & P. P. Mohler (Eds), *Cross-cultural survey methods* (pp. 311–327). Hoboken, New Jersey: Wiley.

Morgan, D. L. (2013). *Integrating qualitative and quantitative methods: A pragmatic approach*. London: SAGE.

Morrison, R. L., Dillman, D. A., & Christian, L. M. (2010). Questionnaire design guidelines for establishment surveys. *Journal of Official Statistics*, *26*(1), 43–85.

MRIA. (2013). *Improving the quality of your online research: Ten questions to ask your online survey provider*. Toronto, Ontario.

Mueller, K., Straatmann, T., Hattrup, K., & Jochum, M. (2012). Effects of personalized versus generic implementation of an intra-organizational online survey on psychological anonymity and response behavior: A field experiment. *Journal of Business and Psychology*, 1–13.

Muñoz-Leiva, F., Sánchez-Fernández, J., Montoro-Ríos, F., & Ibáñez-Zapata, J. Á. (2010). Improving the response rate and quality in web-based surveys through the personalization and frequency of reminder mailings. *Quality & Quantity*, *44*(5), 1037–1052.

Murphy, J., Hamel, L., Harrison, C., & Hammer, H. (2011). AAPOR 2011 membership survey results and methodology. Deerfield, Illinois.

Musch, J., & Reips, U.-D. (2000). A brief history of web experimenting. In M. H. Birnbaum (Ed.), *Psychological experiments on the Internet*, (pp. 61-87). San Diego: Academic Press.

Nadler, R., & Henning, J. (1998). *Web surveys: For knowledge, lead management, and increased traffic*. New York: Perseus.

Naglieri, J. A., Drasgow, F., Schmit, M., Handler, L., Prifitera, A., Margolis, A., & Velasquez, R. (2004). Psychological testing on the Internet: New problems, old issues. *American Psychologist*, *59*(3), 150–162.

Nallan, S. (2012, April 5). Benchmarking for better surveys. Retrieved from http://blog.surveymonkey.com/blog/2012/04/05/benchmarking-for-better-surveys/.

Napoli, P. M., Lavrakas, P. J., & Callegaro, M. (2014). Internet and mobile ratings panels. In M. Callegaro, R. P. Baker, J. Bethlehem, A. S. Göritz, J. A. Krosnick, & P. J. Lavrakas (Eds), *Online panel research: A data quality perspective* (pp. 387–407). Chichester: Wiley.

Neubarth, W. (2010). Drag & drop: A flexible method for moving objects, implementing rankings, and a wide range of other applications. In S. D. Gosling & J. A. Johnson (Eds), *Advanced methods for conducting online behavioral research* (pp. 63–74). Washington, DC: American Psychological Association.

Neuman, W. L. (2009). *Social research methods: qualitative and quantitative approaches* (7th ed.). Boston: Pearson.

Nicolaas, G. (2011). Survey paradata: A review. National Centre for Research Methods: Southampton. Retrieved from http://eprints.ncrm.ac.uk/1719/.

Nicolaas, G. (2013). A probability-based web panel for the UK: What would it look like? Presented at the NCRM Conference: Web surveys for the general population – How, why and when?, London, United Kingdom. Retrieved from http://www.natcenweb.co.uk/genpopweb/documents/UK-prob-based-web-panel-Gerry-Nicolaas.ppt.

Nielsen, J. (1993). *Usability engineering*. Burlington, MA: Morgan Kaufmann.

Nielsen, J. (1997, October 1). How users read on the web. Retrieved from http://www.nngroup.com/articles/how-users-read-on-the-web/.

Nielsen, J. (2000a). *Designing web usability: The practice of simplicity*. Indianapolis: New Riders Press.

Nielsen, J. (2000b). Why you only need to test with 5 users. Retrieved from http://www.nngroup.com/articles/why-you-only-need-to-test-with-5-users/.

Nielsen, J. (2006, April 17). F-shaped pattern for reading web content. Retrieved from http://www.nngroup.com/articles/f-shaped-pattern-reading-web-content/.

Nielsen, J. (2012). Usability 101: Introduction to usability. Retrieved from http://www.nngroup.com/articles/usability-101-introduction-to-usability/.

Nielsen, J., & Budiu, R. (2013). *Mobile usability*. Berkeley, CA: New Riders Press.

Nielsen, J., & Pernice, K. (2009). *Eyetracking web usability*. Berkeley, CA: New Riders Press.

Nielsen, J. S., & Kjær, T. (2011). Does question order influence sensitivity to scope? Empirical findings from a web-based contingent valuation study. *Journal of Environmental Planning and Management*, *54*(3), 369–381.

Nigg, C. R., Motl, R. W., Wong, K. T., Yoda, L. U., McCurdy, D. K., Paxton, R., … Dishman, R. K. (2009). Impact of mixed survey modes on physical activity and fruit/vegetable consumption: A longitudinal study. *Survey Research Methods*, *3*(2), 81–90.

Nunan, D., & Knox, S. (2011). Can search engine advertising help access rare samples? *International Journal of Market Research*, *53*(4), 523–540.

O'Brien, H. L., & Toms, E. (2010). *The development and evaluation of a survey to measure user engagement.* Journal of the American Society for Information Science and Technology, 61(1), 50–69.

O'Brien, H. L., & Toms, E. G. (2008). *What is user engagement? A conceptual framework for defining user engagement with technology.* Journal of the American Society for Information Science and Technology, 59(6), 938–955.

OECD. (2002). *Frascati manual: Proposed standard practice for surveys on research and experimental development* (6th ed.). Paris: OECD. Retrieved from http://www.oecd.org/science/inno/frascatimanualproposed-standardpracticeforsurveysonresearchandexperimentaldevelopment6thedition.htm.

Olson, K., & Parkhurst, B. (2013). Collecting paradata for measurement error evaluation. In F. Kreuter (Ed.), *Improving surveys with paradata: Analytic use of process information* (pp. 43–72). Hoboken, New Jersey: Wiley.

Olson, K., Smyth, J. D., Wang, Y., & Pearson, J. E. (2011). The self-assessed literacy index: Reliability and validity. *Social Science Research*, *40*(5), 1465–1476.

Ongena, Y. P., & Dijkstra, W. (2006). Methods of behavior coding of survey interviews. *Journal of Official Statistics*, *22*(3), 419–451.

ORC Macro. (2003). Report of the results of the asthma awareness survey. Retrieved from http://www.nasn.org/Portals/0/resources/asthma_survey.pdf.

Osborne, J. W. (2012). *Best practices in data cleaning: A complete guide to everything you need to do before and after collecting your data.* Thousand Oaks, California: SAGE.

Oudejans, M., & Christian, L. M. (2010). Using interactive features to motivate and probe responses to open-ended questions. In M. Das, P. Ester & L. Kaczmirek (Eds), (pp. 215–244). *Social and behavioral research and the internet.* New York: Routledge.

Owen, R. (2013). Survey optimisation considerations for Android, Apple and Windows 8 mobile devices. Presented at the Market Research Society (MRS) mobile research conference, London.

Parsons, N. L., & Manierre, M. J. (2013). Investigating the relationship among prepaid token incentives, response rates, and nonresponse bias in a web survey. *Field Methods, 26*(2), 191–204.

Pasek, J., & Krosnick, J. A. (2010). Measuring intent to participate and participation in the 2010 census and their correlates and trends: Comparisons of RDD telephone and non-probability sample internet survey data. Statistical Research Division Study Series, Survey Methodology #2010(15). US Census Bureau. Retrieved from http://www.census.gov/srd/papers/pdf/ssm2010-15.pdf.

Payne, J., & Barnfather, N. (2012). Online data collection in developing nations: An investigation into sample bias in a sample of South African university students. *Social Science Computer Review*, *30*(3), 389–397. doi:10.1177/0894439311407419

Peterson, G. (2012). What we can learn from unintentional mobile respondents. *CASRO Journal, 2012–2013*, 32–35.

Petric, I., & Appel, M. (2007). *The readership currency: Dutch design. How a new methodlogy for AIR measurement opens up new perspectives for the print advertisers and publishers.* Presented at the Worldwide Readership Research Symposium, Vienna, Austria. Retrieved from http://www.nommedia.nl/upload/documenten/2007-wrrs-petric-appel.pdf.

Petrovčič, A., Lozar Manfreda, K., & Petrič, G. (2013). The effect of email invitation characteristics and response reluctance on nonresponse in web forum surveys. Presented at the European Survey Research Association (ESRA), Ljubljana, Slovenia.

Peytchev, A. (2009). Survey breakoff. *Public Opinion Quarterly*, *73*(1), 74–97.

Peytchev, A. (2011). Breakoff and unit nonresponse across web surveys. *Journal of Official Statistics*, *27*(1), 33–47.

Peytchev, A. (2012). Multiple imputation for unit nonresponse and measurement error. *Public Opinion Quarterly*, *76*(2), 214–237.

Peytchev, A., Conrad, F. G., Couper, M. P., & Tourangeau, R. (2010). Increasing respondents' use of definitions in web surveys. *Journal of Official Statistics*, *26*(4), 633–650.

Peytchev, A., Couper, M. P., McCabe, S. E., & Crawford, S. D. (2006). Web survey design: Paging versus scrolling. *Public Opinion Quarterly*, *70*(4), 596–607.

Peytchev, A., & Crawford, S. D. (2005). A typology of real-time validations in web-based surveys. *Social Science Computer Review*, *23*(2), 235–249.

Peytchev, A., & Hill, C. A. (2010). Experiments in mobile web survey design: Similarities to other modes and unique considerations. *Social Science Computer Review*, *28*(3), 319–335.

Pferdekaemper, T., & Batanic, B. (2009). Mobile surveys from a technological perspective. In E. Maxl, N. Döring, & A. Wallisch (Eds), *Mobile market research* (pp. 116–133). Cologne: Herbert von Halem.

Pit, S. W., Vo, T., & Pyakurel, S. (2014). The effectiveness of recruitment strategies on general practitioner's survey response rates: A systematic review. *BMC Medical Research Methodology*, *14*(1), 76.

Pitkow, J., & Recker, M. (1994). Results from the first World Wide Web user survey. *Computer Networks and ISDN Systems*, *27*(2), 243–254.

Półtorak, M., & Kowalski, J. (2013). *Pros and cons of virtual interviewers: Vote in the discussion about surveytainment*, Mannheim, Germany.

Porter, S. R. (2008). Email survey. In P. J. Lavrakas (Ed.), *Encyclopedia of survey research methods*, pp. 231-33. Thousand Oaks, CA: SAGE.

Porter, S. R., & Whitcomb, M. E. (2003a). The impact of contact type on web survey response rates. *Public Opinion Quarterly*, *67*, 579–588.

Porter, S. R., & Whitcomb, M. E. (2003b). The impact of lottery incentives on student survey response rates. *Research in Higher Education*, *44*(4), 389–407.

Porter, S. R., & Whitcomb, M. E. (2005). E-mail subject lines and their effect on web survey viewing and response. *Social Science Computer Review*, *23*(3), 380–387.

Porter, S. R., & Whitcomb, M. E. (2007). Mixed-mode contacts in web surveys: Paper is not necessarily better. *Public Opinion Quarterly*, *71*(4), 635–648.

Postoaca, A. (2006). *The anonymous elect: Market research through online access panels*. Berlin: Springer.

Potaka, L. (2008). Comparability and usability: Key issues in the design of internet forms for New Zealand's 2006 Census of populations and dwellings. *Survey Research Methods*, *2*(1), 1–10.

Poynter, R. (2010). *The handbook of online and social media research: Tools and techniques for market researchers*. Chichester: Wiley.

Poynter, R., Williams, N., & York, S. (2014). *The handbook of mobile market research: Tools and techniques for market researchers*. Chichester: Wiley.

Preece, J. (2001). Sociability and usability in online communities: Determining and measuring success. *Behaviour and Information Technology*, *20*(5), 347–356.

Preece, J., & Maloney-Krichmar, D. (2005). Online communities: Design, theory, and practice. *Journal of Computer-Mediated Communication*, *10*(4).

Presser, S., Rothgeb, J. M., Couper, M. P., Lessler, J. T., Martin, J., & Singer, E. (Eds). (2004). *Methods for testing and evaluating survey questionnaires*. Hoboken, New Jersey: Wiley.

Puleston, J. (2011). Online research – game on!: A look at how gaming techniques can transform your online research. In D. F. Birks, R. Banks, L. Gerrad, A. Johnson, R. Khan, T. Macer, … P. Willis (Eds), *Shifting the boundaries of research* (pp. 20–50). London: Association for Survey Computing.

Puleston, J. (2012). Gamification 101: From theory to practice part I. *Quirk's E-Newsletter*, January.

Puleston, J. (2013). *Online research, game on!* Presented at the NCRM Conference: Web surveys for the general population – How, why and when?, London, United Kingdom. Retrieved from http://www.natcenweb.co.uk/genpopweb/documents/Jon-Puleston.pdf.

Puleston, J., & Rintoul, D. (2012). *Can survey gaming techniques cross continents?* Examining cross cultural reactions to creative questioning techniques. Presented at the Asia Pacific 2012, Shanghai: Esomar.

Raghunathan, T. E., & Grizzle, J. E. (1995). A split questionnaire survey design. *Journal of the American Statistical Association*, *90*(429), 54–63.

Ramos, M., Sedivi, B. M., & Sweet, E. M. (1998). Computerized self-administered questionnaires. In M. P. Couper, R. P. Baker, J. Bethlehem, C. Z. F. Clark, J. Martin, W. L. Nicholls II, & J. M. O'Reilly (Eds), *Computer assisted survey information collection* (pp. 389–408). New York: Wiley.

Rao, K., Kaminska, O., & McCutcheon, A. L. (2010). Recruiting probability samples for a multi-mode research panel with Internet and mail components. *Public Opinion Quarterly, 74*(1), 68–84.

Rao, K., & Pennington, J. (2013). Should the third reminder be sent? The role of survey response timing on web survey results. *International Journal of Market Research, 55*(5).

Rat der Deutschen Markt- und Sozialforschung e.V. (2007). *Richtlinie für Online-Befragungen (Directive for Online Surveys)*.

Reips, U.-D. (2002a). Standards for Internet-based experimenting. *Experimental Psychology, 49*(4), 243–256.

Reips, U.-D. (2002b). Theory and techniques of web experiments. In B. Batanic, U.-D. Reips, & M. Bosnjak (Eds), *Online social sciences* (pp. 229–250). Seattle: Hogrefe & Huber.

Reips, U.-D. (2007). The methodology of internet-based experiments. In A. N. Joinson, K. Y. A. McKenna, T. Postmes, & U.-D. Reips (Eds), *The Oxford handbook of internet psychology* (pp. 373–90). Oxford: Oxford University Press.

Reips, U.-D., & Birnbaum, M. H. (2011). Behavioral research and data collection via the Internet. In K.-P. L. Vu & R. W. Proctor (Eds), *Handbook of human factors in web designs* (2nd ed., pp. 563–585). Boca Raton, FL: Taylor and Francis.

Reips, U.-D., & Funke, F. (2008). Interval-level measurement with visual analogue scales in Internet-based research: VAS Generator. *Behavior Research Methods, 40*(3), 699–704.

Reips, U.-D., & Krantz, J. H. (2010). Conducting true experiments on the Web. In S. D. Gosling & J. A. Johnson (Eds), *Advanced methods for conducting online behavioral research* (pp. 193–216). Washington, DC: American Psychological Association.

Reips, U.-D., & Lengler, R. (2005). The web experiment list: A web service for the recruitment of participants and archiving of Internet-based experiments. *Behavior Research Methods, 37*(2), 287–292.

Reja, U., Lozar Manfreda, K., Hlebec, V., & Vehovar, V. (2003). Open-ended vs close-ended questions in web questionnaires. *Advances in Methodology and Statistics (Metodološki Zvezki), 19*, 159–177.

Revilla, M. (2013). Measurement invariance and quality of composite scores in a face-to-face and a web survey. *Survey Research Methods, 7*(1), 17–28.

Rivara, F. P., Koepsell, T. D., Wang, J., Durbin, D., Jaffe, K. M., Vavilala, M., … Temkin, N. (2011). Comparison of telephone with world wide web-based responses by parents and teens to a follow-up survey after injury. *Health Services Research, 46*(3), 964–981.

Rivers, D. (2007). Sampling for web surveys. *Proceedings of the Joint Statistical Meeting, Survey Research Methods Section*. Salt Lake City: AMSTAT.

Rivers, D. (2010). *AAPOR report on online panels*. Presented at the The American Association for Public Opinion Research (AAPOR) 68th Annual Conference, Chicago, Illinois and at the PAPOR 2010 Annual Conference, San Francisco.

Rivers, D., & Bailey, D. (2009). *Inference from matched samples in the 2008 US national elections*. Presented at the The American Association for Public Opinion Research (AAPOR) 64th Annual Conference, Hollywood, Florida.

Roberts, C. (2013). *Participation and engagement in web surveys of the general population: An overview of challenges and opportunities*. Presented at the NCRM Conference: Web surveys for the general population – How, why and when?, London, United Kingdom.

Roberts, C., Vandenplas, C., & Stähli, M. E. (2014). Evaluating the impact of response enhancement methods on the risk of nonresponse bias and survey costs. *Survey Research Methods, 8*(2), 67–80.

Roe, D. J. (2008). Usabiliity testing. In P. J. Lavrakas (Ed.), Encyclopedia of Survey Research Methods, pp. 933–934. Thousand Oaks, CA: SAGE.

Roman, E. (2011). *Voice-of-the-customer marketing: A revolutionary 5-step process to create customers who care, spend, and stay*. New York: McGraw-Hill.

Rookey, B. D., Hanway, S., & Dillman, D. A. (2008). Does a probability-based household panel benefit from assignment to postal response as an alternative to Internet-only? *Public Opinion Quarterly, 72*(5), 962–984.

Rosenbaum, P. R., & Rubin, D. B. (1983). The central role of the propensity score in observational studies for causal effects. *Biometrika*, *70*(1), 41–55.

Ross, M. W., Månsson, S.-A., Daneback, K., Cooper, A., & Tikkanen, R. (2005). Biases in internet sexual health samples: Comparison of an internet sexuality survey and a national sexual health survey in Sweden. *Social Science & Medicine*, *61*(1), 245–252.

Roster, C. A., Rogers, R. D., Albaum, G., & Klein, D. (2004). A comparison of response characteristics from web and telephone surveys. *International Journal of Market Research*, *46*(3), 359–373.

Rubin, D. B., Stern, H. S., & Vehovar, V. (1995). Handling 'don't know' survey responses: The case of the Slovenian plebiscite. *Journal of the American Statistical Association*, *90*(431), 822–828.

Sackett, P. R. (2009). From the editor. *Industrial and Organizational Psychology*, *2*(1), 1.

Sánchez-Fernández, J., Muñoz-Leiva, F., & Montoro-Ríos, F. J. (2012). Improving retention rate and response quality in web-based surveys. *Computers in Human Behavior*, *28*(2), 507–514.

Saris, W. E. (1991). *Computer-assisted interviewing*. Newbury Park, CA: SAGE.

Saris, W. E. (1998). Ten years of interviewing without interviewers: The telepanel. In M. P. Couper, R. P. Baker, J. Bethlehem, C. Z. F. Clark, J. Martin, W. L. Nicholls II, & J. M. O'Reilly (Eds), *Computer assisted survey information collection* (pp. 409–429). New York: Wiley.

Saris, W. E. (2012). Discussion evaluation procedures for survey questions. *Journal of Official Statistics*, *28*(4), 537–551.

Saris, W. E., & Gallhofer, I. (2007). Estimation of the effects of measurement characteristics on the quality of survey questions. *Survey Research Methods*, *1*(1), 29–43.

Saris, W. E., & Gallhofer, I. (2014). *Design, evaluation, and analysis of questionnaires for survey research* (2nd ed.). Hoboken, New Jersey: Wiley.

Särndal, C.-E., & Lundström, S. (2005). *Estimation in surveys with nonresponse*. Chichester: Wiley.

Sauermann, H., & Roach, M. (2013). Increasing web survey response rates in innovation research: An experimental study of static and dynamic contact design features. *Research Policy*, *42*(1), 273–286.

Schaeffer, D. R., & Dillman, D. A. (1998). Development of a standard e-mail methodology: Results of an experiment. *Public Opinion Quarterly*, *62*(3), 378–397.

Scherpenzeel, A. (2011). Data collection in a probability-based Internet panel: How the LISS panel was built and how it can be used. *Bulletin of Sociological Methodology/Bulletin de Méthodologie Sociologique*, *109*(1), 56–61.

Scherpenzeel, A., & Das, M. (2010). True longitudinal and probability-based Internet panels: Evidence from the Netherlands. In *Social and behavioral research and the internet: Advances in applied methods and research strategies* (pp. 77–104). New York: Routledge.

Scherpenzeel, A., & Toepoel, V. (2012). Recruiting a probability sample for an online panel: Effects of contact mode, incentives, and information. *Public Opinion Quarterly*, *76*(3), 470–490.

Scherpenzeel, A., & Toepoel, V. (2014). Informing panel members about study results. In M. Das, P. Ester, & L. Kaczmirek (Eds), *Social and behavioral research and the Internet. Advances in applied methods and research strategies* (pp. 77–104). New York: Routledge.

Schmidt, S., & Wenzel, O. (2013). *Mobile research performance: How mobile respondents differ from PC users concerning interview quality, drop-out rates and sample structure*. Presented at the General Online Research conference (GOR), Mannheim, Germany.

Schonlau, M., Fricker, R. D., & Elliott, M. N. (2002). *Conducting research surveys via e-mail and the web*. Santa Monica, California: RAND.

Schonlau, M., & Liebau, E. (2012). Respondent driven sampling. *The Stata Journal*, *12*(1), 72–93.

Schonlau, M., Zapert, K., Payne Simon, L., Hayness Sanstand, K., Marcus, S. M., Adams, J., … Berry, S. H. (2004). A comparison between responses from a propensity-weighted web survey and an identical RDD survey. *Social Science Computer Review*, *22*(1), 128–138.

Schouten, B., Calinescu, M., & Luiten, A. (2013). Optimizing quality of response through adaptive survey designs. *Survey Methodology*, *39*(1), 29–58.

Schriver, K. A. (1997). *Dynamics in document design: Creating text for readers*. New York, USA: Wiley.

Schwarz, N. (1996). *Cognition and communication: Judgmental biases, research methods, and the logic of conversation*. Mahwah, New Jersey: Lawrence Erlbaum Associates.

Schwarz, N. (2007). Cognitive aspects of survey methodology. *Applied Cognitive Psychology*, *21*(2), 277–287.

Shannon, D. M., & Bradshaw, C. C. (2002). A comparison of response rate, response time, and costs of mail and electronic surveys. *Journal of Experimental Education*, *70*(2), 179–192.

Sheehan, K. B. (2002). Toward a typology of Internet users and online privacy concerns. *Information Society*, *18*(1), 21–32.

Sheehan, K. B., & Hoy, M. G. (1999). Using e-mail to survey Internet users in the United States: Methodology and assessment. *Journal of Computer Mediated Communication*, *4*(3).

Shih, T.-H., & Fan, X. (2008). Comparing response rates from web and mail surveys: A meta-analysis. *Field Methods*, *20*(3), 249–271.

Shinn, G., Baker, M., & Briers, G. (2007). Response patterns: Effect of day of receipt of an e-mailed survey instrument on response rate, response time, and response quality. *Journal of Extension*, *45*(2).

Shneiderman, B. (1984). Response time and display rate in human performance with computers. *Computing Surveys*, *16*(3), 265–285.

Sikkel, D., & Hoogendoorn, A. (2008). Panel surveys. In E. de Leeuw, J. Hox, & D. A. Dillman (Eds), *International handbook of survey methodology* (pp. 479–499). New York: Lawrence Erlbaum Associates.

Silver, N. (2012, November 10). Which polls fared best (and worst) in the 2012 presidential race? Retrieved from http://fivethirtyeight.blogs.nytimes.com/2012/11/10/which-polls-fared-best-and-worst-in-the-2012-presidential-race/.

Siminski, P. (2008). Order effects in batteries of questions. *Quality & Quantity*, *42*(4), 477–490.

Sinclair, M., O'Toole, J., Malawaraarachchi, M., & Leder, K. (2012). Comparison of response rates and cost-effectiveness for a community-based survey: Postal, internet and telephone modes with generic or personalised recruitment approaches. *BMC Medical Research Methodology*, *12*(1), 1–8.

Singer, E. (2006). Introduction nonresponse bias in household surveys. *Public Opinion Quarterly*, *70*(5), 637–645.

Singer, E., van Hoewyk, J., Gebler, N., Raghunathan, T., & McGonagle, K. (1999). The effect of incentives on response rates in interviewer-mediated surveys. *Journal of Official Statistics*, *15*(2), 217–230.

Sleep, D., & Puleston, J. (2011). *The game experiments: Researching how gaming techniques can be used to improve the quality of feedback from online research*. Presented at Impact: Research Reloaded, Amsterdam: Esomar.

Smith, R. M., & Kiniorski, K. (2003). *Participation in online surveys: Results from a series of experiments*. Presented at the The American Association for Public Opinion Research (AAPOR) 58th Annual Conference, Nashville, Tennessee.

Smith, T. W. (2002). Developing nonresponse standards. In R. Groves, D. A. Dillman, J. L. Eltinge, & R. J. A. Little (Eds), *Survey nonresponse* (pp. 27–40). New York: Wiley.

Smith, T. W. (2011). Refining the total survey error perspective. *International Journal of Public Opinion Research*, *23*(4), 464–484.

Smyth, J. D., Christian, L. M., & Dillman, D. A. (2008). Does 'yes or no' on the telephone mean the same as 'check-all-that-apply' on the Web? *Public Opinion Quarterly*, *72*(1), 103–13.

Smyth, J. D., Dillman, D. A., Christian, L. M., & Mcbride, M. (2009). Open-ended questions in web surveys: Can increasing the size of answer-boxes and providing extra verbal instructions improve response quality? *Public Opinion Quarterly*, *73*(2), 325–337.

Smyth, J. D., Dillman, D. A., Christian, L. M., & O'Neill, A. C. (2010). Using the Internet to survey small towns and communities: Limitations and possibilities in the early 21st century. *American Behavioral Scientist*, *53*(9), 1423–1448.

Smyth, J. D., Dillman, D. A., Christian, L. M., & Stern, M. J. (2006). Comparing check-all and forced-choice question formats in web surveys. *Public Opinion Quarterly*, *70*(1), 66–77.

Smyth, J. D., & Pearson, J. E. (2011). Internet survey methods: A review of strengths, weaknesses, and innovations. In M. Das, P. Ester, & L. Kaczmirek (Eds), *Social and behavioral research and the Internet: Advances in applied methods and research strategies* (pp. 11–44). New York: Routledge.

Snijkers, G., Araldsen, G., Jones, J., & Willimack, D. K. (2013). *Designing and conducting business surveys.* Hoboken, New Jersey: Wiley.

Snijkers, G., & Morren, M. (2010). *Improving the web and electronic questionnaires: The case of audit trails.* Presented at the European Conference on Quality in Official Statistics, Helsinki: Statistics Finland. Retrieved from https://q2010.stat.fi.

Spies, R. A., Carlson, J. F., & Geisinger, K. F. (2010). *The eighteenth mental measurements yearbook.* Lincoln, Nebraska: University of Nebraska Press.

Spijkerman, R., Knibbe, R., Knoops, K., Mheen, D. van de, & Eijnden, R. van den. (2009). The utility of online panel surveys versus computer-assisted interviews in obtaining substance-use prevalence estimates in the Netherlands. *Addiction, 104*(10), 1641–1645.

Stapleton, C. (2011). *The smart(phone) way to collect survey data.* Presented at the The American Association for Public Opinion Research (AAPOR) 66th Annual Conference, Phoenix, Arizona.

Stark, R., & Gatward, R. (2010). *Computer Assisted Interview Testing Tool (CTT): A review of new features and how the tool has improved the testing process.* Ann Arbor, Michigan: University of Michigan. Retrieved from http://www.blaiseusers.org/2010/papers/2a.pdf.

Steinbrecher, M., Roßmann, J., & Bergmann, M. (2013). *The short-term campaign panel of the German Longitudinal Election Study 2009: Design, implementation, data preparation, and archiving.* Retrieved from http://www.gesis.org/fileadmin/upload/forschung/publikationen/gesis_reihen/gesis_methodenberi chte/2013/TechnicalReport_2013-20.pdf.

Steinmetz, S., Bianchi, A., Tijdens, K. G., & Biffignandi, S. (2014). Improving web survey quality: Potential constraints of propensity score adjustments. In M. Callegaro, R. P. Baker, J. Bethlehem, A. S. Göritz, J. A. Krosnick, & P. J. Lavrakas (Eds), *Online panel research: A data quality perspective* (pp. 273–298). Chichester: Wiley.

Stephenson, L. B., & Crête, J. (2011). Studying political behavior: A comparison of internet and telephone surveys. *International Journal of Public Opinion Research, 23*(1), 24–55.

Stettler, K. (2013). Using Web Ex to conduct usability testing of an on-line survey instrument. Presented at the The American Association for Public Opinion Research (AAPOR) 68th Annual Conference, Boston, Massachusetts and at the Quest Workshop 2013, Washington D.C.

Stewart, D. W., & Shamdasani, P. N. (2014). *Focus group: Theory and practice* (3rd ed.). Thousand Oaks, CA: SAGE.

Stieger, S., & Reips, U.-D. (2010). What are participants doing while filling in an online questionnaire: A para-data collection tool and an empirical study. *Computers in Human Behavior, 26*(6), 1488–1495.

Stieger, S., Reips, U.-D., & Voracek, M. (2007). Forced-response in online surveys: Bias from reactance and an increase in sex-specific dropout. *Journal of the American Society for Information Science and Technology, 58*(11), 1653–1660.

Stoop, I. (2005). *Nonresponse in sample surveys: The hunt for the last respondent.* The Hague, Netherlands: Social and Cultural Planning Office.

Stouthamer-Loeber, M., & van Kammen, W. B. (1995). *Data collection and management: A practical guide.* Newbury Park, CA: SAGE.

Strabac, Z., & Aalberg, T. (2011). Measuring political knowledge in telephone and web surveys: A cross-national comparison. *Social Science Computer Review, 29*(2), 175–192.

Sturgis, P., Allum, N., & Smith, P. (2008). An experiment on the measurement of political knowledge in surveys. *Public Opinion Quarterly, 72*(1), 90–102.

Sue, V. M., & Ritter, L. A. (2012). *Conducting online surveys* (2nd ed.). Thousand Oaks, California: SAGE.

Survey Monkey. (2011, August 16). *What day of the week should you send your survey?* Retrieved from https://www.surveymonkey.com/blog/en/blog/2011/08/16/day-of-the-week/.

Svensoon, J. (2013). *Web panel surveys: Can they be designed and used in a scientifically sound way?* Presented at the *59th ISI World Statistics Congress*. Hong Kong, China.

Swoboda, W. J., Mühlberger, N., Weitkunat, R., & Schneeweiß, S. (1997). Internet surveys by direct mailing: An innovative way of collecting data. *Social Science Computer Review*, *15*(3), 242–255.

Tarnai, J., & Moore, D. L. (2004). Methods for testing and evaluating computer-assisted questionnaires. In S. Presser, J. M. Rothgeb, M. P. Couper, J. T. Lessler, E. Martin, J. Martin, & E. Singer (Eds), *Methods for testing and evaluating survey questionnaires* (pp. 319–336). Hoboken, NJ: Wiley.

Taylor, H., Bremer, J., Overmeyer, C., Siegel, J. W., & Terhanian, G. (2001). The record of internet-based opinion polls in predicting the results of 72 races in the November 2000 US elections. *International Journal of Market Research*, *43*(2), 127–136.

Terhanian, G., & Bremer, J. (2012). A smarter way to select respondents for surveys? *International Journal of Market Research*, *54*(6), 751–780.

The International Test Commission. (2006). International guidelines on computer-based and internet-delivered testing. *International Journal of Testing*, *6*(2), 143–171.

Thiele, O., & Kaczmirek, L. (2010). Security and data protection: Collection, storage, and feedback in internet research. In S. D. Gosling & J. A. Johnson (Eds), *Advanced methods for conducting online behavioral research* (pp. 235–253). Washington, DC: American Psychological Association (APA).

Thomas, R. K. (2014). Research quality: Fast and furious ... or much ado about nothing? Sub-optimal respondent behavior and data quality. *Journal of Advertising Research*, *54*(1), 17–31.

Thomas, R. K., & Barlas, F. M. (2014). *Respondents playing fast and loose? Antecedents and consequences of respondent speed of completion.* Presented at the The American Association for Public Opinion Research (AAPOR) 69th Annual Conference, Anaheim, California.

Thomas, R. K., Uldall, B. R., & Krosnick, J. A. (2002). *Reliability and validity of web-based surveys: Effects of response modality, item format and number of categories.* Presented at the The American Association for Public Opinion Research (AAPOR) 57th Annual Conference, Florida, USA.

Thorndike, F. P., Calbring, P., Smyth, F. L., Magee, J. C., Gonder-Frederick, L., Ost, L.-G., & Ritterbrand, L. M. (2009). Web-based measurement: Effect of completing single or multiple items per webpage. *Computers in Human Behavior*, *25*(2), 393–401.

Tijdens, K. G. (2011). Text string matching to measure occupations in web-surveys. Presented at the Data collection for social surveys using multiple modes workshop. Luxembourg.

Tijdens, K. G. (2014). Dropout rates and response times of an occupation search tree in a web survey. *Journal of Official Statistics*, *30*(1), 23–43.

Tippins, N. T. (2009). Internet alternatives to traditional proctored testing: Where are we now? *Industrial and Organizational Psychology*, *2*(1), 2–10.

Tippins, N. T., Beaty, J., Drasgow, F., Gibson, W. M., Pearlman, K., Segall, D. O., & Shepherd, W. (2006). Unproctored internet testing in employment settings. *Personnel Psychology*, *59*(1), 189–225.

Toepoel, V., & Couper, M. P. (2011). Can verbal instructions counteract visual context effects in web surveys? *Public Opinion Quarterly*, *75*(1), 1–18.

Toepoel, V., Das, M., & van Soest, A. (2008). Effects of design in web surveys: Comparing trained and fresh respondents. *Public Opinion Quarterly*, *72*(5), 985–1007.

Toepoel, V., Das, M., & van Soest, A. (2009). Design of web questionnaires: A test for number of items per screen. *Field Methods, 21*(2), 200–213.

Toepoel, V., & Lugtig, P. (2014). What happens if you offer a mobile option to your web panel? Evidence from a probability-based panel of internet users. *Social Science Computer Review*, *32*(4), 544–560.

Tomsic, M. L., Hendel, D. D., & Matross, R. P. (2000). A World Wide Web response to student satisfaction surveys: Comparisons using paper and Internet formats. Presented at the 40th Annual Meeting of the Association for Institutional Research.

Torrance, G. W., Feeny, D., & Furlong, W. (2001). Visual Analog Scales: Do they have a role in the measurement of preferences for health states? *Medical Decision Making*, *21*, 329–34.

Tortora, R. (2009). Recruitment and retention for a consumer panel. In P. Lynn (Ed.), *Methodology of longitudinal surveys* (pp. 235–249). Hoboken, New Jersey: Wiley.

Tourangeau, R. (2004). Experimental design considerations for testing and evaluating questionnaires. In S. Presser, J. M. Rothgeb, M. P. Couper, J. T. Lessler, E. Martin, J. Martin, & E. Singer (Eds), *Methods for testing and evaluating survey questionnaires* (pp. 209–224). Hoboken, NJ: Wiley.

Tourangeau, R., & Bradburn, N. M. (2010). The psychology of survey response. In P. V. Marsden & J. C. Wright (Eds), *Handbook of survey research* (2nd ed., pp. 315–346). Howard House, United Kingdom: Emerald Group Publishing.

Tourangeau, R., Conrad, F. G., & Couper, M. P. (2013). *The science of web surveys*. Oxford: Oxford University Press.

Tourangeau, R., Couper, M. P., & Conrad, F. G. (2003). The impact of the visible: Images, spacing, and other visual cues in web surveys. *Statistical Policy Working Paper 36* (pp. 23–44). Washington, DC: Federal Committee on Statistical Methodology.

Tourangeau, R., Couper, M. P., & Conrad, F. G. (2004). Spacing, position, and order: Interpretive heuristics for visual features of survey questions. *Public Opinion Quarterly*, *68*(3), 368–393.

Tourangeau, R., Couper, M. P., & Conrad, F. G. (2013). 'Up means good': The effect of screen position on evaluative ratings in web surveys. *Public Opinion Quarterly*, *77*(S1), 69–88.

Tourangeau, R., Couper, M. P., & Steiger, D. M. (2003). Humanizing self-administered surveys: Experiments on social presence in web and IVR surveys. *Computers in Human Behavior*, *19*(1), 1–24.

Tourangeau, R., Groves, R. M., Kennedy, C., & Yan, T. (2009). The presentation of a web survey, nonresponse and measurement error among members of web panel. *Journal of Official Statistics*, *25*(3), 299–321.

Tourangeau, R., Rips, L. J., & Rasinski, K. A. (2000). *The Psychology of Survey Response*. Cambridge: Cambridge University Press.

Tourangeau, R., & Yan, T. (2007). Sensitive questions in surveys. *Psychological Bulletin*, *133*(5), 859–883.

Townsend, L. (2012). Flowing with the mainstream: Is mobile market research finally living up to the hype? *Quirk's Marketing Research Review*, July, 36–41.

Trouteaud, A. R. (2004). How you ask counts: A test of internet-related components of response rates to a web-based survey. *Social Science Computer Review*, *22*(3), 385–92.

Truell, A. D., Bartlett, J. E., & Alexander, M. W. (2002). Response rate, speed, and completeness: A comparison of Internet-based and mail surveys. *Behavior Research Methods, Instruments, & Computers*, *34*(1), 46–49.

Tuten, T. L. (1997). Electronic methods of collecting survey data: A review of e-research. *ZUMA-Arbeitsbericht*, *9*, 1–26.

Tuten, T. L., Galesic, M., & Bosnjak, M. (2008). Optimizing response rates and data quality in web surveys: The immediacy effect and prize values. In L. O. Petrieff & R. V. Miller (Eds), *Public opinion research focus* (pp. 149–157). Hauppauge, New York: Nova Publisher.

Valliant, R., Daver, J. A., & Kreuter, F. (2013). *Practical tools for designing and weighting survey samples*. New York: Springer.

van Horn, P., Green, K. E., & Martinussen, M. (2009). Survey response rates and survey administration in counseling and clinical psychology: A meta-analysis. *Educational and Psychological Measurement*, *69*(3), 389–403.

Vannieuwenhuyze, J. T. A. (2014). On the relative advantage of mixed-mode versus single-mode surveys. *Survey Research Methods*, *9*(1), 31–42.

Vannieuwenhuyze, J. T. A., & Loosveldt, G. (2013). Evaluating relative mode effects in mixed-mode surveys: Three methods to disentangle selection and measurement effects. *Sociological Methods & Research*, *42*(1), 82–104.

Vannieuwenhuyze, J. T. A., Loosveldt, G., & Molenberghs, G. (2010). A method for evaluating mode effects in mixed-mode surveys. *Public Opinion Quarterly*, *74*(5), 1027–1045.

Vannieuwenhuyze, J. T. A., Loosveldt, G., & Molenberghs, G. (2012). A method to evaluate mode effects on the mean and variance of a continuous variable in mixed-mode surveys. *International Statistical Review*, *80*(2), 306–322.

Vehovar, V. (1999). Field substitution and unit nonresponse. *Journal of Official Statistics*, *15*(2), 335–350.

Vehovar, V., & Batagelj, Z. (1996). *The methodological issues in WWW surveys*. Presented at the International Conference on Computer-Assisted Survey Information Collection, San Antonio, Texas.

Vehovar, V., Batagelj, Z., Lozar Manfreda, K., & Zaletel, M. (2002). Nonresponse in web suveys. In R. Groves, D. A. Dillman, J. L. Eltinge, & R. J. A. Little (Eds), *Survey nonresponse* (pp. 229–242). New York: Wiley.

Vehovar, V., Berzelak, N., & Lozar Manfreda, K. (2010). Mobile phones in an environment of competing survey modes: Applying metric for evaluation of costs and errors. *Social Science Computer Review*, *28*(3), 303–318.

Vehovar, V., Berzelak, N., Lozar Manfreda, K., & Belak, E. (2009). *Optimising survey costs in mixed mode environment*. Presented at the New Techniques and Technologies for Statistics (NTTS) conference Eurostat February.

Vehovar, V., & Čehovin, G. (2014). *Questionnaire length and breakoffs in web surveys: A meta study*. Presented at the 7th Internet Survey Methodology Workshop. Bolzano, Italy.

Vehovar, V., Čehovin, G., Kavčič, L., & Lenar, J. (2012). *WebSM study: Survey software features overview*. Ljubljana: University of Ljubljana, Faculty of Social Sciences. Retrieved from http://www.websm.org/db/12/15753/.

Vehovar, V., Čehovin, G., & Močnik, A. (2014). *WebSM study: Survey software in 2014*. Retrieved from http://www.websm.org/db/12/17467/.

Vehovar, V., Koren, G., Lozar Manfreda, K., & Berzelak, J. (2005). *What is important when choosing web survey software?* Presented at the Internet Survey Methodology Workshop. Retrieved from http://workshop.websm.org/db/14/118/.

Vehovar, V., Lozar Manfreda, K., & Batagelj, Z. (1999). Web surveys: Can the weighting solve the problem? *Proceedings of the Survey Research Methods Section, American Statistical Association*, pp. 962–967. Alexandria, Virginia: AMSTAT.

Vehovar, V., Lozar Manfreda, K., & Batagelj, Z. (2001). Sensitivity of e-commerce measurement to survey instrument. *International Journal of Electronic Commerce*, *6*(1), 31–52.

Vehovar, V., Lozar Manfreda, K., Koren, G., & Hlebec, V. (2008). Measuring ego-centered social networks on the web: Questionnaire design issues. *Social Networks*, *30*(3), 213–222.

Vehovar, V., Motl, A., Mihelič, L., Berčič, B., & Petrovčič, A. (2012). Zaznava sovražnega govora na slovenskem spletu. *Teorija in Praksa*, *49*(1), 171–189.

Vehovar, V., Petrovčič, A., & Slavec, A. (2014). E-social science perspective on survey process: Towards an integrated web questionnaire development platform. In U. Engel, B Jann, P. Lynn, A. Scherpenzeel & P. Sturgis (Eds) *Improving Survey Methods* (pp. 170–183). London: Taylor and Francis.

Vehovar, V., Sicherl, P., Hüsing, T., & Dolničar, V. (2006). Methodological challenges of digital divide measurements. *The Information Society: An International Journal*, *22*(5), 279–290.

Vehovar, V., Slavec, A., & Berzelak, J. (2011). *Web survey software*. Presented at the 5th Internet Survey Methodology Workshop. Hague, Netherlands.

Vehovar, V., Slavec, A., & Sendelbah, A. (2014). *Investigating respondent multitasking in web surveys: Comparison of self-reports and paradata indicators*. Presented at the 7th Internet Survey Methodology Workshop, Bolzano, Italy.

Vehovar, V., Zaletel, M., & Seljak, R. (2008). Probabilistic methods in surveys and offical statistics. In T. Rudas (Ed.), *Handbook of probability: Theory and applications* (pp. 225–239). Thousand Oaks, CA: SAGE.

Vicente, P., & Reis, E. (2010). Using questionnaire design to fight nonresponse bias in web surveys. *Social Science Computer Review*, *28*(2), 251–267.

Villar, A. (2013). *Feasibility of using web to survey at a sample of addresses: A UK ESS experiment*. Presented at Genpoweb, London. Retrieved from http://www.natcenweb.co.uk/genpopweb/documents/ESS-experiment-Ana-Villar.ppt.

Villar, A., Callegaro, M., & Yang, Y. (2013). Where am I? A meta-analysis of experiments on the effects of progress indicators for web surveys. *Social Science Computer Review*, *31*(6), 744–762.

Vonk, T., van Ossenbruggen, R., & Willems, P. (2006). The effects of panel recruitment and management on research results: A study across 19 online panels. Presented at the ESOMAR Panel Research Conference, Barcelona, November.

Waal, T. de, Pannekoek, J., & Scholtus, S. (2011). *Handbook of statistical data editing and imputation*. Hoboken, New Jersey: Wiley.

Wagner, J., West, B. T., Kirgis, N., Lepkowski, J. M., Axinn, W., & Kruger-Ndiaye, S. (2012). Use of paradata in a responsive design framework to manage a field data collection. *Journal of Official Statistics*, *28*(4), 477–499.

Walker, R. W., Pettit, R., & Rubinson, J. (2009). A special report from the Advertising Research Foundation – The foundations of quality initiative: A five-part immersion into the quality of online research. *Journal of Advertising Research*, *49*(4), 464–485.

Walston, J. T., Lisstiz, R. W., & Rudner, L. M. (2006). The influence of web-based questionnaire presentation. variations on survey cooperation and perceptions of survey quality. *Journal of Official Statistics*, *22*(2), 271–291.

Wansink, B., & Sudman, S. (2002). Predicting the future of consumer panels. *Journal of Database Marketing*, *9*(4), 301–311.

Warren, J. R., & Halpern-Manners, A. (2012). Panel conditioning in longitudinal social science surveys. *Sociological Methods & Research*, *41*(4), 491–534.

WebSM. (2014). Overview of web survey software market. Retrieved from http://www.websm.org/sw.

Weible, R., & Wallace, J. (1998). Cyber research: The impact of the Internet on data collection. *Marketing Research*, *10*(3), 18–31.

Weiner, S. P., & Dalessio, A. T. (2006). Oversurveying: Causes, consequences and cures. In A. I. Kraut (Ed.), *Getting action from organizational surveys. New concepts, technology, and applications* (pp. 294–311). San Francisco: Jossey-Bass.

Wejnert, C., & Heckathorn, D. D. (2008). Web-based network sampling efficiency and efficacy of respondent-driven sampling for online research. *Sociological Methods & Research*, *37*(1), 105–134.

Wells, T., Bailey, J. T., & Link, M. W. (2014). Comparison of smartphone and online computer survey administration. *Social Science Computer Revie*, *32*(2). 238–255.

West, B. T., & Sinibaldi, J. (2013). The quality of paradata: A literature review. In F. Kreuter (Ed.), *Improving surveys with paradata: Analytic uses of process information.* Wiley.

Whitcomb, M. E., & Porter, S. R. (2004). E-Mail contacts. A test of complex graphical designs in survey research. *Social Science Computer Review*, *22*(3), 370–376.

Wiley, J. B., Han, V., Albaum, G., & Thirkell, P. (2009). Selecting techniques for use in an internet survey. *Asia Pacific Journal of Marketing and Logistics*, *21*(4), 455–474.

Wilkerson, J. M., Shenk, J. E., Grey, J. A., Rosser, B. R. S., & Noor, S. W. (2013). Recruitment strategies of methamphetamine-using men who have sex with men into an online survey. *Journal of Substance Use*, 1–5.

Witt, J., Rowland, K., & Wilkinson, C. (2012). Redeveloping the research section of Meningitis UK's website — A case study report. *International Journal of Nonprofit and Voluntary Sector Marketing*, *17*(3), 209–218.

Woolley, P., & Peterson, M. (2012). Efficacy of a health-related Facebook social network site on health-seeking behaviors. *Social Marketing Quarterly*, *18*(1), 29–39.

Wright, G., & Peugh, J. (2012). Surveying rare populations using a probability-based online panel. *Survey Practice*, *5*(3).

Wright, K. B. (2005). Researching Internet-Based Populations: Advantages and Disadvantages of Online Survey Research, Online Questionnaire Authoring Software Packages, and Web Survey Services. *Journal of Computer-Mediated Communication*, *10*(3). Retrieved from http://jcmc.indiana.edu/vol10/issue3/wright.html

Yan, T., Kreuter, F., & Tourangeau, R. (2012). Evaluating survey questions: A comparison of methods. *Journal of Official Statistics*, *28*(4), 503–529.

Yan, T., & Tourangeau, R. (2008). Fast times and easy questions: the effects of age, experience and question complexity on web survey response times. *Applied Cognitive Psychology*, *22*(1), 51–68.

Yeager, D. S., Krosnick, J. A., Chang, L., Javitz, A. S., Levendusky, M. S., Simpser, A., & Wang, R. (2011). Comparing the accuracy of RDD telephone surveys and internet surveys conducted with probability and non-probability samples. *Public Opinion Quarterly*, *75*(4), 709–747.

Zhang, C. (2011). *Impact on data quality of making incentives salient in web survey invitations*. Presented at the American Association for Public Opinion Research (AAPOR) 66th Annual Conference, Phoenix, Arizona.

Zhang, C. (2013). *Satisficing in web surveys: Implications for data quality and strategies for reduction* (A dissertation submitted in partial fulfillment of the requirements for the degree of Doctor of Philosophy (Survey Methodology) in the University of Michigan 2013.). Ann Arbor, Michigan.

Zhang, C., & Conrad, F. G. (2013). Speeding in Web Surveys: The tendency to answer very fast and its association with straightlining. *Survey Research Methods*, 8(2), 127–135.

Zhang, Q., Shao, P., & Fang, J. (2008). Bibliometric Analysis of Current Web Survey Research in China. *Tsinghua Science & Technology*, 13(3), 420–424.

Zuell, C., Menold, N., & Körber, S. (2015). The influence of the answer box size on item nonresponse to open-ended questions in a web survey. *Social Science Computer Review, 33*(1), 115–122.

Žagar, S., & Lozar Manfreda, K. (2012). *Effect of different stimulus on data quality in online panels*. Presented at the 6th Internet Survey Methodology Workshop, Ljubljana, Slovenia.

Author index

Brown-Welty S. 18
Bruijne M. de 197
Brunet I. 50
Buchanan E. A. 125
Buchanan T. 134, 235, 236
Budiu R. 200–201
Buelens B. 239
Buhrmester M. 50
Burchett H. E. 153
Burdein I. 83, 101
Burr M. A. 235
Buskirk T. D. 198

Cai Z. 107
Calinescu M. 237
Callegaro M. 23, 27, 40, 58, 61, 79, 80, 82, 85, 90, 95,
    97, 108, 122, 123, 136, 138, 152, 156, 157, 158,
    168,195, 197, 199, 206, 207, 208, 209, 210, 211,
    213, 237, 240, 241, 242, 248
Cameron D. 149
Campanelli P. 104, 105, 107
Cantor D. 28
Cape P. 101
Carrasco J. A. 86
Carey R. 157
Carini R. 235
Carlson J. F. 65
Carson R. T. 73
Casey T.W. 96
Cechanowicz J. 100
Champion H. 137
Chan P. 211
Chandler D. 122, 123
Chaney B. H. 105
Chaney J. D. 105
Chang C.-Y. 100
Chang L. 24, 38, 58, 103, 148, 180, 213, 235, 236
Chao S. 180
Chen K. 65
Chepp V. 105
Cheung W. 226
Chien Y.-T. 100
Chin T.-Y. 82
Chittenden L. 157
Cho H. 134
Choragwicka B. 137
Chou P.-N. 30
Christian L. M. 24, 26, 27, 29, 40, 59, 69, 83, 103, 148
Christin N. 129
Churchill G. A. Jr. 63, 238, 245
Cialdini R. B. 131
Claridge N. 31
Clayton R. L. 17
Cobanoglu N. 150
Cobben F. 6, 215
Coenders G. 86
Coganoglu C. 20, 150

Coiner T. 103
Comley P. 131, 148, 150, 207
Connor J. 154
Conrad F. G. 51, 65, 67, 69, 71, 73, 76, 81, 82, 85, 97,
    103, 105, 123, 134, 183
Conradt J. 23
Conroy B. 17
Converse J. M. 17
Converse P. D. 39
Cook C. 132, 150, 152, 155
Cooke M. 204
Coombe R. 99, 109
Cooper A. 24
Cooper M. 235
Corbett M. 31
Corning A. 131
Coromina L. 86
Corti L. 125, 128, 189
Couper M. P. 16, 17, 24, 25, 65, 67, 69, 71, 73, 75, 76, 81,
    82, 83, 85, 88, 89, 90, 93, 96, 97, 101, 103, 110, 115,
    122, 125, 131, 132, 134, 135, 151, 152, 195, 197,
    198, 232, 247
Crawford S. D. 24, 71, 81, 88, 92, 101, 07, 108, 153, 197,
    215, 217, 247
Crête J. 24
Crutzen R. 24, 153
Csikszentmihalyi M. 98
Czaja R. F. 238
Čehovin G. 91, 101, 123, 139, 140, 185, 221,
    223, 225

da Costa F. F. 110
Dalessio A. T. 134
Daneback K. 24
Daniel F. 107
D'Arcy H. 24
Das M. 70, 102, 208, 213, 215
Datta R. A. 147
Daver J. A. 183
Dawson C. R. 32
Day B. 153
De Beuckelaer A. 39
de Heer W. 17
de Jong M. 30
de Jongh A. 82
de Leeuw E. 17, 22, 38, 39, 40, 82, 152, 182
de Nooy 251
de Rouvray C. 69
de Ruyter K. 85, 235
Dean E. 30, 105
DeMaio T. 105
Dennis J. M. 69
Dennis M. J. 15
DeRouvray C. 93
Deutskens E. 85, 235, 101, 150, 153, 235
Dietrich B. J. 234
Dijkstra W. 106

Subject index